Australian Marine Life

the plants and animals of temperate waters

Australian Marine Life

the plants and animals of temperate waters

Graham J. Edgar

Dedication

To my parents, Joyce and Allan, for showing me the Reef when young, and as partial compensation for not getting a proper job.

First published in 1997 by
REED BOOKS
a part of Reed Books Australia
35 Cotham Road, Kew, Victoria 3101

National Library of Australia
Cataloguing-in-Publication Data

Edgar, Graham.
Australian Marine Life.

Bibliography.
Includes index.
ISBN 0 7301 0474 5.

1. Marine biology - Australia. I. Title.

574.994

Edited by Beverley Barnes
Designed by Bruno Grasswill
Major photographic contributors:
Rudie Kuiter
Clay Bryce
Kelvin Aitken
Line diagrams: Dave Wright

Printed in Hong Kong by South China Printing

Acknowledgements

I owe a huge debt to the following people for correspondence, identification of specimens, and, in many cases, for commenting on sections of the manuscript. Without their help, and the many authors listed in the bibliography whose published works have been consulted, this book could not have been written.

Lichens: Dr G. Kantvilas
Phytoplankton: Dr G. Hallegraeff
Benthic algae: Professor H.B.S. Womersley, Ms F. Scott, Dr J. Huisman
Seagrasses: Dr H. Kirkman
Sponges: Dr P. Bergquist
Hydrozoans: Mrs J. Watson
Anthozoans: Dr P. Aldenslade
Nematodes: Dr J. Moverley
Pycnogonids: Mr D. Staples
Crustaceans: Dr G.C.B. Poore
Aplacophorans: Dr A. Scheltema
Chitons: Dr K. Gowlett-Holmes
Gastropods, bivalves: Dr W. Ponder, Ms E. Turner
Opisthobranchs: Dr R. Willan
Octopuses: Dr T. Stranks
Bryozoans: Mr P. Bock, Dr J. Walls
Echinoderms, anemones: Mrs L. Marsh
Invertebrates: Dr S.A. Shepherd, Mr C. Handreck
Fishes: Dr P.R. Last, Mr R.H. Kuiter

I also need to thank a number of photographers for their patience and expertise in filming species that I could not: Kelvin Aitken, Gary Bell, Clay Bryce, Neville Coleman, Dave Evans, Gustaaf Hallegraeff, Ken Hoppen, Barry Hutchins, Rudie and Alison Kuiter, Peter Last, Loisette Marsh, Ron Mawbey, Peter Mooney, Barry Munday, Tony Rees, Simon Talbot and Malcolm Wells. The dedication of Dave Wright when drawing the line diagrams also greatly improved the quality of the book.

Many people assisted in the field. Although I cannot acknowledge all, I am especially indebted to Helmut Abt, Neville Barrett, Stuart Dudgeon, Joyce and Allan Edgar, Les and Fran Graham, Richard Holmes, Barry Hutchins, John Keesing, Hugh Kirkman, Peter Last, Ron Mawbey, Scoresby Shepherd, Peter van der Woude, Dave Warth and Malcolm Wells.

The Zoology Department of the University of Tasmania, CSIRO Division of Fisheries and the Tasmanian Department of Primary Industry and Fisheries provided facilities, thereby making the book possible.

To Bill Templeman of Reed Books I also owe a great deal, not least for his considerable patience.

Finally, my thanks go to my family, Christine Crawford, Christopher Edgar, Sophie Edgar and Anna Edgar, for their tolerance and enthusiasm, and for holding the flash.

Author's Note

Changes to the names and distributions of the species listed in this book are updated regularly on the World Wide Web and can be accessed at http://www.utas.edu.au./docs/zoology/edgar.html

PREFACE

Most Australians recognise the beauty and diversity of plant and animal communities in tropical seas, particularly along the Great Barrier Reef. By contrast, relatively few people are aware of the great variety of marine plants and animals living along the southern half of our continent, or know that these temperate species often rival their tropical relatives in colour and ornamentation. The great diversity of marine organisms in the tropics is, in fact, replicated in the south, albeit in a different form. Temperate reefs are not created by corals and contain few coral species, and so they lack the explosion of fishes, molluscs and shrimps that are adapted for life in coral habitats. However, as partial compensation, more than twice as many species of seaweeds and seagrasses are found in temperate Australia as in the tropics, and associated with these plants are thousands of luridly patterned species of crustacean, polychaete and mollusc. These invertebrate species are generally small (less than 10 mm) and live unnoticed by most visitors to the shore. Away from reefs the number of species on soft sediments and in the open water does not differ substantially between tropical and temperate seas.

One important difference between tropical and temperate waters is that nearly all animals in the tropics have a long-lived dispersal phase in their life cycle and occur widely over large geographical areas, while temperate species are generally more localised in distribution. The majority of southern Australian marine species therefore do not occur in other countries, whereas only a small proportion (less than 10 per cent) of species on the Great Barrier Reef are confined to Australian waters. This difference in species distribution has an important consequence for the maintenance of biodiversity, because it indicates that temperate organisms are more vulnerable to extinction. A substantial oil spill in the tropics, for example, would devastate shallow-water communities over a large area but would be unlikely to cause species extinctions, whereas a similar spill in temperate waters could cause loss of species.

Any partnership between a relatively vulnerable fauna and high densities of humans is clearly an uneasy one, which should be carefully monitored; yet the consequences of human activities in temperate Australian waters, including the degradation of virtually all estuaries in the region, are rarely examined from an ecological perspective. Much of this indifference is surely because of a general lack of awareness about the unique and spectacular nature of the plants and animals on our doorstep. Because of this ignorance, only a miserly proportion (less than 1 per cent) of the temperate coastline has been set aside as reserves in order for plant and animal communities to be fully protected from fishing and development. The purpose of this book and a forthcoming volume that describes what little is known about ecological relationships between local species, is to provide a clouded porthole through which more of us may glimpse this wonderful but largely unknown realm.

CONTENTS

INTRODUCTION

Most of the 1200 or so species included in this book are confined to shallow temperate waters and are restricted to Australia. However, because the book is intended as a general guide for divers, fishermen and shore fossickers from Sydney to Perth, the tropical species that commonly reach temperate latitudes on the east and west coasts have also been included. The emphasis in selecting species for the book has been to include representatives from a range of different plant and animal groups, while also providing information on the appearance and distribution of the more noticeable species.

Although the book contains most of the common, conspicuous species found in water depths less than 30 m, it cannot hope to provide a comprehensive coverage, given the huge diversity of organisms in the region. To partially remedy this deficiency, a list of the most useful publications for identifying local species is included in the bibliography. Readers are urged to consult these articles and books, or contact the appropriate specialist at a museum, to definitively identify any species.

A number of scientific terms used in this book are also used in a less restrictive sense in general speech. The more important of these are discussed below, while others are explained the first time they are used in the text, as well as in a separate glossary.

Species

The basic unit of biological classification is the species, a group of organisms that can produce fertile offspring but which cannot interbreed with other organisms. Species can be labelled using either common or scientific names. Common names are usefully applied to well-known groups such as fishes, but generally lack consistency from place to place and have never been used for the majority of inconspicuous species. Common names are included in this book if they are widely used; no attempt has been made to artificially derive common names for poorly-known species.

The conventional scientific way to label each species is to give it a unique Latin name written in italics in two parts, with the first letter of the first word capitalised. An example is *Portunus pelagicus*, a name that refers universally to the animal known as the blue-swimmer crab in New South Wales, the blue manna crab in Western Australia and the sand crab in Queensland. This system was originally applied in the 1750s by the Swedish biologist Carl von Linné (a.k.a. Carolus Linnaeus) and is today known as the Linnaean system of biological nomenclature.

In order to give a scientific name to a new species, a restrictive set of rules now have to be followed, including the designation of a single plant or animal, or strain of bacteria, as the representative or 'type' of that species. The application of these rules is governed by different panels of experts for animals (the International Commission on Zoological Nomenclature), plants (the International Association for Plant Taxonomy) and bacteria (the International Committee for Systematic Bacteriology), and there are some differences in the rules or 'Codes' laid down by each, such as the need to include a Latin description for plants but not animals.

The first word in the species name, e.g. *Portunus*, is also used in the name of closely related organisms and is known as the genus of that species. The genus is often abbreviated (e.g. *P. pelagicus*) in situations where the name is repeated in a short section of text, providing that it is written in full the first time it is used. A question mark can be added to either the genus or species name in situations where there is some uncertainly about the name's accuracy. The position of this question mark is important. *Portunus ?pelagicus*, for example, is used for an crab that definitely belongs to the genus *Portunus* but is perhaps not *Portunus pelagicus*, whereas *?Portunus pelagicus* is used for an animal that is thought to be *Portunus pelagicus* but may be something different. If the genus but not the species name is known, or the species is yet to be scientifically described, the abbreviation sp. (for species) is used (e.g. *Portunus* sp.).

Species authority

Following the first citing of each scientific name, a convention in scientific literature is to add a reference to the author who first described that species (the 'authority'). The value of this reference is that it allows somebody reading about the species to track down the original source of the description. Zoologists often include the date as well as the author of the original description (e.g. Linnaeus, 1766) to enable the full original reference to be quickly found in the Zoological Record, a catalogue of all animal species named in each year. Species that are now placed in a different genus from the one in which they were originally described have the original author's name enclosed in brackets. For example, the species described by Linnaeus as *Cancer pelagicus* is now known as *Portunus pelagicus* (Linnaeus).

Botanists have adopted a slightly different convention by placing the name of the authority for any change in genus after the name of the original describer. The seaweed species *Hormosira banksii* (Turner) Decaisne, for example, was first described by Turner as *Fucus banksii* but later placed in the genus *Hormosira* by Decaisne. The date of the first description is rarely included in botanical names because no catalogue of plant species equivalent to the Zoological Record exists, and there is therefore no easy way to ferret out the original reference.

Higher classification of plants and animals

In addition to species and genus, a number of other categories can be used to hierarchically arrange species into groups with similar characteristics. *Portunus pelagicus* groups with other swimmer crabs in the 'family' Portunidae, which in turn groups with other families of crabs and shrimps in the 'order' Decapoda. The highest categories are the five 'kingdoms' (plants, animals, fungi, protists and bacteria), which are divisible into 'phyla' and then 'classes'. The full classification of the blue swimmer crab is:

Kingdom	Animalia	(animals)
Phylum	Arthropoda	(arthropods)
Class	Malacostraca	(higher crustaceans)
Order	Decapod	(crabs and shrimps)
Family	Portunidae	(swimmer crabs)
Genus	*Portunus*	
Species	*Portunus pelagicus*	(blue swimmer crab)

Any other plant or animal can be classified using the same hierarchical structure; however, botanists tend to use the term 'division' rather than its zoological equivalent term 'phylum'. If a finer structure in classification is needed than provided by the seven categories listed above, the subcategories are denoted by a prefix. The prefix most often used is sub-, to indicate a slightly lower category, such as subclass to denote a category lower than class but higher than order. Occasionally the prefix supra- is used to indicate a slightly higher category, such as supraorder to denote a category higher than order but lower than subclass.

It is important to recognise that there has never been consensus among biologists about the classification of plants and animals into higher categories — the arrangements of various authors differ in the numbers and names of phyla, classes, etc. This is because of the arbitrary nature of how much difference between two groups of organisms constitutes each category and because the traditional method of classifying organisms relies on structural characteristics rather than kinship. One biologist, for example, may consider that differences in the structure of kidneys are more important than differences in the arrangement of the nervous system, while another thinks the opposite. Fortunately, this disorder is now changing because of recent emphasis on the evolutionary history of organisms and the development of molecular techniques that enable relationships between organisms to be established at the DNA level. These techniques should eventually allow a single family tree to be constructed that unambiguously indicates relationships between all species based on their evolutionary history, although the problem of where to break the tree into genus, family, etc., will always remain.

Habitat

In this book the habitats of the various species are described in terms of three key features: habitat type (e.g. sand, reef or open sea), wave exposure and depth. The habitat requirements of many of the species are poorly known, particularly with respect to depth, and so specimens may sometimes be found outside the habitats listed.

Wave exposure cannot be precisely determined without complex measurement and is therefore subjectively defined here. 'Sheltered' habitat occurs at sites in estuaries and in shallow, enclosed coastal bays; 'moderately exposed' habitat is located along sections of the open coast that are protected to some degree and have wave heights rarely exceeding 2 m; 'submaximally exposed' habitat occurs along much of the open coast but not at locations such as those in western Victoria and western Tasmania where large swells almost continuously pound the shoreline (the 'maximally exposed' habitat).

Species that occur throughout moderately, submaximally and maximally exposed habitats are listed as inhabiting exposed habitat; and species that are not given a wave exposure classification are found at all levels of exposure. A number of species extend from shallow estuaries to deep offshore waters but are always found below the area of wave surge along exposed coasts. These are listed as occupying 'sheltered and moderately exposed' habitat.

Distribution

The distribution of species is described in an anticlockwise direction around the southern Australian coastline and Tasmania as precisely as possible.

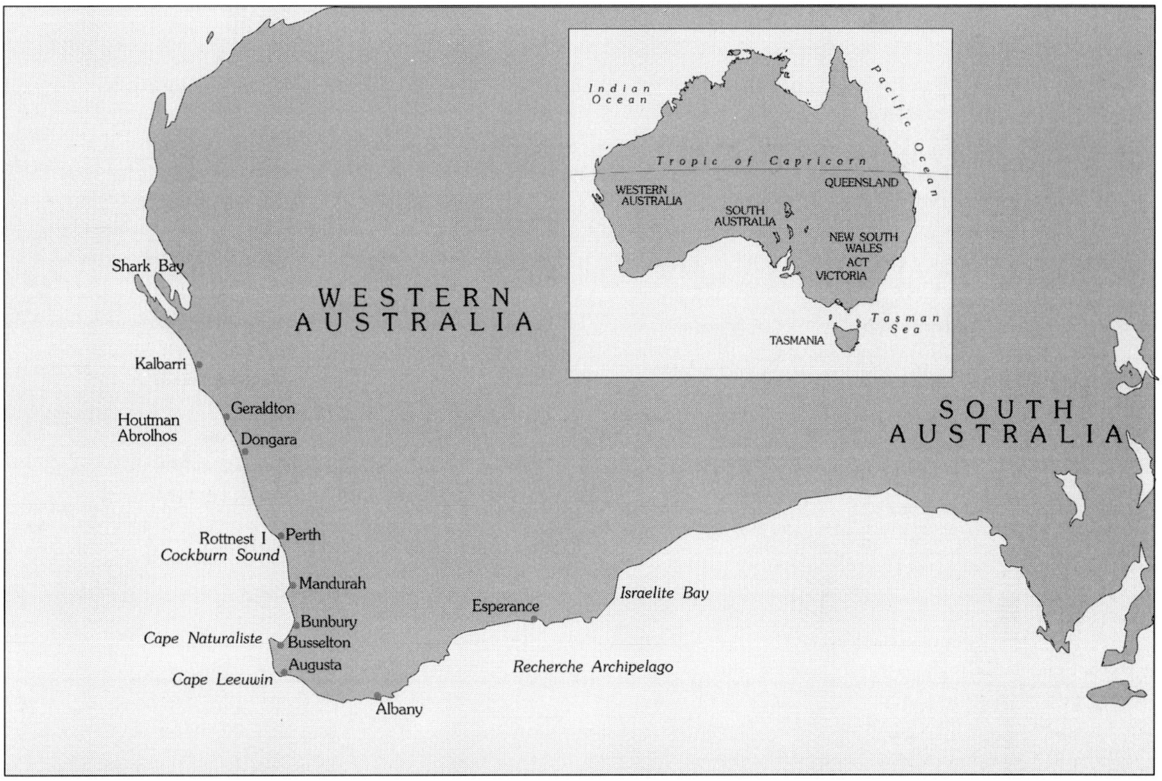

Indian Ocean
Pacific Ocean
Tropic of Capricorn
WESTERN AUSTRALIA
QUEENSLAND
SOUTH AUSTRALIA
NEW SOUTH WALES
ACT
VICTORIA
Tasman Sea
TASMANIA

Shark Bay
WESTERN AUSTRALIA
Kalbarri
Geraldton
Houtman Abrolhos
Dongara
SOUTH AUSTRALIA
Rottnest I
Perth
Cockburn Sound
Mandurah
Esperance
Israelite Bay
Bunbury
Cape Naturaliste
Busselton
Augusta
Recherche Archipelago
Cape Leeuwin
Albany

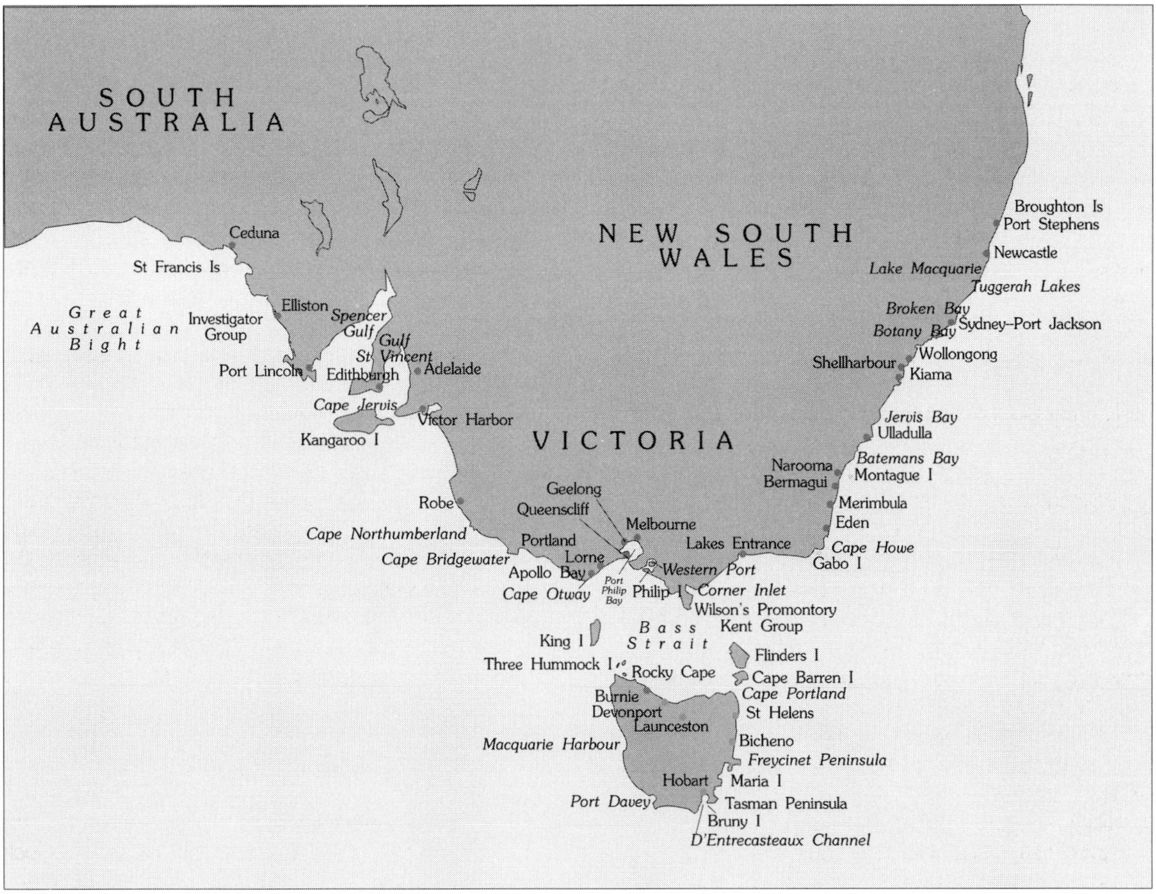

SOUTH AUSTRALIA
Broughton Is
Port Stephens
Ceduna
NEW SOUTH WALES
Newcastle
St Francis Is
Lake Macquarie
Tuggerah Lakes
Elliston
Great Australian Bight
Investigator Group
Spencer Gulf
Gulf St Vincent
Broken Bay
Botany Bay
Sydney–Port Jackson
Wollongong
Shellharbour
Port Lincoln
Edithburgh
Adelaide
Kiama
Cape Jervis
Jervis Bay
Victor Harbor
Ulladulla
Kangaroo I
VICTORIA
Batemans Bay
Narooma
Bermagui
Montague I
Geelong
Robe
Merimbula
Queenscliff
Eden
Melbourne
Cape Northumberland
Portland
Lakes Entrance
Cape Howe
Lorne
Gabo I
Cape Bridgewater
Apollo Bay
Western Port
Port Philip Bay
Philip I
Corner Inlet
Cape Otway
Wilson's Promontory
Bass Strait
Kent Group
King I
Flinders I
Three Hummock I
Rocky Cape
Cape Barren I
Cape Portland
Burnie
Devonport
St Helens
Launceston
Bicheno
Macquarie Harbour
Freycinet Peninsula
Hobart
Maria I
Port Davey
Tasman Peninsula
Bruny I
D'Entrecasteaux Channel

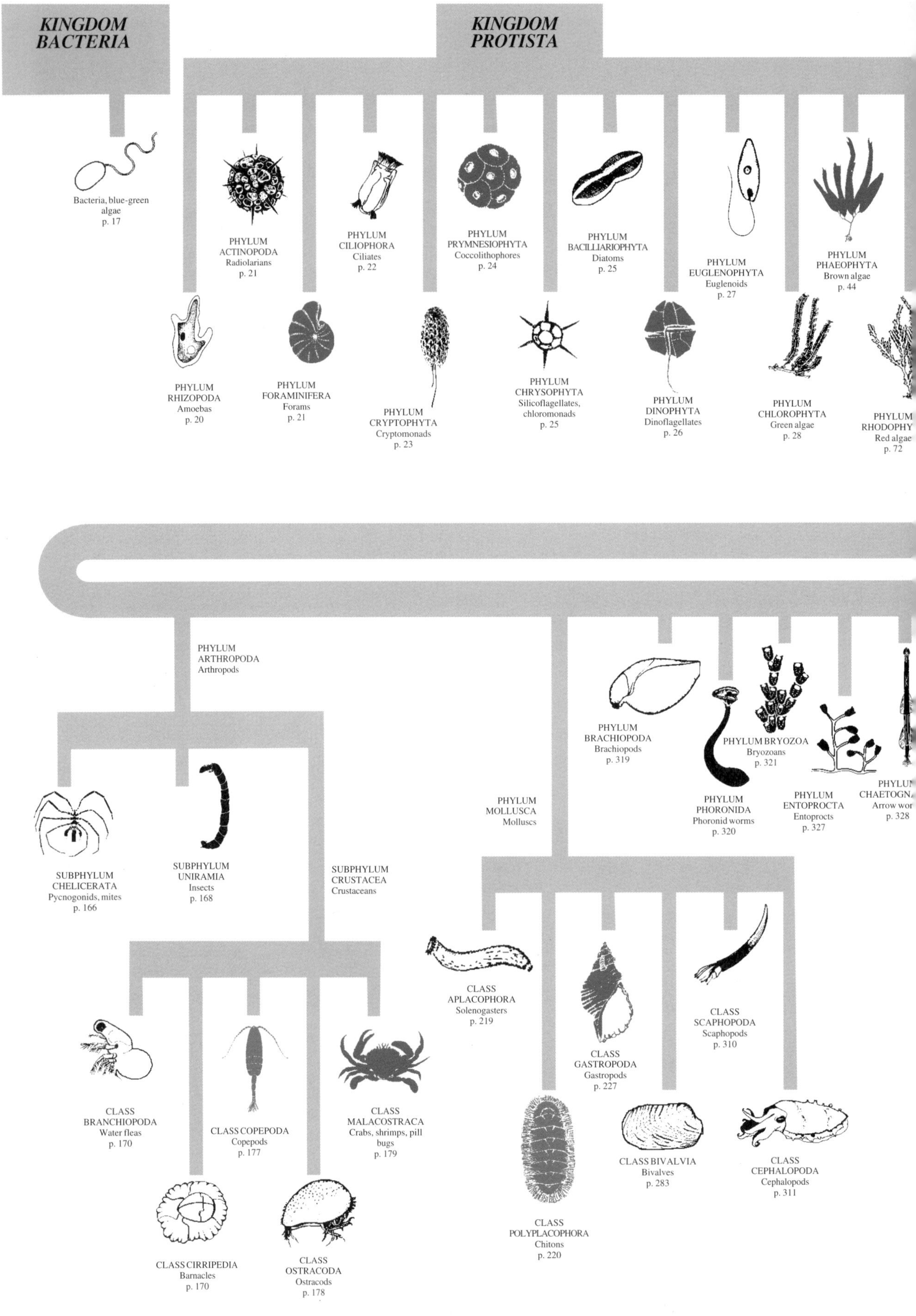

KINGDOM BACTERIA

Bacteria, blue-green algae
p. 17

KINGDOM PROTISTA

PHYLUM ACTINOPODA
Radiolarians
p. 21

PHYLUM CILIOPHORA
Ciliates
p. 22

PHYLUM PRYMNESIOPHYTA
Coccolithophores
p. 24

PHYLUM BACILLIARIOPHYTA
Diatoms
p. 25

PHYLUM EUGLENOPHYTA
Euglenoids
p. 27

PHYLUM PHAEOPHYTA
Brown algae
p. 44

PHYLUM RHIZOPODA
Amoebas
p. 20

PHYLUM FORAMINIFERA
Forams
p. 21

PHYLUM CRYPTOPHYTA
Cryptomonads
p. 23

PHYLUM CHRYSOPHYTA
Silicoflagellates, chloromonads
p. 25

PHYLUM DINOPHYTA
Dinoflagellates
p. 26

PHYLUM CHLOROPHYTA
Green algae
p. 28

PHYLUM RHODOPHY
Red algae
p. 72

PHYLUM ARTHROPODA
Arthropods

SUBPHYLUM CHELICERATA
Pycnogonids, mites
p. 166

SUBPHYLUM UNIRAMIA
Insects
p. 168

SUBPHYLUM CRUSTACEA
Crustaceans

CLASS BRANCHIOPODA
Water fleas
p. 170

CLASS COPEPODA
Copepods
p. 177

CLASS MALACOSTRACA
Crabs, shrimps, pill bugs
p. 179

CLASS CIRRIPEDIA
Barnacles
p. 170

CLASS OSTRACODA
Ostracods
p. 178

PHYLUM BRACHIOPODA
Brachiopods
p. 319

PHYLUM BRYOZOA
Bryozoans
p. 321

PHYLUM PHORONIDA
Phoronid worms
p. 320

PHYLUM ENTOPROCTA
Entoprocts
p. 327

PHYLUM CHAETOGN
Arrow wor
p. 328

PHYLUM MOLLUSCA
Molluscs

CLASS APLACOPHORA
Solenogasters
p. 219

CLASS GASTROPODA
Gastropods
p. 227

CLASS SCAPHOPODA
Scaphopods
p. 310

CLASS POLYPLACOPHORA
Chitons
p. 220

CLASS BIVALVIA
Bivalves
p. 283

CLASS CEPHALOPODA
Cephalopods
p. 311

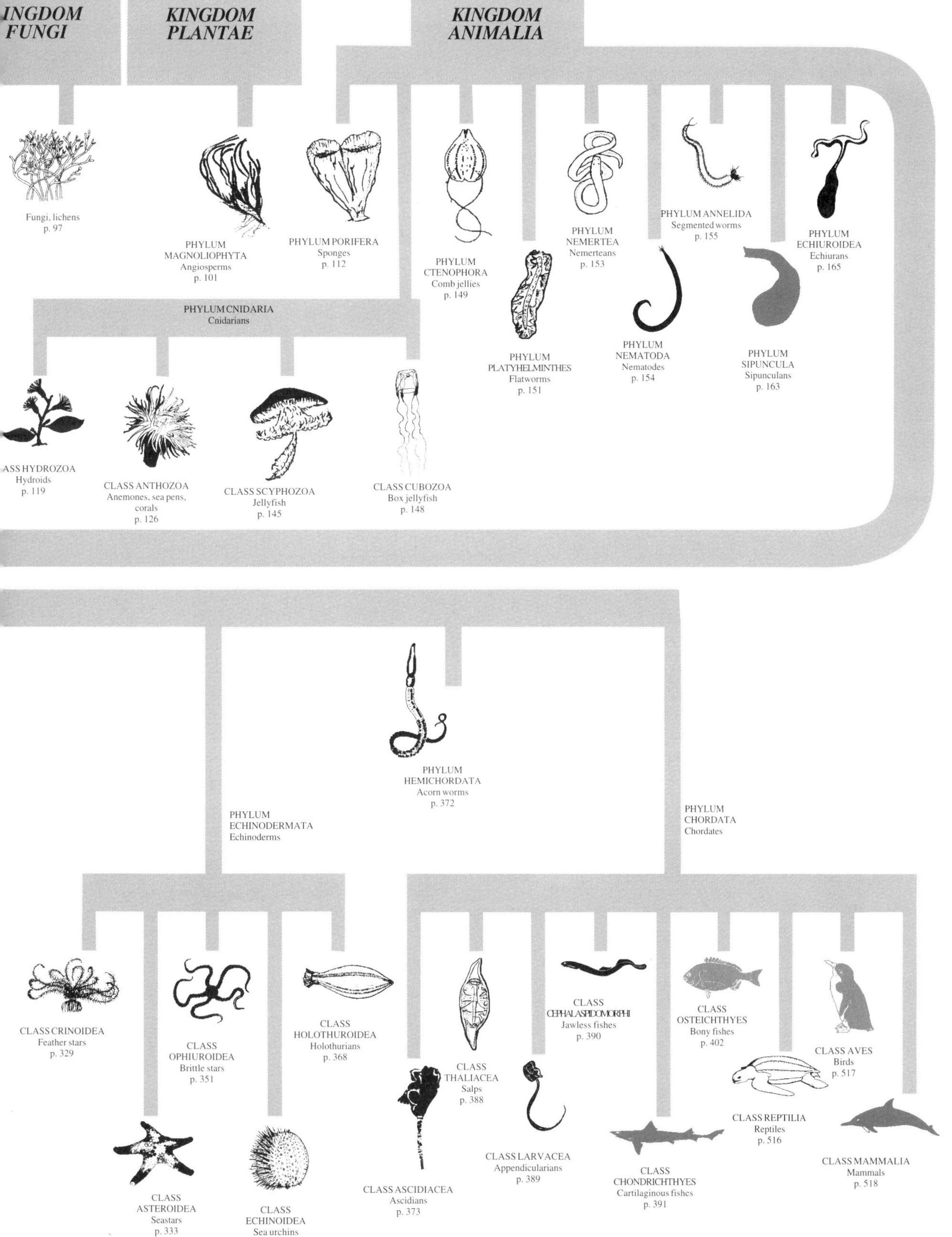

INGDOM FUNGI
KINGDOM PLANTAE
KINGDOM ANIMALIA
Fungi, lichens p. 97
PHYLUM MAGNOLIOPHYTA Angiosperms p. 101
PHYLUM PORIFERA Sponges p. 112
PHYLUM CTENOPHORA Comb jellies p. 149
PHYLUM PLATYHELMINTHES Flatworms p. 151
PHYLUM NEMERTEA Nemerteans p. 153
PHYLUM NEMATODA Nematodes p. 154
PHYLUM ANNELIDA Segmented worms p. 155
PHYLUM SIPUNCULA Sipunculans p. 163
PHYLUM ECHIUROIDEA Echiurans p. 165
PHYLUM CNIDARIA Cnidarians
ASS HYDROZOA Hydroids p. 119
CLASS ANTHOZOA Anemones, sea pens, corals p. 126
CLASS SCYPHOZOA Jellyfish p. 145
CLASS CUBOZOA Box jellyfish p. 148
PHYLUM HEMICHORDATA Acorn worms p. 372
PHYLUM ECHINODERMATA Echinoderms
PHYLUM CHORDATA Chordates
CLASS CRINOIDEA Feather stars p. 329
CLASS ASTEROIDEA Seastars p. 333
CLASS OPHIUROIDEA Brittle stars p. 351
CLASS ECHINOIDEA Sea urchins p. 358
CLASS HOLOTHUROIDEA Holothurians p. 368
CLASS ASCIDIACEA Ascidians p. 373
CLASS THALIACEA Salps p. 388
CLASS LARVACEA Appendicularians p. 389
CLASS CEPHALASPIDOMORPHI Jawless fishes p. 390
CLASS CHONDRICHTHYES Cartilaginous fishes p. 391
CLASS OSTEICHTHYES Bony fishes p. 402
CLASS REPTILIA Reptiles p. 516
CLASS AVES Birds p. 517
CLASS MAMMALIA Mammals p. 518

For seaweeds, fishes and a few other groups, species distributions are accurately known, and it is unlikely that the reader will locate organisms outside their listed range. Very little is known about the distribution of many species, however, and so species in groups such as sponges and bryozoans will have conservative ranges and may occur well outside the listed areas. If no mention of Tasmania is made under 'Distribution' then the species has not been recorded there.

Abundance

A formal abundance ranking for each species is not used in the book because of the difficulty in distinguishing between species that are locally abundant at one or two sites but don't occur elsewhere and species that are found as isolated specimens at numerous sites over a large geographic range. Some indication of the rarity or otherwise of the different species is usually included in the text, but these comments are quite subjective.

KINGDOM MONERA

Prokaryotes, bacteria, cyanobacteria, rickettsia

The monerans or prokaryotes are minute organisms that usually occur as single cells but occasionally aggregate into colonies. They are characterised by the unique chemical composition and construction of cell walls, by the lack of small membrane-enclosed structures (the organelles) within the cells, and by having smaller and less complex genetic material than eukaryotic organisms (i.e. plants, animals, protozoans and fungi). The cells are generally smaller than eukaryotic cells, most of them being 1–5 μm in diameter compared with 10–100 μm for the higher organisms. At present there is no consensus on how to divide monerans into different phyla; the terms bacteria and cyanobacteria are commonly used to distinguish monerans that gain energy from chemicals in their surrounding environment (chemotrophs) from those that utilise the energy of sunlight (phototrophs).

flagellum

cell wall

Bacteria (2 µm)
Pseudomonas sp.
Kingdom Monera

BACTERIA

Bacteria are the most abundant, widespread and smallest-sized group of living organisms on earth (given that viruses are usually considered to be chemical rather than biological structures). Although the negative features of a few species are well known, they are also the most important group and have an overwhelmingly positive role in ecosystems. All plants and animals require bacteria for their survival, yet bacteria would continue to thrive without the higher organisms, as they did for thousands of millions of years before plants and animals evolved. One indispensable feature of bacteria is their ability to break down dead animal and plant material into simple molecules. Another is the ability of the 'nitrogen-fixing bacteria' to convert atmospheric nitrogen into ammonia. Without these processes, which regenerate chemical compounds, plants would quickly run out of nutrients, and without plant food all animals would also disappear.

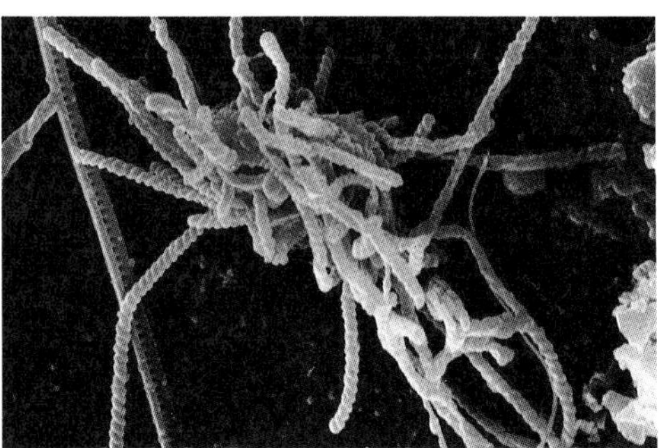

Colony of spiral bacterial cells (cell width 0.5 µm).
A. Rees/CSIRO Division of Fisheries

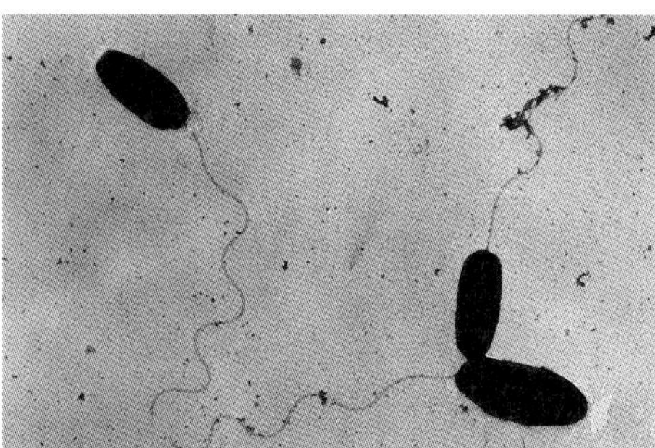

Bacteria (*Pseudomonas* sp.) extracted from gut of crab, Taroona, Tas.

Bacteria and other monerans do not reproduce sexually, although the transfer of genetic material between cells can occur by the uptake of genes from the environment, by direct transfer on contact between cells, and by viral transfer. Reproduction occurs asexually by a process known as binary fission, in which the cells divide. Bacterial cells generally divide every 1–4 hours when environmental conditions are favourable, enabling a colony to increase 100-fold or even 1000-fold within a day. These high reproduction rates obviously cannot be sustained indefinitely; after a short time cell division usually ceases because the bacteria have exhausted some nutrient or generated toxic levels of metabolic waste.

Bacteria found in the marine environment are generally restricted to that habitat, as seawater has strong bactericidal properties and kills most terrestrial and freshwater bacteria within a few hours. The majority of bacteria that scientists have isolated from seawater and marine sediments are rod-shaped organisms with complex (gram-negative) cell walls. Although there are relatively few marine bacterial species, there are a great variety of strains, and they exhibit a much greater variety of metabolic processes than eukaryotic organisms. They occur in huge abundance wherever life can survive, including a number of extreme habitats such as in near-boiling water beside volcanic fissures. Bacteria occur suspended in seawater, attached to rock surfaces, buried in sediments and in the tissues of other organisms. A small handful of mud, for example, may contain more than one thousand billion bacteria. Most bacteria are decomposers, breaking down dead organic matter. Some forms do not need organic material; they oxidise inorganic substances such as ammonia and hydrogen sulphide to produce energy. A few bacteria form symbiotic relationships with higher organisms, including specialised bacteria that live in the guts of some herbivorous fishes, extracting energy from cellulose and breaking it into smaller molecules that can be utilised by the host.

CYANOBACTERIA

Blue-green bacteria, blue-green algae

Cyanobacteria are bacteria that produce oxygen from water using the process of photosynthesis. Like other groups of bacteria, their DNA is not structured into chromosomes enclosed in a nucleus; rather, it is present as fine threads embedded in the central region of the cell. Also, chlorophyll and other photosynthetic pigments are not confined within small organelles known as chloroplasts but are scattered through the outer cytoplasm. The cells are generally small compared with those of plants, although some filaments may be up to 1 mm long. For the past two decades botanists have been arguing with bacteriologists about how the cyanobacteria should be classified; botanists claim that cyanobacteria should be treated with algae because they possess chlorophyll and often form large

Stromatolites, Hamelin Pool, WA

Stromatolites, Hamelin Pool, WA

algae-like structures, whereas bacteriologists claim them as bacteria because of the prokaryotic cell structure. Consensus has swung towards the group being known as cyanobacteria rather than the older cyanophyta, indicating that the bacteriologists' view has prevailed.

Most marine cyanobacteria are attached to the seabed. However, some are planktonic, including species in the genus *Trochodesmium*, which bloom in oceanic water and were responsible for the naming of the Red Sea and the Yellow Sea. On southern Australian shores, cyanobacteria occur commonly as mats or as globular structures but are rarely a dominant feature. The most noticeable species belong to the genus *Rivularia* and produce shiny green gelatinous colonies, which are easily mistaken for green algae. Conspicuous among these is *Rivularia firma*, a species with firm hemispherical colonies up to 20 mm in diameter, which occurs densely scattered across exposed rock platforms. Another common species, *Rivularia atra*, is found in very sheltered conditions and has soft, hollow colonies.

The most impressive cyanobacterial mats known worldwide are those found along the eastern shore of Shark Bay, WA, a location outside the main area covered by this book but with strong temperate influences. At this location, where few grazing animals are present, the cyanobacteria produce a sticky mucous that traps sediment. The trapped sand particles are later bonded using calcium carbonate extracted from seawater, to produce the rounded structures known as stromatolites. The Shark Bay stromatolites fall into three different types, with each type generated by a different community of cyanobacteria. The slowest-growing stromatolites are produced in the upper intertidal zone, primarily by spherical cyanobacteria in the genus *Entophysalis*; these structures are relatively small and coarsely textured. Near low-tide level the stromatolites are layered and have a smooth outer surface; they are produced by a community of cyanobacteria, with the filamentous genus *Schizothrix* dominant. The stromatolites below low-tide level are up to 1 m high, weakly layered and are produced by a microbial community dominated by the genera *Microcoleus* and *Phormidium*, but which also contains diatoms. Growth rates of all types of stromatolites are extremely slow, none of them growing faster than 1 mm per year.

Rivularia ?firma, Coles Bay, Tas.

Rivularia atra, Port Augusta, SA

Stromatolites with a similar shape to those at Shark Bay are known as 3500-million-year-old fossils, indicating that cyanobacteria are among the earliest forms of life. By comparison, the earliest seaweed fossils are about 1000 million years old, and the earliest seagrasses only about 100 million years old. Because gaseous oxygen is released when water molecules are split during photosynthesis, the evolution of the first cyanobacteria marked a watershed in the earth's history. Prior to that time, negligible quantities of oxygen were present in the atmosphere, and the evolution of cyanobacteria was thus a necessary precursor to the evolution of animals.

KINGDOM PROTISTA
Protists

The kingdom Protista contains a mixed collection of single-celled organisms that display a bewildering variety of life cycles and appearances. Traditionally protists have been divided into animal-like organisms known as protozoans, which ingest complex molecules for food (the heterotrophic protists), and plant-like organisms known as algae, which utilise the energy of light (the autotrophic protists). This division breaks down with groups such as the dinoflagellates, which contain equal numbers of plant- and animal-like species, as well as mixotrophic species, which combine both processes. In some classifications, including that used here, the protist kingdom also includes the green, brown and red seaweeds, which have a greater structural affinity with single-celled algae than with the mosses and higher plants. Algae, unlike higher plants, are not differentiated into roots, stems and leaves, and have not developed complex multicellular sex organs.

PHYLUM RHIZOPODA
Amoebas

The amoebas and related species of rhizopod are the simplest of the protists. They have a single-celled body, which lacks flagella and is variable in shape. Amoebas move by forming a bulge known as a pseudopodium ('false foot') in the flexible cell wall in the direction of travel. They then flow the cell contents into this extension and expand it, in the same way that a drip slips down a window. To facilitate this movement, amoebas have an internal microskeleton consisting of very fine filaments and microtubules. Reproduction occurs by cell division rather than sexual means. Most marine rhizopods live freely among sand grains and on reef surfaces, but a few live internally in the guts of vertebrates and invertebrates. They all feed by engulfing food particles between extended pseudopodia.

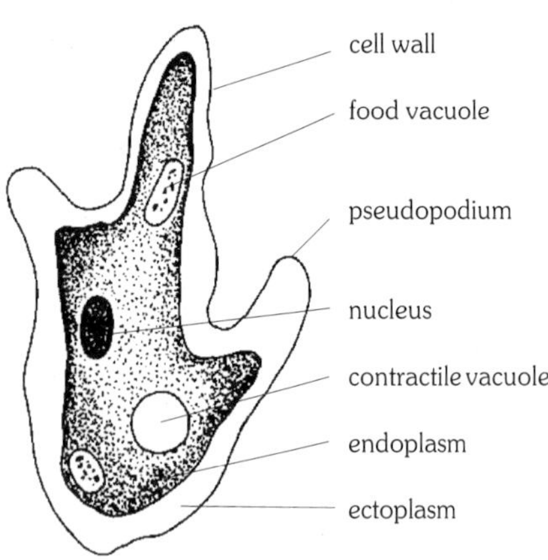

Amoeba (20 µm)
Amoeba sp.
Phylum Rhizopoda

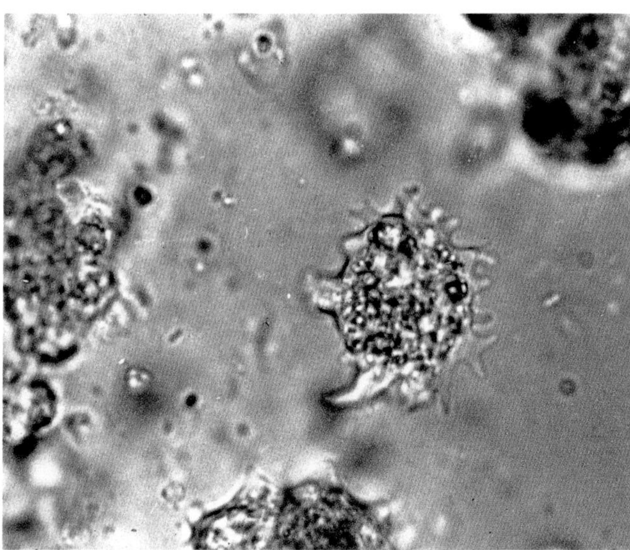

Paramoeba sp. (cell length 30 µm). B. Munday, C. Foster, F. Roubal & R. Lester

PHYLUM ACTINOPODA

Radiolarians, heliozoans, acantharians

The Actinopoda are divided into four classes: Heliozoea, Acantharea, Polycystinea and Phaeodarea, with the latter two classes grouped together and commonly called radiolarians. In all four groups, slender elongations reinforced by supporting rods (the pseudopodia), radiate out from the cell wall. Any microorganisms that come in contact with these pseudopodia become stuck in an adhesive surface secretion. The trapped prey are then engulfed within the cytoplasm and transported to the central

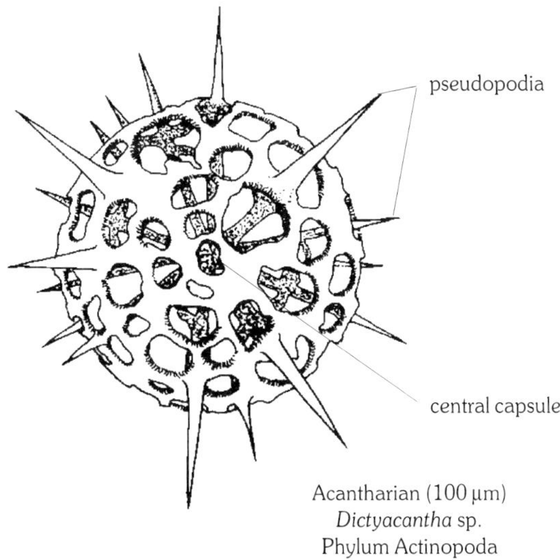

Acantharian (100 μm)
Dictyacantha sp.
Phylum Actinopoda

region of the cell for digestion. Many actinopods (and several other protist groups, including foraminiferans) can also receive nutrition from symbiotic photosynthetic dinoflagellates that are present within the cell.

The pseudopodia of heliozoans are slender, numerous and arranged regularly around the cell. A few heliozoans occur in estuaries and sheltered embayments, but most live in fresh water. Acantharians all drift in the open sea and have radial spines that pass through the centre of the cell and which are constructed from the chemical strontium sulphate. Radiolarians generally have shorter and fewer pseudopodia but are characterised primarily by their distinct outer cell layer, the ectoplasm, which is separated by a membrane from the inner endoplasm layer. They also have intricate shell-like skeletons, which are principally constructed from silica. This glassy skeletal material is relatively inert to chemical attack and dissolves very slowly in deep water, resulting in the shells of polycistinean radiolarians accumulating in large quantities on some seabeds. Such deposits can become fossilised and transform into the siliceous rocks known as cherts. Although radiolarian deposits may extend to several hundred metres depth in the deep sea, radiolarians are comparatively rare in southern Australian waters, and few radiolarian deposits are known in the area. Radiolarian production is highly dependent on silica being upwelled from the seabed to the ocean surface, but Australian waters lack major upwellings and are silica-deficient.

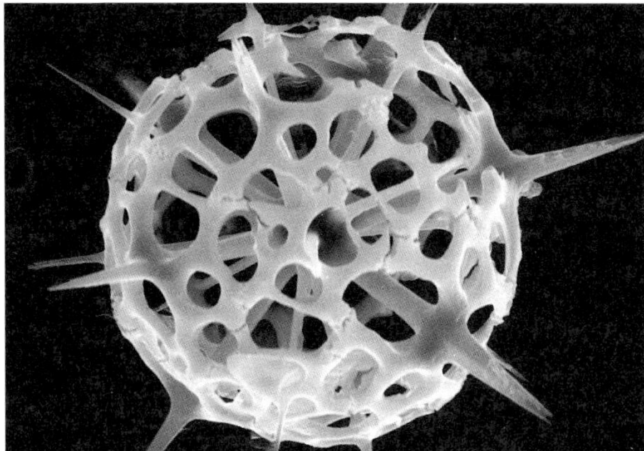

Dictyacantha sp. (acantharian actinopod, cell diameter 100 μm). GUSTAAF HALLEGRAEFF

PHYLUM FORAMINIFERA

Forams

Forams are a diverse, exclusively marine group of protozoans which, apart from a few planktonic species, are found attached to the seabed or plants. They are among the largest of the single-celled protists and normally possess a lobed skeleton (the 'test'), making them easy to identify as a group. The largest species grow to 20 mm and are rounded, reef-dwelling forms belonging to the mainly tropical genus *Marginopora*. The test of forams is constructed from organic material and calcium carbonate and has many perforations through which fine pseudopodia extend, to form a surrounding net-like structure. Small organisms that bump into

Marginopora sp., Recherche Archipelago, WA. CLAY BRYCE

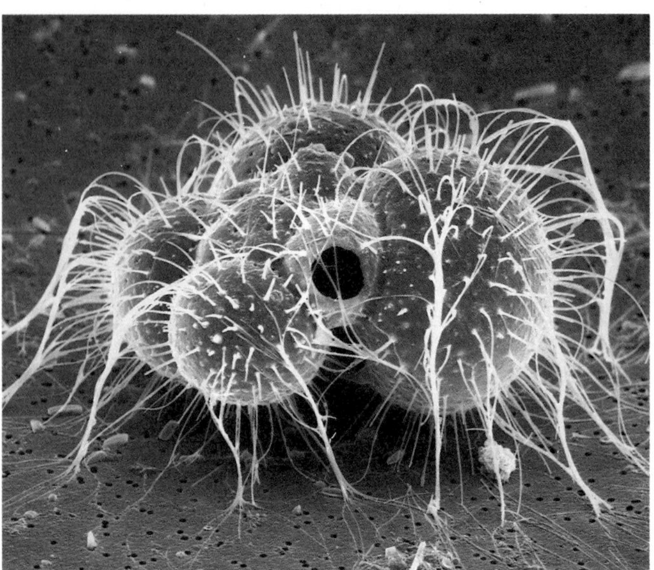
Globigerina bulloides (cell length 150 µm). A. Rees/CSIRO Division of Fisheries

this net become entangled and are eventually digested by secretions from the pseudopodia. The pseudopodia are also used for mobility, as they allow the cell to glide slowly over surfaces. Forams initially have an amoeboid appearance but quickly develop a small test. Rather than extending the test from the edge, as with the shells of molluscs, forams grow by adding a larger chamber to the previous ones, producing the distinctive appearance.

Although few foraminiferan species are planktonic, the genus *Globigerina* occurs in huge densities in the open ocean. A constant rain of tests onto the seabed produces characteristic sediments known as the *Globigerina* ooze, which covers much of the deep sea floor. Over geological time scales these deposits transform into chalk. The particular combination of foram species on the seabed is of great interest to geologists, as oil-bearing rocks often underlie such deposits.

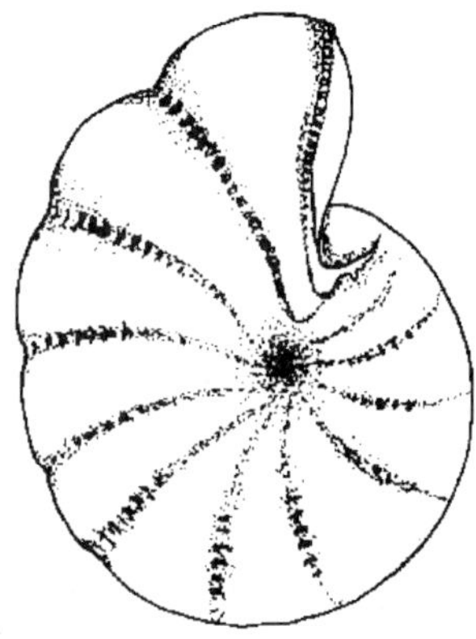
Foraminiferan (500 µm)
Cribrononion oceanicus
Phylum Foraminifera

PHYLUM CILIOPHORA

Ciliates

Ciliates are single-celled protists that are characterised by the presence of one large and at least one small nucleus within the cell. The complexity of ciliates, both in behaviour and in physical appearance, is such that they are probably better considered as organisms lacking cells rather than as akin to the individual cells of multicellular organisms. They lack a hard skeleton, have distinctive forms of asexual and sexual reproduction, and possess numerous short flagella-like structures known as cilia, which beat synchronously and give the phylum its name. Cilia are used for collecting food particles and for locomotion, with some species having the surface covered by cilia and others having them concentrated in tufts or rows. A few species have cilia bonded together into leg-like structures. Embedded within the cell is an elaborate system of fibrils and granules, which are used for coordinating the cilia. The arrangement of this system rather than the cilia themselves is the most important character used when identifying species.

Sexual reproduction in ciliates is an extremely complex procedure known as conjugation. It involves the division and disintegration of many of the smaller nuclei, the swapping of small nuclei between conjoined cells, and the replacement of the large nucleus with a replicated small nucleus that is formed when small nuclei from the two conjoined cells fuse.

Ciliates are prevalent almost everywhere that water is present, including terrestrial and fresh water as well as marine environments, and may be free-living, symbiotic or parasitic. Many symbiotic species live in the guts of larger animals and transform material that is indigestible to the host into food. Ciliates also provide an important link in planktonic food chains, as they feed on bacteria and the smaller phytoplankton species and transfer these small particles into a larger form that can be ingested by invertebrates. Species living among sand grains also provide an important food source for invertebrate animals and include some of the largest ciliates (to 5 mm in length).

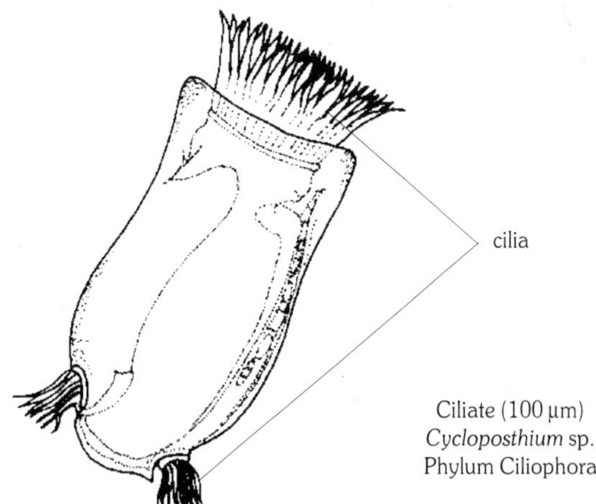

Ciliate (100 µm)
Cycloposthium sp.
Phylum Ciliophora

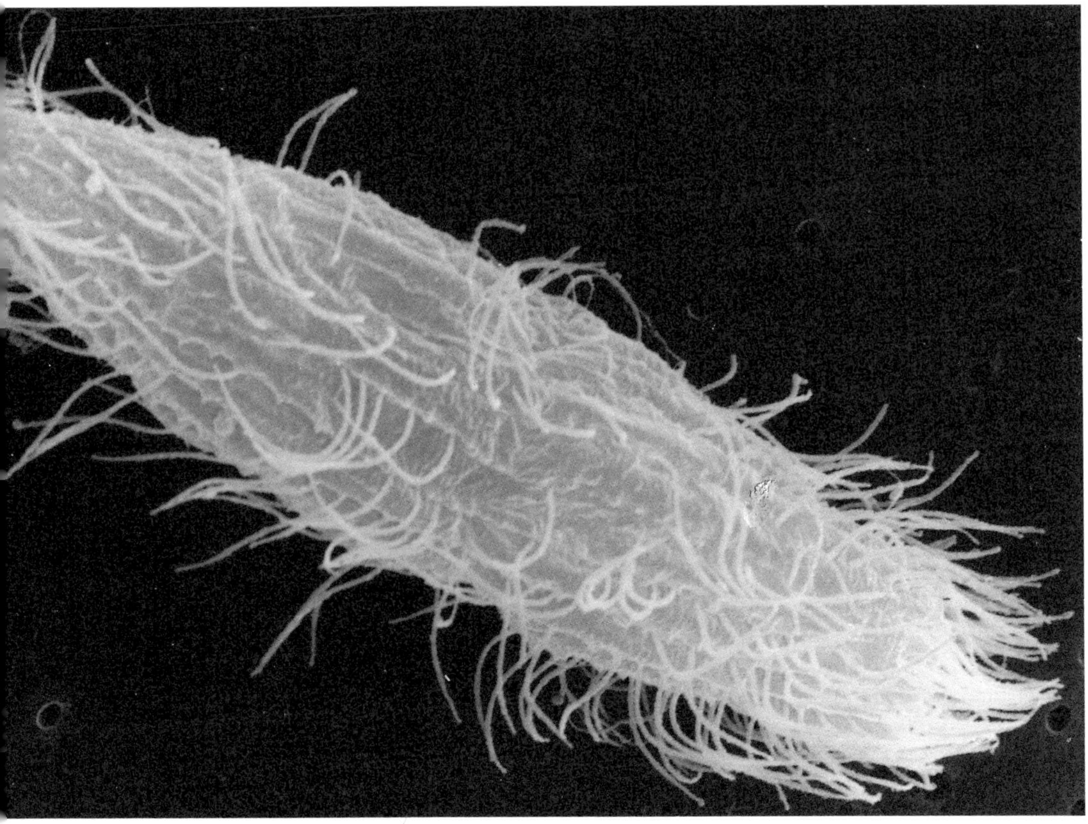

Unidentified ciliate (cell length 80 µm). GUSTAAF HALLEGRAEFF

PHYLUM (DIVISION) CRYPTOPHYTA

Cryptomonads

Cryptomonads are very small (5–20 µm in length), ovoid one-celled algae, which move by flexing paired flagella attached into a furrow at one end of the cell. Most species are planktonic, although a few species are associated with surfaces and some form symbiotic associations with ciliates. Until recently cryptomonads were thought to be relatively rare and unimportant members of the plankton, but their apparent rarity is now thought to be an artefact produced by poor phytoplankton sampling techniques; normal preservative methods cause the cells to burst and be lost from the sample. The production of fish in the sea seems to be highly dependent on how much energy is cycled through food chains involving cryptomonads and dinoflagellates, and how much goes through the diatoms.

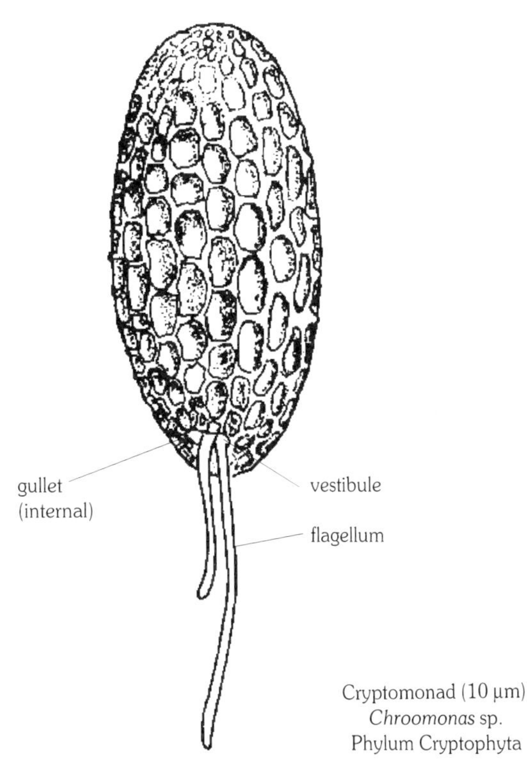

Cryptomonad (10 µm)
Chroomonas sp.
Phylum Cryptophyta

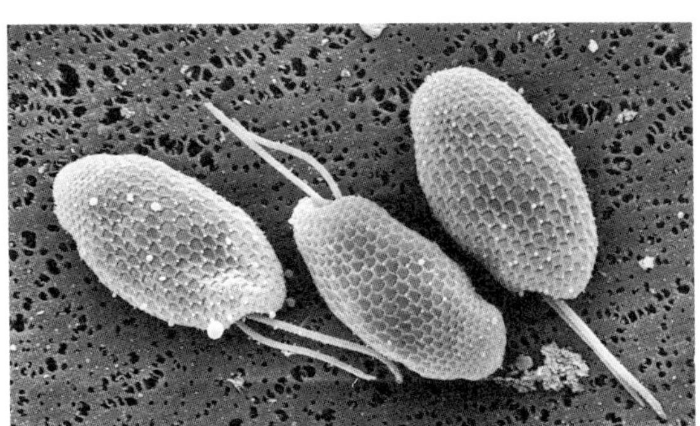

Chroomonas sp. (cryptomonad, cell length 10 µm).
A. REES/CSIRO DIVISION OF FISHERIES

PHYLUM (DIVISION) PRYMNESIOPHYTA

Coccolithophores, prymnesiophytes

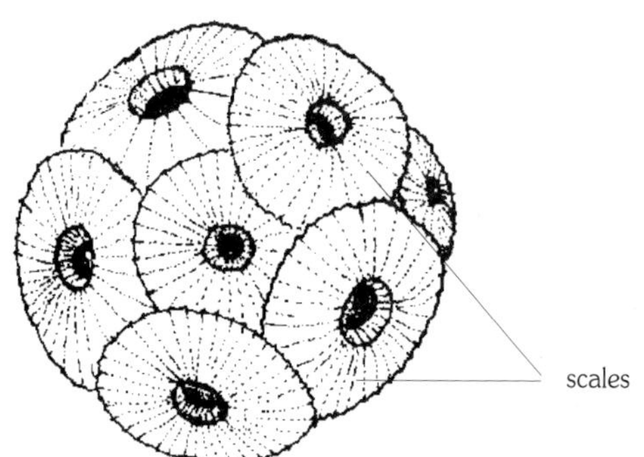

Coccolithophore (10 µm)
Phylum Prymnesiophyta

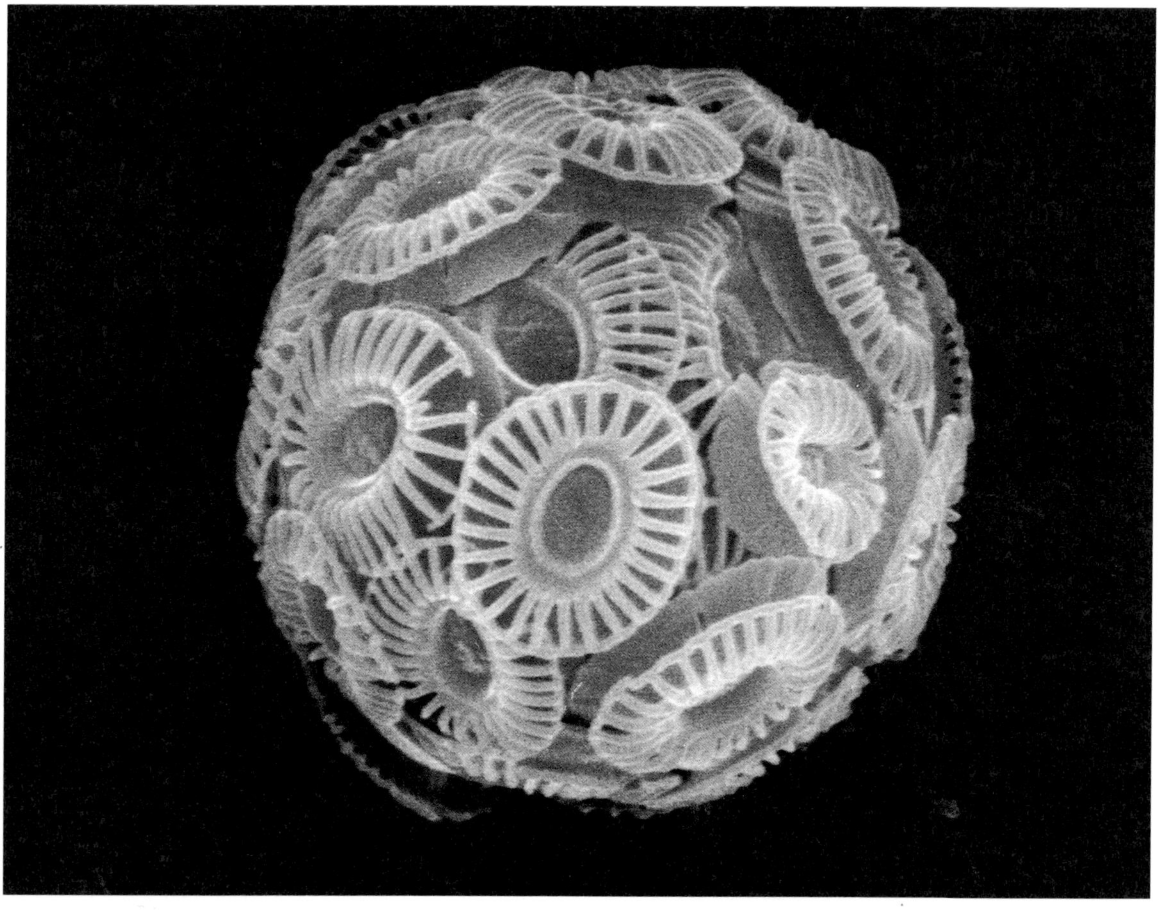

Prymnesiophytes are single-celled algae that differ from cryptophytes largely because they carry a different array of photosynthetic pigments (including fucoxanthin and diadinoxanthin). Most are planktonic marine species with two flagella and an additional thread-like structure, the haptonema. The best known group, coccolithophores, have spherical cells surrounded by an array of delicate calcite scales and are among the most beautiful of unicellular organisms. Like the forams, radiolarians and diatoms, they leave a near-permanent record of their presence in the sediment and, for example, are largely responsible for the chalk beds that form the White Cliffs of Dover. The layered record of coccolithophore scales in marine sediments is also exploited by petroleum specialists to provide clues to the location of oil-bearing strata. The great majority of coccolithophorids are tropical species, but a few are common in temperate Australian waters, including *Emiliania huxleyi*, the species with the widest geographic and temperature range. The non-coccolithophore groups of prymnesiophytes have organic scales that lack calcification, and so these species are difficult to preserve and little known. Because of their preference for oceanic waters, prymnesiophyte species generally have wide distributions, and few (if any) species are restricted to southern Australian waters.

Emiliania huxleyi (coccolithophore, cell diameter 8 µm). A. Rees, P. Bonham/CSIRO Division of Fisheries

PHYLUM (DIVISION) CHRYSOPHYTA

Silicoflagellates, chloromonads, raphidophytes, chrysophytes

Most chrysophytes are freshwater species, with only two groups, the silicoflagellates and the raphidophytes, common in marine waters. Silicoflagellates are single-celled algae that range in size from 20 to 100 μm and have a siliceous skeleton with outward-projecting spines and a single flagellum. Raphidophytes are slightly larger (30–160 μm in length), lack a skeleton and have two flagella. Because they lack hard skeletal material and are difficult to preserve, raphidophytes were considered rare until recently. They are now known to have caused several blooms in inshore coastal waters, including blooms at Port Stephens, NSW, Cockburn Sound, WA, and West Lakes, SA. Silicoflagellates are an important part of the offshore plankton community and reach highest concentrations in subantarctic and antarctic waters. They can seasonally account for up to 10 per cent of the total numbers of phytoplankton in the East Australian Current.

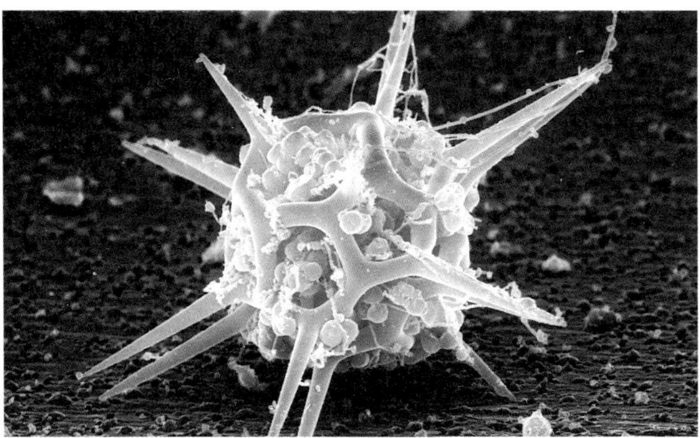

Distephanus sp. (silicoflagellate, cell diameter including spines 60 µm). A. Rees/CSIRO Division of Fisheries

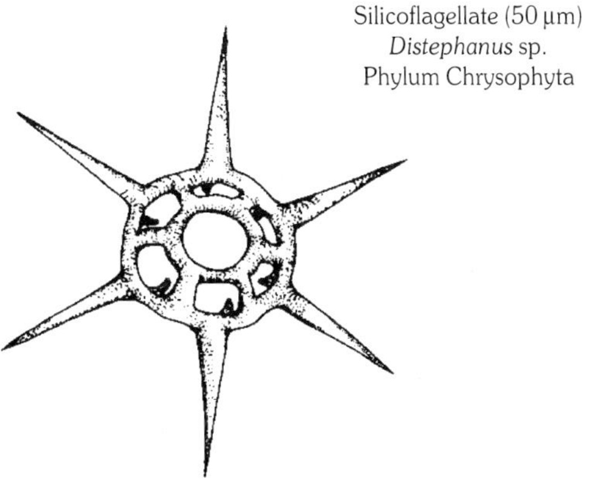

Silicoflagellate (50 µm)
Distephanus sp.
Phylum Chrysophyta

PHYLUM (DIVISION) BACILLIARIOPHYTA

Diatoms

Diatoms are extremely abundant single-celled algae that occur in plankton and attached to surfaces in marine and freshwater environments. Most range in size from 2 to 200 μm, with the larger species up to 4 mm long. These were among the first of all microscopic organisms to be recognised. In Victorian times there was a fad for amateur naturalists to devote leisure hours to investigating and describing diatoms, with the result that about 10 000 species have now been named, including many described by several authors. The most characteristic feature of diatoms is an outer shell constructed from two siliceous valves that fit together with overlapping sides like the halves of a chocolate box. Sometimes these boxes divide and redivide, forming long chains. Diatoms are classified on the basis of valve structure into round forms (the centric diatoms) and forms symmetric about a central line (the pennate diatoms), the latter including boat shapes, triangles, squares and polygons.

Diatoms generally prefer planktonic environments with a greater degree of wave turbulence and mixing than the other phytoplankton groups. They are

Thalassiosira sp. (diatom, cell diameter 60 µm). C. Bolch/CSIRO Division of Fisheries

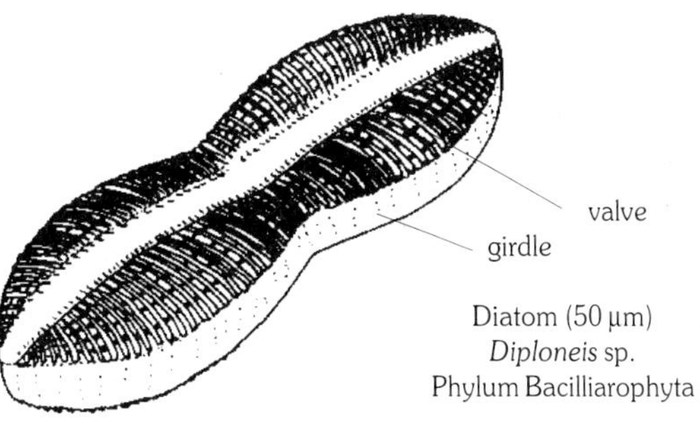

Diatom (50 µm)
Diploneis sp.
Phylum Bacilliarophyta

present in virtually all samples of water and form the most important base of the food chain leading to pelagic fishes and mammals. The shells dissolve extremely slowly after the death of the cell, resulting in a layered history of past environments being continuously built up on the seabed.

PHYLUM (DIVISION) DINOPHYTA

Dinoflagellates

Dinoflagellates characteristically have two flagella, one that encircles the cell in a groove and another that projects from the end of the cell. The spinning of the cell caused by beating of the side flagellum gives the group its name (the Greek *dinos* meaning 'whirling'). While dinoflagellates are grouped with plants, the plant label is used for convenience only; the number of plant-like species that use photosynthetic pigments to utilise energy from sunlight approximately equals the number of animal-like species that consume other single-celled organisms. The phylum Dinophyta also encompasses organisms with a huge range of shapes, internal structures and sizes (2–2000 μm in length). Some species are armoured with distinctive arrangements of cellulose plates, whereas others (the 'unarmoured species') lack such plates. To complicate identification, more than 60 of the approximately

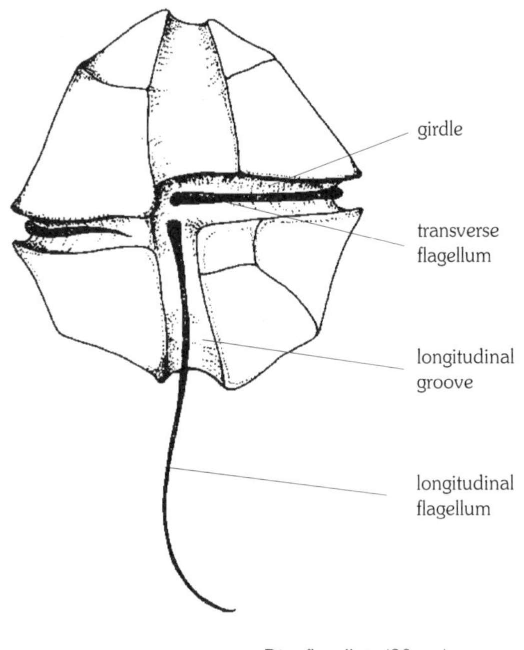

Dinoflagellate (30 µm)
Gonyaulax sp.
Phylum Dinophyta

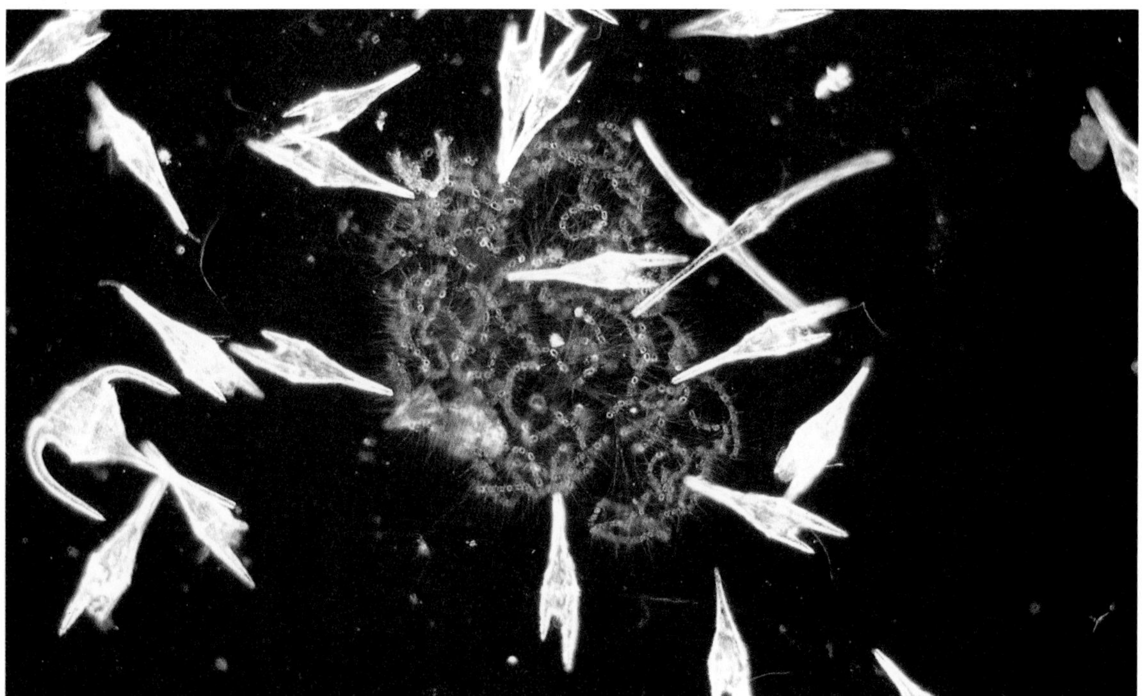

Phytoplankton—large dinoflagellates (three species of *Ceratium*; to 80 µm length) with diatoms (*Chaetoceros* sp.).
A. Rees/CSIRO Division of Fisheries

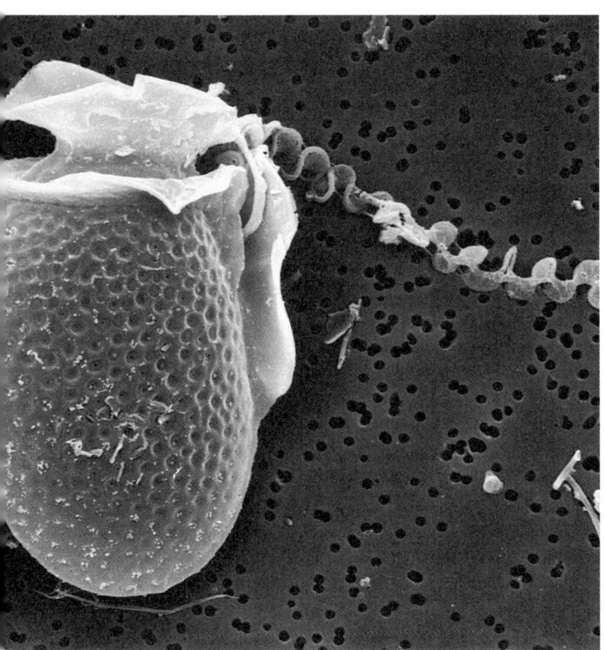

Dinophysis acuminata (dinoflagellate, cell length 35 μm).
A. Rees/CSIRO Division of Fisheries

1200 dinoflagellate species can survive unfavourable conditions for several years in an immobile encysted state, which does not resemble the mobile cell. During encystment, the outer cellulose plates dissolve, the living material becomes concentrated towards the centre of the cell, and a tough protein (known as sporopollenin) forms a cyst wall, usually with outwardly radiating projections.

Most attention on dinoflagellates has been concentrated on their negative environmental effects. Dinoflagellate species can multiply rapidly and aggregate to create blooms when conditions are favourable. Such blooms include the 'red tides' that are capable of killing fish and other marine life over large areas. These harmful effects are due to toxic products produced by the cells and to the using up of most of the available dissolved oxygen. Red tides are so named because of the high density of cells loaded with the red photosynthetic pigment ß-carotene. Toxins produced by dinoflagellates can also be concentrated in the tissues of filter-feeding invertebrates such as mussels and in the tissues of grazing fishes. This does not usually affect the consumer invertebrate but can have a potentially fatal effect on any human or vertebrate predator that eats the contaminated animal. In contrast to the toxic dinoflagellates, other species (known as zooxanthellae) are found in the tissues of animals and are critical to the nutrition of the host species. Reef-building corals, for example, have tissues full of zooxanthellae and can survive only at locations that have sufficient light for the needs of their plant associates.

PHYLUM (DIVISION) EUGLENOPHYTA

Euglenoids

Euglenoids are single-celled organisms that have characteristics of both plants and animals. Like plants, many species have chlorophyll; and like animals they lack a cellulose cell wall, are highly mobile and can utilise external organic compounds for growth. The cells of euglenoids are 15–500 μm long and are characterised by a deep fold, the gullet, at the front end. One to a few long flagella are attached through the gullet wall. An orange light-detecting granule known as the stigma is present within the cell near the gullet, and a single large nucleus is located at the centre or towards the rear of the cell.

Most of the 1000 or so species of euglenoids live in fresh water, although a few are found in soils, in the guts of animals and in the sea. Marine species are common in temperate inshore waters and may occur in high densities at sites polluted by high levels of organic waste. Euglenoids can multiply rapidly when conditions favour growth, by splitting in two down the centre in the process of binary fission; sexual reproduction is unknown in the phylum.

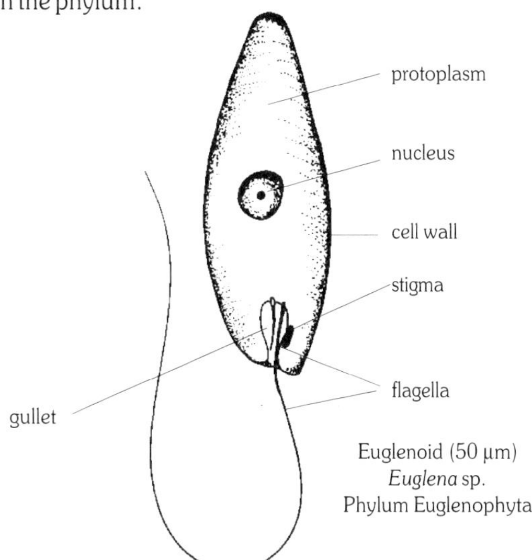

Euglenoid (50 μm)
Euglena sp.
Phylum Euglenophyta

Unidentified euglenoid (cell length 60 μm).
Gustaaf Hallegraeff

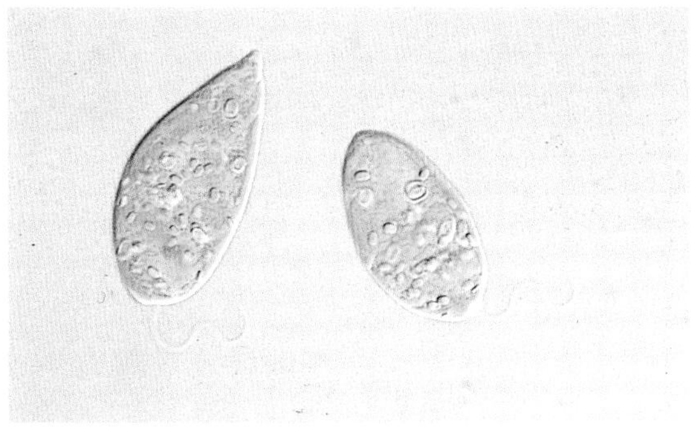

PHYLUM (DIVISION) CHLOROPHYTA

Green algae, green seaweeds

The phylum Chlorophyta includes both attached and planktonic algae, with species occurring in moist terrestrial (e.g. soils) and freshwater environments as well as in the sea. Chlorophytes are usually recognisable by colour and shape, although decaying brown and red seaweeds sometimes also take on a green appearance. Approximately 140 species of attached green algae are known from southern Australian waters, with about 60 per cent of these confined to the region.

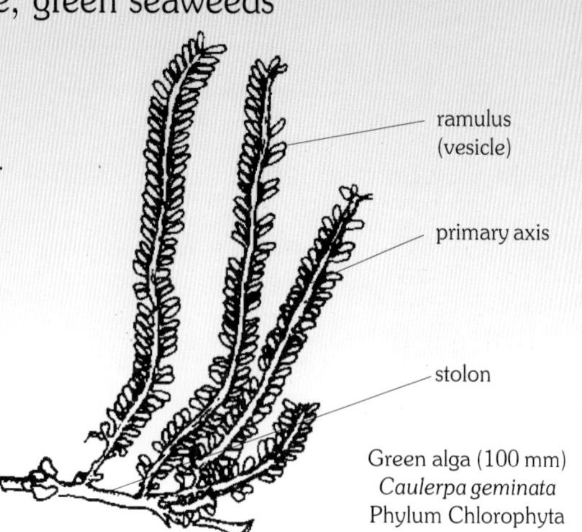

Green alga (100 mm)
Caulerpa geminata
Phylum Chlorophyta

FAMILY ULVACEAE

Included in this family are species with simple plant bodies (known as thalli) constructed in flat or tubular sheets or, less commonly, as filaments that are two cells wide. Classification of species is largely based on the size and arrangement of cells.

Ulva australis Areschoug

Sea lettuce

Habitat: Moderately and submaximally exposed reef, seagrass; 0–5 m depth.
Distribution: Whitford Beach, WA, to Terrigal, NSW, and around Tas.
Maximum size: Thallus length to 300 mm.

Ulva australis, Bicheno, Tas.

About six species of *Ulva* are present in southern Australian waters. They are all broad, two cell-layers thick, leaf-like and commonly called sea lettuce. *Ulva australis* is a common species with several wide fronds arising from a common base and with unruffled edges. It is abundant near low-tide level on moderately exposed rocky shores. Two other local species with unruffled edges are ***Ulva rigida***, a species with a different cell shape and slightly more elongate fronds (the length/width ratio is 2:3 cf. 1.5:2 for *U. australis*), and ***Ulva lactuca***, a comparatively rare species with only a single frond arising from the base.

Ulva taeniata (Setchell) Setchell & Gardner

Sea lettuce

Habitat: Reef, sand; 0–4 m depth.
Distribution: Elliston, SA, to Walkerville, Vic., and around Tas. Also New Zealand and USA.
Maximum size: Thallus length to 1.75 m.

Ulva taeniata has a simple or occasionally branched thallus with long and relatively narrow fronds. The margins are usually strongly ruffled throughout. The species is very common on intertidal rock platforms, developing very long fronds in areas where water streams across the rock. *Ulva taeniata* also develops to a large size in some sheltered bays, particularly in southern Tasmania.

Enteromorpha compressa (Linnaeus) Greville

Habitat: Reef; upper intertidal to 25 m depth.
Distribution: Around Australia.
Also widespread overseas.
Maximum size: Thallus length to 400 mm.

Approximately eight species of *Enteromorpha* occur in southern Australia. They are easily recognised as a group because of their hollow, tubular fronds, but identification of the different species is presently confused. *Enteromorpha compressa* occurs abundantly in the intertidal zone and was until recently confused with ***Enteromorpha intestinalis*** but differs from that species by being branched, usually at the base. Both species are commonly associated with the edges of freshwater soaks and can also be prevalent at polluted sites with high levels of nutrients.

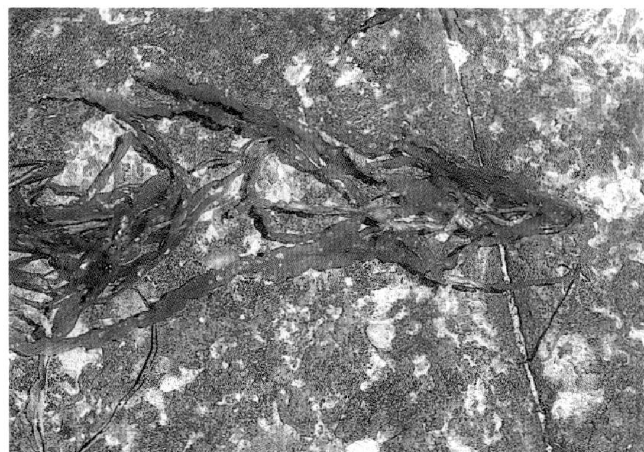

Enteromorpha compressa, Eaglehawk Neck, Tas.

Enteromorpha sp., South Cape Bay, Tas.

Ulva taeniata, Tinderbox, Tas.

FAMILY CLADOPHORACEAE

Species in the family Cladophoraceae have long thin filaments made up of chains of individual cells. In most species the cells are of approximately equal size, and when filaments are branched the branching is from the upper ends of the cells.

Chaetomorpha coliformis (Montagne) Kützing

Habitat: Seagrass, macroalgae, reef; 0–5 m depth.
Distribution: Venus Bay, SA, to Walkerville, Vic., and around Tas.
Also New Zealand and South America.
Maximum size: Thallus length to 600 mm.

Species of *Chaetomorpha* have unbranched filaments. *Chaetomorpha coliformis* is readily identified by its chains of very large, rounded cells (1–4 mm in diameter), which are generally attached to another plant. This species is one of the most abundant epiphytes in a variety of habitats from sheltered bays to wave-exposed coasts. It was known until recently as *Chaetomorpha darwinii*.

Chaetomorpha coliformis, Bicheno, Tas.

Chaetomorpha billardierii, Cloudy Lagoon, Tas.

Chaetomorpha billardierii Kützing

Habitat: Sheltered seagrass, macroalgae, sand; 0–2 m depth.
Distribution: Venus Bay, SA, to Walkerville, Vic., and around Tas. Also New Zealand and South America.
Maximum size: Thallus length to 3 m.

The filaments of *Chaetomorpha* are very long and tangled, and the species forms a loose-lying mass on other plants or the seabed. The individual cells of *C. billardierii* are small (200–400 μm in diameter, 300–1000 μm long), elongate and difficult to distinguish without a microscope. Another common species with a similar appearance, ***Chaetomorpha linum***, differs by having individual cells with length equal to width rather than length approximately twice the width.

Apjohnia laetevirens Harvey

Habitat: Moderately exposed reef; 0–16 m depth.
Distribution: Green Head, WA, to Collaroy, NSW, and northern Tas.
Maximum size: Thallus length to 250 mm.

Apjohnia laetevirens has a distinctive shape, with repeatedly divided branches originating from a single basal segment that is attached to the substrate by fine rhizoids. Each branch has a series of constricted segments in the lower parts. The species is usually found in shaded positions on the sides of overhanging rocks or in crevices.

Apjohnia laetevirens, Canal Rocks, WA

Cladophora feredayi Harvey

Habitat: Moderately exposed reef; 0–16 m depth.
Distribution: Cottesloe, WA, to Port Jackson, NSW, and around Tas. Also New Zealand and the Mediterranean.
Maximum size: Thallus length to 350 mm.

The genus *Cladophora* is a highly diverse one, with 18 species recognised from southern Australia. *Cladophora feredayi* is the species most often seen in reef habitats. It is distinguished from other species by its light green colour, erect rather than tangled form, and the cells towards the base of the plant being much longer than the upper cells (which are 50–100 μm in diameter). Other species of *Cladophora* can form tangled masses of fine filaments over seagrasses and macroalgae in areas polluted by excessive nutrient runoff, thereby smothering and sometimes killing the host plants.

Cladophora feredayi, Bicheno, Tas.

FAMILY ANADYOMENACEAE

This relatively small family is characterised by fronds that are formed from numerous cross-linked segments. The individual cells have more than one nucleus and divide by the formation of an inward-projecting wall.

Struvea plumosa Sonder

Habitat: Moderately exposed reef, sand; 0–35 m depth.
Distribution: Dongara, WA, to Victor Harbor, SA.
Maximum size: Thallus length to 200 mm.

Struvea plumosa is a remarkable-looking plant, the upper part having an oval shape and lace-like appearance. Although the basal structures are similar to *Apjohnia laetevirens*, this species is unlikely to be confused with any other. It occurs most abundantly in deep sheltered bays along the open coast.

Struvea plumosa, Little I, WA

FAMILY VALONIACEAE

Plants in this family lack a central axis and have a thallus formed from the aggregation of large cells, with rows of smaller cells often located between.

Dictyosphaeria sericea Harvey

Habitat: Exposed reef; 0–23 m depth.
Distribution: Rottnest I, WA, to Walkerville, Vic., and northern Tas.
Maximum size:Thallus width to 100 mm.

Dictyosphaeria sericea is the only species in the family found in southern Australia. It is a firm plant with an irregular, lobed appearance and is usually strongly attached to the reef surface by rhizoids. The species is common in shaded situations on the underside of rock overhangs.

Dictyosphaeria sericea, Port Victoria, SA

FAMILY CODIACEAE

Species of Codiaceae have a thallus with a core of fine entwined filaments and an outer layer made up of thousands of cylindrical tubular structures, known as utricles, wedged against each other. Sixteen species in the only genus in the family, *Codium,* are known from southern Australia, with half of these species having a flat or rounded appearance and the other half branched in a repeatedly forked pattern. Identification of species of *Codium* relies largely on the shape and size of the utricles, as well as the general plant shape and coloration.

Codium ?megalophysum Silva

Habitat: Moderately exposed reef; 7 m depth.
Distribution: Busselton, WA. Also South Africa.
Maximum size: Thallus diameter to 50 mm.

The sausage-shaped utricles are particularly large (2 mm in diameter) and easily seen with the naked eye on *Codium ?megalophysum*, whereas in most other local species the utricles are small (normally < 200 μm in diameter) and require a microscope to be clearly distinguished. The only other species known from southern Australia with relatively large utricles (0.4–1.5 mm in diameter) is ***Codium mamillosum***, an uncommon species with a rounded thallus, most often found in deep water. The illustrated Western Australian specimen is probably *C. megalophysum,* an alga previously thought to be restricted to South Africa. Like *C. mamillosum,* the plant is firm when alive but quickly becomes soft and flabby when collected.

Codium ?megalophysum, Busselton, WA

Codium pomoides J. Agardh

Habitat: Exposed reef; 0–20 m depth.
Distribution: Esperance, WA, to Walkerville, Vic., and around Tas.
Maximum size: Thallus diameter to 120 mm.

Codium pomoides has a firm, semi-spherical appearance and is commonly known as the sea apple. It differs from the other spherical species of *Codium, C. mamillosum and C. ?megalophysum*, by possessing much smaller utricles (70–180 μm in diameter). The species occurs commonly on sloping reefs with considerable wave action and is most abundant in Tasmania.

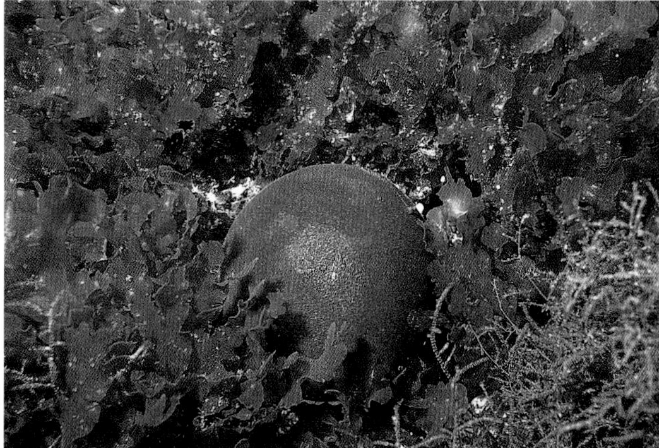

Codium pomoides (with *Jeannerettia lobata*), Ninepin Point, Tas.

Codium dimorphum Svedelius

Habitat: Exposed reef, 0–10 m depth.
Distribution: Eastern Tas.
Also New Zealand and Chile.
Maximum size: Thallus width to 100 mm.

Codium dimorphum, Adventure Bay, Tas.

Codium dimorphum is a firm, flat species of *Codium* with irregular outline and very small utricles (50–100 μm in diameter) that are devoid of hairs. It occurs on wave-swept reefs among stipes of the 'bull kelp' *Durvillaea potatorum* and often is the only large macroalga occurring with the encrusting coralline algal species in this habitat. Like *Durvillaea*, *C. dimorphum* is distributed around the Southern Ocean and seems to just reach Australia in eastern Tasmania.

Codium spongiosum Harvey

Habitat: Sheltered reef; 0–5 m depth.
Distribution: Albany, WA, to Merimbula, NSW. Also widespread overseas.
Maximum size: Thallus width to 500 mm.

Codium spongiosum is a light green species with a lobed appearance and numerous fine hairs covering the surface. The thallus is relatively soft, and the utricles are moderately large (400–500 μm in diameter at tip). This species occurs in slightly more sheltered habitats than the other flat *Codium* species and is sometimes present in estuaries.

Codium spongiosum, Merimbula, NSW

Codium cuneatum Setchell & Gardiner

Habitat: Sheltered reef, shells; 2–12 m depth.
Distribution: Tropical Australia south to Jervis Bay, NSW. Also widespread overseas.
Maximum size: Thallus length to 300 mm.

Codium cuneatum is a dark green species of *Codium* with characteristically flattened branches that expand in size above each fork. Branching commences at the base of the plant, with the final branches very small in comparison with previous branches.

Codium cuneatum, Jervis Bay, NSW

Codium duthieae Silva

Habitat: Moderately exposed reef; 0–25 m depth.
Distribution: Champion Bay, WA, to Walkerville, Vic., and northern Tas. Also South Africa.
Maximum size: Thallus length to 600 mm.

Codium duthieae is a light green species with forked branches. The species is distinguished from others by its long (>1 mm) utricles with thin, rounded ends and can usually be identified in the field by the colour and the branches (3–10 mm) being slightly wider than in most other *Codium* species. The branches are also distinctly flattened rather than round in cross-section near the fork, although not as flattened as in *C. cuneatum*.

Codium duthieae, Canal Rocks, WA

Codium harveyi Silva

Habitat: Moderately to submaximally exposed reef; 0–30 m depth.
Distribution: Shark Bay, WA, to Lake Macquarie, NSW, and around Tas. Also New Zealand.
Maximum size: Thallus length to 300 mm.

Codium harveyi is the medium-green species of *Codium* that is most commonly seen on temperate Australian reefs. Three other common species, ***Codium muelleri***, ***Codium galeatum*** and ***Codium australicum***, have a similar appearance and occur in the same habitat, and can therefore easily be confused with *C. harveyi*. The tips of the utricles of *Codium harveyi* are broadly rounded and sometimes slightly thickened. In comparison, those of *C. muelleri* have a central depression and those of *C. galeatum* are thickened markedly into a cap, whereas *C. australicum* is dark green rather than medium green and differs from *C. harveyi* in the position of a plug in filaments at the base of the utricle.

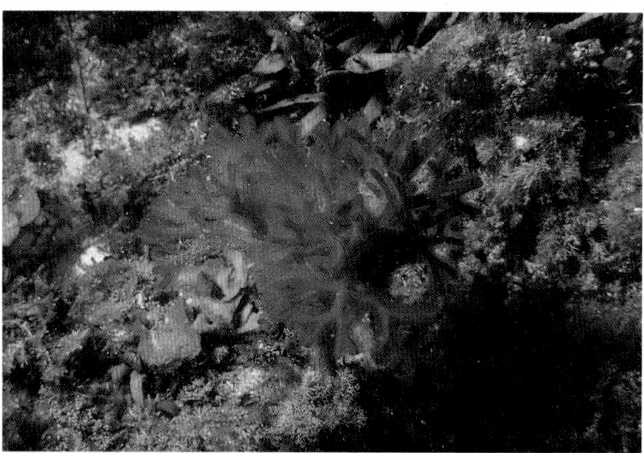

Codium harveyi, Esperance, WA

Codium fragile (Suringar) Hariot

Habitat: Sheltered and moderately exposed reef; 0–2 m depth.
Distribution: Victor Harbor, SA, to Ballina, NSW, and around Tas. Also widespread overseas.
Maximum size: Thallus length to 300 mm.

Codium fragile can generally be recognised by its dark green, forked branches and the furry appearance caused by a profuse covering of hairs. The utricles have pointed rather than rounded ends and are longer (>1 mm cf. 500–700 μm) than in the only other Australian species with pointed utricles, the Western Australian species **Codium spinescens**. *Codium fragile* can occur abundantly in shallow water and will attach and grow on hard material such as bivalve shells as well as on reef surfaces.

Codium fragile, Eaglehawk Neck, Tas.

FAMILY UDOTEACEAE

This family includes a number of genera with quite different appearances but all of them characterised by a dense aggregation of filaments to form a thallus. Many species possess semi-rigid branches due to the secretion of calcium carbonate.

Halimeda cuneata Hering

Habitat: Moderately exposed reef; 0–7 m depth.
Distribution: Tropical Australia to Recherche Archipelago, WA. Also southern Africa.
Maximum size: Thallus length to 150 mm.

Halimeda cuneata, Canal Rocks, WA

Halimeda cuneata has branches of wide, flattened calcified segments connected by flexible, uncalcified nodes. The species is most commonly found in shaded crevices, where it is attached to the rock by numerous fine threads. Although there are many tropical species of *Halimeda*, this is the only species known to reach the southern Australian coast.

Penicillus nodulosus Blainville

Habitat: Sheltered and moderately exposed sand, reef; 0–4 m depth.
Distribution: Tropical Australia south to Rottnest I, WA. Also widespread in the Indo-West Pacific region.
Maximum size: Thallus length to 150 mm.

Penicillus nodulosus is unlikely to be confused with any other algae because of its shaving-brush appearance. The population of this species seems to have declined substantially during the past century; it was formerly extremely abundant on the reef flats at Rottnest Island but has only been recorded once in that area during the past half-century. When conditions are favourable during the summer months, *P. nodulosus* is capable of rapidly colonising large areas of sand using stolons in the same way as the *Caulerpa* species.

Penicillus nodulosus, Cliff Head, WA

Penicillus nodulosus, Cliff Head, WA

FAMILY CAULERPACEAE

Species in this family grow vegetatively from a horizontal stolon and can therefore rapidly occupy large areas of substrate. They are often the dominant plants on reef and sand habitats in southern Australia, in terms of both abundance and number of species. Identification of species of *Caulerpa,* the only genus in the family, relies partly on the branching pattern and on the size and shape of the smallest branches (known as ramuli). Ramuli may be filamentous, flattened or vesiculate (bubble-shaped).

Caulerpa scalpelliformis, Smooth Pool, SA

Caulerpa scalpelliformis
(R. Brown ex Turner) C. Agardh

Habitat: Exposed reef; 0–36 m depth.
Distribution: Whitford Beach, WA, to Jervis Bay, NSW, and around Tas.
Maximum size: Thallus height to 200 mm.

Caulerpa scalpelliformis is the most flattened of the temperate Australian species and has a strongly serrated appearance because of the regular arrangement of the terminal filaments (ramuli) that arise along the sides of the erect fronds. *Caulerpa scalpelliformis* occurs on exposed reefs, most often in association with a variety of other plant species.

Caulerpa remotifolia Sonder

Habitat: Sheltered reef, sand; 0–10 m depth.
Distribution: Gulf St Vincent, SA, to Westernport, Vic., and south to Orford, Tas.
Maximum size: Thallus height to 300 mm.

Caulerpa remotifolia resembles *C. scalpelliformis* but can be distinguished by the narrower ramuli (1–1.5 mm basal diameter cf. 1.5–4 mm) that are less regularly spaced down the main axis, and by the gaps between ramuli exceeding the basal width of ramuli. *Caulerpa remotifolia* occurs on sheltered reefs, sand and stones, and is common only in Port Phillip Bay and the South Australian gulfs.

Caulerpa remotifolia, Ricketts Pt, Vic.

Caulerpa ellistoniae Womersley

Habitat: Exposed reef; 7–68 m depth.
Distribution: Rottnest I, WA, to Kangaroo I, SA.
Maximum size: Thallus height to 250 mm.

Caulerpa ellistoniae has a similar appearance to *C. scalpelliformis* but differs in that the erect axes are branched several times and the ramuli are relatively flat on their lower edge, rather than curved as in *C. scalpelliformis*. *Caulerpa ellistoniae* is a rare deep-water species known from only a few locations.

Caulerpa ellistoniae, Canal Rocks, WA

Caulerpa distichophylla Sonder

Habitat: Moderately exposed sand, reef; 0–7 m depth.
Distribution: Dongara to Albany, WA.
Maximum size: Thallus height to 150 mm.

Caulerpa distichophylla, Marmion Lagoon, WA

Caulerpa distichophylla has erect fronds with ramuli densely packed along the length. The ramuli are shorter (generally 1–2 mm long) than those of the other *Caulerpa* species with flattened ramuli. This species is most commonly found in sand patches on the edge of seagrass beds and seems to colonise wave-disturbed habitats more quickly than other seaweeds or seagrasses.

Caulerpa filiformis (Suringar) Hering

Habitat: Exposed reef; 0–6 m depth.
Distribution: Sydney to Port Stephens, NSW. Also South Africa.
Maximum size: Thallus height to 180 mm.

Caulerpa filiformis has a strap-like shape and is the dominant plant in the lower intertidal zone on many rock platforms in the Sydney area. First recorded in Australia in 1923, the species was probably introduced from South Africa and has been steadily proliferating since then. It is, however, possible that the species occurs naturally and its recent proliferation may be due to a greater tolerance to polluted conditions than other local species. Another species with a simple flattened shape, but which is easily recognised by being considerably smaller (<40 mm high) than *C. filiformis*, also occurs in NSW: ***Caulerpa brachypus*** is a tropical species, which extends to central NSW and also to Rottnest Island, WA.

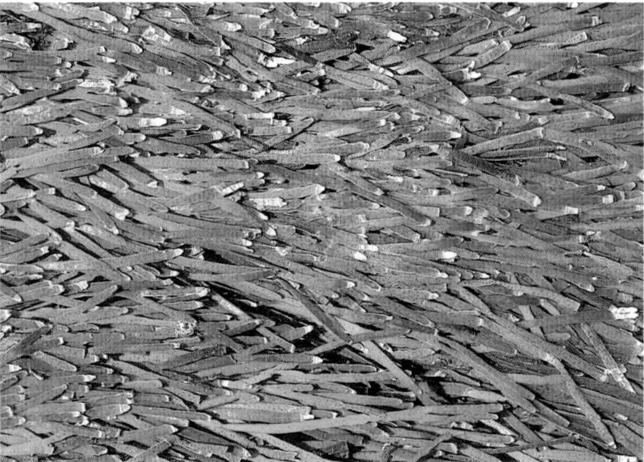

Caulerpa filiformis, Port Stephens, NSW

Caulerpa longifolia C. Agardh

Habitat: Moderately exposed reef; 0–40 m depth.
Distribution: Eucla, WA, to Wilsons Promontory, Vic., and around Tas.
Maximum size: Thallus height to 650 mm.

Caulerpa longifolia can be recognised by the long (5–15 mm), thread-like ramuli that usually occur in five rows along the sides of the erect axes. The species has a shaggy appearance and is most common on the sides of vertical reef faces in areas with good water flow.

Caulerpa longifolia, Tinderbox, Tas.

Caulerpa longifolia forma *crispata*

(Harvey) Womersley

Habitat: Moderately exposed reef; 0–35 m depth.
Distribution: Perth, WA, to Waratah Bay, Vic., and around Tas.
Maximum size: Thallus height to 300 mm.

Although this seaweed is presently classified as a form of *Caulerpa longifolia*, there is some uncertainty about its identity. The plant appears quite different from *C. longifolia* as it is lighter green in colour, has much finer ramuli that are not arranged in rows and is branched at the base. It is presently included under *C. longifolia* because specimens with intermediate characteristics have been collected in southeastern Australia.

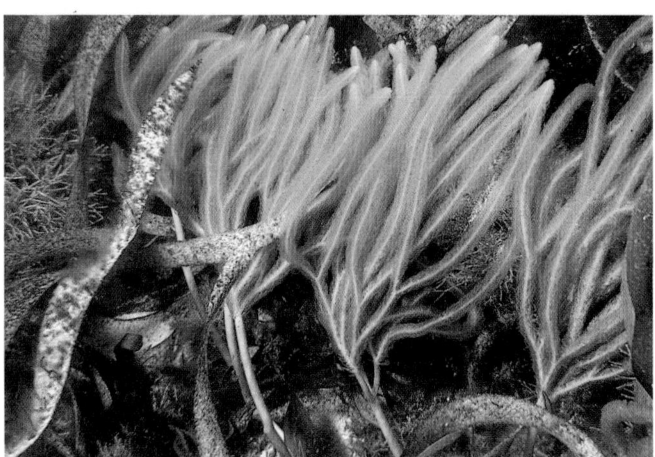

Caulerpa longifolia forma *crispata*, Canal Rocks, WA

Caulerpa trifaria Harvey

Habitat: Sheltered sand, rock; 1–31 m depth.
Distribution: Cottesloe, WA, to Western Port, Vic., and around Tas.
Maximum size: Thallus height to 250 mm.

Caulerpa trifaria has a similar general appearance to *C. longifolia* but grows in sheltered environments and has shorter ramuli (<7 mm) that generally occur in three rather than five rows along the sides of the erect axes. Occasional specimens may have only two rows of ramuli, giving the fronds a flattened appearance. A rare species, ***Caulerpa alternans***, can also be confused with *C. trifaria*, but that species is slender with the fine ramuli distributed sparsely along the axes, and the axes are much branched. *Caulerpa trifaria* is a dominant plant on sand in sheltered bays in southern Tasmania. It sometimes forms a habitat with a fish and invertebrate community similar to that of seagrass beds.

Caulerpa trifaria, Spring Beach, Tas.

Caulerpa brownii (C. Agardh) Endlicher

Habitat: Submaximally exposed reef; 0–42 m depth.
Distribution: Perth, WA, to Walkerville, Vic., and around Tas. Also New Zealand.
Maximum size: Thallus height to 400 mm.

The erect axes of *Caulerpa brownii* are densely covered by short ramuli, which are mostly forked at their bases. This species is most abundant in cooler waters where it sometimes completely covers sloping rock faces in areas with considerable wave action.

Caulerpa brownii, Bunker Bay, WA

Caulerpa obscura Sonder

Habitat: Moderately exposed reef; 0–35 m depth.
Distribution: Yanchep Beach, WA, to Walkerville, Vic., and northern Tas.
Maximum size: Thallus height to 300 mm.

Caulerpa obscura is a very dark green and has a shaggy appearance, with the erect axes resembling miniature pine trees. The erect axes possess secondary axes, to which ramuli 2–10 mm long are densely attached. Another bushy species, ***Caulerpa cliftonii***, superficially resembles *C. obscura*, but the ramuli are branched and attached directly to the main rather than secondary axes, and the basal stolon that runs along the sediment lacks spines.

Caulerpa obscura, Rocky Cape, Tas.

Caulerpa flexilis Lamouroux

Habitat: Exposed reef; 0–40 m depth.
Distribution: Geraldton, WA, to Collaroy, NSW, and around Tas. Also New Zealand.
Maximum size: Thallus height to 300 mm.

Caulerpa flexilis is the most common fern-like species of *Caulerpa* found in southern Australia. It occurs profusely in deep water along the more exposed sections of coast. The erect axes are often heavily grazed or abraded, leaving a mass of stolons on the reef surface as a sign of the plants' presence.

Caulerpa flexilis, Ile des Phoques, Tas.

Caulerpa flexilis var. *muelleri*

(Sonder) Womersley

Habitat: Moderately exposed reef; 0–15 m depth.
Distribution: Geraldton, WA, to Waratah Bay, Vic., and northern Tas.
Maximum size: Thallus height to 400 mm.

Caulerpa flexilis var. *muelleri* has a fern-like shape similar to *C. flexilis* but is brighter green, has a regular fish-bone pattern of branching off the main axis and ramuli that occur densely along these secondary branches without spaces between. Although presently classed as a variety of *Caulerpa flexilis*, it is more likely that *C. flexilis* var. *muelleri* is a distinct species because the shapes of the two plant types do not overlap and the stolons have distinctive colour and spination. The two varieties are also immediately recognisable in the field, even when growing across one another.

Caulerpa flexilis var. *muelleri*, Rocky Cape, Tas.

Caulerpa hedleyi Weber van Bosse

Habitat: Exposed rocky reef; 2–38 m depth.
Distribution: Rottnest I, WA, to Kangaroo I, SA.
Maximum size: Thallus height to 80 mm.

Caulerpa hedleyi is one of the rarer species of southern Australian algae and is largely confined to deep water. It is smaller than the other fern-like algae, with ramuli that are extremely small (200–500 μm long) and densely cover all branches.

Caulerpa hedleyi, Wreck Rock, WA

Caulerpa geminata, Spring Beach, Tas.

Caulerpa geminata Harvey

Habitat: Moderately exposed reef; 0–25 m depth.
Distribution: Dongara, WA, to Bowen, Qld, and around Tas. Also New Zealand.
Maximum size: Thallus height to 150 mm.

Caulerpa geminata is a small species with bubble-like ramuli that can occur paired or irregularly attached to axes. It can be identified by the ovoid ramuli being smaller (2–4 mm long) than those of other local species. While often inconspicuous because of its small size, this is one of the most abundant algae and can cover large areas of rock surface.

Caulerpa geminata, Canal Rocks, WA

Caulerpa hodgkinsoniae, Rocky Cape, Tas.

Caulerpa hodgkinsoniae J. Ag.

Habitat: Moderately and submaximally exposed reef; 4û30 m depth.
Distribution: Robe, SA, to Ballina, NSW, and around Tas.
Maximum size: Thallus height to 250 mm.

Caulerpa hodgkinsoniae differs from *C. geminata* primarily in having larger ramuli (4–10 mm long), which are more elongate and regularly arranged along the erect axes. Some specimens do, however, occur with intermediate characteristics and are difficult to assign to species. *C. hodgkinsoniae* is common in Tasmania and can be a dominant plant in deep water, but seems to be rare off mainland Australia.

Caulerpa cactoides (Turner) C. Agardh

Habitat: Sheltered and moderately exposed sand, mud, reef; 0–38 m depth.
Distribution: Geraldton, WA, to Richmond R, NSW, and northern Tas.
Maximum size: Thallus height to 400 mm.

Caulerpa cactoides has club-shaped ramuli which are larger (10–20 mm long) than on *C. annulata* and tend to be more constricted towards their bases. This species is often a conspicuous plant in open seagrass beds and can also form extensive meadows on sand in sheltered bays.

Caulerpa cactoides, Quarry Bay, WA

Caulerpa racemosa (Forsskål) J. Agardh

Habitat: Exposed reef; 0–4 m depth.
Distribution: Tropical Australia south to Albany, WA.
Maximum size: Thallus height to 100 mm.

Caulerpa racemosa is a pale green plant with elongate swollen ramuli, which are often twisted up the axes. It is probably the most common species of *Caulerpa* seen in the tropics but is also abundant near low-tide level on reefs in the Perth area, particularly at sites with good wave action.

Caulerpa racemosa, Watermans, WA

Caulerpa vesiculifera Harvey

Habitat: Moderately to submaximally exposed reef; 0–25 m depth.
Distribution: Shark Bay, WA, to Phillip I, Vic., and northern Tas.
Maximum size: Thallus height to 350 mm.

Three southern Australian species of *Caulerpa* have elongate, slightly branched forms with numerous small bubble-like ramuli densely arranged around the axes. *Caulerpa vesiculifera* is the largest of these species, in both size of axes and size of vesicles (1–2 mm long). It can be recognised in the field by its pale green colour in contrast to the dark green of *C. simpliciuscula* and *C. papillosa*.

Caulerpa vesiculifera, Flinders I, Tas.

Caulerpa simpliciuscula (Turner) C. Agardh

Habitat: Exposed reef; 0–38 m depth.
Distribution: Dongara, WA, to Walkerville, Vic., and around Tas.
Maximum size: Thallus height to 300 mm.

Caulerpa simpliciuscula is a dark green plant with numerous ovoid ramuli (0.7–1.5 mm long) densely packed around the axes. It is similar in general appearance to ***Caulerpa papillosa***, but the ramuli differ in shape, being ovoid in *C. simpliciuscula* in contrast to having a marked constriction about one-third of the way down in *C. papillosa*.

Caulerpa simpliciuscula, Tinderbox, Tas.

FAMILY BRYOPSIDACEAE

This family contains species with erect primary axes and dense side branches that are constricted at the base.

Bryopsis vestita J. Agardh

Habitat: Exposed reef; 0–4 m depth.
Distribution: Cape Northumberland, SA, to Wilsons Promontory, Vic., and around Tas. Also New Zealand.
Maximum size: Thallus length to 250 mm.

Bryopsis vestita is a common species in rock pools in the spring months along the exposed Tasmanian coast but is not often seen on the mainland. Long branches arise from a common base and have short lateral axes radiating out from all sides. The only other densely tufted species with radial branching, ***Bryopsis foliosa***, occurs in Western Australia and has long secondary branches arising from the main axis.

Bryopsis vestita, Cloudy Bay, Tas.

Bryopsis gemellipara J. Agardh

Habitat: Moderately and submaximally exposed reef; 0–3 m depth.
Distribution: Streaky Bay, SA, to Wilsons Promontory, Vic., and around Tas.
Maximum size: Thallus length to 200 mm.

Bryopsis gemellipara has a similar size and often occurs in the same habitat as *B. vestita* but is immediately recognisable because the side ramuli are all positioned in the one plane. This alga is common during the spring months but is rarely seen in other seasons of the year.

Bryopsis gemellipara, Tinderbox, Tas.

FAMILY POLYPHYSACEAE

This group of algae have long slender axes and whorls of small lateral branches near the ends.

Acetabularia calyculus Lamouroux

Habitat: Shells on sheltered sand; 3–20 m depth.
Distribution: Tropical Australia south to Adelaide, SA, and Newcastle, NSW, Also widespread overseas.
Maximum size: Thallus length to 70 mm.

Acetabularia calyculus occurs in delicate colonies attached to shells or other material scattered among sand. It is immediately recognisable because of the umbrella-like structures at the end of each erect axis, with several whorls of fine hairs below. Like several other tropical species, it survives in the warm waters of the South Australian gulfs but appears to be absent elsewhere in southern waters between Busselton and Newcastle.

Acetabularia calyculus, Busselton, WA

PHYLUM (DIVISION) PHAEOPHYTA

Brown algae, brown seaweeds

Brown algae are nearly all large, multicellular algae. With the exception of a few species that occur in fresh water or are free-floating, they are restricted to rock and other firm habitats in the marine environment. As the name suggests, brown algae are relatively easy to recognise on the basis of their brown coloration, which is caused by the photosynthetic pigment fucoxanthin combined with chlorophyll and other pigments. The group contains most of the large, conspicuous seaweeds seen on rocky shores and in shallow water, and includes the large kelps. The longest and heaviest seaweeds are brown algae, as are the fastest growing of all plants. About 1500 species have been described worldwide, with about 240 known from southern Australian waters.

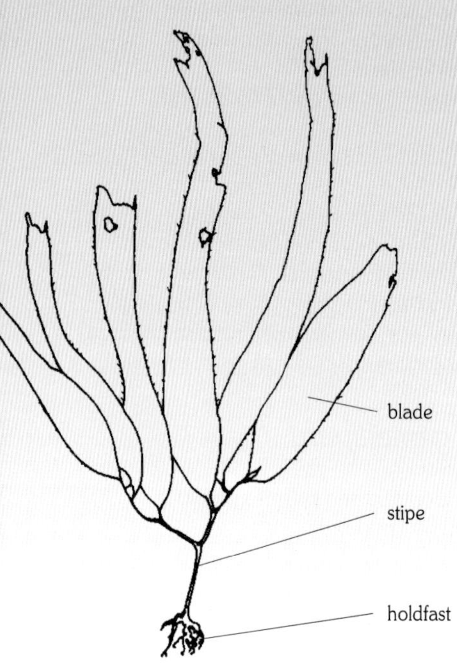

Brown alga (500 mm)
Lessonia corrugata
Phylum Phaeophyta

FAMILY LEATHESIACEAE

This diverse family includes small tufted species and rounded gelatinous forms. It is differentiated from other families on the basis of the form and growth patterns of filaments that make up the thallus.

Leathesia difformis (Linnaeus) Areschoug

Habitat: Moderately exposed reef, algae, seagrass; mid to low intertidal.
Distribution: Point Westall, SA, to Ulladulla, NSW, and around Tas. Also widely distributed overseas.
Maximum size: Thallus width to 80 mm.

Leathesia difformis is a yellow-brown coloured plant of the lower intertidal zone. It superficially resembles another common species, *Colpomenia sinuosa*, but can be distinguished by the presence of a slimy mucoid substance in the interior. Growth is somewhat seasonal, large plants being evident in summer and spring.

Leathesia difformis, Rocky Cape, Tas.

FAMILY CHORDARIACEAE

Species of Chordariaceae usually have a long cylindrical thallus with a slippery feel and which may be either unbranched or irregularly branched.

Cladosiphon filum (Harvey) Kylin

Habitat: Moderately exposed seagrass, macroalgae; 0–26 m depth.
Distribution: Safety Bay, WA, to Nowra, NSW, and around Tas. Also widely distributed overseas.
Maximum size: Length to 500 mm.

Cladosiphon filum and its branched relative ***Cladosiphon vermicularis*** are two of the most common thread-like brown algae in southern Australia. However, several other species with similar appearance also occur in the area, and accurate identification requires a microscope. *Cladosiphon filum* usually grows on the leaves of *Posidonia* and *Amphibolis* seagrasses and is most conspicuous during the warmer months.

Cladosiphon filum, Two Peoples Bay, WA

FAMILY SPLACHNIDIACEAE

This family contains a single species, *Splachnidium rugosum*, which has long gel-filled primary axes radiating out from the central holdfast and small lateral axes. The reproductive structures lie scattered over the surface of the plant.

Splachnidium rugosum (Linnaeus) Greville

Habitat: Exposed rocky shores; mid intertidal.
Distribution: Point Sinclair, SA, to Sydney, NSW, and around Tas. Also South Africa, New Zealand and several subantarctic islands.
Maximum size: Thallus length to 200 mm.

Splachnidium rugosum occurs in the mid intertidal zone and is most conspicuous over summer. During winter the plant is present as a 'microthallus' stage, when it occurs as microscopic threads among the barnacles and tubeworms on rock surfaces.

Splachnidium rugosum, Bicheno, Tas.

FAMILY STYPOCAULACEAE

This family is characterised by densely tufted plants made up of numerous branched filaments arising from a common base. Growth occurs from the apex of each filament.

Halopteris paniculata
(Suhr) Prud'homme van Reine

Habitat: Moderately to submaximally exposed reef; 0–13 m depth.
Distribution: Port Willunga, SA, to Newcastle, NSW, and around Tas. Also New Zealand, Chile and several subantarctic islands.
Maximum size: Thallus length to 300 mm.

Six species of *Halopteris* occur in southern Australia, with *H. paniculata* (formerly known as *H. gracilescens*) being probably the most common. All species have a tufted appearance because the thallus

Halopteris paniculata, Bruny I, Tas.

consists of dense aggregations of fine, branched filaments. Identification of species is based largely on seasonally occurring reproductive structures. The dense twisted spikes at the ends of the branches, as seen in the photograph, occur only on *H. paniculata*.

FAMILY DICTYOTACEAE

Species in this family form a distinctive group, with flattened branches that grow from the tips of the blades and have a regular arrangement of cells in cross-section. Reproductive structures (sporangia) are scattered over the surface of fertile plants. The life cycle consists of two generations of similar-looking plants.

Dilophus marginatus, Ulladulla, NSW

Dictyota dichotoma (Hudson) Lamouroux

Habitat: Reef; 0–25 m depth.
Distribution: Around Australia and widespread overseas.
Maximum size: Thallus length to 200 mm.

Dictyota dichotoma is one of the most widely distributed brown algal species worldwide. It is, however, found in a huge variety of shapes, perhaps representing a complex of several species. The two plants illustrated indicate the range in form. This species is distinguished from less common species of *Dictyota* by its blades with forked branching, smooth margins, lack of surface undulations and medium width (3–8 mm). The plant surface sometimes has an iridescent sheen.

Dictyota dichotoma, North Head, NSW

Dilophus marginatus J. Agardh

Habitat: Moderately and submaximally exposed reefs; 0–8 m depth.
Distribution: Port Stanvac, SA, to Noosa, Qld, and northern Tas.
Maximum size: Thallus length to 150 mm.

Dilophus marginatus is among the most common brown algal species on sand-scoured rock in shallow water along the New South Wales coast. It has forked branching and is easily recognised by the regularly undulated branch surfaces.

Dictyopteris muelleri (Sonder) Reinbold

Habitat: Moderately exposed reefs, algae; 0–37 m depth.
Distribution: Port Gregory, WA, to Walkerville, Vic., and around Tas.
Maximum size: Thallus length to 400 mm.

Dictyopteris muelleri has a similar general shape to *Dictyota dichotoma* but has an obvious midrib in the branches and a spotted appearance because of small tufts of hairs. It is a common species that grows very rapidly in localised areas during late summer, often overgrowing other algae.

Dictyopteris muelleri, Ninepin Pt, Tas.

Padina elegans Koh ex Womersley

Habitat: Moderately exposed reef; 0–5 m depth.
Distribution: Dongara, WA, to Pearson I, SA.
Maximum size: Thallus length to 100 mm.

Although *Padina* is generally considered to be a tropical genus, four species have been recorded from temperate Australian waters and a further three extend down from the tropics to central New South Wales. This genus is highly distinctive, as all species have fan-shaped fronds with concentric markings and rolled edges. Identification of species of *Padina* is difficult, however, as this depends on the cell thickness of the plant and the reproductive structures, which are often absent. The fronds of *P. elegans* are two cells thick, and the species is most common in rock crevices just below low-tide level on the southwestern Australian coast. The species that occurs commonly in Victoria and southern New South Wales, ***Padina fraseri***, has fronds three cells thick.

Padina ?elegans, Busselton, WA

Padina crassa Yamada

Habitat: Sheltered reef; 0–5 m depth.
Distribution: Tropical Australia south to Narooma, NSW. Also Lord Howe I and widespread through the Indo-West Pacific region.
Maximum size: Thallus width to 160 mm.

Padina crassa is a tropical species that can occur in very high densities in sheltered New South Wales estuaries and is also occasionally found along the open coast. The thallus of this alga is made up of 6–10 layers of cells, considerably more than other local *Padina* species.

Padina crassa, Narooma, NSW

Zonaria turneriana, Maria I, Tas.

Zonaria angustata (Kützing) Papenfuss

Habitat: Reefs; 0–22 m depth.
Distribution: Elliston, SA, to Eden, NSW, and around Tas.
Maximum size: Thallus length to 180 mm.

Species in the genus *Zonaria* are the cool-water relatives of species of *Padina*. They are abundant around the southern coastline, and while their genus is easily identified, they are often difficult to identify to species, particularly when the plants are immature. Four species occur along the southern Australian coastline, and a further species, *Zonaria diesingiana*, is common in New South Wales. *Zonaria angustata* has narrower branches (1–2 mm wide) than the other species, with the exception of a comparatively rare deep-water species, ***Zonaria spiralis***, which has thin, spirally twisted branches.

Zonaria ?angustata, Coles Bay, Tas.

Zonaria turneriana J. Agardh

Habitat: Reef; 0–38 m depth.
Distribution: Geraldton, WA, to Port Phillip Heads, Vic., and around Tas. Also New Zealand.
Maximum size: Thallus length to 250 mm.

Zonaria turneriana is one of the species of *Zonaria* most commonly observed along the southern Australian coastline. Mature plants can partly be recognised by the width of the fronds (2–4 mm wide); the fronds of another southern Australian species, ***Zonaria crenata***, are 4–10 mm wide and invariably covered by a dense network of a white hydroid, *Scoresbia daidala*.

Zonaria diesingiana J. Agardh

Habitat: Reef; 0–20 m depth.
Distribution: Green Cape to Coffs Harbour, NSW.
Maximum size: Thallus length to 120 mm.

Zonaria diesingiana plants have a similar size and shape to *Z. turneriana*, the two species differing primarily in the number of cell layers in the thallus (6–8 in *Z. diesingiana* cf. 8–10 in *Z. turneriana*). Like other species of brown algae with flattened fronds, they provide an important refuge from fish predators for numerous small invertebrates.

Zonaria diesingiana, Bass Point, NSW

Lobophora variegata (Lamouroux) Womersley

Habitat: Moderately to submaximally exposed reef; 0–36 m depth.
Distribution: Around Australia. Also widespread overseas.
Maximum size: Thallus length to 140 mm.

Lobophora variegata is a flattened dark brown alga that sometimes possesses an iridescent sheen. It occurs commonly in sheltered situations along the exposed coast and tends to be most erect in the calmest areas. A similar species with a thinner thallus (2 rather than 7 cells thick), ***Distromium flabellatum***, occurs along the southern coast.

Lobophora variegata, Bass Point, NSW

Distromium flabellatum, Maria I, Tas.

Homeostrichus olsenii Womersley

Habitat: Moderately and submaximally exposed reef; 2–38 m depth.
Distribution: Robe, SA, to Split Solitary I, NSW, and around Tas.
Maximum size: Thallus length to 150 mm.

Homeostrichus olsenii is a flattened lobed alga with a thallus 5 cells thick. It has a similar general shape to *Lobophora variegata* but differs in reproductive structures. It can sometimes be distinguished in the field by its matt greyish-brown colour, which is quite different from the shiny dark brown of *L. variegata*. The two species often occur together.

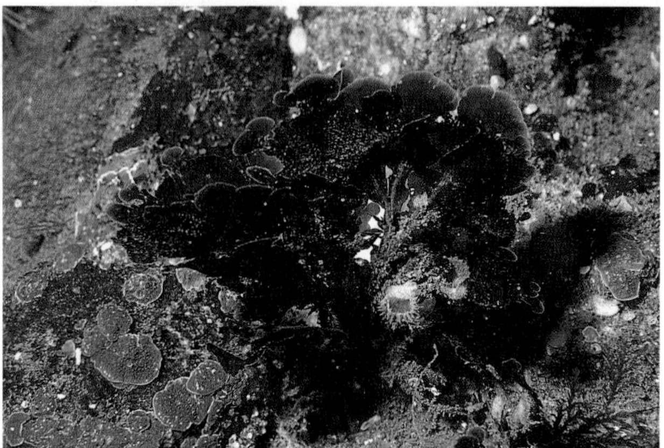

Homeostrichus olsenii, Maria I, Tas.

Carpomitra costata, Bruny I, Tas.

Carpomitra costata (Stackhouse) Batters

Habitat: Moderately and submaximally exposed reef; 0–38 m depth.
Distribution: Kangaroo I, SA, to Port Stephens, NSW, and around Tas. Also widely distributed overseas.
Maximum size: Thallus length to 350 mm.

Carpomitra costata is the only species in the family with branches that are flattened rather than rounded in cross-section. It is a common but inconspicuous plant, mostly seen in shaded locations on exposed reefs.

FAMILY SPOROCHNACEAE

This family contains thin branched algae with crowns of fine hairs at the ends of the branches. They have two generations in the life-cycle, with one large (150–500 mm long plants) and the other filamentous and microscopic.

Sporochnus comosus, Cloudy Lagoon, Tas.

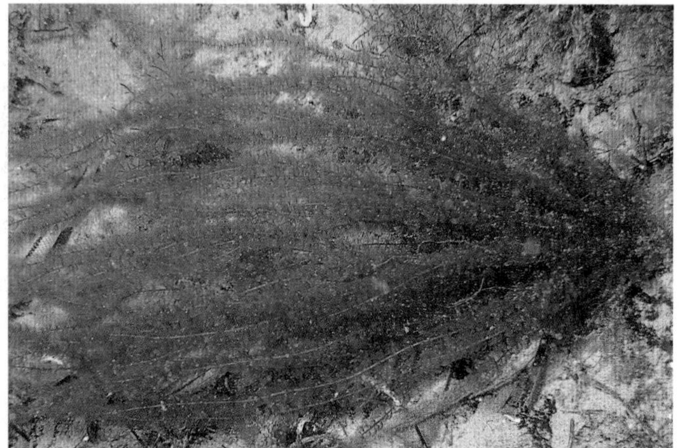

Sporochnus comosus C. Agardh

Habitat: Moderately exposed reef; 0–41 m depth.
Distribution: Dongara, WA, to Calliope River, Qld, and around Tas.
Maximum size: Thallus length to 550 mm.

The five species of *Sporochnus* occurring in southern Australia are characterised by the presence of swollen reproductive structures immediately below tufts of hair on small side-branchlets. The reproductive structures of *S. comosus* have a very small section of branch (known as a pedicel) below them, and the small branchlets (consisting of tufted crown, reproductive structure and pedicel) are arranged densely around long side branches. *Sporochnus comosus* is the most common species in temperate Australian waters.

Perithalia caudata (Labillardière) Womersley

Habitat: Submaximally exposed reefs; 0–18 m depth.
Distribution: West Bay, Kangaroo I, SA, to Wilsons Promontory, Vic., and around Tas.
Maximum size: Thallus length to 1 m.

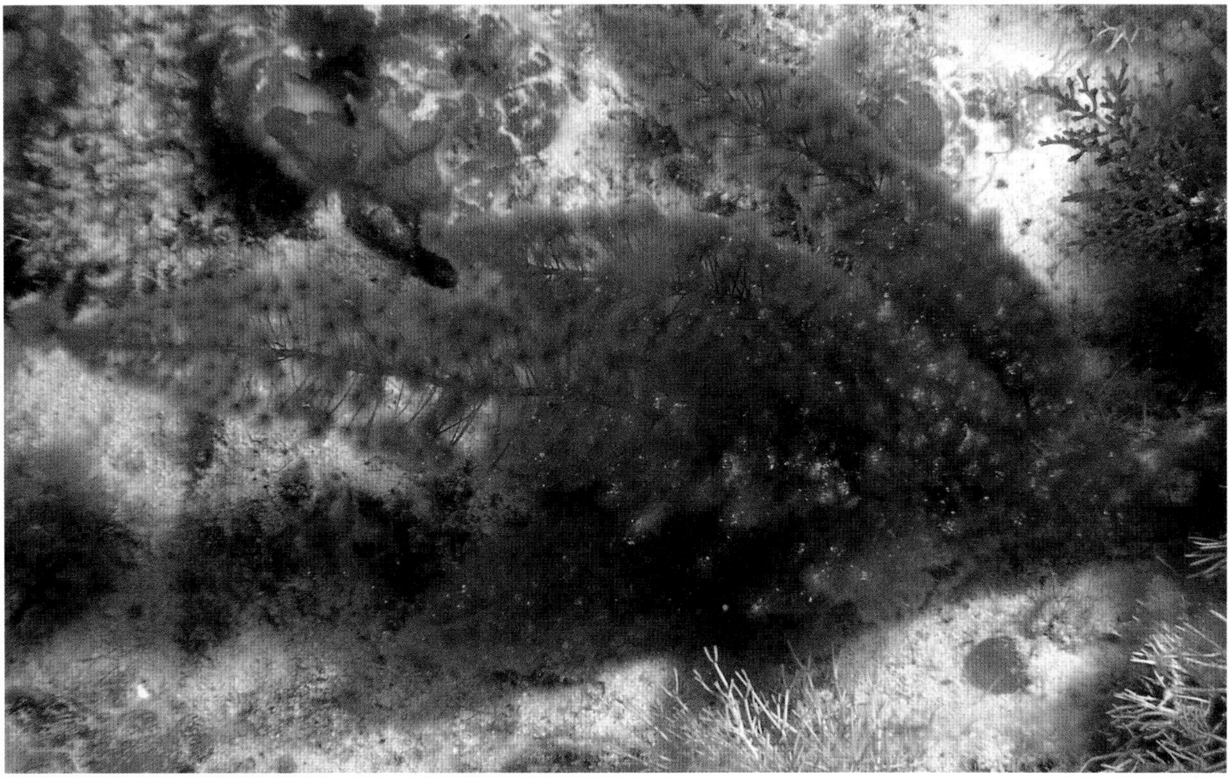

Encyothalia cliftoni, Canal Rocks, WA

Perithalia caudata is a large, densely tufted plant that is common along the exposed southeastern Australian coast. Most of the branches have a small blunt cellular cap on the end, but a few have small (1–3 mm long) tufts of filaments.

Encyothalia cliftoni Harvey

Habitat: Moderately exposed reef; 2–17 m depth.
Distribution: Kalbarri, WA, to Walkerville, Vic.
Maximum size: Thallus length to 1 m.

Encyothalia cliftoni differs from species in the closely related genus *Sporochnus* by having long lateral branches arising from a single main axis and branchlets 5–15 mm long, with prominent tufts of hairs densely distributed around the lateral branches. It is the only species in the genus and is generally found in relatively sheltered areas along the exposed coast.

Perithalia caudata, Flinders I, Tas.

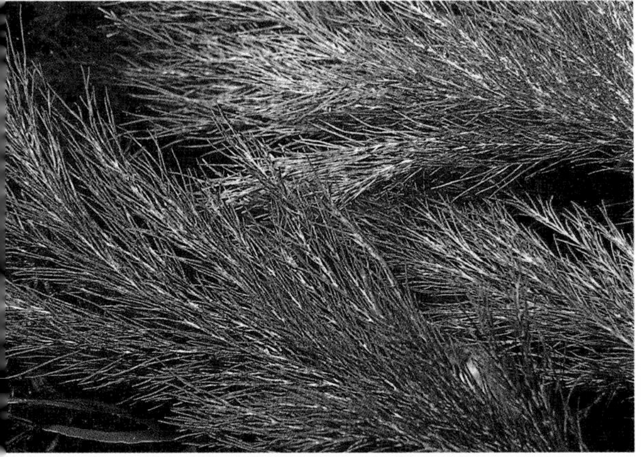

Bellotia eriophorum Harvey

Habitat: Moderately exposed reef, shells; 6–41 m depth.
Distribution: Ceduna, SA, to Walkerville, Vic., and around Tas. Also Noosa Heads, Qld.
Maximum size: Thallus length to 250 mm.

Bellotia eriophorum is immediately recognisable because of the large size of hair tufts and its brushlike appearance. The species generally occurs in waters >12 m depth but can occur in shallower water in Tasmania, where it is usually found growing on old shells in areas of sand.

Bellotia eriophorum, Preservation I, Tas.

FAMILY SCYTOSIPHONACEAE

Species of Scytosiphonaceae have unbranched fronds that may be flattened, tubular or spherical. Growth occurs from cells throughout the plant rather than at the tip.

Scytosiphon lomentaria (Lyngbye) Link

Habitat: Rocky shores, seagrass; low-tide level.
Distribution: Cottesloe, WA, to Sydney, NSW, and around Tas. Also widely distributed overseas.
Maximum size: Thallus length to 760 mm.

Scytosiphon lomentaria is a common inhabitant of rocky shores and in this situation is usually easy to identify because of its unbranched tubular shape. The species does, however, also occasionally occur attached to large marine plants just below low-tide level and could be confused with species such as *Cladosiphon filum*. *Scytosiphon lomentaria* alternates between two phases of its life cycle: during the summer months it mainly occurs inconspicuously as an encrusting plant, but the winter generation has the long tubular shape as shown in the photograph.

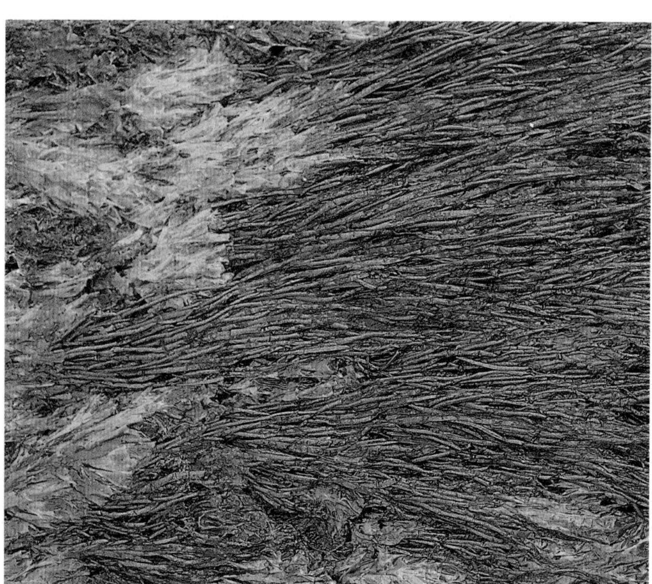

Scytosiphon lomentaria, Bicheno, Tas.

Colpomenia sinuosa
(Mertens ex Roth) Derbes & Solier

Habitat: Sheltered seagrass, reef, macroalgae; intertidal to 1 m depth.
Distribution: Widespread around Australia and overseas.

Colpomenia sinuosa, Albany, WA

Maximum size: Thallus width usually to 150 mm, with compound plants occasionally reaching 1 m in diameter.

Colpomenia sinuosa is the most common species of globular algae found attached to other plants in southern Australia, particularly during the summer months. It also commonly grows on rocks in the lower intertidal zone, where it generally has a more solid, creased appearance and can be confused with *Leathesia difformis*.

Colpomenia peregrina (Sauvageau) Hamel

Habitat: Sheltered seagrass, reef, macroalgae; intertidal to 6 m depth.
Distribution: Albany, WA, to Heron I, Qld, and around Tas. Also widely distributed overseas.
Maximum size: Thallus width to 250 mm.

Colpomenia peregrina is very similar in appearance to *C. sinuosa* but differs slightly in the lighter brown colour, less convoluted appearance and thinner, more

Colpomenia peregrina attached to *Heterozostera tasmanica*, Cloudy Lagoon, Tas.

translucent thallus. It grows prolifically in cooler temperatures than *C. sinuosa* and is most conspicuous in winter. Both species become detached from their host plants during storms and can afterwards form extensive windrows along the shores of sheltered embayments.

FAMILY PUNCTARIACEAE

This family is characterised primarily by cell structure and method of cell division. Plants are unbranched and membranous and generally have an ovoid or tongue-shaped form.

Asperococcus bullosus, Tinderbox, Tas.

Asperococcus bullosus Lamouroux

Habitat: Sheltered and moderately exposed seagrass, algae; 0–22 m depth.
Distribution: Rottnest I, WA, to Port Stephens, NSW, and around Tas. Also widely distributed overseas.
Maximum size: Thallus length to 1 m.

Asperococcus bullosus is a tubular, translucent brown alga that is usually found attached to *Posidonia* or *Amphibolis* seagrass plants. It is larger (plant width 20–100 mm) than a closely related species, ***Asperococcus fistulosus*** (width 2–10 mm), and tends to grow in more exposed conditions.

FAMILY LESSONIACEAE

This is one of four families that are commonly known as kelps and are classified in the order Laminariales. Kelps are characterised by cylindrical stems known as stipes that connect large, leaf-like fronds to a holdfast made up of densely compacted branches (known as haptera). The family Lessoniaceae is distinguished from other kelps by the stipes dividing at the base of the fronds.

Lessonia corrugata Lucas
Strapweed

Habitat: Exposed reef; 0–20 m depth.
Distribution: Around Tas. including King I.
Maximum size: Thallus height to 2 m.

Lessonia corrugata, Bicheno, Tas.

Macrocystis pyrifera (holdfast), Waterfall Bay, Tas.

Macrocystis pyrifera (frond), Waterfall Bay, Tas.

Lessonia corrugata has long straplike blades with numerous longitudinal corrugations. It is a dominant species on exposed reefs in southern Tasmania and generally occurs with *Phyllospora comosa* slightly deeper than a zone of *Durvillaea potatorum* and above a zone of *Ecklonia radiata*.

Macrocystis pyrifera (Linnaeus) C. Agardh

Giant kelp

Habitat: Moderately and submaximally exposed reef; 0–28 m depth.
Distribution: Eastern, southern and western Tas. Also New Zealand, subantarctic islands, South America and the Pacific coast of North America.
Maximum size: Thallus height to 35 m.

Macrocystis pyrifera is the longest marine plant, with exaggerated reports made last century suggesting that it could grow to more than 100 m. This species is also one of the fastest growing organisms, with fronds extending up to 500 mm per day in ideal conditions. In southeastern Tasmanian waters, where it occurs commonly, *M. pyrifera* can be recognised by its size, the ropelike stipes which connect floating fronds to the attached holdfast, and the airfilled vesicles which provide buoyancy. The size and number of beds in Tasmania has dramatically declined during the past thirty years to perhaps only 5 per cent of the original area, and so this species is threatened with local extinction. While a number of theories have been put forward to explain this loss, research indicates that normal levels of dissolved nutrients in Tasmanian waters are barely sufficient for the species' needs and have been declining in recent years.

Macrocystis angustifolia Bory

Giant kelp, string kelp

Habitat: Moderately and submaximally exposed reef; 0–10 m depth.
Distribution: Cape Jaffa, SA, to Walkerville, Vic., and northern Tas. Also occurs in South Africa.
Maximum size: Thallus height to 10 m.

Macrocystis angustifolia is the dwarf relative of the giant kelp *M. pyrifera*. The stipes on *M. angustifolia* arise from numerous places on the holdfast, whereas in *M. pyrifera* the stipes are usually attached to the top of a single major axis that passes through the holdfast. The fronds of *M. angustifolia* are also usually distinctive as they are long, narrow and straight near the growing tip, compared with wide and curved in *M. pyrifera*. Along the northeastern and northwestern Tasmanian coast where the two species potentially overlap, plants often have intermediate features, and

Macrocystis angustifolia (holdfast), Low Head, Tas.

it is possible that the two species are in fact environmental variants of one. Both species are unable to tolerate low nutrient concentrations and occur in dense beds in places with high nutrient input, such as off seal colonies and sewage treatment plants.

FAMILY ALARIACEAE

Kelps in this family have a holdfast connected to a single stipe that remains undivided. The frond has flat side branches at the base, which are initially small but rapidly increase in size.

Ecklonia radiata (C. Agardh) J. Agardh
Common kelp

Habitat: Moderately exposed reefs; 0–44 m depth.
Distribution: Kalbarri, WA, to Caloundra, Qld, and around Tas.
Maximum size: Thallus height to 2 m.

Most people who visit the beach will be aware of *Ecklonia radiata,* the common kelp of the southern coastline. Large quantities are washed ashore on surf beaches and also accumulate in the surf zone. This species appears in a variety of forms, with plants in deep water usually having a long stipe and smooth fronds, whereas shallow-water plants have a short stipe and are often densely covered by spines. *Ecklonia radiata* can tolerate low light conditions and is the deepest growing of the large, dominant algae. It occurs just below low-tide level only in sheltered conditions.

Macrocystis angustifolia (frond). SIMON TALBOT

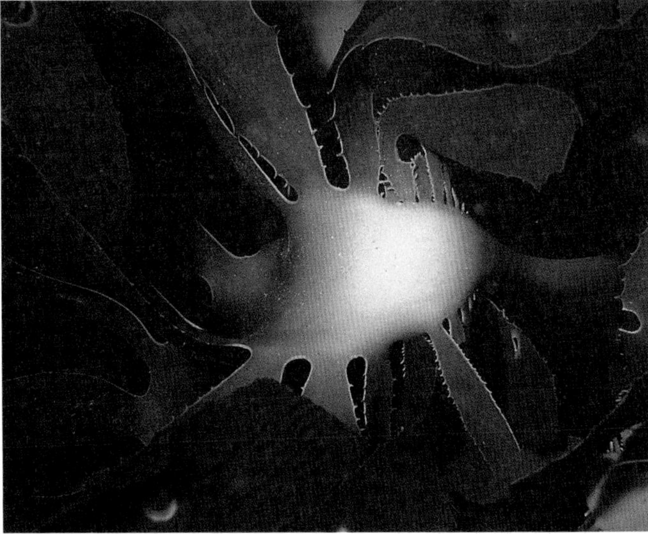
Ecklonia radiata, Bruny I, Tas.

Undaria pinnatifida (Harvey) Suringar

Habitat: Moderately exposed reefs; 0–10 m depth.
Distribution: Marion Bay to Coles Bay, Tas. Also Japan, China, New Zealand and France.
Maximum size: Thallus length to 1 m.

Undaria pinnatifida has a large, green-brown frond with side-branches and a distinctively ruffled stipe. The species was introduced from Asia, presumably on woodchip-transporting boats from Japan, and is now well established in eastern Tasmania. *Undaria pinnatida* is an annual species, which is difficult to detect in late summer and early autumn but which covers large areas of shallow reef in spring. It is a palatable seaweed and is widely eaten in Japan. Commercial harvesting now occurs on a small scale in Tasmania.

Undaria pinnatifida, Spring Beach, Tas.

FAMILY NOTHEIACEAE

This family has only one species, *Notheia anomala*. This plant has an unusual life history, as the female reproductive structures scattered over the plant surface produce mobile female cells rather than eggs. These female gametes need to settle on plants of the same or closely related species (*Hormosira* or *Xiphophora*); otherwise they do not attract sperm and are not fertilised. The fertilised cells produce a single branch, which produces further branches when eggs settle on it and are again fertilised. *Notheia anomala* thus appears to be a highly branched species, but the thallus in fact consists of a colony of numerous single-branched plants.

Notheia anomala Harvey & Bailey

Habitat: Brown algae; lower intertidal.
Distribution: Albany, WA, to Port Stephens, NSW, and around Tas. Also New Zealand.
Maximum size: Thallus length to 200 mm.

Notheia anomala grows semiparasitically on *Hormosira banksii* (Neptune's necklace) and also occasionally on another brown alga, *Xiphophora chondrophylla*. It has a narrow cylindrical thallus, which appears heavily branched. The species occurs very prolifically just above low-tide level along exposed shores.

Notheia anomala attached to *Hormosira banksii*, Flinders, Vic.

FAMILY DURVILLAEACEAE

Species in this family have a massive frond and thick stipe, and are commonly called bull kelps. This name is somewhat misleading, however, as the family differs in life history from the true kelps in the order Laminariales. Species of Durvillaeaceae occur around the Southern Hemisphere in cool temperate and subantarctic waters.

Durvillaea potatorum (Labillardière) Areschoug
Bull kelp

Habitat: Exposed reef; 0–30 m depth.
Distribution: Cape Jaffa, SA, to Bermagui, NSW, and western, southern and eastern Tas.
Maximum size: Thallus length to 8 m.

Durvillaea potatorum has large, bulky fronds, which are extremely heavy. This species is the dominant plant at and just below low-tide level around the exposed Tasmanian and Victorian coasts and can occur at heights of 3 m above low-tide mark at sites where large waves regularly wash up the rock face. Plants are harvested commercially as they drift ashore on King Island and a compound known as sodium alginate extracted. This chemical causes liquids to gel and is used to stabilise ice cream, toothpaste, etc. When dried, bull kelp fronds were also used as containers by Tasmanian Aboriginal tribes to transport water and food, hence the name *potatorum* ('potable') given to the species by a French naturalist who observed the plant in use. A closely related species is ***Durvillaea antarctica***, the dominant species in shallow water at Macquarie Island. Because the fronds of *D. antarctica* have a hollow honeycomb structure, which allows them to float across oceans, specimens regularly drift ashore in southern Tasmania.

Durvillaea potatorum, Bicheno, Tas.

Hormosira banksii, Point Sinclair, SA

FAMILY HORMOSIRACEAE

This family contains only the unusual-looking species *Hormosira banksii*.

Hormosira banksii (Turner) Decaisne
Neptune's necklace

Habitat: Sheltered reef; lower intertidal.
Distribution: Albany, WA, to Arrawarra, NSW, and around Tas. Also New Zealand.
Maximum size: Thallus length to 300 mm.

Because of its pearl necklace shape, *Hormosira banksii* is the most distinctive of Australian algae. The species is restricted to the lower intertidal zone, where it occurs in several different forms that were once thought to be different species. Plants have spherical or cylindrical segments, and most are attached to rock, but others can lie loose among mangrove shoots. Because of the species' high iodine content, Tasmanian schoolchildren were once urged to eat a bead a day to keep goitre away.

FAMILY FUCACEAE

Included in this family are species with flat, branched fronds that are either straplike or tapering. This is a large family on European shores, but only two species are known in southern Australia.

Xiphophora chondrophylla

(R. Brown ex Turner) Montagne ex Harvey

Habitat: Moderately exposed reef; 0–8 m depth.
Distribution: Kangaroo I, SA, to Walkerville ,Vic., and northern Tas. Also New Zealand.
Maximum size: Thallus length to 300 mm.

Xiphophora chondrophylla occurs commonly with other brown algae in the zone immediately below low-tide level. The species is easily recognised because the tough fronds are flattened and repeatedly divided.

Xiphophora chondrophylla, Flinders I, Tas.

Xiphophora gladiata, Muttonbird I, Tas.

Xiphophora gladiata

(Labillardière) Montagne ex Kjellman

Habitat: Submaximally and maximally exposed reef; 0–18 m depth.
Distribution: Western Port, Vic., also eastern, western and southern Tas.
Maximum size: Thallus length to 1 m.

Xiphophora gladiata is a common species in the lower intertidal zone above the band of *Durvillaea potatorum* and can also occur in deeper water between bands of other large algae. It differs considerably from X. *chondrophylla* as its fronds are much longer, curved and dagger-like. The distribution of X. *gladiata* overlaps little (if at all) with X. *chondrophylla* — X. *gladiata* is found along the cooler and more exposed east and west Tasmanian coastlines and X. *chondrophylla* in the warmer Bass Strait region. A single plant attributed to this species was found at Western Port in the nineteenth century.

Phyllospora comosa, Gordon, Tas.

FAMILY SEIROCOCCACEAE

Species of Seirococcaceae have a long flat main axis with flat unbranched lateral fronds densely arranged along the sides. The holdfast is woody and distinctive, with a hemispherical centre and a thickened rim.

Phyllospora comosa (Labillardière) C. Agardh

Habitat: Exposed reefs; 0–20 m depth.
Distribution: Robe, SA, to Port Macquarie, NSW, and around Tas.
Maximum size: Thallus length to 3 m.

Phyllospora comosa is among the most common large algae in shallow water around the wave-swept sections of the southeastern Australian coast. The species often forms a dense band immediately above the region where *Ecklonia radiata* dominates, but this zone has been partly eliminated in New South Wales by dense aggregations of the sea urchin *Centrostephanus rodgersii*, which graze the rock surface bare. *Phyllospora comosa* can be recognised by the sawtooth-edged fronds that arise from flat central axes and the spindle-shaped floats that are attached by small stalks.

Seirococcus axillaris (R. Brown ex Turner) Greville

Habitat: Moderately exposed reef; 1–40 m depth.
Distribution: Fishery Bay, SA, to Walkerville, Vic., and around Tas.
Maximum size: Thallus length to 2 m.

Seirococcus axillaris, Flinders I, Tas.

Seirococcus axillaris has large, flattened branches that have aggregations of reproductive structures densely packed along the inside of branch edges near where the branches fork. The whiplash action of this plant moving backwards and forwards in the swell probably has a detrimental effect on other large macroalgae, as rock adjacent to plants is often clear of other species.

Scytothalia dorycarpa (Turner) Greville

Habitat: Moderately to submaximally exposed reef; 0–44 m depth.
Distribution: Geraldton, WA, to Point Lonsdale, Vic., and Georgetown, Tas.
Maximum size: Thallus length to 2 m.

Scytothalia dorycarpa has a similar general appearance to its relative *Seirococcus axillaris* and occupies a similar habitat but has a more open thallus with reproductive structures that are much larger (10–15 mm long) and fewer in number. A single specimen collected in the nineteenth century from the Tamar Heads is the only record of this species in Tasmania.

Scytothalia dorycarpa, Bunker Bay, WA

FAMILY CYSTOSEIRACEAE

This family is characterised by the terminal branches being used as specialised reproductive structures, known as receptacles. Scattered over the surface of each terminal branch are numerous rounded pits (the conceptacles), which contain male and female structures and release sperm and eggs. Many of the large brown seaweeds found around the coast, particularly in sheltered habitats, are species of Cystoseiraceae.

Platythalia angustifolia, Seven Mile Beach, WA

Cystoseira trinodis, Bicton, WA

Platythalia angustifolia Sonder

Habitat: Exposed reef; 0–5 m depth.
Distribution: Geraldton to Cape Riche, WA.
Maximum size: Thallus length to 800 mm.

Platythalia angustifolia is a large species with distinctive zigzag axes and flat final branches which end as reproductive structures 20–40 mm long and 1–4 mm broad. Its only close relative, ***Platythalia quercifolia***, occurs over the same geographic range but has sharply serrated edges to the receptacles. *Platythalia angustifolia* is the dominant plant in the shallow sublittoral zone on many exposed shores in south Western Australia, particularly on steep slopes.

Cystoseira trinodis (Forsskål) C. Agardh

Habitat: Sheltered reef, shells; 0–3 m depth.
Distribution: Tropical Australia around the southwestern coast to Victor Harbor, SA, and down the eastern coast to Dunalley, Tas. Also widespread overseas.
Maximum size: Thallus length to 1.5 m.

Cystoseira trinodis has chains of up to four small bladder-like structures that form the smallest fronds, and numerous small peg-like processes projecting from branches. The southern Australian form of this species is somewhat different from the more widely distributed tropical form because it lacks leaf-like branches.

Hormophysa cuneiformis (Gmelin) Silva

Habitat: Sheltered reef, shells; 0–5 m depth.
Distribution: Tropical Australia to Mandurah, WA, and Port Stephens, NSW, and northern Spencer Gulf, SA. Also through the Indo-West Pacific region.
Maximum size: Thallus length to 400 mm.

Myriodesma serrulatum, Bunker Bay, WA

Hormophysa cuneiformis, Spencer Gulf, SA

Hormophysa cuneiformis has wings spirally arranged down the axes and a distinctive serrated edge. It is usually confined to tropical regions, but a population exists in the warmer water of northern Spencer Gulf. This isolated population was probably established in former times when the southern Australian coast was warmer and the species widely distributed. The species was known as *Hormophysa triqueta* until recently.

Myriodesma serrulatum

(Lamouroux) Decaisne

Habitat: Moderately exposed reefs; 0–5 m depth.
Distribution: Dongara to Cape Riche, WA.
Maximum size: Thallus length to 300 mm.

Myriodesma serrulatum is one of eight species in the Australian genus *Myriodesma*, with most of these species having localised distributions in southwestern Australia. *Myriodesma serrulatum* differs from the others in having serrated branches 2–4 mm wide. It is often found at sand-scoured sites that are unsuitable for the survival of most other species.

Scaberia agardhii, Esperance, WA

Scaberia agardhii Greville

Habitat: Sheltered and moderately exposed reefs; 0–40 m depth.
Distribution: Houtman Abrolhos, WA, to Sydney, NSW, and north and east Tas. Also Lord Howe I.
Maximum size: Thallus length to 2 m.

Scaberia agardhii is an interesting alga that is often the dominant species in sheltered locations near the edge of seagrass. The branches are long, warty-looking and unmistakable, with a yellow-green hue. Specimens were collected near Sydney in the first half of the twentieth century, but no plants have been found in New South Wales during the past 50 years.

Carpoglossum confluens

(R. Brown ex Turner) Kützing

Habitat: Moderately exposed reef; 1–40 m depth.
Distribution: Elliston, SA, to Walkerville, Vic., and around Tas.
Maximum size: Thallus length to 2 m.

Carpoglossum confluens has long flattened branches (5–15 mm broad), which appear to be segmented because they narrow and widen irregularly. The species occurs abundantly around Tasmania in a similar habitat to *Seirococcus axillaris*. The reef substrate around *C. confluens* plants is often devoid of turfing plants or animals, possibly because of a negative reaction to the slimy mucilaginous material produced by the plant.

Cystophora platylobium (Mertens) J. Agardh

Habitat: Submaximally and maximally exposed reef; 0–48 m depth.
Distribution: Eucla, SA, to Sydney, NSW, and around Tas.
Maximum size: Thallus length to 4 m.

Because of their local diversity and dominance, species in the Australasian genus *Cystophora* can be regarded as the eucalypts of the underwater world. Most of the 23 southern Australian species can be immediately recognised as belonging to this genus by possessing a characteristic zigzag branching pattern. Identification of individual species is generally more difficult and relies on the size and shape of branches, particularly the terminal branches, which are specialised reproductive structures known as receptacles.

Carpoglossum confluens, Tinderbox, Tas.

Cystophora platylobium is perhaps the easiest to identify as it has flattened fronds with the side-branches arising from the edge rather than the face of the main axis, and the receptacles are large (10–30 mm long, 3–10 mm broad) and leaf-shaped. It also has conspicuous gas-filled floats known as vesicles. This species has a different habitat from other *Cystophora* species, as it generally occurs in relatively deep water (>10 m) along wave-swept coasts with kelps and *Phyllospora comosa*.

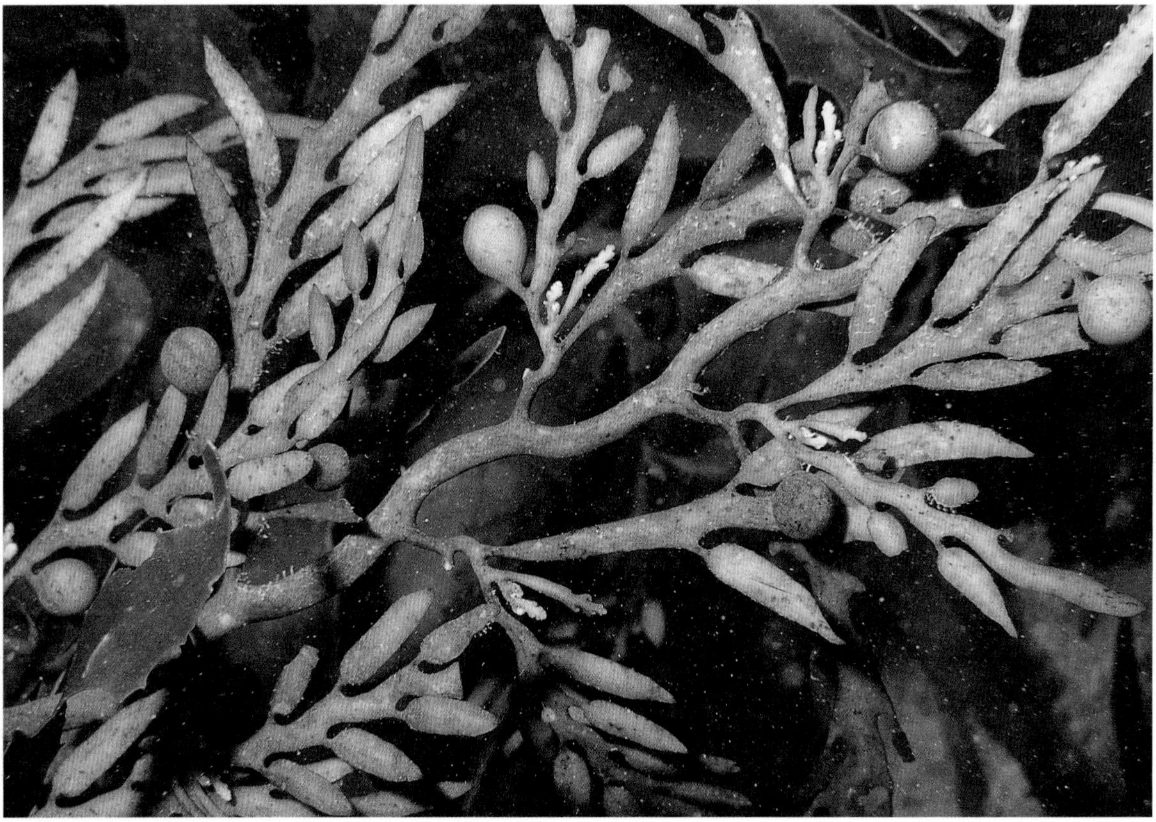

Cystophora platylobium, Rocky Cape, Tas.

Cystophora moniliformis

(Esper) Womersley & Nizamuddin ex Womersley

Habitat: Moderately exposed reefs; 0–28 m depth.
Distribution: Cape Naturaliste, WA, to Port Stephens, NSW, and around Tas. Also Lord Howe I.
Maximum size: Thallus length to 4 m.

Cystophora moniliformis is one of the most common species of *Cystophora* found in southern Australia and is most conspicuous on sand-abraded reefs in shallow water. The lateral branches are zigzag shaped, bushy at the ends, and arise from the edges of a flat (3–20 mm wide) central axis. The final branches are long (5–40 mm), thin (0.5–1 mm wide) and somewhat lumpy, and floats are absent.

Cystophora grevillei, Flinders I, Tas.

Cystophora moniliformis, Swan I, Tas.

Cystophora grevillei

(C. Agardh ex Sonder) J. Agardh

Habitat: Moderately exposed reef, shells; 1–30 m depth.
Distribution: Dongara, WA, to Wilsons Promontory, Vic., and around Tas.
Maximum size: Thallus length to 1.5 m.

Cystophora grevillei is an open-branched species with a main axis almost round in cross-section (2–7 mm in diameter). The branching is regular and ends in very long (20–150 mm), slender (1–3 mm) receptacles and a few large floats. This plant is a deep-water species and is most often seen attached to shells or rocks in sandy areas, with the weight of shells sometimes insufficient to combat the drag and buoyancy of large plants.

Cystophora intermedia J. Agardh

Habitat: Exposed reef; 0–2 m depth.
Distribution: Point Sinclair, SA, to Portland, Vic., and Hogan I, Tas.
Maximum size: Thallus length to 850 mm.

Cystophora intermedia is another in the small group of *Cystophora* species that branch from the edge rather than the face of the main axis. The main axis is ovoid in cross-section and relatively narrow (3–8 mm across), and the receptacles are long (5–20 mm) and thin (0.5–1 mm in diameter). Floats are absent. This species is often the dominant species near low-tide level on exposed coasts in central South Australia, but it is rare east of Victor Harbor, where this zone is occupied by *Durvillaea potatorum*.

Cystophora intermedia, Victor Harbor, SA

Cystophora xiphocarpa Harvey

Habitat: Moderately and submaximally exposed reef; 1–15 m depth.
Distribution: Cape Otway, Vic., and around Tas.
Maximum size: Thallus length to 1 m.

Cystophora xiphocarpa has longer receptacles (20–90 mm long, 3–10 mm wide) than other *Cystophora* species and can be identified on the basis of these large and flat final branches alone. It also lacks floats and is the only species with side fronds that do not branch. Crescent-shaped pits (the conceptacles) are easily seen along the edges of the large receptacles in this species, and it is from the conceptacles that spores are released. *Cystophora xiphocarpa* has been recorded at only one site outside Tasmania and is most abundant on the eastern Tasmanian coast.

Cystophora xiphocarpa, Spring Beach, Tas.

Cystophora racemosa

(Harvey ex Kützing) J. Agardh

Habitat: Moderately and submaximally exposed reef; 2–10 m depth.
Distribution: Geographe Bay, WA, to Queenscliff, Vic.
Maximum size: Thallus length to 1 m.

Cystophora racemosa has flattened receptacles that are similar to those of *C. platylobium* but smaller. The receptacles are 5–30 mm long, 1.5–4 mm wide and leaf-like. The main axis in this species is 2–6 mm wide, with lateral branches arising from the face rather than the edges. Spherical floats (3–10 mm in diameter) are present. This species is most abundant in the western section of its range in mixed beds with other *Cystophora* species.

Cystophora racemosa, Two Peoples Bay, WA

Cystophora pectinata

(Greville & C. Agardh ex Sonder) J. Agardh

Habitat: Moderately and submaximally exposed reef; 4–21 m depth.
Distribution: Perth, WA, to Walkerville, Vic.
Maximum size: Thallus length to 1 m.

Cystophora pectinata has small flat receptacles (5–20 mm long, 1–3 mm broad) densely arranged in a fishbone pattern down the fronds. The species lacks floats and has side-branches arising from the face of the main axis. It is a common species, often found associated with its close relative *C. racemosa*.

Cystophora pectinata, Two Peoples Bay, WA

Cystophora monilifera J. Agardh

Habitat: Moderately exposed and sheltered reef; 0–48 m depth.
Distribution: Nickol Bay, WA, to Sydney, NSW, and south to Freycinet Peninsula, Tas.
Maximum size: Thallus length to 1 m.

Cystophora monilifera is the species most commonly encountered by divers along the southern Australian coastline. It is characterised by receptacles that are long (5–30 mm), thin (0.5–1 mm) and lumpy, and floats that when present are spherical and 3–8 mm in diameter. A characteristic feature of the species is that the smaller branches are aligned in three planes off the side-branches, so that if a branch is viewed down the axis then three lines of smaller branches will be seen at 120° angles to each other.

Cystophora monilifera, Esperance, WA

Cystophora botryocystis Sonder

Habitat: Sheltered and moderately exposed reef; 1–12 m depth.
Distribution: Perth, WA, to Port Phillip Bay, Vic., and northern Tas.
Maximum size: Thallus length to 4 m.

Cystophora botryocystis is an easily recognised species as it has distinctive clusters of round, grapelike floats at the base of dense aggregations of receptacles. The receptacles are 5–20 mm long, 1–1.5 mm wide and club-shaped.

Cystophora botryocystis, Port Victoria, SA

Cystophora brownii (Turner) J. Agardh

Habitat: Moderately and submaximally exposed reef; 0–4 m depth.
Distribution: Dongara, WA, to Victor Harbor, SA, and Waterhouse Point, Tas.
Maximum size: Thallus length to 600 mm.

Cystophora brownii has very small (2–8 mm long), lumpy receptacles that are rigidly arranged along the side-branches in one plane only. Other characteristics of the species are that the side-branches have a strong zigzag pattern and floats are not present. The species is generally found in the turbulent zone just below low-tide level.

Cystophora brownii, Canal Rocks, WA

Cystophora harveyi Womersley

Habitat: Moderately exposed reef; 0–5 m depth.
Distribution: Geographe Bay to Walpole, WA.
Maximum size: Thallus length to 2 m.

Little is known about *Cystophora harveyi*, a recently described species from the shallow subtidal zone in Western Australia. It can be recognised by the dark golden-brown colour, rounded main axis and numerous branch remnants along the main axis from which side-branches have broken off. The receptacles are 2–12 mm long and 0.6–0.8 mm wide, and floats are absent.

Cystophora harveyi, Bunker Bay, WA

Cystophora torulosa

(R. Brown ex Turner) J. Agardh

Habitat: Sheltered reef; lower intertidal zone.
Distribution: Apollo Bay to Wilsons Promontory, Vic., and around Tas. Also New Zealand.
Maximum size: Thallus length to 1.5 m.

Cystophora torulosa is the dominant alga at low-tide level in sheltered areas of Tasmania, such as the D'Entrecasteaux Channel. It is yellow-brown and has long (20–70 mm), cylindrical (2–4 mm wide) receptacles which are characteristic of the species. This alga often occurs just below a band of *Hormosira banksii* or rock platforms.

Cystophora torulosa with *Hormosira banksii*, Coles Bay, Tas.

Cystophora retorta (Mertens) J. Agardh

Habitat: Moderately exposed reef; 0–21 m depth.
Distribution: Nickol Bay, WA, to Crookhaven Heads, NSW, and south to Spring Bay, Tas.
Maximum size: Thallus length to 1.2 m.

Cystophora retorta has long (20–80 mm), thin (1–2 mm) final branches and a characteristically regular branching pattern. Each side-frond branches into two several times in the one plane, with each fork curved at the base. This species is quite similar to ***Cystophora siliquosa***, a less common species with a main axis that is almost square rather than rectangular in cross-section.

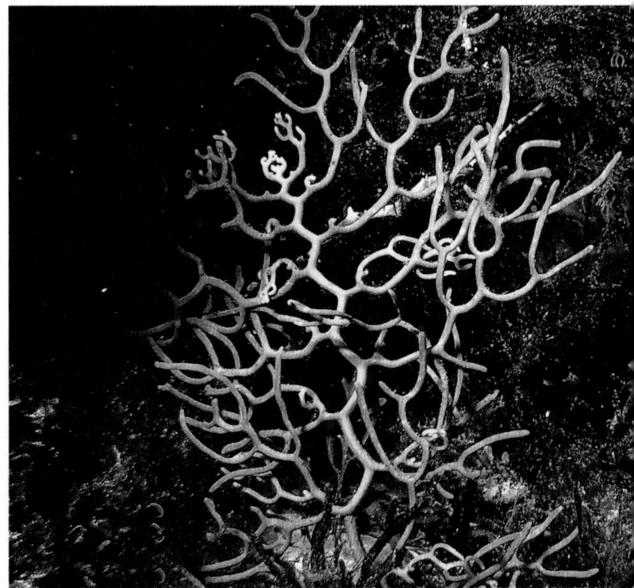

Cystophora retorta, Spring Beach, Tas.

Cystophora retroflexa

(Labillardière) J. Agardh

Habitat: Sheltered reef; 0–12 m depth.
Distribution: Kangaroo I, SA, to Sydney, NSW, and around Tas. Also New Zealand.
Maximum size: Thallus length to 2 m.

Cystophora retroflexa prefers a more sheltered environment than other species of *Cystophora*. It is a large, openly branched species with floats longer (4–10 mm) than broad (3–6 mm) and final branches long (20–60 mm) and thin (1–2 mm). The side-branches have smaller branches arising at irregular intervals from all sides, rather than these branches arising in the one plane.

Cystophora subfarcinata (Mertens) J. Agardh

Habitat: Moderately and submaximally exposed reefs; 0–7 m depth.
Distribution: Nickol Bay, WA, to Wilsons Promontory, Vic., and around Tas.
Maximum size: Thallus length to 2 m.

Cystophora subfarcinata is a dominant plant in the shallow subtidal zone of many areas of the southern coast. It is not characterised by any particular feature, except perhaps for the very pronounced zigzag structure of the main axis, but differs from other plants in a combination of characteristics. The main axis is wide (2–7 mm) and relatively thin (1–2 mm), with lateral branches arising downward from the faces. The side fronds are very dense and branched irregularly rather than in one plane. The final branches are 6–50 mm long and 1–2 mm thick at the widest point, and contain three to five lumps (the conceptacles). Floats are nearly spherical in shape (about 4 mm in diameter) but present on plants in sheltered locations only.

Cystophora retroflexa, Rocky Cape, Tas.

Cystophora subfarcinata, Frenchmans Bay, WA

Cystophora subfarcinata, Cape Jervis, SA

Caulocystis cephalornithos
(Labillardière) Areschoug

Habitat: Sheltered reef; 0–7 m depth.
Distribution: Cape Naturaliste, WA, to Sydney, NSW, and around Tas.
Maximum size: Thallus length to 1 m.

The two species in the genus *Caulocystis* are closely related to species of *Cystophora* but have side fronds radiating in all directions from the main axis rather than from the face or the edge. *Caulocystis cephalornithos* has small torpedo-shaped floats attached to the axis and the side branches. It is one of the most common species on sheltered reefs, where it is often associated with *Scaberia agardhii* and *Cystophora retroflexa*.

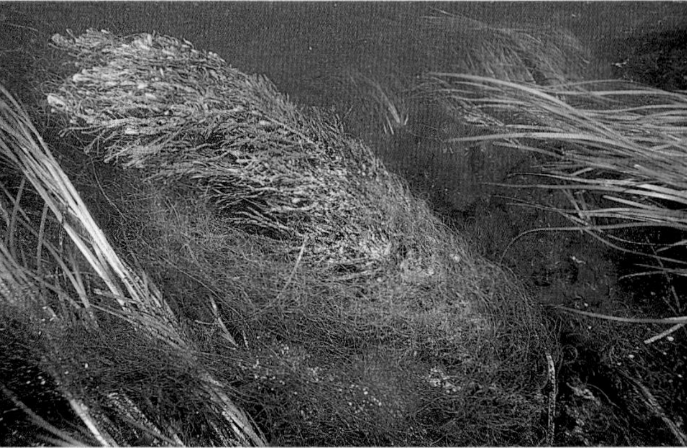
Caulocystis cephalornithos, Cloudy Lagoon, Tas.

Caulocystis uvifera (C. Agardh) Areschoug

Habitat: Sheltered reef; 0–14 m depth.
Distribution: Shark Bay, WA, to Coogee, NSW, and northern and eastern Tas. Also Norfolk I.
Maximum size: Thallus length to 600 mm.

Caulocystis uvifera differs from *C. cephalornithos* primarily by having round rather than cigar-shaped floats. Intergrades between the two seaweeds are moderately common, so there is some doubt that the two species are distinct.

Caulocystis cephalornithos, Rocky Cape, Tas.

Caulocystis uvifera, Georgetown, Tas.

Acrocarpia paniculata (Turner) Areschoug

Habitat: Moderately to submaximally exposed reef; 0–42 m depth.
Distribution: Ceduna, SA, to Port Stephens, NSW, and around Tas. Also Lord Howe I.
Maximum size: Thallus length to 1.5 m.

Acrocarpia paniculata is a robust species of the open coast. Like *Caulocystis cephalornithos* it is related to *Cystophora* but is branched on all sides of the main axis. It differs from *C. cephalornithos* in lacking floats and having smaller (1–10 mm long, 1.5–1 mm wide) receptacles that are densely packed at the ends of the branches.

Acrocarpia paniculata, Rocky Cape, Tas.

Acrocarpia robusta (J. Agardh) Womersley

Habitat: Moderately exposed reef; 0–2 m depth.
Distribution: Cape Naturaliste to Israelite Bay, WA.
Maximum size: Thallus length to 450 mm.

Acrocarpia robusta has several long main axes that each bear a cluster of bushy side-branches towards their ends. Arising from the side-branches are thin ramuli, which are forked at the base and twist up the branch. This species grows in dense patches just below low-tide level.

Acrocarpia robusta, Esperance, WA

FAMILY SARGASSACEAE

The Sargassaceae are closely related to the Cystoseiraceae (described above), but the receptacles are located on specialised branches rather than on vegetative fronds. The family includes only one genus in southern Australia (*Sargassum*) and is a very large one, containing about 200 mainly tropical and subtropical species. In many cases the reproductive fronds of *Sargassum* are produced seasonally; consequently, identification of species of *Sargassum* is often impossible for part of the year because it requires a knowledge of the shape and size of the receptacles.

Sargassum heteromorphum J. Agardh

Habitat: Sheltered reef; 1–10 m depth.
Distribution: Rottnest I, WA, to San Remo, Vic., and northern Tas.
Maximum size: Thallus length to 450 mm.

Sargassum heteromorphum is one of the easiest species of *Sargassum* to identify because of its exceptional shape. The lower section of the plant is flat with wide leaf-like fronds, and this section grades

Sargassum heteromorphum, Flinders I, Tas.

into an upper section of narrow cylindrincal branches. One tropical species, ***Sargassum decurrens***, which occurs as an isolated population in northern Spencer Gulf, is somewhat similar but has larger floats (3–6 mm cf. 1–3 mm).

Sargassum decipiens
(R. Brown ex Turner) J. Agardh

Habitat: Sheltered and moderately exposed reef; 0–13 m depth.
Distribution: Cape Naturaliste, WA, to Western Port, Vic., and around Tas.
Maximum size: Thallus length to 500 mm.

Sargassum decipiens has branched lower fronds, which are slender and stiff and arise from a flattened main axis. The floats are small (1–3 mm in diameter) and spherical. This species can tolerate greater wave action than most other *Sargassum* species. Another southern species, ***Sargassum sonderi***, has the same tongue-like axis at the base of the plant and has similar floats to *S. decipiens*; it differs by possessing small strap-like fronds (30–60 mm long, 2–5 mm broad) at the base of the plant.

Sargassum decipiens (basal fronds), Flinders I, Tas.

Sargassum decipiens, Flinders I, Tas.

Sargassum varians Sonder

Habitat: Sheltered reef; 0–38 m depth.
Distribution: Perth, WA, to Wilsons Promontory, Vic., and northern Tas.
Maximum size: Thallus length to 500 mm.

Sargassum varians is characterised by flat, branched lower fronds that project downwards from the basal axis. The upper branches are thin and cylindrical, while the floats are relatively large (3–10 mm in diameter) and spherical. It occurs commonly in mixed algal beds with other *Sargassum* and *Cystophora* species.

Sargassum varians, Flinders I, Tas.

Sargassum verruculosum
(Mertens) C. Agardh

Habitat: Sheltered and moderately exposed reef; 1–16 m depth.
Distribution: Cape Leeuwin, WA, to Sydney, NSW, and around Tas. Also New Zealand.
Maximum size: Thallus length to 1 m.

Sargassum verruculosum is the most widely distributed of the group of *Sargassum* with branched lower fronds. It has a similar shape to *S. varians* but has a rounded rather than flat main axis and has narrower (1–3 mm cf. 3–6 mm wide) lower side branches. The upper side-branches arise from the main axis in a spiral pattern that is distinctive when seen in the living plant. Only one specimen has been found in New South Wales.

Sargassum fallax Sonder

Habitat: Moderately exposed reef; 0–48 m depth.
Distribution: Houtman Abrolhos, WA, to Ballina, NSW, and around Tas.
Maximum size: Thallus length to 1 m.

Sargassum fallax is the most abundant of the large bushy *Sargassum* species with unbranched, leaf-like lower fronds. This species cannot be distinguished from several other species if the slender reproductive upper branches are missing, and these are generally absent during the winter and spring months. The characteristic features of *S. fallax* are receptacles at the end of the upper branches that are 2–4 mm long and lack spines, basal leaves that are large (40–250 mm long, 5–20 mm wide) and lack a sharply serrated edge, and floats that are 5–10 mm in diameter.

Sargassum fallax (basal fronds), Rocky Cape, Tas.

Sargassum vestitum, Rocky Cape, Tas.

Sargassum verruculosum, Coles Bay, Tas.

Sargassum verruculosum, Cloudy Lagoon, Tas.

Sargassum vestitum
(R. Brown ex Turner) C. Agardh

Habitat: Submaximally and maximally exposed reef; 0–12 m depth.
Distribution: Robe, SA, to Sydney, NSW, and around Tas.
Maximum size: Thallus length to 1.5 m.

Sargassum vestitum is usually the only species of *Sargassum* encountered on heavily wave-exposed reefs. Unlike its close relatives, it can generally be identified solely on the shape of its basal leaves. These are tough, glossy and have a smooth edge. The receptacles occur in dense clusters on the upper branches in late summer and autumn and are 1–5 mm long and spiny. Floats are rarely present.

PHYLUM (DIVISION) RHODOPHYTA

Red algae, red seaweeds

The red algae are a diverse group of predominantly benthic algae that occur in all the world's oceans. Because of the particular combination of pigments carried by these algae to trap light energy, rhodophytes can normally be easily recognised by their red or purple coloration, although in dead specimens and some species in shallow water this colour bleaches to yellow or green as the pigments break down. Compared with the brown and green algae, red algae rarely dominate reef communities in terms of density but often tolerate lower light conditions than other marine plants and are generally the most abundant plants in deep water. Reproduction in red algae varies considerably in the different groups. Some species have a three-phase life cycle, with the plants in the different generations bearing little resemblance to each other. Other species have a life cycle with one generation identical in appearance but carrying twice the number of chromosomes as another generation, and a third generation that is greatly reduced in size. Yet other species have a two-phase life cycle, with the second generation reduced to a specialised reproductive structure on the surface of the parent plant.

Approximately 4500 species are known worldwide, with about 800 species recorded from southern Australia, making this region the largest centre of biodiversity for the group. Because of the large number of species, this book includes only some of the most obvious red algae and therefore cannot be used to accurately identify specimens. Placing names on red algae is generally a much more difficult and confusing process than for the other seaweed groups because it relies largely on characteristics of the reproductive structures rather than overall appearance. Consequently, sheet-like and branched algae can occur together in one genus (e.g. *Sarcothalia*), while superficially similar plants may be very distantly related. For many if not most species, identification requires the microscopic examination of cell arrangement and reproductive structures.

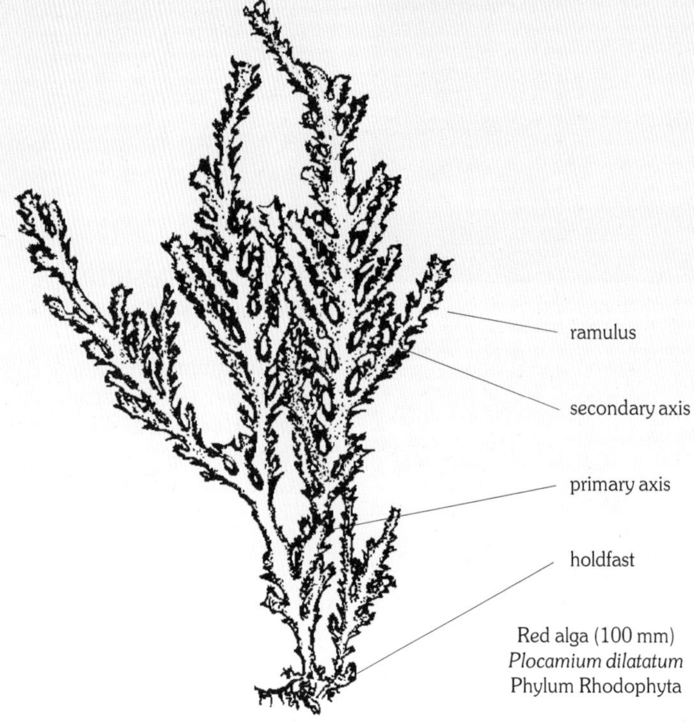

Red alga (100 mm)
Plocamium dilatatum
Phylum Rhodophyta

FAMILY BANGIACEAE

Species in this family have filamentous or flattened thalli that are only one or two cells thick. They grow by division of cells throughout the thallus and are attached to rock or other plants by a holdfast constructed from several filaments.

Porphyra lucasii (R. Brown ex Turner) C. Agardh

Habitat: Sheltered and moderately exposed rocky shores; mid intertidal.
Distribution: Cottesloe, WA, to Sydney, NSW, and around Tas.
Maximum size: Thallus length to 400 mm.

Porphyra lucasii is a delicate purple leafy alga seen between tidemarks on sheltered southern shores during the cooler months. It is rare in the more northerly sections of its range, and only two specimens have been recorded from New South Wales. The species is normally found dried to the rock and is occasionally confused with the green seaweed *Ulva taeniata*. Plants in the genus *Porphyra* are collectively known as 'nori' in Japan and form the basis of a $1 billion food industry there. *Porphyra lucasii* is slightly tougher than the Japanese plants but has the same distinctive taste.

Porphyra columbina Montagne

Habitat: Exposed rocky shores; mid intertidal.
Distribution: Elliston, SA, to Sydney, NSW, and around Tas. Also New Zealand, South America and subantarctic islands.
Maximum size: Thallus length to 400 mm.

Porphyra columbina is a thicker and more robust plant than *P. lucasii* and doesn't crumble easily when dried. It lives on shores with greater wave action than *P. lucasii* and is most prevalent during the winter months.

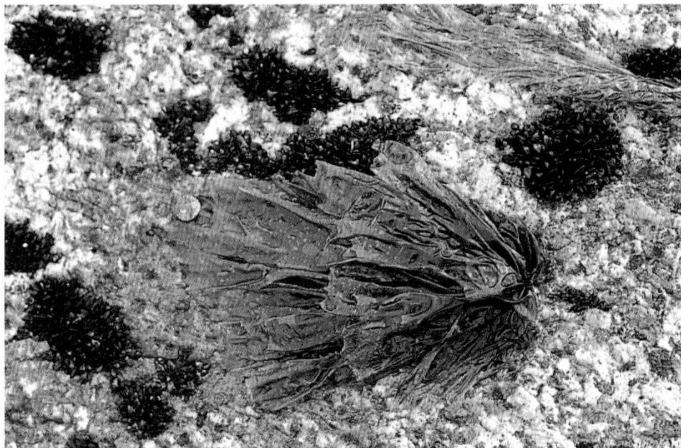

Porphyra columbina, Bicheno, Tas.

Porphyra lucasii, Cloudy Lagoon, Tas.

FAMILY GELIDIACEAE

This family is characterised by plants that grow by the division of a single apical cell on each branch and by a distinctive cellular organisation in the reproductive structures. Species in this family contain large quantities of agar, a gelling agent used extensively in microbiological research.

Pterocladia capillacea (Gmelin) Bornet

Habitat: Moderately and submaximally exposed reefs; 0–16 m depth.
Distribution: Perth, WA, to Stradbroke I, Qld, and around Tas. Also widespread overseas.
Maximum size: Thallus length to 200 mm.

Pterocladia capillacea normally occurs as dense turfs on steeply sloping wave-swept reefs. It has a similar shape to another species, ***Gelidium australe***, but the axes of that species are rounded rather than flattened. Like other closely related species of *Pterocladia* and *Gelidium*, *P. capillacea* contains considerable agar and will form a firm gel if boiled in a small amount of water and left to cool.

Pterocladia capillacea, Bicheno, Tas.

FAMILY PEYSSONNELIACEAE

The family Peyssonneliaceae contains flattened species that partly or completely adhere to rock or plant surfaces and are often calcified. Growth occurs from a row of marginal cells, producing a concentric pattern. This family belongs to a large red algal order, the Gigartinales, which is distinguished by the relatively unspecialised nature of the cell that supports the nucleus after fertilisation.

Sonderopelta coriacea, Waterfall Bay, Tas.

Sonderopelta coriacea Womersley & Sinkora

Habitat: Moderately and submaximally exposed reefs; 3–33 m depth.
Distribution: Ceduna, SA, to Walkerville, Vic., and around Tas. Also New Zealand.
Maximum size: Thallus length to 250 mm.

Sonderopelta coriacea is a dark-red alga that occurs in shaded locations and has a flattened lobe shape. Although very common, the species had long been confused with other similar-looking plants and was scientifically named only in 1981. *Sonderopelta coriacea* is often mistaken for *Peyssonnelia novaehollandiae*, particularly as the two species can occur beside each other on reefs, but is distinguished by the undersurface being covered by a matt of fine white hairs.

Peyssonnelia novaehollandiae, Horseshoe Reef, WA

Peyssonnelia novaehollandiae Kützing

Habitat: Moderately and submaximally exposed reefs; 0–48 m depth.
Distribution: Geraldton, WA, to Coffs Harbour, NSW, and around Tas.
Maximum size: Thallus length to 200 mm.

Peyssonnelia novaehollandiae differs from most other *Peyssonnelia* species by being only partly attached to the reef, rather than attached across all of the plants' undersurface. It occurs in the same habitat as *Sonderopelta coriacea* and has a similar shape, but with a red undersurface that lacks hairs.

FAMILY HALYMENIACEAE

Species in this family have a distinctive cell structure, with filaments in the central section of the plant and ovoid cells in the outer layer. They have a three-stage life history, in which the two conspicuous stages look identical although one carries twice the chromosome number of the other.

Halymenia plana Zanardini

Habitat: Exposed reef; 2–23 m depth.
Distribution: Eucla, SA, to Walkerville, Vic., and around Tas.
Maximum size: Thallus length to 300 mm.

Halymenia plana has a red, broadly flattened, ovate thallus with dark red blotches on the surface. It is not common at any site but is widely distributed along the exposed southern coast in shaded situations under rock overhangs.

Halymenia plana, Bicheno, Tas.

Grateloupia filicina (Lamouroux) C. Agardh

Habitat: Sheltered and moderately exposed reef; 0–3 m depth.
Distribution: Perth, WA, to Wybury Head, Qld, and around Tas. Also widespread overseas.
Maximum size: Thallus length to 250 mm.

Grateloupia filicina is a common species in rock pools on sheltered coasts. It can be recognised by the slippery texture and characteristic shape. The number of side-branches on plants varies considerably between sites, depending on the local level of wave action.

Grateloupia filicina, Tinderbox, Tas.

Gelinaria ulvoidea Sonder

Habitat: Moderately exposed reef; 5–28 m depth.
Distribution: Yanchep, WA, to Walkerville, Vic., and northern Tas.
Maximum size: Thallus length to 750 mm.

Gelinaria ulvoidea is a large rubbery alga with a much branched thallus. The species has a similar appearance to a related species, ***Halymenia floresia***, but can be distinguished by more open branching, secondary axes that narrow near the point of attachment and a thinner and different textured thallus.

Gelinaria ulvoidea, Horseshoe Reef, WA

Polyopes constrictus (Turner) J. Agardh

Habitat: Moderately to submaximally exposed reef; 1–20 m depth.
Distribution: Sleaford Bay, SA, to Twofold Bay, NSW, and around Tas.
Maximum size: Thallus length to 160 mm.

Polyopes constrictus is a wiry alga with slightly flattened forked branches that usually narrow towards the base. It is similar in external appearance to a species that is not closely related, ***Peltasta australis***, and microscopic examination is often needed to distinguish between these plants. *Polyopes constrictus* occurs quite commonly in clumps on shaded areas of reef.

Polyopes constrictus, Bicheno, Tas.

Thamnoclonium dichotomum (J. Agardh) J. Agardh

Habitat: Sheltered and moderately exposed reef; 3–32 m depth.
Distribution: Nickol Bay, WA, to Ballina, NSW, and around Tas.
Maximum size: Thallus length to 300 mm.

Thamnoclonium dichotomum is a reddish-purple alga with a surface that is usually covered by white sponge. The species is easily recognised as it is the only common species with rigid, knobbed and repeatedly divided branches. It is often the dominant plant in low light conditions below the kelp zone.

Thamnoclonium dichotomum, Bicheno, Tas.

FAMILY KALLYMENIACEAE

This family is characterised by a distinctive arrangement of cells forming the female reproductive structure. The cells in the centre of the thallus are ovoid and closely packed or filamentous, while those in the outer layer are filamentous.

Kallymenia cribrosa Harvey

Habitat: Sheltered and moderately exposed reef; 3–40 m depth.
Distribution: Houtman Abrolhos, WA, to Flinders, Vic., and around Tas.
Maximum size: Thallus length to 300 mm.

Kallymenia cribrosa is a beautiful lace-like alga that is moderately common along sheltered open coasts. It has a similar appearance to a close relative that occurs in deeper water, ***Kallymenia cribrogloea***, but the holes in the thallus of that species decrease substantially in size (to 1–2 mm in diameter) toward the margin.

Kallymenia cribrosa, Bruny I, Tas.

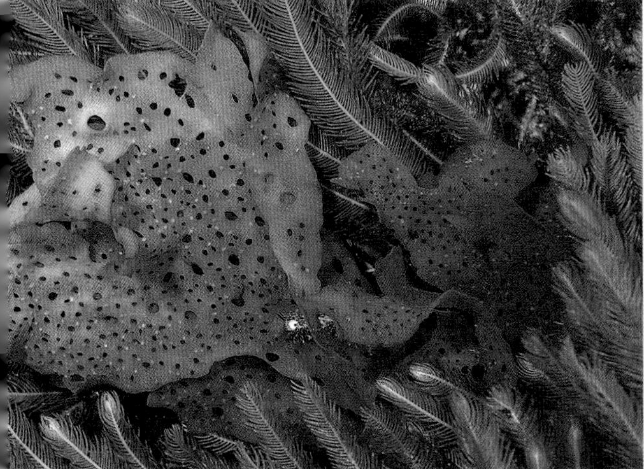

Kallymenia tasmanica Harvey

Habitat: Moderately exposed reef; 4–40 m depth.
Distribution: Gulf St Vincent, SA, to Western Port, Vic., and around Tas.
Maximum size: Thallus length to 300 mm.

Kallymenia tasmanica has a tougher frond and is darker than *Kallymenia cribrosa* and lacks the many perforations. There are, however, a number of other flattened red algae that are not closely related, and therefore microscopic examination of cell arrangement is needed for accurate identification. *Kallymenia tasmanica* occurs in much the same habitat as *K. cribrosa* but is the more common species in Tasmania.

Kallymenia tasmanica, Bruny I, Tas.

Callophyllis rangiferina (Turner) Womersley

Habitat: Moderately to submaximally exposed reef; 3–24 m depth.
Distribution: Champion Bay, WA, to Tathra, NSW, and around Tas.
Maximum size: Thallus length to 250 mm.

Callophyllis rangiferina has a regular, highly branched frond that is flattened in the one plane. The species occurs commonly on southeastern reefs, and detached specimens often wash ashore on beaches.

Callophyllis rangiferina, Ninepin Point, Tas.

Callophyllis lambertii (Turner) J. Agardh

Habitat: Exposed reef; 3–35 m depth.
Distribution: Ceduna, SA, to Walkerville, Vic., and around Tas.
Maximum size: Thallus length to 400 mm.

Callophyllis lambertii has a similar branching pattern to *C. rangiferina* but a more solid appearance because the width of the final branches is greater (>1 mm near their end). Specimens are sometimes found with intermediate characteristics, and it is difficult to assign these to one or the other species. *Callophyllis lambertii* tolerates slightly more exposed conditions than *C. rangiferina*.

Callophyllis lambertii, Bicheno, Tas.

FAMILY PHYLLOPHORACEAE

Species of Phylloporaceae are grouped together on the basis of cell arrangement in the frond, and the presence of chains of spore-producing structures (tetrasporangia) that are located within blister-like protuberances on the frond surface.

Stenogramme interrupta

(C. Agardh) Montagne ex Harvey

Habitat: Moderately exposed reef; 5–33 m depth.
Distribution: Nuyts Reef, SA, to Arrawarra, NSW, and northern and eastern Tas. Also New Zealand and widespread in the Northern Hemisphere.
Maximum size: Thallus length to 150 mm.

Stenogramme interrupta has a flattened frond that forks several times and expands in size out from each fork. Reproductive structures can sometimes be seen forming a line down the centre of branches. The alga is moderately common along the open coast but generally lies close to the reef surface and so is not often noticed.

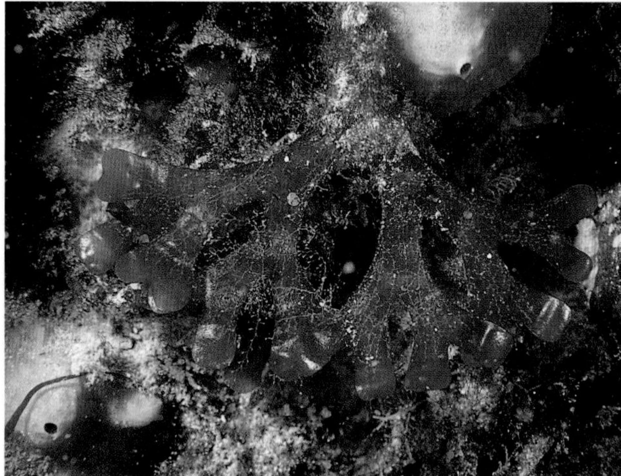

Stenogramme interrupta, Bicheno, Tas.

FAMILY GIGARTINACEAE

This family contains plants that are often flattened and have a rubbery feel. They are distinguished from other families by the method of growth (cells dividing at the end of parallel rows of filaments) and the arrangement of cells in the female reproductive structure (the cell that produces eggs is suspended on a filament of three cells).

Rhodoglossum gigartinoides

(Sonder) Edyvane & Womersley

Habitat: Sheltered and moderately exposed rock, shells; 0–5 m depth.
Distribution: Hamelin Bay, WA, to San Remo, Vic., and around Tas.
Maximum size: Thallus length to 600 mm.

Rhodoglossum gigartinoides, Cloudy Lagoon, Tas.

Rhodoglossum gigartinoides has such a variable appearance that the species has been given nine different scientific names since it was first described in 1855. The plants are usually large, flat and moderately branched, with numerous reproductive structures dotted over the surface. The most characteristic habitat is on rocks surrounded by sand in areas of high tidal current flow.

Gigartina recurva Edyvane & Womersley

Habitat: Sheltered and moderately exposed reef; lower intertidal.
Distribution: Musselroe Bay to Recherche Bay, Tas.
Maximum size: Thallus length to 100 mm.

Gigartina recurva is often the dominant alga on sheltered eastern Tasmanian reefs just above low-tide level. The species has a distinctive twisted shape and a dark purple colour in shaded locations, but bleaches to yellow-green when exposed to the sun. Until recently, this species was thought to be the New Zealand species *Gigartina ancistroclada*.

Gigartina recurva, Taroona, Tas.

FAMILY ARESCHOUGIACEAE

This family is characterised by its reproductive features, including the presence of spore-bearing structures that are scattered through the outer layer of the thallus and which are divided by parallel walls into quarters. Most species in the family are erect and densely branched.

Callophycus dorsiferus (C. Agardh) Silva

Habitat: Moderately exposed reef; 1–8 m depth.
Distribution: Dongara to Cape Leeuwin, WA.
Maximum size: Thallus length to 250 mm.

Callophycus dorsiferus has a distinctive branching pattern with long main axes that have broad midribs bearing flat side-branches. These side-branches are arranged in a crowded fishbone pattern with thin flat branchlets. The species is moderately common on reefs near Perth.

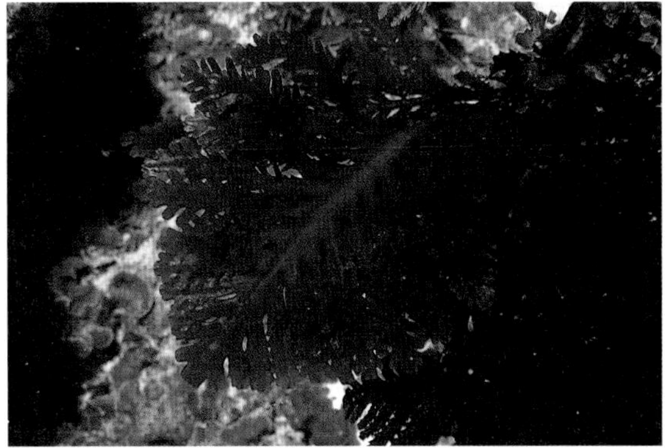

Callophycus dorsiferus, Little I, WA

Callophycus oppositifolius (C. Agardh) Silva

Habitat: Moderately exposed reef; 2–38 m depth.
Distribution: Geraldton, WA, to Yorke Peninsula, SA.
Maximum size: Thallus length to 300 mm.

Callophycus oppositifolius has a similar branching structure to *C. dorsiferus* but the final branches are narrower (0.5–1 mm cf. 1–2 mm broad). Both species are patchily distributed but where they do occur can form dense clumps.

Callophycus oppositifolius, Little I, WA

Erythroclonium sonderi Harvey

Habitat: Moderately exposed reef; 3–40 m depth.
Distribution: Mullaloo, WA, to Robe, SA, and King I, Tas.
Maximum size: Thallus length to 150 mm.

Erythroclonium sonderi is a profusely branched plant that is common off the southern west coast. The branches are composed of small ovoid segments that narrow at the lower end and contain a dense internal matrix of cells.

Erythroclonium sonderi, Horseshoe Reef, WA

FAMILY PLOCAMIACEAE

Species in the family Plocamiaceae have a distinctive appearance because of beautiful geometric arrangements produced by the regular branching pattern. Branches arise from the edges of flat axes, with two or more branchlets alternating in a group on either side of the larger branch. The smallest, tooth-like branchlets are known as ramuli and are often followed in each group by a larger branchlet that may itself regularly branch.

Plocamium angustum
(J. Agardh) Hooker & Harvey

Habitat: Moderately and submaximally exposed reef; 0–50 m depth.
Distribution: Ceduna, SA, to The Entrance, NSW, and around Tas. Also Lord Howe I.
Maximum size: Thallus length to 250 mm.

Plocamium angustum is the most common southern Australian species of *Plocamium*. It has narrow axes (<1 mm) with a regular alternating series of branchlets

Plocamium angustum, Low Head, Tas.

consisting of a short peg-like ramulus followed by a small branched frond. A closely related but less abundant species, ***Plocamium costatum***, has a similar appearance but the axes are wider (1–2 mm) and the reproductive structures different.

Plocamium dilatatum J. Agardh

Habitat: Exposed reef; 3–22 m depth.
Distribution: Victor Harbor, SA, to Port Phillip Bay, Vic., and around Tas.
Maximum size: Thallus length to 250 mm.

Plocamium dilatatum differs from *Plocamium angustum* by having wide (2–4 mm diameter) final branches and short peg-like ramuli with a finely serrated outer edge. The grape-like clusters at the branch junctions (shown in the photo) are reproductive structures, known as stichidia. They occur seasonally on the different species of *Plocamium* but are particularly well developed on *P. dilatatum*. *Plocamium dilatatum* tends to occur in more exposed conditions than the related species and is the only one found commonly on submaximally exposed coasts.

Plocamium dilatatum, Actaeon I, Tas.

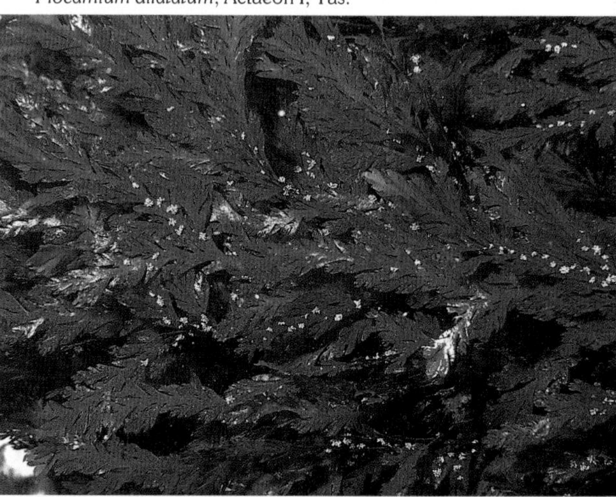

Plocamium patagiatum J. Agardh

Habitat: Exposed reef; 8–26 m depth.
Distribution: Great Australian Bight, SA, to Cape Woolamai, Vic., and around Tas.
Maximum size: Thallus length to 300 mm.

Plocamium patagiatum is easily confused with *P. dilatatum* because the width of axes is similar and the ramuli are occasionally peg-like with a serrated edge. However, *P. patagiatum* normally has narrow, non-serrated ramuli, which alternate with either long side-branchlets or short digitate stumps. This species also often has a matt rather than shiny surface because of a covering of encrusting coralline algae. It is less common than most other species of *Plocamium*.

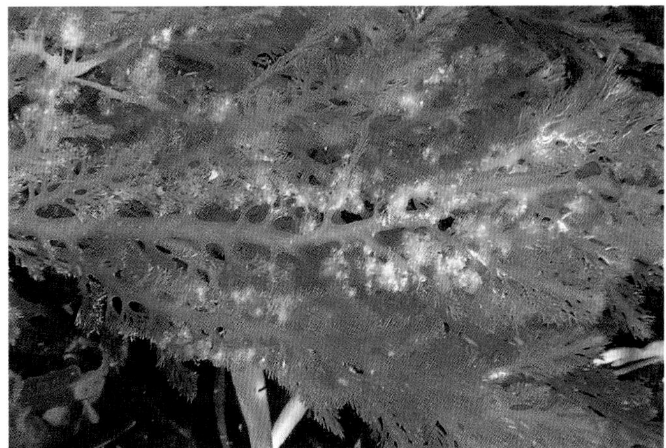

Plocamium mertensii, Canal Rocks, WA

Plocamium patagiatum, Waterfall Bay, Tas.

Plocamium mertensii (Greville) Harvey

Habitat: Moderately exposed reef; 0–50 m depth.
Distribution: Nickol Bay, WA, to Gabo I, Vic., and northern Tas.
Maximum size: Thallus length to 500 mm.

Plocamium mertensii plants vary considerably in shape. The more common form has long branched fronds alternating in pairs from the sides of the axis. Small vegetative structures can usually be seen at the base of the branches. The yellow colour on the photographed specimen is caused by fading and is not a usual characteristic of the species. The other form of *P. mertensii* has an alternating branching series made up of a short, hook-like ramulus followed by the branched frond. This form has a similar appearance to *P. angustum*, except that the branches and ramuli are much wider (>2 mm).

Plocamium preissianum Sonder

Habitat: Moderately and submaximally exposed reef; 2–50 m depth.
Distribution: Geraldton, WA, to Wilsons Prom., Vic., and northern Tas.
Maximum size: Thallus length to 500 mm.

Plocamium preissianum is the most easily recognised species of *Plocamium*, as it is the only wide-axis (>2 mm) species with alternating series of three (or four) rather than two branchlets. The branching series usually consists of a hook-like ramulus followed by one or two small branchlets that are often divided

Plocamium preissianum, Little I, WA

Plocamium mertensii, Actaeon I, Tas.

near the tip and then the larger branched frond. Two other species of *Plocamium* are also present in southern Australia, both with alternating series of three to five branchlets. ***Plocamium cartilagineum*** has axes 1–1.5 mm broad, with two or three fine branchlets followed by the longer branched frond. ***Plocamium leptophyllum*** has extremely narrow axes (0.5 mm) and branchlets in an alternating series of four or five which include one that is strongly curved and hooked.

FAMILY PHACELOCARPACEAE

Plants in this family have long flattened branches with rows of short, tooth-like ramuli of similar length along the edges. The family comprises only one genus.

Phacelocarpus peperocarpus

(Poiret) Wynne, Ardré & Silva

Habitat: Moderately and submaximally exposed reef; 2–40 m depth.
Distribution: Esperance, WA, to Sydney, NSW, and northern Tas.
Maximum size: Thallus length to 500 mm.

Five species of *Phacelocarpus* are recorded from southern Australia, all with the characteristic serrated-edged axes. *Phacelocarpus peperocarpus*, a species formerly called *P. labillardieri,* is by far the most common of these species. It is distinguished by having the ramuli along the edges of the axes longer than the axes are wide and by having the reproductive structures attached to the ends of short stalks between the ramuli. In seasons when the reproductive structures are absent, identification is difficult because a common species in a different family, *Delisea pulchra*, has a similar shape. The reproductive structures of *Delisea pulchra* are located at the end of the branches.

Phacelocarpus peperocarpus, Flinders I, Tas.

FAMILY HYPNEACEAE

Species of Hypneaceae are filamentous and profusely branched. They are chiefly distinguished from other families by the cellular structure of a microscopic phase in the life cycle, after fertilisation of the egg.

Hypnea ramentacea (C. Agardh) J. Agardh

Habitat: Other seaweeds; 0–25 m depth.
Distribution: Dongara, WA, to Walkerville, Vic., and around Tas.
Maximum size: Thallus length to 250 mm.

Hypnea ramentacea is a slender, much branched species that is commonly found growing on other species in moderately exposed conditions. It can usually be identified by the hooked ends of many of the branches.

Hypnea ramentacea, Ninepin Point, Tas.

FAMILY BONNEMAISONIACEAE

This family includes elaborately branched species, which grow by the division of cells at the branch apices. They have a three-phase life cycle, with a microscopic phase and two macroscopic phases which are different in appearance. A feature of these plants is the presence of gland cells in the thallus containing high concentrations of iodine or bromine.

Asparogopsis armata Harvey

Habitat: Reef, other seaweeds; 0–10 m depth.
Distribution: Perth, WA, to Port Stephens, NSW, and around Tas. Also New Zealand and Europe.
Maximum size: Thallus length to 250 mm.

Asparogopsis armata gains the armoured part of its name from the short spines on the lower branches, which are used to cling onto other plants. This phase of the life cycle is found commonly in sheltered and moderately exposed locations and is an important food for blacklip abalone. The species also has a small attached or unattached phase, which is prevalent at a few locations along the open coast. In this phase plants occur as small, red, filamentous balls, which often float near the wave break, turning the sea red. This phase was named *Falkenbergia rufolanosa* and classified in a different order of red algae until recently. *Asparogopsis armata* is thought to have been introduced from Australia to Europe in about 1920 and is prevalent there now.

Asparogopsis armata, Bruny I, Tas.

Delisea pulchra (Greville) Montagne

Habitat: Sheltered and moderately exposed reef; 0–25 m depth.
Distribution: Perth, WA, to Ballina, NSW, and around Tas. Also New Zealand and subantarctic islands.
Maximum size: Thallus length to 600 mm.

Delisea pulchra, Waterfall Bay, Tas.

Delisea pulchra has narrow fishbone axes that resemble, but differ anatomically from, *Phacelocarpus peperocarpus*. The reproductive structures of *D. pulchra* appear as small swellings at the end of the branches but are not always present.

Ptilonia australasica Harvey

Habitat: Moderately and submaximally exposed reef; 3–18 m depth.
Distribution: Robe, SA, to Williamstown, Vic., and around Tas.
Maximum size: Thallus length to 200 mm.

While *Ptilonia australasica* can usually be identified from the shape of the fronds, the most characteristic feature of this species are large, stalked reproductive structures that are attached to the sides of the branches. This species is most common towards the southern end of its range and is one of the more abundant red algae in Tasmania and Victoria.

Ptilonia australasica, Waterfall Bay, Tas.

Ptilonia australasica, Zuidpool Rock, Tas.

FAMILY GRACILARIACEAE

The Gracilariaceae are firm fleshy algae characterised by their reproductive structures and densely packed cells in the centre of the thallus. Included are some of the most commercially valuable seaweed species, which together provide most of the world's agar.

Gracilaria cliftonii, Bunker Bay, WA

Gracilaria cliftonii Withell, Millar & Kraft

Habitat: Moderately exposed rock; 0–7 m depth.
Distribution: Fremantle, WA, to Point Lonsdale, Vic., and northern Tas.
Maximum size: Thallus length to 180 mm.

Gracilaria cliftonii has open, regularly forked branches, which are long, round in cross-section and smooth. The species generally occurs at sand-abraded sites on flat rock and is moderately common. Specimens collected from shaded conditions are a light pink colour, while those exposed to sunlight are yellow.

Gracilaria harveyana J. Agardh

Habitat: Moderately exposed reef; 1–12 m depth.
Distribution: Geraldton, WA, to Fowlers Bay, SA.
Maximum size: Thallus length to 250 mm.

Gracilaria harveyana is a larger, more rigid and densely branched species than *G. cliftonii* and has an irregular branching pattern. Branches in the centre of the clump are a dark red colour, while outer branches are bleached yellow. The plant darkens to almost black on drying. This species is moderately common on the southern west coast but only one questionable specimen has been collected on the south coast (at Fowlers Bay).

Gracilaria harveyana, Bunker Bay, WA

Gracilaria secundata Harvey

Habitat: Sheltered and moderately exposed reef, shells; 0–5 m depth.
Distribution: Vic. to Newcastle, NSW, and around Tas. Also Lord Howe I and New Zealand.
Maximum size: Thallus length to 400 mm.

Gracilaria secundata, Cloudy Lagoon, Tas

Gracilaria secundata is an irregularly branched species of *Gracilaria* with several branches arising after each other from the one side of the main axis. The branches are firm, stiff and round in cross-section. Numerous rounded reproductive structures, the cystocarps, appear as conspicuous bumps when they are seasonally present. The species is common in sand-abraded habitats in estuaries and on moderately exposed reefs, and can survive burial in sand for extended periods.

Curdiea angustata (Sonder) Millar

Habitat: Exposed reef; 2–15 m depth.
Distribution: Encounter Bay, SA, to Sydney, NSW, and around Tas.
Maximum size: Thallus length to 600 mm.

Curdiea angustata has a fleshy, flattened thallus, with both narrow and wide branches arising almost indiscriminately from the edges of large primary branches. The species is easiest to recognise when fertile, as it then has small rounded reproductive structures arranged along the margins. *Curdiea angustata* is common on the eastern south coast; only a single plant has been collected in New South Wales.

Curdiea angustata, Waterfall Bay, Tas.

Melanthalia obtusata J. Agardh

Habitat: Exposed reef; 4–26 m depth.
Distribution: Kangaroo I, SA, to Port Phillip Bay, Vic., and around Tas.
Maximum size: Thallus length to 600 mm.

Melanthalia obtusata is a common dark-purple seaweed with flat fronds 2–4 mm wide, which regularly divide into two. The reproductive structures, when present, appear as swollen lumps on the sides of the plant. This species is tough and leathery, an adaptation that allows it to withstand heavy wave action.

Melanthalia obtusata, Ninepin Point, Tas.

FAMILY CORALLINACEAE
Coralline algae

Species of Corallinaceae can usually be recognised by having a rigid thallus that is reinforced by calcium carbonate. Because the calcium carbonate acts as a cement in many species, this family has an extremely important ecological role. Coral reefs, for example, could not exist without coralline algae binding dead coral together into a solid structure. The Corallinaceae is one of the largest families of red algae and includes branched and encrusting forms. Branched species (known as 'geniculate coralline algae') are constructed from calcareous segments connected at slender, flexible, cartilaginous nodes known as geniculae. The crustose or nongeniculate algae include species that form a thin film over rock and plant surfaces, thread-like species that penetrate other seaweeds, and species that lay down layer after layer, producing a solid mass known as a rhodolith if it is unattached and can roll around freely. Thin encrusting species appear as splashes of pink paint on virtually all shaded rock surfaces. These encrusting species are commonly called 'lithothamnia' after one of the more common genera and are notoriously difficult to identify.

Amphiroa anceps (Lamarck) Decaisne

Habitat: Moderately exposed reef; 0–12 m depth.
Distribution: Around the Australian mainland and northern Tas.
Maximum size: Thallus length to 200 mm.

Amphiroa anceps has regularly divided branches formed from flat calcareous segments that are joined at obvious cartilaginous nodes (the geniculae). It is the most common of the branched coralline algae found on the eastern and southwestern Australian coasts. The branches of plants along the west coast are noticeably wider than those found in the east.

Amphiroa anceps, Esperance, WA

Haliptilon roseum (Lamarck) Garbary & Johansen

Habitat: Exposed reef, seagrass stems, algae; 0–10 m depth.
Distribution: Shark Bay, WA, to Bowen, Qld, and around Tas. Also Lord Howe I and New Zealand.
Maximum size: Thallus length to 120 mm.

Haliptilon roseum is a purple-pink coralline alga with regularly dividing branches. It occurs abundantly around the coast of southern Australia. This species has been known by a variety of different names in the past, including *Corallina cuvieri*. *Haliptilon roseum* differs from true *Corallina* species, including the locally occurring alga ***Corallina officinalis***, by having shorter segments in the major axes (about 0.5 mm cf. about 2 mm) and by sometimes having forked branches.

Haliptilon roseum, Little I, WA

Metagoniolithon stelliferum
(Lamarck) Weber-van Bosse

Habitat: Sheltered and moderately exposed seagrass stems, algae, reef; 0–10 m depth.
Distribution: Shark Bay, WA, to Wilsons Promontory, Vic., and northern Tas.
Maximum size: Thallus length to 150 mm.

Metagoniolithon stelliferum is the most common calcareous alga that lives attached to seagrasses in southern Australia and has a special affinity for the stem of *Amphibolis antarctica*. In some sheltered areas where the growth of this species is particularly prolific, its total weight can equal the weight of seagrass. The plant is branched in a characteristic pattern of whorls, with about six segments radiating from each junction.

Metagoniolithon stelliferum, Little I, WA

Lithophyllum hyperellum Foslie

Habitat: Exposed reef; mid to low intertidal.
Distribution: Central Vic. and eastern, southern and western Tas.
Maximum size: Thallus height to 30 mm.

Lithophyllum hyperellum forms a conspicuous band in the lower intertidal zone on exposed Tasmanian shores, particularly in the south and west. It is easily recognised by the mustard coloration and the granular surface. Numerous small invertebrate species find refuge among the larger clumps.

Lithophyllum hyperellum, Bicheno, Tas.

Synarthrophyton patena
(J.D. Hooker & Harvey) Townsend

Habitat: Exposed algae; 0–36 m depth.
Distribution: SA to Sydney, NSW, and around Tas. Also New Zealand, South Africa and various subantarctic islands.
Maximum size: Thallus width to 15 mm.

Synarthrophyton patena, Muttonbird I, Tas.

Synarthrophyton patena is a distinctive disk-shaped coralline algae with numerous rounded reproductive structures (the conceptacles) in the surface. It is one of only two species in the genus and lives attached to slender branched red algae, particularly *Ballia callitricha*.

Phymatolithon masonianum

Wilks & Woelkerling

Habitat: Exposed reef; 4–20 m depth.
Distribution: Cape Buffon, SA, and around Tas.
Maximum size: Thallus width to 150 mm.

Phymatolithon masonianum is a large plate-like coralline alga that overgrows rock but is not strongly attached. The species is most common in southeastern Tasmania, where it occurs on moderately deep reefs.

Phymatolithon masonianum, Waterfall Bay, Tas.

Sporolithon durum, Quarry Bay, WA

Sporolithon durum

(Foslie) Townsend & Woelkerling

Habitat: Sheltered and moderately exposed reef; 0–30 m depth.
Distribution: Rottnest I, WA, to Botany Bay, NSW.
Maximum size: Thallus width to 110 mm.

A number of different genera of coralline algae can occur free of permanent attachment to the seabed and are collectively known as rhodoliths. *Sporolithon durum* is a large alga with prominent lobes. It often occurs as a rhodolith but is also sometimes attached to reef.

Encrusting coralline algae, Spring Beach, Tas.

FAMILY RHODYMENIACEAE

This family contains species that are grouped largely on the basis of reproductive details (the position of the cell that receives the nucleus from the fertilised egg). They exhibit a great range of shapes and sizes, with some having a firm texture and others gelatinous.

Botryocladia obovata (Sonder) Kylin

Habitat: Moderately exposed reef; 3–10 m depth.
Distribution: Perth, WA, to Vic. and northern Tas.
Maximum size: Thallus length to 200 mm.

The fronds of *Botryocladia obovata* consist of dense clusters of grape-like branches arising radially from the main stem. These branches are filled with sticky gelatinous material when young but develop a hole in the end and become hollow with age.

Botryocladia obovata, Port Victoria, SA

Gloiosaccion brownii Harvey

Habitat: Sheltered and moderately exposed rock, shells; 4–20 m depth.
Distribution: Perth, WA, to Vic. and around Tas.
Maximum size: Thallus length to 300 mm.

Gloiosaccion brownii possesses sausage-shaped fronds that arise from a common base and contain a sticky gelatinous substance. The species occurs commonly attached to shell fragments or small rocks, most often at calm sites in relatively deep water. A similar species that is yet to be scientifically named

Gloiosaccion ?brownii, D'Entrecasteaux Channel, Tas.

occurs in Tasmania. It differs by having reproductive structures grouped in clusters rather than scattered across the thallus.

Rhodymenia australis Sonder

Habitat: Exposed reef; 0–20 m depth.
Distribution: Geraldton, WA, to Coffs Harbour, NSW, and around Tas. Also New Zealand.
Maximum size: Thallus length to 100 mm.

Rhodymenia australis is a common species of red alga found in shaded locations on exposed reefs. It has a flattened thallus with wide, regularly forked branches that have rounded ends. Although the appearance seems to be distinctive, this species cannot be identified without microscopic examination of the cell structure because several other red algal species (e.g. *Stenogramme interrupta*) have a similar shape.

Rhodymenia ?australis, Coles Bay, Tas.

FAMILY CHAMPIACEAE

The Champiaceae are closely related to the Rhodymeniaceae but normally have a filamentous thallus. The branches are distinctively partitioned into numerous segments.

Champia viridis C. Agardh

Habitat: Other algae, seagrass, sheltered and moderately exposed reef; 0–15 m depth.
Distribution: Rottnest I, WA, to Jervis Bay, NSW, and around Tas.
Maximum size: Thallus length to 150 mm.

The branches of *Champia viridis* are subdivided by partitions and have numerous smaller branches radiating out at each junction. This species grows to its largest size when living on rock but is also often found attached to other plants.

Champia viridis, Bicheno, Tas.

FAMILY CERAMIACEAE

This very large family primarily contains filamentous species that are usually thin and delicate; however, in some species the cells in the branches produce fine filaments that wrap around and create a more solid-looking structure. The Ceramiaceae family is closely related to the three families described immediately after it but differs in the cellular arrangement of the microscopic phase of the life cycle that follows fertilisation. This microscopic phase is not enclosed within a special flask-shaped structure.

Ceramium excellens J. Agardh

Habitat: Exposed reef; 8–31 m depth.
Distribution: Great Australian Bight, SA, to Western Port, Vic., and around Tas.
Maximum size: Thallus length to 300 mm.

Ceramium excellens is one of about 15 species of *Ceramium* occurring on southern Australian coasts. They are all filamentous, with cells aligned along the branches in such a way that a banded pattern is produced. The larger species generally occur on rock surfaces and the smaller species attached to seagrasses and large seaweeds. Most species cannot be identified without microscopic examination. *Ceramium*

Ceramium excellens, Bicheno, Tas.

excellens is the longest local species and is distinguished partly by its regular branching in one plane and the axes gradually tapering from about 1 mm diameter near the base to 200 μm near the tips. It is moderately common on deep exposed reefs.

Griffithsia monilis Harvey

Habitat: Sheltered and moderately exposed reef, seagrass; 0–10 m depth.
Distribution: Fremantle, WA, to Redcliff, Qld, and around Tas.
Maximum size: Thallus length to 110 mm.

A characteristic feature of algae in the genus *Griffithsia* is that the branches are constructed from large individual cells, in contrast to most other segmented plants (e.g. *Erythroclonium sonderi*), which have each branch segment made from numerous small cells. The cells of *G. monilis* are particularly large and are arranged in branches that divide at irregular intervals. This species is moderately common along the sheltered open coast and can occur attached to large plants as well as on rock.

Griffithsia monilis, Tinderbox, Tas.

Ballia callitricha (C. Agardh) Montagne

Habitat: Reef; 0–20 m depth.
Distribution: Southern WA to central Vic. and around Tas. Also New Zealand, South America and subantarctic islands.
Maximum size: Thallus length to 250 mm.

Ballia callitricha is a distinctive red alga with stiff ramuli arranged in two or three dense rows along the axes. It is one of the most common algae on exposed reefs in Tasmania, Victoria and southeastern South Australia, occurring in greatest abundance in the colder waters.

Ballia callitricha, Bicheno, Tas.

Euptilota articulata (J. Agardh) Schmitz

Habitat: Exposed reef; 0–12 m depth.
Distribution: Rottnest I, WA, to southern Qld and around Tas. Also Japan.
Maximum size: Thallus length to 350 mm.

Euptilota articulata has repeatedly branched axes, which end in very fine feather-like branchlets arranged in an alternating series in the one plane. Although this species has a delicate appearance, the thallus is quite tough and can withstand considerable wave exposure.

Euptilota articulata, Taroona, Tas.

FAMILY DELESSERIACEAE

This family contains delicate leafy species and includes many of the more beautiful seaweeds. Of the 300 species known worldwide, about 80 are recorded from southern Australia, nearly all of which are restricted to the region.

Hemineura frondosa Harvey

Habitat: Sheltered and moderately exposed reef; 1–14 m depth.
Distribution: Rottnest I, WA, to Vic., and around Tas.
Maximum size: Thallus length to 600 mm.

Hemineura frondosa is a pink alga with numerous lateral branches that often have ruffled edges. A characteristic feature of this species is an obvious central vein towards the end of each branch but which cannot be seen near the branch junction.

Hemineura frondosa, Dennes Pt, Tas.

Claudea elegans Lamouroux

Habitat: Moderately exposed reef; 10–25 m depth.
Distribution: Southern WA, to Western Port, Vic., and northern Tas.
Maximum size: Thallus length to 450 mm.

Claudea elegans has been described as the most beautiful of all algae (by Professor W.H. Harvey, the most prominent nineteenth-century expert on seaweeds). It has a distinctive branching pattern consisting of curved axes bearing lace-like filaments on their outer side and smaller branches with a similar but reduced branching arrangement projecting from the inner side. This species develops best on reefs near sand at locations with good current flow.

Claudea elegans, Twilight Cove, WA

Martensia australis Harvey

Habitat: Exposed reef; 5–25 m depth.
Distribution: Shark Bay, WA, to Coffs Harbour, NSW, and northern Tas. Also Lord Howe I.
Maximum size: Thallus length to 200 mm.

Martensia australis has a flattened frond produced into rounded lobes, with the lower section of each lobe solid and the outer section expanded in a fine lace-like network of interconnecting filaments. The species is widespread but uncommon. Two other smaller (<100 mm thallus length) and more delicate species with similar lace-work on the upper frond also occur around southern Australia. ***Martensia elegans*** has compact fronds with a smooth outer margin, while ***Martensia denticulata*** has more elongate fronds that are forked several times and have a toothed outer margin.

Martensia australis, Terrigal, NSW

Sarcomenia delesserioides Sonder

Habitat: Moderately exposed reef; 4–12 m depth.
Distribution: Southern WA to Western Port, Vic.
Maximum size: Thallus length to 900 mm.

Sarcomenia delesserioides is one the most striking of the southern Australian algae because of its intense purple/green colour. The leaf-like branches that arise in pairs from just within the margins of the axes are also characteristic. The frond in the photographed specimen is broken, a common condition for this delicate species.

Sarcomenia delesserioides, Esperance, WA

Halicnide similans (J. Agardh) J. Agardh

Habitat: Exposed reef; 3–25 m depth.
Distribution: Vic. and around Tas.
Maximum size: Thallus length to 65 mm.

Halicnide similans is a distinctive red alga with veins running across the leaf-shaped fronds and small leafy branches arising from the edge of the main frond. The species occurs commonly on Tasmanian reefs at sites with little light, but is rare on the mainland.

Halicnide similans, Bicheno, Tas.

Dasya extensa, Horseshoe Reef, WA

FAMILY DASYACEAE

Species of Dasyaceae can usually be recognised by the long thin branches that are coated with numerous extremely fine, coloured filaments and by the growth pattern at the apex of the plant (a new growing point continually arises from the side of the preceding growing point and overgrows it).

Dasya extensa Sonder ex Kützing

Habitat: Moderately exposed reef; 0–9 m depth.
Distribution: Dongara, WA, to Western Port, Vic., and northern Tas.
Maximum size: Thallus length to 1 m.

Dasya extensa is a long, pink, cylindrical plant with long side-branches irregularly spaced along the main axis. The branches are flexible and covered by numerous fine hairs, and have a slimy feel. The species is moderately common on reef near sand.

FAMILY RHODOMELACEAE

Like virtually all other red algal families, the Rhodomelaceae are largely characterised by the arrangements of cells in reproductive structures. The axes of these plants are formed from a central cell giving rise to a ring of 4–24 surrounding cells. This is the largest family of red algae in terms of genera, with about 130 so far named.

Cliftonaea pectinata Harvey

Habitat: Moderately exposed reef; 1–12 m depth.
Distribution: Rottnest I, WA, to Kangaroo I, SA.
Maximum size: Thallus length to 140 mm.

Cliftonaea pectinata has very distinctive curved branches with numerous fine filaments packed on the inner surface and smaller curved branches with the same arrangement of filaments arising off the outer surface. This alga occurs commonly in Western Australia, where plants are often bleached yellow in shallow water.

Cliftonaea pectinata, Bunker Bay, WA

Dictymenia harveyana Sonder

Habitat: Sheltered and moderately exposed reef; 0–10 m depth.
Distribution: Southern WA to central Vic. and around Tas.
Maximum size: Thallus length to 300 mm.

Dictymenia harveyana has numerous flat, branched fronds, which arise from the edges of wide axes. The species is moderately common on sheltered reefs, usually at sites with considerable current flow. A closely related species, ***Dictymenia tridens***, has a similar shape except that the branches are less

Dictymenia harveyana, Cloudy Lagoon, Tas.

regularly arranged along the axes, the major axes are not significantly wider than the side-branches, and many of the side-branches are reduced to three-pronged stumps.

Jeannerettia lobata Hooker & Harvey

Habitat: Moderately exposed reef; 3–15 m depth.
Distribution: Kangaroo I, SA, to Vic., and around Tas.
Maximum size: Thallus length to 500 mm.

Jeannerettia lobata is a large red alga that can be recognised by the flat leafy fronds with prominent midribs down the branches. The species occurs abundantly mixed with other red algae in coastal bays.

Jeannerettia lobata, Tinderbox, Tas.

Lenormandia marginata Hooker & Harvey

Habitat: Exposed reef; 1–25 m depth.
Distribution: Rottnest I, WA, to central Vic., and around Tas.
Maximum size: Thallus length to 250 mm.

Lenormandia marginata has flat, leafy, elongate fronds, which branch from the edges, and a characteristic pattern of fine cross-hatched lines over its surface. This alga lies across the rock substrate on southern reefs and is abundant.

Lenormandia marginata, Low Head, Tas.

Lenormandia smithiae
(Hooker & Harvey) Falkenberg

Habitat: Exposed reef; 9–32 m depth.
Distribution: Kangaroo I, SA, to central Vic. and south to Bicheno, Tas.
Maximum size: Thallus length to 200 mm.

Lenormandia smithiae, Bicheno, Tas.

Lenormandia smithiae is a distinctive species with elongate, sponge-covered branches that have a series of pits along the central axis. Branches also arise from this central axis. The species is largely confined to deeper reefs and is uncommon.

Laurencia majuscula (Harvey) Lucas

Habitat: Sheltered and moderately exposed reef, seagrass; 0–10 m depth.
Distribution: Around Australian mainland and Tas. Also widespread in the Indo-West Pacific region.
Maximum size: Thallus length to 200 mm.

Approximately 20 species in the genus *Laurencia* occur in southern Australian waters, all of them characterised by an indentation in the tip of the branches. *Laurencia majuscula* is the bushiest of these species and can be recognised by the soft, highly branched thallus. It occurs abundantly on sand-scoured rock along the New South Wales coast and is moderately common elsewhere. The species is occasionally found attached to other plants. Old and senescing branches often have an iridescent sheen.

Laurencia majuscula, Narooma, NSW

Laurencia clavata Sonder

Habitat: Sheltered and moderately exposed reef; 0–5 m depth.
Distribution: Dongara, WA, to Phillip I, Vic. and around Tas.
Maximum size: Thallus length to 150 mm.

Laurencia ? clavata, Ricketts Pt, Vic.

The branches of *Laurencia clavata* differ from those of other local *Laurencia* species because they narrow in size at their bases, are very open and arise from all sides of the axes. This species has a dark red colour when shaded but becomes bleached in sunlight. It is moderately common in bays along the southern coast.

Osmundaria prolifera Lamouroux

Habitat: Moderately and submaximally exposed reef; 1–14 m depth.
Distribution: Perth, WA, to Gulf St Vincent, SA.
Maximum size: Thallus length to 500 mm.

Osmundaria prolifera is a leathery alga that is abundant along the southwestern Australian coast. The tough, twisted branches with smaller branches arising from the centre are characteristic. The thallus is purple in shaded conditions but is bleached yellow when exposed to sunlight.

Osmundaria prolifera, Canal Rocks, WA

KINGDOM FUNGI

Fungi were until recently thought of as plants that lack chloroplasts, the cellular structures in which photosynthesis occurs, and because of this loss, their plant structure had been greatly modified to allow the absorption of complex organic chemicals from the external environment. They are now considered a distinctive kingdom of organisms in their own right, with unique nutritional, structural and reproductive features. They feed by releasing powerful enzymes that decompose food externally, and the products of digestion are then absorbed through the body wall. Some species feed on decomposing plant and animal material and are known as saprobes. Other fungi are parasitic, receiving nutrition from living hosts. The third group of fungi, the symbionts, also absorb nutrients from a living plant or animal but reciprocate in a way that benefits the host, such as providing important chemicals that are not otherwise available to the host.

Fungi typically have a filamentous structure, with the bulk of the organism consisting of a network of extremely thin threads known as hyphae. Rather than increasing the width of the hyphae during growth, fungi direct nutrients to the tips of the hyphae to maximise the rate of extension and thus maximise the surface area of the organism that can be used for absorption. When conditions are favourable, fungi also channel much of their nutrition towards the production of minute asexual spores, which are released in huge quantities and

Filamentous fungi associated with seagrass debris, Ulladulla, NSW

produce identical clones to the parent. Spores are produced by sexual means only rarely, most often when environmental conditions deteriorate. Sexual reproduction involves the fusion of cells from two different fungi and the subsequent division of the nucleus by meiosis.

The above description of fungi applies to the great majority of species, but not to the yeasts, a group of unicellular organisms that are the most common fungi in marine waters. Yeasts belong to several different lineages of fungi and reproduce asexually by simple cell division. Sexual reproduction is unknown for many yeasts and perhaps does not occur. Because of their small size, yeasts are rarely considered an important group of marine organisms. Plating techniques used to count bacteria nevertheless indicate that densities in water samples often exceed one million cells per litre. Whether these high numbers mean that yeasts have an ecologically significant function is not yet known. Filamentous fungi are ecologically important, as they speed up the decomposition of dead plant and animal material.

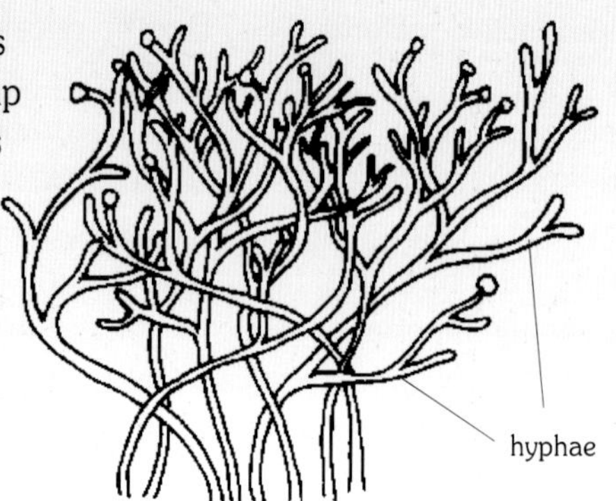

Fungi (1 mm)
Kingdom Fungi

LICHENS

Lichens are remarkable organisms that have a thallus formed from a partnership between at least one species of fungi and at least one species of green algae or, less commonly, cyanobacteria. Most of the lichen thallus consists of a lattice of fungal hyphae that form a water retention and storage area. Numerous photosynthetic algal cells are entangled among the hyphae just below the surface in the part of the thallus receiving greatest light. Fungal hyphae are either pressed against or penetrate the plant cells, receiving food from them and transporting this nourishment throughout the organism. The relationship is considered symbiotic because the fungus in return provides the algal cells with a favourable environment.

Reproduction among lichens is mainly by vegetative means, although many of the common intertidal lichens produce small cup-shaped fruiting bodies known as apothecia, which release fungal spores. These spores can produce new lichens only if they happen to fall on the appropriate algal partner.

Classification of lichens is based on the species of fungi present, although this poses problems in the rare cases where one species of fungus associates with more than one species of algae, creating different-looking lichens. More than 25 000 species of lichens are known worldwide, with about 2300 recorded from Australia. Lichens are generally found on land, where they are particularly common on tree trunks, twigs and rocks, but lichens are also often associated with rock surfaces on sea shores, especially high in the intertidal zone on cool temperate coasts. Individual rocks at the upper tidal levels in Tasmania may be covered by communities that include more than ten types of lichen.

Nearly all lichens on southern Australian shores have encrusting thalli. Among the more common species are black paint-like lichens in the genus *Verrucaria*, yellow, orange or red lichens in the genus *Caloplaca*, the yellow outwardly-radiating species *Xanthoria ligulata*, a grey lichen with black apothecia (*Tylothalia patiensis*) and a grey lichen with grey apothecia (*Ochrolechia* sp.). The black tufted lichen (*Lichina confinis*) is very abundant near high-tide level on cooler shores and is extensively grazed by littorinid molluscs. Virtually nothing is known about the distributions and habitat requirements of intertidal lichens.

Caloplaca sp. (orange) and *Verrucaria* sp. (black), Bicheno, Tas.

Caloplaca spp. (orange and yellow) and *Verrucaria* sp. (black), Bicheno, Tas.

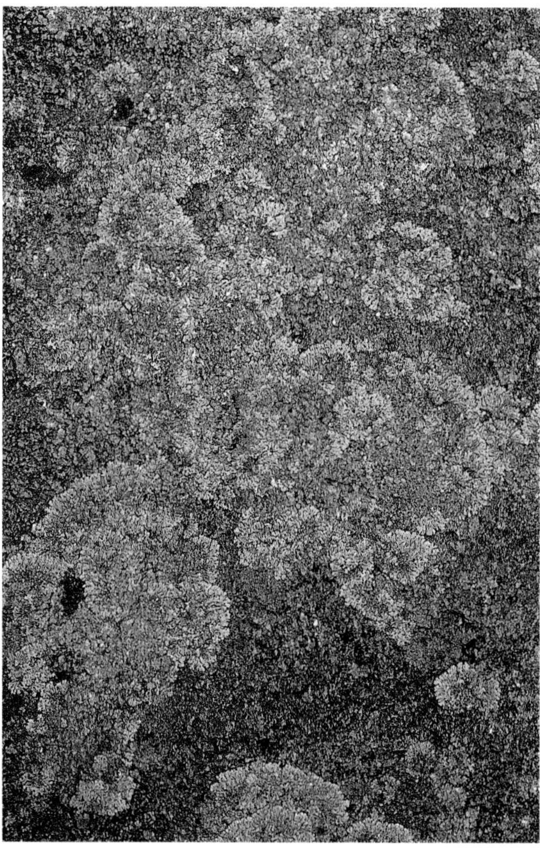

Xanthoria ligulata, Esperance, WA

Tylothalia patiensis, Cloudy Bay, Tas.

Ochrolechia ?parella (grey) and *Caloplaca cribrosa* (yellow), Cloudy Bay, Tas.

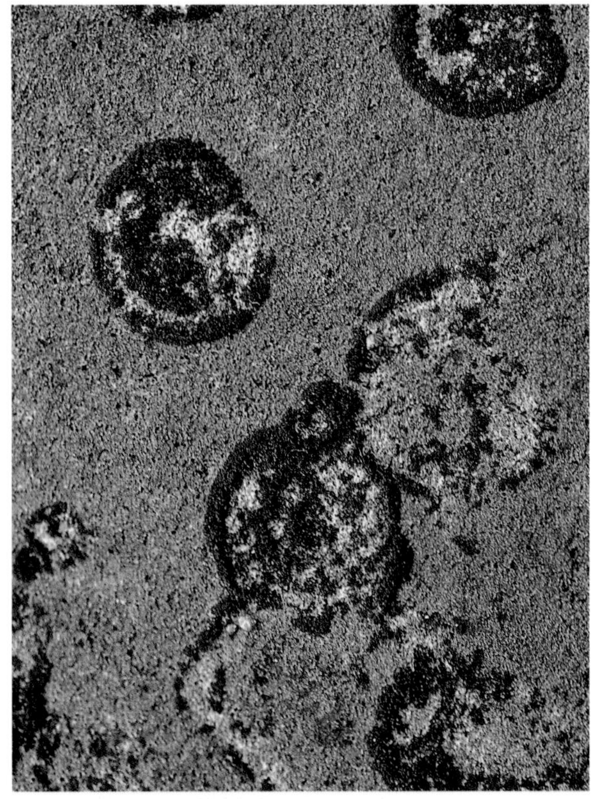

Lichina confinis, Cloudy Bay, Tas.

KINGDOM PLANTAE

Land plants

The plant kingdom, as defined here, includes the mosses, ferns, conifers and flowering plants. Species in these groups are solely terrestrial (confined to land), with the exception of a few flowering plants that have returned in comparatively recent times to the sea and fresh water. Plants have evolved a number of adaptations, such as a coating of waxy cuticle on leaves to prevent desiccation and microscopic pores through the cuticle to allow carbon dioxide and oxygen to diffuse in and out, to cope with the drying effects of the atmosphere and to provide structural support.

PHYLUM MAGNOLIOPHYTA

Angiosperms

This phylum includes the flowering plants, most of which can be recognised by the presence of leaves, stems and roots. They reproduce sexually using specialised structures that are usually formed into flowers. Seeds are produced after fertilisation and enclosed within a fruit. Although most flowering plants are confined to land, a few families have become specialised for life underwater or on the fringes of the sea and estuaries. Marine plants are commonly divided into three groups, seagrasses, mangroves and saltmarsh plants. These groupings have little relevance as far as scientific classification is concerned, because each contains several families that are often more closely related to land and freshwater plants than to each other.

SEAGRASSES

Seagrasses are flowering plants adapted for life submerged in a marine or estuarine environment. Like flowering plants on land they produce flowers and seeds. The flowers and seeds are, however, small, seasonal and difficult to observe in many species; consequently the identification of seagrasses relies largely on leaf, root and rhizome characteristics. Two quite different groups of flowering plants have representatives commonly called seagrasses; most seagrasses belong to the order Potamogetonales, while the genus *Halophila* and the tropical genera *Enhalus* and *Thalassia* belong to the order Hydrocharitales. About 60 species are known worldwide, with one-third of these restricted to southern Australia.

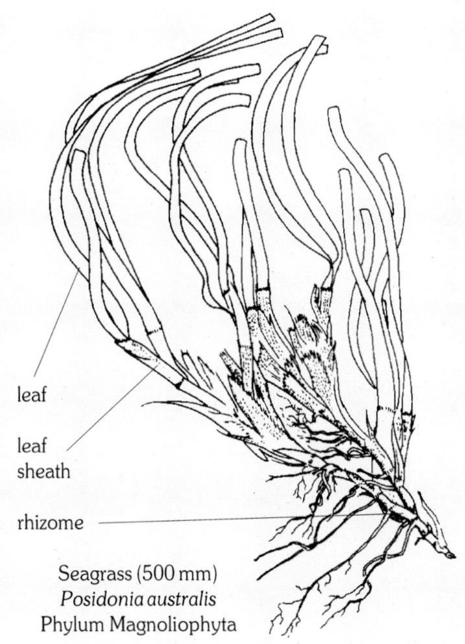

Seagrass (500 mm)
Posidonia australis
Phylum Magnoliophyta

FAMILY HYDROCHARITACEAE

Species in this family are distinguished from other seagrasses by floral characteristics and the absence of a tongue-like membrane between leaf blade and leaf sheath. Four species are known in southern Australia.

Halophila australis Doty & Stone

Habitat: Sheltered sand, mud; 0–23 m depth.
Distribution: Dongara, WA, to Sydney, NSW, and around Tas.
Maximum size: Leaf length to 70 mm.

Halophila species possess ovate leaves with stalk-like petioles. These arise from branched stems called stolons that lie half buried in the sand. The identities of the two common southern Australian species, *H. australis* and *H. ovalis*, were confused until recently because of their similar appearance and because of the great variation in leaf size and shape of individual plants within a population. The leaves of *H. australis* are narrower than the leaves of *H. ovalis*, with a ratio of leaf length to width generally 1:3 to 1:4 compared with 1:1.5 to 1:2 for *H. ovalis*. As well, *H. australis* usually has a slightly greater number of cross-veins on each leaf (commonly 14–16, compared with 10–12), which meet the central vein at a more acute angle. The key character that separates the two species is the position of the female flowers; in *H. ovalis* they are borne on the stolons, and in *H. australis* on branches between the leaf pairs. *Halophila australis* occurs commonly in estuaries and sheltered embayments, often at the edge of patches of *Heterozostera tasmanica*.

Halophila ovalis (R. Brown) J.D. Hooker

Habitat: Sheltered and moderately exposed sand; 0–10 m depth.
Distribution: Tropical Australia south to Cowaramup Bay, WA, and Twofold Bay, NSW. Also widespread in the Indo-West Pacific region.
Maximum size: Leaf length to 40 mm.

Halophila ovalis, Terrigal, NSW

Halophila australis, Princess Royal Harbour, WA

Halophila ovalis has a tropical distribution that barely overlaps with that of the temperate species *H. australis*. It also prefers slightly more exposed conditions. This seagrass often forms extensive beds which, in tropical areas, are an important food source for dugongs.

Halophila decipiens Ostendfield

Habitat: Estuarine sand, silt; 0–3 m depth.
Distribution: Tropical Australia south to Albany, WA, and Mallacoota, Vic. Also widespread in the tropics.
Maximum size: Leaf length to 25 mm.

This is a small species that occurs in a few estuaries in eastern and western Australia. It can be distinguished from other species by its leaf margin which has very fine serrations; the species also differ from *H. australis* and *H. ovalis* in growing to only a small size (leaves to 25 mm) and having few cross-veins (5–9). *Halophila decipiens* in south western Australia is possibly an annual species, relying on seed set each year, as it has not yet been collected during the winter or spring months.

Halophila decipiens, Oyster Harbour, WA

FAMILY POTAMOGETONACEAE

Species of Potamogetonaceae have long, narrow leaves and a spike-like flower. They lack a tongue-like membrane at the base of the leaves and have pollen grains that are rounded. Most species in the family occur in fresh water, but a few are found in estuaries. Some authors do not consider these plants to be true seagrasses.

Ruppia sp., Moulting Lagoon, Tas.

Ruppia megacarpa Mason

Habitat: Estuaries, coastal salt lakes; 0–2 m depth.
Distribution: Peel Inlet, WA, to Jervis Bay, NSW, and around Tas. Also New Zealand.
Maximum size: Height to 2.0 m.

Ruppia megacarpa is a robust perennial species that tolerates a wide range of salinities and can occur in both freshwater-dominated estuaries and coastal lagoons where salinities greatly exceed marine conditions. The species has erect stems that are very long, narrow (0.5–2 mm in diameter) and branched. The leaf blades arise from short sheaths at the end of the branches and are 50–200 mm long with an indented tip.

FAMILY POSIDONIACEAE

This family contains a single genus of seagrass species (*Posidonia*) that is distinguished by bean-shaped fruits and clusters of flowers on spike-like structures. Species in the genus generally also have distinctive strap-like leaves that are very tough. All but one of the nine species of *Posidonia*, the Mediterranean *Posidonia oceanica*, are restricted to Australia, where they are the dominant plants on soft sediments along much of the southern and southwestern coasts.

Posidonia australis Hooker
Southern strapweed

Habitat: Sheltered sand, mud; 0–15 m depth.
Distribution: Shark Bay, WA, to Lake Macquarie, NSW, and along the northern coast of Tas.
Maximum size: Leaf length to 450 mm, width to 20 mm.

Posidonia australis with fruit, Marmion Lagoon, WA

Posidonia australis bed, Shark Bay, WA. CLAY BRYCE

Leaf bases and fibrous leaf sheaths of *Posidonia angustifolia*, Marmion Lagoon, WA

The genus *Posidonia* has two major species groups in Australia: the '*Posidonia australis* group', consisting of *P. australis, P. angustifolia* and *P. sinuosa*; and the '*Posidonia ostenfeldii* group' consisting of five other species. The three species in the *P. australis* group have long, wide (5–20 mm) leaves and can all form pure beds of a single species or can occur mixed with others. *P. australis* has wide (10–15 mm), flat leaves, which grow rapidly and so generally have rounded unbroken ends in contrast to the ragged ends of other species. It is the only species of *Posidonia* recorded from Victoria, New South Wales or Tasmania and seems to tolerate greater extremes of temperature and salinity than related species. In New South Wales it is confined to estuaries, except for areas of Jervis Bay.

Posidonia angustifolia Cambridge & Kuo

Habitat: Moderately exposed sand; 2–35 m depth.
Distribution: Houtman Abrolhos, WA, to Port MacDonnell, SA.
Maximum size: Leaf length to 1.2 m, width to 6 mm.

Posidonia angustifolia differs from *P. australis* in having narrower leaves (usually 4–6 mm) and differs from *P. sinuosa* in the structure of the leaf sheaths. When growing close to other species it can also usually be recognised by the leaves being thin, easily broken and generally coated with dense epiphytes. It is often the dominant species of *Posidonia* in deeper water.

Posidonia sinuosa Cambridge & Kuo

Habitat: Moderately exposed and sheltered sand; 0–15 m depth.
Distribution: Shark Bay, WA, to Kingston, SA.
Maximum size: Leaf length to 1.2 m, width to 11 mm.

Posidonia sinuosa is the most common seagrass that forms meadows off southwestern Australia. It is most accurately identified using the appearance of the sheaths at the base of the leaves. Its leaf sheaths are brown to dark reddish-brown and relatively smooth like those of species in the *P. ostenfeldii* group,

Posidonia sinuosa, Princess Royal Harbour, WA

whereas the sheaths of *P. australis* and *P. angustifolia* are pale yellow to grey and disintegrate into a tangle of hair-like fibres. Rhizomes of *P. sinuosa* also are firmly rooted in the sand and can usually be removed only with difficulty, whereas those of *P. australis* lie horizontally at a depth of 10–20 cm and those of *P. angustifolia* are just below the surface at 5–15 cm depth.

Posidonia denhartogi Kuo & Cambridge

Habitat: Exposed sand; 1–10 m depth.
Distribution: Perth, WA, to Backstairs Passage, SA.
Maximum size: Leaf length to 1.0 m, width to 2 mm.

The five species in the *Posidonia ostenfeldii* group have thick, tough leaves, with the centre of each leaf much thicker than near the edges. These seagrasses have a deep root system and very tough leaves, so can withstand stronger wave action than species in the *P. australis* group. All species in the *P. ostenfeldii* group have overlapping distributions centred on the south coast of Western Australia. ***Posidonia ostenfeldii*** is the easiest to identify because its leaves are round in cross-section, with a diameter of only 1–1.5 mm near the base. The leaves of *P. ostenfeldii* superficially resemble *Syringodium isoetifolium* but are much tougher and not easily broken. *Posidonia ostenfeldii* grows to a length of 1.35 m and occurs on white sand in relatively deep water between Cape Leeuwin and Israelite Bay, WA. *Posidonia denhartogi* also has a very thin leaf (1–2 mm diameter) but this is flattened. It is usually found on the edge of sand blowouts or other disturbed areas and is a comparatively rare species.

Posidonia denhartogi, Two Peoples Bay, WA

Posidonia coriacea with fruit, Marmion Lagoon, WA

Posidonia coriacea Cambridge & Kuo

Habitat: Exposed sand; 1–30 m depth.
Distribution: Shark Bay, WA, to Backstairs Passage, SA.
Maximum size: Leaf length to 1.2 m, width to 7 mm.

Posidonia coriacea, P. kirkmani and *P. robertsonae* are all similar in appearance and difficult to differentiate in the field. The leaves of *P. coriacea* are generally narrower (2.5–7 mm) than the other two species. *Posidonia coriacea* is common among the seagrass beds off Perth and usually occurs on the edge of patches of other seagrasses. It has not been recorded between Cape Leeuwin and Israelite Bay, the region in which *P. kirkmani* is present.

Posidonia robertsonae Kuo & Cambridge

Habitat: Exposed sand; 1–18 m depth.
Distribution: Cape Leeuwin to Israelite Bay, WA.
Maximum size: Leaf length to 1.8 m, width to 12 mm.

Posidonia robertsonae, Two Peoples Bay, WA

Posidonia robertsonae can sometimes be distinguished from the closely related ***Posidonia kirkmani*** because the leaves tend to be narrower. However, identification of these species can only be accurately done by microscopic examination. The leaves of *P. robertsonae* are scalloped rather than smooth when viewed in cross-section because of corrugations in the cell walls. The two species often occur together on white sand in exposed areas.

FAMILY CYMODOCEACEAE

The family Cymodoceaceae includes genera with a range of shapes but grouped together because of the structure of the flower and the presence of a membrane where the leaf joins the sheath.

Syringodium isoetifolium (Ascherson) Dandy

Habitat: Moderately exposed sand; 0–8 m depth.
Distribution: Tropical Australia south to Cockburn Sound, WA, and Moreton Bay, Qld. Also widespread in the Indo-Pacific region.
Maximum size: Leaf height to 300 mm.

Syringodium isoetifolium, Little I, WA

Syringodium isoetifolium has narrow tubular leaves, which grow quickly and rarely have attached epiphytes. It is an opportunistic species, rapidly colonising disturbed edges of seagrass meadows, and is often found in association with *Heterozostera tasmanica* or *Halophila ovalis*.

Thalassodendron pachyrhizum den Hartog

Habitat: Exposed reefs; 0–40 m depth.
Distribution: Geraldton to Cape Arid, WA.
Maximum size: Leaf length to 200 mm.

Thalassodendron pachyrhizum, Canal Rocks, WA

Thalassodendron pachyrhizum has flat leaf blades that arise in clusters from woody stems and have small marginal serrations and rounded apices. The stems are rarely branched and arise regularly at every fourth internode along the rhizomes. The rhizomes and stems both display patterns of circular marks, which are remnant scars from the positions of detached leaves. This species is common on sand-abraded reefs among macroalgae at depths greater than 20 m.

Amphibolis antarctica, Flinders, Vic.

Amphibolis antarctica

(Labillardière) Sonder & Ascherson ex Ascherson

Habitat: Moderately exposed sand, reef; 0–23 m depth.
Distribution: Carnarvon, WA, to Wilsons Promontory, Vic., and south to Maria I, Tas.
Maximum size: Leaf length to 50 mm, stem height to 1.5 m.

The two species of *Amphibolis* have woody, branched stems arising at irregular intervals from rhizomes. The stems have a regular arrangement of circular leaf scars and are very tough and wiry. They can easily stop the outboard motor of a small boat passing across the bed. The leaves are small relative to the stems, flat with smooth margins, and have a blunt apex with two marginal teeth. The leaves of *A. antarctica* are also usually twisted through 180° in the upper half and occur in clusters of eight to ten. Both species in the genus are restricted to southern Australia and have an interesting mode of reproduction. Among the leaves, they produce small seedlings with miniature grappling hooks. The grappling hooks on detached seedlings snag onto other plants, thereby giving the plant a chance to produce roots and anchor properly before the next storm. *Amphibolis antarctica* can occur on the edge of blowouts or mixed with *A. griffithii* but more often occurs by itself in very dense beds. Such monospecific beds are particularly extensive in Shark Bay, where they form the dominant habitat and cover 3700 square kilometres.

Amphibolis antarctica bed, Shark Bay, WA. CLAY BRYCE

Amphibolis griffithii (J. Black) den Hartog

Habitat: Moderately exposed sand, reef; 0–40 m depth.
Distribution: Champion Bay, WA, to Victor Harbor, SA.
Maximum size: Leaf length to 100 mm, stem height to 1.1 m.

Amphibolis griffithii, Two Peoples Bay, WA

Amphibolis griffithii has a similar general appearance to *A. antarctica* but differs in the structure and arrangement of the leaves. Compared to *A. antarctica*, the leaf blades are straight rather than twisted, twice the length and in lower numbers per cluster (4–5), and with the sheaths at the base of the leaves directly attached to the stem. *Amphibolis griffithii* occupies only part of the range of *A. antarctica* and appears to be less tolerant of environmental extremes.

FAMILY ZOSTERACEAE

Species of Zosteraceae form a distinctive family of narrow-leafed plants. The small flowers are arranged in rows on modified leaves, with the edges of the leaf curved up and partly enclosing the flowers.

Heterozostera tasmanica

(Martens ex Ascherson) den Hartog

Habitat: Sheltered and moderately exposed sand, silt; 0–31 m depth.
Distribution: Dongara, WA, to Port Stephens, NSW, and around Tas. Also Chile.
Maximum size: Leaf length to 1.5 m.

Heterozostera tasmanica, Cloudy Lagoon, Tas.

Heterozostera tasmanica with flowers, Rocky Cape, Tas.

Heterozostera tasmanica has a similar leaf shape to the three southern Australian species of *Zostera*, and all are commonly called eelgrass. *Heterozostera tasmanica* can sometimes be separated from the other species on the basis of its branching pattern, with the leaves having dark wiry bases that arise vertically from the rhizomes, whereas the leaves of *Zostera* species are often curved parallel with the sediment near their bases. Nevertheless, the only reliable way to separate these plants is to observe a cross-section of the rhizome with a hand-lens or microscope: *Heterozostera tasmanica* has four to twelve veinlike vascular bundles arranged in a circle, whereas *Zostera* species have only two. *Heterozostera tasmanica* is the species of eelgrass most commonly observed subtidally by divers and is particularly abundant in estuaries.

Zostera mucronata den Hartog

Habitat: Sheltered mud, sand; 0–2 m depth.
Distribution: Swan River Estuary, WA, to Port Clinton, SA.
Maximum size: Leaf length to 200 mm.

Species in the genus *Zostera* have long, thin leaves (1–5 mm wide) and are the dominant seagrasses in intertidal habitats. Their external appearance is almost

Zostera mucronata, Fremantle, WA. DAVE EVANS

identical to *Heterozostera tasmanica* but these two genera differ greatly in the internal structure of the rhizome. The three southern Australian species of *Zostera* are chiefly separated from each other on the basis of leaf characteristics, the number of roots at each node and, most easily, their distribution. The structural characters intergrade considerably between species, with leaf apex shape and the number of roots per node also varying considerably even within populations. *Zostera mucronata* generally has three tooth-like projections at the end of the leaves (the central vein and the leaf edges end in distinct points) and only two roots at each node. It is the dominant seagrass on the intertidal flats in the South Australian gulfs east to Port Gawler.

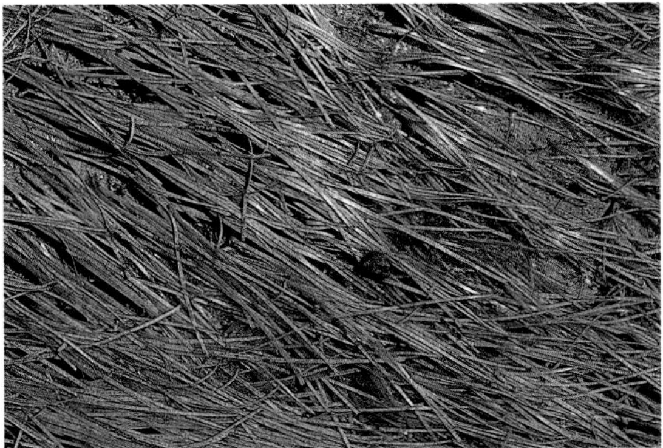

Zostera muelleri, Ricketts Pt, Vic.

Zostera muelleri Irmisch ex Ascherson

Habitat: Sheltered mud, sand; 0–4 m depth.
Distribution: Yorke Peninsula, SA, to Sussex Inlet, NSW, and around Tas. Also New Zealand.
Maximum size: Leaf length to 600 mm.

Zostera muelleri has at least two roots at each node; the leaf apex is usually notched in the centre, and the leaf blade has three longitudinal veins. The species forms extensive beds near low-tide level in Victorian and Tasmanian estuaries and bays. It provides a habitat for a variety of fish and invertebrate species and major feeding grounds for a number of wading birds, including swans.

Zostera capricorni Ascherson

Habitat: Sheltered mud, sand; 0–7 m depth.
Distribution: Mallacoota, Vic., to Qld. Also New Zealand.
Maximum size: Leaf length to 500 mm.

Zostera capricorni, Middle Harbour, NSW

Zostera capricorni, North Head, NSW

Zostera capricorni has a blunt leaf apex, and the blade has four to five longitudinal veins. This seagrass commonly occurs as meadows in the shallows of estuaries and coastal lagoons in New South Wales, where it often occurs immediately shoreward of the strap-like seagrass *Posidonia australis*.

MANGROVES

Mangrove plants comprise the few shrubs and trees that live in the extremely harsh environment between low and high tide levels on sheltered shores. They are thus characterised by their height and habitat rather than by being closely related to each other, and in fact Australian mangrove species belong to about 16 different families of plants. Mangroves are usually thought of as tropical plants, and so Australia is somewhat unusual in having one mangrove species forming dense tidal forests in temperate areas. The Victorian forests of *Avicennia marina* occur at much higher latitudes than mangroves on other continents. A second species, *Aegiceras corniculatum*, also extends into the temperate Australian region.

Mangrove species have acquired a number of adaptations for survival in waterlogged, oxygen-deficient, extremely saline muds. The root systems of mangroves are greatly modified to allow oxygen transport to the cells, either by the roots sitting above the sediment surface or by having vertical branches, the pneumatophores, projecting above the mud. These modified roots allow oxygen to enter and pass into an extensive internal system of air spaces within the root. Mangroves also need to rid themselves of salt as they live in an environment where, during hot, drying weather, the salt concentration in ponded water around the stems sometimes exceeds twice the level in normal seawater. Species found in temperate waters partly do this by excreting salt in the form of crystals onto leaf surfaces, which are lost as the leaf is shed. Mangroves are also adapted to allow the germination and development of seeds on mudflats. They produce very large leafed seeds that quickly root and develop into saplings if embedded in mud.

Avicennia marina (Forsskål) Vierhapper
Grey mangrove

Habitat: Sheltered mud; intertidal.
Distribution: Around mainland Australia.
Maximum size: Tree height to 10 m (25 m in tropics).

Avicennia marina is the only common mangrove species in southern Australia. It can be recognised by the oval leaves, which are pointed at the apex, and numerous peg-like pneumatophores that project from the mud close to the tree. The grey mangrove is primarily a tropical species, with plants along the southern coast stunted and growing to only about 3 m. The species is also patchily distributed in the south, occurring only at Bunbury, Streaky Bay, Spencer Gulf and Gulf St Vincent in the region between Shark Bay and Western Port.

Avicennia marina, Port Stephens, NSW

Avicennia marina, Port Augusta, SA

Aegiceras corniculatum (Linnaeus) Blanco
River mangrove

Habitat: Sheltered mud; intertidal.
Distribution: Tropical Australia south to Shark Bay, WA, and Merimbula, NSW.
Maximum size: Tree height to 4 m.

Aegiceras corniculatum differs from *Avicennia marina* by lacking pneumatophores and by having a rounded leaf. It flowers in spring in New South Wales, slightly

Aegiceras corniculatum flowers, Hexham, NSW

earlier than the grey mangrove, and is less common than that species. In central and southern New South Wales, river mangroves rarely grow larger than the size of a bush and tend to occur well up estuaries.

SALTMARSH PLANTS

Saltmarsh plants are the smaller grasses and shrubs that live on sheltered intertidal sandflats and mudflats. In these areas, few species are usually present, but these species can occur in very high densities. Saltmarsh plants are distinguishable from mangroves primarily on the basis of size, and from other plants by having the roots occasionally submerged in saline water. Saltmarsh plants do not compete well with mangroves and therefore tend to be more characteristic of temperate rather than tropical shores. When these two groups of plants occur together, mangroves are usually seaward of the saltmarsh plants, except for *Sarcocornia quinqueflora*, which may overlap. Shrubs in the genus *Melaleuca* often occur landward of the saltmarsh.

Approximately 50 species in southern Australia can be described as saltmarsh plants, with a small proportion of these also occurring inland. Like the mangroves, saltmarsh species belong to a great range of families.

Sarcocornia quinqueflora, Port Augusta, SA

Sarcocornia quinqueflora

(Bunge ex Ungern-Sternberg) A.J. Scott
Beaded glasswort

Habitat: Sheltered mud; intertidal.
Distribution: Around the Australian mainland and Tas.
Maximum size: Stem length to 300 mm.

Sarcocornia quinqueflora is a succulent saltmarsh plant that lacks leaves and has distinctive stems composed of small segments. A similar species with wider (4–5 mm, cf. 3–4 mm) segments that are blue-grey, ***Sarcocornia blackiana***, is also present in southern Australia but is less common. Both species are highly salt-adapted, often forming a distinct zone at the seaward edge of saltmarshes and occupying the landward edge of mudflats at sites where mangroves are absent.

KINGDOM ANIMALIA

This kingdom includes all multicellular organisms that feed by the ingestion of food particles. Plants and fungi differ by taking in molecules from the external environment across cell walls, rather than by internally digesting large pieces of food.

PHYLUM PORIFERA

Sponges

Sponges are a common, conspicuous and diverse group of about 6000 multicellular animals that generally live attached to marine reefs; about 100 species are present in fresh water. They lack true tissue and organs and therefore have a level of structural organisation that is intermediate between other invertebrate groups and the protozoans. Yet, although sponge cells are relatively unspecialised, the sponges themselves are far from functionally limited and often have complex life-histories. Some species are free-standing and possess a definite shape, whereas other species form a thin encrusting layer over rock surfaces, and some species occur in both encrusting and erect forms, depending on the extent of wave action.

Sponges are specially adapted for a stationary filter-feeding life. They have an outer layer of cells one cell deep, an internal layer of cells one cell deep within feeding chambers, and an intricate internal matrix of organic and mineral supporting elements and floating cells. The usual skeletal elements are a network of fibrous protein known as spongin (the material present in prepared bath sponges) and small rod-shaped and multipointed spicules made of either calcium carbonate or silica, which are embedded in the internal matrix. The surface of the sponge is perforated by numerous pores (the ostia) through which water is drawn and a few large openings (the oscules) through which water is expelled. The openings are connected by a system of canals to chambers that are lined by 'collar cells', so called because of a round collar-like structure on the surface. Within the collar is a single whip-like flagellum, which beats in time with other flagella, producing a flow of water through the body of the sponge. The flagella also produce microcurrents near the cell wall which cause incoming food particles to come into contact with the cell surface, where they can be trapped. The rate of water flow through a sponge is surprisingly high; most sponges pass their own volume of water in less than ten seconds, and so thousands of litres a day can be pumped and filtered by sponges on a square metre of reef.

Because sponges are filter feeders, they flourish best at sites with strong currents or wave action. They grow less rapidly than seaweeds and therefore tend to be dominant in caves and deep water and are less common on shallow sunlit reefs where the seaweeds dominate. The great abundance of sponges on reefs possibly reflects a lack of predators. A few specialised opisthobranchs, crustaceans, echinoderms and fish are known to feed on sponges; however, these animals form a small part of the marine fauna. Most carnivorous animals avoid sponges because of their poor nutritional value, the prevalence of splinter-like spicules and a potent array of toxic chemicals produced by sponge cells.

Sponges are generally hermaphroditic, meaning that individuals each produce both sperm and eggs. Sperm from a neighbouring animal is drawn into the sponge or attaches to the sponge surface, where contact is made with an egg, which develops into a larva. The surface of the larva eventually acquires a covering of flagella, enabling it to swim. After leaving the sponge and settling on a suitable substrate, the outer flagellated layer is shed or broken down. Many sponges also reproduce asexually by producing new animals from pieces broken off the parent sponge.

Although nearly 1000 species of sponges have been recorded from southern Australia, only the most common and distinctive species can usually be identified. Nearly all records of sponges in the region were made in the nineteenth century, and many of the names have been inappropriately used. The good species names are themselves difficult to apply to recent material because the original published descriptions were based on preserved specimens that were often distorted. Identification of sponges relies largely on the type and shape of spicules or other structural material and the positions of spicules within the sponge body. Identification is complicated by the ability of some sponges to incorporate sand and other external matter into the body, including spicules that are distinctively shaped but belong to other sponge species.

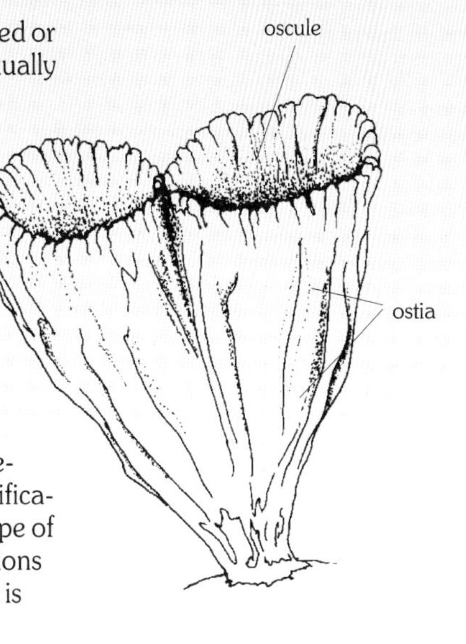

Sponge (200 mm)
Phylum Porifera

Sycon sp.

Habitat: Exposed reef; 0–20 m depth.
Distribution: SA to Vic. and around Tas.
Maximum size: Length to 30 mm.

This is one of several species in southern Australia belonging to the class of sponges (Calcarea) with spicules made from calcium carbonate rather than silica. Species in this genus can often be recognised by the tubular shape, a pattern of fine cross-hatched lines over the surface and small, round openings in the ends.

Sycon sp., Port Davey, Tas.

?*Leucosolenia* sp., Bruny I, Tas.

?*Leucosolenia* sp.

Habitat: Seaweeds; 1–20 m depth.
Distribution: WA to Vic. and around Tas.
Maximum size: Length to 8 mm.

?*Leucosolenia* sp. is a small sponge that is commonly found in groups attached to seaweeds. It has a calcareous skeletal network and a distinctive circular tuft of spicules around the large oscule opening.

Tethya australis Bergquist & Kelly Borges, 1991

Habitat: Reef; 1–26 m depth.
Distribution: SA to Vic. and northern Tas. Also New Zealand.
Maximum size: Diameter to 25 mm.

Species of *Tethya* are generally easy to identify to genus, as they often have a golfball shape and irregular projections that anchor the sponge to the reef surface. *Tethya australis* is the most common solitary species of *Tethya* in southeastern Australia. It has a smooth, rounded shape with up to ten supporting pedicels to anchor it to the rock surface. It also sometimes has buds extending out 2–10 mm on long filaments from the surface. The external colour is usually pink and the interior yellow.

Tethya ingalli Bowerbank, 1859

Habitat: Reef; 2–15 m depth.
Distribution: Southwestern WA.
Maximum size: Diameter to 40 mm.

Tethya ingalli has a similar appearance to *T. australis* and is distinguished chiefly by the arrangement of spicules, including the absence of a dense crust of very small spicules in the outermost layer. The species is common in southern Western Australia.

Polymastia sp.

Habitat: Sheltered and moderately exposed reef, sand; 5–12 m depth.
Distribution: Eastern Tas.
Maximum size: Height above sediment to 60 mm.

Tethya australis, Rocky Cape, Tas.

Tethya ?ingalli, Two Peoples Bay, WA

Polymastia sp., Flinders I, Tas.

Sponges in the genus *Polymastia* have a large base, which is often buried in sediment, with numerous prominent oscule projections extending above. These sponges are commonly associated with pockets of sediment on reef and sand along the reef edge.

Chondrilla australiensis Carter, 1873

Habitat: Moderately exposed reef; 2–15 m depth.
Distribution: WA to central NSW.
Maximum size: Width to 2 m.

Chondrilla australiensis is a common encrusting sponge, occurring in greatest abundance in southern Western Australia and New South Wales. It can be recognised by the smooth, shiny surface, pale interior and the presence of only one type of siliceous spicule (spheres with outward-pointing spines). A cavity is often located between the sponge and the reef, providing a refuge for large numbers of brittle stars, molluscs, shrimps and other animals.

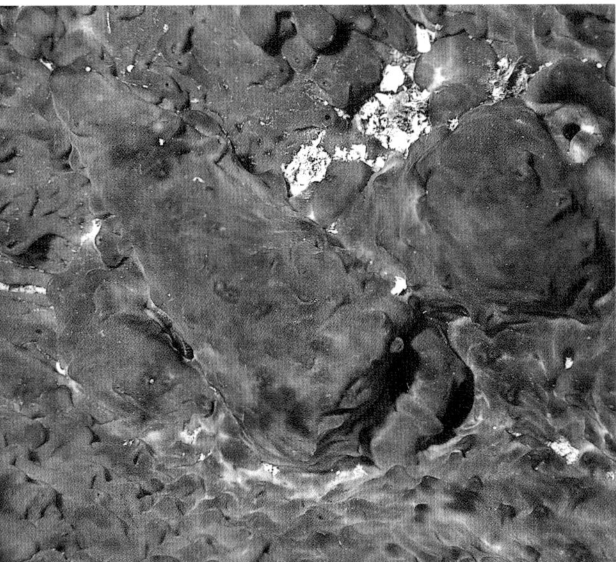

Chondrilla ?australiensis, Two Peoples Bay, WA

Echinoclathria laminaefavosa (Carter, 1885)

Habitat: Exposed reef; 5–40 m depth.
Distribution: Fremantle, WA, to Broughton I, NSW, and around Tas.
Maximum size: Length to 500 mm.

Echinoclathria laminaefavosa is a common sponge on reefs along exposed coasts and reaches greatest abundance in southern New South Wales. The species can usually be recognised by its large size, honeycomb surface and dull orange-brown to cream colour. The shape is variable and includes hand-shaped, lobed and rounded forms.

Echinoclathria laminaefavosa, Bass Point, NSW

Echinoclathria leporina (Lamarck, 1814)

Habitat: Exposed reef; 10–40 m depth.
Distribution: Port Phillip Bay, Vic., to Broughton I, NSW.
Maximum size: Length to 230 mm.

Echinoclathria leporina is a distinctive, orange, fan-shaped sponge with oscules arranged in a regular pattern over the surface. It is one of most abundant species on deep New South Wales reefs and was known as *Ophlitaspongia tenuis* until recently.

Echinoclathria leporina, Bass Point, NSW

Mycale mirabilis (Lendenfeld, 1887)

Habitat: Exposed reef; 4–47 m depth.
Distribution: Vic. to Torres Strait, Qld, and around Tas. Also widepread in the Indo-West Pacific region.
Maximum size: Length to 250 mm.

Mycale mirabilis usually has a flat shape with finger-like processes, but a variety of other forms, including sponges with spiny surface projections, have also been assigned to this species. The most characteristic features are the soft texture and yellowish-cream coloration. Copious amounts of slime are given off by this animal when removed from water.

Carteriospongia caliciformis, Ninepin Pt, Tas.

Mycale mirabilis, Bass Point, NSW

Carteriospongia caliciformis Carter, 1885

Habitat: Moderately exposed reef; 5–35 m depth.
Distribution: Port Lincoln, SA, to eastern Vic., and around Tas.
Maximum size: Diameter to 300 mm.

Carteriospongia caliciformis is one of the more easily identified sponges because of its concentric bowl-like shape. Unlike the majority of sponges, this species lacks spicules and has only the fibrous skeleton of spongin for support. It occurs commonly on deeper reefs, particularly in areas of high current flow. The irregular pink/green appearance of this sponge may be caused by green symbiotic algae growing on the surface. Related tropical species gain much of their nutrition from symbiotic microorganisms embedded in the outer layer.

Spongia sp.

Habitat: Exposed reef; 8–16 m depth.
Distribution: NSW.
Maximum size: Diameter to 150 mm.

Species of *Spongia* have a soft, elastic surface, which is usually pigmented black, brown or grey, with a white interior. Two types of spongin fibre are present internally: a few primary fibres with a central axis of foreign material and more numerous secondary fibres entwined around them. *Spongia* sp. occurs commonly under overhangs on exposed reefs along the southern New South Wales coast.

Spongia sp., Bass Point, NSW

Thorecta sp.

Habitat: Moderately exposed reef; 5 m depth.
Distribution: Eastern Tas.
Maximum size: Length to 100 mm.

A large number of species in the genus *Thorecta* are recorded from southern Australia. They are generally large sponges with sand embedded in the outer cell layer and with a fleshy skeleton of spongin fibres. The primary fibres have a central core of sand and other debris, while the secondary fibres lack a core. Species with cylindrical, flanged, exhalent openings, as in the illustrated animal, are moderately common.

Thorecta sp., Maria I, Tas.

Darwinella sp.

Habitat: Moderately exposed reef; 18 m depth.
Distribution: Northern Tas.
Maximum size: Length to 100 mm.

Darwinella sp., Rocky Cape, Tas.

Species of *Darwinella* are characterised by a skeleton of spongin fibres that lack embedded sand and by the presence of distinctive two-, three- or four-pronged spicules made of spongin. Local species in this genus often occur as encrustations on reefs and have a surface folded into irregular lobes.

Dendrilla rosea Lendenfeld, 1883

Habitat: Moderately exposed reef; 3–22 m depth.
Distribution: Adelaide, SA, to Sydney, NSW, and around Tas. Also widespread in the Indo-West Pacific region.
Maximum size: Length to 400 mm.

Dendrilla rosea is one of the most commonly observed sponges in southern Australia. It is typically a bright pink sponge with a deeply ruffled surface and can occur erect, branched or encrusting over other sessile animals. The internal skeleton of this and other members of the genus consists of repeatedly branched spongin fibres.

Dendrilla rosea, Flinders I, Tas.

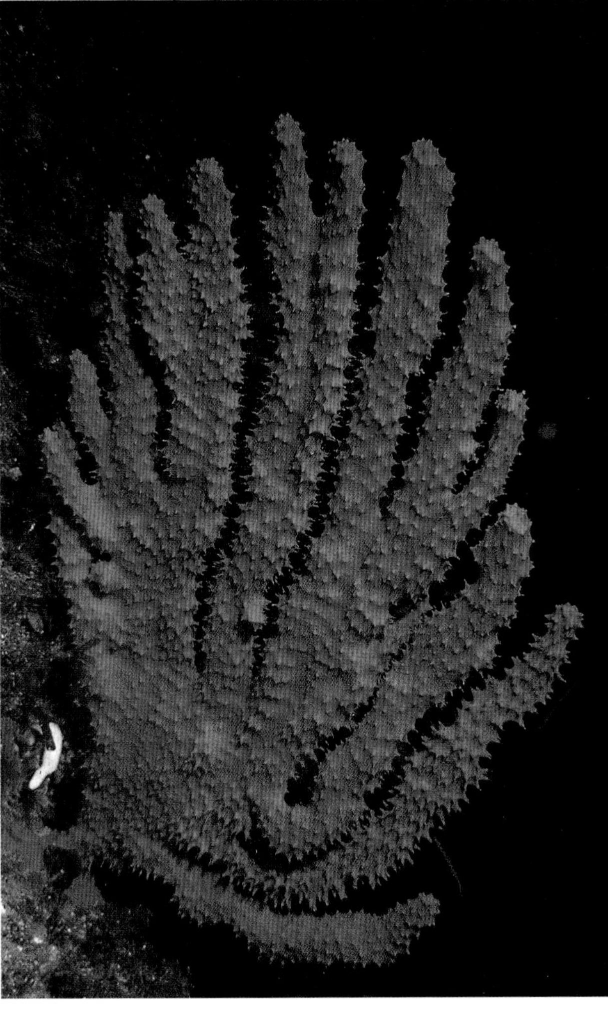

Aplysina lendenfeldi Bergquist, 1980

Habitat: Exposed reef; 8–30 m depth.
Distribution: Vic. to central NSW and around Tas.
Maximum size: Length to 150 mm.

Aplysina lendenfeldi is a cigar-shaped species with a short stalk and large exhalent opening at the uppermost end. It is usually light orange or yellow but quickly changes to dark brown or purple on removal from seawater. Like most other local sponge species, it has been recorded from very few localities but probably has a wide distribution.

Siphonochalina sp.

Habitat: Exposed reef; 20–35 m depth.
Distribution: Eastern Tas.
Maximum size: Length to 150 mm.

Species in the genus *Siphonochalina* have long tubular extensions with rough exteriors and a smooth internal lining. The illustrated species is one of the more common sponges on deep Tasmanian reefs.

?*Aplysina lendenfeldi*, Erith I, Tas.

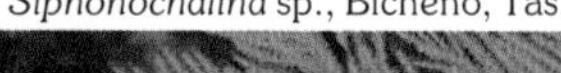

Siphonochalina sp., Bicheno, Tas.

PHYLUM CNIDARIA

Cnidarians

(including bluebottles, anemones, corals, jellyfish)

Cnidarians are structurally more complex than sponges and protozoans but are relatively unspecialised compared with other animal groups. The body wall is composed of two layers of cells, an outer ectoderm layer and inner endoderm layer, separated by a layer of gelatinous material known as the mesogloea. In many jellyfish the mesogloea layer is extremely thick and comprises most of body.

Cnidarians have two distinct body forms, polyps and medusae. Polyps have a tubular body attached at the base to the seabed, or to each other in a colony, with tentacles surrounding the mouth at the upper end. Medusae have a free-swimming hemispherical body, with tentacles surrounding the centrally located mouth on the undersurface. In some species these body forms occur in different generations — the polyp generation reproduce vegetatively on the seabed and release medusae, and the medusoid generation reproduce using sexual means and release planulae, which settle on the rocks to form new polyp colonies. Other species of cnidarians have lifecycles that are completed as polyp or medusa alone.

A characteristic feature of cnidarians is the presence of stinging cells known as nematocysts in the tentacles and body wall. Each nematocyst cell contains a coiled thread that can be pressurised and ejected from the cell for defensive purposes or for capturing prey. Some nematocyst threads have barbed ends and are connected to poison sacs, while others are sticky and entangle prey.

Class Hydrozoa

Hydroids, hydras and siphonophores

Hydrozoans generally have a two-phase life cycle in which the hydroid phase is most conspicuous. Most hydrozoan medusa are very small (generally <2 mm in diameter) and short lived, but, by contrast, large hydrozoans such as the bluebottle or Portuguese man o' war can have colonies several metres long. Many of the species are able to lay down a primitive external skeleton during the polyp stage, either a wall constructed from the protein chitin called the perisarc or in the hydrocorallines a calcareous wall. More than 3000 species are known worldwide, about 200 species having been recorded from southern Australia. Many are microscopic and rarely seen.

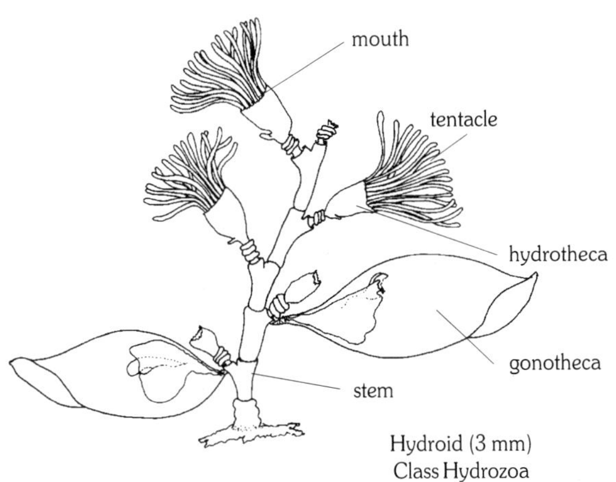

Hydroid (3 mm)
Class Hydrozoa

Order Hydroida

Hydroids

Hydroids are relatively small animals that usually form extended colonies attached to rocks or plants. They typically have branched stems arising from a network of vein-like structures known as stolons running along the substratum, with all parts of the colony enclosed within a chitinous wall, the perisarc. Attached to the branches are cup-shaped feeding polyps with a central mouth surrounded by tentacles. Small planktonic animals such as copepods are stung by the array of nematocysts along the tentacles and then transferred into the gastric cavity for digestion. A relatively small number of reproductive polyps that are often protected in vase- or club-shaped structures are seasonally present on the hydroid colony. Small medusae are released from these reproductive polyps by asexual budding.

Gymnangium superbum (Bale, 1882)

Habitat: Sheltered and moderately exposed reef; 2–15 m depth.
Distribution: Southern WA to Vic. and around Tas.
Maximum size: Colony height to 100 mm.

Gymnangium superbum is the largest and most distinctive of several feather-shaped hydroid species present in southern Australia. It has golden-coloured plumes that cover the sides of rock faces. Fertile specimens, which occur during the summer months, can be recognised by the presence of small, white, cup-shaped reproductive structures attached to the central axis.

Gymnangium superbum, Bicheno, Tas.

Gymnangium ascidioides (Bale, 1882)

Habitat: Moderately and submaximally exposed reef; 8–15 m depth.
Distribution: Vic. and eastern Tas.
Maximum size: Colony height to 60 mm.

Gymnangium ascidioides, Bicheno, Tas.

Gymnangium ascidioides has a similar shape to *G. superbum* but is a smaller, less common species with a reddish-brown colour. The species prefers sites along the open coast in areas with reasonable current flow.

Stereotheca elongata (Lamouroux, 1816)

Habitat: Moderately exposed and sheltered seagrass, macroalgae; 0–6 m depth.
Distribution: WA to NSW and around Tas. Also New Zealand and South Africa.
Maximum size: Colony height to 80 mm.

Stereotheca elongata is one of the more common hydroids found living on other plants, with an particular affinity for *Amphibolis* seagrasses. While the species has a similar colony shape to a variety of others, the individual polyps are easily recognised when seen under a microscope. The feeding polyps are attached in an alternating series up the branch, with the bottom half of each polyp connected to other polyps, and the free half curved with a sharply toothed outer margin.

Stereotheca elongata, Marmion Lagoon, WA

Ralpharia magnifica, Zuidpool Rock, Tas.

Ralpharia magnifica Watson, 1980

Habitat: Sheltered reef; 3–20 m depth.
Distribution: SA to Vic. and around Tas.
Maximum size: Polyp height to 100 mm.

Ralpharia magnifica is a very large hydroid (polyps up to 50 mm in diameter) that occurs in groups of two to 100 separated polyps. At the base of the polyps is a tangled mass of filaments embedded in soft coral on the reef surface. *Ralpharia magnifica* can be confused with another species, ***Tubularia ralphi***, which has smaller (<15 mm in diameter), more entangled polyps. Both species are fertile during summer and early autumn.

Halopteris campanula (Busk, 1852)

Habitat: Reef, jetty piles; 4–110 m depth.
Distribution: SA to Qld and around Tas. Also New Zealand, Japan and South Africa.
Maximum size: Colony height to 200 mm.

Halopteris campanula is a common species usually seen in dense, entangled colonies. It occurs in greatest abundance on deepwater reefs along the exposed coast and also occasionally occurs in shallow sheltered bays. The species has a delicate structure, with a distinctive orange or yellow colour.

Halocordyle disticha (Goldfuss, 1820)

Habitat: Moderately exposed reef; 3–12 m depth.
Distribution: Perth, WA, to NSW but absent from Vic. Also widespread overseas.
Maximum size: Colony height to 100 mm.

Halopteris campanula, Munro Bight, Tas.

Halocordyle disticha, Horseshoe Reef, WA

Halocordyle disticha has dark axes, which contrast with the much lighter coloured polyps. The polyps are widely and evenly spaced, each one having a complex structure like a miniaturised *Ralpharia magnifica*. This hydroid is often noticed by divers in the Sydney and Perth regions.

Solanderia fusca (Grey, 1868)

Habitat: Moderately and submaximally exposed reef; 3–30 m depth.
Distribution: WA to Qld and northern Tas.
Maximum size: Colony height to 300 mm.

Solanderia fusca has a fan-shaped appearance similar to that of gorgonians (see pages 140-143) but, in contrast with gorgonians, generally occurs in areas with wave surge. Individual polyps are quite different from those of gorgonians, with each polyp supported on spiky, grooved ledges. Two other hydroids (***Clathrozoon wilsoni*** and *Plumularia procumbens*) are also large, brown and fern-shaped and can be confused with *Solanderia fusca* if the individual polyps are not examined. *Clathrozoon wilsoni* grows to a larger size than *S. fusca*, occurs on deep reefs, and has dark brown, untidy-looking colonies.

Plumularia procumbens Spencer, 1891

Habitat: Moderately and submaximally exposed reef; 3–200 m depth.
Distribution: St Francis I, SA, to eastern Vic. and around Tas.
Maximum size: Colony height to 300 mm.

Plumularia procumbens has a dark gorgonian-shaped skeleton, with small polyps arising from fine, white secondary axes. The species is common in shallow water in southern Tasmania but is generally restricted to deeper reefs on the Australian mainland.

Solanderia fusca. PETER LAST

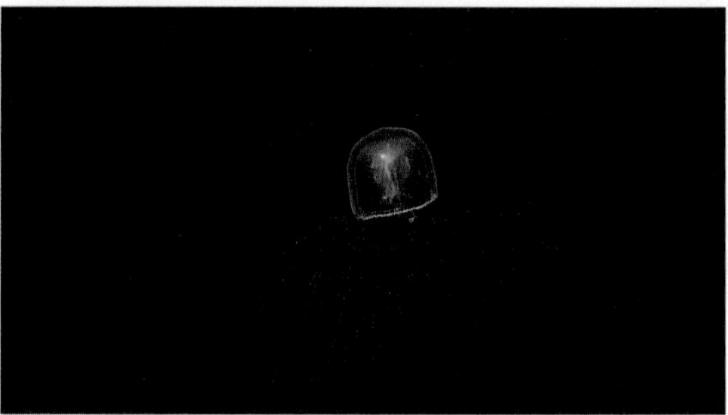

Turritopsis nutricula, Bathurst Channel, Tas.

Turritopsis nutricula (McCrady, 1856)

Habitat: Sheltered bays; 0–10 m depth.
Distribution: WA to NSW and around Tas. Also widespread overseas.
Maximum size: Medusa height to 15 mm.

The polyp stage of the life cycle of *Turritopsis nutricula* form inconspicuous colonies up to 40 mm in height on algae and rock in sheltered bays. The medusae are, however, quite noticeable because of their relatively large size and bright red gonads. They are released in large numbers by polyps in shallow water in summer and autumn.

Plumularia procumbens, Low Head, Tas.

Aequorea eurhodina Péon & Lesueur, 1809

Habitat: Open sea; 1–30 m depth.
Distribution: Eastern Tas. to southern NSW
Maximum size: Diameter to 200 mm.

Aequorea eurhodina is a hydrozoan with an extremely large, saucer-shaped medusa that floats in the open ocean. The medusa can be readily recognised by the numerous radial canals around the periphery of the bell. There is some doubt about the identity of this animal. The original scientific description of a Bass Strait specimen was poor, and it is possible that this southeastern Australian jellyfish is the same as the cosmopolitan species *Aequorea forskalea.*

Aequorea eurhodina, Montague I, NSW. Rudie Kuiter

Velella velella (Linnaeus, 1758)

By-the-wind-sailor

Habitat: Ocean surface.
Distribution: Around the Australian mainland and Tas. Also widespread overseas.
Maximum size: Disc diameter to 40 mm.

Velella velella is a highly distinctive species that was once classed with the bluebottle *Physalia physalis* in the order Siphonophora, but which is now grouped with the hydroids. Each polyp has a disc-shaped float with a low, sheet-like sail on the upper surface. The underside of the float has a fringe of feeding tentacles arranged around the margin, numerous reproductive structures inside this fringe and a centrally located mouth. The by-the-wind-sailor seasonally occurs in large numbers on the ocean surface and is often accompanied by *Physalia physalis* and other species of drifting, blue-coloured invertebrates. One of these invertebrates is *Porpita porpita* , a closely related hydrozoan with a disc-shaped float but which lacks a sail and has longer marginal tentacles.

Velella velella, Coffs Harbour, NSW. Gary Bell/Ocean Wide Images

Order Limnomedusae

Limnomedusids are a group of marine and freshwater hydrozoans with four to six radial canals and tentacles arranged in sets around the margin of the saucer-shaped bell. The medusoid stage is relatively large and conspicuous. In contrast, the polyp stage is not known for most species but generally seems to be poorly developed and have few or no tentacles.

Olindias phosphorica (Delle Chiaje, 1841)

Habitat: Sheltered bays, seagrass, algae; 0–20 m depth.
Distribution: Tropical Australia south to southern WA and southern NSW. Also widespread overseas.
Maximum size: Medusa diameter to 35 mm.

Olindias phosphorica is one of the most striking sea creatures, with corkscrew tentacles and brilliant red and green colours. It has a painful sting and can move by either swimming or crawling. The crawling motion is caterpillar-like and involves the use of special suckers attached to the tentacles.

Olindias phosphorica, Esperance, WA. RUDIE KUITER

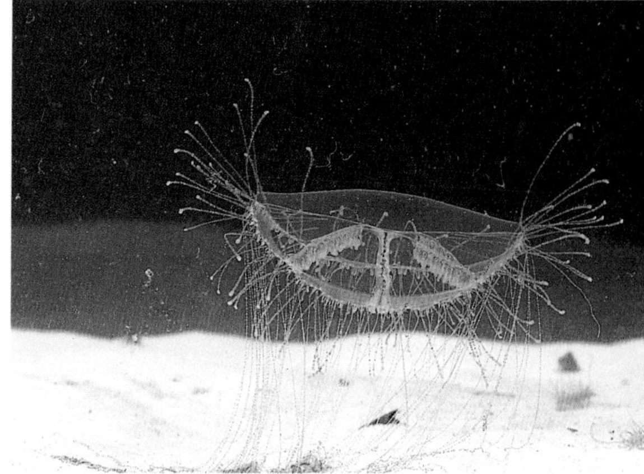

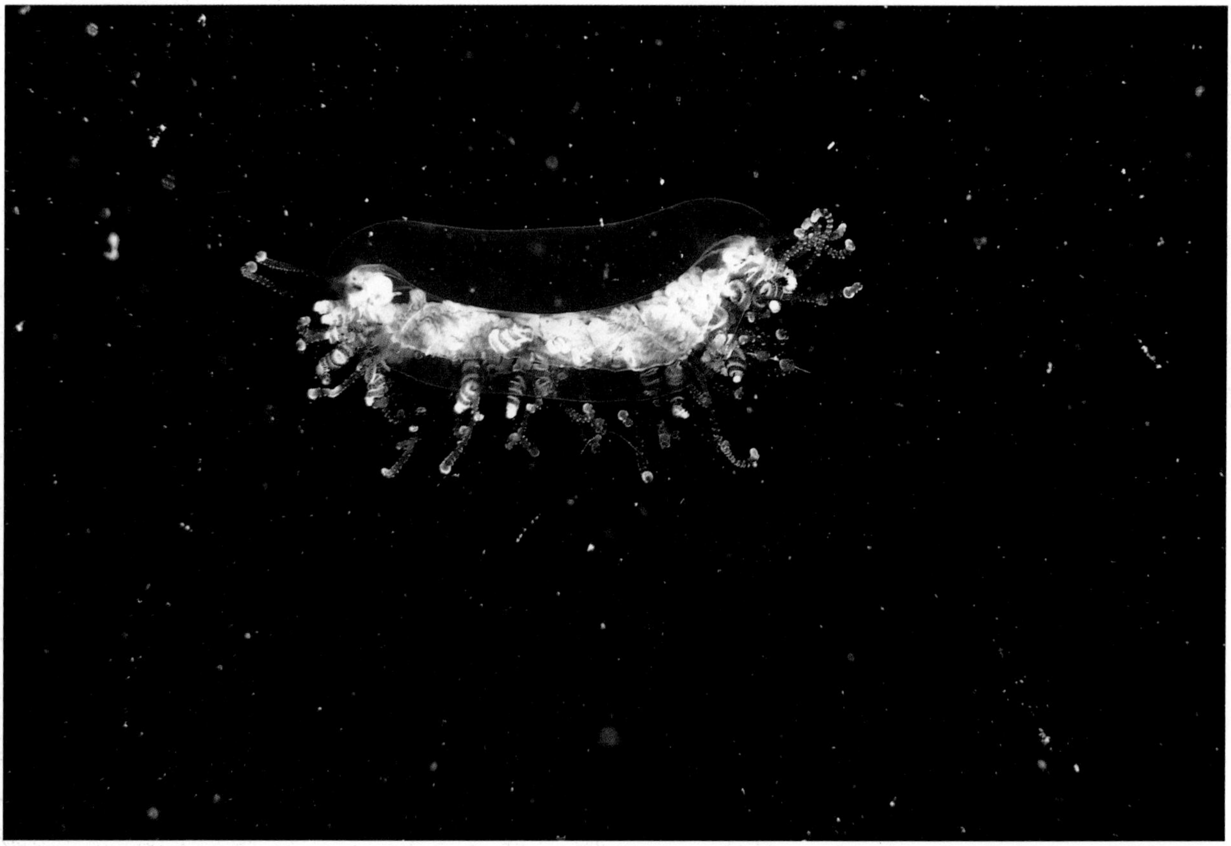

Olindias singularis, Albany, WA. CLAY BRYCE

Olindias singularis Browne, 1904

Habitat: Sheltered bays; 0–15 m depth.
Distribution: Tropical Australia south to SA and southern NSW. Also widespread in the Indo-West Pacific region.
Maximum size: Medusa diameter to 36 mm.

Olindias singularis has a saucer-shaped bell with 28–86 tentacles around the margin and orange gonads attached to each of the radial canals. The species is very common in late summer and is responsible for many of the stings on bathers in the South Australian gulfs.

Order Siphonophora

This order comprises species with colonies of polyps that are individually specialised for feeding, defence, float production and reproduction. The medusae are also highly specialised and are generally directly attached to the polyps in the colony. Most species of siphonophore float passively on the ocean surface, but some are active swimmers and a few are bottom dwellers.

Physalia physalis (Linnaeus, 1766)
Bluebottle, Portuguese man o' war

Habitat: Ocean surface.
Distribution: Around Australia and Tas. Also widespread overseas.
Maximum size: Float length to 300 mm, tentacles to 10 m.

Few people who live around the coast would be unaware of the common bluebottle, *Physalia physalis*, an oceanic species with a very painful sting. When driven ashore in large numbers by prevailing onshore winds, as occurs frequently in late summer, the virulence of stings from this species can clear beaches of swimmers. The traditional treatment of stings has been to apply vinegar or methylated spirits after threads are removed by forceps or by flushing with water; this process can cause remaining tentacles to discharge, and so current practice is to apply cold packs for the relief of skin pain and to seek medical advice if necessary.

Physalia physalis washed up after storm, Cloudy Bay, Tas.

Each bluebottle is a colony of specialised animals rather than a single individual, with some animals specialised for food capture, others for digestion, others for reproduction and one to produce the gas-filled float. Some colonies have floats aligned at 45° left of the wind and others at 45° to the right. This difference in float direction probably aids survival of the species, as it prevents all colonies drifting in the same direction and being stranded together.

The southern Australian bluebottle is considered by some authorities to be different from the Portuguese man o' war, in which case the name ***Physalia utriculus*** is appropriate.Rather than having several large tentacles of about equal size as in the Portuguese man o' war, the bluebottle has a single prominent fishing tentacle that is usually a darker blue colour than the thinner tentacles nearby. The sting is also less virulent than the sting of northern Australian and overseas animals.

Physalia physalis, Watermans, WA. CLAY BRYCE

Class Anthozoa

Anemones, corals, sea pens

Anthozoans occur as polyps or colonies of polyps and lack a medusoid stage. Most are short and relatively wide across the mouth compared with the hydrozoans, and unlike the hydrozoans they have the body cavity divided by inward-projecting partitions of the body wall, known as mesenteries; the mesenteries are covered by digestive cells and are also the sites where gonads are located. Anthozoans can reproduce by budding miniature animals from the body wall. They can also reproduce sexually, producing a mobile planula larva after fertilisation of the egg. This planula is capable of dispersing some distance away from the parents. Some species have direct development, producing juveniles that are initially retained within the body cavity. About 6500 species are known world-wide, with most occurring in the tropics. Approximately 200 species are recorded from southern Australia.

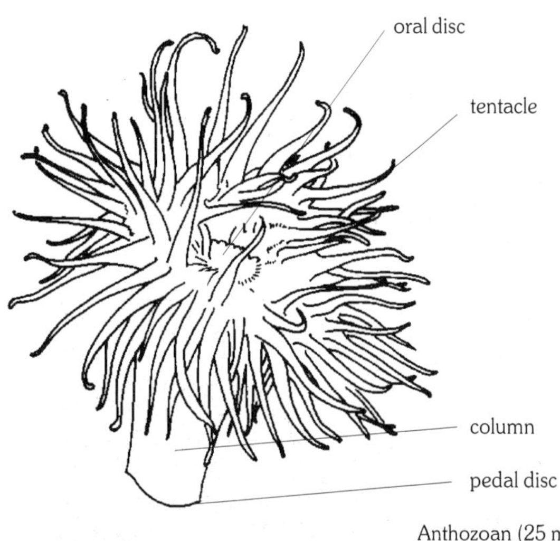

Anthozoan (25 mm)
Class Anthozoa

Order Actiniaria

Anemones

Anemones are the most conspicuous cnidarians on temperate rocky shores. They occur as solitary individuals and have a central body cavity partitioned by complete and incomplete mesenteries, a centrally located mouth, and hollow tentacles radiating in one or more rows from around the mouth. Because the body is supported by water pressure, they are not able to support themselves or operate tentacles at low-tide.

Actinia tenebrosa Farquhar, 1898

Waratah anemone

Habitat: Rocky shores; mid intertidal to 5 m.
Distribution: Shark Bay, WA, to Heron I, Qld, around Tas. Also New Zealand.
Maximum size: Diameter to 40 mm.

Actinia tenebrosa is the most noticeable anemone on southern shores. It is generally seen during low-tide in its contracted shape, when it appears as a dark red blob with a lighter red spot where the mouth is located. Its beauty becomes apparent only when the tide comes in and the tentacles unfurl. Young waratah anemones emerge through the mouth as fully formed replicas of the adult.

Actinia tenebrosa, Port Stephens, NSW

Actinia tenebrosa contracted (with *Brachidontes rostratus*), Eaglehawk Neck, Tas.

Oulactis muscosa (Drayton, 1846)

Habitat: Sheltered and moderately exposed rockpools; mid to low intertidal.
Distribution: Spencer Gulf, SA, to southern Qld and around Tas. Also New Zealand.
Maximum size: Diameter to 80 mm.

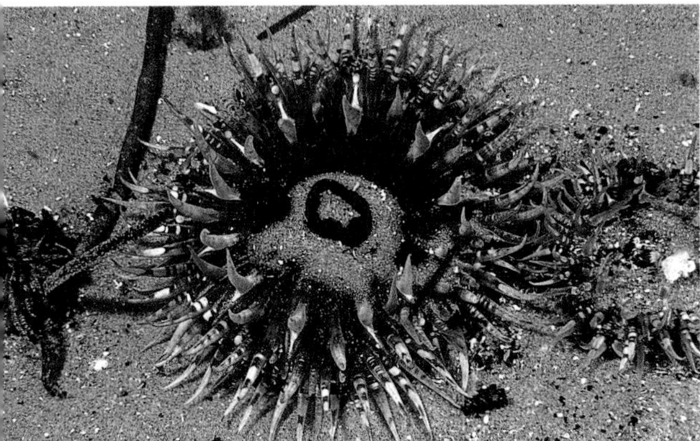
Oulactis muscosa, Tinderbox, Tas.

Oulactis muscosa has blotched grey tentacles and a cream column with dark spots. These spots are rarely seen because the animal usually remains buried in sand with only the tentacles and part of the upper body surface showing. This species feeds largely on small mussels after they have been dislodged by wave action.

Oulactis macmurrichi (Lager, 1911)

Habitat: Rockpools; mid to low intertidal.
Distribution: Perth, WA, to Coffin Bay, SA.
Maximum size: Diameter to 80 mm.

Oulactis macmurrichi is virtually impossible to distinguish from *O. muscosa* on the basis of shape and also has similar behaviour and habitat preferences, so may not be a distinctive species. Its column has a darker coloration than that of its eastern relative.

Oulactis macmurrichi, Marmion Lagoon, WA

Aulactinia veratra (Drayton, 1846)

Habitat: Rockpools; low intertidal.
Distribution: Rottnest I, WA, to southern Qld and around Tas.
Maximum size: Diameter to 70 mm.

Aulactinia veratra has a dark green column with long tentacles of a lighter green. Its usual habitat is water-filled crevices near low-tide level on the open coast, where it often occurs in extremely high densities.

Aulactinia veratra, Bicheno, Tas.

Anthothoe albocincta (Hutton, 1878)

Habitat: Moderately exposed and sheltered reef; 0–40 m depth.
Distribution: Ceduna, SA, to NSW and around Tas. Also New Zealand.
Maximum size: Diameter to 30 mm.

Anthothoe albocincta is one of the more easily recognised anemone species as it has a distinctively striped orange and white column and up to 200 short white tentacles. It is abundant on rock surfaces but can reach even higher densities on jetty pylons. When disturbed, this species releases groups of stinging cells through holes in the body wall. These stinging cells are generally harmless to humans.

Anthothoe albocincta, Tathra, NSW

Phlyctenactis tuberculosa
(Quoy & Gaimard, 1833)
Swimming anemone

Habitat: Moderately exposed and sheltered reef, macroalgae, seagrass; 0–35 m depth.
Distribution: Southwestern WA to Byron Bay, NSW, and around Tas.
Maximum size: Diameter to 150 mm.

Phlyctenactis tuberculosa is the largest anemone commonly seen in southern Australian waters. Its body consists of numerous reddish-brown vesicles striped with blue, and it also has many long orange tentacles. The species can move rapidly either by crawling or by drifting with the current. During the day this anemone looks like a collapsed bag of baked beans, but during the night it moves high on plant fronds and shows considerable agility in catching floating prey.

Phlyctenactis tuberculosa, Maria I, Tas.

Phlyctenanthus australis Carlgren, 1950

Habitat: Exposed reef; 1–35 m depth.
Distribution: Ceduna, SA, to Sydney, NSW, and around Tas.
Maximum size: Diameter to 100 mm.

Phlyctenanthus australis has a superficial similarity in shape to *Phlyctenactis tuberculosa* and a confusingly similar name. *Phlyctenanthus australis* remains permanently attached to the reef and has a bulbous blue-grey column and up to 100 reddish-brown tentacles.

Phlyctenanthus australis, Bicheno, Tas.

? *Tealia* sp.

Habitat: Sheltered and moderately exposed reef; 8–50 m depth.
Distribution: Eastern and southern Tas.
Maximum size: Diameter to 80 mm.

This is one of the largest anemones, with most of the observed animals being about 100 mm long. The species is known from sheltered locations with good tidal current flow. Although few specimens have been recorded, the anemone is possibly common on deep reef habitats.

? *Tealia* sp., Bathurst Harbour, Tas.

Epiactis australiensis Carlgren, 1950

Habitat: Sand; 0–30 m depth.
Distribution: Gulf St Vincent, SA, to Vic. and northern Tas.
Maximum size: Diameter to 25 mm.

Two species of *Epiactis* are recorded from southern Australian waters, although the affinities and geographic distribution of each are not yet clearly known. *Epiactis australiensis* has a long, smooth cylindrical column with rounded structures at the base and up to sixty pale tentacles with purplish tips. It is usually found buried in sand but attached to shells or rock.

Epiactis ?thomsoni, Port Victoria, SA

Epiactis? australiensis, Rocky Cape, Tas.

Epiactis thomsoni (Coughtrey, 1874)

Habitat: Sheltered and moderately exposed rocks; 0–10 m depth.
Distribution: SA.
Maximum size: Diameter to 30 mm.

Epiactis thomsoni is a slightly larger species than *E. australiensis* and is usually found under rocks. Its colour pattern is extremely variable, although red and pink shades usually predominate. The tentacles generally have a stripe along the upper surface.

Actinothoe glandulosa Carlgren, 1954

Habitat: Moderately exposed reef; 0–12 m depth.
Distribution: Southwestern WA.
Maximum size: Diameter to 15 mm.

Actinothoe glandulosa is a small pale anemone with a white oral area and white tentacles. It is one of the most common species on temperate Western Australian reefs and generally occurs in clusters of several individuals.

Actinothoe glandulosa, Quarry Bay, WA

Heteractis malu (Haddon & Shackleton, 1893)

Habitat: Moderately exposed sand; 4–18 m depth.
Distribution: Tropical Australia south to Perth, WA. Also widespread in the Indo-West Pacific region.
Maximum size: Diameter to 100 mm.

Heteractis malu is a large tropical anemone that occurs very commonly on the edges of seagrass beds off Perth. The species was known as *Radianthus concinnata* until recently, but that name has been subsumed under the name of the more widely distributed tropical species. *Heteractis malu* has a wide body and numerous small tentacles regularly arranged around the edge, and so is unlikely to be confused with other species. Small transparent shrimps often live among the tentacles.

Heteractis malu, Marmion Lagoon, WA

Dofleina armata Wassilieff, 1908

Habitat: Sheltered sand, mud; 0–20 m depth.
Distribution: Tropical Australia south to Perth, WA.
Maximum size: Diameter to 200 mm.

Dofleina armata is one of the largest Australian anemones and is certainly the most dangerous. Contact with this species will produce an extremely painful wound that may take up to a month to heal. It is relatively common on fine silt sediments in Cockburn Sound but is more prevalent in the tropics, where it often occurs intertidally among mangroves. The long arms (up to 500 mm) can be striped or plain, with a scale-like surface structure, and usually terminate in a slightly swollen purple tip.

Dofleina armata, Woodmans Point, WA

?*Boloceroides* sp.

Habitat: Sheltered seagrass; 0–5 m depth.
Distribution: Southeastern Tas.
Maximum size: Diameter to 15 mm.

This anemone is common in *Heterozostera tasmanica* seagrass beds in southern Tasmania and is probably more widely distributed. During both day and night it climbs along seagrass leaves, searching for prey with its tentacles.

?*Boloceroides* sp., Cloudy Lagoon, Tas.

Order Corallimorpharia
Jewel anemones

This order contains solitary and colonial animals that superficially look like anemones but are more closely related to the corals. They generally have a swollen tip to the tentacles and do not produce a calcareous skeleton.

Corynactis australis Haddon & Duerden, 1896

Habitat: Exposed reef; 2–30 m depth.
Distribution: Port Phillip Bay, Vic., to NSW and around Tas. Also New Zealand.
Maximum size: Diameter to 15 mm.

Corynactis australis lives in shaded situations along the wave-exposed coast, the largest colonies often occurring at the entrance to seacaves. The various polyps within a colony are joined to a common sheet-like base, and several colonies often adjoin each other at a site. The boundaries between adjoining colonies are generally easy to distinguish because of differences in coloration between colonies, making underwater rockwalls in some places a spectacular combination of pinks, purples, oranges and browns. Polyps often vary greatly in shape between sites, perhaps indicating that several species are presently being confused as one. All possess a characteristic knob on the end of the tentacles.

Corynactis australis, Rocky Cape, Tas.

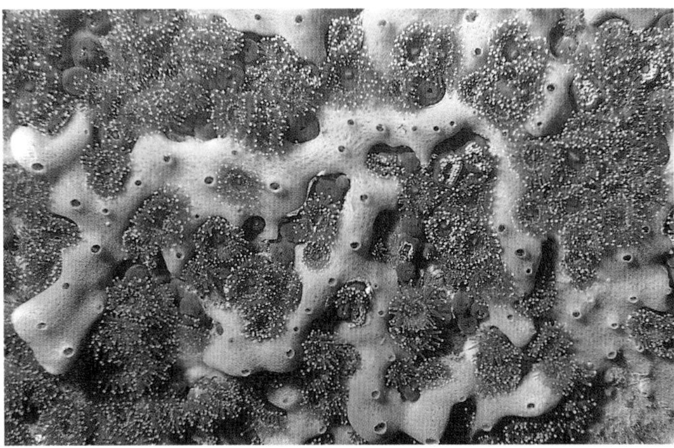

Corynactis australis, Tathra, NSW

Order Zoanthidea
Zoanthids

Zoanthids are a group of mainly colonial species that resemble small anemones; they have smooth tentacles that occur in one or two rings. The colonial species are connected by stolons and can occur in very dense colonies on rock or on sessile invertebrates such as sponges and gorgonians.

Zoanthus robustus Carlgren, 1950

Habitat: Moderately exposed reef; 1–10 m depth.
Distribution: Ceduna, SA, to central Vic.
Maximum size: Length to 60 mm.

Zoanthus robustus occurs in large aggregations on flat reef near the edge of sand. Its colour pattern varies little throughout the geographical range: the column being a khaki-green and tentacles a lighter yellow-green.

Zoanthus robustus, Cape Jervis, SA

Zoanthus praelongus Carlgren, 1954

Habitat: Moderately exposed reef; 1–12 m depth.
Distribution: Perth to Esperance, WA.
Maximum size: Length to 80 mm.

Zoanthus praelongus is found in a similar environment to *Z. robustus* but is a more elongate species and is coloured a brighter green than its relative. The species feeds mainly at night. During the day most animals, including those illustrated, have their tentacles retracted inside the body cavity.

Zoanthus praelongus, Quarry Bay, WA

Isaurus cliftoni (Gray, 1857)

Habitat: Moderately exposed reef; 1–7 m.
Distribution: Tropical Australia south to Esperance, WA.
Maximum size: Length to 90 mm.

Isaurus cliftoni, Two Peoples Bay, WA

Isaurus cliftoni prefers similar environmental conditions in southern Western Australia to *Zoanthus praelongus*, and these two species often live next to one another. *Isaurus cliftoni* can be identified by the more elongate body and blotchy colour pattern.

Epizoanthus sabulosus Cutress, 1971

Habitat: Moderately exposed reef; 5–12 m depth.
Distribution: Esperance, WA, to Port Phillip Bay, Vic.
Maximum size: Length to 8 mm.

Epizoanthus sabulosus is a common species of zoanthid in southern Australia that grows on encrusting sponge. It has a white, sand-encrusted column and dark tentacles.

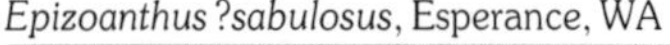

Epizoanthus ?sabulosus, Esperance, WA

Parazoanthus sp.

Yellow zoanthid

Habitat: Exposed reef; 2–60 m depth.
Distribution: Cape Northumberland, SA, to Jervis Bay, NSW, and around Tas.
Maximum size: Height to 20 mm.

Although this yellow zoanthid is one of the most conspicuous animals on coastal reefs and is known by most divers, it still has no scientific name. It is usually easy to recognise because of the colour and the dense colonial form, and also because of the small red spot on one end of the mouth and orange lines radiating from the mouth to the yellow tentacles. The species cannot compete for space with algae on well-lit reefs and is therefore generally restricted to dark rock faces under overhangs. It grows on encrusting sponge.

Parazoanthus sp., Bathurst Channel, Tas.

?*Parazoanthus* sp.

Habitat: Sheltered reef; 5–20 m depth.
Distribution: Southern Tas.
Maximum size: Height to 10 mm.

This white zoanthid is relatively common in southern Tasmania and probably has a much wider distribution. It is often associated with *Dactylochalina australis*, the white encrusting sponge that is in turn associated with the red alga *Thamnoclonium dichotomum*.

?*Parazoanthus* sp., Bathurst Channel, Tas.

Palythoa heideri Carlgren, 1954

Habitat: Exposed reef; 0–10 m depth.
Distribution: Kalbarri to Rottnest I, WA.
Maximum size: Diameter to 25 mm.

Although most zoanthids in the genus *Palythoa* are restricted to the tropics, *Palythoa heideri* is common on the reefs off Perth. The species is easily recognised by the very small size of the 70 or so tentacles in relation to the width of the body and the radially furrowed oral disk. A second *Palythoa* species, ***Palythoa densa***, occurs in the same area as *P. heideri* but has fewer tentacles (about 40) and is fawn to pale green.

Palythoa heideri, Jurien Bay, WA. CLAY BRYCE

Order Scleractinia
Stony corals

Scleractinians are anemone-like animals with a hard calcareous skeleton laid down outside the living polyp. They include the reef-building corals, an extremely important group in tropical areas but relatively inconspicuous in temperate waters. Coral reefs generally form only when winter water temperatures exceed 18°C and light levels are high. Three reef-building (hermatypic) corals are known from southern Australia. A number of non-reef-building (ahermatypic) species, which generally occur as solitary individuals, also occur in the region.

Plesiastrea versipora (Lamarck, 1816)

Habitat: Moderately exposed reef; 0–30 m depth.
Distribution: Around Australia and northern Tas. Also widespread in the Indo-West Pacific region.
Maximum size: Colony width to 3 m, polyps to 3 mm in diameter.

Plesiastrea versipora is the most widespread of the southern Australian reef-building corals. It is generally easily recognised because of its green and brown colour and the distinctive array of large circular pits in which the polyps are located. The green coloration is caused by vast numbers of symbiotic dinoflagellates (known as zooxanthellae) living embedded in the coral tissue. Zooxanthellae trap the energy of sunlight and convert it into chemical energy, which is used by the host coral.

Plesiastrea versipora, Horseshoe Reef, WA

Coscinaraea marshae, Marmion Lagoon, WA

Coscinaraea marshae Wells, 1962

Habitat: Moderately exposed reef; 1–40 m depth.
Distribution: Houtman Abrolhos, WA, to Pearson I, SA.
Maximum size: Colony width to 500 mm.

Coscinaraea marshae is a reef-building coral with a circular shape and a regular arrangement of high concentric ridges running around the inside of the colony. It is usually found growing flat on the seabed on clear deep-water reefs, where it may be abundant.

Coscinaraea mcneilli Wells, 1962

Habitat: Moderately exposed reef; 0–33 m depth.
Distribution: Houtman Abrolhos, WA, to Byron Bay, NSW.
Maximum size: Colony width to 500 mm.

Coscinaraea mcneilli, Twilight Cove, WA

Coscinaraea mcneilli lacks the obvious ridges of its relative *C. marshae* and has a less regular shape. Both species prefer clear, deep-water habitats and are most abundant on offshore reefs.

Culicia tenella Dana, 1846

Habitat: Moderately and submaximally exposed reef; 2–238 m depth.
Distribution: Perth, WA, to Solitary I, NSW, and around Tas.
Maximum size: Polyp width to 5 mm.

Culicia tenella is not often noticed but is common on rock surfaces with little light and is very abundant on the walls of submarine caves. The individual polyps are arranged in a regular pattern, with colonies often radiating out from a central point. The colour of this species shows considerable variation. A related species found along the southern coastline, ***Culicia hoffmeisteri***, has fewer septa (20–24) than *C. tenella* (36–48).

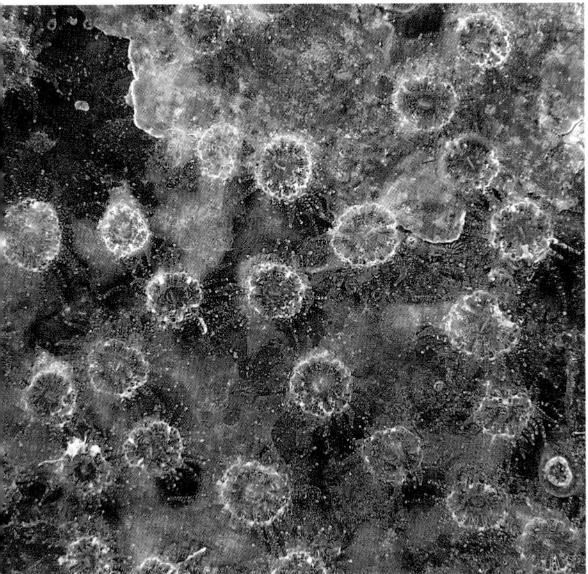

Culicia sp., Bicheno, Tas.

Scolymia australis (Milne Edwards & Haime, 1849)

Habitat: Moderately and submaximally exposed reef; 0–17 m depth.
Distribution: Rottnest I, WA, to Port Phillip Bay, Vic. Also Qld and Lord Howe I.
Maximum size: Polyp width to 56 mm.

Scolymia australis is a large solitary coral, which is often noticed by divers because of the bright green or brown polyps. It is common under rock ledges along the western south coast but becomes less common towards the east of its range.

Scolymia australis, Investigator Group, SA

Balanophyllia bairdiana Edwards & Haime, 1848

Habitat: Moderately and submaximally exposed reef; 5–70 m depth.
Distribution: Port Phillip Bay, Vic., to southern Qld and around Tas.
Maximum size: Polyp width to 20 mm.

Balanophyllia bairdiana is a common solitary coral in low-light habitats. It has a conical shape that tapers towards the base and is pink, orange or white. The transparent tentacles have coloured banks of nematocysts and generally remain contracted during daylight.

Balanophyllia bairdiana, Ile des Phoques, Tas.

Order Ceriantharia
Tube anemones

Tube anemones have anemone-like bodies and live in sand-encrusted mucous tubes on soft sediments. The body is not directly attached to the tube and rapidly retracts down it if disturbed. Tube anemones have two sets of tentacles, one set encircling the mouth and a set of much longer tentacles around the edge of the disk. They are most closely related to the black corals (order Antipatharia).

Pachycerianthus sp.
Purple-tipped tube anemone

Habitat: Sheltered sand; 5–25 m depth.
Distribution: Southwestern WA.
Maximum size: Length of tentacles to 100 mm.

Pachycerianthus sp. is common on soft sediment in Cockburn Sound and in the lower Swan Estuary. Its major characteristics are the purple inner tentacles and the purple tip to the long outer tentacles. The tube can extend for more than 300 mm into the sand.

Pachycerianthus sp., Woodmans Point, WA

Pachycerianthus delwynae Carter, 1995

Habitat: Sheltered sand; 3–15 m depth.
Distribution: Central NSW.
Maximum size: Length of tentacles to 100 mm.

Pachycerianthus delwynae, Terrigal, NSW

Pachycerianthus delwynae has a regular pattern of pale bands down the brown outer tentacles. When not feeding, these tentacles are often coiled in a tight corkscrew arrangement near the tips. The inner tentacles are a pale yellowish brown to cream colour, and the oral disc is purplish brown. This tube anemone has recently been scientifically named on the basis of specimens collected in Sydney Harbour, where it is extremely common. The species may be widely distributed around southern Australia because animals with a similar appearance are commonly seen by divers as far as Perth, where they are as abundant as the purple-tipped tube anemone.

Pachycerianthus longistriatis Carter, 1995
Habitat: Sheltered sand; 4–12 m depth.
Distribution: Sydney Harbour, NSW.
Maximum size: Length of tentacles to 100 mm.

Pachycerianthus longistriatis commonly occurs in Sydney Harbour alongside *P. delwynae*. It is readily distinguished from that species because the long outer tentacles have pale longitudinal stripes rather than a cross-banding pattern. These outer tentacles can be either purple or pale brown and do not coil at the tips; the inner tentacles are cream, and the oral disc is brown.

Pachycerianthus longistriatus, North Head, NSW

Order Antipatharia
Black corals

The black corals are a group of tree-like or whip-like species that occur most conspicuously in deep water on tropical and subtropical reefs. Each colony has a rigid central axis made from horny material, surrounded by a thin layer of light-coloured living tissue. Polyps occur embedded in this surface tissue, and each have six or occasionally eight unbranched tentacles. The horny skeletons of several of the larger black coral species glisten when polished and are used for jewellery.

Antipathes sp.

Habitat: Exposed reef; 20–40+ m depth.
Distribution: Southern WA.
Maximum size: Colony length to 1.5 m.

Most Australian black corals can be recognised by the high degree of branching and by a white coating of polyps and body tissue over the dark internal skeleton. *Antipathes* sp. is a large plant-like species which is sometimes brought up in trawls and also occasionally seen by divers. It lives on deep reefs in areas of good current flow. The brittle star ***Astrobrachion adhaerens*** often occurs entwined in its branches.

Antipathes sp., Torbay Heads, WA. NEVILLE COLEMAN/ UNDERWATER GEOGRAPHIC

Order Alcyonacea

Octocorals, soft corals, gorgonians, sea whips

Members of the order Alcyonacea have polyps with eight feathery tentacles, each tentacle possessing a hollow central canal interconnecting with the stomach cavity. Alcyonaceans are grouped with the seapens (order Pennatulacea) in the subclass Octocorallia, so are commmonly called octocorals. Octocorals are found most abundantly in tropical waters, but a large number of species, with a wide variety of forms, are also present along temperate coasts. They occur as colonies, which are attached to the seabed and may be encrusting, erect or branched. These colonies are supported by an internal arrangement of knobbly, calcareous structures known as sclerites, the shape of which is of critical importance in distinguishing between species; sclerites can occur free within polyp tissue or connected to form a calcareous central axis which may also contain horn.

The order Alcyonacea includes soft corals, gorgonians and several less prominent groups. Until recently, a number of these groups were classified in separate orders but they are linked by species with intermediate characteristics. Identification of temperate Australian octocorals is difficult and is hindered by the application of numerous incorrect names in the past. Information provided here relies largely on the assistance of Phil Alderslade (Museum and Art Gallery of the Northern Territory), as it is substantially based on his studies in progress.

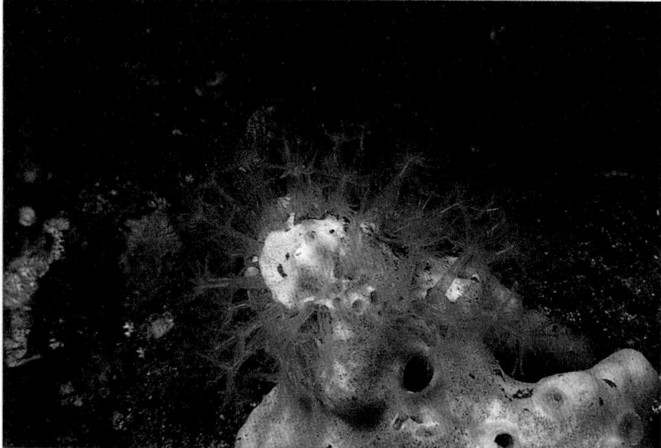

Clavularia sp., Bathurst Channel, Tas.

Clavularia sp.

Habitat: Sheltered reef; 4–16 m depth.
Distribution: Tas.
Maximum size: Polyp length to 15 mm.

Clavularia belongs to a group of alcyonaceans commonly known as stoloniferans, a group characterised by polyps that arise from a narrow basal strip called the stolon. Nothing much is known about stoloniferans in southern Australia. This species has narrow transparent polyps and a basal stolon that is comparatively thin and buried under the encrusting white sponge in the illustration.

Erythropodium hicksoni (Utinomi, 1971)

Habitat: Sheltered to moderately exposed reef; 2–15 m depth.
Distribution: Vic. to central NSW and around Tas.
Maximum size: Polyp height to 10 mm.

Erythropodium hicksoni occurs in large grey sheets on boulders in sheltered habitats and is very common in Bass Strait, eastern Tasmania and southern New South Wales. Like most other species of soft coral, each colony consists of numerous polyps embedded in a fleshy mass. The name *Parerythropodium membranaceum* has been applied to this and other species in the past but is unlikely to refer to any local soft coral; it properly belongs to a deep-water South African species.

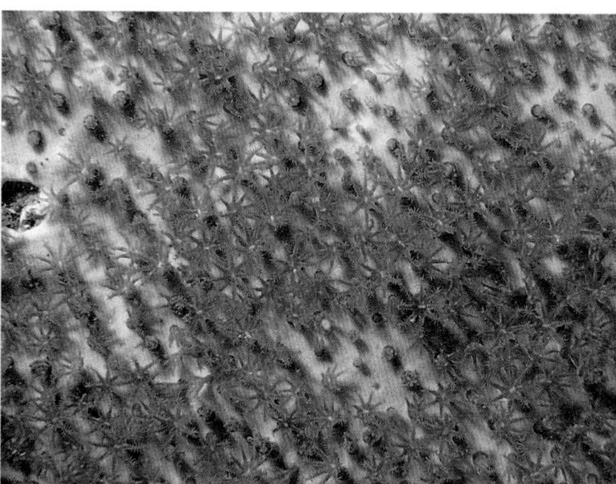

Erythropodium hicksoni, Zuidpool Rock, Tas.

Capnella erecta Verseveldt, 1977

Habitat: Moderately to submaximally exposed reef; 3–30 m depth.
Distribution: Cape Jaffa, SA, to Gabo I, Vic., and around Tas.
Maximum size: Colony height to 200 mm.

Capnella erecta is a large, openly branched species of soft coral that occurs commonly in deeper Victorian and Tasmanian waters. The colour can differ substantially between sites, varying from the blue-grey of the illustrated specimen to yellow.

Capnella erecta, Ile des Phoques, Tas.

Capnella ?johnstonei, Ile des Phoques, Tas.

Capnella ?johnstonei Verseveldt, 1977

Habitat: Moderately to submaximally exposed reef; 10–275 m depth.
Distribution: Portland, Vic., to Eden, NSW, and around Tas.
Maximum size: Colony height to 150 mm.

Capnella ?johnstonei has a similar general shape and sometimes occurs in close proximity to *C. erecta*. It is distinguished by differences in the shape of the sclerites and usually appears to have a denser arrangement of branches.

Capnella gaboensis Verseveldt, 1977

Habitat: Reef; 5–30 m depth.
Distribution: Waldegrave I, SA, to Port Stephens, NSW, and Erith I, Tas.
Maximum size: Colony height to 150 mm.

Capnella gaboensis is the most abundant soft coral seen along the central and southern NSW coast. It has a distinctively lobed shape and grey surface colour, with the coloration darkening significantly when the polyps expand.

Capnella gaboensis, Merimbula, NSW

Capnella sp. 1

Habitat: Exposed reef; 3–10 m depth.
Distribution: Mullaloo to Rottnest I, WA.
Maximum size: Colony height to 75 mm.

Capnella sp. 1 is a small, grey, erect species, with a dense covering of polyps over the surface. It is the

Capnella sp. 1, Wreck Rock, WA

most common soft coral on shallow reefs in the vicinity of Perth, where it generally occurs under overhanging ledges.

Capnella sp. 2

Habitat: Exposed reef; 12–18 m depth.
Distribution: Canal Rocks, WA.
Maximum size: Colony height to 75 mm.

Capnella sp. 2 is a blue-grey species that occurs as a round, flat colony with relatively small lobes projecting from the upper surface. The species has so far been found at only a single location in southwestern Australia.

Capnella sp. 2, Canal Rocks, WA

Carijoa sp. 1

Habitat: Sheltered and moderately exposed reef; 2–20 m depth.
Distribution: Southern WA to Gulf St Vincent, SA, and NSW to Qld.
Maximum size: Colony length to 250 mm.

Species of *Carijoa* form colonies by a process of budding, with side polyps arising as outgrowths from the canal of a long central polyp. The colony is often supported by a skeleton of calcareous sclerites partially fused into tubes. This species occurs commonly in sheltered clear-water sites and is abundant on many jetty pylons. It has a rigid skeletal network and large white polyps, which obscure the base when expanded. The colony is nearly always coated by an orange sponge. *Carijoa* sp. 1 has been called *Carijoa* (and *Telesto) multiflora*, but the classification of Australian telestaceans is so confused at present that no scientific name can be reliably applied to this distinctive species.

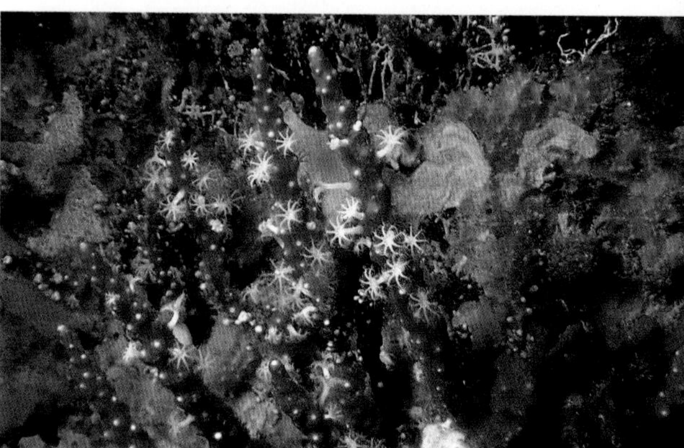

Carijoa sp. 1 (polyps contracted), Busselton, WA

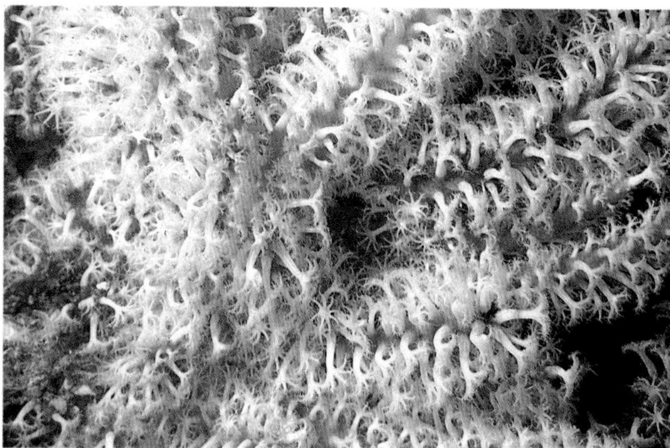

Carijoa sp. 1 (polyps expanded), Busselton, WA

Carijoa sp. 2

Habitat: Moderately exposed reef; 8–50 m depth.
Distribution: SA to NSW and northern Tas.
Maximum size: Colony length to 250 mm.

The polyps of *Carijoa* sp. 2 are large and pink, and the axes much thinner than those of *Carijoa* sp. 1. This species is extremely abundant on deep reef walls in areas with good current flow in Bass Strait. It has sometimes been called *Carijoa* (and *Telesto) smithi*.

Carijoa sp. 2, Rocky Cape, Tas.

Mopsella zimmeri Kükenthal, 1908

Habitat: Exposed reef; 2–50 m depth.
Distribution: WA to NSW and northern Tas.
Maximum size: Colony height to 1 m.

Gorgonians are erect octocorals, readily recognised by their plant-like shape. They have a rigid central axis made from various combinations of crystalline calcium carbonate, calcareous sclerites, and a horn-like material known as gorgonin. This central axis is surrounded by small living polyps and connective tissue and is attached firmly to a hard surface by creeping branches or an adhesive disc. *Mopsella zimmeri* is the most abundant species of gorgonian seen in shallow water along the southeastern Australian coast. It develops most profusely on the edges of steep dropoffs and at the entrances to caves, particularly in areas with strong currents. A number of different colour forms are known, with yellows, oranges and reds predominant.

Mopsella zimmeri, Erith I, Tas.

Mopsella klunzingeri Kükenthal, 1908

Habitat: Exposed reef; 4–30 m depth.
Distribution: Houtman Abrolhos, WA, to Portsea, Vic.
Maximum size: Colony height to 500 mm.

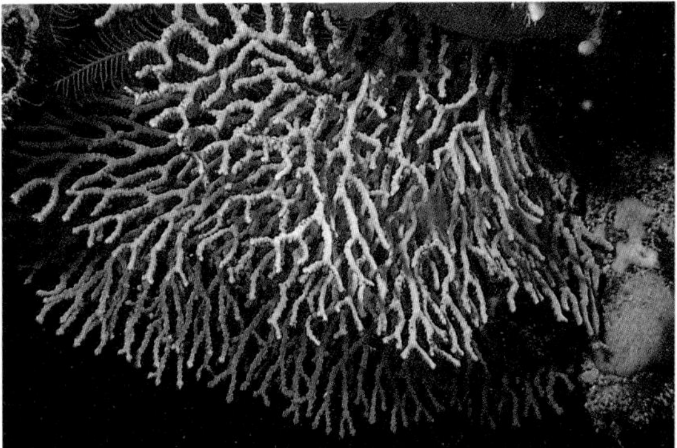

Mopsella klunzingeri, Little I, WA

Mopsella klunzingeri is a pink fan-shaped species that occurs commonly along the southern Australian coast and reaches highest density in Western Australia. It has sclerites similar in shape to those of *M. zimmeri*, so these two gorgonians may prove to be forms rather than distinct species. The chief distinguishing character of *M. klunzingeri* is that the branches are open and, unlike *M. zimmeri*, rarely rejoin each other.

Mopsella sp.

Habitat: Exposed reef; 12–30 m depth.
Distribution: NSW.
Maximum size: Colony height to 500 mm.

This species is very common in moderately deep water along the southern New South Wales coast. It is closely related to *Mopsella zimmeri* but has sclerites of a slightly different shape. The background coloration is consistently dark red with white polyps, whereas *M. zimmeri* can be any of a variety of colours.

Mopsella sp., Bass Point, NSW

Acabaria sp.

Habitat: Reef; 8–40 m depth.
Distribution: Northern Tas.
Maximum size: Colony height to 120 mm.

Species of *Acabaria* are yellow, pink or cream and have fragile branches that usually develop most profusely in deep-water sites. The axes are irregularly branched and have swollen nodes made of sclerites in a gorgonin matrix alternating with thinner sections of fused sclerites, giving the colony a lumpy appearance. This genus has not been studied recently, and the number of species occurring in southern Australia is unknown. Animals similar to the illustrated specimen are common throughout southeastern Australian waters.

Acabaria sp., Three Hummock I, Tas.

Melithaeid sp.
Bramble coral

Habitat: Sheltered reef; 5–20 m depth.
Distribution: Southern Tas.
Maximum size: Polyp length to 5 mm.

This is an unusual species of melithaeid, with short white polyps arranged regularly along the branches. These branches are very thin and often lie clear of the reef substratum. The species occurs commonly in the Port Davey area of Tasmania but may also occur in habitats elsewhere with little light.

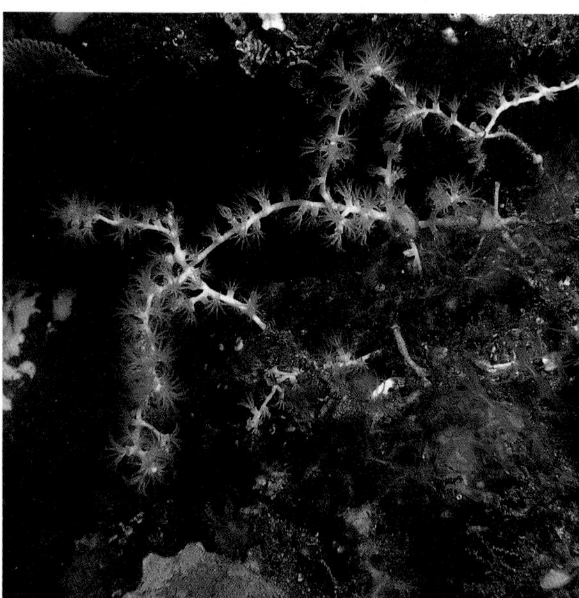

Melithaeid sp., Bathurst Channel, Tas.

Isidid sp. 1
Indeterminate gorgonian

Habitat: Sheltered reef, shells; 6–50 m depth.
Distribution: SA to Vic. and around Tas.
Maximum size: Colony height to 250 mm.

This is a delicate pink gorgonian that has been confused for many years with *Mopsea whiteleggei*, a New South Wales species found below normal diving range. It is the most common gorgonian on moderately deep reefs in Tasmania and Victoria and also grows on shells in sandy areas with strong current flow. This species is currently being assessed as part of a biological study of the group.

Isidid sp. 1, D'Entrecasteaux Channel, Tas.

Isidid sp. 1, Rocky Cape, Tas.

Isidid sp. 2

Plumed gorgonian

Habitat: Sheltered reef, shells; 4–220 m depth.
Distribution: Vic. and Tas.
Maximum size: Colony height to 300 mm.

Isidid sp. 2 is a pink fishbone-shaped species that cannot be distinguished from Isidid sp. 1 by external appearance but differs in the shape of scerites. It is found in depths exceeding 60 m through most of its range but enters relatively shallow water in southern Tasmania.

Isidid sp. 2, Bathurst Channel, Tas.

Primnoella australasiae (Gray, 1849)

Habitat: Exposed reef; 8–270 m depth.
Distribution: Ceduna, SA, to Sydney, NSW, and around Tas.
Maximum size: Colony height to 700 mm.

Primnoella australasiae is the common sea whip observed on deep reefs around southeastern Australia. The polyps form compacted whirls around the horny central stem when not feeding. This species is used as a platform by several filter-feeding invertebrate species, such as anemones and basket stars, to escape the region of low current flow and low plankton supply near the seabed.

Primnoella australasiae, D'Entrecasteaux Channel, Tas.

Order Pennatulacea
Sea pens

Sea pens have a long primary polyp that forms a stalk and secondary polyps arranged in rows for food capture and for pumping water. The stalk has four canals which expand when filled with water, giving the colony the flexibility to extend upright for feeding and, when needed, to contract into the sediment. Many sea pens luminesce when touched and will produce coloured pulses of light that radiate along the colony.

Sarcoptilus grandis (Gray, 1870)

Habitat: Sand and silt, 8–30 m depth.
Distribution: Eucla, WA, to southern Qld and around Tas.
Maximum size: Length to 400 mm.

Sarcoptilus grandis, Bathurst Channel, Tas.

Sarcoptilus grandis is a common inhabitant in the deeper channels of sheltered bays. It is the largest sea pen in southern Australian waters and can be recognised by the kidney-shaped leaves (about 30) arranged in a row on each side of the body. The bulbous stalk of this species remains buried in the sediment and is about the length of the leafy section above. A predatory mollusc (*Armina* sp.) feeds on *S. grandis* and can often be observed in the near vicinity.

Cavernularia obesa Milne Edwards & Haime, 1857

Habitat: Sheltered sand, mud; 4–30 m depth.
Distribution: Central NSW.
Maximum size: Length to 250 mm.

Cavernularia obesa is abundant in Sydney Harbour and other bays in the region but not often seen because it remains hidden under sand during much of the day. The individual polyps on this species are extremely large and feathery.

Cavernularia sp.

Habitat: Sheltered sand, mud; 8–25 m depth.
Distribution: Cockburn Sound, WA.
Maximum size: Length to 350 mm.

This sea pen occurs commonly in Cockburn Sound and in the lower reaches of the Swan estuary. The species seems to be most closely related to a Mediterranean species, *Cavernularia pusilla*. It has a distinctive appearance, with polyps directly attached to the orange or pink stalk, and it luminescences brilliantly when touched.

Cavernularia obesa, North Head, NSW

Cavernularia sp., Bicton, WA

Class Scyphozoa
Jellyfish

Scyphozoans are generally medusoid in shape, with the polyp stage either inconspicuous or absent. The medusae have a four-rayed symmetry and a complex arrangement of nerves, muscles and sense organs around the edge of the bell to coordinate movement. Tentacles (when present) are located around the margin of the bell; conspicuous oral arms, which can be mistaken for large tentacles, are also generally present under the centre of the bell. The mouth is usually situated at the base of the oral arms and leads into a central stomach with four compartments. Numerous fine canals run from the stomach to the edge of the bell. The gonads are most often crescent-shaped organs located in the four compartments to the stomach.

The polyp, called the scyphistoma, is shaped like an inverted vase with feeding tentacles around the fringe; during favourable conditions the scyphistoma divides transversely into a stack of medusae, which then separate and swim away.

Approximately 250 species of scyphozoans are known, many of them being widespread oceanic species. Only about ten species occur regularly along the temperate Australian coast.

Order Semaeostomeae

Scyphozoans in this order generally have tentacles hanging from the margin of the bell and the corners of the mouth extended into four frilly lobes; most species are shaped like a large inverted bowl with a scalloped margin. This tends to be the most common order of jellyfish in cool temperate and polar regions.

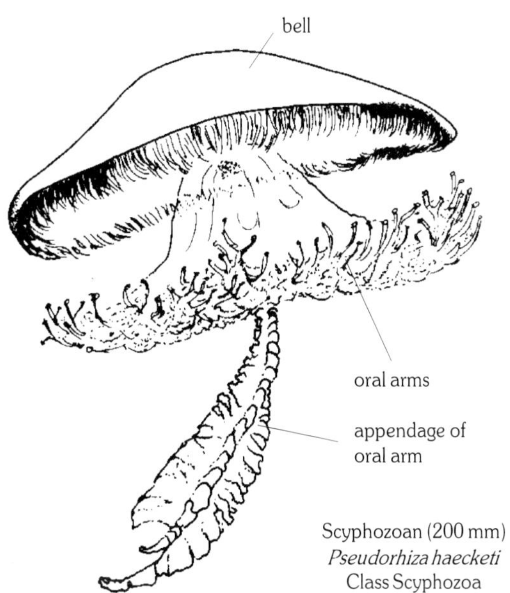

Scyphozoan (200 mm)
Pseudorhiza haecketi
Class Scyphozoa

Cyanea capillata (Linnaeus, 1746)
Lion's mane jellyfish

Habitat: Ocean; 0–20 m depth.
Distribution: WA to northern Qld and around Tas. Also widespread overseas.
Maximum size: Bell width to 1 m.

Cyanea capillata is an oceanic species that becomes more abundant and reaches its largest size in southern waters. It has a flat-topped body, which is much thicker in the middle than at the edges, with eight deep lobes in the margin and a small cleft with a sense organ in the centre of each lobe. The tentacles are numerous and very fine, extending to a great distance when the animal is feeding. This is the largest of all jellyfish, with the disc-shaped bell sometimes exceeding 1 m in polar waters and the tentacles exceeding 10 m in length. The larger animals are often host to juvenile fish.

Cyanea capillata, Bathurst Channel, Tas.

Pelagia noctiluca (Forsskål, 1775)

Habitat: Ocean; 0–200 m depth.
Distribution: Around Australia, including Tas. Also widespread overseas.
Maximum size: Bell width to 100 mm.

Pelagia noctiluca is one of the easiest of jellyfish to identify, with purple streaks to the bell, four long oral arms, a phosphorescent body and eight tentacles, which are sometimes broken. It is primarily an oceanic species but is also common in coastal waters, particularly along the southern NSW coast. The species lacks a scyphistoma stage; its planula larvae develop directly into medusae.

Pelagia noctiluca, Jervis Bay, NSW

Aurelia aurita (Linnaeus, 1746)
Moon jellyfish

Habitat: Ocean, estuaries; 0–40 m depth.
Distribution: WA to northern Qld and around Tas. Also widespread overseas.
Maximum size: Bell width to 400 mm.

Aurelia aurita is a large saucer-shaped species with four transparent oral arms that extend to the margins of the bell. Numerous fine branched canals radiate from the stomach to the margin. The margin is divided into eight or sixteen lobes and has eight sensory organs and a multitude of short, thin tentacles attached. Four white, circular gonads can usually be seen through the body wall. The species occurs commonly in oceanic waters and sheltered estuaries.

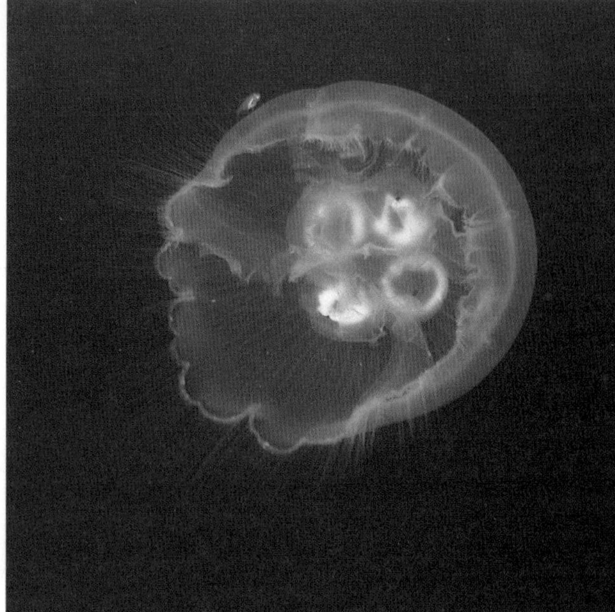

Aurelia aurita, Binalong Bay, Tas.

Chrysaora sp.

Habitat: Open water; 0–20 m depth.
Distribution: Gulf St Vincent, SA, to Port Phillip Bay, Vic.
Maximum size: Bell width to 80 mm.

Chrysaora sp. has eight marginal sense organs, with each pair separated by a section of bell with six tentacles. The upper surface of the bell is covered by dense brown flecks, which coalesce towards the centre and along the radii. The central stomach is connected to sixteen separated pouches. This species is not as common as several other large jellyfish species. It has been reported to give moderately severe stings.

Chrysaora sp., Portsea, Vic. Rudie Kuiter

Order Rhizostomeae

Rhizostomeans lack tentacles but are easily recognised by the massive oral arms below the mouth which carry nematocysts and fulfil the food-capture role of tentacles. The underside lacks an obvious mouth, but the oral arms have many small openings through which food passes to the stomach. Species in this order are the dominant scyphozoans in tropical and warm temperate regions and in estuaries.

Catostylus mosaicus (Quoy & Gaimard, 1824)

Habitat: Estuaries, ocean; 0–25 m depth.
Distribution: Port Phillip Bay, Vic., to Torres Strait, Qld.
Maximum size: Bell width to 350 mm.

Catostylus mosaicus, an animal commonly called the jelly blubber, is the most common species along the eastern Australian coast. Large swarms appear in summer in many estuaries (e.g. Pittwater and Tuggerah Lakes). The species can be recognised by its eight three-winged arms and the conspicuous internal cross that is apparent through the top of the bell. The brown coloration of animals in the Sydney region is caused by the presence of large numbers of symbiotic algae in the body tissue.

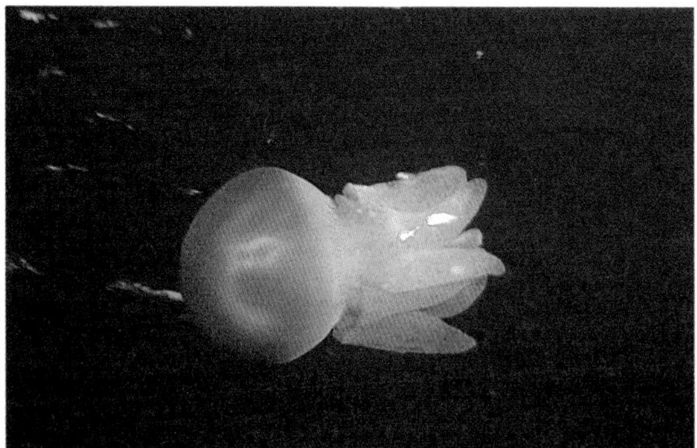

Catostylus mosaicus, Maroubra, NSW. RUDIE KUITER

Pseudorhiza haeckeli (Haacke, 1884)

Habitat: Ocean; 0–30 m depth.
Distribution: Northern Territory around WA to Vic. and northern Tas.
Maximum size: Bell width to 300 mm.

The most characteristic feature of *Pseudorhiza haeckeli* is a long paddle-shaped appendage that projects below one of the mouth-arms. The bell is covered by numerous warty-looking clumps of nematocysts and is divided into eight equal parts, with each part having six rounded lobes around the margin. The species is most common in offshore waters, but animals may also be seen stranded along the coast.

Pseudorhiza haeckeli, Tomahawk, Tas. SIMON TALBOT

Phyllorhiza punctata von Lendenfeld, 1884

Habitat: Estuaries, ocean; 0–30 m depth.
Distribution: Tropical Australia south to southern WA and Sydney, NSW. Also through the Indo-West Pacific region.
Maximum size: Bell width to 500 mm.

Phyllorhiza punctata is a large and spectacular species that is common in Western Australian and New South Wales estuaries during summer. It can usually be identified from its bell, which is brown, hemispherical and covered by a regular pattern of white spots. The mouth arms have characteristic trailing filaments that end in knobs.

Phyllorhiza punctata, Bicton, WA

Class Cubozoa

Order Cubomedusae

Box jellies, cubomedusans

Cubomedusans have a rounded box-like shape with four flattened sides and a tentacle or group of tentacles attached to the bottom four corners of the bell. The upper section of the tentacles near the point of attachment has few if any nematocysts and is much thicker than the stinging section. Cubomedusan species are all strong swimmers and have painful stings. The order contains mainly tropical species, including the deadly box jelly *Chironex fleckeri*. The order Cubomedusae is now generally considered to contain species sufficiently different from the scyphozoans to be placed in a class of its own, the Cubozoa.

manubrium
gonad
bell
tentacle

Cubozoan
Carybdea rastoni
(100 mm)
Class Cubozoa

Carybdea rastoni Haacke, 1886

Habitat: Off sheltered and moderately exposed sand beaches, seagrass; 0–20 m depth.
Distribution: Southern WA to NSW and south to Bicheno, Tas. Also widespread in the Indo-West Pacific region.
Maximum size: Bell height to 35 mm.

Carybdea rastoni is the only species of box jelly recorded from southern Australia. It aggregates in extremely high densities above sandy seabed during daylight hours. At night the individual animals disperse, moving diagonally from the seabed to the water surface and back again. The sting of this species is not very noticeable on hands or arms but very painful if contact is made with a sensitive area such as the lips or genitals.

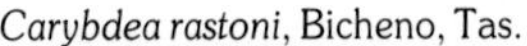

Carybdea rastoni, Bicheno, Tas.

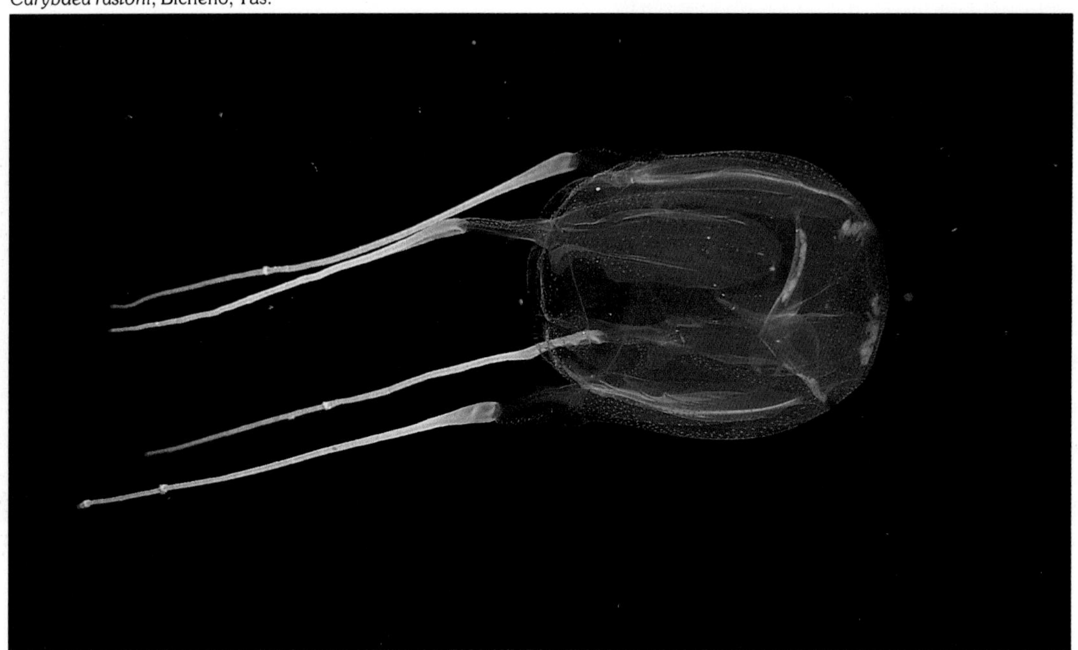

PHYLUM CTENOPHORA

Comb jellies

Ctenophores are an exclusively marine group of delicate gelatinous animals. They resemble cnidarians and were once included in the same phylum, but lack stinging cells and are now thought to be only superficially similar. Most of the 100 or so species are transparent, free-swimming animals with ovoid or flattened shapes; however, small, flat, inconspicuous species in the genus *Coeloplana*, which creep along the seabed, are also common in southern Australia.

Ctenophores are characterised by the presence of eight rows of comb-like plates containing fused cilia. They are the largest animals to use cilia for locomotion, the beating rows of cilia often luminescing brilliantly. Ctenophores usually also possess a pair of long tentacles that can be retracted into pouches and are used in food capture. Despite a lack of stinging cells, the tentacles are able to capture large crustaceans and even small fishes because of adhesive cells that strongly grip on contact. Captured prey are drawn into tube-like internal cavities via the mouth and are digested there. Indigestible material is partly ejected through the mouth and partly through excretory pores at the opposite end of the body.

Individual ctenophores release both sperm and eggs, which are fertilised externally. The resultant embryo develops differently from the embryo of cnidarians, an indication that the two phyla are not closely related. The larvae are free-swimming and resemble the parents. Ctenophore numbers can rapidly build up in coastal lagoons, suggesting that they have high reproductive and growth capacities when conditions are favourable. Swarms of a variety of oceanic species also irregularly occur around the southern Australian coasts when driven inshore by prevailing winds and currents.

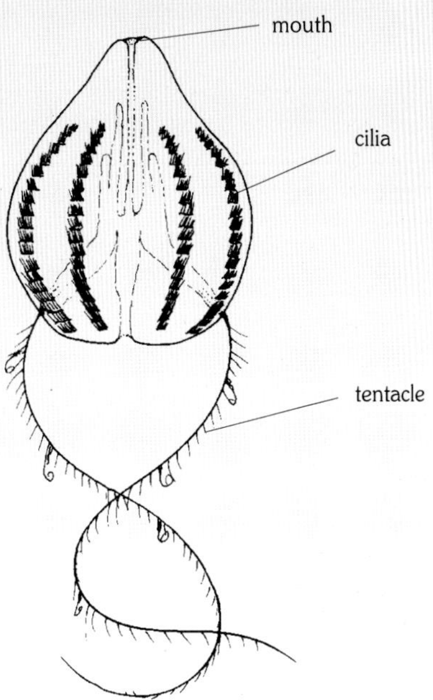

Ctenophore (20 mm)
Hormiphora sp.
Phylum Ctenophora

Leucothea sp.

Habitat: Ocean; 0–25 m depth.
Distribution: Vic. to central NSW and around Tas.
Maximum size: Bell height to 90 mm.

Leucothea sp. is one of the largest ctenophores. It has two long external tentacles, four long ciliated appendages known as auricles within the body and an external surface that is covered by papillae. This ctenophore occurs abundantly along the eastern coast of Tasmania throughout the year and is moderately common elsewhere. The species is sometimes attacked by groups of toothbrush leatherjackets when it crosses shallow reefs.

Leucothea sp., Waterfall Bay, Tas.

Bolinopsis sp., Terrigal, NSW

Bolinopsis sp.

Habitat: Estuaries, ocean; 0–20 m depth.
Distribution: NSW.
Maximum size: Bell height to 70 mm.

Bolinopsis sp. has four full rows and four half-rows of cilia down the outside of the bell and four leaf-like auricles with ciliated margins inside. The species occurs in huge numbers in many New South Wales estuaries, with large aggregations also occasionally appearing along the coast during periods of still weather.

Beroe cucumis, D'Entrecasteaux Channel, Tas.

Beroe cucumis Fabricius, 1780

Habitat: Open ocean; 0–20 m depth.
Distribution: WA to NSW and around Tas.
Maximum size: Bell height to 150 mm.

Beroe cucumis has a shape reminiscent of a cardinal's hat. It lacks tentacles, and has a wide opening at the base and eight rows of cilia that extend to about three-quarters of the distance to the mouth. This species is moderately common in Tasmania but becomes progressively rarer towards the north.

PHYLUM PLATYHELMINTHES

Flatworms, platyhelminths

The platyhelminths are a group of about 25 000 known species with soft, flattened bodies that lack segmentation and are symmetrical about a central line. They have a definite head with sensory organs, and most have a large internal gastrovascular cavity for digesting food. This cavity is connected externally by a single opening on the underside, acting as both mouth and anus, and the cavity structure is an important feature used in the classification of species. One group of small marine species, the acoelan flatworms, lack a definite gut but have a mouth leading directly into a network of digestive cells. Platyhelminths have no need for blood vessels as cells all lie close enough to either the outer body surface or the gastrovascular cavity to directly receive oxygen for respiration and to excrete metabolic wastes.

Almost all flatworms possess both male and female sexual organs and transfer sperm between individuals. Free-living platyhelminths usually produce juveniles with a similar appearance to the adult, whereas juvenile stages of the many parasitic species are often tadpole- or worm-shaped. The life cycles of parasitic flatworms can be extremely complex, with a succession of stages inhabiting different hosts.

The phylum Platyhelminthes has four major classes, three of which are exclusively parasitic. Species in the class Monogenea are primarily external parasites of fishes. The flukes (class Trematoda) are all internal parasites, living mainly in vertebrate animals when adult and in molluscs when juvenile, and also having a short free-living ciliated larval stage known as the miracidium. The tapeworms (class Cestoda) are internal parasites of vertebrates when adult and often have an intermediate stage inhabiting vertebrate prey of the larger host.

The fourth main class, Turbellaria, contains free-living platyhelminths that primarily live in the sea. A few species can swim freely in water, but most glide across the seabed propelled by beating cilia on the undersurface. Nearly all turbellarians are less than 10 mm long, so are rarely noticed, but are very common in mud and anaerobic sand. The few brightly coloured species noticed by divers belong to the order Polycladida and are comparatively rare. These polyclad turbellarians are generally carnivorous, often feeding on a limited range of soft coral, bryozoan or other sessile invertebrate animals; however, a few species are closely associated with large mobile invertebrates. About 25 species of polyclad have been recorded from temperate Australian waters, but many unnamed species are also present.

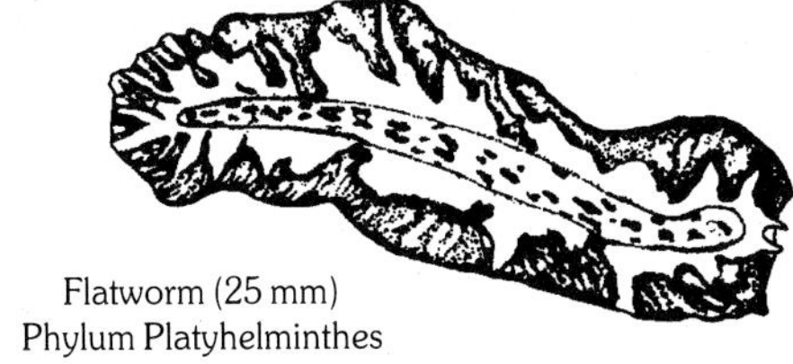

Flatworm (25 mm)
Phylum Platyhelminthes

Callioplana marginata Stimpson, 1857

Habitat: Reef; 0–20 m depth.
Distribution: Tropical Australia south to Merimbula, NSW. Also through the Indo-West Pacific region.
Maximum size: Length to 50 mm.

Callioplana marginata is a large, distinctive flatworm with a dark body surrounded by orange and white trim and two large tentacles positioned close to each other near the front margin. Because of its size and bright coloration, this flatworm is often noticed by divers along the New South Wales coast.

Callioplana marginata, Narooma, NSW

Thysanozoon sp.

Habitat: Reef; 2–10 m depth.
Distribution: NSW.
Maximum size: Length to 30 mm.

Several species of *Thysanozoon* occur in temperate Australian waters, most of them undescribed. They are easily identified as a group because of the warty papillae which cover the upper surface of the body, but species identification is difficult and requires the sectioning of preserved specimens.

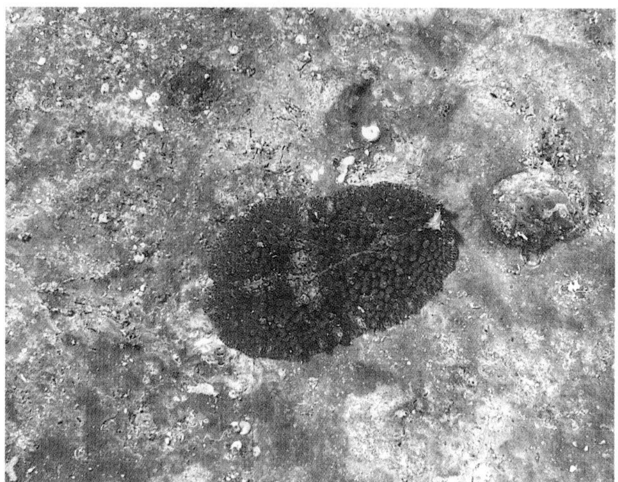

Thysanozoon sp., Norah Head, NSW

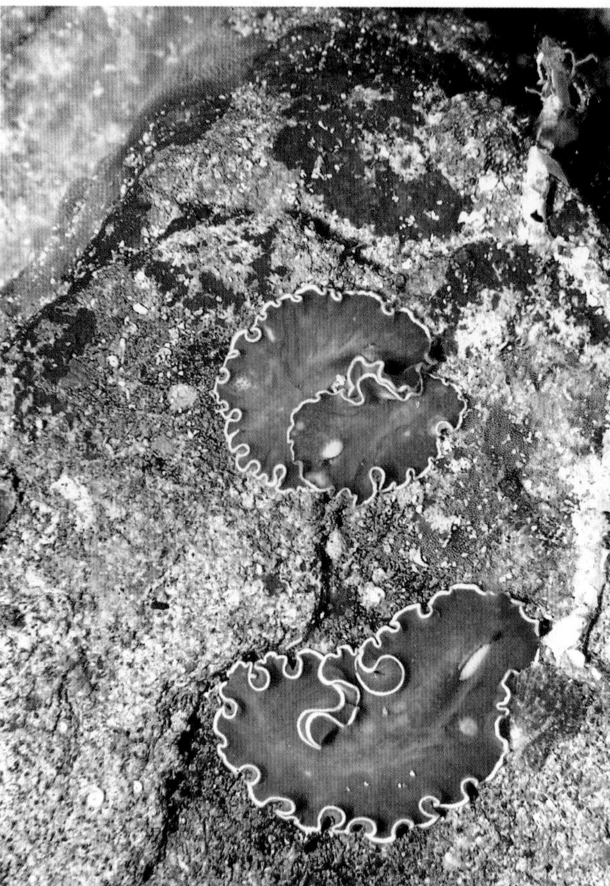

Pseudoceros lividus, Kangaroo I, SA. RUDIE KUITER

Pseudoceros lividus Prudhoe, 1981

Habitat: Reef; 4–8 m depth.
Distribution: Kangaroo I, SA.
Maximum size: Length to 30 mm.

Pseudoceros lividus is one of the most colourful species of flatworm seen in southern Australia and has a bright blue body with light margin. The species is found under rocks within a relatively small area of South Australia.

Notoplana australis (Schmarda, 1859)

Habitat: Sheltered and moderately exposed shores; low intertidal.
Distribution: SA to Sydney, NSW, and around Tas. Also New Zealand.
Maximum size: Length to 40 mm.

Notoplana australis is a large brown flatworm that occurs very commonly under boulders and among oysters on sheltered shores. This is the only local flatworm to have been studied in any detail; it was found near Sydney to have a planktonic larval stage lasting for about three weeks.

Notoplana australis, Rocky Cape, Tas.

PHYLUM NEMERTEA

Nemerteans, proboscis worms, ribbon worms

Nemerteans are worm-like animals that range in size from a few millimetres to tens of metres long. They can generally be recognised by a smooth, muscular body, which has a slippery feel because of the secretion of mucous and the presence of minute cilia. Large species are often flattened, distinctively patterned and readily break into pieces if handled. The head end of the body has a mouth on the underside and, in some species, light-sensitive ocelli (consisting of retinal cells, pigments and nerve fibres) on the upper surface. The most characteristic feature of nemerteans is a large proboscis. This usually remains within the body cavity but can be everted through the mouth or a nearby hole to entangle or, when piercing barbs are present, to spear prey. Nemerteans actively hunt a variety of other animals, most commonly polychaetes, flatworms, molluscs and crustaceans.

Most nemerteans live under rocks, in sand or among seaweeds in shallow water; a few species float in the open ocean, and others live in fresh water and among damp leaf litter. They generally reproduce by shedding eggs and sperm after two animals approach; the fertilised egg develops either directly into a young worm or into a distinctive free-living larva. Approximately 1000 species are known worldwide, with about 20 species recorded from southern Australia. Many local species are yet to be scientifically named.

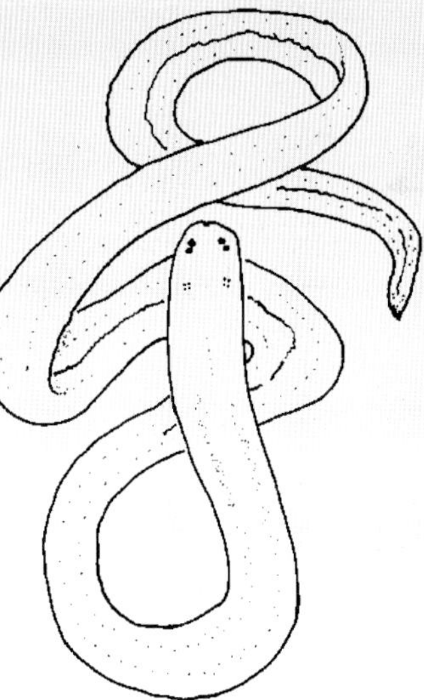

Nemertean (100 mm)
Ischyronemertes sp.
Phylum Nemertea

Unidentified nemertean, Merimbula, NSW

Unidentified nemertean, Cloudy Lagoon, Tas.

Unidentified nemertean, Rocky Cape, Tas.

PHYLUM NEMATODA

Nematodes, roundworms

Nematodes are unsegmented worm-like animals with cylindrical bodies that taper towards each end and are covered by a thick layer of cuticle. At one end of the body they have a small mouth surrounded by lips, with bristles and sensory organs nearby. About 20 000 species have been named, a small proportion of the total as at least ten times that number probably exist. They occur in virtually all moist environments, including damp soils and plant and animal tissue as well as freshwater and marine habitats. Marine species are usually small (0.5–3 mm in length), while the largest mammalian parasitic nematodes are more than a metre long.

Male and female nematodes join together in copulation, and subsequently the female generally releases huge numbers of fertilised eggs. There are, however, a few exceptional species, whose young develop within the female body. Newly hatched nematodes have a similar appearance to adults. They undergo four moults involving the shedding of an outer layer of cuticle before reaching maturity.

sensory bristle
mouth
anus

Nematode (2 mm)
Prochromadorella sp.
Phylum Nematoda

Although parasitic species are also common, most marine nematodes live freely among sediment and seaweeds. They occur in enormous densities in soft sediments, where they wriggle with a characteristic snake-like motion among the sand grains. The densities in clean sand are generally in the order of 100 000 per square metre, but densities in areas with high organic enrichment can reach tens of millions per square metre. Because of their abundance, nematodes have an important role breaking down dead plant and animal material in marine ecosystems. Some marine species are carnivorous, but most feed on detritus.

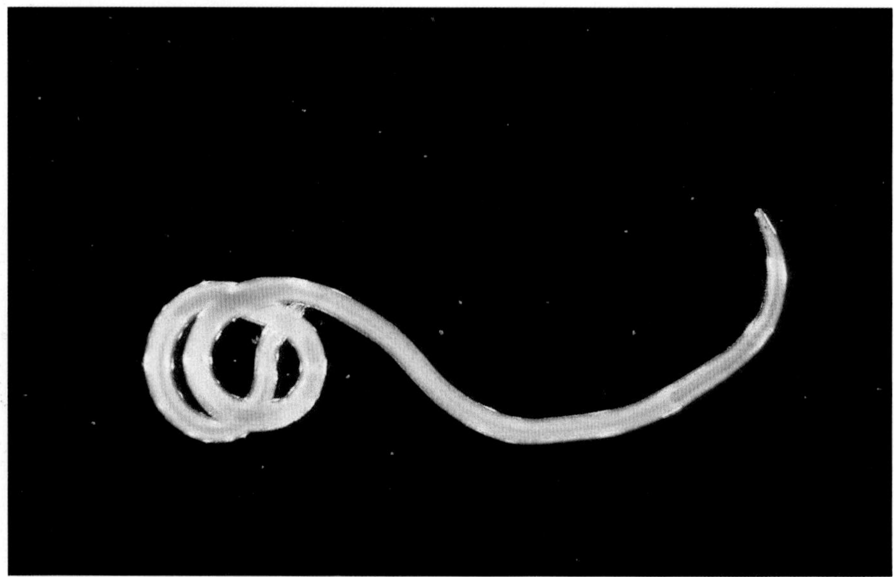

Nematode (*Metoncholaimus* sp.), Sandy Bay, Tas.

PHYLUM ANNELIDA

Segmented worms

Annelids are soft-bodied cylindrical animals with the body divided into numerous segments. They range in size from less than 1 mm to the giant earthworms more than 3 m long. Enclosed within the body is a gut surrounded by a fluid-filled cavity and separate muscle layers running around and parallel with the body. Because of hydrostatic pressure, contraction of the outer longitudinal muscle layer causes a shortening and thickening of the body; contraction of the circular muscle layer causes the opposite effect. Movement of most annelid species is aided by the flexing of lobes and bristles projecting from the sides of each segment. About 20 000 species in the phylum have been scientifically named, a small proportion of the total numbers.

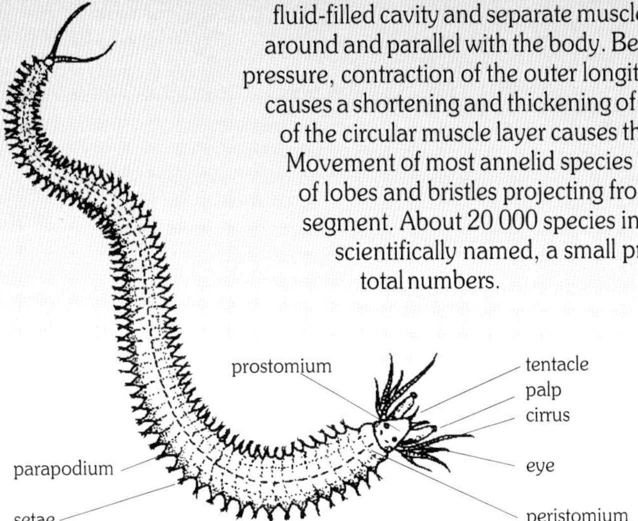

Polychaete (20 mm)
Nereis sp.
Phylum Annelida

Class Oligochaeta

Oligochaete worms

Oligochaetes are elongate, cylindrical animals with highly segmented bodies and no large external appendages. Most body segments have inconspicuous side bristles (the setae), except in the head region (known as the prostomium). Included in this class are the earthworms and numerous freshwater species, as well as many small marine forms. Oligochaetes are particularly prevalent in shallow sediments with a high content of organic material, including sediments polluted by sewage or other organic waste.

Most aquatic oligochaetes possess a pair of testes towards the front of the body, and a pair of ovaries in the next segment. During mating, partners align head-to-tail and transfer sperm, which is then stored in special receptacles, the spermathecae. A cocoon is later produced from the clitellum, a glandular area of skin two segments long in marine species. Eggs and sperm are released into the cocoon as the worm wriggles forward, and the cocoon with the fertilised eggs inside is then left behind. The eggs, which are few in number (1–20) and relatively large, produce a newly hatched worm that is a miniature replica of the adult. A few species can reproduce asexually, either by fragmenting or by budding off small individuals from the sides.

Olavius albidus (Jamieson, 1977)

Habitat: Moderately exposed sand; 0–12 m depth.
Distribution: Rottnest I, WA, to Capricorn Group, Qld.
Maximum size: Length to 13 mm.

Olavius albidus is one of several abundant species of oligochaete found off Australian beaches. Very few marine sites in Australia have been examined for oligochaetes, yet *O. albidus* has been found at most of these. The species lacks a gut and has up to 76 segments.

Olavius albidus, Rottnest I, WA. Clay Bryce

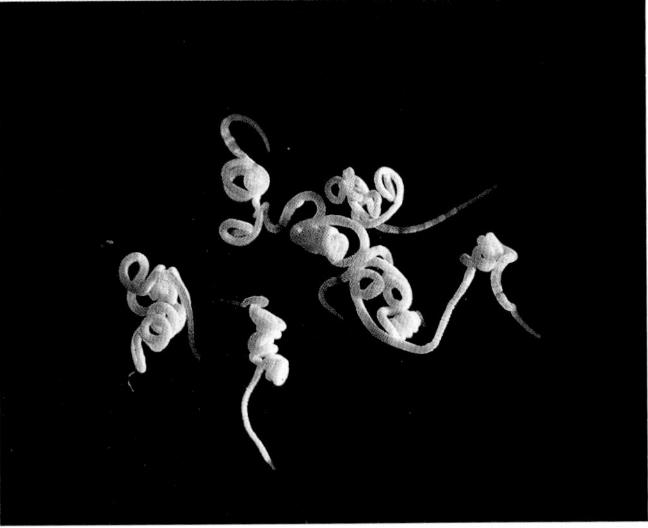

Class Hirudinea

Leeches

Leeches have flattened or cylindrical bodies that usually taper towards the head and have a small sucker surrounding the mouth and a larger sucker at the rear. Unlike other annelids described in the previous and subsequent sections, they have no setae (bristles) or parapodia. Most leeches have the body divided into 33 segments; however, many species have superficial constrictions in the surface layer, obscuring the true internal segmentation. An important feature in the identification of leeches is the arrangement of pairs of eyespots on the upper surface of the head.

Leeches are hermaphrodites, laying large eggs in a cocoon secreted from the clitellum in the same way as oligochaetes (described above). This cocoon may be attached to the seabed or carried around by the parent. Juveniles of a few species attach themselves to the underside of the adult after leaving the cocoon. Most of the 300 or so species of leech occur in fresh water with the others living on land and in the sea. Contrary to popular belief, not all leeches are parasitic — some are scavengers and others predatory. The blood-sucking leeches expand their bodies to such an extent during feeding that their body weight may increase tenfold.

Branchellion sp.

Habitat: Fishes; 4–25 m depth.
Distribution: NSW.
Maximum size: Length to 70 mm.

Branchellion sp. is a gregarious, parasitic species that occurs commonly between the spiracles and eyes of the electric ray *Hypnos monopterygium*. This leech can be recognised by the thick, dark, cylindrical body with feathery, gill-like processes along the sides. It uses a muscular proboscis and secretions rather than jaws to obtain food and often removes much of the pigment layer from the host's skin while feeding. *Branchellion* sp. belongs to a family of fish parasites (Piscicolidae) that are unusual among leeches in having the largest sucker at the head end.

Branchellion sp., Camp Cove, NSW. RUDIE KUITER

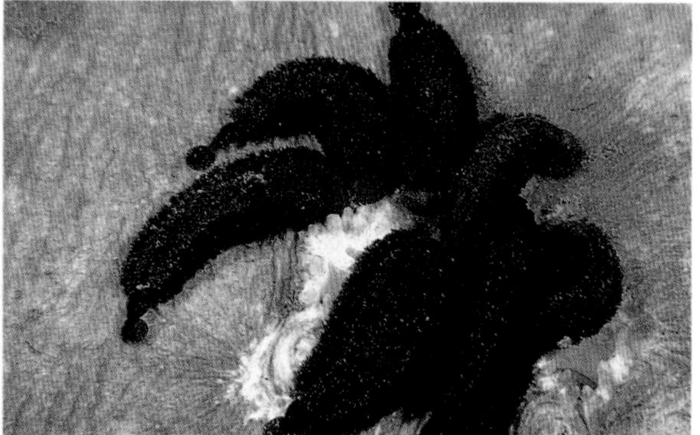

Class Polychaeta

Polychaete worms

This is the largest class of annelid worms, and almost exclusively contains marine species. In many areas of soft sediment polychaetes are the dominant macroscopic animal group, in terms of both numbers of species and numbers of individuals. Polychaetes are characterised by long, obviously segmented bodies with paddle-shaped projections from the side body walls, known as parapodia. The parapodia are often filled with blood vessels for gas exchange and have bundles of spines (the setae or chaetae) attached. As the name polychaete suggests, these chaetae are arranged in many ways on individuals and between species. The animals themselves also exhibit a huge variety of sizes and shapes.

Polychaetes traditionally have been divided into two subclasses, the Errantia (free-living polychaetes) and the Sedentaria (tube-dwelling polychaetes). These categories do not relate to separate evolutionary lineages, and are not now used in a formal sense, but remain commonly used to describe polychaetes with similar habits. The errant polychaetes generally move freely through sediments or over the seabed, or swim in the water column. Their bodies are composed of numerous similar-looking segments. The head is usually clearly defined and divided into two regions: the prostomium with eyes, palps and sensory tentacles, and the peristomium or mouth region. Many species capture prey in chitinous jaws, which are quickly everted with the front section of the gut. The errant polychaetes include ragworms (Nereidae), sea mice (Aphroditidae) and scale worms (Polynoidae).

Sedentary polychaetes have highly differentiated bodies and usually live in secreted tubes attached to the seabed. They include such families as fanworms (Sabellidae, Serpulidae and Spirorbidae), lugworms (Arenicolidae) and bamboo worms (Maldanidae). Many of these species are filter feeders, while others feed on organic material deposited in the sediment.

The sexes of polychaetes are nearly always separate, with eggs and sperm released externally, producing a distinctively shaped planktonic larvae, the trochophore. This reproductive stategy is, however, far from invariate, and the life histories of some species are quite bizarre. A number of species brood young, while others bud off juveniles from special body segments. Species in several families seasonally transform either the whole body or the rear section into reproductive vessels packed with eggs and sperms. These 'epitokes' swim near the sea surface on particular nights, releasing the reproductive contents. They have prominently beating setae and large eyes and often dart around divers at night when attracted to torchlight.

The recent use of sophisticated techniques when classifying polychaetes has shown, unfortunately, that many of the scientific names traditionally used for Australian polychaetes are wrongly applied. Identification of polychaete species nearly always requires microscopic dissection of setae and close examination of the appendages in the head region and jaws. However, even this may not be enough for some species. For example, scientists using molecular techniques have recently found that *Capitella capitata*, one of the most highly studied of all European polychaete species, is actually a complex of a number of species that cannot be distinguished by appearance.

FAMILY POLYNOIDAE
Scale worms

Worms in the family Polynoidae have compact flattened bodies with large oval scales attached in pairs to the upper surface of each body segment. They are active predators, feeding on smaller invertebrates captured by everting a spiny proboscis. Most species are found in cracks and under rocks on reefs; a number live associated with larger invertebrates, particularly echinoderms.

Lepidonotus melanogrammus

(Haswell, 1883)

Habitat: Moderately exposed reef; 0–20 m depth.
Distribution: WA to NSW and around Tas.
Maximum size: Body length to 50 mm.

Lepidonotus melanogrammus possesses 12 pairs of scales on the upper body surface, each with a smooth margin and S-shaped markings, and with cream coloration near the point of attachment and purple-brown pigmentation in the outer section. The species occurs commonly under rocks and is nearly always found near brittle stars.

FAMILY SYLLIDAE

Syllids comprise an extremely diverse but poorly studied family. They can usually be recognised by having a pair of long jointed appendages (the cirri) on each body segment, and similar cirri on the head. Most species are small; the larger species often have colourful and distinctive patterning.

Lepidonotus melanogrammus, Jervis Bay, NSW

?*Odontosyllis* sp.

Habitat: Sheltered reef, silt; 0–7 m depth.
Distribution: Vic. to NSW and around Tas.
Maximum size: Body length to 100 mm.

This is a long and very slender polychaete with an orange body, a white patch behind the head and a pair of yellow spots high on each segment. It is commonly seen by divers at night in a range of sheltered habitats, remaining hidden under rocks and among shell fragments during the day.

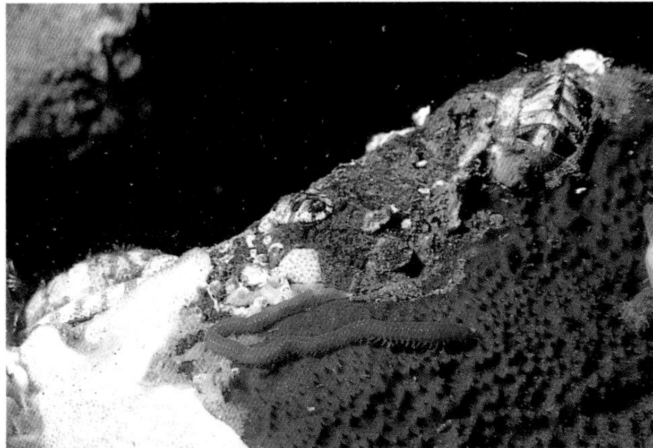

?*Odontosyllis* sp., Cloudy Lagoon, Tas.

FAMILY NEREIDAE
Ragworms

Nereids are elongate highly-segmented worms with two pairs of eyes, a pair of large palps, and several pairs of tentacles of different length attached to the head. Many species are active carnivores, others feed on algae, and a few are filter feeders. They occur commonly under rocks and among algae on reefs and are also abundant in muddy sediments.

Perinereis sp.

Habitat: Sheltered and moderately exposed reef, sand; 0–3 m depth.
Distribution: WA.
Maximum size: Body length to 80 mm.

A number of species of *Perinereis* occur in southern Australia; they differ from other nereids primarily in the shape of the eversible pharynx. The illustrated animal can be recognised by the feathery setae to be

Perinereis sp., Princess Royal Harbour, WA.

the reproductive epitokous or heteronereis stage. These swim at night for perhaps an hour near the water surface shedding gametes; they then drop to the seabed dead. The free-swimming animals provide a feast for fishes, while the bodies are quickly consumed by crabs and other scavengers.

FAMILY ONUPHIDAE

This family contains large, highly segmented species that usually live in thick-walled or shelly tubes. Five long tentacles and two short rounded palps are generally present on the head, and numerous gills prominently arranged behind. The proboscis can be rapidly everted through the mouth and has two strong jaws with which large animals can inflict a painful wound if carelessly handled.

Diopatra dentata Kinberg, 1865

Habitat: Coarse sand; 0–6 m depth.
Distribution: NSW.
Maximum size: Body length to 100 mm.

Diopatra dentata is a tube-dwelling species that occurs abundantly along the New South Wales coast. Arising from the front end of the body are five long tentacles, each with a ringed base, and two short palps. The animal has the ability to quickly withdraw into its tube, so is rarely seen. Half-exposed *Diopatra* tubes are, however, a conspicuous feature of sheltered habitats. The walls of these tubes are composed of a fibre matrix with embedded shells and stones.

Diopatra ?dentata tubes, Terrigal, NSW

Diopatra sp., Rockingham, WA

FAMILY EUNICIDAE

Eunicids have elongate bodies with two bulbous palps and one to five tentacles on the head, and a distinctive arrangement of spines on the eversible pharynx. Most species live on reefs and other hard substrates in shallow water, where they feed on smaller invertebrates; some burrowing and tube-dwelling species are also known.

Eunice sp.

Habitat: Reef; 0–30 m depth.
Distribution: Vic., NSW and Tas.
Maximum size: Body length to 350 mm.

Eunice sp. is a very large, iridescent, reddish-brown polychaete in the family Eunicidae and has a white bar on the fourth body segment. Five ringed antennae are present at the front of the head and an additional pair of tentacles are located a segment behind. This polychaete is abundant under rocks and among attached animals on New South Wales reefs. It is sometimes called *Eunice aphriditois* but is more likely to be *Eunice tentaculata*, or neither of these species names may correctly apply.

Eunice sp, Terrigal, NSW

FAMILY OPHELIIDAE

Species in the family Opheliidae lack prominent parapodia and have simple setae, and therefore superficially resemble oligochaete worms. Their bodies are short and tapered and often have a long groove on the underside. They are among the most common polychaetes associated with sediments rich in organic material.

Armandia intermedia Fauvel, 1902

Habitat: Sheltered and moderately exposed sand, mud; 0–20 m depth.
Distribution: WA to southern Qld and around Tas.
Maximum size: Body length to 15 mm.

Armandia intermedia is the most abundant species in the family Opheliidae found in southern Australia and is very common among decaying seagrass vegetation. It can be specifically identified only by looking at the arrangement of microscopic structures, particularly the number of filament-like gills along the sides.

Armandia intermedia, Port Phillip Bay, Vic. RUDIE KUITER

FAMILY PECTINARIIDAE

Species in the family Pectinariidae construct rigid tapered tubes by cementing sand grains together. The bodies of the living animals are cone-shaped and fit snugly within the tube. They have a distinctive comb of stout spines and numerous small tentacles at the front of the head. The comb is used for burrowing and the tentacles for capturing and manipulating food particles.

Pectinaria sp.

Habitat: Exposed sand; 3–15 m depth.
Distribution: Eastern Tas.
Maximum size: Body length to 50 mm.

This is one of several poorly known pectinariids found in clean sand off temperate coastal beaches. The narrow tip of the tube protrudes just above the sediment surface while the head is buried in sand. They feed on small particles of detritus.

Pectinaria sp., Spring Beach, Tas.

FAMILY TEREBELLIDAE

Terebellids have soft bodies divided into two parts and a dense tuft of tentacles that can contract but not be withdrawn into the mouth. The body usually remains concealed within a tube in the sediment or in rock crevices, and the tentacles are normally extended over the seabed. Food particles are captured by cilia and transported embedded in mucous along grooves in the lower edge of the tentacles to the mouth.

Eupolymnia koorangia Hutchings & Glasby, 1988

Habitat: Sheltered and moderately exposed reef, seagrass; 0–100 m depth.
Distribution: Around the Australian mainland and Tas.
Maximum size: Body length to 70 mm.

Eupolymnia koorangia is the largest of several local terebellid species with a generally similar appearance. It is very widely distributed and occurs commonly under rocks and in shallow seagrass beds.

Eupolymnia koorangia, Coles Bay, Tas.

FAMILY SABELLIDAE

Sabellid worms live in tubes made of sand or mud, but not calcium carbonate. Their bodies are cylindrical, taper towards the rear, and appear relatively smooth because only inconspicuous setae are present on most of the body segments. All species in the family are filter feeders, trapping minute particles in an large extendible tentacular crown.

Sabellastarte sp.

Habitat: Exposed reef; 0–30 m depth.
Distribution: WA to NSW and around Tas.
Maximum size: Body length to 50 mm.

Sabellestarte sp. is a tube-dwelling species with two fans of white or purple tentacles projecting from the front of the body. Like other members of the family Sabellidae, the tentacles are rapidly withdrawn into the tube if the animal is disturbed. This polychaete was once thought the same as the Northern Hemisphere species *Sabellastarte indica,* but probably is distinct. It occurs abundantly on reefs in areas of good current flow.

Sabellastarte sp., Bathurst Channel, Tas.

Spirographis spallanzani Vivani, 1805

Habitat: Silt; 1–20 m depth.
Distribution: Cockburn Sound, WA, to Port Phillip Bay, Vic. Also Europe.
Maximum size: Body length to 200 mm.

Spirographis spallanzani is a large sabellid polychaete with banded tentacles arranged in a distinctive spiral. The species has been introduced into Australia from Europe and now occurs in huge densities across large sections of Corio Bay and western Port Phillip Bay. Because of the great colonising and particle-filtering capacity of these animals, the species is probably having an adverse effect on populations of native filter-feeding invertebrates.

?*Myxicola infundibulum* (Renier, 1804)

Habitat: Silt; 0–12 m depth.
Distribution: Fremantle, WA, to Port Phillip Bay, Vic.
Maximum size: Body length to 150 mm.

?*Myxicola infundibulum* has a solid body buried in sediment and a crown of exposed tentacles. The tentacles are webbed and feathery near their bases but lack side filaments at the tips. This sabellid polychaete is common in the silty sediments of Cockburn Sound and has also been recorded from Port Phillip Bay. There is some doubt about its name because, although virtually identical in appearance with *Myxicola infundibulum*, that name describes a species living in the Northern Hemisphere. The species has perhaps been introduced into Australia in the same way as *Spirographis spallanzani*.

?*Myxicola infundibulum*, Bicton, WA

Spirographis spallanzani, Princess Royal Harbour, WA

FAMILY SERPULIDAE

Species in the family Serpulidae are closely related to the Sabellidae as they also have two tentacular fans extending from tubes. They differ largely because their tubes are made from calcium carbonate and they possess an operculum, a cup-shaped structure on a stalk, which is used for sealing the tube when the tentacles are withdrawn.

Serpula sp.

Habitat: Exposed reef; 3–15 m depth.
Distribution: NSW.
Maximum size: Body length to 40 mm.

Serpula sp. is a colourful species with a bright red fan and is similar in appearance to the European species *Serpula vermicularis*. It occurs commonly along the New South Wales coast.

Serpula sp., Merimbula, NSW

Protula sp., Princess Royal Harbour, WA

Protula sp.

Habitat: Sheltered reef, jetty pylons; 1–5 m depth.
Distribution: Southern WA.
Maximum size: Body length to 30 mm.

Protula sp. resembles *Serpula* sp. but has a whiter tentacular fan and an inconspicuous operculum. The species is moderately common on jetty pylons and occasionally seen on sheltered reefs.

Filograna implexa Berkeley, 1828

Habitat: Sheltered and moderately exposed reef; 1–25 m depth.
Distribution: WA to NSW and around Tas. Also widespread overseas.
Maximum size: Body length to 4 mm.

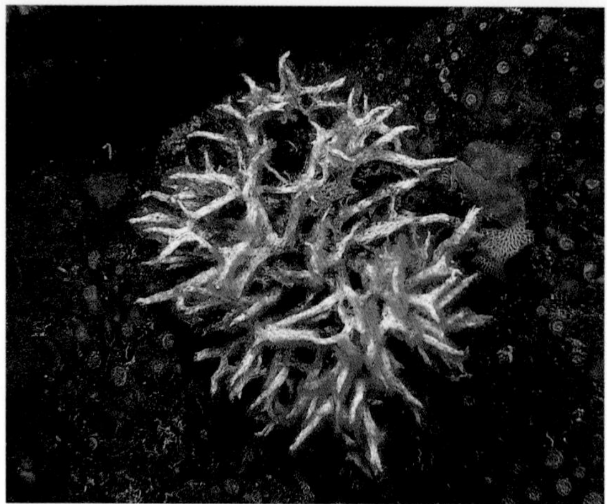

Filograna implexa, Rocky Cape, Tas.

Filograna implexa, Merimbula, NSW

Filograna implexa forms colonies of quite variable shape, ranging from delicate branched structures located in the open to masses of encrusting tubes under rocks. The tubes of this serpulid are white and heavily calcified, while the tentacles range in colour from bright red to white. The species is common around the southern coast.

Galeolaria caespitosa Lamarck, 1818

Habitat: Reef; mid intertidal.
Distribution: Perth, WA, to Hervey Bay, Qld, and around Tas.
Maximum size: Body length to 20 mm.

Galeolaria caespitosa is the most conspicuous Australian polychaete because it occurs in such high densities that the calcareous tubes form a distinct band on many southeastern and southern Australian shores. The tubes often overgrow each other, particularly along the central New South Wales coast, where they can form thick encrustations known as Sydney coral. The living animal has black tentacles and an operculum with 9–11 movable spines projecting from the centre.

Galeolaria caespitosa, Rocky Cape, Tas.

Galeolaria caespitosa, Cloudy Lagoon, Tas.

FAMILY SPIRORBIDAE

Spirorbids form a distinct group of polychaetes that live in spirally-coiled calcareous tubes and possess an operculum, but which are sometimes classed within the family Serpulidae (see previous family). They are small (usually about 1mm in diameter) and can occur extremely high densities on seaweed fronds and rock surfaces. They also often occur attached to animals with hard surfaces, such as the exoskeletons of crabs and rock lobsters.

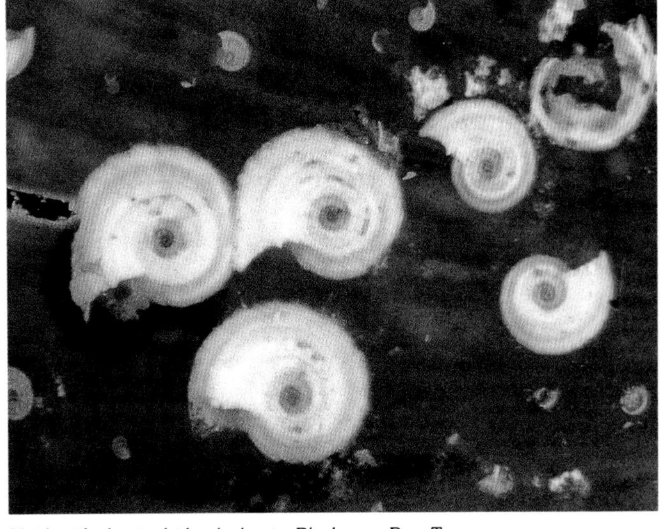

Unidentified spirorbid polychaete, Blackmans Bay, Tas.

PHYLUM SIPUNCULA

Peanut worms, sipunculans

Sipunculans are unsegmented, leech-like animals that are well described by their common name of peanut worm. About 330 species are known, all from marine or estuarine habitats. They have a cylindrical body with a fat trunk section that continues into a slender, extensible proboscis known as the introvert. The introvert, which can be fully withdrawn into body, ends in a mouth surrounded by a crown of tentacles. Rows of hooks or spines are sometimes present on the introvert below the tentacles, and the trunk surface may be covered by tiny protuberances known as papillae.

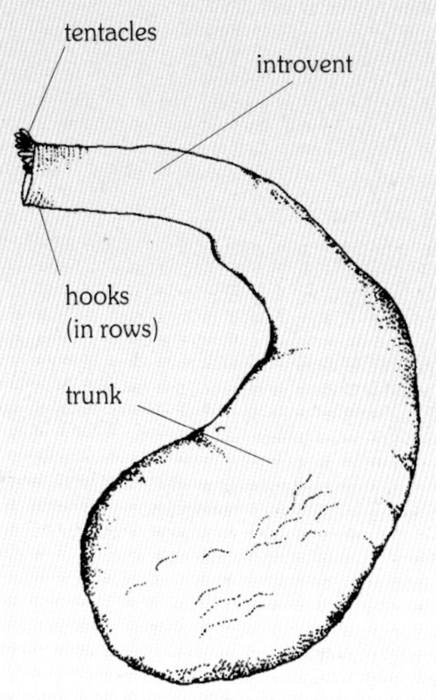

Sipunculan (50 mm)
Phascolosoma noduliferum
Phylum Sipuncula

Sipunculans range in size from a few millimetres to half a metre, with most 10–50 mm long. They occur in a variety of habitats; some species excavate temporary burrows in sand or mud or among the rhizomes of seagrasses, some live in crevices or burrows that they bore themselves in soft rock, and others inhabit discarded mollusc shells. The trunk usually remains protected within the burrow while the introvert, which can be extended for up to 10 times the trunk's length in some species, fossicks about searching for food. If the exposed introvert is eaten by a predator, as often happens, it can be regenerated. Sipunculans associated with sediment generally feed on organic material extracted from sand or mud, while the reef dwellers use the tentacles to trap small food particles on the reef surface or suspended in water.

Sipunculans have separate sexes, which can only be distinguished by slight differences in internal anatomy. Eggs and sperm are released externally. After fertilisation, the egg transforms into a ciliated larva which resembles the trochophore larva of a polychaete.

Phascolosoma noduliferum Stimpson, 1855

Habitat: Sheltered and moderately exposed reef, silt; 0–1340 m depth.
Distribution: Hopetoun, WA, to Port Stephens, NSW, and around Tas.
Maximum size: Trunk length to 65 mm.

Phascolosoma noduliferum is the most common species of sipunculan found along the New South Wales coast. It is a moderate-sized species with a brown body and numerous rounded papillae over the surface. Large numbers are often found together under rocks.

Phascolosoma noduliferum, Port Stephens, NSW

Phascolosoma annulatum Hutton, 1879

Habitat: Sheltered and moderately exposed reef, silt; 0–500 m depth
Distribution: Ceduna, SA, to Kilcunda, Vic., and around Tas. Also New Zealand.
Maximum size: Trunk length to 50 mm.

Phascolosoma annulatum differs from *P. noduliferum* by having darker papillae on the surface of the body, with these papillae aggregating into a dark collar at the front of the trunk and also forming a dark patch at the rear. The two species have similar habitat requirements and can occur under the same rock. *Phascolosoma annulatum* is the more common species in southern Australian waters

Phascolosoma annulatum, Cloudy Lagoon, Tas.

PHYLUM ECHIUROIDEA

Echiurans

Echiurans are soft-bodied worm-like animals that look somewhat similar to their closest relatives, the sipunculans. They have a sausage-shaped body that remains concealed under sediment or among rocks and a long, protrusible proboscis that is usually extended across the seabed. The proboscis may be forked or have a spoon-shaped end and is used for respiration and to trap detrital food particles. When disturbed the proboscis retracts quickly, but, unlike the introvert of a sipunculan, cannot be withdrawn fully into the body cavity of the animal. Below the base of the proboscis is a small mouth. This receives particles of food passed by beating cilia along a groove that extends along the proboscis. Below and behind the mouth are usually a pair of curved setae that assist in locomotion and hold the animal in place within the burrow. Echiurans are divided into species that have sexes of similar appearance and species in which the male is very small and lives internally within the female. Both types release eggs into the water; these develop into ciliated trochophore larvae of a similar shape to the larvae of polychaetes and molluscs. Approximately 130 species are known worldwide, with three species recorded from southern Australia, only one of which is common.

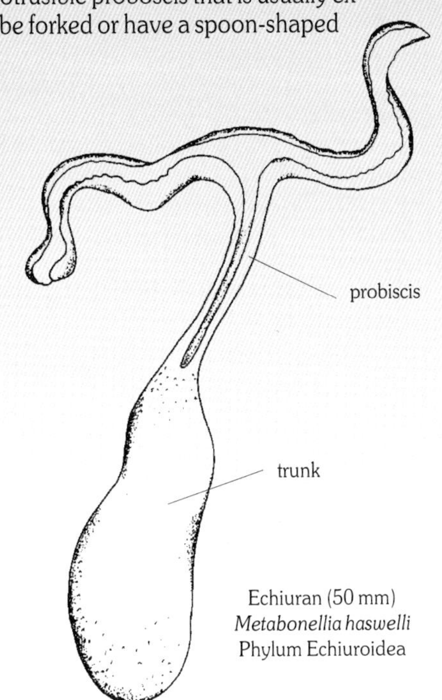

Echiuran (50 mm)
Metabonellia haswelli
Phylum Echiuroidea

Metabonellia haswelli (Johnston & Tiegs, 1920)

Habitat: Sheltered rocky reefs; 0–10 m depth.
Distribution: Fremantle, WA, to Sydney, NSW, and around Tas.
Maximum size: Trunk length to 70 mm, proboscis can extend to 500 mm.

Metabonellia haswelli cannot be confused with any other known Australian species, with its bright green body and forked proboscis. This species hides under rocks, extending its rubber band-like proboscis out at night to catch food. The male is extremely reduced in size and lacks a proboscis, appearing as an poorly defined tadpole about 5 mm long attached to the internal organs of the female. The sexual identity of an animal is not fixed at birth but depends on whether it settles as a larva on rock, in which case it becomes female, or on the extended proboscis of a female, in which case it moves inside and becomes male.

Metabonellia haswelli, Esperance, Tas.

PHYLUM ARTHROPODA

Arthropods

This is by far the largest phylum of free-living animals; it includes many millions of species, most of which are terrestrial insects and mites. Arthropods are characterised by a segmented body that is symmetrical around a central line and numerous jointed limbs. The other major feature is an external body wall that is strengthened by a structural protein (chitin), supplemented in some species by deposits of calcium carbonate, to form an external skeleton. The rigid chitinous plates have soft joints at regular intervals and are connected by internal muscles, allowing the body to flex and limbs to move. Because of the rigidity of the exoskeleton, arthropods cannot increase in size once the body wall has hardened. They therefore grow by a series of moults, the animal escaping through a crack in the old exoskeleton and then rapidly increasing in size by taking in water or air before the new exoskeleton hardens.

The arthropods are here divided into three subphyla: Chelicerata, Uniramia and Crustacea. Some authorities raise these groupings to the level of separate phyla because it is now thought unlikely that they are derived from the same worm-like ancestor.

Subphylum Chelicerata

Chelicerates

The Chelicerata are arthropods without antennae and with the body divided into two regions, the head/thorax region (known as the prosoma) and the abdominal opisthosoma. Included in the subphylum are spiders, harvestmen, scorpions and mites; the pycnogonids are also considered chelicerates although not closely related to the other groups. Nearly all chelicerate species live on land, but the pycnogonids, the horseshoe crabs (a class containing five species restricted to the Northern Hemisphere) and some mites are marine.

Class Pycnogonida

Sea spiders, pycnogonids

Pycnogonids have a spider-like appearance and four, or (in a few species found overseas) five or six, pairs of legs that generally end in claws. Located at the front of the body is a sucking proboscis with mouth at the end, two or occasionally four pairs of eyes positioned on a rounded knob, and usually three pairs of appendages, the chelifores, palps and ovigers. The trunk is greatly reduced in size and the abdomen appears as a small stump at the rear of the body. Because of the extreme reduction of the trunk, the gonads and part of the gut extend into the legs. An interesting feature of pycnogonids is that they lack excretory and respiratory organs; waste products are released and oxygen diffuses directly across cell walls.

This class contains more than 1000 described species, none of which occur on land or in fresh water. Most species are small (<10 mm) and rarely noticed. Pycnogonids occur in virtually all seabed habitats, from intertidal rock pools to deep-sea sediments. Many species can be found on clumps of tufted seaweed in shallow water. Some pycnogonids feed by inserting their proboscis into anemones, hydroids or bryozoans and sucking out the internal fluids of the prey. The life cycles of pycnogonids vary substantially from species to species and may include particular specialisations for life in association with only one or two hosts. Many females deposit eggs that are picked up and brooded by the male using the ovigers. The first larval or 'protonymphon' stage lacks legs and is usually either carried by the male or lives parasitically within the body of hydroids or other animals. The nymphs moult several times, adding an extra pair of legs during the moult, before attaining the adult shape.

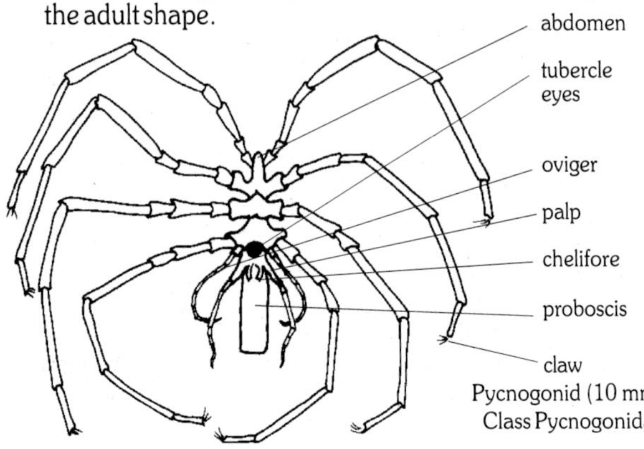

Pycnogonid (10 mm)
Class Pycnogonida

Pseudopallene ambigua Stock, 1956

Habitat: Exposed reef; 8–126 m depth.
Distribution: Investigator Group, SA, to Sydney, NSW, and around Tas.
Maximum size: Length to 30 mm.

Pseudopallene ambigua is abundant on coastal reefs, most often in association with the bryozoan *Orthoscuticella ventricosa*. It is the only pycnogonid species regularly seen by divers and is occasionally found swimming in open water. The species can be recognised by its bright yellow colour, occasionally with red markings, and long, smooth legs.

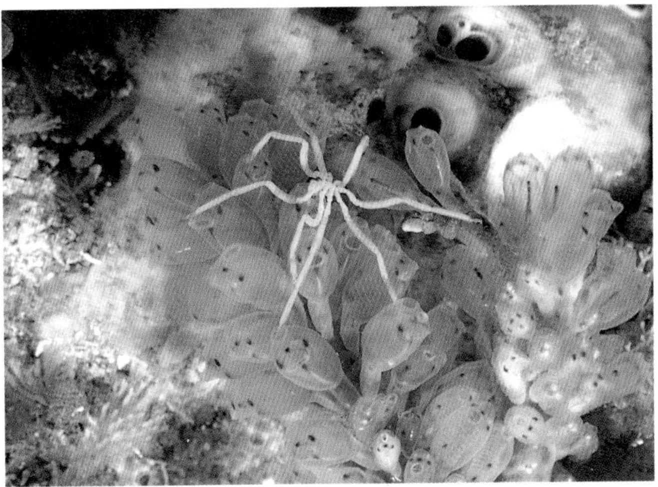

Pseudopallene ambigua, Ile des Phoques, Tas.

Anoplodactylus evansi Clark, 1963

Habitat: Exposed reef; 0–20 m depth.
Distribution: Victor Harbor, SA, to Tweed Heads, Qld, and around Tas.
Maximum size: Length to 20 mm.

Anoplodactylus evansi has a distinctive banded colour pattern, with predominantly red (in adults) or blue (in juveniles) trunk and legs and blue bands at the end of the segments and yellow between. The species is moderately common on shallow reefs. It ranges widely over plants and sessile animals, rarely stopping for long in one place.

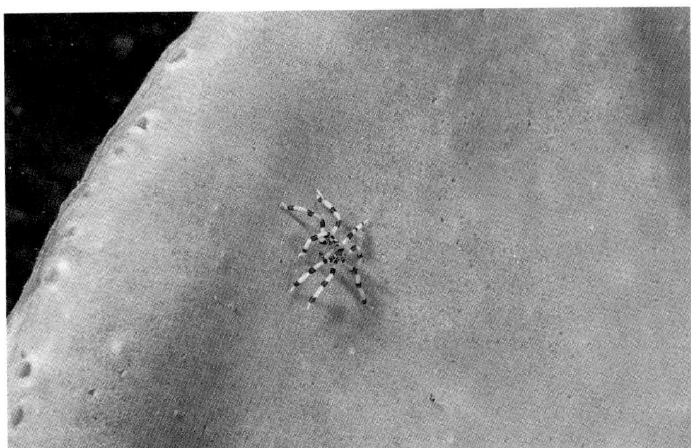

Anoplodactylus evansi, Ile des Phoques, Tas.

Pallenopsis gippslandiae Stock, 1954

Habitat: Reef; 6–555 m depth.
Distribution: Eastern Vic. to Double I, Qld, and eastern and southern Tas.
Maximum size: Length to 50 mm.

Pallenopsis gippslandiae is a large, thin-legged pycnogonid with prominent spines on the legs. The illustrated pycnogonid and similar animals that occur on shallow southern Tasmanian reefs are likely to be this species. There is some uncertainty because the original scientific description of *P. gippslandiae* was based on deep-water (>60 m) specimens.

Pallenopsis gippslandiae, Bathurst Channel, Tas.

Nymphon aequidigitatum, Bathurst Channel, Tas.

Nymphon aequidigitatum Haswell, 1884

Habitat: Exposed reef; 0–20 m depth.
Distribution: Gulf St Vincent, SA, to Byron Bay, NSW, and around Tas.
Maximum size: Length to 35 mm.

Nymphon aequidigitatum is a common species that is usually found associated with encrusting sponges on the underside of boulders, but which also occurs in a variety of other microhabitats. The species has extremely long, thin legs and is a pale straw colour, or occasionally pink or orange.

Class Arachnida
Arachnids

Arachnids are distinguished from other chelicerates by having six pairs of appendages: chelicerae and pedipalps near the front of the head and four pairs of walking limbs. The body is divided into two major regions, which may be either joined by a narrow waist, as in spiders, or completely fused, as in mites. In most orders, the cephalothorax region is protected by a large plate, the carapace.

Order Acarina
Mites

This is the largest group of chelicerates, with about 30 000 species scientifically named and perhaps an additional million species remaining to be discovered. Because most mites are less than 1 mm in length and live well hidden, the huge diversity of these species has been recognised only in recent years. Mites differ from other arachnids by having the cephalothorax and abdomen fused together into a seamless structure. The front of the body projects forward and carries the chelicerae and pedipalps.

While mites are generally considered terrestrial animals, one family, the Halacaridae, has diversified in shallow waters. Recent collections at Rottnest Island, for example, have revealed at least 70 species in that area. Halacarids are primarily associated with seaweeds and sandy sediments and include algal-feeding and carnivorous forms. They lack a planktonic stage in the life cycle. Crawling larvae with three pairs of legs emerge from the egg and develop directly into adults after two or three moults.

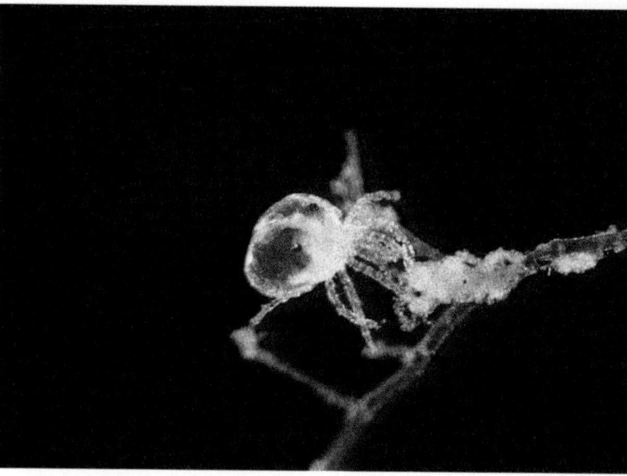
Halacarid mite, Sandy Bay, Tas.

The most abundant terrestrial family of mites, the Oribatidae, is also represented by a few intertidal and shallow subtidal species. Oribatids are usually larger than halacarids and have a much more swollen body.

Subphylum Uniramia

This large subphylum contains arthropods with unbranched appendages and a single pair of antennae. They use a system of tubes (trachea) to pass air to different parts of the body and have a complex organ (the Malpighian tubules) for the excretion of waste products. Most uniramians are insects, but this subphylum also includes centipedes, millipeds and related groups.

Phalanisus plebeius, Broughton I, NSW

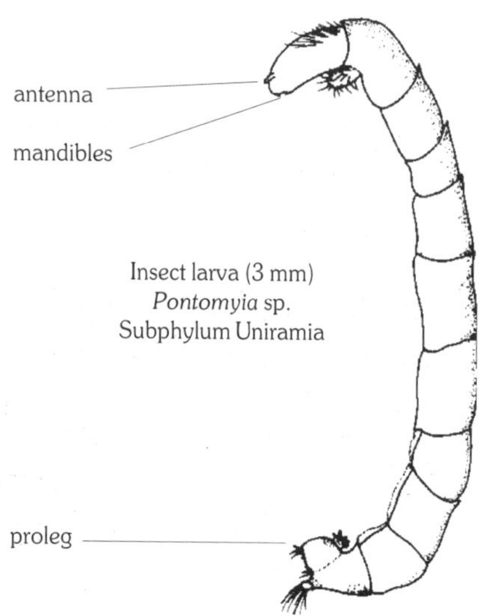

Insect larva (3 mm)
Pontomyia sp.
Subphylum Uniramia

Class Insecta

Insects

Insects are characterised by a body divided into three sections, the head, the thorax and the abdomen, and three pairs of legs attached to the thorax. The adults of most species have one or two pairs of wings and compound eyes. This is by far the largest class of animals, with recent estimates suggesting that perhaps 10 million species are included, nearly half of which are beetles. However, despite such huge diversity and having colonised most land and freshwater habitats, they are virtually absent from the sea.

Three small groups of insects, namely water striders, caddis flies and midges, have colonised marine habitats in Australia. The water strider genus *Halobates* is commonly found on the surface of tropical seas but does not extend into temperate areas south of Sydney or Shark Bay. The caddis fly *Philanisus plebeius* is, however, a temperate species that is common in New South Wales and also occurs in New Zealand. Adults of this species deposit eggs through pores in the body of the intertidal sea star *Patiriella exigua*, and initial development begins in its body cavity. Later larval stages live freely in shallow water. The most important group of marine insects around southern Australian coasts are chironomid midges. Larval midges in the genus *Pontomyia* are very common in algal and seagrass habitats in estuaries and sheltered bays to a depth of about 10 m. Adults can be found sitting on intertidal rocks.

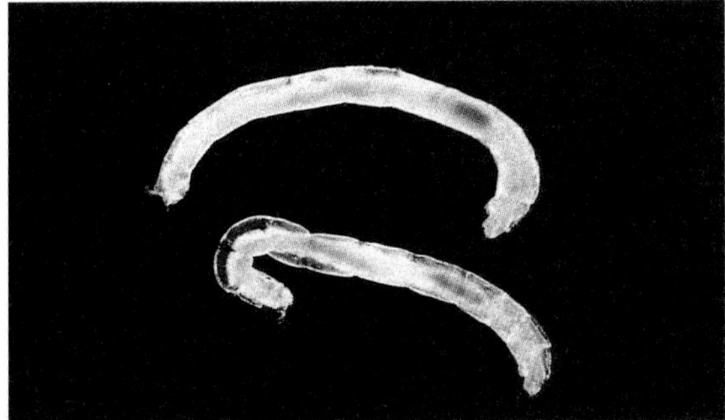

Pontomyia sp., D'Entrecasteaux Channel, Tas.

Subphylum Crustacea

Crustaceans

Crustaceans are a large group of predominantly marine species, which differ from other arthropods by having two pairs of antennae in front of the mouth. The limbs also usually divide into two branches except when they are used for walking, in which case one of the branches is generally lost. The body is subdivided into head, thorax and abdomen, a basic body plan that may be obscured by the first thoracic segments being fused with the head and a large fold from the body wall, the carapace, extending back from the head to protect the front section of the thorax.

A variety of different reproductive strategies are used by crustaceans. A few species (notably many barnacles) have male and female organs within the one animal, but the majority of crustaceans have separate sexes. Some species change sex as they develop. Most crustacean groups have a planktonic larval stage that differs greatly in appearance from the adult. The most common larval form is a nauplius, a rounded animal with three pairs of appendages, including large antennae used for swimming.

Crustaceans occur in virtually all marine and most freshwater environments; they are usually the dominant animal group in plankton and among seaweeds and can be dominant in sediments. They range in size from copepods and cladocerans, which are mostly less than 1 mm long, to crabs with a maximum legspan in excess of 2 m. About 40 000 species have been scientifically named; however, this represents only a small proportion of species, as total numbers are likely to exceed 100 000.

Cladoceran (*Podon* sp.), Sandy Bay, Tas.

Class Branchiopoda

Order Cladocera

Water fleas, cladocerans

The class Branchiopoda contains the order Cladocera and three freshwater orders. Cladocerans are small, transparent crustaceans with a bivalved carapace that usually encloses the thorax and abdomen and is often extended into a conspicuous spine at the rear. The second pair of antennae are very large and used for swimming, while the first antennae are greatly reduced. Four to six pairs of limbs project from the thorax; these are used for filtering food particles from the water in most species and for grasping prey in others. Cladocerans occur predominantly in freshwater ponds, lakes and estuaries, but a few species occur in the open sea. Many populations consist of self-

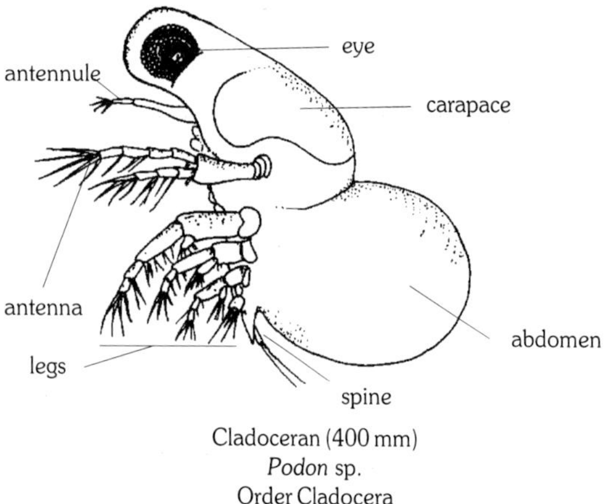

Cladoceran (400 mm)
Podon sp.
Order Cladocera

reproducing females; males appear during periods of deterioration in the environment in order to help produce fertilised eggs. The eggs have thick walls and can survive in a harsh environment for long periods.

Class Cirripedia

Barnacles

This class of crustaceans comprises about 1000 species, most of them occurring fixed to rock or other hard surfaces when adult, although there are also a few parasitic forms. The young (larval) barnacles generally pass through several nauplius stages that

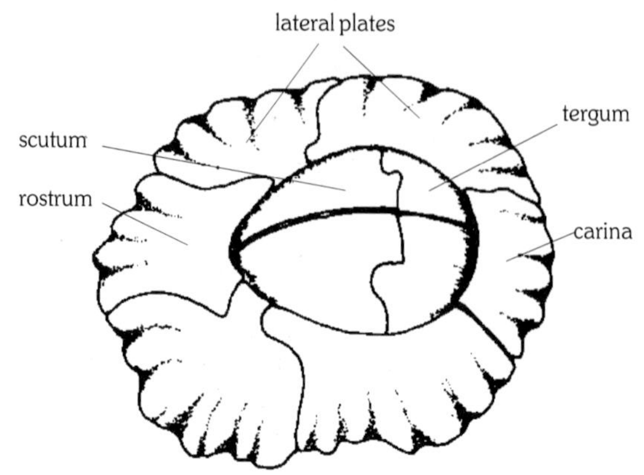

Barnacle (10 mm)
Chthamalus antennatus
Class Cirripedia

resemble the larvae of several other crustacean groups. Each nauplius eventually moults into a cypris, a free-swimming, six-limbed larva with an appearance similar to an ostracod because the body is enclosed by two carapace valves. On settling, the cypris cements itself onto a suitable substrate head down, and the body becomes highly distorted and modified for a stationary existence. The limbs transform into long, feathery cirri, which beat through the water, directing food particles into the upwardly directed mouth. The head disappears, and the carapace hardens and transforms into a shell that surrounds the rest of the body. Two additional pairs of hardened plates, the scuta and terga, seal the entrance to the shell, but can open rhythmically to allow the cirri to protrude. These plates provide protection from desiccation and predators. Virtually all barnacles have both male and female sex organs. Fertilisation of most shore barnacles occurs when sperm are passed between adjacent individuals using an extremely long penis. Barnacles separated by long distances are either not fertilised or fertilise themselves.

Two major groups of barnacles are found in southern Australia, the Lepadomorpha (goose barnacles) and the Balanomorpha (acorn barnacles). Goose barnacles have long, rubbery stalks and often attach themselves to objects floating in the open sea. They gain their common name from a European legend based on the resemblance of the food-gathering cirri to the feathers of birds. This legend, which was widely accepted through the Middle Ages, stated that barnacles drifting ashore attached to logs were the egg cases of geese. These birds migrate south each winter and did not appear to nest on land.

Acorn barnacles have rigid sides formed from four, six or eight calcareous plates and include the great majority of cirripede species.

Ibla quadrivalvis (Cuvier, 1817)

Habitat: Sheltered and moderately exposed reef; mid intertidal.
Distribution: Albany, WA, to central NSW and around Tas.
Maximum size: Length to 30 mm.

Ibla quadrivalvis is a small stalked barnacle that commonly occurs in large numbers under rocks and occasionally appears in aggregations on jetty pylons. It has a long stalk covered by small horny spines and four small terminal plates forming a claw-like structure. This barnacle is usually associated with the tubeworm *Galeolaria caespitosa*.

Ibla quadrivalvis, Taroona, Tas.

Lepas pectinata Spengler, 1793

Habitat: Floating molluscs, wood, pumice.
Distribution: Tropical Australia south to Cape Le Grande, WA, and central NSW. Widespread overseas.
Maximum size: Length to 25 mm.

Lepas pectinata is one of several species of barnacles in the genus *Lepas* that live attached to drifting objects and are occasionally washed ashore. The outer side-plates of *L. pectinata* are narrower than those of other species, and it is a small species with a relatively wide body. Other common goose barnacles are ***Lepas anatifera***, which has a long stalk and smooth sides, ***Lepas anserifera***, which has a short stalk and ridged side-plates with orange margins, and ***Lepas fascicularis***, a species with blue side-plates.

Lepas pectinata attached to *Janthina janthina*, Marmion Lagoon, WA. Clay Bryce

Lepas australis Darwin, 1851

Habitat: Floating objects in the open sea.
Distribution: Cottesloe, WA, to NSW and around Tas. Also New Zealand and widespread in subantarctic seas.
Maximum size: Length to 70 mm, including 35 mm stalk.

Lepas australis resembles *Lepas anatifera* but has wider and more rounded, relatively brittle plates. It is commonly washed ashore on cool southern shores attached to wood and other objects. This goose barnacle has also been found attached to the feathers of a penguin.

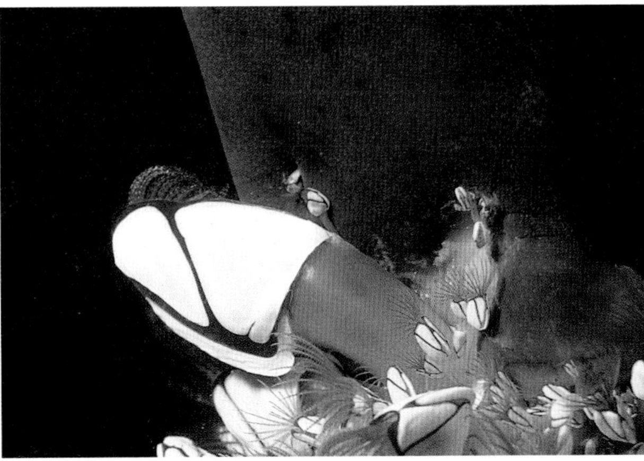

Lepas australis, Cloudy Bay, Tas.

Smilium peronii Gray, 1825

Habitat: Stones, shells; 0–135 m depth.
Distribution: Houtman Abrolhos, WA, to southern Qld. Also Indonesia.
Maximum size: Length to 30 mm.

Smilium peronii is a lepadomorph barnacle with a short stalk and thin covering over the plates. It is related to several deep-water species but differs from these by lacking calcareous scales on the stalk. This barnacle is common in Western Port, Vic., where it grows to a large size on stones and shells in channels with strong current flow. Large individuals are rarely seen elsewhere in shallow water.

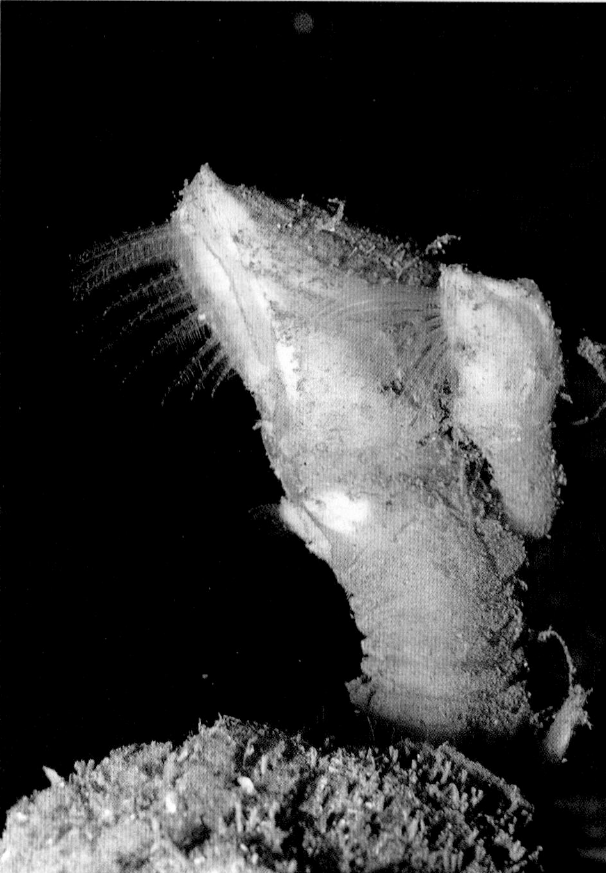

Smilium peronii, Western Port, Vic. RUDIE KUITER

Catomerus polymerus (Darwin, 1854)

Habitat: Exposed shores; mid intertidal.
Distribution: Great Australian Bight, WA, to Tweed Heads, NSW, and around Tas.
Maximum size: Diameter to 30 mm.

Catomerus polymerus is the most easily recognised species of Australian barnacle because of its flat shape and the numerous plates that diminish in size towards the edge of the shell. This barnacle is extremely abundant on southeastern reefs with breaking surf. It usually grows on rock surfaces and on shells of the mussel *Brachidontes rostratus*.

Catomerus polymerus, Bicheno, Tas.

Chthamalus antennatus Darwin, 1854

Habitat: Exposed shores; mid to high intertidal.
Distribution: Discovery Bay, Vic., to northern NSW and around Tas.
Maximum size: Diameter to 12 mm.

Chthamalus antennatus has an off-white shell with six plates and numerous grooves towards the bottom of the outer surface. The species occurs abundantly on moderately exposed shores, usually at a slightly higher level than other barnacle species.

Chthamalus antennatus, Rocky Cape, Tas.

Chamaesipho tasmanica

(Foster & Anderson, 1986)

Habitat: Exposed shores; mid to high intertidal.
Distribution: Point Sinclair, SA, to Byron Bay, NSW, and around Tas.
Maximum size: Diameter to 8 mm.

Chamaesipho tasmanica has four shell plates that are virtually impossible to distinguish because they are fused together with the plates of adjoining barnacles. This small barnacle occurs in honeycomb-like aggregations and is extremely abundant on moderately exposed shores. The species was known until recently as *Chamaesipho columna*, but that name now applies to a closely related New Zealand species.

Chamaesipho tasmanica, Coles Bay, Tas.

Tetraclitella purpurascens (Wood, 1815)

Habitat: Moderately exposed shores; mid intertidal.
Distribution: Kalbarri, WA, to Moreton Bay, Qld, and around Tas. Also New Zealand.
Maximum size: Diameter to 25 mm.

Tetraclitella purpurascens is a flat, grey barnacle with characteristic radial ribs, which are best developed on solitary animals. The species is relatively uncommon on open rock surfaces but is abundant in shaded habitats where it remains moist during low-tide.

Tetraclitella purpurascens, Taroona, Tas.

Tetraclitella purpurascens, Bicheno, Tas.

Tesseropora rosea, Merimbula, NSW

Tesseropora rosea (Krauss, 1848)

Habitat: Exposed shores; mid intertidal.
Distribution: Fremantle, WA, and Inverloch, Vic., to southern Qld. Also Kermadec I, New Caledonia and South Africa.
Maximum size: Diameter to 30 mm.

Tesseropora rosea is a high, four-plated barnacle, which usually erodes rapidly, exposing pink shell and causing a series of grooves to form down the outside. This species is extremely abundant on virtually all exposed New South Wales shores, but is rarely seen elsewhere. A record of this species at Fremantle, the only sighting on the west coast, has been confirmed recently.

Epopella simplex, Spring Beach, Tas.

Epopella simplex (Darwin, 1854)

Habitat: Moderately exposed shores; low intertidal.
Distribution: Green Head, WA, to central NSW and around Tas.
Maximum size: Diameter to 12 mm.

Epopella simplex is a high-sided, white, conical barnacle, which resembles a volcano in shape and has four plates. It occurs in small groups under rocks and is less common than the other barnacles described here.

Austrobalanus imperator, Port Stephens, NSW

Austrobalanus imperator (Darwin, 1854)

Habitat: Exposed shores; low intertidal.
Distribution: NSW and Qld.
Maximum size: Diameter to 20 mm.

Austrobalanus imperator is a large barnacle with an obvious purple tint because of internal shell colouring. It is one of the dominant barnacle species on exposed shores along the central and northern New South Wales coasts.

Elminius modestus Darwin, 1854

Habitat: Sheltered rocks, wood; mid to high intertidal.
Distribution: Southern WA to NSW and around Tas. Also New Zealand and Europe.
Maximum size: Diameter to 12 mm.

Elminius modestus has a white to grey shell with four strongly ridged plates. This barnacle was first collected by Charles Darwin during his voyage on the *Beagle* and was described by him. It is abundant on virtually all solid surfaces in southern Australian estuaries and has been introduced into Europe on ships' hulls.

Elminius modestus, Kelso, Tas.

Elminius covertus Foster, 1981

Habitat: Sheltered rocks, wood; mid to high intertidal.
Distribution: Bunbury, WA, to Coffs Harbour, NSW, and around Tas.
Maximum size: Diameter to 15 mm.

Elminius covertus occurs in much the same sheltered estuarine habitat as *E. modestus* but can be distinguished by the less strongly ridged plates and reddish-brown basal colour with cream ridges. Another characteristic feature is six pairs of black dots that can be seen along the fleshy edge to the aperture when feeding. It occurs abundantly in many southern Australian estuaries. Two small estuarine NSW species, ***Hexaminius popeiana*** and ***Hexaminius foliorum***, may also be confused with *E. convertus* or *E. modestus*, but they have six side plates, including one small pair.

Elminius covertus with *Elminius modestus* (centre of group at upper right), Dunalley, Tas.

Elminius flindersi, Spencer Gulf, SA

Elminius flindersi Bayliss, 1994

Habitat: Sheltered rocks, wood; mid to high intertidal.
Distribution: Ceduna to Gulf St Vincent, SA.
Maximum size: Diameter to 10 mm.

Elminius flindersi is a greyish-white barnacle that resembles *E. modestus* but has less strongly ridged side-plates and opercular plates of a different shape. It occurs abundantly through much of South Australia. A number of other species of *Elminius* that were previously confused with *E. modestus* have also been described recently from South Australia. These species all have weaker and more numerous ribs. They are ***Elminius adelaidei***, a light-grey species commonly found growing on mangrove trees near Adelaide, ***Elminius placidus***, a grey species with light and dark bands from Spencer Gulf, and ***Elminius erubescens,*** a species so far found only near Adelaide with a translucent reddish-purple shell.

Balanus variegatus Darwin, 1854

Habitat: Sheltered reef, wood; 0–4 m depth.
Distribution: Carnarvon, WA, to northern NSW. Also New Zealand.
Maximum size: Height to 25 mm.

Balanus variegatus has six white, curved plates, with purple cross-hatched markings over the shell. The species occurs in sheltered embayments and open estuaries, where it lives on rock, jetty pylons, old bottles, etc.

Balanus variegatus, Merimbula, NSW

Balanus trigonus, Terrigal, NSW

Balanus trigonus Darwin, 1854

Habitat: Sheltered and moderately exposed reef, wood; 0–150 m depth.
Distribution: Tropical Australia south to Rockingham, WA, and Vic. Also widespread overseas.
Maximum size: Height to 15 mm.

Balanus trigonus resembles *B. variegatus* but has purple lines rather than cross-hatched markings down the shell. The species is common along moderately exposed coasts on a variety of rock and other substrates, including the shells of crabs. Unlike most other common barnacles, this barnacle is generally found subtidally rather than on intertidal shores. Another barnacle with purple vertical lines on the shell but with a square rather than acutely angled opening, ***Balanus amphitrite***, occurs abundantly as a fouling species higher up estuaries.

Austromegabalanus nigrescens, Bicheno, Tas.

Austromegabalanus nigrescens (Lamarck, 1818)

Habitat: Exposed rocky shores; intertidal to 9 m depth.
Distribution: Cape Leeuwin, WA, to northern NSW and eastern Tas.
Maximum size: Height to 50 mm.

Austromegabalanus nigrescens can be distinguished from other Australian shore barnacles by its large size and the bright blue mantle that can normally be seen within the shell. The species is very common at low-tide level on central and southern coasts of New South Wales at sites with heavy wave exposure but is less common elsewhere. It has become well established along exposed eastern Tasmanian shores only since 1960, probably as a result of a general increase in coastal water temperatures. A closely related species in Chile, *Austromegabalanus psittacus*, is commercially harvested for human consumption.

Class Copepoda
Copepods

Copepods are small crustaceans (most species < 1 mm long) that lack a carapace and have the body divided into head, thorax and abdomen. The head usually has a single central eye and two antennae, the first of which is much longer than the second. The thorax is six-segmented, each segment having a pair of limbs with two branches. The abdomen lacks appendages other than filaments projecting from the rear. This basic body plan, which derives from the ancestral crustacean, is not generally apparent, however, as the first and sometimes second thoracic segments are fused with the head. A more obvious way of subdividing the copepod body is into a cephalosome, which includes the head and one or two thoracic segments, followed by the metasome and then the narrower urosome at the rear.

The class Copepoda is divided into three major orders, Calanoida, Cyclopoida and Harpacticoida, plus seven minor orders, including the aberrant parasitic groups Monstrilloida and Caligoida.

Calanoid copepods are the most abundant group of planktonic animals living in inshore and oceanic waters, where they provide a critical link in marine food chains leading to pelagic fishes. Most are easily recognised by the very long first antennae which are generally about as long as the body and have 18–25 segments. In males one of the antennae is generally modified to allow for grasping of females during copulation. Calanoid copepods also have a single egg sac attached under the rear of the body in females; and the thorax is much wider than the abdomen. They usually feed on phytoplankton.

Calanoid copepods, Sandy Bay, Tas.

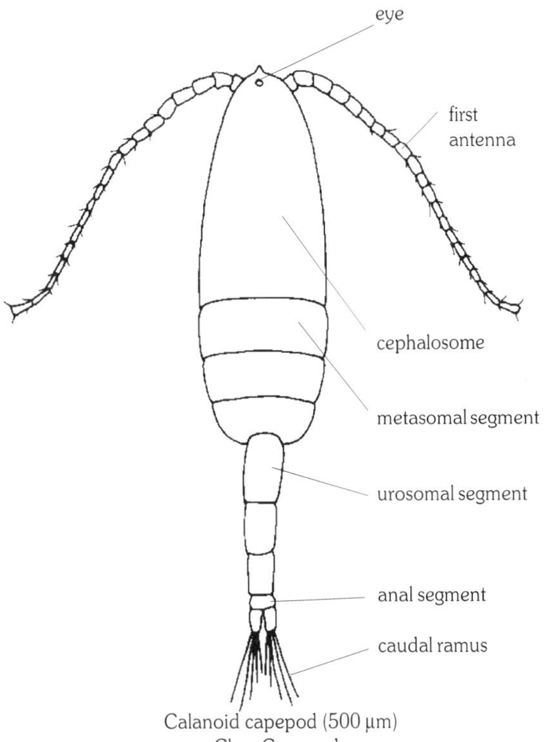

Calanoid capepod (500 µm)
Class Copepoda

Cyclopoid copepods are the predominant group of copepods living in freshwater lakes and ponds. They are also abundant in estuaries but diminish in importance offshore. Most species are planktonic, but many bottom-dwelling species are also known. Cyclopoids are distinguished by moderately long first antennae (6–17 segments), which are generally held at right angles to the body and have a slight S-shaped bend. Females carry two clusters of eggs, which project from the sides at the rear of the

Cyclopoid copepod (*Oithona* sp.), Bathurst Channel, Tas.

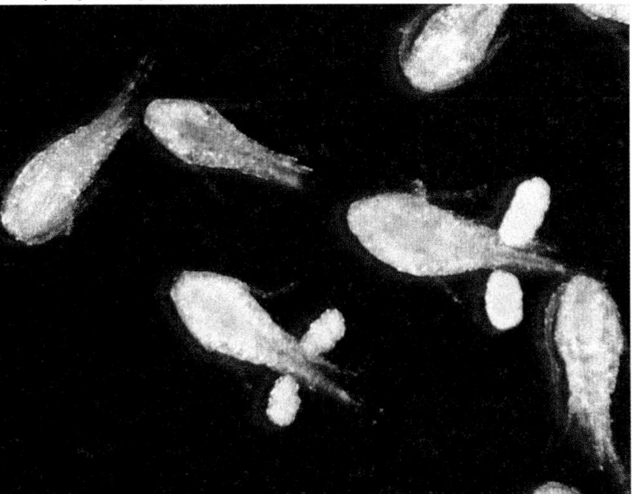

body, and like the calanoid copepods, the thorax is much wider than the abdomen.

Harpacticoid copepods are nearly all bottom-dwelling species. They are often the most abundant group of animals living on sediments and among plants in marine and freshwater environments. In contrast to the other dominant group of small animals living in the same habitats, the nematodes, harpacticoid copepods are an important source of food for juvenile fishes. They can be recognised by the short (4–10 segments), concave first antennae; the abdomen is not obviously narrower than the thorax, and the female has a single egg sac. Harpacticoid copepods usually feed on bacteria, single-celled algae and other microbes associated with the seabed.

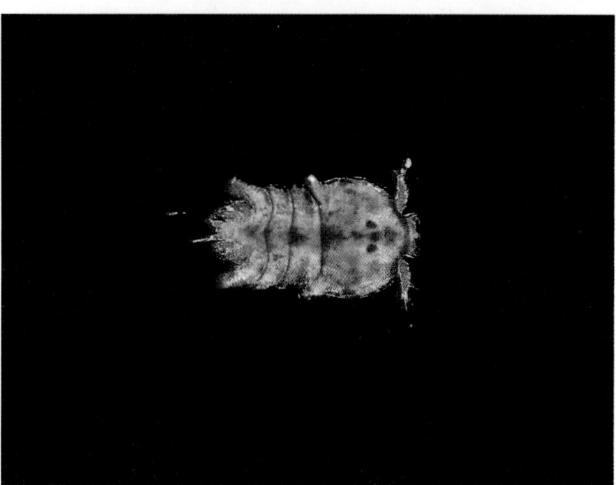

Unidentified harpacticoid copepod, Gordon, Tas.

Class Ostracoda

Ostracods, seed shrimps

Ostracods are small crustaceans, usually about 1 mm in length, with a bivalved carapace that can completely enclose the body. The body is not noticeably segmented and has a reduced complement of limbs compared with other crustaceans. They have two large antennae, three pairs of mouthparts and two pairs of trunk limbs, with the end of the abdomen often developed into a claw-like structure.

Most ostracods live on the seabed, although a considerable number of planktonic and freshwater species are also known. One unusual New Zealand species can be found crawling over leaf litter on land. The habitat of the animal is generally reflected in the structure of its carapace, with planktonic species possessing the most fragile shells. Ostracod carapaces are highly resistant to disintegration, and so are found in large numbers as fossils extending back more than 500 million years. The bivalved carapace is present on even the youngest ostracods, which are otherwise similar to the nauplius stage of other crustacean groups.

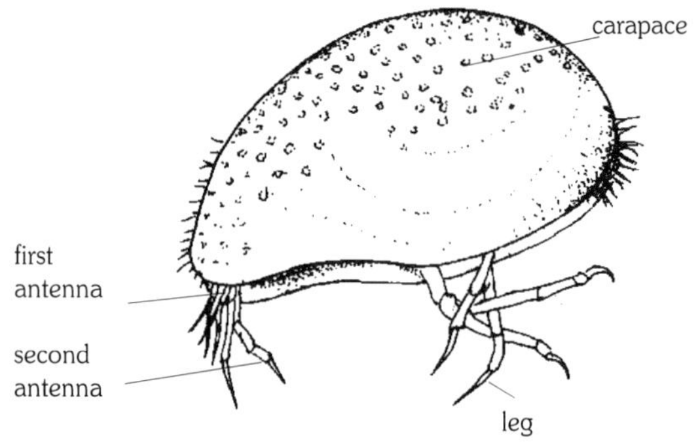

Ostracod (1 mm)
Class Ostracoda

Unidentified ostracod, Tinderbox, Tas.

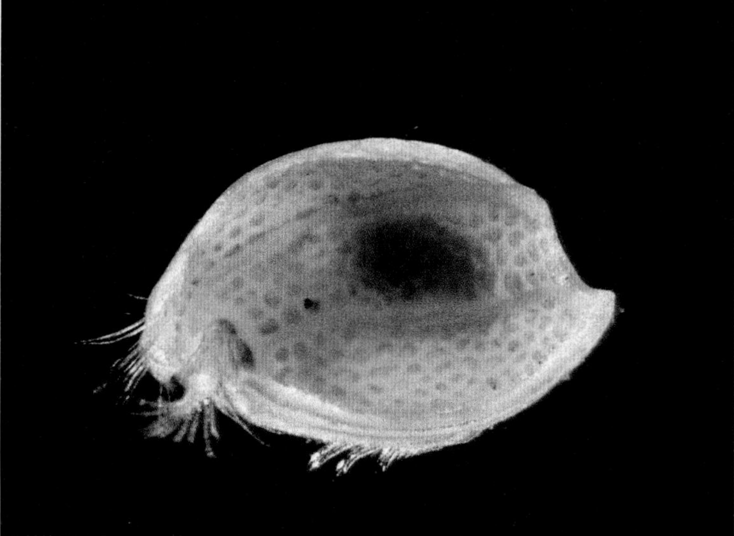

Class Malacostraca

Malacostracans, higher crustaceans

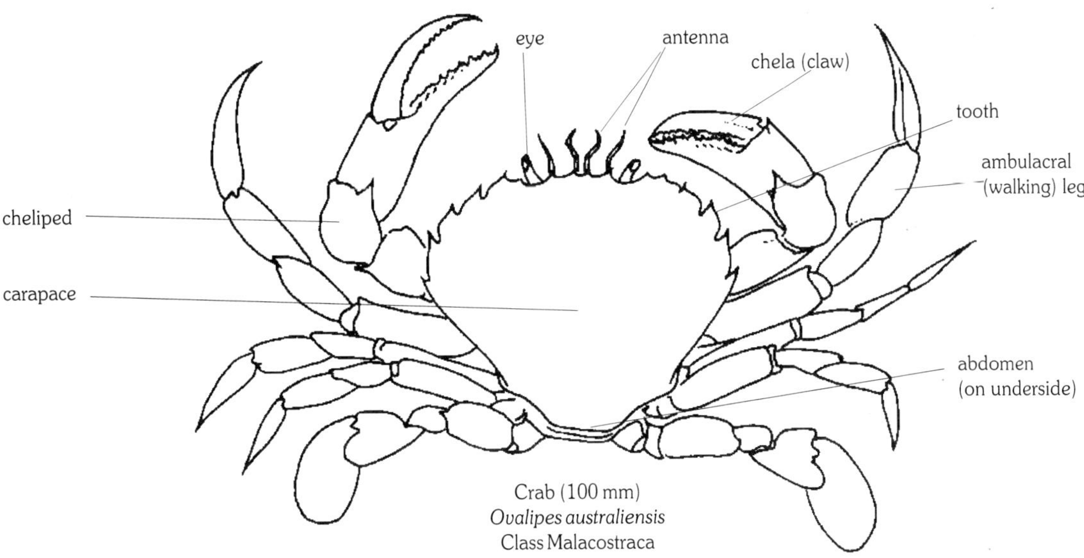

Crab (100 mm)
Ovalipes australiensis
Class Malacostraca

The class Malacostraca includes most of the familiar crustaceans, such as lobsters, crabs, shrimps, slaters and sand-hoppers. These groups all have the same body plan: a head made up of six fused segments, a thorax with eight segments, and an abdomen with six or seven segments plus a terminal process, the telson. They generally have forked first antennae, flattened limbs under the abdomen (the pleopods) and paired compound eyes, which may be stalked or attached directly to the head. The openings of the male and female genital ducts are on the eighth and sixth thoracic segments, respectively.

Order Nebaliacea

Nebaliaceans, leptostracans

Nebaliaceans differ from other malacostracans by having seven rather than six segments in the abdomen. They can also be recognised by the presence of long second antennae, stalked eyes and a large carapace that enfolds the thorax and first few segments of the abdomen. Although numerous fossil forms have been scientifically named, fewer than 20 living species are known.

Nebalia sp.

Habitat: Marine plants, sand, silt; 0–15 m depth.
Distribution: WA to Vic. and around Tas.
Maximum size: Body length to 5 mm.

This very common nebaliacean has bright red eyes and flattened thoracic limbs, each with a large outer flap. The second antennae of the male are longer than the body, whereas in females they are comparatively short. The species occurs in great abundance among accumulations of decaying plant material on the seabed.

Nebalia sp., Tinderbox, Tas.

Order Stomatopoda

Mantis shrimps, prawn killers

Stomatopods are among the most distinctive of crustaceans, as the second thoracic segment bears large inward-folding claws that are either spined (as in a preying mantis) or hammer-like. They are further distinguished by having eyes and first antennae attached to separate movable segments of the head, filamentous gills attached to the limbs under the abdomen, and a carapace that covers but is not attached to most of the thorax. All species are predatory, using spined claws to spear or hammer-like claws to stun prey. Most live in burrows they construct themselves in soft sediments.

Like the rock lobsters, the larval stages of stomatopods are long and complex. Females generally carry the eggs or lay them in the burrow, and the newly hatched larva is bottom-dwelling. After one or two moults, the larva commences a planktonic existence and looks quite different from the adult. This 'alima' stage, so named because the larva of one species was mistakenly given the genus name *Alima*, is usually slender, with a long spine projecting from the head and two spines from the rear corners of the carapace. After several months at sea, the alima metamorphoses during a moult into the typical burrowing adult form.

Squilla laevis, Rottnest I, WA. Clay Bryce

Squilla laevis (Hess, 1865)

Habitat: Sheltered sand, silt; 0–20 m depth.
Distribution: WA to NSW and around Tas.
Maximum size: Body length to 120 mm.

Lysiosquilla perpasta, Cloudy Lagoon, Tas.

Squilla laevis is one of two large stomatopods occasionally seen by divers at night or taken by dredge along southern coasts. It has six spines on the last segment of the large claw and three large spines on each side margin of the telson. The other species, ***Squilla miles***, has a telson with about eight small spines on each side.

Lysiosquilla perpasta Hale, 1924

Habitat: Sand; 0–20 m depth.
Distribution: SA, Vic. and around Tas.
Maximum size: Body length to 35 mm.

Lysiosquilla perpasta is a small sand-coloured stomatopod with numerous speckles over the body surface. Judging by the density of vertical stomatopod burrows in sand, this species is extremely abundant in southeastern waters. However, because it rarely comes to the surface, few animals are seen or captured.

Order Cumacea

Cumaceans

Cumaceans are tadpole-shaped crustaceans with a long, narrow abdomen, reduced eyes merged together, and a carapace that is fused with the first three or four thoracic segments. The carapace curls around the thorax, forming a respiratory chamber on each side, and females have a brood chamber underneath. Females can usually be distinguished from males because they lack pleopods, the small paired limbs under the abdomen. As in the next four orders, which are classed together as 'peracarids', juveniles develop directly from eggs hatched in the brood chamber and have the same body form as the adult.

Cumaceans are small (most 2–5 mm) and inhabit marine or estuarine habitats. Nearly all are adapted for living near the surface of sediment, although a number of species with short spines (family Nannastacidae) are associated with seaweeds in southern Australia. On particular nights, large numbers of males in reproductive condition swim near the water surface.

Order Tanaidacea
Tanaids

The carapace of tanaids is small and covers the first two thoracic segments. Tanaids have seven thoracic limbs, with the first pair (the chelipeds) usually large and clawed. The abdomen generally has five segments, although some or all of these can be fused, plus a flattened terminal segment (the pleotelson) with two long filaments (the uropods) at the rear. Tanaids are usually 2–5 mm long and therefore in the mid-range of sizes for crustaceans.

Tanaids are divided into two groups of about equal importance. The tanaidomorph tanaids have cylindrical bodies, an undivided first antennae and a single, cone-shaped genital opening between the hind legs of males. Nearly all species in this group live on the surface of reefs or among marine plants and are extremely abundant there. The males often have extremely long, claw-like chelipeds and a quite different appearance from the females.

The second group of tanaids, the apseudomorphs, have flattened bodies, first antennae almost always forked and, in males, a pair of genital openings near the bases of the hind legs. Apseudomorphs generally live in soft sediments and will be found in nearly all samples collected there. They are the dominant macroscopic animals on mudflats in some Australian estuaries and can reach densities well in excess of 5000 per square metre.

Cumacean (*Leptocuma* sp.), Dongara, WA

Apseudes sp.

Habitat: Sheltered reef, seaweed; 0–10 m depth.
Distribution: Vic. and eastern Tas.
Maximum size: Length to 5 mm.

Apseudes sp. has a solid, cream body with large, branched first antennae and five abdominal segments, which are extremely hairy. This is one of the largest local species of apseudomorph tanaids and also among the most abundant.

Zeuxo sp.

Habitat: Seaweed on sheltered reefs; 0–7 m depth.
Distribution: Vic. and eastern Tas.
Maximum size: Length to 5 mm.

Zeuxo sp. is one of a number of tanaidomorph tanaids in the genus *Zeuxo* that have brown blotches on the body and are distinguished by the shape of their mouthparts. These species are extremely abundant among seaweeds on sheltered reefs, with hundreds often occurring on a single plant.

Apseudes sp., Tinderbox, Tas.

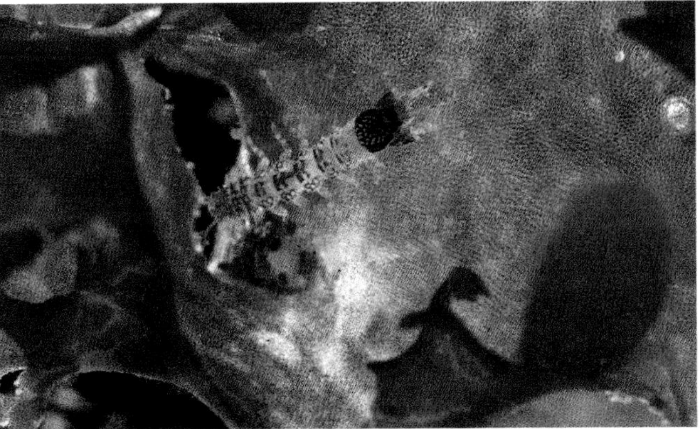

Zeuxo sp., Sandy Bay, Tas.

Order Mysidacea

Mysids, opossum shrimps

Mysids are moderately-sized crustaceans with a carapace that extends over most of the thorax but fuses with only the first three or four segments. Although superficially looking like shrimps, they are easily distinguished because of two rounded structures used for balance (the statocysts) that are prominently placed at the base of the uropods, the flattened appendages projecting from the tail. They also have first antennae that are branched into two, and second antennae with a large leaf-like projection near the base.

Mysids are generally found in swarms living just above the seabed and are often mistaken by divers for schools of juvenile fish. The largest aggregations tend to occur over pockets of sand on reefs, but swarms are also common in a range of other habitats. Many mysid species feed on fine particles produced by the decomposition of kelps and seagrasses. They are therefore an important link between the sea-floor and open-water food webs, as they are in turn eaten in large numbers by pelagic fishes.

Paramesodopsis rufa Fenton, 1985

Habitat: Moderately exposed reef, sand; 0–12 m depth.
Distribution: Vic. and around Tas.
Maximum size: Length to 14 mm.

Paramesodopsis rufa is a slender, orange mysid with very large eyes and a short, rounded projection between their eyes (the rostrum) that does not cover the eyestalks. The species is extremely abundant on sand at the edge of reef. It feeds mainly on small crustaceans but also ingests some plant material.

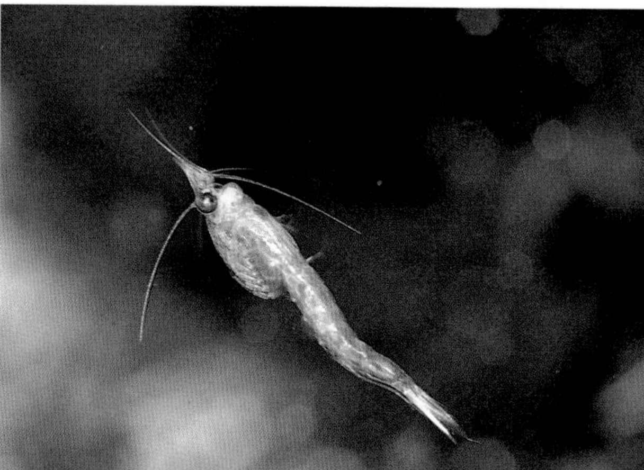

Paramesodopsis rufa, Portsea, Vic. Rudie Kuiter

School of mysids, Frankston, Vic. Rudie Kuiter

Mysidetes halope, Ile des Phoques, Tas.

Mysidetes halope O'Brien, 1986

Habitat: Exposed reef; 5–30 m depth.
Distribution: Southern and eastern Tas.
Maximum size: Length to 25 mm.

Mysidetes halope is a red mysid with extremely large eyes and a short rostrum that does not overlap the eyes. This mysid has an unusual habitat because it lives deep in the back of seacaves where there is virtually no visible light. Other species in this genus occur in deep water.

Order Isopoda

Isopods, slaters, pill bugs

Isopods are a large group of crustaceans that lack a carapace and have the first and occasionally second segments of the thorax fused to the head. Other features are gills associated with the abdominal pleopods (limbs), the first pair of antennae not being forked and the first two pairs of legs not often ending in claws. Although one suborder of freshwater species (the Phreatoicidea) is flattened from side to side, isopods can usually be distinguished from the closely related amphipods because they are nearly all flattened from top to bottom.

Isopods are more often noticed than other peracarids (i.e. Cumacea, Tanaidacea, Mysidacea and Amphipoda) because of their greater average size (2–20 mm). Their basic body plan is extremely adaptable, enabling them to inhabit an unusually large range of habitats. Numerous species are found in fresh water, among leaf litter on land, as parasites of fishes and crustaceans, and as borers in wood, as well as on the sea floor where they reach their greatest diversity. The order is subdivided into nine suborders, which include the freshwater Phreatoicidea and the terrestrial Oniscidea (slaters and woodlice). The largest suborder is the Flabellifera, a group of marine crustaceans generally with oval bodies and a tailfan made up of a central triangular telson with two pairs of side appendages, the uropods. This suborder contains marine pill bugs, fish parasites and scavenging species which quickly congregate on dead animal material and are commonly known as 'sea lice'. The Valvifera are another large group, distinguished by the presence of two valve-like uropods that can shut to enclose the respiratory appendages under the abdomen. Large, green valviferans known as sea-centipedes are occasionally seen in seagrass beds and among seaweeds. The suborder Asellota consists of actively moving species that have narrow uropods at the rear of the abdomen instead of at the sides. Other important suborders are the Epicaridea, soft and highly distorted crustaceans that live parasitically on decapod crustaceans, and the Anthuridea, a group of long, cylindrical animals with short antennae and clawed first legs, which can occur in high densities in sediments and among seaweeds.

Zuzara venosa (Stebbing, 1876)

Habitat: Under rocks; 0–5 m depth.
Distribution: SA to Vic. and around Tas.
Maximum size: Length to 20 mm.

Zuzara venosa is a distinctive flabelliferan isopod; the uropods are very large, and in males the last thoracic segment is greatly extended in a central process. The species occurs in high densities under rocks in shallow water.

Zuzara venosa, Flinders, Vic. RUDIE KUITER

Euidotea bakeri Collinge, 1917

Habitat: Moderately exposed seagrass, seaweed, reef; 0–17 m depth.
Distribution: Onslow, WA, to Montague I, NSW, and around Tas.
Maximum size: Length to 23 mm.

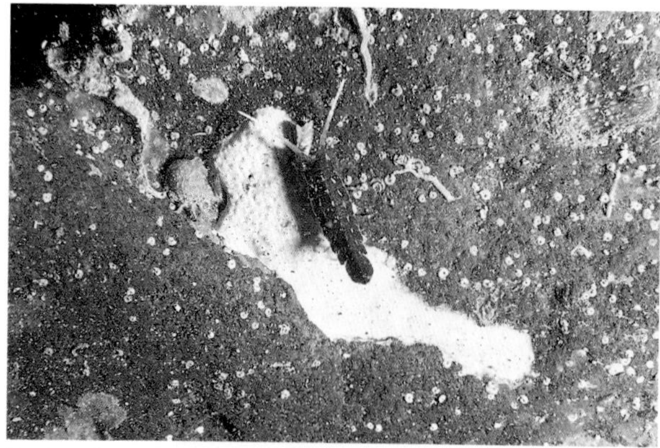
Euidotea bakeri, Cape Portland, Tas.

Euidotea bakeri is a relatively short and squat member of the valviferan family Idoteidae, with stout second antennae and a ridge along the back. It occurs abundantly in a variety of different habitats but is most often found in seagrass beds and under rocks on reefs.

Paridotea ungulata Pallas, 1772
Sharp-tailed sea centipede

Habitat: Sheltered seagrass, seaweed; 0–3 m depth.
Distribution: Spencer Gulf, SA, to Nadgee Reserve, NSW, and around Tas. Also New Zealand, South Africa and South America.
Maximum size: Body length to 43 mm.

Paridotea ungulata is a relatively large isopod with green or brown body that varies with the colour of the host plant. It differs from a closely related species, ***Paridotea munda***, by having sharp tips rather than rounded processes at the end of the last body segment (the pleotelson). This species is extremely abundant among green seaweeds such as sea lettuce (*Ulva* sp.) and seagrasses, and is sometimes noticed by waders because of its swimming ability. The animal holds the long second antennae together in front of the head when swimming from plant to plant.

Paridotea ungulata, Cloudy Lagoon, Tas.

Ligia australiensis (Dana, 1853)

Habitat: Under rocks; high intertidal.
Distribution: Southern WA to NSW and around Tas.
Maximum size: Length to 13 mm.

Ligia australiensis has a flattened, oval body with two large eyes and long antennae. The species is extremely abundant near high-tide level, where it is found under rocks and in crevices during the day. Animals run quickly for the nearest shelter if rocks are overturned. A related species, ***Ligia exotica***, has been introduced into Australia and now occurs at very high densities on the shores of the Hawkesbury estuary at Bobbin Head, NSW. *L. exotica* has acute projections extending backward from the sides of the last segment. Its full distribution in this country is not known.

Ligia australiensis, Bicheno, Tas.

Order Amphipoda
Amphipods, beach hoppers

The Amphipoda is a very large order containing about 8000 named species and many times that number of undescribed forms. They are moderately sized (usually 1–5 mm) and similar to the isopods in having the first and sometimes second thoracic segments fused with the head. They usually differ from isopods by having a body flattened from side to side, by having small gills attached to the bases of the thoracic legs and by often having first antennae with a small side branch.

Species in the largest suborder, Gammaridea, typically have two pairs of clawed limbs behind the head, followed by five pairs of walking legs, the first two or three of which have the tips directed backwards. Under the abdomen are three pairs of flattened, forked pleopods for swimming, followed by three pairs of spine-like appendages (the uropods). A small leaf-like telson is attached to the top of the last segment. Gammaridean amphipods are rarely noticed but are the dominant macroscopic group living on reef surfaces. More than 50 species can occur associated with individual seaweeds or clumps of bryozoans. About 20 families are also adapted for living in sediments. Gammarideans are consumed in great quantities by larger animals and are the dominant component in the diets of small (0.1 to 100 g) inshore fishes.

After the gammarideans, the next largest suborder of amphipods, Caprellidea, contains the skeleton shrimps and whale lice. Skeleton shrimps are elongate animals with a large pair of claws held in a praying mantis-like fashion; legs are often lacking from the thoracic segments, leaving the gills prominently exposed. Skeleton shrimps seasonally occur in huge numbers on branched seaweeds in shallow water, with several thousand animals sometimes occurring on a single plant. The whale lice have a short, flat body with strong claws on the ends of the legs. They occur parasitically attached to the skin of whales and dolphins, particularly on the head of the host.

The other two suborders of amphipods are the Hyperiidea, a group of planktonic crustaceans that feed on salps and jellyfish and have large rounded heads with huge eyes, and the Ingolfiellidea, a group of minute worm-like crustaceans that live among sand grains.

Caprella species

Habitat: Reef; 0–100 m depth.
Maximum size: Length to 20 mm.

This is by far the largest genus of caprellid amphipods, with more than 150 species known worldwide and at least 20 species present in southern Australian waters. It is characterised by the head being fused with the first abdominal segment, large claws on the next segment, gills but no legs on the next two segments, followed by three segments with six-articulated legs. Species of *Caprella* commonly occur in huge numbers on algae.

Caprella sp.1. Rudie Kuiter

Caprella acanthogaster with numerous small ischyrocerid amphipods, Maria I, Tas.

Amaryllis sp.

Habitat: Moderately exposed reef; 2–15 m depth.
Distribution: Vic. to NSW and northeastern Tas.
Maximum size: Length to 6 mm.

Amaryllis sp. is a distinctive red gammaridean amphipod with a yellow stripe down the back and white lines along the margins of the segments. The species is occasionally noticed by divers moving over sponges and other sessile animals on reefs. This is the most famous of all amphipods, as it is the only one to have been featured on a postage stamp.

Amaryllis sp., Montague I, NSW. Alison Kuiter

Talorchestia sp.

Habitat: Exposed beach; high intertidal.
Distribution: Vic. and around Tas.
Maximum size: Length to 15 mm.

Talorchestia sp. belongs to a family of gammaridean amphipods (Talitridae) adapted for living in moist conditions on land and which move about by hopping. Species in the family are somewhat unusual in having the first pair of antennae generally much shorter than the second. *Talorchestia* sp. occurs in sand at the high-tide level and is rapidly attracted to any drift seaweed in order to feed. Surprisingly high numbers can be found by turning over rotting kelp, particularly at night.

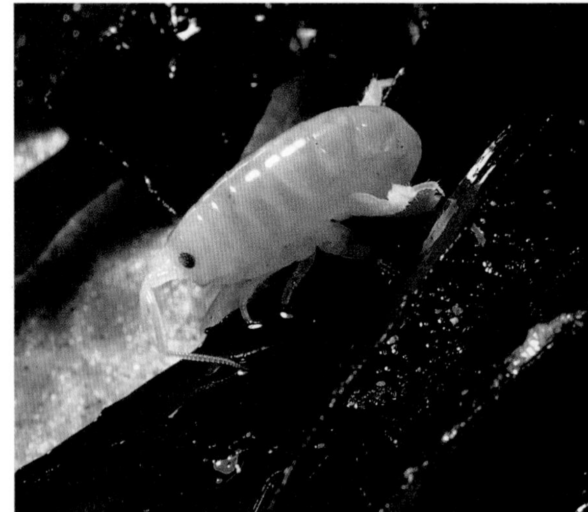

Talorchestia sp., Bicheno, Tas.

Ampithoe sp.

Habitat: Seaweeds, sessile animals; 0–8 m.
Distribution: NSW.
Maximum size: Length to 10 mm.

Many of the most common large gammaridean amphipods living among seaweeds belong to the family Ampithoidae, a group that includes *Ampithoe* sp. and is characterised by the presence of two minute pairs of hooks at the end of the body. Virtually none of the local species in this family have been scientifically named. Many ampithoids consume the larger brown algae and are in turn an important food source for fishes.

Ampithoe sp., Clovelly, NSW

Ceradocus serratus Bate, 1862

Habitat: Under rocks; 0–16 m.
Distribution: Port Phillip Bay, Vic., to Sydney, NSW, and around Tas.
Maximum size: Length to 14 mm.

Ceradocus serratus is characterised by the arrangement of spines around the segments towards the end of the body and a very short basal segment on the second antennae. Like most other members of the family Melitidae, it also has a short branch on the first antennae and long, easily broken projections (third uropods) on the last body segment. This species is often noticed briefly by divers when rocks are overturned.

Austropheonoides sp. (family Amphilochidae), Waterfall Bay, Tas.

Ceradocus serratus, Ricketts Pt, Vic. Rudie Kuiter

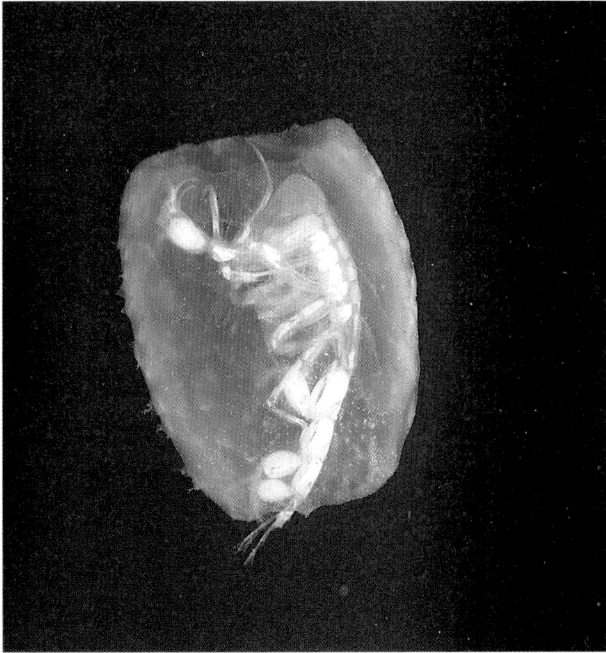

Hyperiid amphipod. Rudie Kuiter

Order Euphausiacea

Krill, euphausiids

Euphausiids are an exclusively marine group of crustaceans that resemble mysids (order Mysidacea) and shrimps (order Decapoda). They have a carapace that fuses all thoracic segments with the head but leaves the gills exposed. The first six pairs of thoracic limbs are similar in structure, except in a few species that have one pair greatly enlarged. Branched gills are situated at the bases of thoracic segments, while luminous organs (the photophores) are located on the second and seventh thoracic segments and the first few abdominal segments. The abdomen has five pairs of hairy pleopods, which are used for swimming. Euphausiids lack the balancing organs that typify the mysids, and they have a nauplius as the first larval stage.

Many species of euphausiid congregate in large swarms near the ocean surface. These swarms of 'krill' attract large carnivorous animals, particularly in southern waters, and are the most important food source for many whales, seals, pelagic fishes and sea birds. The largest krill species, the Antarctic *Euphausia superba*, is also netted for human and livestock consumption. Catches of this species are increasing and now exceed 300 000 tonnes per year, possibly removing a substantial proportion of the food available to their natural predators. Most euphausiids feed on small phytoplankton, which they capture using a dense comb of hair located along the thoracic legs.

Nyctiphanes australis Sars, 1885

Habitat: Coastal waters; 0–400 m depth.
Distribution: Great Australian Bight, SA, to northern NSW and around Tas. Also New Zealand.
Maximum size: Length to 16 mm.

Nyctiphanes australis is a small species of krill with seven thoracic limbs and a short recurved process at the end of the first segment of the antennule (first antennae). It occurs in very large swarms off the southeastern Australian coast and during spring and summer provides most of the total quantity of planktonic crustaceans off southeastern Tasmania. Animals grow rapidly through several larval stages, reaching maturity at about three months and rarely living for longer than one year. Unlike most other euphausiids, this species is found in inshore rather than oceanic waters and feeds on small organic particles associated with the seabed. It is itself an important component in the diets of jack mackerel, barracouta, tuna and muttonbirds. Large swarms occasionally become stranded ashore in sheltered coastal bays.

Nyctiphanes australis, Portsea, Vic. RUDIE KUITER

Order Decapoda

Decapods (prawns, shrimps, lobsters, crabs)

Decapods are so named because the five rear pairs of thoracic limbs are generally enlarged and used as walking legs (Greek *deka* meaning 'ten', and *pous* 'foot'), whereas the first three pairs of thoracic limbs are highly modified as mouthparts. Decapods are also characterised by a large carapace that fuses the head and thorax and forms an extensive cavity around the sides of the body. Enclosed within this cavity are usually seven rows of complexly branched gills. These are aerated by a flow of water propelled by the beating of flaps on one of the pairs of mouthparts (the maxillae). The evolution of an extensive gill system has enabled species in the order to reach a larger size than other crustacean groups.

FAMILY PENAEIDAE

Prawns, shrimps

Penaeids are commonly known as prawns in Australia but are called shrimps in most other parts of the world. They can be distinguished from other families of shrimps by having claws on the first three pairs of walking legs and a second abdominal segment that is overlapped by the first. Unlike the other major group of shrimps, the carids (which includes the five families, listed below), eggs are released by the female rather than carried under the body.

Penaeus plebejus Hess, 1885

Eastern king prawn

Habitat: Sand, silt; 0–220 m depth.
Distribution: Lakes Entrance, Vic., to North Reef, Qld, and south to Georges Bay, Tas.
Maximum size: Length to 300 mm.

Penaeus plebejus is one of several prawns found along the eastern coast. It is a grooved prawn, with a distinctive groove running alongside the rostrum to the rear of the carapace. The species also has 10–11 teeth on the upper and 1 tooth on the lower surface of the rostrum, and the pleopods and outer edge of the tail are blue. Eastern king prawns migrate from coastal waters into estuaries as planktonic post-larvae. They then grow rapidly over the next 9–12 months, before migrating into offshore waters where they spawn. This is the most important commercial species of prawn in New South Wales.

Penaeus plebejus, Church Pt, NSW

Penaeus latisulcatus Kishinouye, 1896

Western king prawn

Habitat: Sand, silt; 0–90 m depth.
Distribution: Tropical Australia south to Gulf St Vincent, SA, and Ballina, NSW. Also widespread in the Indo-West Pacific region.
Maximum size: Length to 200 mm.

Penaeus latisulcatus is a large grooved prawn that resembles *P. plebejus* and is common on the western seaboard. It can be distinguished from the eastern species by the lack of black speckling and the narrower markings on the lower sides of the abdomen. The western king prawn occurs abundantly in the South Australian gulfs, near Perth and in Shark Bay. The largest animals are about four years old.

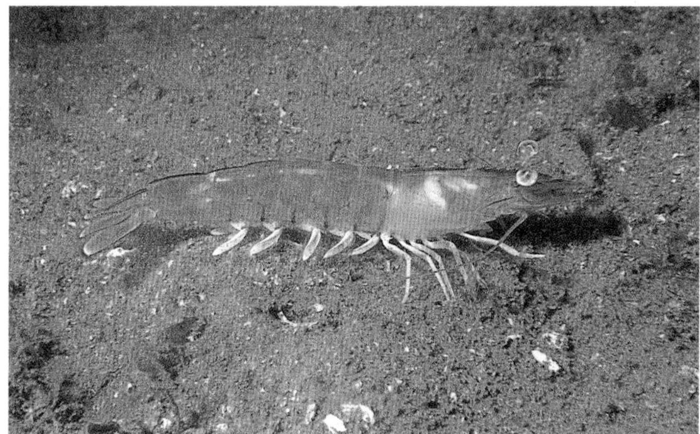

Penaeus latisulcatus, Bicton, WA

Metapenaeus dalli Racek, 1957

Western school prawn

Habitat: Sheltered sand, silt; 0–33 m depth.
Distribution: Darwin, NT, to Mandurah, WA. Also Indonesia.
Maximum size: Length to 85 mm.

Metapenaeus dalli, Bicton, WA

Metapenaeus dalli is a relatively small prawn, with the groove along the upper carapace stopping at the last tooth. Two closely related species, the eastern school prawn ***Metapenaeus macleayi*** and the greentail prawn ***Metapenaeus bennettae***, extend from eastern Victoria to Hervey Bay in eastern Australia. The eastern school prawn can be recognised by four pairs of conspicuous spines on the side of the central triangular telson in the tail, and the greentail prawn by numerous patches of fine hairs on the abdomen and green tips to the tail. All three species are common in shallow water in estuaries and generally prefer a soft, muddy bottom.

FAMILY PALAEMONIDAE

Palaemonid shrimps

This and the following four families are grouped together as carid shrimps. Carids have pincers on the first two pairs of legs (but not the third), a second abdominal segment that overlaps the first, and eggs carried under the abdomen. Palaemonids are further distinguished by having the second pair of chelipeds (legs with nippers) usually considerably larger than the first, and by the normal complement of six segments in the second pair of legs.

Macrobrachium intermedium, Merimbula, NSW

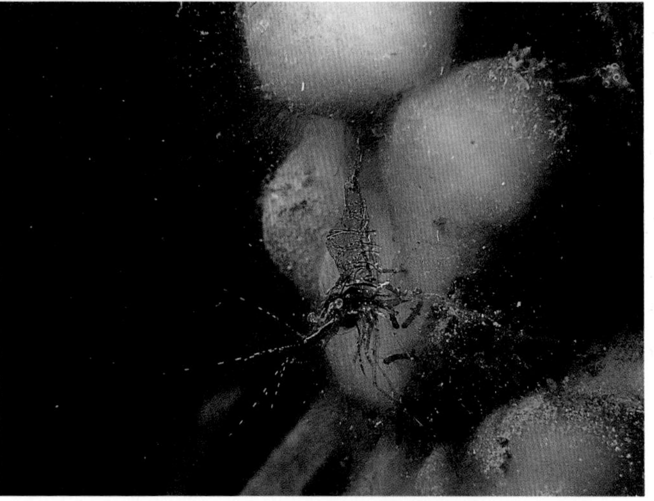

Macrobrachium intermedium

(Stimpson, 1860)

Habitat: Sheltered seagrass, reef; 0–17 m depth.
Distribution: Perth, WA, to Port Molle, Qld, and around Tas.
Maximum size: Length to 60 mm.

Macrobrachium intermedium is distinguished by a short spine below the eye and a second spine lower down, its tip just reaching the front carapace edge. The body is transparent with dark red spots on the upper surface and thin stripes below. This shrimp occurs in very high densities in coastal and estuarine seagrass beds and also among seaweeds on sheltered reefs.

Macrobrachium sp.

Habitat: Sheltered seagrass, reef; 0–17 m depth.
Distribution: Gulf St Vincent, SA, to eastern Vic. and around Tas.
Maximum size: Length to 60 mm.

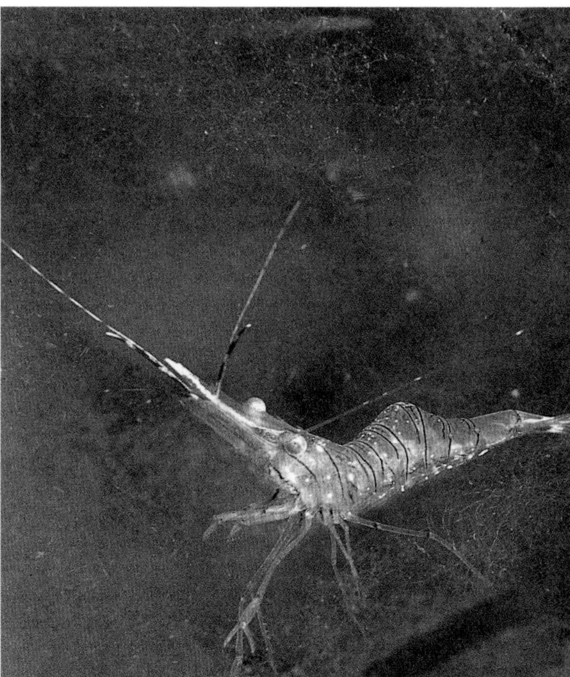

Macrobrachium sp., Cloudy Lagoon, Tas.

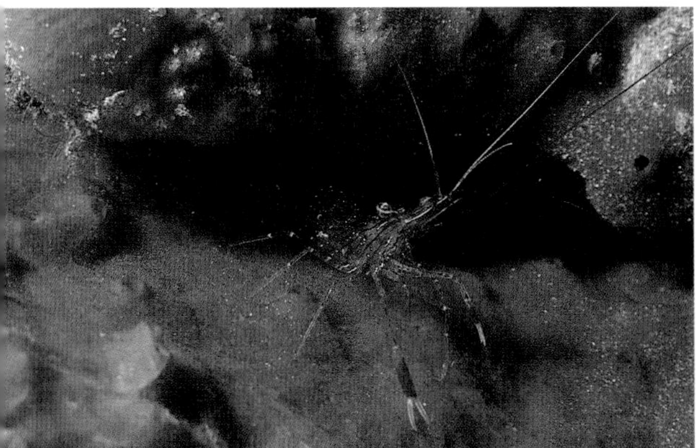

Palaemon serenus, Cloudy Lagoon, Tas.

This *Macrobrachium* species resembles *M. intermedium* and until recently was confused with it but differs by having the tip of the lower spine below the eye falling well short of the front edge of the carapace. Also, the dark stripes extend around the abdomen rather than being confined to the lower body. *Macrobrachium* sp. is abundant in estuaries and prefers slightly less-saline conditions than *M. intermedium*, although in many areas the two species overlap.

Palaemon serenus (Heller, 1868)

Habitat: Sheltered and moderately exposed reef; 0–15 m depth.
Distribution: SA to NSW and around Tas.
Maximum size: Length to 60 mm.

Palaemon serenus is a transparent shrimp when alive, with oblique red lines on the carapace and flecks of red over the abdomen. The second pair of legs are long and have an obvious red collar on the claws. This species can be found sheltering in large numbers in cracks between rocks on coastal reefs.

FAMILY RHYNCHOCINETIDAE
Hinge-back shrimps

The hinge-back shrimps are so named because they possess an articulated rostrum that can be moved up and down independently of the head. Nearly all species live in recesses in the reef and are brightly coloured. The local species have two teeth on the top of the carapace behind the articulation of the rostrum.

Rhynchocinetes rugulosus (Stimpson, 1860)

Habitat: Reef; 0–20 m depth.
Distribution: Central Vic. to northern NSW and northeastern Tas.
Maximum size: Length to 60 mm.

Rhynchocinetes rugulosus has a complex pattern of spots and bands along the back and prominent bands on the legs. This shrimp occurs abundantly in crevices on exposed reefs in New South Wales and is commonly seen by divers at night.

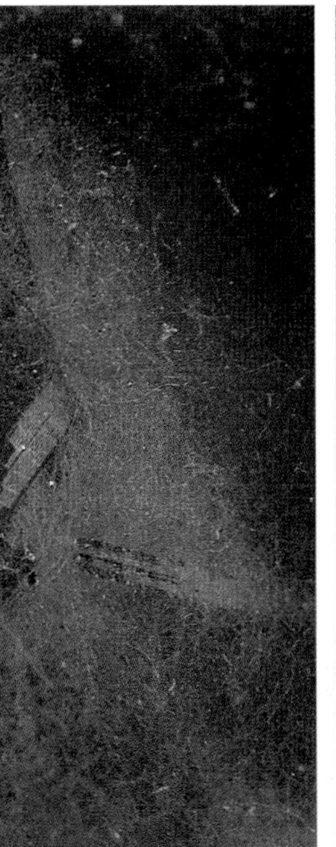

Rhynchocinetes rugulosus, Terrigal, NSW

Rhynchocinetes australis Hale, 1941

Habitat: Reef; 4–22 m depth.
Distribution: Esperance, WA, to central Vic. and northern Tas.
Maximum size: Length to 60 mm.

Rhynchocinetes australis is the close relative of *R. rugulosus* found in southern waters. It differs structurally from *R. rugulosus* by lacking a gill at the base of the third walking leg (present on the first two) but is more easily recognised by having stripes rather than bands on the upper segments of the legs. Southern hinge-back shrimps nevertheless exhibit a range of different colour patterns, and it is therefore possible that several species are involved.

Rhynchocinetes australis, Rocky Cape, Tas.

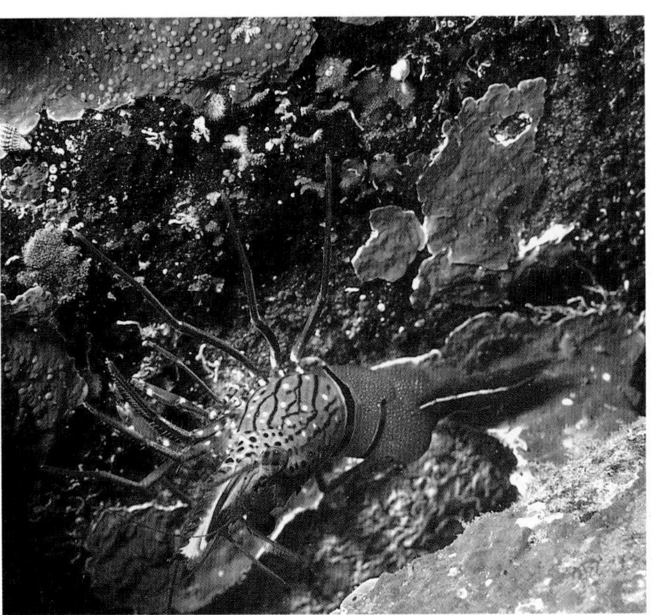

Rhynchocinetes kuiteri, Adventure Bay, Tas.

Rhynchocinetes kuiteri Tiefenbacher, 1983

Habitat: Exposed reef; 4–35 m depth.
Distribution: Portsea to Wilsons Promontory, Vic., and around Tas.
Maximum size: Length to 50 mm.

Rhynchocinetes kuiteri is patterned quite differently from the other local *Rhynchocinetes* species, as two bands cross the abdomen and stripes are present down the last segments before the tail. This species is generally found on deep exposed reefs, where it remains hidden in cracks in the rock during the day.

FAMILY HIPPOLYTIDAE
Hippolytid shrimps

Species of hippolytid shrimp often have a hump-backed appearance because of a pronounced bend in the abdomen at the rear of the third segment. The wrist of the second pair of legs is subdivided into additional segments, making these limbs appear to have more than the six segments typical of decapods.

Hippolyte australiensis (Stimpson, 1860)

Habitat: Seaweed on exposed reef; 0–15 m depth.
Distribution: Perth, WA, to NSW and around Tas.
Maximum size: Length to 38 mm.

Hippolyte australiensis is a small shrimp with a smooth upper edge to the rostrum and two notches underneath. The species lives in association with tufted algae and usually takes on the red or green colour of the host plant. It occurs in great abundance around the southeastern coast. A related species with three spines on the upper edge of the rostrum and

Hippolyte australiensis, Blackmans Bay, Tas.

often with tufts of hairs on the back, *Hippolyte caradina*, is equally common among marine plants in sheltered habitats.

Alope australiensis (Baker, 1907)

Habitat: Exposed reef; 0–2 m depth.
Distribution: St Francis I, SA, to NSW.
Maximum size: Length to 27 mm.

Alope australiensis can be recognised by the very long last pair of mouthparts, which project forward and resemble legs. Its body is a transparent greenish colour with red spots and red banding on the legs. This species is abundant in rockpools near low-tide level along the New South Wales coast.

Tozeuma kimberi (Baker, 1904)

Habitat: Seagrass; 0–6 m depth.
Distribution: SA and Vic.
Maximum size: Length to 45 mm.

Tozeuma kimberi is an unusual shrimp with a long rostrum, which is cut into numerous teeth on the underside. The most obvious feature is a black spot resembling an eye on the fifth abdominal segment. This shrimp lives attached to seagrass but is uncommon, and so its habits are little known.

Alope australis, Ulladulla, NSW

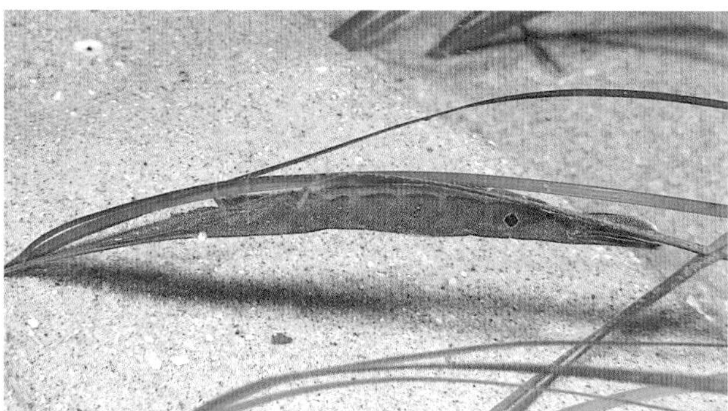

Tozeuma kimberi, Flinders, Vic. RUDIE KUITER

FAMILY ALPHEIDAE
Snapping shrimps, pistol shrimps

Alpheid shrimps have a relatively large first pair of legs; both legs are usually massive, but one side is much larger than the other. The largest claw often has a small peg on the last segment which produces a loud click as it slots into a socket when the claw is snapped shut. This is thought to have a twofold purpose: the force of the clicking action stuns nearby animals, while the sound can be used to signal potential competitors and mates.

Alpheus novaezealandiae, D'Entrecasteaux Channel, Tas.

Alpheus novaezealandiae Miers, 1876

Habitat: Sheltered and moderately exposed reef; 0–26 m depth.
Distribution: Around mainland Australia and Tas. Also Lord Howe I. and New Zealand.
Maximum size: Length to 70 mm.

Alpheus novaezealandiae is dark purple with white markings on the sides. The nippers on both the snapping and grasping chelipeds are very long in comparison with those of other species. This shrimp commonly occurs under rocks and among sponges, ascidians and other attached animals.

Alpheus euphrosyne Miers, 1876

Habitat: Sheltered mud, seagrass, reef; 0–24 m depth.
Distribution: Around mainland Australia and Tas. Also New Zealand, Indonesia and Thailand.
Maximum size: Length to 60 mm.

Alpheus euphrosyne can usually be recognised by its green coloration and fine red speckles over the body. This is by far the most abundant shallow-water alpheid shrimp in southern Australia, particularly at muddy locations, where it lives in burrows or under rocks.

Alpheus euphrosyne, Ricketts Pt, Vic.

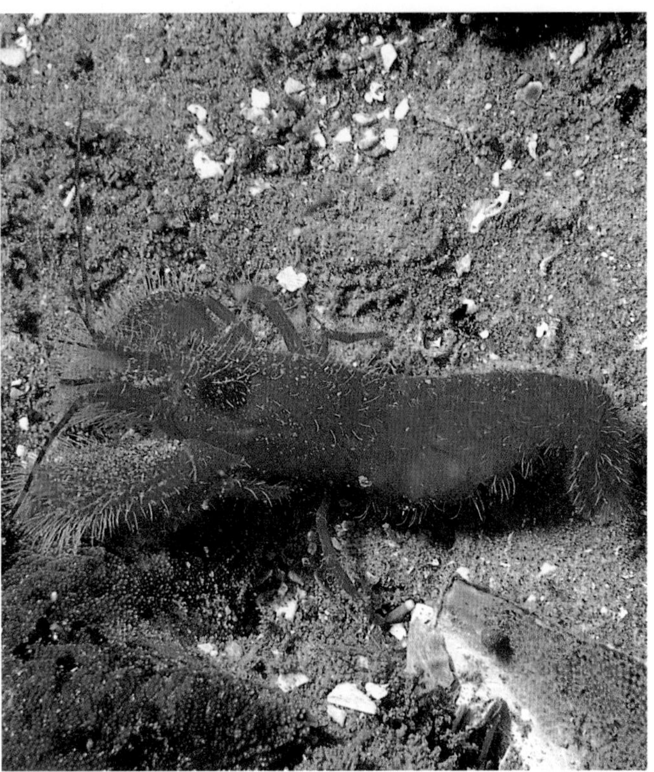

Alpheus villosus, Ricketts Pt, Vic.

Alpheus villosus Miers, 1876

Habitat: Sheltered reef; 0–45 m depth.
Distribution: Perth, WA, to Eden, NSW, and northern Australia. Also South Africa, Philippines and Mauritius.
Maximum size: Length to 60 mm.

Alpheus villosus is a distinctive, bright orange shrimp with numerous hairs on the body and reduced eyes. The species occurs in Australia in two forms, a tropical form associated with corals and a temperate form associated with the underside of rocks. Neither form is recorded from the east coast between Eden and Torres Strait.

FAMILY PANDALIDAE
Pandalid shrimps

In this family of carid shrimps, the first pair of legs is slender and often lacks claws. The second pair is also slender and, like the hippolytids and alpheids (described above), has the wrist subdivided into additional segments. Included in this family are a number of deepwater species that have recently been exploited and marketed as 'royal red prawns'.

Chlorotocella leptorhynchus (Stimpson, 1860)

Habitat: Sheltered seagrass, seaweed; 0–10 m depth.
Distribution: Albany, WA, to Vic. and around Tas.
Maximum size: Length to 25 mm.

Chlorotocella leptorhynchus is a slender, semi-transparent species with a very long rostrum and a red stripe under the body. It locally occurs in very high abundances, which can exceed a hundred animals per square metre in seagrass and macroalgal beds.

Chlorotocella leptorhynchus, Bathurst Channel, Tas.

FAMILY STENOPODIDAE
Cleaner shrimps

This family is characterised by the third pair of legs being much larger than the first two and all three pairs having pincers at the end. They also have the second abdominal segment overlapped by the first. Many stenopids pick parasites off the backs and mouths of visiting fishes at permanent 'cleaner stations'.

Stenopus hispidis (Olivier, 1811)
Banded cleaner shrimp

Habitat: Exposed reef; 0–25 m depth.
Distribution: Tropical Australia south to Rottnest I, WA, and southern NSW. Also widespread in the Indo-West Pacific region.
Maximum size: Length to 90 mm.

Stenopus hispidis is a slender shrimp that is easily recognised by the red and white banding pattern extending along the body and long third legs. Females pair with smaller males to set up cleaner stations at the entrances to caves and crevices. The species is very common on tropical coral reefs and moderately common along the central New South Wales coast.

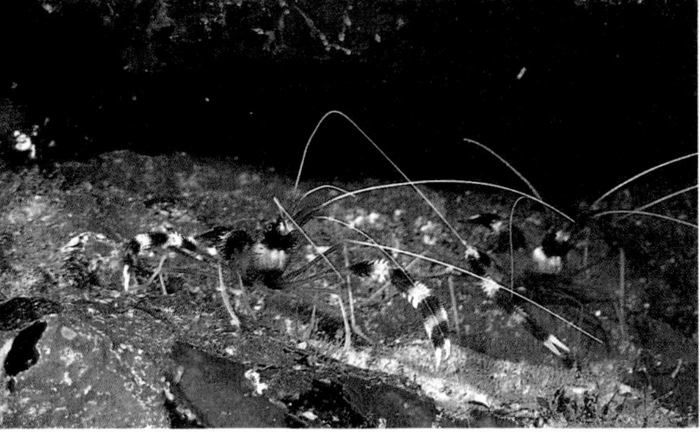
Stenopus hispidis, Montague I., NSW. RUDIE KUITER

FAMILY PALINURIDAE
Rock lobsters, spiny lobsters, crayfish, langouste

Rock lobsters differ from true lobsters by lacking pincers on the first pair of walking legs. They have cylindrical bodies, a moderately long pair of first antennae (antennules) and an extremely long pair of second antennae. As with all the following crustacean families, the pleopods (flattened limbs) under the abdomen are reduced in size and used for carrying eggs rather than for swimming or respiration. Members of this family and the Scyllaridae have an extremely long-lived transparent larvae of an unusual flattened shape with long legs. This 'phyllosoma' stage floats offshore in the near-surface plankton and moults approximately 11 times before transforming into a settlement stage resembling the adult.

Panulirus cygnus George, 1962
Western rock lobster

Habitat: Exposed reef, seagrass; 0–180 m depth.
Distribution: North West Cape to Cape Naturaliste, WA.
Maximum size: Carapace length to 200 mm.

Panulirus cygnus possesses forked antennules between the larger antennae; this allies the species with the tropical rock lobsters, rather than with the southern rock lobsters, which have antennules ending in fine filaments and a knob. The western rock lobster is the most valuable fishery species in Australia, with a total annual catch valued at more than $200 million. Juvenile rock lobsters drift for 9–11 months many hundreds of kilometres offshore among Indian Ocean plankton. They then move shoreward and settle in great abundance on shallow coastal reefs (0–20 m depth), where they forage at night among seaweeds and on adjacent seagrass habitats. Western rock lobsters migrate offshore into deeper water (30–150 m depth) at about five years of age and remain there for up to 20 years, spawning once or twice each year.

Panulirus cygnus, Seven Mile Beach, WA

Jasus edwardsii (Hutton, 1875)
Southern rock lobster, crayfish

Habitat: Exposed reef; 0–200 m depth.
Distribution: Dongara, WA, to Coffs Harbour, NSW, and around Tas. Also New Zealand.
Maximum size: Carapace length to 230 mm.

Jasus edwardsii is distinguished by two long spines ('horns') projecting forward from the front of the carapace beside the eyes. It has an orange-red colour in shallow water, gradually changing to a reddish-purple or lighter colour at depth. This species is extremely important to the South Australian and Tasmanian fishing industries, with a total catch of about 5000 tonnes per year. After a larval stage (thought to last for 8–9 months) the animals settle in large numbers in narrow crevices on shallow reefs. Growth is quite variable between sites, with the largest animals living for more than 20 years. The scientific name of this species has changed in recent times; it was originally classed with the South African species *J. lalandii*, then given its own name *J. novaehollandiae*, and is now regarded as the same as the New Zealand species *J. edwardsii*.

Jasus edwardsii, Tinderbox, Tas.

Jasus verreauxi, Seal Rocks, NSW. RUDIE KUITER

Jasus verreauxi (Milne Edwards, 1834)
Eastern rock lobster

Habitat: Exposed reef; 0–220 m depth.
Distribution: Port MacDonnell, SA, to Tweed Heads, NSW, and northeastern Tas.
Maximum size: Carapace length to 262 mm.

Jasus verreauxi has a short rostral projection between the horns at the front of the carapace, and the abdominal segments are smooth on top. The body is green and the legs red-brown. This rock lobster is moderately common along the New South Wales coast but is not often seen by divers, particularly during the cooler months when most animals migrate offshore. The commercial fishery for this species (about 100 tonnes per year) is very small in comparison with the other two temperate Australian species.

FAMILY SCYLLARIDAE
Shovel-nosed lobsters, slipper lobsters

Scyllarids are closely related to the palinurids (rock lobsters) but have a flattened body and short, wide antennae. Most species in the family are tropical or confined to deep water.

Ibacus alticrenatus, Bermagui, NSW. RUDIE KUITER

Ibacus alticrenatus Bate, 1888
Wollongong bug

Habitat: Sand, mud; 20–500 m depth.
Distribution: Kalbarri, WA, to Newcastle, NSW, and around Tas. Also New Zealand.
Maximum size: Carapace length to 75 mm.

Ibacus alticrenatus is reddish-brown, with yellow hairs covering the surface and a series of teeth diminishing in size down the edges of the carapace. It resembles the Balmain bug ***Ibacus peronii***, a species with much the same Australian distribution, but can be distinguished by the wider slot in the side of the carapace towards the front. Both species live in the deeper waters of coastal bays on a soft silt bottom and are moderately common.

Scyllarus sp.

Habitat: Exposed reef; 15–30 m depth.
Distribution: Eastern Tas.
Maximum size: Carapace length to 25 mm.

Scyllarus sp. is a small, reef-dwelling scyllarid, with spines on the midline, a strongly serrated margin around the flattened antennae and blue bands on the legs. The species is occasionally encountered by divers in sea caves on deep reefs but is uncommon. Other small species in the genus *Syllarus* with blue bands on the legs are also encountered by divers from Perth to Sydney, and it is not known whether one or more species are involved.

Scyllarus sp., Ile des Phoques, Tas.

FAMILY CALLIANASSIDAE
Ghost shrimps, marine yabbies

Callianassids have a pale, shrimp-like body with large claws on the first pair of legs (chelipeds). The claw on one side is generally much larger than on the other. The rostrum is inconspicuous, and the eyes are located on top of flattened stalks. Callianassids are commonly known as 'yabbies' in New South Wales, although this term is more widely applied to freshwater crayfish. They are burrowers in soft sediment, where they feed on organic particles.

Trypaea australiensis (Dana, 1852)

Habitat: Sheltered mud; low intertidal.
Distribution: Port Phillip Bay, Vic., to Low Isles, Qld.
Maximum size: Length to 65 mm.

Trypaea australiensis is the most distinctive of the temperate callianassids because of the dense fringe of long hairs on the first antennae and because the large nipper (the cheliped) is relatively slender and has a prominent hook on the second segment. This is also the most common ghost shrimp on intertidal mudflats in eastern Australia, reaching densities of many hundreds per square metre. Large numbers are caught by fishermen for use as bait.

Trypaea australiensis, Bermagui, NSW. RUDIE KUITER

Callianassa ceramica, Cloudy Lagoon, Tas.

Callianassa ceramica Fulton & Grant, 1906

Habitat: Sheltered sand, mud; 0–2 m depth.
Distribution: Mandurah, WA, to Wilsons Promontory, Vic., and around Tas.
Maximum size: Length to 80 mm.

Callianassa ceramica is a large species with one nipper substantially larger than the other, and with a strongly serrated lower margin on the second segment of the cheliped (the limb that ends in the large nipper). This is the most common ghost shrimp found on sandflats along the southern coast and is largely responsible for the numerous small mounds covering these flats near low-tide level.

FAMILY LAOMEDIIDAE

The laomediids are closely related to the callianassids but have a pointed rostrum, cylindrical eyestalks and left and right chelipeds which are usually approximately equal in size. The most characteristic feature is that the flattened uropods at the end of the body have a suture across both pairs of flaps.

Laomedia healyi, Pittwater, NSW

Laomedia healyi Yaldwyn & Wear, 1970

Habitat: Mangroves, mud; intertidal.
Distribution: Western Port, Vic., to northern Qld.
Maximum size: Length to 60 mm.

Laomedia healyi has a smooth, red-brown carapace with a triangular rostrum and a tiny spine projecting over each eye. The species is normally associated with mangroves and lives in burrows or under rocks.

FAMILY DIOGENIDAE
Diogenid hermit crabs

Hermit crabs differ from other crustaceans by generally having an asymmetrical abdomen that is soft and partly coiled in order to fit gastropod shells; as the hermit crab grows, it needs to periodically find a new home, and at some sites there is intense competition between animals for the limited number of shells available. Diogenids can be recognised by having the left claw equal in size or larger than the right. This family includes nearly all the large and colourful hermit crab species.

Paguristes frontalis, Busselton, WA

Paguristes frontalis (Milne Edwards, 1836)

Habitat: Moderately exposed reef; 0–8 m depth.
Distribution: Cape Naturaliste, WA, to Wilsons Promontory, Vic.
Maximum size: Length to 80 mm.

Paguristes frontalis is a large, moderately common hermit crab, distinguished from others by its size, lack of hairs, enlarged left claw and tubercles of different size on the movable 'finger' of the right cheliped. Animals living in southeastern Australia are a bright orange-red, while those in the southwest are purple-brown.

Paguristes frontalis, Port Victoria, SA

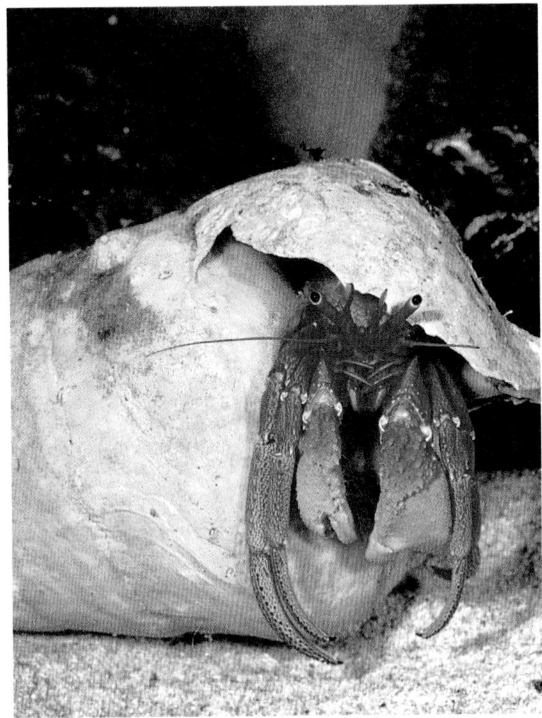

Paguristes purpureantennatus, Mullaloo, WA. CLAY BRYCE

Paguristes purpureantennatus Morgan, 1987

Habitat: Moderately exposed reef; 0–10 m depth.
Distribution: Geraldton to Albany, WA.
Maximum size: Length to 80 mm.

Paguristes purpureantennatus resembles *P. frontalis* but has purple rather than orange-red antennae and the right claw has the movable finger densely covered in small tubercles. The species is common in a variety of habitats in southwestern Australia. Large animals most often inhabit the shells of *Campanile symbolicum*, while juveniles utilise a number of different shells.

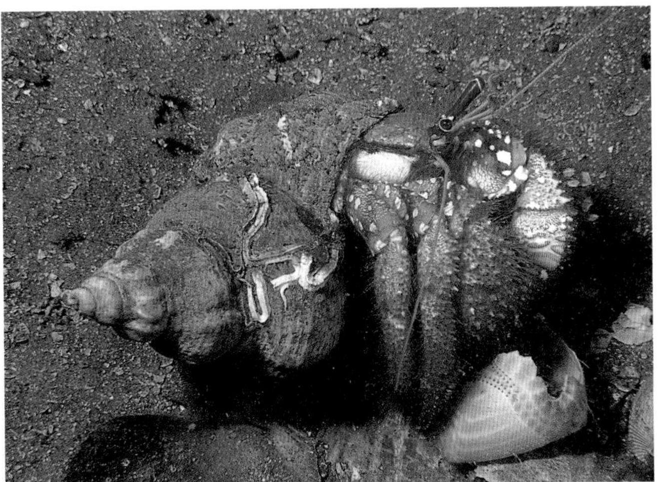

Trizopagurus strigimanus, Tinderbox, Tas.

Trizopagurus strigimanus (White, 1847)

Habitat: Reef; 0–220 m depth.
Distribution: Bunbury, WA, to Sydney, NSW, and around Tas.
Maximum size: Length to 130 mm.

Trizopagurus strigimanus differs from other southern Australian hermit crabs by having a ridged, sound-producing organ on the palm of both claws. It is a large red animal with blue eyes and numerous tufts of hair in the lower part of the chelipeds and legs. The species is common on shallow Tasmanian reefs but is uncommon in divable depths around the mainland.

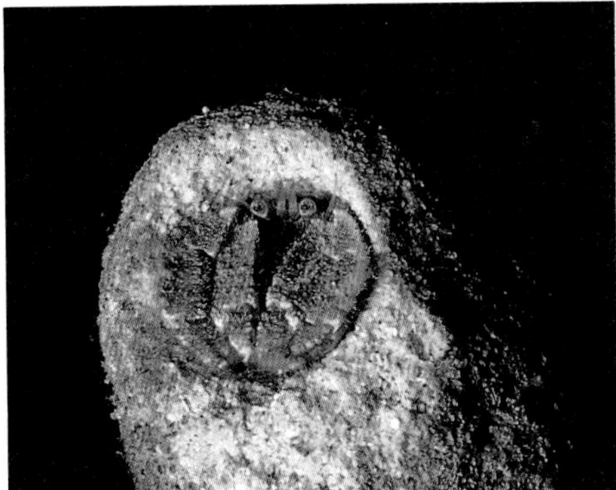

Cancellus typus, Portsea, Vic. RUDIE KUITER

Cancellus typus (Milne Edwards, 1836)

Habitat: Reef; 0–90 m depth.
Distribution: Cervantes, WA, to Sydney, NSW, and around Tas.
Maximum size: Length to 45 mm.

Cancellus typus is an unusual hermit crab with a straight body and symmetrical tail fan. It lives in a hole excavated in soft stone, which is sealed by its equal-sized claws and the first pair of walking legs.

FAMILY PAGURIDAE
Pagurid hermit crabs

The pagurid hermit crabs differ from the diogenids by having the right claw larger than the left. The large rearmost pair of mouthparts, the third maxillipeds, have a large gap between their bases, whereas in diogenid hermit crabs the third maxilliped bases are close together. Most pagurids are small and inconspicuous, and a number of species in southern Australia remain to be scientifically named.

Pagurus sinuatus (Stimpson, 1858)

Habitat: Sheltered reef, sand; 0–5 m depth.
Distribution: Houtman Abrolhos to Albany, WA, and Merimbula to Sydney, NSW.
Maximum size: Length to 60 mm.

Pagurus sinuatus has hairy claws and walking legs mottled red-brown, yellow and white. As with other members of the family, the right claw is much larger than the left. This species is very common in sheltered bays and near the mouths of estuaries in Western Australia and New South Wales but has not yet been found in the southern states.

Pagurixus handrecki Gunn & Morgan, 1992

Habitat: Sheltered reef, sand, seagrass; 0–42 m depth.
Distribution: Rottnest I, WA, to Lakes Entrance, Vic., and around Tas.
Maximum size: Length to 6 mm.

Pagurixus handrecki is distinguished from several other local species in the genus *Pagurixus* by the longitudinal red stripes on a white background on the legs. Related species with reddish bands on the

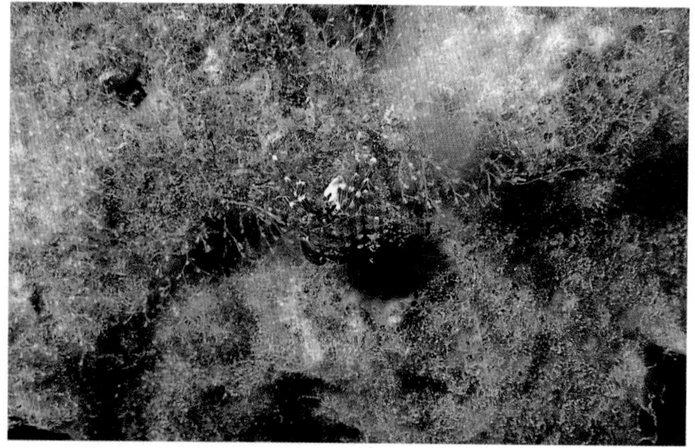

Pagurixus handrecki, Edithburgh, SA

Pagurus sinuatus, Princess Royal Harbour, WA

walking legs are ***Pagurixus amsa*** in Western Australia and ***Pagurixus jerviensis*** in southern New South Wales. *Pagurixus handrecki* is by far the most common species of hermit crab found along the southern coast but is generally overlooked because of its small size. It lives in a variety of microhabitats, including among shell sediments, plants and in crevices on reefs.

FAMILY PORCELLANIDAE
Porcelain crabs

Porcellanids have a crab-like appearance but differ from the true crabs by having an inconspicuous last pair of legs and a small tail fan. They can also be recognised by the long antennae and large flattened claws. The family is very diverse in the tropics but the number of species diminishes south along the Australian coast. They usually feed unselectively by trapping edible particles in long combs of hair attached to the mouthparts.

Petrocheles australiensis, Portsea, Vic. RUDIE KUITER

Petrocheles australiensis Miers, 1876

Habitat: Moderately and submaximally exposed reef; 0–10 m.
Distribution: Great Australian Bight, WA, to Wilsons Promontory, Vic., and northern Tas.
Maximum size: Carapace width to 25 mm.

Petrocheles australiensis is unusual among the porcellanids for its large size and the numerous spines on the body and claws. It is a common species on reefs just below low-tide level but usually remains concealed in rock crevices and is not often seen.

Petrolisthes elongatus, Dunalley, Tas.

Petrolisthes elongatus Milne Edwards, 1840

Habitat: Sheltered reef; low intertidal to 12 m.
Distribution: Vic. and around Tas. Also New Zealand.
Maximum size: Carapace width to 7 mm.

Petrolisthes elongatus is a small green-brown porcellanid with a smooth carapace. The species occurs under rocks near low-tide level and is extremely abundant in sheltered bays around Tasmania.

FAMILY LOMISIDAE
Hairy stone crabs

This family contains a single species, which resembles the porcellanid crabs but has hairy rather than smooth antennae, and short bristles covering its body.

Lomis hirta, Flinders, Vic.

Lomis hirta (Lamarck, 1810)

Habitat: Moderately exposed reef; 0–5 m depth.
Distribution: Bunbury, WA, to Mallacoota, Vic., and around Tas.
Maximum size: Carapace width to 25 mm.

Lomis hirta has a very distinctive appearance caused by its brown hairy body and blue antennae. It lives under flat-bottomed rocks in the lower intertidal zone and is locally common.

FAMILY GALATHEIDAE
Squat lobsters, craylets, lobster krill

Galatheids resemble lobsters but have an abdomen that is bent up under the body. The last leg is small and hidden and can be used for cleaning the respiratory chamber. A few galatheid species form large, coherent swarms at particular times of the year, but this behaviour has not been noticed among the Australian species.

Munida haswelli Henderson, 1885

Habitat: Sand, shells; 8–420 m depth.
Distribution: Eucla, WA, to Eden, NSW, and around Tas.
Maximum size: Body length to 30 mm.

Munida haswelli, Sandy Bay, Tas.

Munida haswelli is a small, brown species with a prominent central spine between the eyes, as well as two side spines. Other characteristics of the species are the very long claws and prominent eyes. This galatheid lives among broken shells and other coarse sediments and is common in southeastern Tasmania but rarely occurs elsewhere in shallow depths.

Galathea australiensis Stimpson, 1858

Habitat: Exposed reef, sponges, bivalves; 0–40 m depth.
Distribution: Shark Bay, WA, to Port Stephens, NSW, and around Tas.
Maximum size: Body length to 15 mm.

Galathea australiensis differs from *Munida haswelli* by having shorter claws and a rostrum that is triangular with three teeth on the sides. The species is extremely common among large attached invertebrates, such as sponges, bivalves and ascidians, where it is often mistaken for a juvenile rock lobster.

Galathea australiensis, Edithburgh, SA

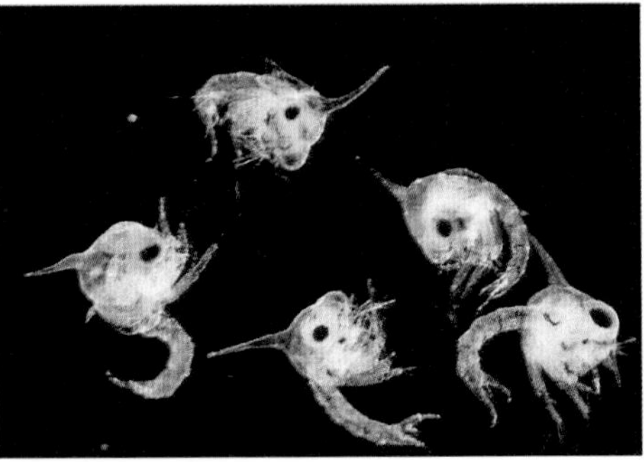

Crab zoea larvae, Sandy Bay, Tas.

FAMILY DROMIIDAE
Sponge crabs

The dromiids receive their common name of sponge crab from the habit of most species of cultivating a living sponge (or occasionally ascidians) on the top of the carapace. The last pair of legs are small with claw-like ends and are used for manipulating the associated sponge. This is generally considered the most primitive of the crab families; some species retain traces of a tail fan.

Cryptodromia octodentata, Edithburgh, SA

Cryptodromia octodentata (Haswell, 1882)

Habitat: Sheltered reef, jetty pylons; 0–60 m depth.
Distribution: Great Australian Bight, WA, to Western Port, Vic.
Maximum size: Carapace width to 75 mm.

Cryptodromia octodentata has a rounded carapace with four or five inconspicuous teeth on the side margins towards the front. The most distinctive feature is a dense covering of tufted bristles on the carapace and legs. This species and ***Dromidiopsis globosa***, another large dromiid with a pink body covering and row of bristles along the front of the carapace, are the most commonly seen species on jetty pylons in South Australia and Victoria.

Petalomera lateralis (Gray, 1831)

Habitat: Sheltered reef, jetty pylons; 0-220 m depth.
Distribution: North West Cape, WA, to Low Isles, Qld, and around Tas. Also NZ, Japan and China.
Maximum size: Carapace width to 25 mm.

Petalomera lateralis is a sponge-carrying crab with two large teeth either side of a smaller central tooth between the eyes. The walking legs have low, rounded ridges running down them, and the claws are a light orange colour with white tips. This crab is common under rocks on reefs and on jetty pylons, but is not often noticed.

FAMILY CANCRIDAE
Edible crabs

Cancrid crabs have an oval carapace with indentations around the margin that resemble finger marks in a pie crust. The family includes many species of edible crab in the northern Pacific and Atlantic oceans and has a long fossil history. The single species found in the southern Pacific, *Cancer noveaehollandiae*, appears to have changed little since the southern and northern continents were separated.

Petalomera lateralis, Ricketts Pt, Vic.

Cancer novaezealandiae (Jacquinot, 1853)

Habitat: Sheltered reef, sand; 0–20 m depth.
Distribution: Central Vic. and eastern and southern Tas. Also New Zealand.
Maximum size: Carapace width to 190 mm.

Cancer novaezealandiae has large claws and a distinctively shaped carapace that is typical of the family. This crab occurs commonly in the lower Derwent estuary and D'Entrecasteaux Channel but is not often seen because it moves about at night. The

Cancer novaezealandiae, Cloudy Lagoon, Tas.

species has probably been introduced into Tasmania from New Zealand, as it had not been recorded in this country before the early twentieth century.

FAMILY LEUCOSIIDAE
Pebble crabs

Leucosiids are readily indentified by the rounded, pebble-shaped bodies which are often produced at front, the small eyes and the relatively long claws, which are rounded in cross-section. Species in this family have an unusually shaped mouth, which narrows toward the front, an adaptation that allows them to breathe while buried in sand.

Philyra laevis Bell, 1855

Habitat: Sand, mud, seagrass; 0–10 m depth.
Distribution: Albany, WA, to Wilsons Promontory, Vic. and around Tas.
Maximum size: Carapace width to 25 mm.

Philyra laevis has a rounded grey carapace with four small white dots on the upper surface and a slight ridge above the rear margin. The male is very much larger than the female. This pebble crab is abundant on intertidal mudflats and sandflats in sheltered bays along the southern coast.

Philyra laevis, Albany, WA

Philyra undecimspinosa (Kinahan, 1856)

Habitat: Sand, mud; 0–75 m depth.
Distribution: SA to Newcastle, NSW, and around Tas.
Maximum size: Carapace width to 30 mm.

Philyra undecimspinosa differs from *P. laevis* by having a central spine and two side spines on the relatively straight rear margin of the carapace, and by the male having much longer claws, with the first segment of the cheliped longer than the width of the body. The species is much less common in shallow water than *P. laevis*. Pebble crabs mate immediately after the female has moulted, and, in anticipation, males often cling to the female for several days prior to that time.

Ebalia intermedia Miers, 1886

Habitat: Sheltered sand, mud; 0–60 m depth.
Distribution: Cottesloe, WA, to Westernport, Vic., and around Tas.
Maximum size: Carapace width to 14 mm.

Ebalia intermedia can be recognised by the rear margin of the carapace, which is straight and overlapped by a large central spine. The front of the body extends between the eyes and has four rounded spines. This species is common on coarse sediments in the channels of sheltered bays but because of its small size is not often noticed.

Ebalia intermedia, Tinderbox, Tas.

Philyra undecimspinosa, Cloudy Bay, Tas.

Leucosia pubescens, Bicton, WA

Leucosia pubescens Miers, 1877

Habitat: Sheltered rocks, silt; 0–5 m depth.
Distribution: Tropical WA south to Perth. Also widespread in the Indian Ocean.
Maximum size: Carapace width to 25 mm.

Leucosia pubescens has a light brown carapace that narrows at the front, and has three spines between the eyes, a series of darker markings in a grid pattern across the back and prominent tubercles at the base of the claws. The species is common in the lower reaches of the Swan River near Fremantle.

FAMILY MAJIDAE
Spider crabs

The majids, or spider crabs, have triangular or occasionally rounded carapaces covered by spines, hairs and knobs. Algae, sponges or hydroids from the surrounding environment are usually attached to these projections, providing the animal with excellent camouflage. This family of about 600 species includes the world's broadest crab, *Macrocheira kaempferi*, a deepwater Japanese species with a legspan that can exceed 2 m.

Naxia aurita (Latreille, 1825)

Habitat: Sheltered seagrass, seaweeds; 0–15 m.
Distribution: Houtman Abrolhos, WA, to Western Port, Vic., and around Tas.
Maximum size: Carapace width to 40 mm.

Naxia aurita is a moderate-sized spider crab with a pear-shaped body and orange chelipeds with blue trim. Two related species differ by having the second last segment of the legs expanded terminally to form a claw and by having large spines (***Naxia spinosa***) and tubercles (***Naxia tumida***) on the upper surface of the carapace. All three species occur in sheltered vegetated habitats along the southern coast, with *N. aurita* the most common.

Naxia aurita, Princess Royal Harbour, WA

Notomithrax ursus (Herbst, 1788)

Habitat: Moderately exposed reef; 0–20 m.
Distribution: Discovery Bay, Vic., to NSW and around Tas.
Maximum size: Carapace width to 40 mm.

Notomithrax ursus has a carapace that is usually obscured by dense growths of algae, sponges or hydroids attached to hooked hairs and tubercles. The claws are reddish-orange with light-coloured tips and have two granulose ridges along the segment before the hand. The species is common in rock pools in the lower intertidal zone but is not often noticed.

Notomithrax ursus, Eaglehawk Neck, Tas.

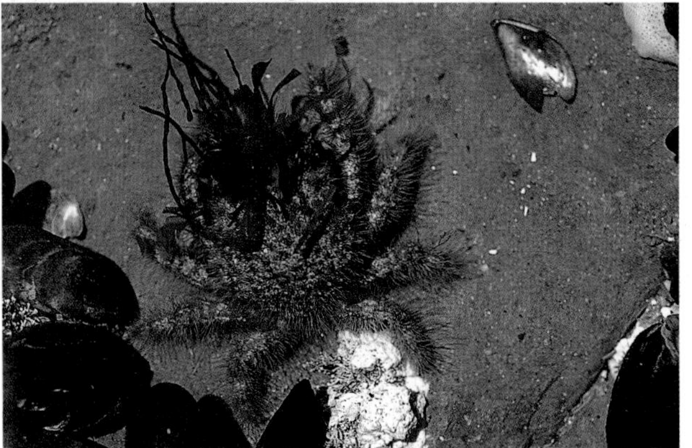

Notomithrax minor, Ile des Phoques, Tas.

Notomithrax minor (Filhol, 1885)

Habitat: Exposed reef; 0–125 m.
Distribution: Port Phillip Bay, Vic., to Gladstone, Qld, and around Tas. Also New Zealand.
Maximum size: Carapace width to 40 mm.

Notomithrax minor resembles its relative *N. ursus* in shape and in the covering of algae and sessile animals over the body. It differs by having spines on the upper carapace in addition to tubercles and hooked hairs, and by having nine rather than six spines along the side of the carapace below the large spine associated with the eye. The species is moderately common in caves and crevices on exposed reefs.

Leptomithrax gaimardii (adult male), Port Lincoln, SA

Leptomithrax gaimardii (Milne Edwards, 1834)

Habitat: Exposed reef, sand; 0–820 m.
Distribution: Albany, WA, to Sydney, NSW, and around Tas.
Maximum size: Carapace width to 125 mm.

Leptomithrax gaimardii can generally be recognised by its orange colour, massive size and legs considerably longer than the carapace. The species normally occurs in deep water, but local aggregations form in shallow water in particular seasons of the year.

Leptomithrax gaimardii aggregation, D'Entrecasteaux Channel, Tas. RON MAWBEY

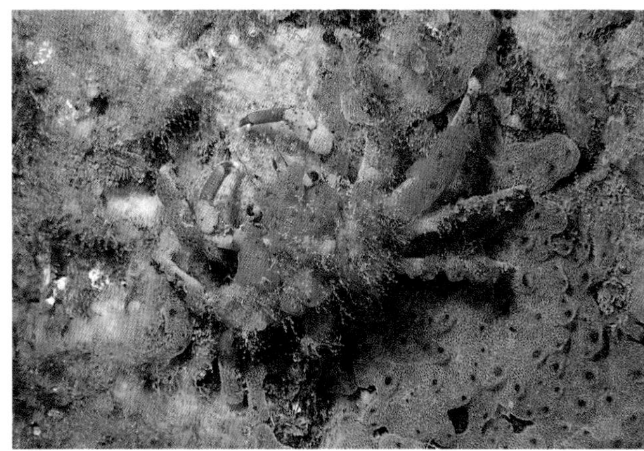

Schizophrys aspera, Edithburgh, SA

Schizophrys aspera Milne Edwards, 1834

Habitat: Sheltered rock, jetty pylons; 0–15 m depth.
Distribution: Tropical Australia and South Australian gulfs. Also widespread in the Indo-West Pacific region.
Maximum size: Carapace width to 50 mm.

Schizophrys aspera has an orange-red carapace that is normally covered by encrusting growths of sponges, ascidians and hydroids. The claws are relatively slender, smooth towards the end, and have white tips. This crab is generally considered a tropical species, but it also occurs commonly on jetty pylons in the South Australian gulfs.

Hyastenus elatus Griffin & Tranter, 1986

Habitat: Sheltered rock, jetty pylons; 0–54 m depth.
Distribution: Tropical Australia south to Fremantle, WA, and Botany Bay, NSW. Also Indonesia.
Maximum size: Carapace width to 80 mm.

Hyastenus elatus, Port Stephens, NSW

Hyastenus elatus has a pear-shaped carapace with two long rostral projections, which are nearly as long as the body, and two shorter projections from the rear sides. The species is nearly always heavily encrusted with sponges and other sessile animals. It occurs commonly in Sydney Harbour.

FAMILY HYMENOSOMATIDAE

Hymenosomatids are closely related to majid spider crabs but have smooth, flat-topped carapaces. Most species live among marine plants, and some occur in estuaries. All species are small.

Halicarcinus ovatus Stimpson, 1858

Habitat: Sheltered and moderately exposed seagrass, seaweed; 0–60 m.
Distribution: Geraldton, WA, to Port Stephens, NSW, and around Tas.
Maximum size: Carapace width to 13 mm.

Halicarcinus ovatus is characterised by three short spines of equal size on the front margin between the eyes. It has an almost rounded carapace, which bends at a blunt point on the front of each side, and is extremely variable in colour pattern. This species is by far the most abundant hymenosomatid found around the southern coasts, although ***Halicarcinus rostratus***, a species with one long spine between the eyes, can be equally common in deeper estuaries.

Halicarcinus ovatus, Victor Harbor, SA

FAMILY PORTUNIDAE
Swimming crabs

Crabs in the family Portunidae have the last segment of the hind legs flattened; this segment is paddle-shaped in the strongly swimming species (e.g. *Ovalipes australiensis)*, whereas in reef-dwelling species (e.g. *Carcinus maenas*) it is only slightly widened. Portunids are the most active of crabs, and nearly all of the 300 species do not hesitate to use their claws to defend themselves.

Carcinus maenas (Linnaeus 1758)
Common shore crab

Habitat: Sheltered rock, mud, sand, seaweed; 0–5 m depth..
Distribution: Swan River, WA, Coorong, SA, Anglesea, Vic., to Eden, NSW, and eastern Tas. Also Europe, Brazil and North America.
Maximum size: Carapace width to 65 mm.

Carcinus maenas, Ricketts Pt, Vic.

Carcinus maenas has a greenish-grey body with three teeth between the eyes and four teeth around the front of the side margin. The hindlegs are less flattened than on almost all other members of the family Portunidae. This species occurs abundantly under stones and in crevices at shallow estuarine sites. It was introduced into Australia from Europe in the nineteenth century and has also been introduced into North America. The species is an active predator and has probably affected the populations of a number of local animal species.

Ovalipes australiensis Stephenson & Rees, 1968
Surf crab, sand crab

Habitat: Sand; 0–34 m depth.
Distribution: Perth, WA, to Wide Bay, Qld, and around Tas.
Maximum size: Carapace width to 105 mm.

Ovalipes australiensis is readily identified by the two red oval patches towards the rear of a light grey carapace, and coarse granules near the front. This is a widespread, pugnacious species, which occurs abundantly in shallow water off sandy beaches.

Ovalipes australiensis, Cloudy Lagoon, Tas.

Thalamita sima Milne Edwards, 1834

Habitat: Sheltered reef, sand; 0–34 m depth.
Distribution: Tropical Australia south to central SA and Sydney, NSW. Also widespread in the Indo-West Pacific region.
Maximum size: Carapace width to 90 mm.

Thalamita sima has five strong teeth on each side of the carapace, with the first the broadest and bluntest. Between the eyes the carapace is relatively straight with a central notch and two lobes. This tropical species is common under rocks in sheltered habitats near Perth.

Thalamita sima, Bicton, WA

Thalamita admete (Herbst, 1803)

Habitat: Sheltered reef, sand; 0–12 m depth.
Distribution: Tropical Australia south to Perth, WA, and Sydney, NSW. Also widespread in the Indo-West Pacific region.
Maximum size: Carapace width to 40 mm.

Thalamita admete has a mottled carapace with four lobes on the margin between the eyes and four or five teeth around the front of the sides. The species is moderately common in Sydney Harbour but probably arrives as larvae from more tropical areas and does not breed there.

Thalamita admete, North Head, NSW

Nectocarcinus integrifrons, Cloudy Lagoon, Tas.

Nectocarcinus integrifrons (Latreille, 1825)
Red swimmer crab

Habitat: Sheltered seagrass, seaweed; 0–20 m depth.
Distribution: Fremantle, WA, to Port Stephens, NSW, and around Tas. Also New Zealand.
Maximum size: Carapace width to 80 mm.

Nectocarcinus integrifrons is a bottom-dwelling species with flattened hind limbs, a purple-brown front half of the carapace and light brown rear, and a smooth front margin between the eyes. This crab is extremely abundant in sheltered seagrass beds and has an unusual diet for a portunid crab, as it feeds mainly on seagrass material. Portunid crabs often pair together before mating and may remain in this position for several days.

Nectocarcinus tuberculosus

Milne Edwards, 1860

Red swimmer crab

Habitat: Exposed reef; 0–20 m depth.
Distribution: Albany, WA, to Sydney, NSW, and around Tas.
Maximum size: Carapace width to 90 mm.

Nectocarcinus tuberculosus has a reddish-brown carapace with black fingers on the chelipeds. The species is distinguished from its closest relative, *Nectocarcinus integrifrons*, by having a small notch at the front of the carapace midway between the eyes. This species is common on exposed coasts, whereas *N. integrifrons* prefers more sheltered sites.

Nectocarcinus tuberculosus, Bathurst Channel, Tas.

Portunus pelagicus (Linnaeus, 1766)

Blue swimmer crab, blue manna crab, sand crab

Habitat: Sheltered sand, seagrass; 0–60 m depth.
Distribution: Tropical Australia south to Cape Naturaliste, WA, and Eden, NSW, and the South Australian gulfs. Also widespread in the Indo-West Pacific region and the Mediterranean Sea.
Maximum size: Carapace width to 210 mm.

Portunus pelagicus can be distinguished from other large crabs in southern Australia by the long spine projecting from each side of the carapace, the smoothly curved rear of the body and the bluish coloration. Female crabs (known as jennies) are less

Portunus pelagicus, Cliff Head, WA

brightly coloured than males and have a prominent spot at the base of the claws. Blue swimmer crabs are caught in large numbers by professional and recreational fishers. They settle as juveniles in very shallow sandy habitats and grow rapidly, reaching maturity after one year. This crab has reached the Mediterranean in recent times by migrating through the Suez Canal.

Portunus tenuipes (de Haan, 1833)

Habitat: Sheltered reef, sand; 0–36 m depth.
Distribution: Tropical Australia south to Perth, WA. Also widespread in the Indo-West Pacific region.
Maximum size: Carapace width to 70 mm.

Portunus tenuipes is one of the smaller species in the largely tropical genus *Portunus*. It is distinguished by having three teeth on the front margin between the eyes, a long spine at the centre of each side, which is preceded by a series of relatively small spines, and a blunt projection on each of the rear corners. Although primarily a tropical species, this crab is moderately common near Perth.

Portunus tenuipes, Bicton, WA

FAMILY XANTHIDAE
Stone crabs

Xanthid crabs are very solid crabs which are common on rock and coral reefs. They can usually be recognised by having an oval body that is widest towards the front, and indentations around the front margin. Many species have dark tips to the claws. The family Xanthidae is very large and includes the world's second heaviest crab, the deepwater southern Australian species *Pseudocarcinus gigas*.

Actaea peronii (H. Milne Edwards, 1834)

Habitat: Exposed reef; 0–150 m depth.
Distribution: Southern WA to Port Stephens, NSW, and around Tas.
Maximum size: Carapace width to 25 mm.

Actaea peronii, Rocky Cape, Tas.

Actaea peronii has a distinctive appearance because of its bright orange-red colour, knobbled carapace and numerous spines covering the lower regions of the legs. The species occurs commonly under rocks on the reefs of southeastern Australia but is rare in the western section of the south coast.

FAMILY MENIPPIDAE

Menippids have a xanthid crab shape (as described above) but, in contrast to species in that family, have long second pleopods and the males have seven rather than five abdominal segments.

Ozius truncatus Milne Edwards, 1834

Habitat: Exposed reef; 0–5 m depth.
Distribution: Perth, WA, to southern Qld.
Maximum size: Carapace width to 60 mm.

Ozius truncatus is a solid, slow-moving crab, which occurs commonly under rocks at lower tidal levels. It has a dark grey-brown carapace with a margin that is relatively straight between the eyes and then rounded with four broad teeth. The claws are massive and have dark brown fingers.

Ozius truncatus, Port Stephens, NSW

FAMILY PILUMNIDAE
Hairy shore crabs

Pilumnids, or hairy shore crabs, were once included in the family Xanthidae, as were the menippids and goneplacids. Pilumnids can usually be distinguished from related families by having numerous long hairs on the carapace and legs.

Heteropilumnus fimbriatus
(Milne Edwards, 1834)

Habitat: Sheltered reef; 0–20 m depth.
Distribution: Gulf St Vincent, SA, to Western Port, Vic., and around Tas.
Maximum size: Carapace width to 15 mm.

Heteropilumnus fimbriatus is a flattened, yellow-brown species, easily recognised by the dense fringe of hair on the front margin of the carapace and along the legs. The species is moderately common under flat rocks in shallow water.

Heteropilumnus fimbriatus, Ricketts Pt, Vic.

Pilumnus tomentosus Latreille, 1825

Habitat: Sheltered rock; 0–550 m depth.
Distribution: Albany, WA, to Newcastle, NSW, and around Tas.
Maximum size: Carapace width to 40 mm.

Pilumnus tomentosus, Ricketts Pt, Vic.
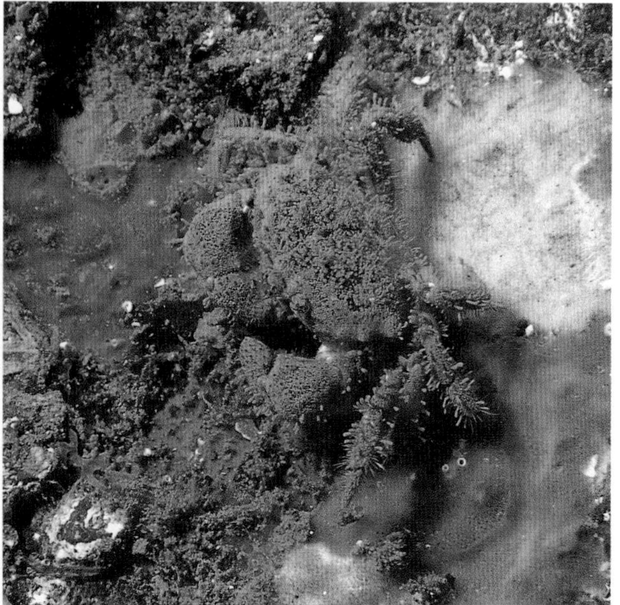

Pilumnus tomentosus is one of nine species in the genus *Pilumnus* found in temperate Australian waters. It is characterised by a relatively sparse covering of long hairs on the carapace, three prominent teeth that lack spines on the sides, tubercles across most of the surface of the claws, and body and legs that are usually coated with some mud or debris. This is the most frequently seen member of the genus. It is moderately common under rocks.

FAMILY GONEPLACIDAE
Goneplacid crabs

Goneplacids are closely related to the xanthid crabs but can usually be distinguished by the rectangular body. The family contains relatively few species, with only one commonly encountered in southern Australia.

Litocheira bispinosa Kinahan, 1856

Habitat: Sheltered and moderately exposed reef, sand, seagrass; 0–30 m.
Distribution: Albany, WA, to Western Port, Vic., and around Tas.
Maximum size: Carapace width to 15 mm.

Litocheira bispinosa superficially resembles a grapsid crab in shape, as it has a square carapace with a sharp spine towards the front of each side. The body is a mottled purple-brown, with the legs banded in similar colours. This crab is moderately common under rocks and among shelly sands.

Litocheira bispinosa, D'Entrecasteaux Channel, Tas.

FAMILY GRAPSIDAE
Shore crabs

Grapsids normally have smooth, rectangular carapaces with spines usually present in the side margin behind the front corner. They are well adapted for life out of water and include nearly all crabs encountered on rocky shores.

Cyclograpsus granulosus (Milne Edwards, 1853)

Habitat: Under rocks on sheltered and moderately exposed shores; mid intertidal.
Distribution: SA to Mallacoota, Vic., and around Tas.
Maximum size: Carapace width to 35 mm.

Cyclograpsus granulosus has a mottled grey-brown carapace with a smooth side margin. It occurs in huge abundances under cobbles and stones high on the shore and is particularly prevalent on boulder beaches. The largest animals have been found to be about three years old.

Cyclograpsus granulosus, Eaglehawk Neck, Tas.

Cyclograpsus audouinii Milne Edwards, 1837

Habitat: Under rocks on sheltered and moderately exposed shores; mid intertidal.
Distribution: Shark Bay, WA, to Hervey Bay, Qld. Also New Guinea.
Maximum size: Carapace width to 40 mm.

Cyclograpsus audouinii, Elliston, SA

Cyclograpsus audouinii is difficult to distinguish from *C. granulosus*, and for many years these species were confused. The best way to distinguish between them is the presence of a tuft of hairs at the base of the walking legs on *C. audouinii*. Both species occur in similar habitat and are abundant, although *C. audouinii* prefers a warmer climate.

Paragrapsus gaimardii (Milne Edwards, 1837)

Habitat: Sheltered reef, sand; 0–10 m depth.
Distribution: Kangaroo I, SA, to Lakes Entrance, Vic., and around Tas.
Maximum size: Carapace width to 45 mm.

Paragrapsus gaimardii can be recognised by the two notches in the side margin towards the front of the carapace. The body has a greenish hue with black spots, and the tips of the legs are generally yellow. The species is abundant in sheltered bays and estuaries, where it is usually found under rocks or in shallow burrows. Large numbers move about at night in shallow water, often following the tide.

Paragrapsus gaimardii, Cloudy Lagoon, Tas.

Paragrapsus laevis, Moonee Moonee, NSW

Paragrapsus laevis (Dana, 1852)

Habitat: Under rocks; mid intertidal.
Distribution: Warnambool, Vic., to Moreton Bay, Qld, and south to Marion Bay, Tas.
Maximum size: Carapace width to 35 mm.

Paragrapsus laevis has a carapace with similar notches to *P. gaimardii*, but the shell is slightly more rounded and has a dark mottled rather than spotted pattern. The species is locally common under rocks in the intertidal zone of estuaries.

Paragrapsus quadridentatus (Milne Edwards, 1837)

Habitat: Sheltered and moderately exposed reef; 0–10 m depth.
Distribution: Discovery Bay to Mallacoota, Vic., and around Tas.
Maximum size: Carapace width to 30 mm.

Paragrapsus quadridentatus, Cloudy Lagoon, Tas.

Paragrapsus quadridentatus has a flat, rounded carapace with a single notch on the side margin towards the front. The base colour of the animal is fawn with a greenish tint and with a spattering of small black spots. This crab is locally common under rocks in the lower intertidal zone.

Helograpsus haswellianus (Whitelegge, 1889)

Habitat: Mud; high intertidal.
Distribution: Port River, SA, to Townsville, Qld, and around Tas.
Maximum size: Carapace width to 30 mm.

Helograpsus haswellianus resembles *Paragrapsus quadridentatus* because of the single notch on the side margin of the carapace, but the body is more inflated, the claws are larger and the legs thinner. The species lives in burrows or under rocks on mudbanks and may occur a long way up tidal creeks.

Helograpsus haswellianus, Snug, Tas.

Leptograpsus variegatus (Fabricius, 1793)
Swift-footed crab

Habitat: Exposed shores; intertidal.
Distribution: North West Cape, WA, to Rockhampton, Qld, and south to Tasman Peninsula, Tas. Also New Zealand and South America.
Maximum size: Carapace width to 80 mm.

Leptograpsus variegatus is an active crab that occurs abundantly on rock platforms, particularly along the New South Wales coast. It is characterised by purple chelipeds on adults, rounded carapace margins, and parallel grooves running obliquely across the shell. The species is harvested intensively along the New South Wales coast for use as fish bait.

Leptograpsodes octodentatus
(Milne Edwards, 1857)

Habitat: Under rocks on exposed shores; high intertidal.
Distribution: Houtman Abrolhos, WA, to Wilsons Promontory, Vic., and south to Eaglehawk Neck, Tas.
Maximum size: Carapace width to 60 mm.

Leptograpsodes octodentatus has an oval carapace that is wider than long. Three small teeth diminishing in size posteriorly are present towards the front of the side margin. This species lives at higher tidal levels than other shore crabs and is often found under rocks in pools greatly diluted by fresh water.

Leptograpsodes octodentatus, Eaglehawk Neck, Tas.

Brachynotus spinosus (Milne Edwards, 1853)

Habitat: Under rocks on sheltered and moderately exposed shores; intertidal.
Distribution: SA to Mallacoota, Vic., and around Tas.
Maximum size: Carapace width to 15 mm.

Leptograpsus variegatus, Eaglehawk Neck, Tas.

Brachynotus spinosus, Rocky Cape, Tas.

Brachynotus spinosus is a small species with a squarish carapace and three strong teeth on each side. The eyes are distinctive, as they are jet black with fine white spots. This crab is moderately common under rocks at all tidal levels.

Plagusia chabrus (Linnaeus, 1758)
Red bait crab

Habitat: Exposed reef; 0–8 m depth.
Distribution: Rottnest I, WA, to Newcastle, NSW, and around Tas. Also New Zealand, South Africa and Chile.
Maximum size: Carapace width to 70 mm.

Plagusia chabrus differs from the other local grapsid crabs by living subtidally on reefs rather than on intertidal shores. It is easily recognised by its large size, red coloration, deeply indented teeth around the front of the body and the covering of felt that extends in rows down the legs. The species feeds mainly on encrusting animals such as bryozoans, sponges and hydroids.

Plagusia chabrus, Ile des Phoques, Tas.

Sesarma erythrodactyla Hess, 1865

Habitat: Mudflats; mid intertidal.
Distribution: Western Port, Vic., to Qld.
Maximum size: Carapace width to 25 mm.

Sesarma erythrodactyla is a greenish-black crab with bright orange-red tips to the claws when mature. The carapace is rectangular and has inconspicuous parallel ridges running obliquely in from the rear sides. This is a burrowing species that occurs abundantly in mangroves and is often associated with the semaphore crab *Heloecius cordiformis* (described below).

Sesarma erythrodactyla, Moonee Moonee, NSW

FAMILY OCYPODIDAE
Ghost crabs, stalk-eyed crabs

Ocypodid crabs are semi-terrestrial and they burrow into sand and mud. They have distinctive stalked eyes, which can be raised or laid sideways in grooves. Nearly all species in the family live in the tropics, where they occur abundantly in mangroves and on sandy beaches.

Ocypode cordimana Desmarest, 1825
Ghost crab

Habitat: Sand; high intertidal.
Distribution: Tropical Australia south to Kimberley, WA, and Sydney, NSW.
Maximum size: Carapace width to 35 mm.

Heloecius cordiformis, East Gosford, NSW

Ocypode cordimana is a light grey crab with a rounded carapace and large ovoid eyes at the end of short eyestalks. It lives in deep burrows above high-tide level, in some cases more than 100 m inland, and is the source of the holes on central New South Wales beaches. Animals found in temperate areas are generally much smaller than those in the tropics. At night the crab moves out of the burrows and scavenges for food deposited by the tide.

Heloecius cordiformis (Milne Edwards, 1837)
Semaphore crab

Habitat: Mud; mid intertidal.
Distribution: Port Phillip Bay, Vic., to Brisbane, Qld, and eastern Tas.
Maximum size: Carapace width to 25 mm.

Heloecius cordiformis has a wide carapace, which is rounded in cross-section, and distinctively bent claws, which are purple on adults and pale orange on juveniles. The eyes are very long and almost reach the sides of the carapace when laid flat. This is the most abundant crab found between tidemarks in mangrove forests and muddy estuaries. It is commonly called the semaphore crab because adult males often stand near their burrows signalling with their claws.

Ocypode cordimana, Terrigal, NSW

Macrophthalmus latifrons (Haswell, 1882)

Habitat: Mud; low intertidal.
Distribution: Gulf St Vincent, SA, to Wilsons Promontory, Vic., and eastern Tas.
Maximum size: Carapace width to 25 mm.

Macrophthalmus latifrons has a yellowish-brown carapace with two notches in the side margin towards the front. It also has legs fringed with hair, and eyestalks set well apart. The species is abundant in burrows at low-tide level in muddy estuaries but is not often seen because it rarely moves to the burrow entrance.

Macrophthalmus latifrons, Kettering, Tas.

FAMILY MICTYRIDAE
Soldier crabs

Mictyrids have rounded, blue-grey bodies and flattened chelipeds. They form large armies of tens of thousands of animals on estuarine shores, and so are commonly known as soldier crabs. If disturbed, they bury rapidly into the sediment using a spiral motion.

Mictyris platycheles Milne Edwards, 1852
Soldier crab

Habitat: Sand, mud; mid intertidal.
Distribution: Port Phillip Bay, Vic., to Moreton Bay, Qld, and around Tas.
Maximum size: Carapace width to 15 mm.

Mictyris platycheles has a blue body with prominent purple side-bulges towards the rear. The species occurs in huge abundance near the entrance of estuaries in locations where sandflats are merging into

Mictyris platycheles, Cloudy Lagoon, Tas.

mudflats. Each animal processes large quantities of sand in order to extract a relatively small amount of unicellular algal and detrital food.

Mictyris longicarpus Latreille, 1806
Soldier crab

Habitat: Sand, mud; mid intertidal.
Distribution: Wilsons Promontory, Vic., to northern Qld.
Maximum size: Carapace width to 15 mm.

Mictyris longicarpus resembles *M. platycheles* in shape but has a brighter blue carapace and purple bands on the joints of the legs. The two species have similar habitat preferences and often occur together on sandflats in southern New South Wales.

Mictyris longicarpus, Bermagui, NSW. RUDIE KUITER

FAMILY PINNOTHERIDAE
Pea crabs

Pinnotherids are commonly called pea crabs because of their soft, smooth, rounded body and their habit of living in shells. The female spends its life in the mantle cavity of bivalves or in the body cavities of other invertebrates, while the smaller male sometimes accompanies the female but can also move between hosts.

Pinnotheres hickmani (Guiler, 1950)

Habitat: Bivalves; 0–2 m depth.
Distribution: Shark Bay, WA, to Mallacoota, Vic., and around Tas.
Maximum size: Carapace width to 10 mm (female).

Pinnotheres hickmani is difficult to distinguish from a number of almost identical species of pea crab inhabiting bivalves in southern Australia. The female is rounded, with small eyes that are close together, and has weak walking legs. Males have a more flattened appearance and are about half the size of the female. The most common host is the blue mussel *Mytilus edulis*, which usually has a more swollen shape when infested. The relationship between crab and bivalve is sometimes described as symbiotic, but it is difficult to see much benefit for the host.

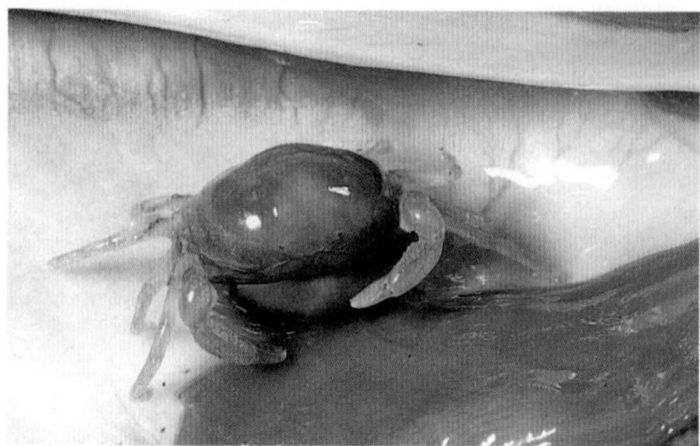
Pinnotheres hickmani, Cloudy Lagoon, Tas.

PHYLUM MOLLUSCA

Molluscs

The phylum Mollusca includes species with a huge range of body forms, such as squid, clams, snails and chitons. Despite this diversity of appearance, all molluscs have bodies structured on the same basic pattern. They have a head and muscular foot, which are separated from a section of the body known as the visceral mass containing the digestive, reproductive and excretory organs. A sheet of skin (the mantle) arises from the body wall and grows over the visceral mass. The space between the mantle and the visceral mass is known as the mantle cavity and is the usual location for gills. A calcareous shell secreted by the mantle is also often present, although in several mollusc groups this is reduced, internal or absent.

Seven classes are presently recognised: six of them recorded from shallow Australian seas and the seventh (Monoplacophora) confined to deep water. With a total of about 80 000 known species, molluscs form one of the largest phyla.

Class Aplacophora

Aplacophorans, solenogasters

Aplacophorans have a worm-like body with a thick covering of cuticle that has spiny spicules embedded throughout, giving the animals a silvery appearance. A slit-like mouth and an area called the oral shield, on which there are no spicules, are located at the head end of the body. The foot is reduced or absent. The anus opens into a cavity at the rear of the body, and this cavity sometimes contains reduced gills. Some species have small radula teeth, an important feature because it provides the major evidence that these animals should be classified as molluscs. Most species burrow into the sediment in oceanic depths and feed on protozoans and other microscopic organisms or, for species in one order, cnidarians. About 300 species are presently known in the family.

Aplacophoran (5 mm)
Falcidens sp.
Class Aplacophora

Falcidens poias Scheltema, 1995

Habitat: Moderately exposed seagrass; 3–4 m depth.
Distribution: Rottnest I. WA.
Maximum size: Length to 5 mm.

Only a single species of aplacophoran has been recorded from shallow southern Australian waters; however, other species are probably also present but have been overlooked because of their small size. *Falcidens poias* was found in rhizomes of the seagrass *Posidonia sinuosa* at Rottnest Island. Other *Falcidens* species have been collected from depths greater than 30 m in Bass Strait.

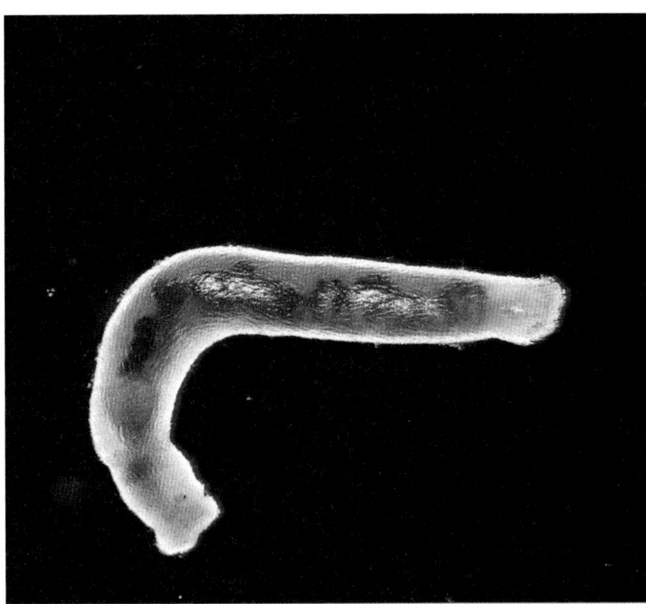

Falcidens poias, Rottnest I, WA

Class Polyplacophora

Chitons

Chitons are a conspicuous group of molluscs that are well adapted for life on wave-swept rock surfaces and which also commonly occur under rocks and in crevices. Although individual species are often very abundant in intertidal and shallow waters, only about 600 species are known worldwide, with nearly one-quarter of these occurring in Australia. The body plan of chitons varies little among species, with the basic structure consisting of an oval body covered by eight overlapping plates or valves. All valves except the tail valve overlap projections (known as sutural laminae) from the front of the next valve. Valves in most species also have marginal projections (insertion plates) that underlie the mantle. Most chitons have distinctive arrangements of grooves, granules or ridges across the valves, and the locations of these features are important when identifying species. The highest section of the valve is called the 'dorsal' (or central or jugal) region; the raised fan-shaped area that includes the outer margin is known as the 'lateral' region; and the intermediate triangular area is the 'pleural' region. Around the edges of the valves is an area of tough mantle called the girdle, which often has numerous embedded spines or a covering of scales. Some species have eye-like light-sensitive organs, complete with lens, retina and optic nerve, which are located in pits in the shell.

The undersurface of a chiton consists largely of a muscular foot that is separated by a groove from the rest of the body including the head. Within the groove are between four and 80 gills with rows of cilia. The cilia have a synchronous beat, producing a respiratory current that is drawn in under the front of the animal when the girdle is slightly raised and then expelled out behind the foot. The head lacks eyes and tentacles but has an obvious mouth with associated radula teeth. Chitons use the radula to rasp encrusting plant and animal material from the rock surface and convey it to the gut. A few species known to be carnivores raise their girdles and clamp down on small invertebrates which shelter underneath.

Chitons move slowly, and most species are more active after dusk than during the day. The majority of species live under rocks or in crevices because animals in the open may be attacked by wrasses and other fishes. Female chitons generally deposit eggs externally after nearby males have released sperm; however, several southern Australian species brood their young in the groove between foot and girdle. Spawning in some species is synchronised with a particular phase of the moon or with the tide.

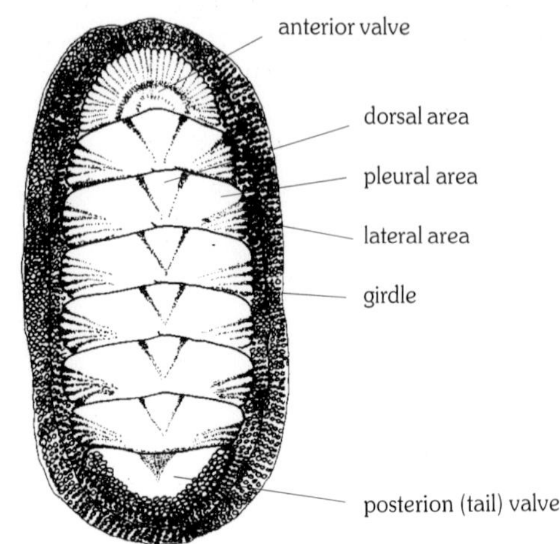

Chiton (50 mm)
Ischnochiton cariosus
Class Polyplacophora

FAMILY ISCHNOCHITONIDAE

Ischnochitonids are elongate chitons with the tail valve longest, and usually with the lateral and pleural areas of the shell valves separated by a clearly defined diagonal rib. The outermost margins of the valves where they are attached to the girdle (the insertion plates) are very narrow, and there are more than eight slits in the margin of the tail valve. This chiton family is very diverse, with more than 30 species recorded from southern Australia.

Ischnochiton australis (Blainville, 1825)

Habitat: Under rocks on reef; 0–8 m depth.
Distribution: Great Australian Bight, SA, to southern Qld and around Tas.
Maximum size: Length to 90 mm.

Ischnochiton australis, Norah Head, NSW

Ischnochiton australis is a dark green chiton with large girdle scales, several diagonal ridges across the lateral area and fine longitudinal ridges in the pleural area. It is the largest of the many southern Australian species of *Ischnochiton* and is abundant under rocks and rubble on reefs. This chiton can move relatively rapidly when disturbed and will also sometimes drop off overturned rocks and curl into a ball.

Ischnochiton lineolatus (Sowerby, 1840)

Habitat: Under rocks on sheltered and moderately exposed shores; 0–15 m depth.
Distribution: Normalup, WA, to Burleigh Heads, Qld, and around Tas.
Maximum size: Length to 50 mm.

Ischnochiton lineolatus has a white background colour, a fawn girdle and generally brown or black longitudinal streaks in the dorsal area. The lateral areas have closely packed ridges made of fine beads, and the pleural and dorsal areas have extremely fine ridges set in a zigzag pattern. The species is abundant and is usually found under rocks embedded in sand.

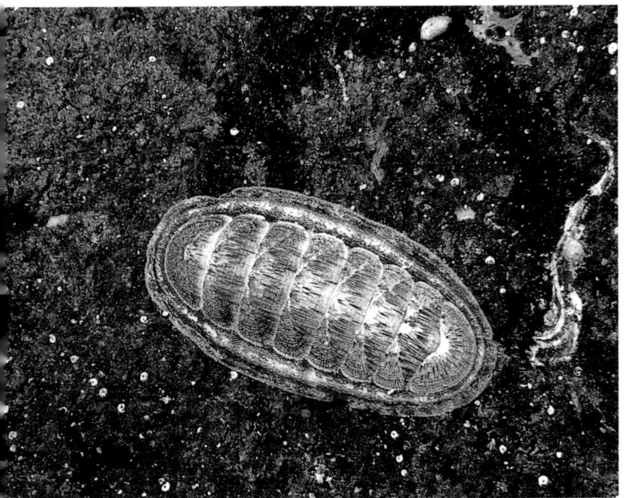

Ischnochiton lineolatus, Low Head, Tas.

Ischnochiton elongatus (Blainville, 1825)

Habitat: Under rocks on sheltered and moderately exposed shores; 0–10 m depth.
Distribution: Shark Bay, WA, to NSW and around Tas.
Maximum size: Length to 35 mm.

Ischnochiton elongatus superficially resembles *I. lineolatus* but lacks the dark streaks and has smaller girdle scales and finer ridges in the pleural area. The patterning is extremely variable, with the most common form having a dark background with a pale

Ischnochiton elongatus, Ricketts Pt, Vic.

stripe down the centre. This is one of the most abundant species of chiton found under rocks along much of the Victorian and Tasmanian coasts, and most often occurs under boulders embedded in sand.

Ischnochiton variegatus
(H. Adams & Angus, 1864)

Habitat: Under rocks on sheltered and moderately exposed reef; 0–5 m depth.
Distribution: Esperance, WA, to Mallacoota, Vic., and northern and eastern Tas.
Maximum size: Length to 30 mm.

Ischnochiton variegatus usually has a mottled brown, white or green coloration and pale girdle with brown bands. The species is often difficult to distinguish from several other *Ischnochiton* species; it differs from *I. elongatus* partly by having stronger riblets in the lateral areas, and from *I. lineolatus* by lacking the fine zigzag ridges in the dorsal areas and by having smaller girdle scales. *Ischnochiton variegatus* is locally abundant under rocks in lower intertidal habitats.

Ischnochiton variegatus, Flinders, Vic.

Ischnochiton contractus (Reeve, 1847)

Habitat: Under rocks on sheltered sand; 0–6 m depth.
Distribution: Dampier, WA, to Port Phillip Bay, Vic., and the Furneaux Group, Tas.
Maximum size: Length to 45 mm.

Ischnochiton contractus has the lateral areas of the valves covered by very small granules, and fine longitudinal and zigzag grooves in the pleural and dorsal areas, respectively. The colour pattern is extremely variable and can include creams, greens, browns, pinks and blues. The species occurs in small aggregations on the undersides of hard objects on sand.

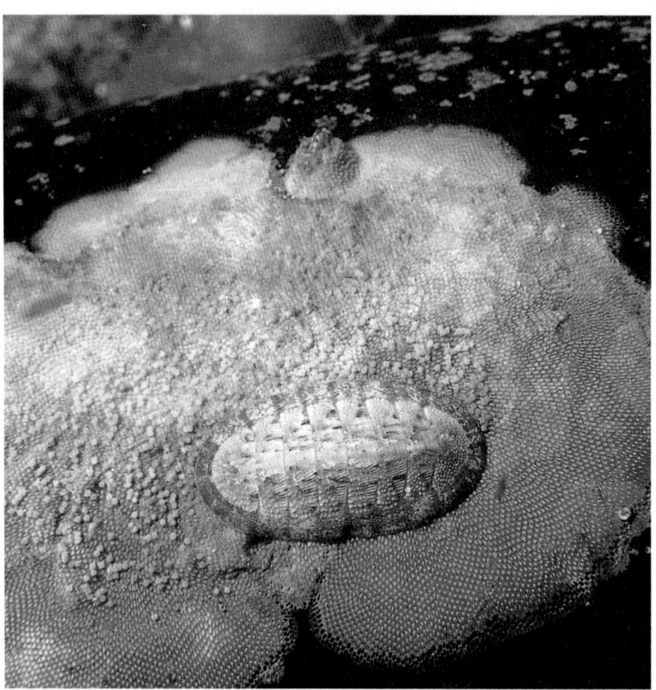

Ischnochiton contractus, Princess Royal Harbour, WA

Ischnochiton torri Iredale & May, 1916

Habitat: Under rocks on sheltered and moderately exposed sand, seagrass, reef; 0–10 m depth.
Distribution: Southern WA to Cape Patterson, Vic., and northern Tas.
Maximum size: Length to 42 mm.

Ischnochiton torri is easily recognised by its distinctive pattern of an orange girdle, chocolate-brown shell and white streaks concentrated in the dorsal region. The species is common and seems to prefer the undersurface of rocks embedded in sand near seagrass beds. This species moves rapidly if rocks are overturned and feeds mainly on drifting plant debris.

Ischnochiton cariosus (Pilsbry, 1892)

Habitat: Under rocks on sheltered and moderately exposed reef; 0–30 m depth.
Distribution: Albany, WA, to northern NSW and around Tas.
Maximum size: Length to 50 mm.

Ischnochiton cariosus has ridges formed from large beads in the lateral area and numerous thin longitudinal grooves in the pleural area. The species can also be recognised by the characteristic girdle scales, which are divided into two groups: large inner scales and smaller outer scales. Its coloration can include cream, yellow and brown.

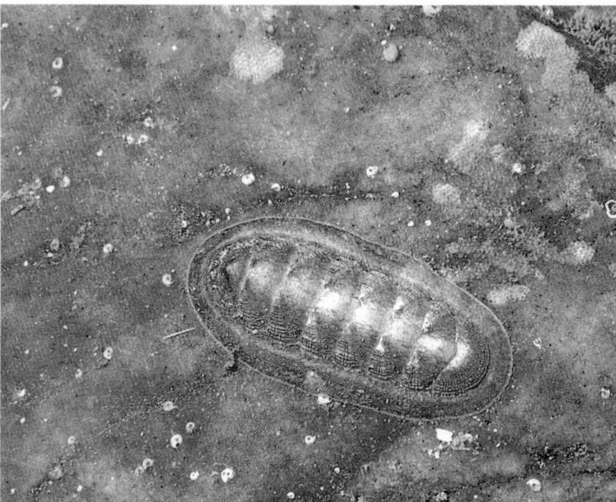

Ischnochiton cariosus, Rocky Cape, Tas.

Stenochiton longicymba Blainville, 1825

Habitat: Seagrass; 0–12 m depth.
Distribution: Dongara, WA, to western Vic. and northern Tas.
Maximum size: Length to 45 mm.

Ischnochiton torri, Port Victoria, SA

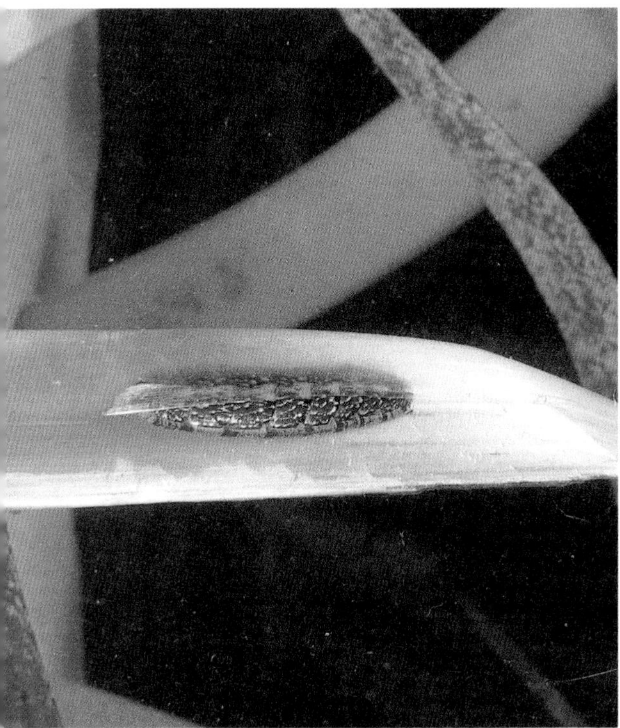

Stenochiton longicymba, Albany, WA. CLAY BRYCE

Stenochiton longicymba is an interesting elongate chiton, which occurs attached to leaf sheaths of the seagrass *Posidonia australis*. It occurs commonly in its restricted habitat but is normally seen only if deliberately searched for. Two other smaller and less elongate species of *Stenochiton* are associated with other southern Australian seagrasses: ***Stenochiton pilsbryanus*** occurs at the base of the leaves (but not the sheaths) of several *Posidonia* species and *Heterozostera tasmanica*, while ***Stenochiton cymodocealis*** lives at the base of the leaves of *Amphibolis antarctica* and (rarely) *Amphibolis griffithii*.

Callochiton crocina (Reeve, 1847)

Habitat: Under rocks on exposed reefs; 0–20 m depth.
Distribution: Southern WA to southern Qld and around Tas. Also New Zealand.
Maximum size: Length to 60 mm.

Callochiton crocina is a smooth chiton that is usually red with paired cream markings on the girdle at the four corners of the body. The species feeds by grazing encrusting algae and generally lives on reefs under rocks, in dark crevices or on the underside of the plate-like red alga *Sonderopelta coriacea*. Large specimens are occasionally found on rocks among sand and on rare occasions live freely on sand. This is one of the few chitons known to brood eggs in the mantle cavity.

Callochiton crocina, Bass Point, NSW

Eudoxoplax inornata (Tenison Woods, 1881)

Habitat: Under rocks on moderately exposed reefs; 0–10 m depth.
Distribution: SA and Vic. and around Tas.
Maximum size: Length to 75 mm.

Eudoxoplax inornata is a large chiton that is easily recognised by its red colour, low elevation and smooth valves. The species is moderately common under rocks on reefs in the D'Entrecasteaux Channel, southeastern Tas, but is rare through the rest of its range.

Eudoxoplax inornata, Gordon, Tas.

Callistochiton antiquus (Reeve, 1847)

Habitat: Under rocks on sheltered and moderately exposed reef; 2–10 m depth.
Distribution: Cape Naturaliste, WA, to Cooktown, Qld, and northern Tas.
Maximum size: Length to 40 mm.

Callistochiton antiquus is a brown species that is often heavily eroded; each valve has two prominent diagonal ridges made up of nodules, and longitudinal ridges are present in the pleural areas. The species prefers the underside of stones on reefs in slightly silty habitat and is not found on sand.

Callistochiton antiquus, Quarry Bay, WA

FAMILY MOPALIDAE

Species in this chiton family can usually be recognised by the wide leathery girdle with numerous bristles. The front section of the valves where they are inserted under the preceding valve is large, and there are no slits around the edge of the tail valve where it underlies the girdle.

Plaxiphora albida (Blainville, 1825)

Habitat: Exposed rocky shores; low intertidal.
Distribution: Southern WA to southern Qld and around Tas.
Maximum size: Length to 100 mm.

Plaxiphora albida is a large chiton that occurs at high densities in areas of reef with wave surge. It has large valves with conspicuous wavy green lines in juveniles but which become heavily eroded in adults, and a leathery girdle covered with bristles. The underside of the valves is coloured a distinctive torquoise blue. This species grazes encrusting algae, the individual chitons returning daily to the same site on the rock after feeding forays.

Plaxiphora albida, Bicheno, Tas.

FAMILY SCHIZOCHITONIDAE

This family contains relatively large chitons that are mainly carnivorous. There are flattened ridges on the valves and a deep excavation in the tail valve. The girdle bears small or blunt spines and has a slit at the rear.

Lorica volvox (Reeve, 1847)

Habitat: Exposed reef; 1–10 m depth.
Distribution: Southern WA to NSW and around Tas.
Maximum size: Length to 100 mm.

Lorica volvox is distinguished by its large size, relatively high shell and rows of fine granules in the lateral areas and on the head valve. The basal colour is generally cream with dark brown or ochre markings. The species is moderately common under large flat rocks in areas with good water flow.

Lorica volvox, Coles Bay, Tas.

FAMILY CHITONIDAE

The family Chitonidae includes several different groups of species, all characterised by a fine comb-like pattern around the edges of the valves where they underlie the girdle. Most species have a girdle constructed from dense, bead-like scales. Some species have well-developed light-sensitive organs arranged in a regular pattern across the valves.

Chiton pelliserpentis Quoy and Gaimard, 1836

Habitat: Sheltered and moderately exposed rocky shores; mid to low intertidal.
Distribution: Cape Conran, Vic., to central NSW and eastern Tas. Also New Zealand.
Maximum size: Length to 65 mm.

Chiton pelliserpentis is mottled greenish-brown with dark markings in the dorsal area. The scientific name for the species alludes to the snakeskin-like appearance of its girdle, which has alternating grey and brown bars and large scales that detach easily. This chiton is one of the most conspicuous and abundant animals in the intertidal zone, particularly on sheltered southeastern Tasmanian reefs. Animals generally return to the same scars in the rock during the day after foraging away at night. The valves of individuals living high in the intertidal zone, particularly in New South Wales, are usually heavily eroded.

Chiton pelliserpentis, Port Stephens, NSW

Chiton glaucus Gray, 1828

Habitat: Sheltered rocky shores; low intertidal.
Distribution: Southeastern Tas. Also New Zealand.
Maximum size: Length to 30 mm.

Chiton glaucus is an olive-green species with smooth valves and a peaked ridge along the centre. During the day it remains hidden under boulders, but at night large numbers appear moving about the tops of reefs. The species is believed to have been introduced from New Zealand to Tasmania early in the twentieth century. *Chiton glaucus* and *C. pelliserpentis* are now the most conspicuous chitons on intertidal shores in southeastern Tasmania.

Chiton pelliserpentis, Eaglehawk Neck, Tas.

Chiton glaucus, Tinderbox, Tas.

Rhyssoplax calliozona (Pilsbry, 1894)

Habitat: Under rocks on sheltered and moderately exposed reef; 1–60 m depth.
Distribution: Esperance, WA, to Vic. and Tas.
Maximum size: Length to 70 mm.

Several brightly coloured species belonging to the genus *Rhyssoplax* occur in southern Australian waters, with *R. calliozona* distinguished by having very fine diagonal grooves in the lateral areas and strong longitudinal grooves in the pleural areas. A related species found in much the same region (South Australia, Victoria and Tasmania), ***Rhyssoplax diaphora***, has higher valves, numerous fine longitudinal ridges across the lateral areas and more colourful markings. *Rhyssoplax calliozona* is most commonly found on the undersurface of rocks embedded in sand.

Rhyssoplax calliozona, Rocky Cape, Tas.

Rhyssoplax jugosa (Gould, 1846)

Habitat: Under rocks on exposed reef; 1–15 m depth.
Distribution: Point Hicks, Vic., to northern NSW.
Maximum size: Length to 50 mm.

Rhyssoplax jugosa is a bright but variably coloured species that differs from *R. calliozona* by having longitudinal grooves across the lateral areas; it differs from its close relative, *R. diaphora*, by having strong longitudinal grooves extending fully rather than part-way across the pleural areas. It is one of the most commonly observed chitons on reefs along the New South Wales coast.

Rhyssoplax jugosa, Terrigal, NSW

Onithochiton quercinus (Gould, 1846)

Habitat: Exposed reef; 0–5 m depth.
Distribution: Houtman Abrolhos to Esperance, WA, and southern NSW to Mackay, Qld.
Maximum size: Length to 80 mm.

Onithochiton quercinus has low, flat valves, which are generally covered by wavy markings, and a wide, leathery girdle, which lacks scales but is covered by very fine spicules. An interesting feature of this species is the presence of light-sensitive organs (the 'shell eyes'), which appear as rows of small black spots across the valves. This chiton is common in the lower intertidal zone on rock platforms in New South Wales and Western Australia, the animals at exposed sites often having heavily eroded shells.

Onithochiton quercinus, Terrigal, NSW

FAMILY ACANTHOCHITONIDAE

Acanthochitonids are a varied group of chitons with girdles containing numerous embedded spicules. Their valves are often reduced in size and have large insertion plates. Most species in the family feed on other invertebrates.

Cryptoplax striata (Lamarck, 1819)

Habitat: Under rocks on reef; 0–20 m depth.
Distribution: Southern WA to Cape Paterson, Vic., and around Tas.
Maximum size: Length to 120 mm.

Cryptoplax striata is a flexible chiton with a very large, cream to yellow-brown, spicule-covered girdle that changes in length and width as the animal crawls about. The valves are small and ridged and are connected on juveniles but become separated as each individual develops. A close relative with a wider girdle, ***Cryptoplax mystica***, occurs in New South Wales.

Cryptoplax striata, Gordon, Tas.

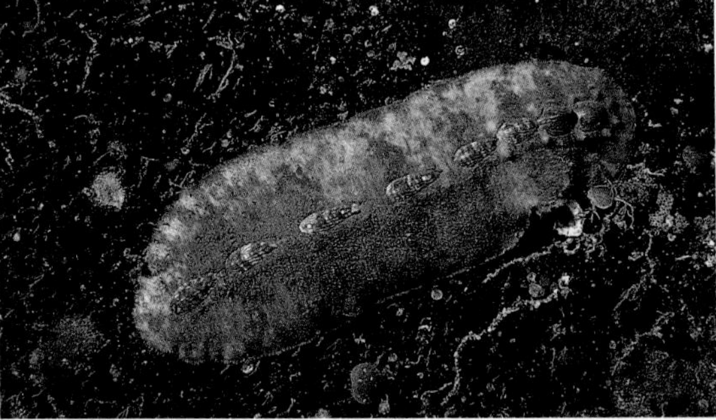

Class Gastropoda

Gastropods, univalves

The gastropods form the largest and most ubiquitous class of molluscs, including abalone, limpets, periwinkles, cowries, tritons, whelks and many other families. Approximately 70 000 species are known at present. Most species have a large, right-handed, spirally coiled shell into which the animal can fully withdraw, the entrance then being sealed by a rounded structure known as the operculum, which is attached to the foot. However, some gastropods are slug-like in appearance, while others have the shell greatly reduced or, in one small group of opisthobranchs, twinned in a way that resembles bivalves (class Bivalvia). A distinguishing characteristic of gastropods is that most of the body rotates through 180° relative to the head early in the life of the animal, resulting in the nervous and circulatory systems becoming twisted.

Although a few families have male and female organs within the one animal and in other families there is a change from male to female late in life, in most the sexes are separate and fixed from birth. The developmental process differs greatly between gastropod groups. In some species eggs are released in large numbers and fertilised externally, while in others the male internally introduces sperm to the female using an intromittent organ, and fertilised eggs are attached to the seabed or, in rare cases, fully develop within the female. Most gastropods have two planktonic larval stages, a ciliated lantern-like trochophore stage, followed by a veliger stage when the mollusc develops a small shell and long ciliated lobes. Once the veliger settles, it quickly transforms into the shelled form typical of the adult.

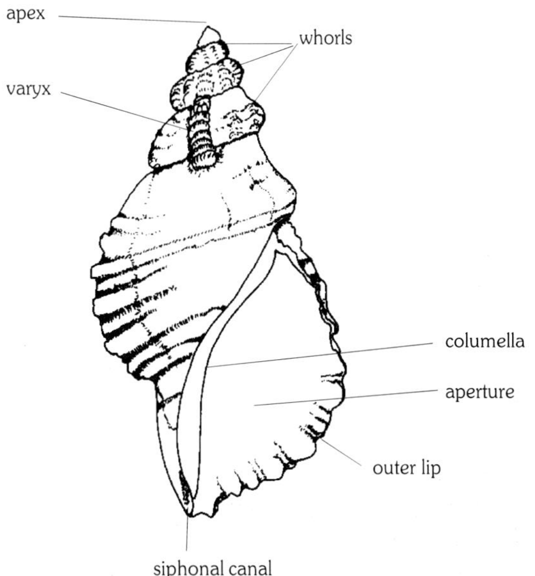

Gastropod (150 mm)
Cabestana spengleri
Class Gastropoda

Gastropods also exhibit a huge array of feeding strategies that capitalise on the plasticity of their radula teeth. The majority are grazers, possessing a ribbon-like radula with rows of chitinous teeth that scrape plant and animal material off hard surfaces. Some species are scavengers, while others are predators, including the infamous cone shells which harpoon prey with their radula and have caused human deaths. The shape and arrangement of the radula is distinctive within species and is an important character in the classification of molluscs.

Subclass Prosobranchia

Prosobranchs

The prosobranchs differ from gastropods in other subclasses largely on the basis of internal anatomy. They have a single pair of tentacles projecting from the head, with eyes at the base, and generally possess an operculum. The subclass includes most of the commonly encountered species with spirally coiled shells. The majority are marine, although numerous terrestrial (land-dwelling) and freshwater species also exist.

FAMILY HALIOTIDAE
Abalone, earshells

Abalone are distinguished by the low spire and very large ear-shaped aperture. A row of respiratory holes is present on the left side of the shell near the margin, with the innermost holes gradually filling up with the pearly shell lining (nacre). The foot is extremely large, enabling the animal to clamp rigidly onto rock in areas of wave action.

Haliotis rubra Leach, 1814
Blacklip abalone

Habitat: Exposed reef; 0–40 m depth.
Distribution: Fremantle, WA, to northern NSW and around Tas.
Maximum size: Length to 200 mm.

Haliotis rubra is a large reddish abalone with a black-edged foot and numerous fine spiral ridges around the shell that are crossed by irregular radiating ribs.

Haliotis rubra, Bicheno, Tas.

The shells on larger animals are often heavily eroded and partly covered by algae and sessile animals. The blacklip abalone is the third most valuable fishery species in Australia, generating an annual catch worth about $100 million. Although animals tend to aggregate in crevices, this is also the most conspicuous of the large gastropods on most shallow southeastern Australian reefs. Some authorities consider southwestern animals to be a separate species, ***Haliotis conicopora***, because they grow to a larger size than eastern animals and have a darker and less obviously ribbed shell.

Haliotis rubra (conicopora form), Rocky Cape, Tas.

Haliotis laevigata (Donovan, 1808)

Greenlip abalone

Habitat: Moderately exposed reef; 0–30 m depth.
Distribution: Cape Naturaliste, WA, to Cape Liptrap, Vic., and northern Tas.
Maximum size: Length to 200 mm.

Haliotis laevigata is the largest of the Australian abalone. It is easily recognised by the smooth light-coloured shell, green tentacles and green edge to the foot. The species prefers more sheltered conditions than the other large abalone, and congregates on the edge of reefs and boulders near sand or seagrass beds. Greenlip abalone provides about one-fifth of the total commercial abalone catch and is widely considered the best-tasting of Australian abalone.

Haliotis laevigata, Rocky Cape, Tas.

Haliotis scalaris Leach, 1814

Habitat: Moderately exposed reef; 0–50 m depth.
Distribution: Southern WA to Cape Liptrap, Vic., and northern Tas.
Maximum size: Length to 120 mm.

Haliotis scalaris resembles *H. rubra* but is a smaller animal and has a wide groove around the outside of the shell next to the row of holes. The other characteristic feature of the species is a wide spiral ridge running around the shell between the row of holes and the spire. This ridge is best seen on the inside of

Haliotis scalaris, Esperance, WA

the shell, where it forms an obvious groove. The internal groove of animals east of central South Australia is not as sharply defined as in western animals, and the eastern animals were called ***Haliotis emmae*** until recently. *Haliotis scalaris* is normally found under boulders or in narrow crevices.

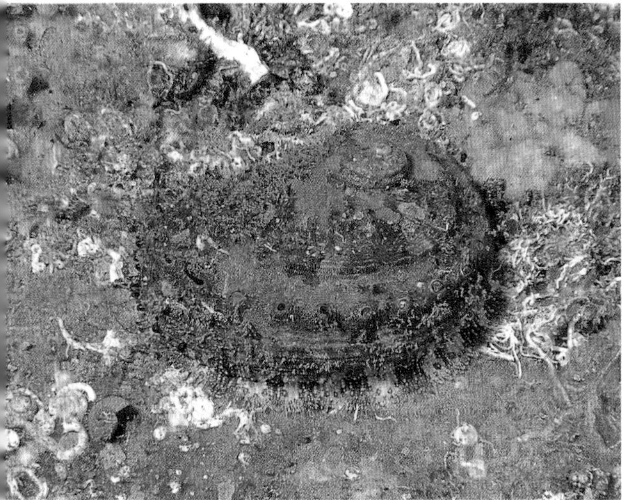

Haliotis scalaris (emmae form), Rocky Cape, Tas.

Haliotis roei Gray, 1827

Roe's abalone

Habitat: Moderately and submaximally exposed reef; 0–3 m depth.
Distribution: Shark Bay, WA, to western Vic.
Maximum size: Length to 120 mm.

The shell surface of *Haliotis roei* has numerous fine ridges but lacks the diffuse outward-radiating ribs of most other abalone. It is most abundant at low-tide level in wave-swept areas, with the shells of animals in the most exposed locations often heavily eroded. The species naturally occurs in extremely high densities on limestone rock platforms near Perth and is exploited by both commercial and recreational fishers. It is able to occur in such high densities only because it does not rely on the limited food growing in the immediate vicinity but feeds mainly on drifting macroalgae.

Haliotis roei, Port Lincoln, SA

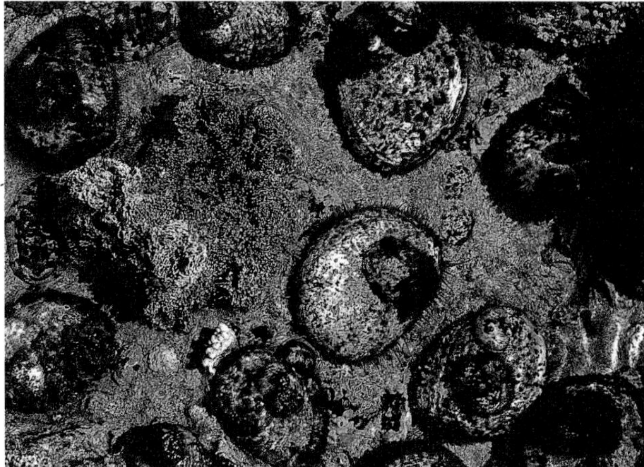

Haliotis roei, Watermans, WA

Haliotis elegans Phillipi, 1874

Habitat: Moderately exposed reef; 4–33 m depth.
Distribution: Jurien Bay to Esperance, WA.
Maximum size: Length to 70 mm.

Haliotis elegans is a small abalone with numerous distinctive spiral ridges and a more elongate shell than other local species. It is found in caves and under rock slabs, mainly on limestone reefs, and is one of the rarer abalone species.

Haliotis elegans, Rottnest I, WA. CLAY BRYCE

Haliotis semiplicata Menke, 1843

Habitat: Moderately exposed reef; 4–18 m depth.
Distribution: Fremantle to Esperance, WA.
Maximum size: Length to 70 mm.

Haliotis semiplicata is an uncommon species found under rocks. It can be confused with juvenile blacklip abalone *H. rubra* but has a relatively straight rather

Haliotis semiplicata, Albany, WA. CLAY BRYCE

than rounded outer lip. On the inside of the shell there is an indistinct spiral groove in the same position as the groove on *H. scalaris*.

Haliotis coccoradiata Reeve, 1846

Habitat: Moderately and submaximally exposed reef; 0–10 m depth.
Distribution: Mallacoota, Vic., to northern NSW.
Maximum size: Length to 65 mm.

Haliotis coccoradiata is the New South Wales counterpart in shape to *H. semiplicata.* It has a slightly elongate shell with radial and spiral ridges and is a red-brown colour (the black and white markings on the illustrated animal are caused by encrusting invertebrates). The species is common but is often mistaken for juvenile blacklip abalone *H. rubra*. It remains concealed under rocks during the day.

Haliotis coccoradiata, Norah Head, NSW

FAMILY FISSURELLIDAE
Keyhole limpets, slit limpets

Fissurellids have a limpet-like shell with a hole in the apex, or notch or groove in the margin, to assist the exit of water from the mantle cavity. Nearly all species graze algae off rocks.

Scutus antipodes Montfort, 1810
Elephant snail

Habitat: Reef; 0–20 m depth.
Distribution: Southern WA to NSW and around Tas. Also New Zealand.
Maximum size: Length to 100 mm.

Scutus antipodes is a large black slug-like animal with a white trough-shaped shell located under folds of skin on its upper surface. Because of its distinctive appearance and the large numbers found under rocks near low-water mark, the elephant snail is one of the better-known gastropods. At night it moves out from under rocks to forage on drift algae. The species is fully protected in Tasmania.

Scutus antipodes, Flinders, Vic.

Cosmetalepas concatenatus
(Crosse & Fischer, 1864)

Habitat: Moderately and submaximally exposed reef; 0–15 m depth.
Distribution: Houtman Abrolhos, WA, to southern NSW and northeastern Tas.
Maximum size: Length to 22 mm.

Cosmetalepas concatenatus has a white rounded shell with numerous fine pits and a nearly circular hole. It avoids sunlight so lives under rocks or in crevices, and is not often seen alive.

Amblychilepas nigrita (Sowerby, 1834)

Habitat: Under rocks on sheltered and moderately exposed reef; 0–70 m depth.
Distribution: Geraldton, WA, to southern Qld and around Tas.
Maximum size: Shell length to 25 mm.

Amblychilepas nigrita is a keyhole limpet with an elongate saddle-shaped shell that is much smaller than the animal. The species is common under rocks and moves rapidly if exposed to sunlight.

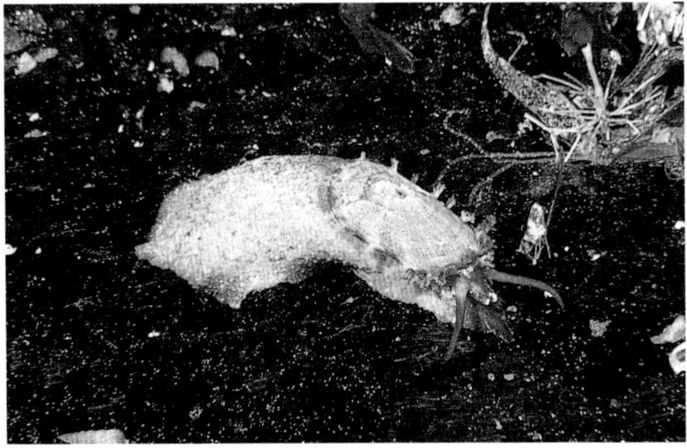

Amblychilepas nigrita, Flinders, Vic. RUDIE KUITER

Amblychilepas javanicensis has a more rounded shell than *A. nigrita*, and the hole is pear-shaped rather than round. Shells are often washed ashore, but the animals themselves are not often seen. This species is recorded to occur under rocks; however, it seems to predominantly live partly buried under sand attached to seagrass (*Heterozostera tasmanica*) rhizomes.

Amblychilepas javanicensis, Bicheno, Tas.

Amblychilepas javanicensis (Lamarck, 1822)

Habitat: Moderately exposed seagrass; 0–16 m depth.
Distribution: Houtman Abrolhos, WA, to southern Qld and around Tas.
Maximum size: Shell length to 25 mm.

Diodora lineata, Norah Head, NSW

Diodora lineata (Sowerby, 1835)

Habitat: Under rocks on sheltered and moderately exposed reef; 0–10 m depth.
Distribution: Port Phillip Bay, Vic., to southern Qld.
Maximum size: Length to 50 mm.

Diodora lineata is a distinctive keyhole limpet with a high oval shell, round hole and prominent knobbly radial ridges. In contrast with many other keyhole limpets, the animal can conceal itself completely within the shell and moves relatively slowly.

Cosmetalepas concatenatus, Flinders, Vic.

Notomella bajula (Hedley, 1913)

Habitat: Under rocks on moderately exposed reef; 0–38 m depth.
Distribution: Southern WA to NSW and around Tas.
Maximum size: Length to 15 mm.

Notomella bajula has a small white shell with numerous fine radial ribs crossed by slightly weaker concentric ridges. It is a slit limpet, and therefore related to the keyhole limpets and abalone, but has a slit in the front of the shell, serving the same respiratory and excretory function as the holes in the other groups. The slit in *Notomella bajula* extends for about one-third of the distance to the spire and leads into a slight groove on the shell. The other relatively common slit limpet, ***Notomella candida***, has a relatively short slit in the front of the shell that extends for only about one-sixth of the way to the spire and has fewer and stronger ribs.

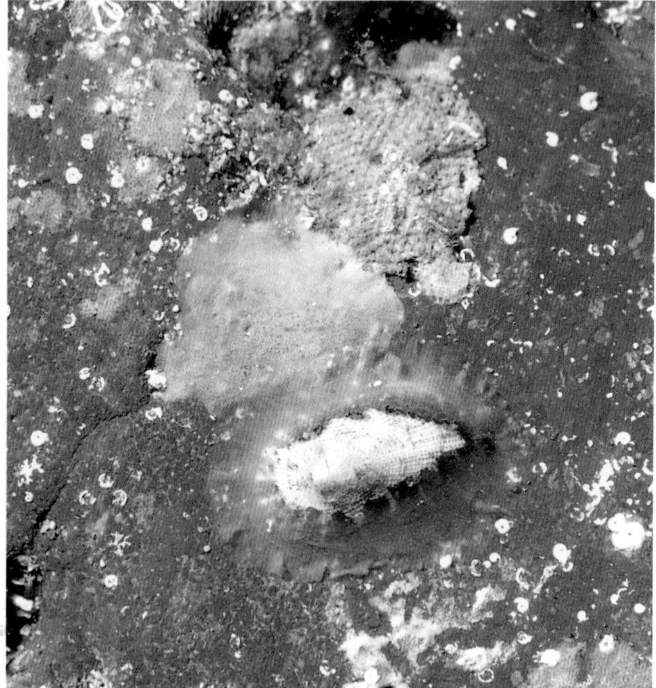

Notomella bajula, Merimbula, NSW

Clypidina rugosa (Quoy & Gaimard, 1834)

Habitat: Exposed rocky shores; mid to low intertidal.
Distribution: Southern WA to NSW and around Tas.
Maximum size: Length to 18 mm.

Clypidina rugosa is a small, white, high-spired species with about 15 major radiating ribs and two or three minor ribs between. Small concentric ridges are also present around the shell. Although classified with the slit limpets, *C. rugosa* has only a small notch at the front end, which is most visible on the undersurface. The species is one of the most widespread and abundant gastropods living on the shore. Ecological studies in the Sydney area indicate that the largest animals are about three years old.

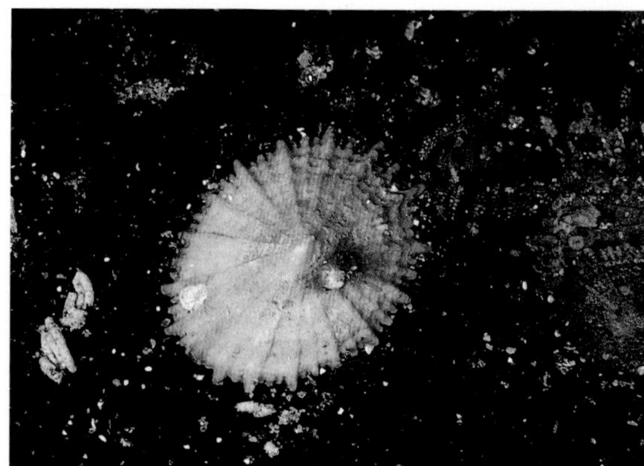

Clypidina rugosa, Terrigal, NSW

FAMILY PATELLIDAE
Patellid limpets, true limpets

Patellid limpets have a low conical shell, which lacks perforations, and they have a fine network of gills surrounding the foot rather than a single feathery gill. The species are adapted for living on wave-swept shores and so possess a strongly muscular foot.

Patella peronii Blainville, 1825

Habitat: Exposed rocky shores; low intertidal.
Distribution: Shark Bay, WA, to NSW and around Tas.
Maximum size: Length to 40 mm.

Patella peronii is a variable limpet that occurs abundantly near low-tide level. It can usually be recognised by the numerous strong ribs (up to 24) covered by sharp scales with smaller ridges between. The ribs are dull white and the grooves dark-coloured; however, this pattern is usually obscured by shell erosion and growths on the surface. The undersurface of the shell is white with a light orange tint at the apex.

Patella peronii, Eaglehawk Neck, Tas.

Patella chapmani Tenison Woods, 1876

Habitat: Exposed reef; 0–5 m depth.
Distribution: Dongara, WA, to NSW and around Tas.
Maximum size: Length to 40 mm.

Patella chapmani is the easiest of limpets to recognise because of its distinctive eight-rayed shape. The star pattern is most pronounced at sites with heavy wave exposure, and animals are also flatter at these sites. The species is extremely abundant in New South Wales, where it occurs most commonly on flat coralline-algal encrusted rock just below low-tide level.

Patella chapmani, Ulladulla, NSW

Patella laticostata Blainville, 1825

Habitat: Exposed rocky shores; low intertidal.
Distribution: Shark Bay, WA, to Port Lincoln, SA.
Maximum size: Length to 110 mm.

Patella laticostata is a massive species, by far the largest limpet in Australia. The shell is covered by numerous (about 50) cream-coloured ribs, with dark areas between. Larger animals are, however, heavily eroded on the top of the shell, and so the ribs are seen only around the edge. The species is common near low-tide level in southern Western Australia, but population numbers appear to be declining because of increasing fishing pressure.

Patella laticostata, Albany, WA

Cellana tramoserica (Holten, 1802)

Habitat: Exposed rocky shores; mid to low intertidal.
Distribution: Southern WA to southern Qld and northeastern Tas.
Maximum size: Length to 50 mm.

Cellana tramoserica is an orange-brown limpet with dark radiating stripes or crescent-shaped markings. Because of its size and abundance in the mid intertidal zone, this species has been studied more intensively than almost any other intertidal animal. Dense populations of limpets are important in controlling the growth of algae on many rock platforms because of the intensity of their grazing activity. Animals return to the same home spot after each feeding excursion, using chemical sensors to retrace their mucous trail.

Cellana tramoserica, Point Sinclair, SA

Cellana solida (Blainville, 1825)

Habitat: Exposed rocky shores; low intertidal.
Distribution: Great Australian Bight, SA, to southern Qld and around Tas.
Maximum size: Length to 80 mm.

Cellana solida grows to a much larger size than *C. tramoserica* and has fewer radiating ribs (about 26 cf. 36) and an orange margin. The two species occupy much the same habitat on rocky shores, with *C. solida* dominant in Tasmanian waters and *C. tramoserica* on the mainland. *Cellana solida* is now protected in Tasmania, after heavy exploitation of localised populations for export as an abalone substitute.

Cellana solida, Eaglehawk Neck, Tas.

FAMILY ACMAEIDAE
Acmaeid limpets

Species in this family are very closely related in form and habits to the patellid limpets. They are distinguished by the presence of a single large feathery gill on the left side of the mantle cavity.

Patelloida alticostata (Angas, 1865)

Habitat: Exposed rocky shores; mid to low intertidal.
Distribution: Geraldton, WA, to northern NSW and around Tas.
Maximum size: Length to 40 mm.

Patelloida alticostata is easily mistaken for another common limpet, *Patella peronii*, but generally occurs at a higher level on the shore and has fewer and stronger ribs. Its major distinguishing characteristic is the presence of black crescent-shaped markings in grooves low down on the shell; however, these may be indistinct or obscured on large specimens. Large animals are generally over five years old.

Patelloida alticostata, Tinderbox, Tas.

Patelloida latistrigata (Angas, 1865)

Habitat: Exposed rocky shores; upper to mid intertidal.
Distribution: Eastern SA to Coolangatta, Qld, and around Tas.
Maximum size: Length to 18 mm.

Patelloida latistrigata is a small limpet with a variable shape that enables it to occupy small depressions in rock; it is therefore rarely noticed, despite being the most abundant limpet on many southeastern

Patelloida latistrigata, Eaglehawk Neck, Tas.

Australian rock platforms. It usually has about 12 large ribs with dark markings between and is speckled with black towards the centre of the shell. The species is often found beside the small barnacle *Chaemosipho tasmanica*.

Patelloida victoriana (Singleton, 1937)

Habitat: Submaximally and maximally exposed reef; 0–10 m depth.
Distribution: Spencer Gulf, SA, to Wilsons Promontory, Vic., and around Tas.
Maximum size: Length to 45 mm.

Patelloida victoriana has a reddish-brown shell covered by very fine radiating ribs and a white eroded top. When observed alive, the shell is seen to be covered by the same pink encrusting coralline algae as grows on nearby rock. The species occurs most abundantly on flat rock in areas swept by fronds of the giant seaweed *Durvillaea potatorum*.

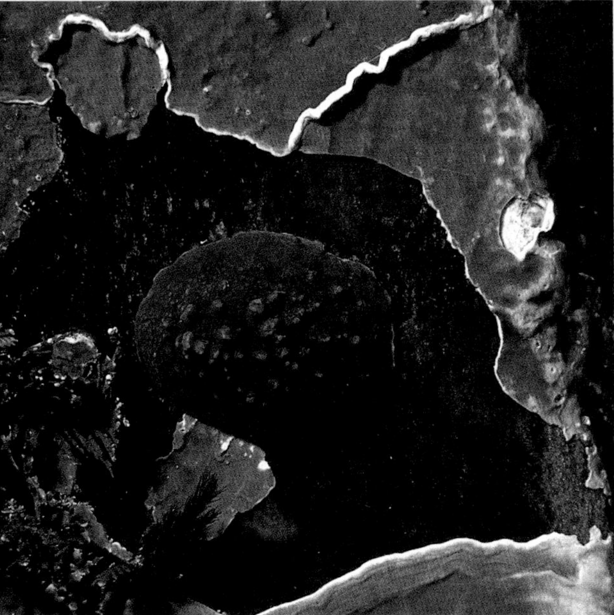

Patelloida victoriana, Port Davey, Tas.

Patelloida mimula (Iredale, 1924)

Habitat: Sheltered shells, rock; high intertidal.
Distribution: Tropical Australia south to Lakes Entrance, Vic.
Maximum size: Length to 20 mm.

Patelloida mimula is a common species in sheltered bays and estuaries along the eastern coast, where it is nearly always found attached to the Sydney rock oyster. The outer shell is greenish-brown, often with an indistinct cross.

Patelloida insignis (Menke, 1843)

Habitat: Sheltered and moderately exposed reef; 0–5 m depth.
Distribution: Geraldton, WA, to central Vic. and around Tas.
Maximum size: Length to 30 mm.

Patelloida insignis is a moderately high limpet with a Maltese Cross pattern on the upper surface and a predominantly white undersurface with a dark centre. The species is very common on open rock surfaces just below low-tide level.

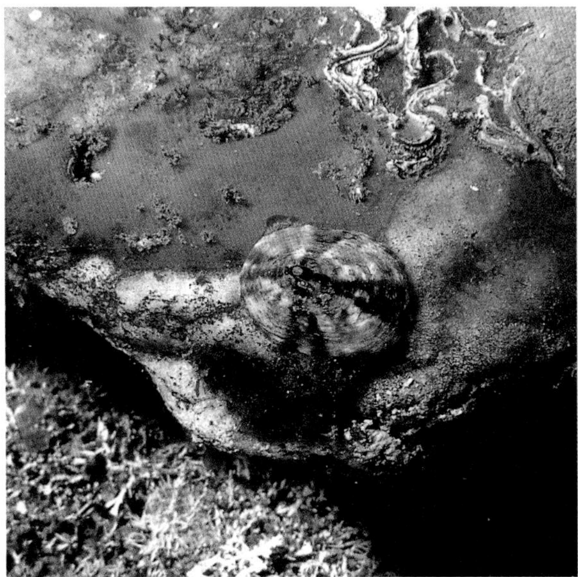

Patelloida insignis, Rocky Cape, Tas.

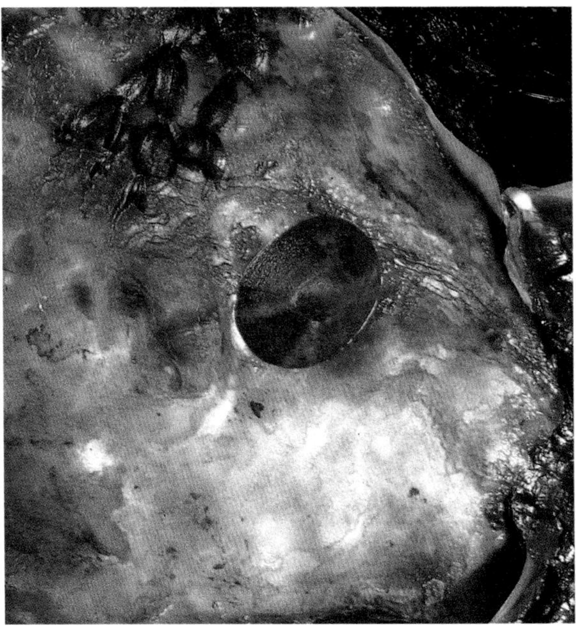

Patelloida mimula, Moonee Moonee, NSW

Notoacmea flammea (Quoy & Gaimard, 1834)

Habitat: Under rocks on sheltered reef; 0–5 m depth.
Distribution: Fremantle, WA, to Sydney, NSW, and around Tas.
Maximum size: Length to 17 mm.

Notoacmea flammea is a small, relatively flat limpet with a thin shell. Numerous dark lines radiate out from the pointed spire, with cross-hatching also present on many specimens, particularly those from Tasmania, such as the animal illustrated. The species is commonly found under rocks in sheltered estuaries and bays and is sometimes attached to other molluscs.

Notoacmea flammea, Tinderbox, Tas.

Notoacmea mayi (May, 1923)

Habitat: Exposed reef; high to mid intertidal.
Distribution: Eastern SA to Cape Liptrap, Vic., and around Tas.
Maximum size: Length to 25 mm.

Notoacmea mayi is a small dark limpet with a smooth surface and an apex close to the margin of the shell; this apical area is usually heavily eroded. The species occurs abundantly in Tasmania, where it forms aggregations on vertical rock surfaces below high-tide level.

Notoacmea petterdi (Tenison Woods, 1876)

Habitat: Exposed reef; high to mid intertidal.
Distribution: Eastern SA to Noosa Heads, Qld, and around Tas.
Maximum size: Length to 22 mm.

Notoacmea mayi, Cloudy Bay, Tas.

Notoacmea petterdi, Bicheno, Tas.

Notoacmea petterdi occurs in much the same habitat as *N. mayi* but is unlikely to be confused with that species because the apex is near the centre and the shell surface has radial ridges. The interior of the shell of *N. petterdi* is distinctive, with a dark stripe running around the edge of the shell and a dark brown central area.

FAMILY TROCHIDAE
Top shells

Top shells, or trochids, are generally conical-shaped and round in cross-section and have an pearly internal lining of nacre. The shells are sealed by a thin horny operculum. The family includes many small grazing species in southern Australia and also several large species in the tropics with shells that are used for making buttons and jewellery. Trochids have separate sexes, which expel sperm and gametes into the water column for fertilisation. The planktonic larvae generally drift for about a week before settling. The names of species in this family are unstable, as there is little consensus among biologists about many of the generic names.

Granata imbricata (Lamarck, 1816)

Habitat: Under rocks; 0–20 m depth.
Distribution: Geraldton, WA, to Wilsons Promontory, Vic., and northern Tas.
Maximum size: Length to 35 mm.

Because of its very large aperture, *Granata imbricata* superficially resembles a small abalone. The shell is cream with numerous fine spiral ridges and a pearly interior. The species is commonly found in small aggregations under rocks on exposed reefs.

Granata imbricata, Albany, WA. CLAY BRYCE

Stomatella impertusa (Burrow, 1815)

Habitat: Under stones on sheltered and moderately exposed reef; 0–7 m depth.
Distribution: Southern WA to NSW and around Tas.
Maximum size: Length to 25 mm.

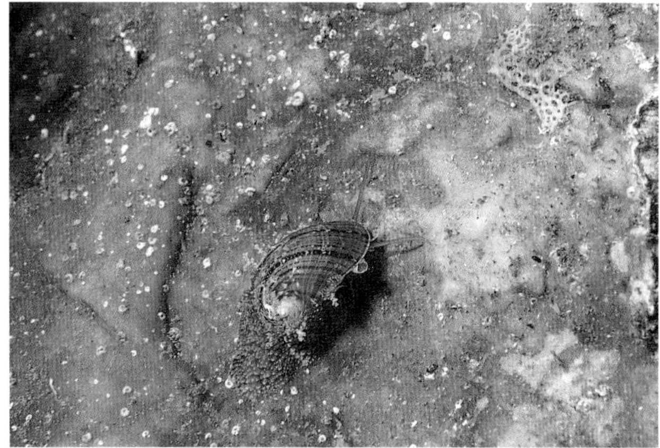

Stomatella impertusa, Portsea, Vic.

Stomatella impertusa is often confused with juvenile abalone, but the species lacks respiratory holes in the shell and has a very large foot that cannot retract fully. It occurs in aggregations under rocks and will move very rapidly towards darkened spaces if the rock is overturned. Part of the foot can be shed if the animal is threatened.

Clanculus undatus (Lamarck, 1816)

Habitat: Exposed reef; 0–15 m depth.
Distribution: Cape Naturaliste, WA, to NSW and around Tas.
Maximum size: Width to 31 mm.

Clanculus undatus is by far the largest of the many southern Australian species of *Clanculus*, a genus that can be recognised by the shell being squat and rounded in shape, with a beaded spiral sculpture, and having one or more prominent teeth on the columella. *Clanculus undatus* has numerous rows of fine granules around the shell and a red-brown basal colour with darker spots. The animals remain in crevices and under rocks during the day but move about quite rapidly in the open at night.

Clanculus undatus, Bicheno, Tas.

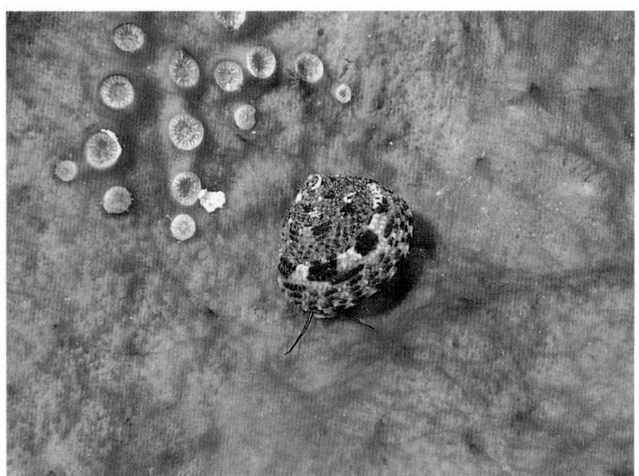

Clanculus flagellatus, Esperance, WA

Clanculus flagellatus (Phillipi, 1848)

Habitat: Under rocks on moderately exposed reef; 0–10 m depth.
Distribution: Fremantle, WA, to Vic. and around Tas.
Maximum size: Width to 12 mm.

Clanculus flagellatus has eight rows of spiral beads around the last whorl, six rows around the previous whorl, and a colourful pattern of dark and white markings on a pale reddish-brown background. It occurs commonly under rocks but is rarely noticed because of its small size.

Calliostoma armillata (Wood, 1828)

Habitat: Moderately and submaximally exposed reef; 0–30 m depth.
Distribution: Fremantle, WA, to NSW and around Tas.
Maximum size: Height to 35 mm.

Calliostoma armillata, Bicheno, Tas.

Calliostoma armillata has a pretty shell, with virtually no variation in colour or pattern throughout its range. It lives in the open, grazing on algae-encrusted rock, and is most common below the kelp zone on eastern Tasmanian reefs.

Cantharidus lepidus (Wood, 1828)

Habitat: Sheltered and moderately exposed seagrass, macroalgae; 0–7 m depth.
Distribution: North West Cape to Esperance, WA.
Maximum size: Height to 16 mm.

Despite its small size, *Cantharidus lepidus* plays an important role in the ecology of *Amphibolis* and *Posidonia* seagrass communities in Western Australia because it can occur in huge densities. It is, for example, an important food source for juvenile western rock lobsters. The species has straight sides to the shell, a height approximately equal to width and a distinctive purple, red and white pattern along the fine spiral ridges.

Cantharidus lepidus, Cliff Head, WA

Odontotrochus indistinctus Wood, 1828

Habitat: Sheltered seagrass, algae; 0–4 m depth.
Distribution: Eastern Vic. to central Qld.
Maximum size: Height to 20 mm.

Odontotrochus indistinctus resembles *Cantharidus lepidus* except that its spiral ridges are beaded. It is the most common top shell living among beds of the seagrass *Posidonia australis* in New South Wales estuaries and has been known until recently as *Thalotia comtessi*.

Thalotia conica (Gray, 1827)

Habitat: Sheltered seagrass, algae; 0–25 m depth.
Distribution: Geraldton, WA, to Wilsons Promontory, Vic., and south to Triabunna, Tas.
Maximum size: Height to 23 mm.

Thalotia conica is a small reddish-brown species with dark beads around its spiral ridges and an inner tooth on the side of the aperture. The species occurs commonly in southern seagrass beds and is also occasionally found on seaweeds in sheltered rockpools.

Thalotia conica, Little I, WA

Odontotrochus indistinctus, Merimbula, NSW

Prothalotia lehmani, Little I, WA

Prothalotia lehmani (Menke, 1843)

Habitat: Moderately exposed seagrass, algae; 0–8 m depth.
Distribution: Kalbarri, WA, to SA.
Maximum size: Height to 15 mm.

Prothalotia lehmani differs from other species by having wavy white and green lines down the shell, and each whorl is widest about two-thirds of the way down. The species also differs from most other seagrass-associated top shells by usually occurring as individuals rather than in aggregations.

Phasianotrochus eximius (Perry, 1811)

Habitat: Moderately and submaximally exposed seaweed; 0–8 m depth.
Distribution: Dongara, WA, to NSW and around Tas.
Maximum size: Height to 40 mm.

Phasianotrochus eximius can be distinguished from several other elongate conical species in the genus *Phasianotrochus* by the relatively thin lip, acutely pointed spire, iridescent green aperture and thin spiral lines around the shell. The khaki green of the live shell turns red on beach-washed specimens because of the partial breakdown of the shell pigment. The species occurs abundantly on seaweeds in pools and protected bays on exposed coasts.

Phasianotrochus eximius, Bicheno, Tas.

Phasianotrochus irisodontes

(Quoy & Gaimard, 1834)

Habitat: Sheltered seagrass, seaweed; 0–5 m depth.
Distribution: Geraldton, WA, to Cape Liptrap, Vic., and around Tas.
Maximum size: Height to 15 mm.

Phasianotrochus irisodontes can usually be identified by its greenish shell, the iridescent sheen to the interior and the squat rounded appearance compared with other species of *Phasianotrochus*. Very high abundances of this species occur on seagrasses and brown seaweeds in sheltered bays and estuaries. The shells were used by Tasmanian Aboriginal tribes for making necklaces.

Phasianotrochus irisodontes, Tinderbox, Tas.

Austrocochlea constricta Lamarck, 1822

Habitat: Sheltered and moderately exposed rocky shores, mangroves, mudflats, seagrass; mid to upper intertidal.
Distribution: Albany, WA, to Coffs Harbour, NSW, and around Tas.
Maximum size: Height to 25 mm.

Austrocochlea constricta is a conspicuous gastropod along the shores of most southern estuaries. The whorls of this species have prominent spiral ridges, which give it a grooved appearance, and its shell height is greater than or equal to its width. It has a offwhite shell colour.

Austrocochlea constricta, Cloudy Lagoon, Tas.

Austrocochlea porcata (Adams, 1851)

Habitat: Rocky shores; mid intertidal.
Distribution: Geraldton, WA, to Townsville, Qld, and northern and eastern Tas.
Maximum size: Height to 25 mm.

Austrocochlea porcata has a shell similar in shape to *A. constricta* but with broken ridges and parallel oblique bands of black and white extending onto the spire. The species is abundant in bays and rockpools in southeastern Australia.

Austrocochlea porcata, Bass Point, NSW

Austrocochlea brevis, Cloudy Lagoon, Tas.

Austrocochlea brevis Parsons & Ward, 1994

Habitat: Sheltered rock, seagrass and sand; upper to mid intertidal.
Distribution: Around Tas.
Maximum size: Height to 22 mm.

Austrocochlea brevis has been confused with *A. constricta* and *A. porcata* until recently, but can be recognised by the broken ridges around the whorls and the undulating bands of dark pigment low on the shell, which coalesce on the spire below the eroded tip. This species is found abundantly in sheltered bays and estuaries; it has so far been recorded only from Tasmania but is also likely to occur in Victoria.

Austrocochlea concamerata (Wood, 1828)

Habitat: Exposed reef; upper to mid intertidal.
Distribution: Cape Naturaliste, WA, to NSW and around Tas.
Maximum size: Height to 25 mm.

Austrocochlea concamerata is easily confused with other *Austrocochlea* species but occurs in more exposed conditions and has a rounded shell, the

Austrocochlea concamerata (right) and *A. porcata*, Port Stephens, NSW

height less than or equal to the width. The colour pattern varies little throughout the range and is black with yellow spots regularly spaced on the spiral ridges. The species is gregarious and occurs in large aggregations under rocks during the day.

Austrocochlea odontis (Wood, 1828)

Habitat: Sheltered and moderately exposed reef; 0–5 m depth.
Distribution: SA to Cape Liptrap, Vic., and around Tas.
Maximum size: Height to 15 mm.

Austrocochlea odontis has a rounded blue-black shell with a checkerboard pattern of small white spots. It also has a bright green edge to the aperture, a feature shared with a closely related species, ***Austrocochlea adelaidei***, which also occurs in shallow subtidal waters but has a brown or grey shell with coarser markings.

Austrocochlea odontis, Rocky Cape, Tas.

FAMILY TURBINIDAE
Turban shells

Turban shells, or turbinids, are closely related to trochids but have a solid calcareous rather than thin horny operculum, and the shells are generally large and solid with rounded whorls.

Phasianella australis (Gmelin 1788)

Pheasant shell, painted lady

Habitat: Sheltered algae, seagrass, reef; 0–5 m depth.
Distribution: Geraldton, WA, to Wilsons Promontory, Vic., and around Tas.
Maximum size: Height to 100 mm.

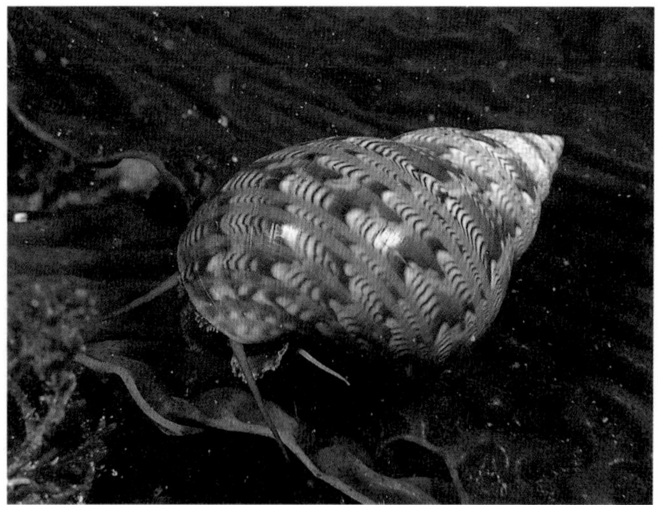

Phasianella australis, Portsea, Vic. RUDIE KUITER

Phasianella australis is an abundant gastropod, well known to most shell collectors because of its relatively large size and pretty combination of stripes, blotches and chevrons. It occurs most commonly on marine plants just below low-tide level along sheltered open coast.

Phasianella ventricosa (Swainson, 1822)

Habitat: Moderately exposed algae, reef; 0–6 m depth.
Distribution: Southern WA to central NSW and around Tas.
Maximum size: Height to 40 mm.

Phasianella ventricosa has a more rounded and swollen shell than *P. australis,* with the spire relatively short compared with the size of the last whorl. It is also smaller and less common than its relative and prefers a more exposed habitat.

Phasianella ventricosa, Port Noarlunga, SA

Turbo undulatus (Lightfoot, 1786)

Warrener, periwinkle

Habitat: Exposed reef; 0–10 m depth.
Distribution: Hopetoun, WA, to NSW and around Tas.
Maximum size: Height to 50 mm.

Turbo undulatus has a smooth, round shell with a low spire and mottled green markings. It can occur in huge aggregations on southern reefs, and in such situations denudes the reef of large seaweeds. The species is harvested commercially in Tasmania and is considered one of the more tasty gastropods.

Turbo undulatus, Port Davey, Tas.

Turbo jourdani Kiener, 1839

Habitat: Exposed reef; 0–40 m depth.
Distribution: Geraldton, WA, to central SA.
Maximum size: Height to 200 mm.

Turbo jourdani is one of the largest gastropods living in temperate Australian waters, and so can usually be easily recognised by its size as well as the reddish-brown colour. It rarely enters shallow water but is common in depths of 20–30 m along the southern Western Australian coast.

Turbo jourdani, Canal Rocks, WA

Turbo torquatus Gmelin, 1791

Habitat: Exposed reef; 0–20 m depth.
Distribution: Port Gregory, WA, to eastern SA and NSW.
Maximum size: Height to 90 mm.

Turbo torquatus has a relatively low shell with several raised ridges spiralling around each whorl. On western specimens the ridges are quite angular with the whorls undercut below, so this form has sometimes been considered a different species, *T. whitleyi*. Both forms are abundant in rockpools on exposed shores.

Turbo torquatus, Jervis Bay, NSW

Astralium aureum (Jonas, 1844)

Habitat: Sheltered and moderately exposed reef, sand, seagrass; 0–5 m depth.
Distribution: Cape Naturaliste, WA, to southern NSW and around Tas.
Maximum size: Width to 18 mm.

Astralium aureum has a low, cream-coloured shell, which is generally eroded, with knobbled transverse ridges across the whorls. The species is patchily distributed but occurs gregariously in a large range of shallow habitats.

Astralium aureum, Tinderbox, Tas.

Astralium squamiferum, Princess Royal Harbour, WA

Astralium squamiferum (Koch, 1844)

Habitat: Sheltered seagrass; 0–5 m depth.
Distribution: Port Gregory, WA, to southern NSW and northern Tas.
Maximum size: Width to 30 mm.

Astralium squamiferum has a very low shell with outward projections from the whorls, giving it a star-shaped appearance when seen from above. The species is common in estuaries, where it is often found grazing microscopic algae from the surface of seagrass leaves.

Astralium tentoriformis (Jonas, 1845)

Habitat: Exposed reef; 0–12 m depth.
Distribution: Southern NSW to central Qld.
Maximum size: Height to 45 mm.

Astralium tentoriformis has a conical shell with slight folds along the side and distinctive bluish marks on the margins of the operculum. It is one of the few gastropods commonly found on the bare, coralline algal-encrusted reefs along the New South Wales coast.

Astralium tentoriformis, Merimbula, NSW

FAMILY NERITIDAE
Nerites

Species of nerite are easily recognised by the rounded, slipper-like appearance of the shell and the semi-circular aperture. The family is diverse and widespread on tropical shores, but only a single species is found on the southern Australian coast.

Nerita atramentosa Reeve, 1855

Habitat: Sheltered and moderately exposed rocky shores; mid to high intertidal.
Distribution: North West Cape, WA, to southern Qld. Also Lord Howe I and New Zealand.
Maximum size: Height to 28 mm.

Nerita atramentosa is a herbivorous species with a black shell, white apex and white margin around the aperture. It occurs in great abundance high in the intertidal zone, usually in clusters under rocks.

Nerita atramentosa, Eaglehawk Neck, Tas.

FAMILY LITTORINIDAE
Periwinkles

Periwinkles, or littorinids, have squat spiral shells and lack a siphonal canal, so the outer lip is smoothly rounded. The operculum is horny and tight fitting, enabling the animals to survive long periods between tides without significant loss of water. Almost all periwinkles are associated with intertidal rocks, some species living at such high levels that they receive splash but never become submerged. They graze on microscopic algae and lichens.

Bembicium nanum (Lamarck, 1822)

Habitat: Moderately and submaximally exposed reef; high to mid intertidal.
Distribution: Southern WA to southern Qld and around Tas.
Maximum size: Height to 10 mm.

Bembicium nanum is an abundant species at high shore levels along the southeastern coast. The species has a conical shape, the height less than the width, with brown wavy lines running obliquely across the lower whorls and orange coloration near the apex.

Bembicium nanum, Eaglehawk Neck, Tas.

Bembicium auratum (Quoy & Gaimard, 1834)

Habitat: Sheltered mud, sand, seagrass, mangrove; mid to high intertidal.
Distribution: Port Lincoln, SA, to Yeppon, Qld, and around Tas.
Maximum size: Height to 20 mm.

Bembicium auratum grows to a larger size than *B. nanum* and is chiefly distinguished by the higher shell and the nodular ridges down the sides giving the edges of the whorls a wavy appearance. It is often the most conspicuous gastropod in sheltered bays and occurs abundantly near high-tide level.

Bembicium auratum, Bayview, NSW

Bembicium melanostomum (Gmelin, 1791)

Habitat: Sheltered mud, sand; mid to high intertidal.
Distribution: Port Phillip Bay and Western Port, Vic., and around Tas.
Maximum size: Height to 20 mm.

Bembicium melanostomum has less obvious nodules on the sides than *B. auratum* and five to seven spiral grooves around the periphery of the last whorl (cf. 7–12 in *B. auratum*). The interior also differs in colour, as it is dark and the columella is tinged with orange. A very close relative, ***Bembicium vittatum***, which is chiefly distinguished on internal anatomy, occurs in South Australia and Western Australia. These two species are both abundant in estuaries.

Bembicium melanostomum, Snug, Tas.

Nodilittorina unifasciata (Gray, 1826)

Habitat: Exposed rocky shores; high intertidal.
Distribution: North West Cape, WA, to southern Qld and around Tas. Also New Zealand.
Maximum size: Height to 16 mm.

Nodilittorina unifasciata is the most abundant mollusc living high on temperate Australian shores. Clusters of this pale blue species occur in slight depressions on the rock, with the largest individuals recorded as far as 10 m above high-tide level. The species feeds predominantly on lichens scraped from the rock surface.

Nodilittorina unifasciata, Taroona, Tas.

Nodilittorina praetermissa (May, 1908)

Habitat: Exposed rocky shores; high intertidal.
Distribution: Kangaroo I, SA, to southern NSW and around Tas.
Maximum size: Height to 16 mm.

Nodilittorina praetermissa has similar habits and appearance to *N. unifasciata* and is more abundant than its relative in cool Tasmanian waters. It differs by having a more swollen shell and brown zigzag stripes

Nodilittorina praetermissa, Taroona, Tas.

across the whorls. Where the two species occur together, *N. praetermissa* usually occurs slightly lower on the rockface.

Nodilittorina australis (Quoy & Gaimard, 1826)

Habitat: Exposed rocky shores; high intertidal.
Distribution: Kimberley to Esperance, WA.
Maximum size: Height to 20 mm.

Nodilittorina australis can be distinguished from other southern littorinids by the fine ridges around the whorls and the pointed spire. It tends to be solitary rather than gregarious like related species.

Nodilittorina australis, Cape Leeuwin, WA

Nodilittorina pyramidalis

(Quoy & Gaimard, 1833)

Habitat: Exposed rocky shores; high intertidal.
Distribution: Tropical Australia south to Fremantle, WA, and Point Hicks, Vic. Also through the Indo-West Pacific region.
Maximum size: Height to 18 mm.

Nodilittorina pyramidalis has a distinctive pointed shell with large rounded nodules forming ridges around the whorls. The species lives at a higher level than other littorinids and is rarely found on flat rock surfaces, preferring sandstone that has been weathered into a honeycomb structure.

Nodilittorina pyramidalis, Merimbula, NSW

Littoraria luteola (Quoy & Gaimard, 1833)

Habitat: Mangroves, mud; high intertidal.
Distribution: Merimbula, NSW, to Torres Strait, Qld.
Maximum size: Height to 23 mm.

Littoraria luteola has a sharply spired shell with a dark mottled appearance. It occurs abundantly on the leaves and trunks of mangrove trees in New South Wales but can also be found wandering across soft sediments in estuaries.

Littoraria luteola, Moonee Moonee, NSW

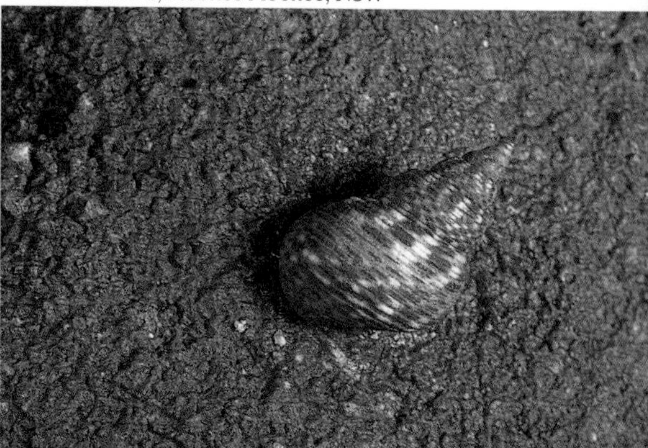

FAMILY TURRITELLIDAE
Screw shells

Turritellids have tall, narrowly tapered shells with numerous whorls. They have a thin, rounded outer lip and horny operculum but lack a siphonal canal.

Maoricolpus roseus (Quoy & Gaimard, 1834)

Habitat: Silt, sand; 3–50 m depth.
Distribution: Eastern Tas. to southern NSW. Also New Zealand.
Maximum size: Height to 90 mm.

Maoricolpus roseus is a large brown screw shell with a pointed tip. It was introduced from New Zealand to Tasmania about 80 years ago with live shipments of oysters and now occurs in massive aggregations. The species poses a threat to local species because living and dead shells have carpeted the seabed in places such the D'Entrecasteaux Channel, greatly altering the habitat. It has also been gradually extending its range northwards and has reached southern New South Wales. The numbers of the native screw shell ***Gazameda gunnii*** seem to decline following the arrival of *Maoricolpus roseus* in an area. *Gazameda gunnii* is smaller, with a more mottled appearance and has fine beads forming ridges around the shell.

Maoricolpus roseus, Tinderbox, Tas.

FAMILY BATILLARIDAE
Mudwhelks

This family consists of species with solid elongate shells made up of many spiral whorls. The aperture has a short siphonal canal and an outer lip that is often flared.

Pyrazus ebeninus (Brugiere, 1792)
Hercules club whelk

Habitat: Sheltered mudflats; low intertidal.
Distribution: Lakes Entrance, Vic., to Port Curtis, Qld.
Maximum size: Height to 110 mm.

Pyrazus ebeninus is an abundant species that can be found on most estuarine mudflats and among mangroves on the eastern coast; it is the source of the large tracks crisscrossing these areas. This is the largest of the local species of mudwhelks and the only one with a widely flared aperture.

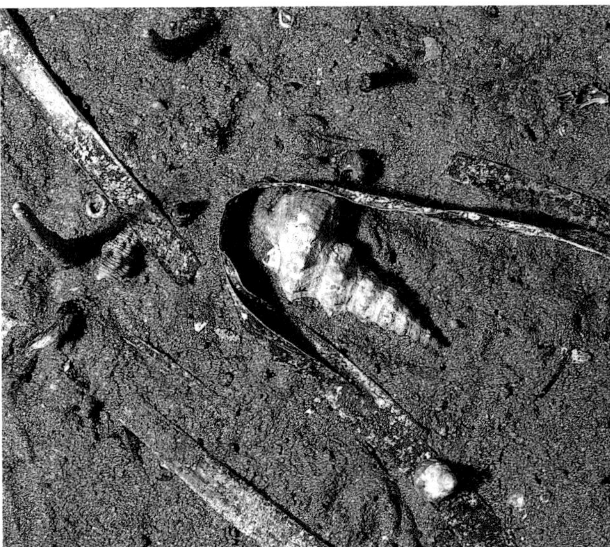

Pyrazus ebeninus, Merimbula, NSW

Batillaria australis (Quoy & Gaimard, 1834)

Habitat: Sheltered mud, sand, seagrass; 0–4 m depth.
Distribution: Perth, WA, to southern Qld and northern Tas.
Maximum size: Height to 45 mm.

Batillaria australis is a brown mudwhelk with nodular ridges around the whorls and raised folds running obliquely across them. It occurs abundantly in the same locations as *Pyrazus ebeninus*, but also extends into shallow subtidal depths. In Western Australia the species has been found only in the Swan estuary and Cockburn Sound and has possibly been introduced there.

Batillaria australis, Ulladulla, NSW

FAMILY CAMPANILIDAE

Campanilids differ from the mud whelks more in anatomy than shell shape. The shells of campanilids can, however, be recognised by the thin outer lip, chalky surface and rectangular aperture. The family has a long fossil history, but only a single species survives today.

Campanile symbolicum (Quoy & Gaimard, 1834)

Habitat: Sheltered sand, seagrass; 0–10 m depth.
Distribution: Geraldton to Esperance, WA.
Maximum size: Height to 200 mm.

Campanile symbolicum is a large, white, sharply spired gastropod with a prominent siphonal canal leading out from the aperture. The species is found abundantly in patches of sand and seagrass close to reef along the southwestern coast. This interesting gastropod has been called a living fossil because it is the only surviving species in a family that was dominant and widespread in Early Tertiary seas, some 60 million years ago. A few fossil campanilids grew to more than a metre long.

Campanile symbolicum, Albany, WA

FAMILY VERMETIDAE
Worm shells

Worm shells are unlikely looking gastropods, possessing an irregularly coiled shell that can be mistaken for the tube of a polychaete worm. Most species feed by secreting a string of mucus that traps plankton, but a few species can also do this using their gill. A second family of worm-like gastropods, the slit worm shells (family Siliquariidae), is occasionally seen in southern Australia and can be recognised by the presence of a slit or groove along the side of the shell. Although superficially similar in appearance, the two families are not closely related.

Serpulorbis sipho (Lamarck, 1818)

Habitat: Exposed reef; 0–30 m depth.
Distribution: WA to Qld and around Tas. Also widespread in the Indo-West Pacific region.
Maximum size: Width to 120 mm.

Serpulorbis sipho is the most common worm shell found along the southern coast, differing from related species by having the last few whorls irregularly coiled and fine ridges running longitudinally along the shell.

Serpulorbis sipho, Jervis Bay, NSW

FAMILY HIPPONICIDAE
Bonnet limpets

Bonnet limpets are cap-shaped molluscs that lack an operculum and live attached to hard surfaces such as stones and shells. They feed predominantly on fecal pellets and other detritus.

Hipponix conicus (Schumacher, 1817)

Habitat: Other molluscs; 0–12 m depth.
Distribution: WA to Qld and around Tas. Also widespread in the Indo-West Pacific region.
Maximum size: Width to 25 mm.

Hipponix conicus occurs in groups on the shells of large gastropods and bivalves, with a preference for *Campanile symbolicum*, abalone, whelks and razor clams as hosts. The male is smaller than the female and lives attached to the top of her shell. Both sexes have a long proboscis, which is extended to capture algae or other large food particles. A related species, ***Antisabia foliacea***, has a rounded shell like *Hipponix conicus* but has a rooftile-like pattern over the shell and is found gregariously under stones.

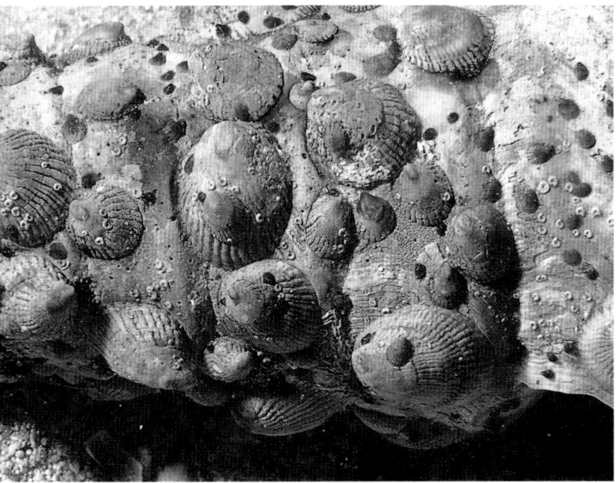

Hipponix conicus, Albany, WA

FAMILY JANTHINIDAE
Violet snails

The few species in this family have thin rounded shells with a low spire and deep blue or purple coloration, which is most intense on the lower half of the whorls. They are pelagic, floating upside down across the open ocean attached to a float of solidified bubbles.

Janthina janthina (Linnaeus, 1758)

Habitat: Ocean surface.
Distribution: WA to Qld and eastern Tas. Widespread overseas.
Maximum size: Height to 30 mm.

Janthina janthina has an almost spherical shell with a low flat spire. Depending on prevailing winds, the species can be blown ashore in huge numbers; such events occur most often during the summer months in southern Australia. Each animal begins life as a male released alive from the parent and later transforms into a female. The species feeds on floating cnidarians. The living animal with attached barnacles is illustrated on page 171.

Janthina janthina, Bicheno, Tas.

FAMILY NATICIDAE
Moon snails

Moon snails have a smooth swollen shell with a very low spire and a tight-fitting horny or calcareous operculum. They are active predators on sandflats, feeding largely on bivalves. Females produce collar-shaped eggmasses, which are a conspicuous feature of estuarine sandflats.

Polinices conicus (Lamarck, 1822)
Moon shell, sand snail

Habitat: Sheltered sand; 0–5 m depth.
Distribution: Around Australia and Tas.
Maximum size: Height to 42 mm.

Polinices conicus is common on intertidal sandflats, where it can be found half-buried in sand at the end of distinctive trails. It differs from several closely related species by having a pear-shaped rather than round shell, with a brown or orange band along the top of each whorl. The species is an important predator of bivalves in estuaries. Captured bivalves are held by folds of the body and a round hole drilled through the shell. The gastropod's proboscis is then inserted through the hole, enzymes released, and the partially digested flesh of the prey broken up and ingested with the aid of radular teeth.

Polinices conicus, Cloudy Lagoon, Tas.

FAMILY LAMELLARIIDAE
Lamellarias

Lamellarias are often confused with opisthobranchs as they have a fragile, internal shell that is completely covered by fleshy lobes of the body. The shell has a small spire and large aperture and most closely resembles the shell of juvenile cowries.

Lamellaria australis, Flinders, Vic.

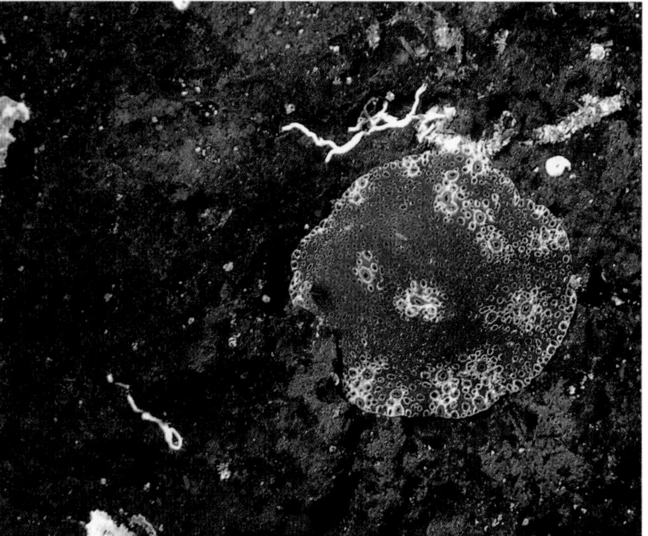

Lamellaria australis (Basedow, 1905)

Habitat: Reef; 2–10 m depth.
Distribution: Southern WA to Vic.
Maximum size: Length to 50 mm.

Lamellaria australis has a bright red or orange body, which is usually covered by numerous rings and spots, including a large yellow spot in the centre of the body. This is the most common lamellariid seen on shallow southern Australian reefs and one of the largest.

FAMILY CYPRAEIDAE
Cowries

Mature cowry shells are glossy and rounded, with a long, narrow, finely toothed aperture on the flat underside. Juvenile cowries have a more typical gastropod shape but produce a huge last whorl which envelops previous whorls and generates the distinctive cowry appearance. Most of the approximately 200 species in the family are medium-sized animals confined to the tropics. A number of large and medium-sized species keenly sought by shell collectors are, however, restricted to southern waters.

Cypraea hesitata Iredale, 1916

Habitat: Sand, silt; 15–200 m depth.
Distribution: Bass Strait, Vic., to Capricorn Group, Qld, and eastern Tas.
Maximum size: Length to 120 mm.

Cypraea hesitata is one of the largest and most beautiful cowries, easily recognised by the rounded humpback shape and chestnut flecks on a white background. The pure white form of this cowry was

Cypraea hesitata, D'Entrecasteaux Channel, Tas.

named *Cypraea howelli* but is a colour variant rather than representing a different species. *Cypraea hesitata* is generally collected only by trawler or in scallop dredges, although a population in the D'Entrecasteaux Channel near Hobart occurs in relatively shallow water. ***Cypraea armeniaca***, a related but more rounded species found in the Great Australian Bight in depths greater than 40 m, is one of the most sought after and valuable of shells.

Cypraea angustata Gmelin, 1791

Habitat: Under rocks on reef; 0–12 m depth.
Distribution: Gulf St Vincent, SA, to Eden, NSW, and around Tas.
Maximum size: Length to 30 mm.

A group of closely related species of small cowries known as the *Notocypraea* complex occurs in southern Australian waters, and mollusc specialists do not agree about which are species and which are merely varieties. *Cypraea angustata* and *C. comptoni* are the most frequently found of these cowries and both are common under rocks throughout their ranges. *Cypraea angustata* has a dark, rounded shell with dark spots around the edges and a white base; the colour of the living animal is red or brown. The most closely related cowry is ***Cypraea declivis***, which has a relatively high, white or fawn shell that is usually speckled with numerous chestnut spots and a white or grey mantle.

Cypraea hesitata (*howelli* form), D'Entrecasteaux Channel, Tas.

Cypraea comptoni Gray, 1847

Habitat: Under rocks on reef; 0–15 m depth.
Distribution: Cape Leeuwin, WA, to southern NSW and around Tas.
Maximum size: Length to 25 mm.

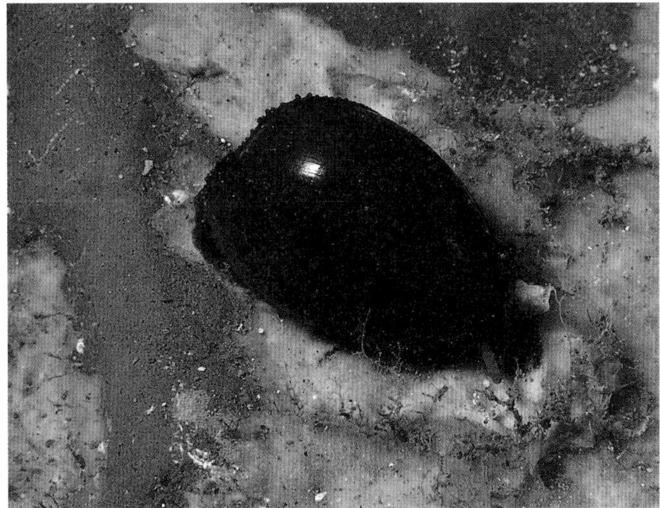

Cypraea angustata, D'Entrecasteaux Channel, Tas.

Cypraea comptoni has an orange mantle with an orange-brown shell that is crossed by two faint bands. A few black spots are generally located on the edges of the shell. A pure white cowry similar to this species and which may or may not be distinct, has been named ***Cypraea subcarnea***; its habitat is very restricted compared with the habitats of others in the group, as it has been found only near low-tide level on exposed shores. Another related species, ***Cypraea piperata***, resembles *C. comptoni* but has a different radula tooth arrangement and generally has four broken bands and a splattering of very fine speckles across the shell. The other cowry in the *Notocypraea* complex, the southern Western Australian species ***Cypraea pulicaria***, has a pale orange shell with brown spots forming four indistinct bands around the shell.

Cypraea comptoni, Bathurst Channel, Tas.

Cypraea comptoni, Maria I, Tas.

Cypraea friendii Gray, 1831

Black cowry

Habitat: Moderately to submaximally exposed reef, sponges, seagrass, sand; 3–180 m depth.
Distribution: Port Maud, WA, to western Vic.
Maximum size: Length to 130 mm.

Cypraea friendii is one of a group of sponge-eating cowries that are classed together in the subgenus *Zoila* and are restricted to Australia. All species in this group have direct larval development and consequently form localised populations, which can vary substantially in appearance over a short geographical distance. They are highly desired by shell collectors because of this variation as well as the large size and handsome markings of the shells. *Cypraea friendii* is the most common of the *Zoila* species and can be identified by the lack of teeth on the inner margin of the aperture (a few protuberances are present at one end). It has extremely variable markings and shape, although most specimens have a light brown basal colour and darker brown spots and blotches. Specimens collected from the Perth region are relatively narrow and dark compared with those collected from South Australia or deep water. In South Australia there are now legal restrictions (bag limits and a restricted season for harvesting) to ease the pressure that collectors have put on this species.

Cypraea friendii, Esperance, WA

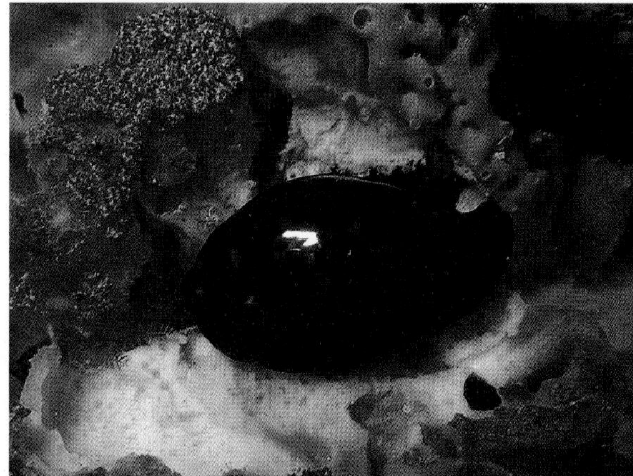

Cypraea friendii (dark form), Little I, WA

Cypraea venusta Smith, 1880

Habitat: Sponges on moderately to submaximally exposed reef and sand; 5–180 m depth.
Distribution: Shark Bay to Great Australian Bight, WA.
Maximum size: Length to 80 mm.

The general appearance of *Cypraea venusta* almost falls within the range of variation of *C. friendii,* but *Cypraea venusta* can be best identified by the presence of five to seven teeth at one end of the inner margin of the aperture and three to four protuberances at the other. Specimens found in shallow water can also be recognised by general appearance, as they are rounded, with a tan base and with dark smudges across the shell. The species lives on the host sponge on which it feeds.

Cypraea reevei Sowerby, 1832

Habitat: Moderately to submaximally exposed reef; 5–25 m depth.
Distribution: Houtman Abrolhos, WA, to Port Lincoln, SA.
Maximum size: Length to 45 mm.

Cypraea venusta, Little I, WA

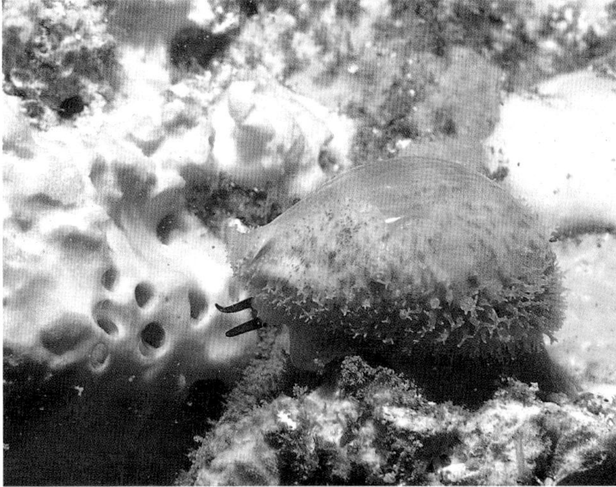
Cypraea reevei, Recherche Archipelago, WA. CLAY BRYCE

Cypraea reevei is an enigmatic cowry with a rounded shape and small dents over the surface. It is not common but has a preference for the underside of large limestone slabs in areas of good water movement.

FAMILY OVULIDAE
Spindle cowries, egg cowries

The spindle cowries are a group of well-camouflaged gastropods that live and feed on gorgonians and soft corals. They are related to the true cowries but lack teeth on the aperture. Most occur in the tropics, but several extend down the east and west coasts to temperate waters, and a few are known only from southern locations.

Phenacovolva philippinarum
(Sowerby, 1848)

Habitat: Gorgonians on exposed reef; 3–25 m depth.
Distribution: Tropical Australia south to Esperance, WA, and central Qld. Also widespread in the Indo-West Pacific region.
Maximum size: Length to 35 mm.

Phenacovolva philippinarum, Esperance, WA. CLAY BRYCE

Phenacovolva philippinarum is one of the largest of the spindle cowries and has a long projecting shell. It is not often seen because of camouflage that closely matches its host gorgonian (*Mopsella* species).

Prosimnia semperi (Weinkauff, 1881)

Habitat: Gorgonians on exposed reef; 5–30 m depth.
Distribution: Tropical Australia south to Cape Leeuwin, WA, and Merimbula, NSW. Also widespread in the Indo-West Pacific region.
Maximum size: Length to 12 mm.

Prosimnia semperi is a common species associated with gorgonians but is seen only if deliberately searched for. The colour of this species is variable and includes pinks, reds and yellows, depending on the colour of the host gorgonian. The prominent spots on the mantle resemble polyps and help to break up the outline.

Prosimnia semperi, Port Stephens, NSW

FAMILY CASSIDAE
Helmet shells

Helmet shells gain their common name from a fanciful resemblance to Roman helmets. The shells are usually solid, smooth and brightly coloured, with an expanded shield on the inside of the aperture forming a relatively flat undersurface. They are all carnivorous, feeding mainly on sea urchins.

Semicassis pyrum, Bicheno, Tas.

Semicassis pyrum (Lamarck, 1822)

Habitat: Exposed sand; 3–480 m depth.
Distribution: Fremantle, WA, to NSW and around Tas. Also New Zealand and South Africa.
Maximum size: Height to 70 mm.

Semicassis pyrum is a smooth helmet shell with a cream basal colour and light brown blotches. It stays buried under sand during the day and moves about at night searching for prey. The species is normally collected in trawls along the southern Australian coast but enters shallow water off sandy beaches in Tasmania.

Semicassis semigranosum (Lamarck, 1822)

Habitat: Exposed sand, silt; 1–400 m depth.
Distribution: Fremantle, WA, to Portsea, Vic., and around Tas.
Maximum size: Height to 60 mm.

Semicassis semigranosum, Tinderbox, Tas.

Semicassis semigranosum can be easily recognised by the rows of fine beads around the upper part of the shell and the lack of distinct markings. It occurs commonly along the southern coast.

FAMILY CYMATIIDAE
Tritons, trumpet shells

Tritons have medium to large shells with a moderately long siphonal canal and a brown shell covering known as the periostracum. These species lay down a thick outer lip in the shell between growth spurts. Previous outer lips appear as a series of very strong ribs (known as varices) crossing the whorls.

Charonia lampas (Linnaeus, 1758)

Habitat: Exposed reef; 0–200 m depth.
Distribution: Jurien Bay, WA, to Swain Reefs, Qld, and around Tas. Also New Zealand, South Africa, Japan and Europe.
Maximum size: Height to 150 mm.

Charonia lampas is one of the largest of the temperate gastropods and is a close relative of the giant triton *C. tritonis* of the tropics. A distinctive feature of the species is a series of black markings around the outer but not inner lip of the aperture. It feeds on sea urchins and sea stars, immobilising prey with toxic saliva extruded from the proboscis.

Cabestana spengleri (Perry, 1811)

Habitat: Sheltered and moderately exposed reef; 0–20 m depth
Distribution: SA to southern Qld and around Tas.
Maximum size: Height to 150 mm.

Cabestana spengleri is a common southeastern Australian triton that can be recognised by the strong ridges and nodular shoulders. It preys almost exclusively on ascidians and is usually found near them. A smaller, relatively broad species with a dark, hairy periostracum, ***Cabestana tabulata***, occurs in much the same habitat along the southern coast from Fremantle to New South Wales.

Cabestana spengleri, Ulladulla, NSW

Charonia lampas, Ile des Phoques, Tas.

Cymatium parthenopeum (von Salis, 1793)

Habitat: Reef; 0–18 m depth
Distribution: Lancelin, WA, to northern NSW and northern Tas.
Maximum size: Height to 150 mm.

Cymatium parthenopeum has a strongly ridged shell like *Cabestana spengleri* but with fewer ridges and black and white markings around the aperture. The foot of the living animal is also distinctive, as it is cream with round brown spots. Juveniles differ from adults by having a dense covering of hairs over the shell and a more swollen shape. The species is not appreciated by New South Wales oyster growers because it is a major predator of bivalves.

Cymatium parthenopeum, Terrigal, NSW

Cymatium parthenopeum (juvenile), Bass Point, NSW

Argobuccinium pustulosum (Lightfoot, 1786)

Habitat: Moderately and submaximally exposed reef; 3–20 m depth
Distribution: Eastern SA to central Vic. and around Tas. Also New Zealand, South Africa and South America.
Maximum size: Height to 100 mm.

Argobuccinium pustulosum is one of the smaller Australian tritons, with a rounded fawn shell, white aperture and thin dark-brown stripes that follow the whorls. It occurs most commonly along the eastern Tasmanian coast but is not abundant.

Argobuccinium pustulosum, Bathurst Channel, Tas.

Ranella australasia (Perry, 1811)

Habitat: Moderately and submaximally exposed reef, silt; 0–200 m depth
Distribution: Houtman Abrolhos, WA, to northern NSW and around Tas.
Maximum size: Height to 110 mm.

Ranella australasia has a brown shell with a high spire, low ridges around the whorls and relatively wide aperture. Animals along the southern coast are less often seen than those on New South Wales reefs but grow to a larger size. Specimens are also occasionally trawled from the edge of the continental shelf.

Ranella australasia, Bass Point, NSW

Sassia verrucosa (Reeve, 1844)

Habitat: Moderately exposed reef; 0–15 m depth.
Distribution: Southern WA to southern NSW and around Tas.
Maximum size: Height to 25 mm.

Sassia verrucosa, Waterfall Bay, Tas.

Sassia verrucosa is a small species of triton with a spire just more than half the length of the shell and with strong ribs crossed by ridges to give a lattice-like effect over the shell surface. The species is common in cryptic habitats such as under rocks and among encrusting plants and animals. A closely related species, ***Sassia eburnea***, with finer sculpture and generally a pink top to the spire, is moderately common in Victoria and Tasmania.

FAMILY MURICIDAE
Murex shells

Muricids constitute a diverse family of often spectacularly sculptured shells that have a small rounded aperture, prominent spines or knobs and a short to very long siphonal canal. Like the cymatiids (described above), the outer lip thickens and produces spines between periods of growth, resulting in a history of shell growth being discernible from the positions of spines and thick ridges across the whorls.

Dicathais orbita (Gmelin 1791)
Cartrut shell

Habitat: Reef; 0–10 m depth.
Distribution: Barrow I, WA, to southern Qld and around Tas. Also New Zealand.
Maximum size: Height to 75 mm.

Dicathais orbita, Ulladulla, NSW

Dicathais orbita, Cloudy Bay, Tas.

Dicathais orbita is one of the most abundant gastropods both intertidally and subtidally along southern coasts. The shell shape varies with location, but the widest shells with deep grooves occur in New South Wales, and pear-shaped shells with low ridges occur in exposed habitats. The species is an important predator on rock platforms, controlling population numbers of barnacles and mussels in many areas. The largest animals in studies in Western Australia were found to be about 20 years of age.

Agnewia tritoniformis (Blainville, 1832)

Habitat: Moderately and submaximally exposed reef; 0–25 m depth.
Distribution: Port Fairy, Vic., to central NSW and around Tas. Also New Zealand.
Maximum size: Height to 30 mm.

Agnewia tritoniformis, Ile des Phoques, Tas.

Agnewia tritoniformis has a grey shell with ribs and ridges forming a cross-hatched sculpture across the surface and dark depressions between. The species can occur in high abundances under individual rocks and is most common along the southern New South Wales coast.

Lepsiella vinosa (Lamarck, 1822)

Habitat: Moderately and submaximally exposed rocky shores; mid to high intertidal.
Distribution: Cockburn Sound, WA, to Vic. and around Tas.
Maximum size: Height to 20 mm.

Lepsiella vinosa is an abundant species among the tubeworms and barnacles on which it feeds in the mid intertidal zone. The shell shape is extemely variable but always has a number of offwhite ridges on each whorl crossed by ribs and with dark grooves between. Two related species with similar shapes are also common: ***Lepsiella flindersi***, a species found from low-tide level to 10 m depth, has a larger and wider shell with fewer ribs and ridges, while ***Lepsiella reticulata*** has an light brown coloration overall and nodulose ridges with dark spots on the nodules.

Lepsiella vinosa, Taroona, Tas.

Pterynotus undosus Vokes, 1993

Habitat: Sheltered and moderately exposed reef; 2–30 m.
Distribution: Perth to Eucla, WA.
Maximum size: Height to 55 mm.

Pterynotus undosus is a strongly sculptured murex with thin fluted folds projecting from the ribs. Until recently it was considered a form of a widespread species, ***Pterynotus triformis***, but that species name has now been restricted to animals found from Esperance, WA, to southern New South Wales, with a relatively smooth rather than undulating margin along the shell folds. Another closely related species of murex is ***Pterynotus duffusi***, a Victorian and New South Wales species with relatively long spines on the shoulders.

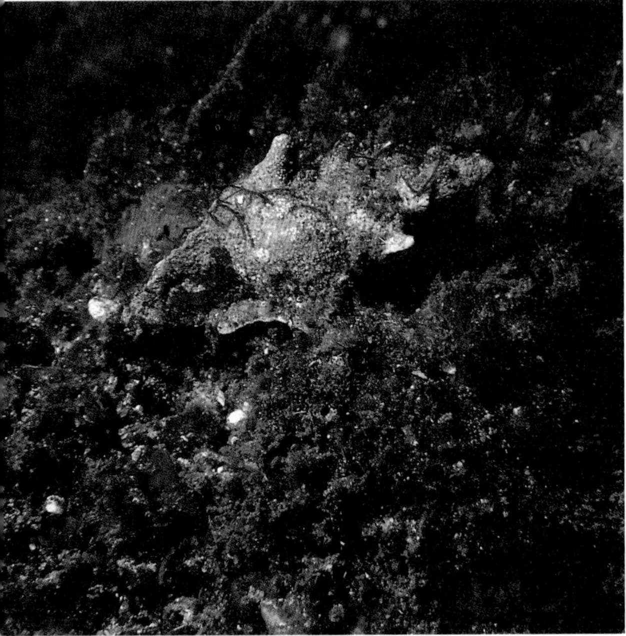

Pterynotus undosus, Princess Royal Harbour, WA.

Chicoreus denudatus (Perry, 1811)

Habitat: Exposed reef, silt; 0–100 m depth.
Distribution: SA to NSW and northern Tas.
Maximum size: Height to 50 mm.

The shell of *Chicoreus denudatus* has fine ridges around the whorls and winged ribs that are relatively low compared with many other murex shells. The species is generally found under rocks during the day but also occurs on soft sediments. It is more commonly found by divers in southern New South Wales than along the southern coast.

Morula marginalba (Blainville, 1832)

Habitat: Exposed rocky shores; mid intertidal.
Distribution: Merimbula, NSW, to Qld.
Maximum size: Height to 25 mm.

Morula marginalba is easily recognised by the offwhite shell with raised black bumps. It is one of the most abundant gastropods on New South Wales rock platforms and is an important predator of barnacles and other invertebrates. The species was probably responsible for the mosaic of dead *Chaemosipho tasmanica* barnacles in the illustration.

Chicoreus denudatus, Merimbula, NSW

Morula marginalba, Merimbula, NSW

FAMILY FASCIOLARIIDAE
Tulip shells, spindle shells

Tulip shells have an oval aperture, moderately to extremely long siphonal canal, solid operculum, relatively long spire and sculpture of numerous ridges running along the whorls. The head and foot of the animal are often bright red.

Pleuroploca australasia (Perry, 1811)

Habitat: Sheltered and moderately exposed reef, sand; 0–100 m depth.
Distribution: Esperance, WA, to NSW and around Tas.
Maximum size: Height to 150 mm.

Pleuroploca australasia is a common species of tulip shell along the southeastern coast. The shell is large, with prominent nodules on the shoulders and a dark brown periostracum, and varies considerably between sites. The species is generally found in crevices on reefs during the day but moves onto sand in search of invertebrate prey at night.

Pleuroploca australasia egg mass, D'Entrecasteaux Channel, Tas.

Pleuroploca australasia, D'Entrecasteaux Channel, Tas.

Fusinus australis (Perry, 1811)

Habitat: Sheltered and moderately exposed sand, reef; 1–30 m depth.
Distribution: Geraldton, WA, to Lakes Entrance, Vic.
Maximum size: Length to 110 mm.

Fusinus australis resembles *Pleuroploca australasia* except that it is smaller, with a longer siphonal canal, and lacks the angular, nodulose shoulders on the whorls. It occurs most commonly in small aggregations on sand near seagrass along the western section of the southern coast.

Fusinus australis, Princess Royal Harbour, WA

Fusinus novaehollandiae (Reeve, 1848)
New Holland spindle

Habitat: Sand, silt; 5–150 m depth.
Distribution: SA to southern NSW and around Tas.
Maximum size: Length to 200 mm.

Fusinus novaehollandiae is a spectacular looking spindle shell with an extremely long siphonal canal. It occurs in deep water through most of its range but is also common in relatively shallow depths in southeastern Tasmanian bays.

Fusinus novaehollandiae, Sandy Bay, Tas.

FAMILY BUCCINIDAE
Whelks

Buccinid whelks range in size from small to very large animals and encompass a great variety of shell forms. They are distinguished as a group largely because of their distinctive arrangement of radula teeth. Some species have an external appearance very close to that of trumpet shells.

Penion mandarinus (Duclos, 1831)

Habitat: Sheltered and moderately exposed sand, silt, reef; 0–600 m depth
Distribution: Great Australian Bight, SA, to Trial Bay, NSW, and around Tas.
Maximum size: Height to 180 mm.

Penion mandarinus is a large whelk that can easily be mistaken for *Pleuroploca australasiae* but has a cream rather than red foot and lacks folds on the columella. The shape of the shell is quite variable, causing

Penion mandarinus, Bicheno, Tas.

P. mandarinus to have been given a variety of names in the past. The species is common only in the southernmost part of its range and is most often seen by divers on soft sediment beside reef. It is a voracious predator of molluscs.

Penion maxima (Tryon, 1881)

Habitat: Sand, silt, reef; 5–200 m depth
Distribution: Eastern Vic. to southern Qld and around Tas.
Maximum size: Height to 250 mm.

Penion maxima has a long siphonal canal compared with that of *P. mandarinus* and has angular nodules on the shoulders of the whorls. Through most of its range it occurs in deep water and may be collected by trawlers, but in southern Tasmania it enters comparatively shallow water.

Penion maxima, Bathurst Channel, Tas.

Cominella lineolata (Lamarck, 1809)

Habitat: Sheltered sand; 0–5 m depth.
Distribution: Hopetoun, WA, to NSW and around Tas.
Maximum size: Height to 30 mm.

Cominella lineolata is an abundant species on intertidal and shallow subtidal sandflats and in sheltered rockpools. The most common form of this variable species is smooth and cigar-shaped covered by a checkerboard pattern. Other forms have various combinations of stripes and blotches, and smooth or weakly nodulose shoulders.

Cominella lineolata with egg mass, Ricketts Pt, Vic.

Cominella eburnea (Reeve, 1846)

Habitat: Sheltered sand; 0–10 m depth.
Distribution: Southern WA to southern NSW and around Tas.
Maximum size: Height to 30 mm.

Cominella eburnea, Portsea, Vic.

Cominella eburnea differs from *C. lineolata* by having prominent nodules on the shoulders and a narrower aperture. The shell is usually a light brown colour with dark brown blotches partly obscured by the periostracum. This gastropod is very common on sand near reef in South Australia and Victoria but is only moderately common in other states.

FAMILY NASSARIDAE
Dog whelks

Dog whelks, or nassarids, are small ovoid molluscs with a medium spire, short siphonal canal and horny operculum. Many species also have a distinctive flattened shield extending across the underside of the shell from the inside of the aperture. They are predominantly scavengers on sandflats and can occur in very high abundances.

Nassarius pauperatus (Lamarck, 1822)

Habitat: Sheltered sand, mud; 0–3 m depth.
Distribution: Geraldton, WA, to Sydney, NSW, and around Tas.
Maximum size: Height to 20 mm.

A number of species in the genus *Nassarius* occur in southern Australia, with *Nassarius pauperatus* by far the most common. Adults have an enamel-coated inner edge to the aperture, numerous nodules on the shell surface at the positions where ridges and ribs cross, and brown bands at the centre and bottom of the whorls. The species occurs in huge numbers on sandflats, where it rapidly tracks and scavenges dead animal material, as well as consuming algae between carnivorous feasts.

Nassarius pauperatus, Cloudy Lagoon, Tas.

Nassarius particeps (Hedley, 1915)

Habitat: Sheltered sand, mud; 0–8 m depth.
Distribution: Dampier Archipelago, WA, to NSW.
Maximum size: Height to 25 mm.

Nassarius particeps is an abundant and important scavenger in warm-temperate areas. The species can be identified by the fine brown stripes around the shell and the distinctive black-spotted foot. It is sometimes considered a subspecies of the wide-ranging tropical species *Nassarius glans* but has a more rounded shape and lacks teeth at the bottom of the outer lip.

Nassarius particeps, Norah Head, NSW

FAMILY CONIDAE
Cone shells

Cone shells are easily recognised by their conical outline, long narrow aperture, thin outer lip and relatively low spire. They feed using a radula consisting of a few harpoon-like teeth, which are connected to poison sacs; prey are speared, immobilised by venom and then engulfed by the mollusc. Several tropical species possess highly specialised venoms that are used for paralysing fish but which are also potentially lethal to other vertebrates, including humans. However, temperate species are not known to be responsible for any serious human injuries. All of the approximately 300 species in the family are included in the genus *Conus*.

Conus anemone (Lamarck, 1810)

Habitat: Sheltered and moderately exposed reef; 0–15 m depth.
Distribution: Port Gregory, WA, to central NSW and around Tas.
Maximum size: Height to 70 mm.

Conus anemone is the only cone shell found commonly along the southern Australian coast. It is drably coloured compared with its tropical relatives, having a blotched pattern on a cream base. The colour is, however, more variable than in most other cone shells and may be brown, pink, orange, yellow, white or grey. The species is usually found under rocks during the day but moves out at night to harpoon polychaete worms.

Conus anemone with eggs, Flinders, Vic.

Conus dorreensis with eggs, Rottnest I, WA. CLAY BRYCE

Conus dorreensis Peron, 1807

Habitat: Moderately and submaximally exposed reef; 0–10 m depth.
Distribution: Monte Bello Is to Albany, WA.
Maximum size: Height to 50 mm.

Conus dorreensis has shoulders with prominent nodules and a distinctive yellow-green band edged with black around the shell. The species is restricted to Western Australia and is found commonly among coralline-algal turf in depressions on intertidal rock platforms.

FAMILY MITRIDAE
Mitres

Mitres lack an operculum and have elongate shells with moderate-length spires and narrow apertures. The columella can be seen on the inside of the aperture to possess several strong folds. Species in the family live in sand and under rocks in shallow water and feed on other invertebrates.

Mitra glabra Swainson, 1821

Habitat: Moderately exposed reef; 0–12 m depth.
Distribution: Fremantle, WA, to central NSW and around Tas.
Maximum size: Height to 90 mm.

Mitra glabra is a long, tapered species of mitre with a light brown shell masked by a dark brown epidermis and with a white interior. The species hides under rocks or in sand during the day and hunts for sipunculans and polychaete worms at night.

Mitra glabra, Rocky Cape, Tas.

Mitra chalybeia Reeve, 1844

Habitat: Moderately exposed reef; 0–8 m depth.
Distribution: Shark Bay to Albany, WA.
Maximum size: Height to 60 mm.

Mitra chalybeia resembles *M. glabra* except for a slightly shorter spire. It is readily identified by the distinctive pattern of fine lines around the shell and pale bands at the top of the whorls. The species is common in shaded habitats on shallow reefs along the lower west coast.

Mitra chalybeia, Little I, WA

FAMILY VOLUTOMITRIDAE

Volutomitrids resemble mitres but can be distinguished externally because they possess an operculum. The two families are primarily separated because of different arrangements of the radula teeth.

Waimatea obscura (Hutton, 1873)

Habitat: Moderately exposed reef; 0–60 m depth.
Distribution: SA to Cape Liptrap, Vic., and around Tas. Also New Zealand.
Maximum size: Height to 18 mm.

Waimatea obscura can be identified by the characteristic brown bands around the shell and the white wavy markings at the top of the whorls. The species is abundant among seaweed and bryozoans on the reef surface but is not often noticed because of its small size. It was known as *Proximitra pica* until recently.

Waimatea obscura, Waterfall Bay, Tas.

FAMILY VOLUTIDAE
Volutes

Volutes are second only to the cowries in being sought by collectors because of their large size and beautiful patterning. They are somewhat similar in appearance to the mitres but are larger and wider and have different dentition. Volutes lack a planktonic larval stage, and so members of localised populations interbreed only among themselves. This often results in genetic differences between populations over short geographic distances, which can correspond with distinctive patterns on their shells. Volutes generally remain buried under sand during the day and move about on the surface at night.

Amoria undulata (Lamarck, 1804)
Wavy volute

Habitat: Sheltered and moderately exposed sand; 0–200 m depth.
Distribution: Southern WA to southern Qld and around Tas.
Maximum size: Height to 90 mm.

Like other volute species, *Amoria undulata* shows considerable variation in pattern but usually has an orange background with thin brown wavy lines down the shell. It is the only volute species commonly found living on sand in shallow water around the southeastern Australian coast.

Amoria undulata, Bicheno, Tas.

Cymbiola magnifica (Shaw & Nodder, 1808)
Magnificent volute

Habitat: Moderately and submaximally exposed reef, sand; 0–150 m depth.
Distribution: Mallacoota, Vic., to Capricorn Group, Qld.
Maximum size: Height to 360 mm.

Cymbiola magnifica is regularly seen by divers along the New South Wales coast and is collected by trawlers in moderate numbers. The rounded shell is orange to light brown with three dark brown bands broken up by fine zigzag reticulations. Specimens found in shallow water, such as the one illustrated, are generally heavily eroded, with the pattern clearly defined only on the undersurface.

Cymbiola magnifica, Bass Point, NSW

Ericusa fulgetra (Sowerby, 1825)
Lightning volute

Habitat: Sheltered and moderately exposed sand; 0–260 m depth.
Distribution: Recherche Archipelago, WA, to SA.
Maximum size: Height to 150 mm.

Ericusa fulgetra, Edithburgh, SA

Ericusa fulgetra is an elongate volute with a rounded tip to the spire and characteristic dark wavy stripes down the shell. The width and shape of these stripes varies greatly from site to site, and it is often possible to relate a shell pattern to a restricted location. The species is uncommon except in localised areas of the South Australian gulfs. Numbers in these areas are probably declining because of overcollecting.

Aulacina nivosa (Lamarck, 1804)

Snowy volute

Habitat: Moderately exposed sand; 0–20 m depth.
Distribution: Kimberley to Fremantle, WA.
Maximum size: Height to 90 mm.

The shell of *Aulacina nivosa* has pointed but not projecting shoulders and characteristic bands that are made up of short, aligned, wavy stripes. It is the most common species of volute found by divers on the central west coast and often occurs in groups.

Aulacina nivosa, Mullalloo, WA

Melo miltonis Gray, 1834

Southern bailer

Habitat: Moderately and submaximally exposed reef, sand, seagrass; 0–20 m depth.
Distribution: Houtman Abrolhos, WA, to western SA.
Maximum size: Height to 450 mm.

Melo miltonis is the largest shelled mollusc to occur on the southern coast. It is one of a group of volutes known as bailer shells because of their value to indigenous people for holding water. Like other bailer shells, *M. miltonis* remains concealed under sand for much of the time and moves about searching for molluscs at night and on overcast days. The illustrated animal has captured a *Campanile symbolicum*.

Melo miltonis, Rottnest I, WA. Clay Bryce

Subclass Pulmonata

Pulmonates

The pulmonates are air-breathing gastropods that lack gills but use the mantle cavity as a lung. This method of respiration is more efficient in air than water, and so virtually all species are associated with the intertidal zone or found on land. In the majority of species the shell is well developed and spirally coiled, but limpet-like and slug-like pulmonates are also common. Most species are herbivorous, grazing microscopic plant material off hard surfaces or grains of sand.

FAMILY AMPHIBOLIDAE

A family of small species with rounded shells, low spire and horny operculum. They are restricted to high intertidal mudflat and mangrove habitats, where they feed unselectively by passing large quantities of sediment through their gut and retaining organic particles.

Salinator fragilis (Lamarck, 1822)

Habitat: Sheltered sand, mud; high intertidal.
Distribution: WA to Qld and around Tas.
Maximum size: Height to 18 mm.

Salinator fragilis is a small, round species that occurs in countless millions on estuarine sandflats, with highest numbers often just inside the area where salt-tolerant land plants grow. The species can drift on the water surface with tidal currents by taking air into the

Salinator fragilis, Cloudy Lagoon, Tas.

mantle cavity. A closely related species, ***Salinator solidus***, differs by having a more solid shell with a higher spire, zigzag marks on the whorls, and an operculum with a horny lump on the inside. *Salinator solidus* occurs in the same habitat type as *S. fragilis*.

FAMILY SIPHONARIIDAE
Pulmonate limpets, siphons

Siphonariids have a limpet-like shape and are often confused with the true limpets. They can be recognised by having a distinct groove on the undersurface of the shell, leading obliquely from the apex to the right front margin. This groove enhances the flow of air into the mantle cavity.

Siphonaria diemenensis Quoy & Gaimard, 1833

Habitat: Sheltered and moderately exposed rocky shores; mid to high intertidal.
Distribution: Southern WA to central NSW and around Tas.
Maximum size: Length to 28 mm.

Siphonaria diemenensis occurs abundantly in sheltered habitats on rocks and wood pylons. Its dark shell surface is sculptured by numerous white radiating ribs; the apex of large shells is generally heavily eroded.

Siphonaria zelandica Quoy & Gaimard, 1833

Habitat: Exposed rocky shores; mid to high intertidal.
Distribution: Broome, WA, to Keppel Bay, Qld.
Maximum size: Length to 25 mm.

Siphonaria zelandica, Terrigal, NSW

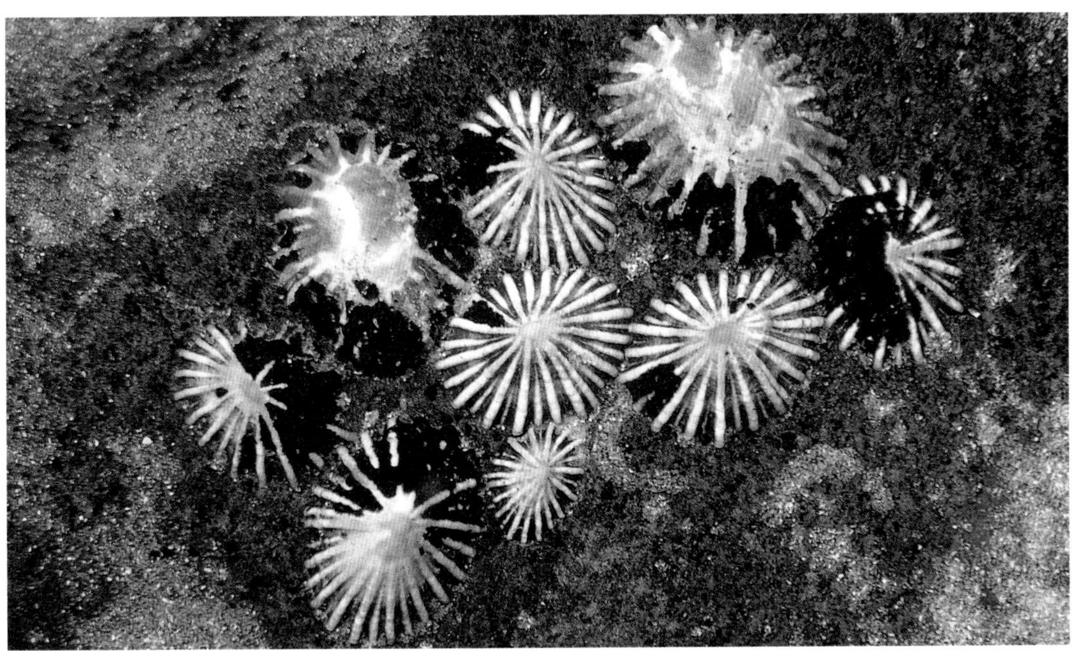
Siphonaria diemenensis, Swan I, Tas.

Siphonaria zelandica has a flatter shell than *S. diemenensis*, and the grooves between the ridges are a lighter colour. It has the lowest number of radial ribs (about 18) of all the southern siphonariid limpets. The species occurs on open rock surfaces in slightly more exposed conditions than those preferred by *S. diemenensis*.

Siphonaria tasmanica Tenison Woods, 1876

Habitat: Exposed rocky shores; mid intertidal.
Distribution: Eastern SA to Wilsons Promontory, Vic., and around Tas.
Maximum size: Length to 23 mm.

Siphonaria tasmanica differs in appearance from other southern pulmonate limpets because it is marked by concentric light and dark bands. The apex is generally eroded but when present is a reddish colour. The species is abundant, particularly on vertical rock faces along moderately exposed coasts.

Siphonaria tasmanica, Taroona, Tas.

Siphonaria funiculata Reeve, 1856

Habitat: Exposed rocky shores; mid to high intertidal.
Distribution: Eastern SA to Burnett Heads, Qld, and around Tas.
Maximum size: Length to 20 mm.

Siphonaria funiculata is closest in appearance to *S. diemenensis* but has much more numerous and regular radial ribs. It is slightly less abundant than the other species but can still occur in very high numbers on rock faces.

Siphonaria funiculata, Coles Bay, Tas.

Siphonaria jeanae Jenkins, 1984

Habitat: Exposed rocky shores; mid to high intertidal.
Distribution: Kalbarri, WA, to Ceduna, SA.
Maximum size: Length to 15 mm.

Siphonaria jeanae is the smallest of the southern siphonariid limpets and has an average of about 27 radial ribs, approximately the same number as *S. diemenensis*. The ribs are pale blue-grey, and the space between them brown. This species usually occurs on steep to vertical rocky shores.

Siphonaria jeanae, Cape Leeuwin, WA.

FAMILY ONCHIDIIDAE
Air-breathing sea slugs

This family contains slug-like pulmonates with a thick-leathery mantle covering the back. The head is small, with short tentacles and eyes.

Onchidella patelloides (Quoy & Gaimard, 1832)

Habitat: Moderately exposed rocky shores; mid intertidal.
Distribution: SA to NSW and northern Tas. Also New Zealand.
Maximum size: Length to 25 mm.

Onchidella patelloides is a greenish-brown slug-like animal with a scalloped border and with small granules on the upper surface. It is an inconspicuous species that commonly lives in rock crevices and among *Galeolaria* tubes, creeping out in large numbers to feed at night and on overcast days.

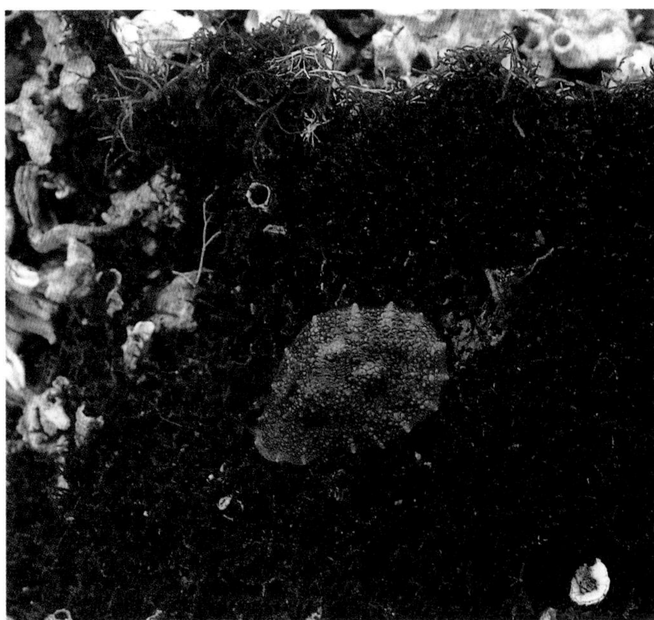

Onchidella patelloides, Coles Bay, Tas.

Subclass Opisthobranchia
Sea slugs

The name opisthobranch means 'rearward gill', a feature that distinguishes species in this subclass from the other gastropods. A more obvious feature of the subclass is that the shell is reduced, internal or lost, a characteristic but not diagnostic feature because slug-like prosobranch and pulmonate gastropods also occur in southern Australia, and some of the bubble-shells can fully withdraw the animal into the shell. Species of opisthobranch exhibit a huge range in body forms, from animals with limpet-like, gastropod-like or bivalve-like shells, to the majority of sea slugs with no shell at all. They also encompass a huge range in body size, from microscopic animals that move between sand grains to giant sea hares that weigh several kilograms. Nearly all opisthobranchs have a large head, which is often flattened for burrowing, a pair of small eyes, a pair of forward-pointing oral tentacles and a pair of tubular tentacles placed just behind the eyes (the rhinophores). Many species also have large lobes extending upwards from the foot (parapodia) and rows of spindle-shaped processes from the upper body surface (cerata). The cerata can contain extensions of the gut and digestive gland and are partly used for defence. All opisthobranchs have both male and female organs, exchanging sperm between individuals. They produce huge quantities of eggs, which are generally embedded in a jelly-like substance and stuck to the substrate.

FAMILY BULLIDAE

The family Bullidae contains a single genus, *Bulla*, with several similar-looking species. Their bodies are orange to brown in colour and have two posterior lobes to the head. They can fully retract their bodies into the shell when threatened but lack an operculum. The shells are glossy with sunken spires and have large apertures.

Bulla quoyii Gray in Dieffenbach, 1843
Botany Bay bubble shell

Habitat: Sheltered sand, mud; 0–10 m depth.
Distribution: Carnarvon, WA, to northern NSW and around Tas. Also New Zealand.
Maximum size: Height to 50 mm.

Bulla quoyii, Terrigal, NSW

Bulla quoyii is the only large bubble shell found in southern Australia. It is easily recognised by the smooth, mottled-brown shell with sunken spire and thin outer lip. The species is abundant in estuaries and coastal bays at sites with a layer of fine silt on sand. Animals remain hidden in the sediment during daylight and move onto the surface at night to feed on algae.

FAMILY BULLINIDAE

The family Bullinidae has few species, nearly all of which are confined to the tropics. They have a solid shell with a medium-sized spire and a large foot that can be fully withdrawn into the shell, the entrance then being sealed by an operculum.

Bullina lineata (Gray, 1825)

Habitat: Sheltered sand, reef; low intertidal.
Distribution: Tropical Australia south to Cowaramup, WA, and Bermagui, NSW. Also widespread in the Indo-West Pacific region.
Maximum size: Height to 20 mm.

Bullina lineata has a solid, spirally grooved shell with a characteristic pattern of pink lines. The appearance of the living animal is also distinctive, as the foot is wide and thin with a light blue margin. Two black eye spots are located on folds that project in front of the shell. *Bullina lineata* feeds on polychaete worms, which it generally finds on patches of sand on the intertidal rock platform. The species is very sporadic in occurrence; it can be found in moderate abundance in particular rockpools for perhaps a month in summer and then will not be seen again in the area for several years.

FAMILY PHILINIDAE

More than 100 species of philinids are known worldwide. Most have a similar external appearance: a flat, white body with two side lobes and a large head lobe. Identification of species depends largely on the thin internal shell. This is translucent with a very large aperture that restricts the whorled part of the shell to one corner.

Philine angasi (Crosse & Fischer, 1865)

Habitat: Sheltered sand, mud; 0–100 m depth.
Distribution: Cockburn Sound, WA, to southern Qld and around Tas. Also New Zealand.
Maximum size: Length to 80 mm.

Philine angasi is the only species of philinid in southern Australian to occur abundantly in estuaries.

Bullina lineata, Bermagui, NSW. RUDIE KUITER

Philine angasi, Cloudy Lagoon, Tas.

It generally lives under a shallow layer of sand but occasionally also wanders across the surface at night. The species is a specialised predator of bivalves.

FAMILY GASTROPTERIDAE

Species in this family have two large wing-like extensions of the foot (parapodia) with which they can swim if necessary. Most species also have a small internal shell, although this is occasionally absent. The family is not large but includes temperate and tropical species whose habitats vary from the intertidal zone to the deep sea.

Sagaminopteron ornatum

Tokioka & Baba, 1964

Habitat: Moderately exposed reef; 0–20 m depth.
Distribution: Around Australia. Also widespread in the Indo-West Pacific region.
Maximum size: Length to 25 mm.

Sagaminopteron ornatum has a small internal shell and a purple body with wide orange-margined side lobes, making it one of the most distinctive of all opisthobranchs. The species is generally found living on the bottom in the vicinity of a grey sponge, but can also swim, which it does rarely by flapping the side lobes in a slow bat-like motion. Although this sea slug is not abundant, it is well known to divers because the bright coloration attracts attention.

FAMILY AGLAJIDAE

Aglajids have a cylindrical body and two very large parapodia that fold over the top and extend behind as a pair of tails, one longer than the other. They also have a very small internal shell. Most are rarely noticed because of small size, although they can be abundant on sand in shallow, sheltered habitats. A large number of species occur in the tropics, with a few extending southwards along the east and west

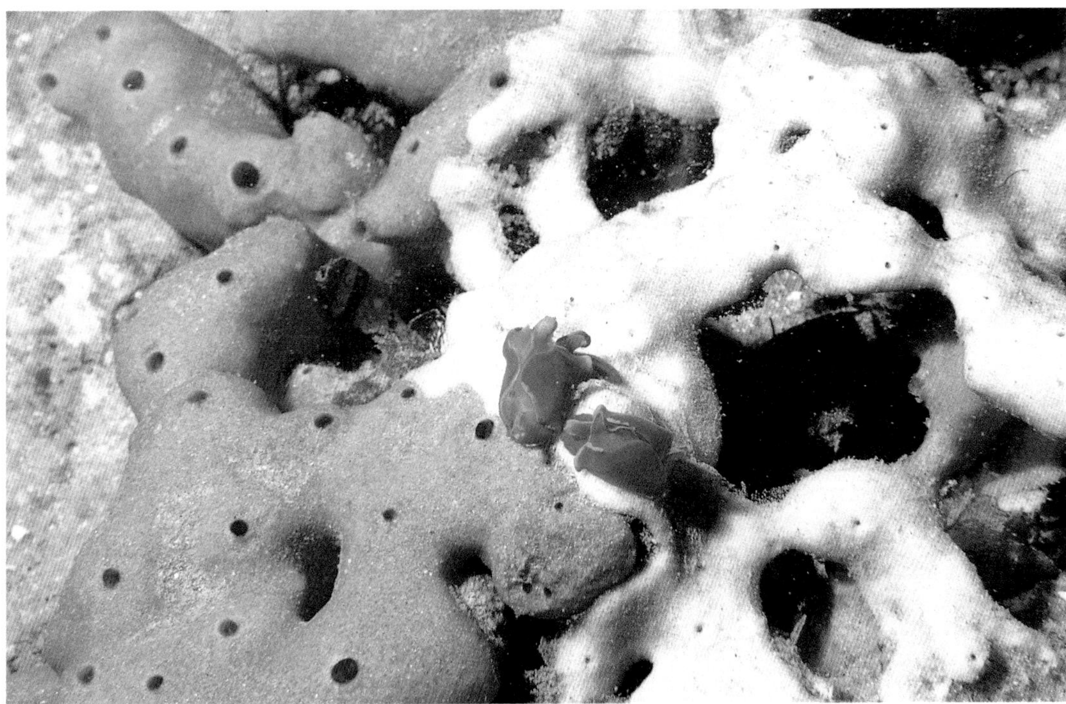

Sagaminopteron ornatum, Port Noarlunga, SA

coasts and at least one large species, the mottled-brown ***Philinopsis troubridgensis***, restricted to southern Australia. All aglajids feed on other invertebrates, with polychaete worms and molluscs being the most important prey.

Chelidonura hirundinina

(Quoy & Gaimard, 1824)

Habitat: Sheltered sand; 0–3 m depth.
Distribution: Tropical Australia south to Rottnest I, WA, and Merimbula, NSW. Also widespread in the Indo-West Pacific region.
Maximum size: Length to 20 mm.

Chelidonura hirundinina occurs abundantly during the summer months in sand patches on shallow sheltered reefs and near the entrance to large estuaries. It has a distinctive pattern of yellow, blue and green stripes on a black background.

Chelidonura hirundinina, Merimbula, NSW

FAMILY APLYSIIDAE
Sea hares

Aplysiids receive their common name from their side-on appearance. The oral tentacles that extend in front of the head bear a resemblance to the nostrils of mammals, and the pair of rolled tentacles (the rhinophores) just behind the eye spots resemble the large ears of a hare. Most species also have a short tail, parapodial flaps that extend up from the foot over the body, and a small internal shell. Sea hares have a prodigious reproductive talent, the larger animals laying tens of millions of eggs in spaghetti-like filaments during their lifetime. They usually mate in large groups, forming clusters of animals or long chains with each individual acting as male to the animal in front and female to the animal in rear. They also grow extremely rapidly; some species weigh more than a kilogram when mature yet have only a one-year life cycle. All investigated sea hares have been found to be herbivorous, feeding mainly on seaweeds but also seagrass and blue-green algae. Nearly all southern Australian aplysiids release a purple ink when threatened.

Aplysia parvula Mörch, 1863

Habitat: Exposed reef, seagrass; 0–20 m depth.
Distribution: Around the Australian mainland and Tas. Also widespread overseas.
Maximum size: Length to 100 mm.

The background coloration of *Aplysia parvula* can be yellow, green, brown or red, depending on the colour of the host seaweed on which the animal is feeding. The species is, however, easily recognised by the black trim to the parapodia and the black tips to the oral tentacles and rhinophores. It also is a relatively small sea hare, whose parapodia commence a long way back along the body. Like many other opisthobranchs, *A. parvula* is sporadic in appearance, being extremely abundant at some sites for several months and then not being seen again for several years.

Aplysia parvula, Eaglehawk Neck, Tas.

Aplysia dactylomela Rang, 1828

Habitat: Moderately exposed seagrass, reef, sand; 0–15 m depth.
Distribution: Tropical Australia south

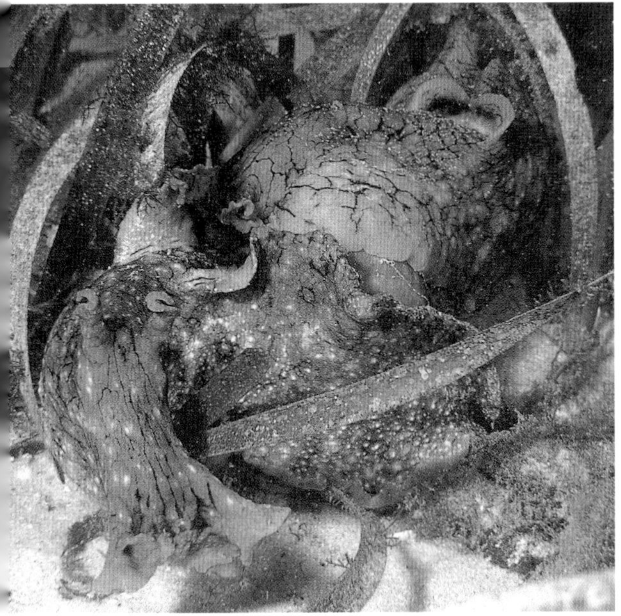

Aplysia dactylomela (mating pair), Jervis Bay, NSW

to Albany, WA, and Western Port, Vic. Also widespread overseas.
Maximum size: Length to 250 mm.

Aplysia dactylomela has an olive background colour with black rings and a network of fine black lines over the body. It is the most common of the larger sea hares along the New South Wales coast and is abundant in coastal embayments but very rarely enters estuaries.

Aplysia sydneyensis Sowerby, 1869

Habitat: Sheltered and moderately exposed reef, sand; 0–20 m depth.
Distribution: Southern WA to southern Qld and around Tas.
Maximum size: Length to 150 mm.

Aplysia sydneyensis, Southport Lagoon, Tas.

Aplysia sydneyensis resembles *A. dactylomela* but can be distinguished by the presence of irregularly edged brown blotches on the sides of the body and brown streaks on the head. Fine black lines overlie the basic pattern but these never form rings. *Aplysia sydneyensis* occurs commonly in southeastern waters.

Aplysia gigantea Sowerby, 1869

Habitat: Sheltered and moderately exposed reef, sand; 0–20 m depth.
Distribution: Esperance to Shark Bay, WA.
Maximum size: Length to 600 mm.

Aplysia gigantea has a brown body with mottled sides and a short tail. This is by far the largest opisthobranch known in Australia and one of the largest worldwide. Specimens are often found on beaches after storms in late summer and autumn.

Aplysia gigantea, Trigg Reef, WA. Clay Bryce

Bursatella leachii (Blainville, 1817)

Habitat: Moderately exposed seagrass, reef, sand; 3–22 m depth.
Distribution: Tropical Australia south to Albany, WA. Also widespread in the Indo-West Pacific region.
Maximum size: Length to 100 mm.

Bursatella leachii is easily recognised by the distinctive covering of light-coloured hairs and tufted processes on the body. The background colour is black, with small, vivid green-blue spots.

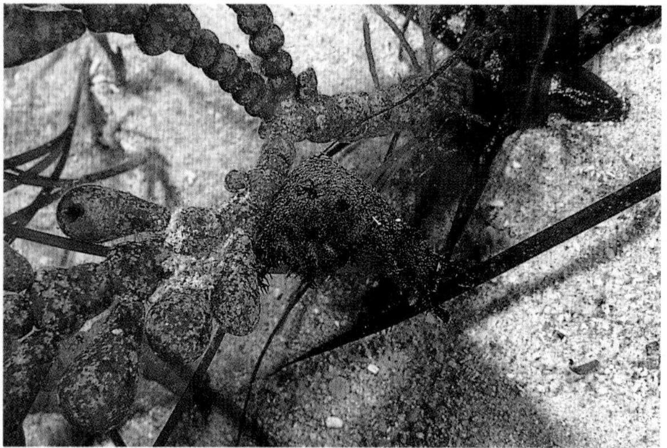

Bursatella leachii, Little I, WA

FAMILY OXYNOIDAE

Oxynoids have a fragile, internal, ovoid shell, a long muscular tail and fleshy parapodial lobes that extend out from the foot. Most species in this and related families, including Elysiidae and Stiligeridae, are specialised associates of a few green algal species. They feed on the algae using dagger-shaped teeth, which pierce the plant cells, releasing the cell contents. Most species are very difficult to detect among the host plant because of their small size and green coloration.

Oxynoe viridis (Pease, 1861)

Habitat: Moderately exposed green seaweed; 0–20 m depth.
Distribution: Around Australia. Also widespread through the Indo-West Pacific region.
Maximum size: Length to 25 mm.

Oxynoe viridis, Ricketts Pt, Vic. RUDIE KUITER

Oxynoe viridis occurs commonly on clumps of *Caulerpa geminata* and *Caulerpa cactoides* along the southern coast but is rarely seen unless deliberately searched for because the rounded body resembles the bubble-shaped vesicles of the associated plant. The long tail is readily sacrificed if the animal is threatened.

FAMILY ELYSIIDAE

Elysiids are small shell-less opisthobranchs. They have elongate bodies, wing-like parapodia on the sides, prominent rhinophores and usually a groove across the foot behind the head region. Most species in this family remain undetected in their algal habitats; some have only recently been discovered and are yet to be given scientific names.

Elysia expansa, Houtman Abrolhos, WA. CLAY BRYCE

Elysia expansa (O'Donoghue, 1924)

Habitat: Moderately exposed green seaweed; 0–5 m depth.
Distribution: Houtman Abrolhos to Rottnest I, WA. Also New Caledonia.
Maximum size: Length to 30 mm.

Elysia expansa has an olive-green body with dark tips to the rhinophores and a thin black line along the margin of the parapodia. The parapodia are very large in comparison with those of other species in the family and have a ruffled appearance. The species occurs commonly along the southern west coast, where it feeds on species of *Caulerpa*.

Elysia sp.

Habitat: Moderately exposed seaweed; 5–10 m depth.
Distribution: Central NSW.
Maximum size: Length to 20 mm.

Elysia sp. is one of numerous poorly known elysiids found along the Australian coast. The colour patterns on these species are generally distinctive.

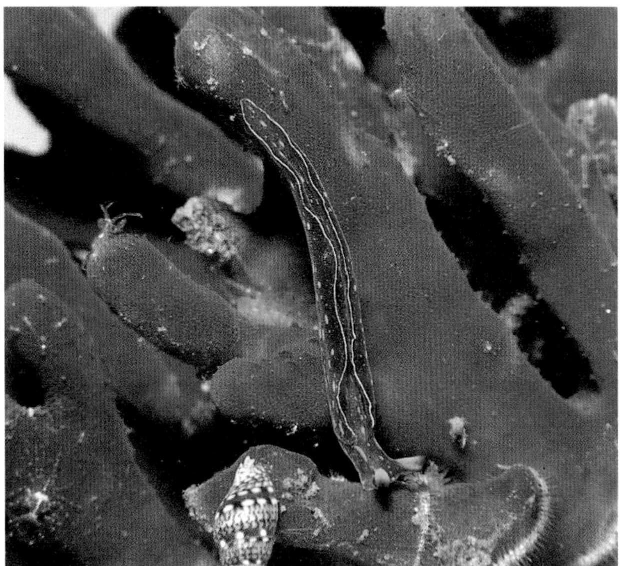

Elysia sp., Clovelly, NSW. RUDIE KUITER

FAMILY STILIGERIDAE

This is a small family of sap-sucking opisthobranchs that have prominent rhinophores, an anus on the upper surface and numerous spindle-shaped cerata. The cerata contain extensions of the digestive gland and can also store intact cells of consumed plants that continue to photosynthesise, producing additional food for the animal. They also provide a defence against predators because of the toxic compounds contained within.

Stiliger smaragdinus Baba, 1949

Habitat: Moderately exposed green seaweed; 0–22 m.
Distribution: Mullaloo, WA, to southern NSW. Also Japan.
Maximum size: Length to 75 mm.

Stiliger smaragdinus is the largest known Australian opisthobranch that feeds on the cell contents of green algae. The animal is lime-green in colour and has its upper surface obscured by rows of cerata. On the rare occasions when the species has been seen, it has usually been associated with the alga *Caulerpa cactoides*.

Stiliger smaragdinus, Little I, WA

FAMILY TYLODINIDAE

The most obvious feature of tylodinids is a flattened limpet-like shell into which the animal can just withdraw. They lack jaws but have radular teeth. Six species are known in the family.

Tylodina corticalis (Tate, 1889)

Habitat: Moderately exposed reef; 0–60 m depth.
Distribution: Recherche Archipelago, WA, to southern Qld and around Tas.
Maximum size: Length to 100 mm.

Tylodina corticalis, Recherche Archipelago, WA. CLAY BRYCE

Tylodina corticalis is the only species in the family recorded from Australia. The animal is bright chrome yellow with a wide foot, and the shell is oval-shaped and covered by a thick brown protective layer (the periostracum) with strong radial ridges. The species is widely distributed through southern Australia but is not abundant and is very rarely seen outside the autumn months. It feeds on a yellow sponge (*Pseudoceratina* sp).

FAMILY UMBRACULIDAE

The family Umbraculidae contains two species with limpet-like shells and anatomical similarities to the tylodinids. Differences between them relate to the development of the gill, the location of the penis, and the location of tentacles on the head.

Umbraculum sinicum (Gmelin, 1793)

Umbrella shell

Habitat: Moderately exposed reef; 0–20 m depth.
Distribution: Tropical Australia south to Houtman Abrolhos, WA, and southern NSW. Also widespread in the Indo-West Pacific region.
Maximum size: Length to 150 mm.

Umbraculum sinicum has a large, firm rounded body covered by numerous wart-like protuberances. The shell is usually covered by plants and encrusting animals and is much too small to accommodate the body. The species is difficult to detect because of the disruptive covering but occurs in intertidal rock pools and, more commonly, on shallow reefs.

Umbraculum sinicum, Port Stephens, NSW

FAMILY PLEUROBRANCHIDAE
Side-gilled slugs

The family Pleurobranchidae is closely related to the Tylodinidae and Umbraculidae. Species have a single gill plume on the right side of the body, strong jaws, rows of numerous small teeth in the radula and usually a small internal shell. They generally feed on sessile (permanently attached) invertebrates such as sponges, hydroids and ascidians.

Berthellina citrina (Rüppell & Leuckart, 1828)

Habitat: Moderately exposed reef; 0–60 m depth.
Distribution: Around the Australian mainland and Tas. Also widespread overseas.
Maximum size: Length to 50 mm.

Berthellina citrina has a cylindrical shape and uniform colour, which can be either yellow or orange. Two prominent rhinophores, which are fused at their base, project out from under the front of the mantle. The species feeds on sponges and is moderately common throughout southern Australia.

Berthellina citrina, Busselton, WA

Pleurobranchaea maculata, Bathurst Channel, Tas.

Pleurobranchaea maculata
(Quoy & Gaimard, 1832)

Habitat: Sheltered and moderately exposed reef, silt; 0–200 m depth.
Distribution: Southern WA to southern Qld and around Tas. Also New Zealand.
Maximum size: Length to 100 mm.

Pleurobranchaea maculata is a light grey sea slug with a network of fine brown lines over the surface and an aardvark-like head. It occurs abundantly in coastal bays, where it moves rapidly scouting for anemones and other soft-bodied invertebrate prey.

FAMILY POLYCERIDAE

This and the following six families belong to the order Nudibranchia, a group of opisthobranchs with external gills arranged along both sides of the body or in a cluster towards the back of the upper body surface. Nudibranchs are a highly diverse order with at least 300 species occurring in Australia, and many more species yet to be discovered. The family Polyceridae includes slender nudibranchs with retractable rhinophores and large gills on the upper surface that can be contracted into a bunch but not withdrawn below the body surface. They differ from several closely related families in the arrangement of their radula teeth. Nearly all of the many species of polycerids are restricted to the tropics.

Tambja verconis (Basedow & Hedley, 1905)

Habitat: Moderately exposed reef; 2–36 m depth.
Distribution: Southern WA to central NSW and around Tas. Also New Zealand.
Maximum size: Length to 130 mm.

Tambja verconis is one of the most distinctive and abundant of the southern nudibranchs. It has a yellow body with sky-blue markings, gills and rhinophores — a pattern that remains constant throughout the species' range. This nudibranch apparently feeds solely on the green bryozoan *Bugula dentata* and is present at virtually all locations where that bryozoan occurs.

FAMILY DORIDIDAE
Dorids

The family Dorididae contains more species than other nudibranch families; however, most are drably coloured and therefore rarely noticed by divers or shore fossickers. The family is divided into genera largely on the basis of the radula teeth and reproductive system. All dorids so far investigated have been found to feed on sponges.

Tambja verconis (mating pair), Rocky Cape, Tas.

Aphelodoris varia, Port Stephens, NSW

Aphelodoris varia (Abraham, 1877)

Habitat: Moderately exposed reef; 0–30 m.
Distribution: Jervis Bay to Cape Byron, NSW.
Maximum size: Length to 76 mm.

Aphelodoris varia is a flaccid, elongate nudibranch with a mottled brown upper surface that partly continues onto the flat white margin, and rhinophores and gills that are usually blue-grey. The taste of the body when licked has been described as peppery. The species is very common along the New South Wales coast during the late summer months, when groups of 10–20 animals can be found mating.

Neodoris chrysoderma (Angas, 1864)

Habitat: Reef, seagrass; 0–30 m.
Distribution: Cape Naturaliste, WA, to Hastings Point, NSW, and around Tas.
Maximum size: Length to 50 mm.

Neodoris chrysoderma, Terrigal, NSW

Neodoris chrysoderma is easily recognised with its yellow body, large white papillae on the back and orange rhinophores and gills. It is one of the more abundant nudibranchs and is found in a variety of habitats.

FAMILY CHROMODORIDIDAE
Chromodorids

This large family includes many of the brightly coloured nudibranchs, with more than 100 species recorded from Australia. Although the majority are found in the tropics, many are restricted to the temperate western and eastern Australian coasts, and a few are found in southern waters. Chromodorids feed on sponges and are generally able to extract toxic chemicals from the sponges for use in their own defence. Without this defensive mechanism it is doubtful that they would have evolved such conspicuous colour patterns.

Ceratosoma amoena, Jervis Bay, NSW

Ceratosoma amoena (Cheeseman, 1886)

Habitat: Exposed reef; 0–30 m.
Distribution: Southern NSW to North Stradbroke I, Qld. Also Lord Howe I, Norfolk I and New Zealand.
Maximum size: Length to 60 mm.

Ceratosoma amoena has a distinctive series of round orange spots on the upper surface and rectangular markings along the margin. The rhinophores and gills are deep red. The species is abundant on coastal New South Wales reefs and occurs in highest densities in depths greater than 10 m.

Ceratosoma brevicaudatum Abraham, 1876

Habitat: Moderately exposed reef; 0–100 m depth.
Distribution: Houtman Abrolhos, WA, to Cape Byron, NSW, and around Tas.
Maximum size: Length to 150 mm.

Ceratosoma brevicaudatum is the most frequently noticed nudiboranch species along the southern coast because of its great abundance, large size and vivid coloration. The pattern varies slightly between locations but always has a pink–orange background with numerous red, white-edged spots. The body is firm, with a long tail.

Ceratosoma brevicaudatum, Busselton, WA

Chromodoris epicuria (Basedow & Hedley, 1905)

Habitat: Moderately exposed reef; 0–30 m.
Distribution: Cape Naturaliste, WA, to Western Port, Vic., and around Tas.
Maximum size: Length to 50 mm.

Chromodoris epicuria, Bicheno, Tas.

Chromodoris epicuria has a light coloured body, usually with a row of orange spots around the outer margin and fine orange spots on the back. Animals living in the western part of the range generally have a pink background, whereas those from Tasmania are white. The species is moderately common and is often associated with the sponge *Aplysilla rosea*.

Chromodoris tasmaniensis (Bergh, 1905)

Habitat: Moderately exposed reef; 0–30 m.
Distribution: Portland, Vic., to Port Hacking, NSW, and around Tas.
Maximum size: Length to 50 mm.

Chromodoris tasmaniensis has a row of red spots around the margin and scattered red spots across the centre of a white body, with red lines around the rims of the rhinophore and gill cavities. This nudibranch lives in a similar habitat to *C. epicuria* but is slightly less common.

Chromodoris tasmaniensis, D'Entrecasteaux Channel, Tas.

Chromodoris splendida (Angas, 1864)

Habitat: Moderately exposed reef; 0–25 m.
Distribution: Southern NSW to Mooloolaba, Qld.
Maximum size: Length to 60 mm.

Chromodoris splendida is one of the most commonly sighted nudibranchs on New South Wales reefs. It is readily identified by the large red spots on the top of the body and the yellow band around the edge of the mantle.

Chromodoris splendida, Terrigal, NSW

Chromodoris westraliensis, Little I, WA

Chromodoris westraliensis

(O'Donoghue, 1924)

Habitat: Moderately exposed reef; 0–18 m.
Distribution: Rockingham to Point Quobba, WA.
Maximum size: Length to 60 mm.

Chromodoris westraliensis is the most common nudibranch seen in the Perth region, particularly on reefs just below low-tide level. The colour pattern varies little throughout the species' range and is immediately recognisable because of two pale blue patches prominent on the back, red gills and rhinophores, and orange and black stripes along the margin.

Hypselodoris bennetti, Merimbula, NSW

Hypselodoris bennetti (Angas, 1864)

Habitat: Exposed reef; 0–34 m.
Distribution: Southern NSW to Cape Moreton, Qld.
Maximum size: Length to 60 mm.

Hypselodoris bennetti has a distinctive blue body, red spots on the upper surface, red streaks on the rhinophores and gills, and a yellow margin. It occurs commonly in shallow water in the Sydney region.

Glossodoris atromarginata (Cuvier, 1804)

Habitat: Sheltered and moderately exposed reef, sand; 0–28 m.
Distribution: Tropical Australia south to southern NSW. Also widespread in the Indo-West Pacific region.
Maximum size: Length to 50 mm.

Glossodoris atromarginata has a repeatedly ruffled margin with a thin black strip along the edge. The body is generally a cream to lemon colour, and the rhinophores and gills are edged in black. The species is most often found on a broken rubble bottom near the entrance to sheltered bays.

Glossodoris atromarginata, Norah Head, NSW

FAMILY DENDRODORIDIDAE
Dendrodorids

Species in this family have soft bodies and lack radula teeth, jaws and tentacles around the mouth. They use their long oral tube to secrete saliva and later suck in the partially digested food, which is usually sponge.

Dendrodoris peculiaris, Rocky Cape, Tas.

Dendrodoris peculiaris (Abraham, 1877)

Habitat: Sheltered and moderately exposed reef; 0–40 m depth.
Distribution: Cape Naturaliste, WA, to Wilsons Promontory, Vic., and northern Tas.
Maximum size: Length to 50 mm.

Dendrodoris peculiaris is a very flat species that can easily be mistaken for a flatworm when its gills are retracted (as in the illustrated animal). It is brown to yellow in colour, with round, cream papillae on the upper surface and numerous, fine white spicules visible through the body wall near the margin. A more brightly coloured relative, ***Dendrodoris carneola***, has a narrower and more solid body with a granular surface. Both species are common under rocks in the lower intertidal and shallow subtidal zone.

FAMILY FACELINIDAE

Facelinids are distinguished by long bodies with numerous clusters of thin-walled cerata that project from the upper margins. Most species feed on hydroids and soft corals.

Pteraeolidia ianthina (Angas, 1864)
Blue dragon

Habitat: Exposed reef; 0–27 m.
Distribution: Tropical Australia south to Gulf St Vincent, SA, and Jervis Bay, NSW. Also widespread in the Indo-West Pacific region.
Maximum size: Length to 150 mm.

Pteraeolidia ianthina is the largest nudibranch seen on exposed reefs. The species is easily recognised by the elongate body shape and fans of long cerata

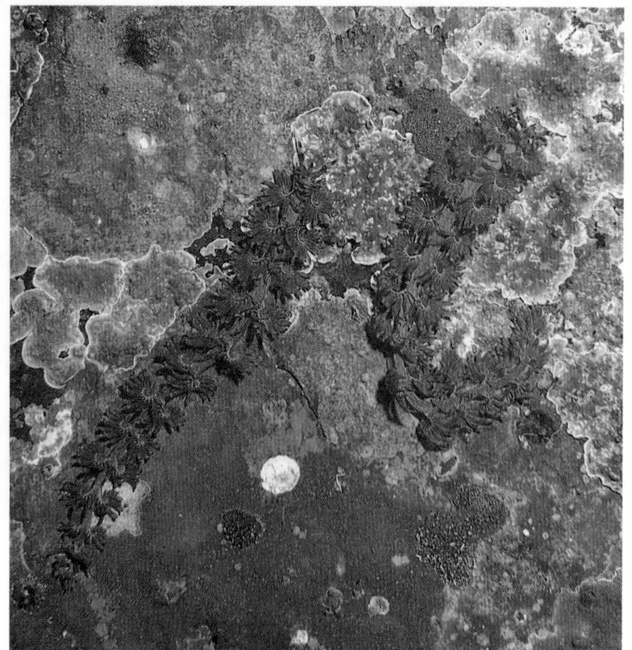

Pteraeolidia ianthina, Bass Point, NSW

(horn-like projections) down the back. When feeding on soft corals, it does not digest the photosynthetic cells (zooxanthellae) embedded in the soft coral tissue but transports them to the cerata, where they continue to photosynthesise and produce food to supplement the normal hydroid diet. *Pteraeolidia ianthina* is the only nudibranch known in which the adult will remain beside and protect its eggmass.

Austraeolis ornata (Angas, 1864)

Habitat: Sheltered and moderately exposed reef; 0–20 m depth.
Distribution: Houtman Abrolhos, WA, to Moreton Bay, Qld, and around Tas.
Maximum size: Length to 35 mm.

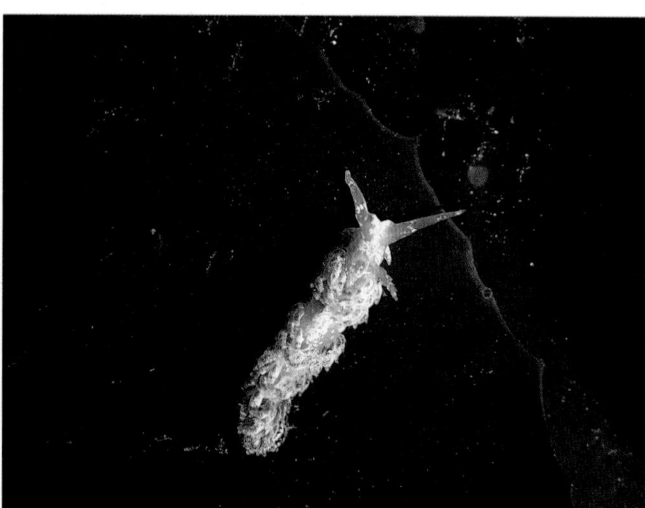

Austraeolis ornata, Southport Lagoon, Tas.

Austraeolis ornata has a orange body flecked with white and blue spots and numerous cerata arranged in small groups down the body. These cerata are quite fragile and will break off if the animal is handled roughly. The species occurs commonly in intertidal rock pools and shallow water, where it glides over the bottom looking for hydroids.

Spurilla macleayi (Angas, 1864)

Habitat: Reef; 0–3 m depth.
Distribution: Albany, WA, to northern NSW and around Tas.
Maximum size: Length to 35 mm.

Spurilla macleayi resembles *Austraeolis ornata* but can be distinguished by the shorter and stouter cerata, which are more densely aggregated down the body, and the less attenuated tail. The species is moderately common but not often seen. It is thought to feed on small anemones.

Spurilla ? macleayi, Port Stephens, NSW

FAMILY FLABELLINIDAE

Flabellinids are related to facelinids but generally have much narrower bodies and are less aggressive. They also differ in the arrangement of the radular teeth, as they have three teeth rather than a single tooth in each row.

Flabellina rubrolineata (O'Donoghue, 1929)

Habitat: Sheltered and moderately exposed reef; 2–32 m.
Distribution: Tropical Australia south to eastern Vic. Also widespread in the Indo-West Pacific region.
Maximum size: Length to 42 mm.

Flabellina rubrolineata is a noticeable species because of its bright pink-purple colour and characteristic shape. It is primarily a tropical species but is also common in the deeper estuaries along the central New South Wales coast. The diet consists of large hydroid species, particularly *Halocordyle disticha*.

Flabellina rubrolineata, Port Stephens, NSW

FAMILY ARMINIDAE

Arminids comprise a large family of nudibranchs with the body produced into a thin veil at the front and usually with longitudinal ridges down the back. A number of similar-looking but poorly known species belonging to the genera *Armina* and *Dermatobranchus* occur around southern Australia. They feed on sea pens or soft corals.

Armina sp.

Habitat: Sheltered silt; 5–18 m.
Distribution: Southern Tas.
Maximum size: Length to 50 mm.

Armina sp. is a strongly lined species of nudibranch with orange tentacles and black bands across the body. It feeds on the sea pen *Sarcoptilus grandis* in Tasmania, and so is usually found either on the tentacles of that species or buried in soft sediment nearby.

Armina sp., Bathurst Channel, Tas.

Class Bivalvia

Bivalves, pelycypods, lamellibranchs

Bivalves are highly modified molluscs, which possess two valves joined at the margin by an elastic ligament and associated hinge teeth. Most species can retract fully within the valves, which are closed by the contraction of strong adductor muscles that directly connect the two valves. The shell opens as a result of the elasticity of the hinge ligament. Bivalves lack a head and radula teeth and have a well-developed foot that is generally utilised for burrowing. A highly developed gill system is used for feeding as well as respiration in most species. The beating of rows of cilia causes water currents to be drawn in the inhalant siphon and passed across the gills, where small food particles are extracted and sorted. The particles are then passed via labial palps onto the mouth located near the front of the foot, while water moves out through the exhalant siphon. Because of their reliance on the complex gill system, bivalves cannot feed or respire in air and so have never colonised land.

Bivalves are extremely well adapted for life in soft sediments and are often the dominant group of large animals in this habitat type. Some live buried in sand or mud with just the tips of the inhalent and exhalent siphons reaching the sediment surface. Other species attach themselves to hard substrates by means of byssal threads secreted by the foot. A few species bore into soft rock or wood. In contrast, some scallops and limids are active swimmers, moving in short spurts by quickly expelling a jet of water behind the shell.

Approximately 10,000 species of bivalve are known. They are classified at family and higher levels largely on the basis of hinge structure and the shape and complexity of the gills. Species and genera are largely identified on the basis of the shape of the shell

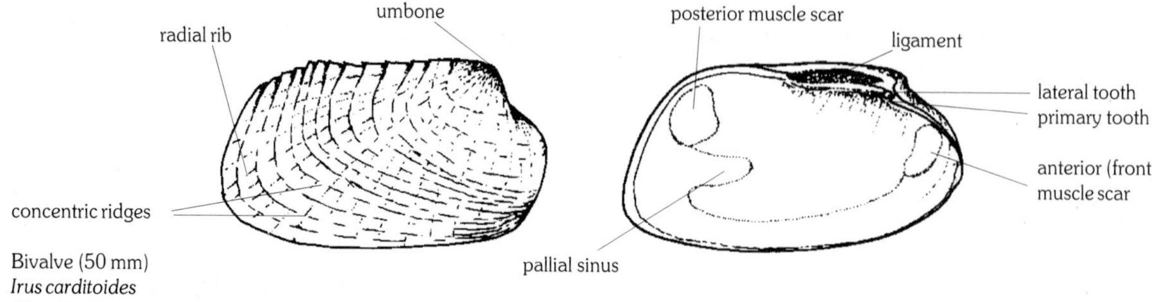

Bivalve (50 mm)
Irus carditoides
Class Bivalvia

and hinge teeth and the positions of marks on the inside of the shell that correspond with muscle attachment points.

FAMILY SOLEMYIDAE
Date shells

Solemyids have a fragile shell with a distinctive horny periostracum overlapping the ends of the shell and splitting along radial lines. A large proportion of species in the family have a much-reduced gut or none at all and obtain nutrition from chemical-transforming (chemosynthetic) bacteria embedded in their tissues. Solemyids mainly occur in oxygen-deficient muds.

Solemya australis Lamarck, 1818

Habitat: Moderately exposed mud, sand, seagrass; 0–10 m.
Distribution: Fremantle, WA, to Andersons Inlet, Vic., and south to Bicheno, Tas.
Maximum size: Length to 57 mm.

Solemya australis can be immediately distinguished from other southern Australian shells by its elongate, internally nacreous shell and outwardly radiating lines that cross the dark brown periostracum. The species generally occurs in mud just below low-tide level and is not often seen.

Solemya australis, Bicheno, Tas.

FAMILY ARCIDAE
Arks

Arks have large solid shells with a series of numerous small vertical teeth in the hinge, increasing in size towards the extremities. The ligament has alternate bands of hard and soft tissue. Most species have a thick brown periostracum that is sometimes produced into hairy tufts. The family is an ancient one, with numerous fossils dating as far back as the Jurassic period (200–145 million years ago).

Anadara trapezia (Deshayes, 1840)
Sydney cockle

Habitat: Sheltered mud, sand, seagrass; 0–2 m.
Distribution: Port Phillip Bay, Vic., to southern Qld, with an isolated population at Albany, WA.
Maximum size: Length to 75 mm.

Anadara trapezia, Merimbula, NSW

Anadara trapezia is a heavy ark shell with thick radiating ribs. In estuaries with suitable conditions it occurs abundantly on the surface of mud. The presence of fresh-looking fossil shells on southern Australian, northern Tasmanian and New Zealand shores indicates that the species was recently very common throughout the region. *Anadara trapezia* is sometimes taken for human consumption, although relatively little flesh is obtained from a large weight of collected shells.

Barbatia pistachia (Lamarck, 1819)

Habitat: Moderately exposed reef; 0–30 m depth.
Distribution: Kimberley, WA, to Qld and around Tas.
Maximum size: Length to 70 mm.

Barbatia pistachia has a cream-coloured shell stained with brown and numerous fine radiating ribs crossed by very fine ridges. The lower margin is concave and the end margins covered by a narrow band of brown hairs. The species locally occurs in very high abundance in areas with strong current flow.

Barbatia pistachia, Gordon, Tas.

FAMILY NUCULANIDAE
Beaked nut shells

Beaked nut shells, or nuculanids, have a hinge that includes numerous fine teeth extending in a series each side of the central depression to which the ligament attaches. The internal surface of the shell is not nacreous, as in the closely related family Nuculidae (nut shells), and the valves often project at the rear into a beak-like structure.

Nuculana crassa (Hinds, 1843)

Habitat: Exposed sand; 5–60 m depth.
Distribution: Southern WA to NSW and around Tas.
Maximum size: Length to 30 mm.

Nuculana crassa, Cloudy Bay, Tas.

Nuculana crassa can be recognised by the distinctive beak at the rear of the shell and the concentric ridges around the valves. The species is widespread and moderately commonly in southern Australia, reaching greatest abundance in southern Tasmania. Living animals sit just below the surface of sand and feed on fine food particles.

FAMILY GLYCYMERIDAE
Dog cockles

Glycymerids are readily recognised because the shells are solid and rounded and possess a semi-circular row of strong teeth and associated grooves around the top of the shell. The family is related to the arks but has fewer teeth in the hinge line.

Glycymeris radians (Lamarck, 1819)

Habitat: Sheltered and moderately exposed sand; 2–30 m depth.
Distribution: Albany, WA, to NSW and around Tas.
Maximum size: Length to 40 mm.

Glycymeris radians, Princess Royal Harbour, WA

Glycymeris radians is a common species in sheltered bays along the southern coast. It has a solid rounded shell with 30–40 radial ribs and is a dark brown colour that lightens toward the umbone (the protuberance of each valve above the hinge).

Glycymeris striatularis (Lamarck, 1819)

Habitat: Exposed sand; 5–30 m depth.
Distribution: Port Gregory, WA, to southern Qld and around Tas.
Maximum size: Length to 45 mm.

Glycymeris striatularis is common in shallow water behind the wave break off exposed surf beaches. It differs from *G. radians* by having slightly wider ribs and fine brown zigzag markings in concentric rows towards the top of the shell. A third glycymerid species that is most common in New South Wales, ***Glycymeris grayana*** (formerly *G. flammeus*), has large brown zigzag splashes across the shell.

Glycymeris striatularis, Cloudy Bay, Tas.

FAMILY MYTILIDAE
Mussels

Mussel shells are angular at one end, rounded at the other and longer than wide. They are usually attached in groups to rock with byssal threads and have an external ligament. Mussels also have a thick dark periostracum, which may be hairy and adheres strongly to the shell.

Mytilus edulis Linnaeus, 1758
Blue mussel

Habitat: Sheltered and moderately exposed reef, wood pylons; 0–15 m depth.
Distribution: Perth, WA, to NSW and around Tas. Also widespread overseas.
Maximum size: Length to 120 mm.

Mytilus edulis is a large fan-shaped mussel with a bluish-black exterior and bluish-white interior. It is the only local mussel raised commercially and is commonly served in restaurants. There has been confusion about the name of this mussel as it was originally thought to be a species restricted to Australia and called *Mytilus planulatus*. The blue mussel is, however, virtually identical to the common blue mussel of Europe, so now carries the older name.

Mytilus edulis, Cloudy Lagoon, Tas.

Xenostrobus pulex (Lamarck, 1819)

Habitat: Moderately and submaximally exposed rocky shores; mid intertidal.
Distribution: Yanchep, WA, to NSW and around Tas.
Maximum size: Length to 25 mm.

Xenostrobus pulex is a mat-forming mussel that lives in dense populations on exposed rock platforms. The shiny black shell is relatively small and inflated, with the umbone positioned at the end of a steep ridge.

Xenostrobus pulex with predatory *Lepsiella vinosa*, Coles Bay, Tas.

Modiolus cottoni Laseron, 1956

Habitat: Sheltered and moderately exposed reef; 2–10 m depth.
Distribution: Fremantle, WA, to southern NSW and around Tas.
Maximum size: Length to 85 mm.

Modiolus cottoni is one of the largest southern species of mussel. It has a fan-shaped shell, yellow-brown exterior, white interior and a characteristic group of brown hairs around the lower margin. The species is locally common but not often seen.

Modiolus cottoni, Bathurst Channel, Tas.

Modiolus albicostus Lamarck, 1819

Habitat: Reef; 1–50 m depth.
Distribution: Southern WA to NSW and around Tas.
Maximum size: Length to 130 mm.

Modiolus albicostus is an extremely large species that can be identified by the shiny dark brown exterior and white interior. Shells are commonly washed up on beaches, but living animals are rarely seen.

Modiolus albicostus, Cloudy Lagoon, Tas.

Brachidontes rostratus (Dunker, 1857)

Habitat: Moderately and submaximally exposed rocky shores; mid intertidal.
Distribution: Southern WA to southern NSW and around Tas.
Maximum size: Length to 40 mm.

Brachidontes rostratus occurs in dense mats in much the same habitat as *Xenostrobus pulex* and is equally as abundant. It can be recognised by the purple

Brachidontes rostratus, Eaglehawk Neck, Tas.

coloration, the relatively long, flat shell with a rounded lower margin, and the regular rounded ribs which are best developed towards the lower margin of the shell.

Brachidontes erosus (Lamarck, 1819)

Habitat: Sheltered reef and rocks; mid intertidal to 4 m depth.
Distribution: Albany, WA, to San Remo, Vic., and northern Tas.
Maximum size: Length to 70 mm.

Brachidontes erosus resembles *B. rostratus* but has fewer and deeper grooves in the valves. The species is commonly found high in the intertidal zone embedded in a spongy green seaweed; it has also been recorded subtidally, attached to rocks in muddy bays.

Brachidontes erosus, Elliston, SA

Amygdalum beddomei Iredale, 1924

Habitat: Sheltered and moderately exposed sand; 3–280 m.
Distribution: Southern WA to southern Qld and around Tas.
Maximum size: Length to 50 mm.

Amygdalum beddomei, Tinderbox, Tas.

Amygdalum beddomei is the most distinctive of the southern mussels. The species has a fragile fingernail-shaped shell, iridescent internal sheen and network of fine brown lines on the exterior. It sits on the sediment in moderate depths among a cluster of byssal threads extruded by the animal.

Trichomya hirsuta, Port Stephens, NSW

Trichomya hirsuta (Lamarck, 1819)

Habitat: Exposed reef; 0–15 m.
Distribution: Great Australian Bight, SA, to southern Qld and Flinders I, Tas.
Maximum size: Length to 60 mm.

Trichomya hirsuta has a bearded appearance, with numerous finely barbed hairs on the lower half of the shell. It is a common species intertidally as well as subtidally, particularly along the New South Wales coast.

Musculista senhousia (Benson, 1842)

East Asian bag mussel

Habitat: Sheltered mud, wood; 0–20 m depth.
Distribution: Swan River Estuary, WA, and Tamar estuary, Tas. Also East Asia, California, New Zealand.
Maximum size: Length to 30 mm.

Musculista senhousia is a recent invader of Australia, having been first collected near Perth in 1982. Since arriving, it has increased in numbers to become one of the more common molluscs in the Swan estuary. The species can be recognised by its small size, inflated shape and iridescent green/brown colour with radiating reddish lines. It generally occurs just below low-tide level in aggregated clumps, with the individuals attached together by byssal threads.

Musculista senhousia, Bicton, WA

FAMILY PINNIDAE
Razor clams

Razor clams have large, flat, wedge-shaped shells, which are embedded in sediment with the narrow end downward. Byssal threads are extruded from the shell tip, providing substantial anchorage. The shell exterior has a horny sheen, while the interior is nacreous.

Pinna bicolor Gmelin, 1791
Razor clam

Habitat: Sheltered sand; 0–10 m.
Distribution: Tropical Australia around the southwest to Gulf St Vincent, SA, and down the east coast to NSW. Also widespread in the Indo-West Pacific region.
Maximum size: Length to 500 mm.

Pinna bicolor is the largest bivalve found on the south coast. It is fan-shaped with the tip embedded in sand or mud. The popular name 'razor clam' indicates the hazard these bivalves pose to bare-footed bathers. The species occurs gregariously and can be extremely abundant near low-tide mark in the South Australian gulfs. Shells in that area are usually colonised by diverse communities of plants and animals. The flesh of the razor clam can be eaten and was once sold in South Australia, although the amount of edible meat is trivial compared with the size of the shell.

Pinna bicolor, Princess Royal Harbour, WA

Atrina tasmanica (Tenison Woods, 1876)

Habitat: Moderately exposed sand; 5–40 m.
Distribution: Port Lincoln, SA, to southern NSW and northern and eastern Tas.
Maximum size: Length to 240 mm.

Atrina tasmanica, Port Lincoln, SA

Atrina tasmanica resembles *Pinna bicolor* but is smaller, more translucent and has 10–14 radiating ribs with fingernail-shaped spines. It occurs commonly in water depths below 20 m but rarely enters shallower water.

FAMILY PTERIIDAE
Pearl oysters

Shells in this family are flattened, with triangular wing-like projections from both ends of the hinge. The interior of the shell has a pearly lustre.

Electroma georgiana (Quoy & Gaimard, 1835)

Habitat: Sheltered seagrass, seaweed; 0–20 m depth.
Distribution: Southern WA to southern NSW and around Tas.
Maximum size: Length to 40 mm.

Electroma georgiana is an extremely thin bivalve that lives attached to marine plants. The shell is winged and translucent and is often marked by radiating brown or green stripes. The species grows very rapidly, causing population explosions in localised areas until the shells are eventually dislodged by wave action and washed in abundance onto local beaches. Despite its small size, *Electroma georgiana* is closely related to the giant pearl oysters of the tropics.

Electroma georgiana, Cloudy Lagoon, Tas.

FAMILY MALLEIDAE
Hammer oysters, finger oysters

This family can be distinguished by shells with a nacreous interior and the presence of a triangular pit beside the hinge. It includes both the distinctive hammer oysters and the sponge-dwelling finger oysters.

Malleus meridianus Cotton, 1930
Southern hammer oyster

Habitat: Sheltered and moderately exposed reef, sand; 0–200 m depth.
Distribution: Fremantle, WA, to Gulf St Vincent, SA.
Maximum size: Length to 150 mm.

Malleus meridianus is one of an interesting group of bivalves known as the hammer oysters, with long narrow wings in the upper part of the shell and a glossy blue and black central interior. The species is common on broken rubble in sheltered habitats along the southern Australian coast but is usually well camouflaged and not often noticed.

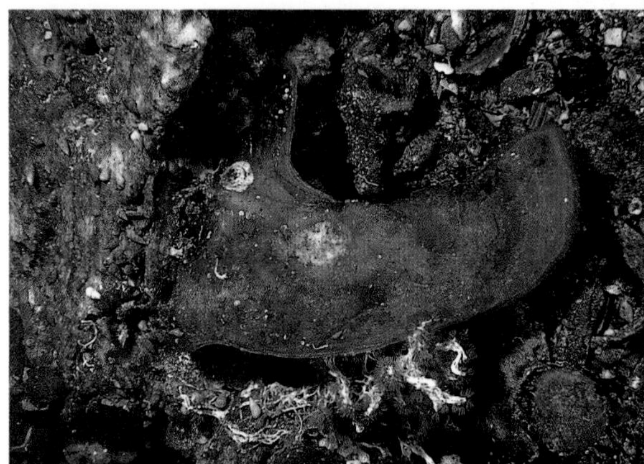

Malleus meridianus, Esperance, WA

Vulsella spongiarum, Coles Bay, Tas.

Vulsella spongiarum Lamarck, 1819

Habitat: Exposed reef, sand; 2–30 m depth.
Distribution: Fremantle, WA, to Mallacoota, Vic., and around Tas.
Maximum size: Length to 45 mm.

Vulsella spongiarum has an elongate shell with approximately parallel sides and rounded ends. The pit beside the hinge is deep and very pronounced. This abundant bivalve occurs embedded among sponges and may be detected by its gaping valves.

FAMILY PECTINIDAE
Scallops, fan shells

Scallops have a distinctive shell shape with conspicuous wings. They are highly regarded as food and are commercially harvested and cultivated throughout much of the world.

Pecten fumatus Reeve, 1852

Commercial scallop, king scallop

Habitat: Sand; 0–80 m depth.
Distribution: Shark Bay, WA, to central Qld.
Maximum size: Length to 145 mm.

Pecten fumatus has a left (i.e. uppermost) valve that is flat, a right valve that is ashtray-shaped and 12–16 radial ribs. It differs from other local species in that the wings are mirror images of each other. Larval scallops drift among plankton for up to six weeks. They then settle and fix themselves to a hard substrate, detaching and moving onto sediment when they reach about 6 mm in length. Growth studies indicate that animals reach about 70 mm after two years but then grow slowly, and that the largest animals are about 15 years old. As indicated by its common name, this has traditionally been the main species targeted by scallop fishermen. Most inshore populations have been devastated by overharvesting and habitat degradation during the past half-century, and fishermen have needed to move further and further offshore in search of commercial scallop beds.

Pecten fumatus, Bathurst Channel, Tas.

Mesopeplum tasmanicum

(Adams & Angas, 1863)
Tasmanian scallop

Habitat: Exposed reef; 15–70 m depth.
Distribution: Yorke Peninsula, SA, to Twofold Bay, NSW, and around Tas.
Maximum size: Length to 62 mm.

Mesopeplum tasmanicum differs from other southern scallops in having five strong radial ribs with secondary riblets between, and dissimilar sculpturing on the two valves. The colour pattern is quite variable, ranging from mottled cream to orange and purple. The species occurs attached to deeper reefs and is possibly quite common below normal diving depths.

Mesopeplum tasmanicum, Bicheno, Tas.

Equichlamys bifrons (Lamarck, 1819)

Queen scallop

Habitat: Sheltered and moderately exposed sand, seagrass; 0–36 m depth.
Distribution: Ceduna, SA, to southern NSW and around Tas.
Maximum size: Length to 110 mm.

Equichlamys bifrons is distinguished by the 7–9 strong rounded ribs. The colour is usually a light purple on the exterior and dark purple inside. Adults are good swimmers and generally occur in groups, which move

Equichlamys bifrons (juvenile), Esperance, WA

about. The species was once commercially fished in Tasmania in the D'Entrecasteaux Channel, but this fishery is now restricted to a short season for amateur divers.

Scaeochlamys livida (Lamarck, 1819)

Habitat: Exposed reef; 0–15 m depth.
Distribution: Shellharbour, NSW, to Qld.
Maximum size: Length to 75 mm.

Scaeochlamys livida is a relatively small scallop with about 11 strong radial ridges that each carry a series of raised scales. It is occasionally found by divers along the New South Wales coast attached to the undersurface of rocks or on shell debris.

Equichlamys bifrons, D'Entrecasteaux Channel, Tas.

Chlamys asperrimus (Lamarck, 1819)
Doughboy scallop

Habitat: Exposed reef, sand; 1–136 m depth.
Distribution: Shark Bay, WA, to southern Qld and around Tas.
Maximum size: Length to 110 mm.

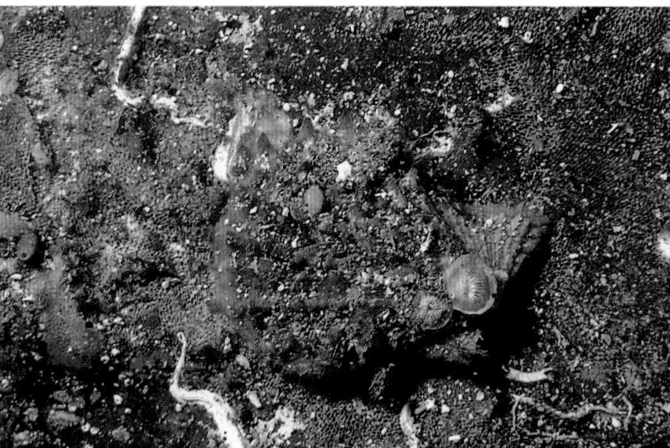
Scaeochlamys livida, Bass Point, NSW

The shell of *Chlamys asperrimus* has 20–26 major radial ribs, which are finely scaled. Shell colour is variable, with purple, pink and orange predominant. This coloration is usually obscured on living animals by a covering of sponge, with the row of blue eyes around the edge of the shell and orange mantle often the first features noticed underwater. The species occurs abundantly attached to reefs, jetty pylons and sponges. An immense mobile population of dwarf animals 20–40 mm in length is present in the deeper waters of Bass Strait.

FAMILY SPONDYLIDAE
Thorny oysters

Thorny oysters are very closely related to scallops, differing most obviously in the long spines that occur profusely on the shell.

Spondylus tenellus Reeve, 1856
Thorny oyster

Habitat: Moderately and submaximally exposed reef; 2–30 m depth.
Distribution: Southern WA to NSW and south to Maria I, Tas.
Maximum size: Length to 60 mm.

Chlamys asperrimus, Esperance, WA

Spondylus tenellus is a spectacular pink bivalve, shaped like a swollen scallop with short wings and with numerous long spines projecting out from the valves. It lives on broken reef in areas of good current flow but is not common.

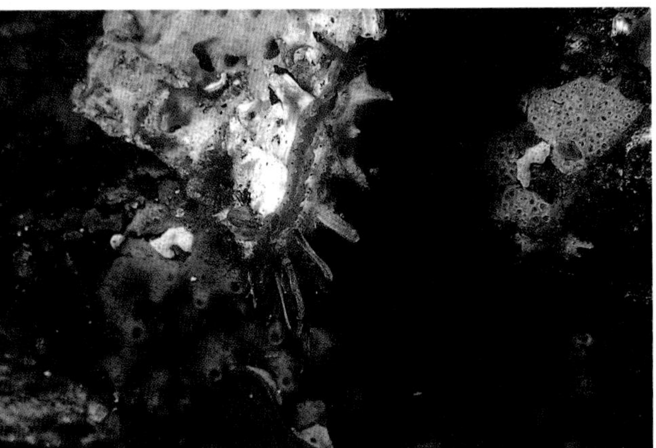

Spondylus tenellus, Busselton, WA

Spondylus tenellus, Rocky Cape, Tas.

FAMILY ANOMIIDAE
Jingle shells, windowpane shells

Jingle shells are related to the scallops but have thin flattened shells of an irregular shape. The lower valve has a hole, through which byssal threads pass.

Anomia trigonopsis Hutton, 1877

Habitat: Sheltered and moderately exposed reef; 0–100 m depth.
Distribution: Southern WA to NSW and northern Tas. Also New Zealand.
Maximum size: Length to 90 mm.

Anomia trigonopsis, Narooma, NSW

Anomia trigonopsis has a thin shell with the left (upper) valve free and the right valve attached and conforming in shape to a hard object. Almost all valves that are washed ashore are therefore the left valve. The shell is usually translucent and shiny and varies in colour from orange to bluish-green. The species is very abundant.

FAMILY LIMIDAE
File shells

File shells have ears projecting from the ends of the hinge line and white, radially ribbed valves that gape along the sides when closed. The mantle bears numerous brightly coloured tentacles, which play an important sensory role for swimming species.

Lima lima Linnaeus, 1758

Habitat: Moderately and submaximally exposed reef; 2–30 m depth.
Distribution: Around Australia including Tas. Also widespread overseas.
Maximum size: Length to 65 mm.

Lima lima has a shell with one long, relatively straight margin and the other curved in an arc that includes the lower edge. The shell surface is a cream colour, with 26–32 scaly radial ribs. The tentacles protruding from the margin of living animals are pink and white. The species usually lives in groups associated with sponges and is generally found under rocks.

Lima lima, Bass Point, NSW

Lima lima, Spencer Gulf, SA

Limatula strangei, Ulladulla, NSW

Limatula strangei (Sowerby, 1872)

Habitat: Moderately and submaximally exposed reef; 2–15 m depth.
Distribution: Southern WA to southern Qld and around Tas.
Maximum size: Length to 38 mm.

Limatula strangei differs in shape from *Lima lima* by having the two long sides of the shell approximately similar, 16–22 radial ribs on the valves, and concentric ridges across the ribs rather than prickly scales. It also has prominent marginal tentacles and is a reasonable swimmer, although it generally lives concealed under rocks.

FAMILY OSTREIDAE
Oysters

Oysters have two unequal valves, with the left or lower valve usually deep and attached to a hard substrate, and the right valve flat. The hinge lacks teeth.

Ostrea angasi Sowerby, 1871
Mud oyster, flat oyster

Habitat: Sheltered and submaximally exposed silt, sand; 1–30 m depth.
Distribution: Fremantle, WA, to NSW and around Tas.
Maximum size: Length to 180 mm.

Ostrea angasi is a large, rounded oyster with a cup-shaped lower valve and a flat or slightly concave right valve that fits within. Juveniles grow attached to stones or shells, but older animals live free on soft sediment. The species is virtually indistinguishable from the European oyster *Ostrea edulis*, renowned among gourmets. *Ostrea angasi* was once harvested in large numbers, but the population crashed during the nineteenth century, possibly because of an epidemic caused by a parasitic protozoan *Bonamia* sp. The mud oyster is now cultivated on shellfish farms in a minor way.

Ostrea angasi, D'Entrecasteaux Channel, Tas.

Saccostrea glomerata, Port Stephens, NSW

Saccostrea glomerata

(Gould 1850)
Sydney rock oyster

Habitat: Sheltered rocky shores, mangroves; mid intertidal.
Distribution: Port Phillip Bay, Vic., to southern Qld. Also New Zealand.
Maximum size: Length to 100 mm.

Saccotrea glomerata is perhaps the most widely recognised bivalve along the New South Wales coast because of its abundance and well-documented palatability. It dominates space at the mid levels of sheltered shores to such a degree that oysters grow on each other and the shells of adjoining animals become distorted. The upper valve of the Sydney rock oyster is bluish-white and slightly convex, while the lower valve is cup-shaped and strongly sculptured with thick ribs. The upper shell has a series of narrow pits along the edge leading away from the hinge. The species has long been called *Saccostrea commercialis* but is now thought to be the same as a New Zealand species.

Crassostrea gigas (Thunberg, 1793)

Pacific oyster

Habitat: Sheltered rocky shores; low intertidal.
Distribution: Central NSW and northern and eastern Tas. Also Japan and widespread overseas.
Maximum size: Length to 250 mm.

Crassostrea gigas grows to a larger size than *S. glomerata*, has a flaky rather than smooth exterior, and lacks the row of pits associated with the hinge. The species was introduced to Tasmania from Japan for aquaculture purposes and is now the second most valuable bivalve in Australia after the tropical pearl oyster. The Pacific oyster bred more prolifically than expected when released around Tasmania and is now a pest along rocky shores in many of the larger estuaries in that state. A wild population is also well established in Port Stephens, NSW, and there are concerns that, because of its faster growth rate, the species may outcompete the local Sydney rock oyster and eventually dominate sheltered New South Wales shores.

Crassostrea gigas, Cloudy Lagoon, Tas.

FAMILY TRIGONIIDAE
Brooch shells

Brooch shells are characterised by a widely flanged and corrugated hinge and bright internal sheen. They are often called living fossils because they belong to a subclass of bivalves whose fossils are abundant throughout the world. This subclass was presumed to be long extinct until live animals were found by a French exploring expedition at the beginning of the nineteenth century. Several other species in the genus *Neotrigonia* have been found in offshore Australian waters since that first discovery of *Neotrigonia margaritacea*.

Neotrigonia margaritacea (Lamarck, 1804)

Habitat: Sheltered and moderately exposed sand; 4–70 m depth.
Distribution: Vic. to NSW and around Tas.
Maximum size: Length to 50 mm.

Neotrigonia margaritacea is distinguished from other species in the genus by 22 strong radial ribs lined with prominent scales. The species occurs in abundance among coarse sand and shell grit in deep waters and is also common in the channels of Western Port, Vic., and D'Entrecasteaux Channel, Tas., where there is fast current flow.

Neotrigonia margaritacea, D'Entrecasteaux Channel, Tas.

FAMILY LUCINIDAE

Lucinids usually have rounded white shells without periostracum. Two central teeth are present in the hinge, with lateral (side hinge) flanges present on the right valve and corresponding grooves on the left.

Anodontia perplexa (Cotton & Godfrey, 1938)

Habitat: Sheltered sand; 0–5 m depth.
Distribution: Southern WA to central Qld.
Maximum size: Length to 25 mm.

Anodontia perplexa has a fragile white shell, which is almost spherical and with a rounded umbone. The species occurs in high densities in very sheltered bays and is particularly common in the upper regions of the South Australian gulfs.

Anodontia perplexa, Spencer Gulf, SA

Divalucina cumingi (Adams & Angas, 1863)

Habitat: Moderately exposed sand; 0–14 m depth.
Distribution: Around Australia, including Tas.
Maximum size: Length to 30 mm.

Divalucina cumingi has a white, flattened, rounded shell with a distinctive sculpture of two sets of concentric ridges crossing each other. The species is moderately common buried in white sand at shallow depths.

Divalucina cumingi, Bicheno, Tas.

FAMILY ERYCINIDAE

Erycinids are small species with an often transparent shell and a long strap-shaped foot. They generally live confined in rock crevices or among attached plants or animals.

Scintilla sp., Esperance, WA

Scintilla sp.

Habitat: Moderately and submaximally exposed reef; 3–15 m depth.
Distribution: Southern WA.
Maximum size: Length to 20 mm.

Scintilla sp. is a fragile white species that is easily recognised when alive because of the long white foot and transparent finger-like processes that project from the mantle covering the shell. It occurs commonly under rocks in the Esperance region and moves rapidly across the substrate when disturbed.

Ephippodonta lunata, Albany, WA. CLAY BRYCE

Ephippodonta lunata Tate, 1886

Habitat: Moderately exposed reef, sponge; 0–10 m depth.
Distribution: Southern WA to central SA.
Maximum size: Length to 10 mm.

Ephippodonta lunata has a pair of white, flat semi-circular shells joined by a small hinge. The mantle lobes associated with each shell join together to cover the animal except for a small central slit through which the foot and part of the gills protrude. The species lives associated with sponges and is found occasionally on the underside of rocks.

Lasaea australis, Cloudy Lagoon, Tas.

Lasaea australis (Lamarck, 1819)

Habitat: Sessile invertebrates; mid intertidal.
Distribution: Southern WA to NSW and around Tas.
Maximum size: Length to 5 mm.

Lasaea australis is a very small bivalve that lives in great abundance among mussel byssal threads or *Galeolaria* worm tubes. The shell is white with pink markings and has a few concentric ridges.

FAMILY CARDITIDAE
Carditas

Carditas have a shell sculptured with large radial ribs that often bear prominent scales, an external ligament and one or two strong central teeth in the hinge. Some species have a cavity along the edge of the shell, in which the young develop.

Cardita incrassata Sowerby, 1825

Habitat: Sheltered and moderately exposed silt, sand; 2–10 m depth.
Distribution: Tropical Australia south to Albany, WA.
Maximum size: Length to 50 mm.

The shell of *Cardita incrassata* has 15–17 very strong ribs, which project slightly over the lower edge. The external colour is variable but usually has a pink tinge, and the interior is white. The species is locally common on rubble bottom in southwestern Australia.

Cardita incrassata, Woodmans Point, WA

FAMILY CRASSATELLIDAE
Crassatellas

Crassatellas generally have a rectangular shell with a pointed umbone and fine concentric ridges. The cartilages attach into a pit on each hinge, and the lateral teeth are small.

Eucrassatella kingicola (Lamarck, 1805)

Habitat: Moderately exposed sand, seagrass; 10–22 m depth.
Distribution: SA to southern NSW and around Tas.
Maximum size: Length to 75 mm.

Eucrassatella kingicola is a large, moderately common bivalve with a very solid shell. The outer surface on the valve is brown and the interior white with brown muscle scars. A number of concentric ridges occur close to the umbone but disappear towards the outer margin. An even larger species, ***Eucrassatella donacina***, occurs from central Western Australia to South Australia.

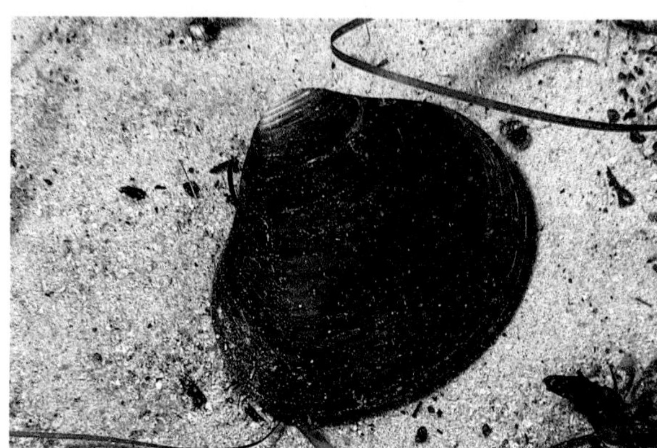

Eucrassatella kingicola, Bicheno, Tas.

FAMILY CARDIIDAE
Cockles

Members of the family Cardiidae can be recognised by their heart-shaped shells when viewed side on with the valves together. They have two central teeth and two flanged lateral teeth in each valve and an external ligament. Species in this family are the true cockles, and nearly all are tropical. A number of unrelated Australian species (e.g. species of *Katylesia*) are also commonly known as 'cockles'.

Fulvia tenuicostata (Lamarck, 1819)
Thin-ribbed cockle

Habitat: Sheltered sand, mud; 0–30 m depth.
Distribution: Fremantle, WA, to northern NSW and around Tas.
Maximum size: Length to 60 mm.

Fulvia tenuicostata is a rounded, thin-shelled cockle with 48–60 fine ribs. The colour of large shells is usually cream with some pink near the umbone, while small specimens may have brighter splashes of red. The species is common throughout its range but generally occurs as individuals rather than in dense beds.

Fulvia tenuicostata (juvenile), North Head, NSW

Fulvia tenuicostata, Cloudy Lagoon, Tas.

FAMILY MACTRIDAE
Trough shells

Mactrids have shells with a rounded triangular shape, long flanged lateral teeth and small central teeth shaped in a Λ-configuration. Beside the central teeth is a depression in which an internal ligament attaches.

Mactra pura Reeve, 1854

Habitat: Moderately exposed sand; 0–20 m depth.
Distribution: Point Samson, WA, to Vic. and northern Tas.
Maximum size: Length to 55 mm.

Like most species in the family Mactridae, *Mactra pura* has wide flanges on the hinges and these flanges extend a long way back from the internal ligament. *Mactra pura* has a pure white, moderately inflated shell with a light periostracum near the lower margin. It occurs commonly just below the surface of clean sand in shallow water.

Mactra pura, Flinders, Vic.

Mactra rufescens Reeve, 1854

Habitat: Exposed sand; 0–12 m depth.
Distribution: Shark Bay, WA, to NSW and around Tas.
Maximum size: Length to 65 mm.

Mactra rufescens is a large species with numerous concentric ridges across the shell, a cream to light mauve exterior and glossy white interior. It is occasionally washed ashore on ocean beaches in large numbers after storms and lives in sand just behind the wave break.

Mactra rufescens, Cloudy Bay, Tas.

Spisula trigonella (Lamarck, 1819)

Habitat: Sheltered sand, mud; 0 –1 m depth.
Distribution: Around Australia including Tas.
Maximum size: Length to 24 mm.

Spisula trigonella is a small triangular species with a high rounded umbone and with one straight edge. Its cream shell colour is usually masked by a brown periostracum. This bivalve locally occurs in huge densities at low-tide level in the muddy sand of estuaries and near river mouths.

Spisula trigonella, Western Port, Vic.

Lutraria rhynchaena Jonas, 1844

Habitat: Sheltered sand, mud; 2–20 m depth.
Distribution: Southern WA to NSW and northern Tas.
Maximum size: Length to 112 mm.

Lutraria rhynchaena is one of the largest temperate bivalves, easily recognised by the elongate oval valves, which gape at the ends when shut, and the

Lutraria rhynchaena, Portsea, Vic.

large pit in the hinge. It usually lives deeply buried in the silt of estuaries, with the two siphons projecting from the sediment surface.

FAMILY MESODESMATIDAE
Wedge shells

Mesodesmatids are closely related to the mactrids and have a similar tooth arrangement, except that the right valve has a small oblique central tooth with corresponding Λ-shaped socket in the left valve, and the internal ligament attaches onto a narrow process that extends below the central teeth. They also have separated inhalent and exhalent siphons (the mactrids have the siphons fused together).

Anapella cycladea (Lamarck, 1819)

Habitat: Sheltered sand, mud; intertidal.
Distribution: Around Australia, including Tas.
Maximum size: Length to 30 mm.

Anapella cycladea, Cloudy Lagoon, Tas.

Anapella cycladea occurs abundantly in the same habitat as *Spisula trigonella* and, although belonging to a different family, is easily confused with that species. The hinges of the two species are the main distinguishing characteristic; *Anapella cycladea* lacks cross-grooving on the wide hinge teeth and has an obvious central downward-projecting process to which the ligament is attached.

Paphies elongata (Reeve, 1854)

Habitat: Exposed sand; mid to low intertidal.
Distribution: Fremantle, WA, to NSW and around Tas.
Maximum size: Length to 25 mm.

Paphies elongata has a small, white triangular shell covered by a brown periostracum. The species is very common on surf beaches, where it can be detected by pockmarks in the sand left in the wake of receding waves. It also sometimes crawls on the sand surface and uses wave energy to carry it up and down the shore, following the tide.

Paphies elongata, Cloudy Bay, Tas.

FAMILY SOLENIDAE
Razor shells

Solenids have a distinctive shell shape reminiscent of an old cut-throat razor. The shell gapes at both ends, has an external ligament and lacks lateral teeth.

Solen correctus Iredale, 1924
Eastern razor shell

Habitat: Sheltered and moderately exposed sand; 0–18 m depth.
Distribution: Southern NSW to Qld.
Maximum size: Length to 80 mm.

Solen correctus has a shell typical of the family, with pink markings along the sides. Large numbers of shells are found washed up on beaches, indicating that the species is common. The species can bury into sand with great rapidity and so is rarely collected alive.

Solen correctus, Port Stephens, NSW

Solen vaginoides (Lamarck, 1818)

Southern razor shell

Habitat: Sheltered and moderately exposed sand; 0–10 m depth.
Distribution: Fremantle, WA, to NSW and around Tas.
Maximum size: Length to 84 mm.

Solen vaginoides is the close southern relative of *S. correctus*, differing chiefly by having an obvious curve to the shell. It generally lives buried below the sediment surface with only the siphon tips showing and is abundant in large sheltered bays.

Solen vaginoides, D'Entrecasteaux Channel, Tas.

FAMILY TELLINIDAE
Tellins

Species in the family Tellinidae have ovate or elongate shells with an external ligament and two central teeth in each valve. Lateral teeth are usually present but are much reduced in length compared with those of the mactrids (trough shells). In most species the shells are slightly bent at the rear.

Tellina deltoidalis Lamarck, 1818

Habitat: Sheltered sand, mud, seagrass; low intertidal.
Distribution: Fremantle, WA, to southern Qld and around Tas.
Maximum size: Length to 45 mm.

Tellina deltoidalis can be recognised by the abrupt bend at one end of the shell and the chalky white colour. It occurs in great abundance at a depth of a few centimetres in muddy sands on the shores of estuaries.

Tellina deltoidalis, Cloudy Lagoon, Tas.

Tellina margaritina Lamarck, 1818

Habitat: Sheltered sand, mud; 0–15 m depth.
Distribution: Southern WA to Vic. and around Tas.
Maximum size: Length to 34 mm.

Tellina margaritina (formerly known as *T. mariae*) is somewhat similar in appearance to *T. deltoidalis* but is oval in shape and lacks the obvious bend in the shell. The two species are often found together near the entrance to estuaries.

Tellina albinella Lamarck, 1818

Habitat: Exposed sand; 0–10 m depth.
Distribution: Southern WA to NSW and around Tas.
Maximum size: Length to 60 mm.

Tellina margaritina, Cloudy Lagoon, Tas.

738 *Tellina albinella*, Bruny I., Tas.

Tellina albinella has a thin, glossy shell with a pointed umbone and distinctive shape. The valves are marked by numerous fine concentric ridges, which often border crescents of orange or pink. The species is quite common just below the sand surface off ocean beaches, often in the vicinity of river mouths.

FAMILY DONACIDAE
Pipis

Pipis have solid triangular valves that lack a bend; they have two central teeth and usually two small lateral teeth. The hinge is small and located in a groove.

Donax deltoides Lamarck, 1818

Pipi, Goolwa cockle

Habitat: Exposed sandy beach; low intertidal.
Distribution: Around Australia.
Maximum size: Length to 60 mm.

Donax deltoides is a distinctive species of wedge-shaped bivalve with a white and light pink exterior and purple interior. Pipis are well known to surf fishers and are marketed for bait in South Australia and New South Wales. The species occurs in great abundance just below the sand surface on ocean beaches and is harvested in large quantities; in some states there are legal restrictions on the capture of this species.

Donax deltoides, Smooth Pool, SA

FAMILY PSAMMOBIIDAE
Sunset shells

Psammobiids generally have long oval-shaped shells with obvious periostracum and a ligament in a deep groove. Generally there are two central teeth (although some have one, and others three) and the lateral teeth are absent or greatly reduced.

Soletellina biradiata (Wood, 1815)

Habitat: Sheltered sand, mud; 0–3 m depth.
Distribution: Kalbarri, WA, to NSW and around Tas.
Maximum size: Length to 65 mm.

Soletellina biradiata, Cloudy Lagoon, Tas.

Soletellina biradiata has a thin oval shell characterised by the flaky brown periostracum around the lower margin. The colour is variable but most often is a pink-tinged brown with two pale rays extending from the umbone to the rear margin. The species occurs abundantly just below low-tide level in sheltered bays.

Gari livida (Lamarck, 1818)

Habitat: Moderately exposed sand; 0–70 m depth.
Distribution: Southern WA to NSW and around Tas.
Maximum size: Length to 45 mm.

Gari livida is a delicate white bivalve with several wide purple rays that radiate from the umbone and are visible through the shell. The lower margin of the shell is slightly rounded. The species is common in sand or shellgrit off coastal bays.

Gari livida, Cloudy Bay, Tas.

FAMILY VENERIDAE
Venus shells

Venerids form the largest family of bivalves that are commonly found along the southern coast. They have large, solid, often-brightly coloured valves with three central teeth in the hinge; lateral teeth are greatly reduced or absent.

Circe scripta (Linnaeus, 1758)

Habitat: Sheltered silt, sand; 3–15 m depth.
Distribution: Tropical Australia south to central NSW.
Maximum size: Length to 50 mm.

Circe scripta, Pittwater, NSW

Circe scripta has a flat, rounded shell, usually cream to light brown, with two to four brown radial rays. The species is occasionally found in the Sydney region, where it lives in areas of current flow in the deeper estuaries.

Dosinia incisa (Reeve, 1850)

Habitat: Moderately exposed sand, silt; 2–12 m depth.
Distribution: Tropical Australia south to Cockburn Sound, WA.
Maximum size: Length to 65 mm.

Dosinia incisa is a large white bivalve with a flat rounded shell that is concave on one side of the umbone. Shells of this species are common on fine sediments in Cockburn Sound near Perth, but living animals are rarely seen.

Dosinia incisa, Rockingham, WA

Dosinia caerulea Reeve, 1850

Habitat: Sand, silt; 5–15 m depth.
Distribution: Queenscliff, Vic., to southern Qld and around Tas.
Maximum size: Length to 70 mm.

Dosinia caerulea resembles *D. incisa* but has finer concentric ridges around the valve, a more swollen shell and a purple or orange tinge to the umbone. It lives moderately deep (≃100 mm) in sand and has long extendible siphons that reach the sediment surface. While *D. caerulea* is the species most often seen around Tasmania and the southern east coast, several other species in the genus also occur in temperate waters. ***Dosinia victoriae***, a smaller species with much fewer and wider concentric ridges, is the most common species in South Australia.

Dosinia caerulea, Cloudy Lagoon, Tas.

Dosinia caerulea, Cloudy Lagoon, Tas.

Katelysia scalarina (Lamarck, 1818)

Habitat: Sheltered sand, silt; low intertidal.
Distribution: Augusta, WA, to southern NSW and around Tas.
Maximum size: Length to 40 mm.

Katelysia scalarina has a series of concentric ridges around the shell, a cream external colour with fine brown zigzag lines sometimes present, and a purple blotched interior. The species is extremely abundant on intertidal sandflats in estuaries and is harvested commercially. ***Katelysia peroni***, an almost identical but less abundant species, has a shell that is rounded rather than straight on the long edge behind the hinge.

Katelysia scalarina, Princess Royal Harbour, WA

Katelysia scalarina, Cloudy Lagoon, Tas.

Katelysia rhytiphora Lamy, 1937

Habitat: Sheltered sand; low intertidal to 4 m depth.
Distribution: Albany, WA, to southern NSW and around Tas.
Maximum size: Length to 60 mm.

Katelysia rhytiphora, Cloudy Lagoon, Tas.

Katelysia rhytiphora occurs mixed with *K. scalarina* on estuarine sandflats and is nearly as abundant. Differentiating between these bivalves requires close inspection, as the concentric ridges on the shell of *K. rhytiphora* are crossed by very fine scratches, but not on *K. scalarina*. Both species are marketed commercially as 'cockles'.

Tawera lagopus (Lamarck, 1818)

Habitat: Moderately exposed sand; 0–36 m depth.
Distribution: Southern WA to NSW and around Tas.
Maximum size: Length to 40 mm.

Tawera lagopus has numerous concentric ridges on the outside of the shell and a row of fine serrations around the outer margin where the valves contact each other. The valves are marked by brown blotches arranged in radiating bands. A related species, ***Tawera gallinula***, has stronger concentric ridges and a mauve interior. Both species are moderately common on sand off sheltered ocean beaches.

Tawera lagopus, Cloudy Lagoon, Tas.

Eumarcia fumigata (Sowerby, 1853)

Habitat: Sheltered sand, mud; 0–5 m depth.
Distribution: Southern WA to southern Qld and around Tas.
Maximum size: Length to 45 mm.

Eumarcia fumigata has a smooth shiny shell with streaky radial markings, which are most clearly defined on juveniles. The interior of the shell is characteristically yellow with purple along the edge close to the hinge. The species is moderately common in fine sand below low-tide level in estuaries.

Eumarcia fumigata, Cloudy Lagoon, Tas.

Tapes dorsatus (Lamarck, 1818)

Habitat: Sheltered sand, silt; 0–15 m depth.
Distribution: Tropical Australia south to southern NSW.
Maximum size: Length to 90 mm.

Tapes dorsatus is a large cockle with valves circled by numerous flat concentric ridges. The shell surface is generally a light brown colour with fine zigzag markings and with a white or slightly yellow interior. The species is very common in many New South Wales estuaries, including Sydney Harbour.

Tapes dorsatus, North Head, NSW

Paphia crassisulca (Lamarck, 1818)

Habitat: Moderately exposed sand, silt; 3–10 m depth.
Distribution: Tropical Australia south to Albany, WA, and NSW.
Maximum size: Length to 55 mm.

Paphia crassisulca is a solid bivalve with a slightly indented lower margin and a regular arrangement of flattened concentric ridges. Shells of this species are commonly seen on rubble sediments in southwestern Australia, but little is known about the habits of living animals.

Paphia crassisulca, Woodmans Point, WA

Venerupis galactites (Lamarck, 1818)

Habitat: Sheltered and moderately exposed sand, silt, seagrass; 0–15 m depth.
Distribution: Perth, WA, to NSW and around Tas.
Maximum size: Length to 50 mm.

Venerupis galactites has a white shell with obvious concentric growth lines that are crossed by fine radial scratches. The species occurs commonly on gravelly sand, particularly among seagrasses.

Venerupis galactites, Ricketts Pt, Vic.

Venerupis anomala (Lamarck, 1818)

Habitat: Sheltered sand, mud, reef; 0–5 m depth.
Distribution: SA to southern Qld and around Tas. Also New Zealand.
Maximum size: Length to 25 mm.

Venerupis anomala is a white bean-shaped bivalve that is small, rounded and fragile. It has more numerous concentric growth lines than *V. galactites* but only microscopic radial scratches. The species is locally common on rubbly sand in the larger bays and also occurs under stones.

Venerupis anomala, Flinders, Vic.

Bassina pachyphylla (Jonas, 1839)

Habitat: Exposed sand; 0–10 m depth.
Distribution: Central SA to NSW and around Tas.
Maximum size: Length to 50 mm.

Bassina pachyphylla is one of the most easily identified bivalves because of its very solid shell with characteristic frills that extend off the growth lines at one end. The external colour is light brown with darker radiating bands, and the interior is white. The species is common behind the surf line on ocean beaches and is sometimes washed up alive after heavy swells.

Bassina pachyphylla, Cloudy Bay, Tas.

Bassina pachyphylla, Cloudy Bay, Tas.

Bassina disjecta (Perry, 1811)

Frilled venus

Habitat: Sheltered and moderately exposed sand, silt; 4–40 m depth.
Distribution: Bluff Point, WA, to NSW and around Tas.
Maximum size: Length to 63 mm.

Bassina disjecta is perhaps the prettiest of Australian bivalves, with its light pink wings and white basal colour. The species is found in moderate numbers, most often on a coarse sand bottom in deep sheltered bays with good current flow.

Bassina disjecta, D'Entrecasteaux Channel, Tas.

FAMILY CLEIDOTHAERIDAE

Cleidothaerids have a solid, cup-shaped right valve that is attached to rock and a flat left valve that sits across the rim. The left valve has one large central tooth that fits into a pit in the right valve.

Cleidothaerus albidus Lamarck, 1819

Habitat: Exposed reef; 1–10 m depth.
Distribution: Rottnest I, WA, to NSW and around Tas.
Maximum size: Length to 50 mm.

Cleidothaerus albidus is easily mistaken for an oyster but is quite different in internal anatomy. It occurs abundantly attached to reef in shallow water along moderately exposed coasts.

Cleidothaerus albidus, Tinderbox, Tas.

FAMILY HIATELLIDAE

This family includes rock- and mud-boring species that have irregular-shaped valves with one or two weak primary teeth. The ends of the valves gape rather than seal closely together.

Panopea australis Sowerby, 1833

Habitat: Sheltered sand, silt; 0–38 m depth.
Distribution: SA to NSW and around Tas.
Maximum size: Length to 93 mm.

Panopea australis, D'Entrecasteaux Channel, Tas.

Panopea australis is a very large white bivalve with gaping ends, a single tooth on each valve, and obvious muscle scars on the interior of the shell. The species is rarely collected alive, as it lives deeply embedded in the sediment.

FAMILY PHOLADIDAE
Angel wings, piddocks

Species in the family are borers of soft rock, wood and firm mud. The two valves are thin and white and accompanied by accessory plates also made of shell, which protect the beaks and ligaments.

Barnea australasiae (Sowerby, 1849)

Angel wing

Habitat: Bores into stiff mud or soft stone; 0–5 m depth.
Distribution: Kalbarri, WA, to Qld and around Tas.
Maximum size: Length to 70 mm.

Barnea australasiae (above) and *Barnea obturamentum*, Dunalley, Tas.

The shell of *Barnea australasiae* is aptly termed 'angel wing' and has a very distinctive shape. The living animal is very large in comparison with the shell and uses the two wings as scrapers for digging into soft rock. It lives deep in holes bored in friable rock or hard mud, with just the siphons protruding from the entrance. Very high abundances of the species occur at shallow depths in suitable habitat but are rarely seen. The species is edible.

Barnea obturamentum (Hedley, 1893)

Habitat: Bores into stiff mud or soft stone; 0–8 m depth.
Distribution: SA to NSW and around Tas.
Maximum size: Length to 50 mm.

Barnea obturamentum differs from *B. australasiae* by having a shell that ends in a point because of a concavity in the margin. It occurs in a similar habitat to *B. australasiae* but is less commonly washed up on beaches.

Barnea obturamentum, Cloudy Lagoon, Tas.

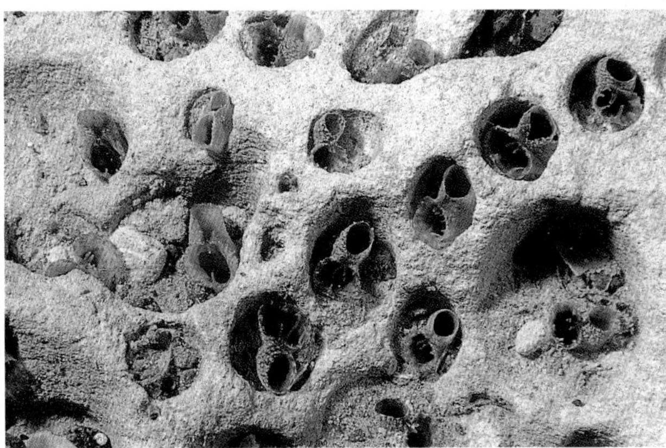

Barnea sp., Dunalley, Tas.

FAMILY TEREDINIDAE
Ship worms, teredos

A large number of specialised wood-boring bivalves known as teredos and shipworms occur in tropical Australian waters, and at least 15 occur in the temperate region. They have a planktonic larval stage and then settle on wood and commence burrowing. The various species are all worm-like, with very small shells at the head end and a pair of siphons and a pair of spade- or feather-like structures known as pallets protruding from the posterior. The pallets seal the entrance to the hole at low-tide and are the most important feature used in identification.

Bankia australis (Calman, 1920)
Southern shipworm

Habitat: Wood; 0–3 m depth.
Distribution: WA to Qld and around Tas.
Maximum size: Length of shell to 10 mm.

Bankia australis is the most abundant shipworm in Victorian and Tasmanian waters. Its pallet is nearly twice as long as the shell and looks like a string of serrated-edged cups of diminishing size placed inside each other.

Class Scaphopoda
Scaphopods, tusk shells

The class Scaphopoda is a relatively small one containing about 400 species, most of them living in deep offshore waters. The body is contained within a curved tubular 'tusk shell' that tapers towards one end and is embedded in sand. The head and a wedge-shaped foot can be extended from the wide end of the shell, while the narrow end projects above the sand surface to allow a respiratory current to pass in and out. Scaphopods feed on microscopic organisms such as foraminiferans, which they capture using club-shaped tentacles associated with the head. The sexes are separate, releasing either sperm or eggs into the water for fertilisation. Several species occur in shallow depths around the southern Australian coastline. All are small (less than 30 mm) and rarely seen. Species in the most common genus, *Cadulus*, have a smooth shell, which is usually swollen in the centre.

Bankia australis burrows, Cloudy Lagoon, Tas.

shell
tentacle
foot

Scaphopod (100 mm)
Dentalium sp.
Class Scaphopoda

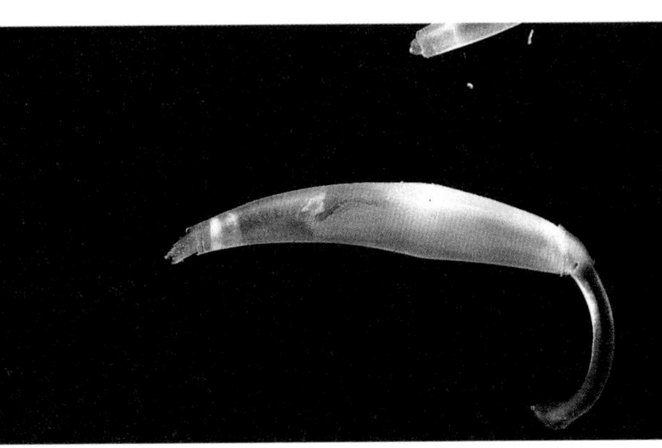

Cadulus sp., Cervantes, WA. CLAY BRYCE

Class Cephalopoda

Cephalopods (squid, octopus, cuttlefish)

Cephalopods (literally 'head-foot') are soft-bodied molluscs that are characterised by the head being partially (squid) or completely (octopus) fused with the foot and by possessing eight or ten long arms with powerful suction discs. Species in the tropical genus *Nautilus* have a shell; all others have only a reduced shell or it is lacking. Shelled forms were, however, one of the dominant invertebrate groups in ancient seas, and nautiloid and belemnoid cephalopods in particular left an extensive fossil record. The sexes of cephalopods are separate, with the male having one tentacle specially adapted for passing a packet of sperm into the mantle cavity of the female.

Cephalopods are more active than other marine invertebrates and have developed complex sensory and nervous systems that allow them to respond quickly to outside influences. They are considered the most intelligent of invertebrates because of their rapid learning ability, adapting new behavioural patterns with the flexibility of some mammals. Their eyes are extremely complex and, although formed from different structural elements, provide a similar level of visual detail to the eyes of vertebrate animals. Cephalopods also have special nerve-activated pigment cells in their outer body layer, enabling them to change colour rapidly to blend in with the environment or to communicate with potential mates or enemies.

The diets of many fishes, seals, whales and seabirds collected at sea are composed almost entirely of cephalopods, indicating that the class is extremely abundant in the open ocean. This is somewhat surprising, given the relatively few specimens collected in fishing nets. Cephalopods are obviously adept at escaping from nets, presumably because they can forcibly eject water from the mantle cavity through a funnel-shaped siphon and thereby move rapidly by a form of jet propulsion. When undisturbed, squids normally move by undulating the fleshy fins on each side of the body, while octopuses move by crawling over the bottom using their arms. When threatened by predators, cephalopods use the arms in defence and can bite with powerful jaws, which form a sharp beak at the centre of the undersurface of the head. They can also eject a cloud of dark ink from the anus, creating a phantom shape about the same size as the escaping animal.

Cuttlefish (200 mm)
Sepia plangon
Class Cephalopoda

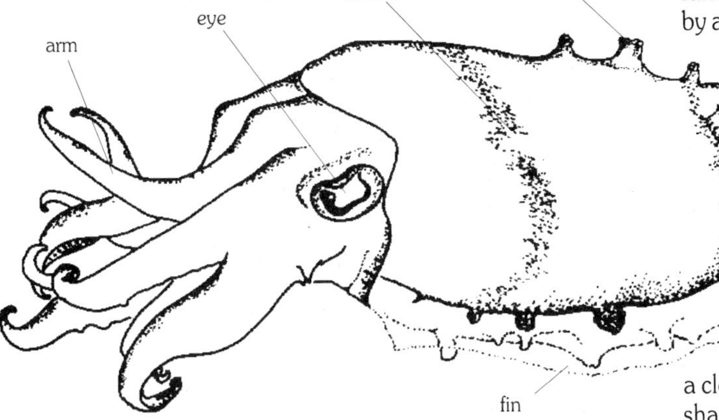

FAMILY OCTOPODIDAE
Octopuses

The octopuses are a well-defined family of cephalopods, with a sack-like body and eight arms that are covered by suckers. Most live alone, foraging about at night and remaining hidden during the day in lairs that can be identified by a pile of discarded shells near the entrance. Eggs are generally attached to rock and guarded and ventilated by the female.

Hapalochlaena maculosa (Hoyle, 1883)
Blue-ringed octopus

Habitat: Sheltered and moderately exposed reef, sand; 0–30 m depth.
Distribution: Southern WA to southern Qld and northern Tas.
Maximum size: Length to 120 mm.

Hapalochlaena maculosa is readily identified by the characteristic neon blue rings that glow strongly when the animal is irritated, but they are quite pale when the animal is resting and therefore may not be immediately apparent. The blue-ringed octopus is one of the more infamous sea creatures because of the powerful nerve toxin that is injected with saliva if the animal is strongly provoked and bites. Two human fatalities and about 15 incidents of envenomation have been attributed to this species during the past 50 years. Despite its reputation, the species is not usually aggressive, remaining hidden among broken rock and shell during the day and venturing out from these refuges to feed at night. The female lays about 50 eggs in late autumn and carries them around under her arms for about six months. Once the eggs have hatched, the female dies. Young rapidly grow to maturity and mate in early autumn. The males then die, and the females continue on with the eggs.

Octopus berrima Stranks & Norman, 1992

Habitat: Reef, seagrass, sand; 5–267 m depth.
Distribution: Great Australian Bight, SA, to Eden, NSW, and around Tas.
Maximum size: Length to 400 mm.

Octopus berrima, Eaglehawk Neck, Tas. SIMON TALBOT

Hapalochlaena maculosa, Erith I, Tas.

Octopus berrima occurs commonly in southern Australia. The species is characterised by very long narrow arms with thin webbing at the base, a small skin fold beside each eye and a dense arrangement of fine tubercles over the upper surface. The colour is usually a light brown but darkens considerably when the animal is stimulated, and there is often a white bar extending between the eyes. This octopus has only recently been scientifically named because it was confused with a similar long-armed species, ***Octopus australis***, which is found along the east coast north of Jervis Bay. However, it differs from the eastern species by having finer tubercles over the body surface and a ridge running partway rather than fully around the lower sides. Female *Octopus berrima* take care of 50–130 eggs for about 100 days in summer, and hatched animals grow to maximum size over the next two years.

Octopus tetricus Gould, 1852

Gloomy octopus

Habitat: Reef; 0–30 m depth.
Distribution: Eden, NSW, to Moreton Bay, Qld.
Maximum size: Length to 800 mm.

Octopus tetricus is the large species of octopus most commonly seen along the New South Wales coast. It has long arms that are unequal in length and slender at the tips. The undersides of the arms are rust red in colour, and the body and upper arms mottled grey and brown. The species is also officially recognised to occur in southwestern Australia from Shark Bay to Esperance, although this southwestern population is probably a closely related but distinctive species.

Octopus tetricus, Tathra, NSW

Octopus ? tetricus, Esperance, WA

Octopus pallidus Hoyle, 1885

Pale octopus

Habitat: Sand; 0–275 m depth.
Distribution: Great Australian Bight, SA, to southern NSW and around Tas.
Maximum size: Length to 350 mm.

Octopus pallidus is the most distinctive of the southern octopuses because of the comparatively large body, short solid arms and reddish brown to orange coloration. This species often raises the skin on the body in relatively long, spiky protuberances. It occurs

Octopus pallidus, Portsea, Vic. RUDIE KUITER

Octopus maorum, Maria I, Tas.

commonly on sand among sponges, gorgonians and other attached invertebrates. Moderate numbers are captured commercially in Tasmania using plastic pots that are placed on the sandy bottom for several days and retrieved with newly settled inhabitants.

Octopus maorum Hutton, 1880
Maori octopus

Habitat: Exposed reef, sand; 0–549 m depth.
Distribution: Great Australian Bight, SA, to Lakes Entrance, Vic., and around Tas.
Maximum size: Length to 1.2 m.

Octopus maorum is the largest of the southern octopuses, reaching a weight of 9 kg. It can be recognised by the dark red colour, smooth skin, long arms of unequal length and the head being separated from the body by a distinct constriction. For a long time this species was known as *Octopus flindersi*, but recent work indicates that Australian animals are the same as the New Zealand-named species *Octopus maorum*. This octopus is a major predator of rock lobsters and is caught incidentally in lobster pots in sufficient quantities to be commercially important in its own right in South Australia.

Octopus maorum, Portsea, Vic. RUDIE KUITER

Octopus kaurna Stranks, 1990
Sand octopus

Habitat: Sand, seagrass; 0–49 m depth.
Distribution: Great Australian Bight, SA, to eastern Vic. and around Tas.
Maximum size: Length to 420 mm.

Octopus kaurna, Tinderbox, Tas. RON MAWBEY

Octopus kaurna, Maria I, Tas.

Octopus kaurna is the most common sand octopus seen in temperate waters. It remains buried under sand during the day and moves into the open at night to feed. The species is distinguished from other octopuses by the characteristic pattern of rounded tubercles on the upper surface, extremely long, thin arms, webbing at the bases of the arms and relatively small suckers. However, the general appearance is highly variable, as animals can quickly change patterns and extend or contract their bodies.

Octopus sp.
Pygmy octopus

Habitat: Kelp holdfasts; 5–15 m depth.
Distribution: Eastern Tas.
Maximum size: Length to 60 mm.

This undescribed species of *Octopus* has so far been found living only within holdfasts of giant kelp (*Macrocystis pyrifera*). It is very common in this restricted habitat, where several individuals generally occupy the base of a single large plant.

Octopus sp., Bicheno, Tas. RUDIE KUITER

FAMILY ARGONAUTIDAE
Argonauts, paper nautiluses

This is an open-water family of octopus-like animals, the sexes differing remarkably in appearance. The female is large and produces a papery shell from membranes on two modified arms. She lives within the shell and broods her eggs there. The male is very small and has one very long mating arm (the hectocotylus), which breaks off in the female's mantle cavity after copulation. This broken arm was once thought to be a parasitic worm and given the scientific name *Hectocotylus*.

Argonauta nodosa, Portsea, Vic. RUDIE KUITER

Argonauta nodosa Solander, 1786
Paper nautilus

Habitat: Open ocean; 0–50 m depth.
Distribution: WA to NSW and around Tas. Also widespread in the Indo-West Pacific region.
Maximum size: Shell length to 350 mm.

Argonauta nodosa has a slender body with arms of unequal length. The egg case is white with nodular radial ridges on the sides and a wide grooved keel around the edge. A less abundant species also occasionally found in southern Australia, ***Argonauta argo***, has a narrower keel and ridges on the sides of the shell that divide but are not broken into nodules. Both species generally inhabit oceanic waters but occasionally move into coastal shallows in large numbers to release their eggs and die.

FAMILY SEPIIDAE
Cuttlefish

Cuttlefish have an oval body with narrow fins around the edges, a relatively large head, eight short arms and two long tentacular arms. The most characteristic feature of the family is the internal shell along the back. These 'cuttlebones' are surfboard-shaped with a strong spine at the rear, and are buoyant so wash ashore in large numbers. The identification of species has traditionally been based on the shape of the cuttlebone, and so it is often difficult to identify species from the appearance of the living animal.

Sepia apama Gray, 1849
Giant cuttle

Habitat: Reef, seagrass; 0–50 m depth.
Distribution: Point Cloates, WA, to Sydney, NSW, and south to Tasman Peninsula, Tas.
Maximum size: Length to 800 mm.

Sepia apama is the most abundant and by far the largest local species of cuttlefish. The species can usually be recognised by the raised skin flaps, and it has three flat skin folds behind eye. Mature animals are often curious to the point of aggressively approaching and confronting divers. The cuttlebone of this species is broad with a small spine and has a white-grey upper surface, in contrast to the pink of most other species.

Sepia plangon Gray, 1849
Mourning cuttle

Habitat: Sheltered seagrass, reef; 2–10 m depth.
Distribution: Southern NSW to southern Qld.
Maximum size: Length to 100 mm.

The mantle of *Sepia plangon* is proportionately longer than on the other species and extends to between the eyes. Animals often have a bluish tinge around the eyes. The cuttlebone is slender with a groove on the lower surface and a small spine. The species grows to only a small size and is usually confined to estuaries.

Sepia plangon, North Head, NSW

Sepia apama, Terrigal, NSW

Sepia apama (juvenile), Jervis Bay, NSW

Sepia sp., Terrigal, NSW

Sepia sp.
Red cuttle

Habitat: Sheltered and moderately exposed reef; 5–25 m depth.
Distribution: NSW.
Maximum size: Length to 200 mm.

Although the red cuttle has often been seen by divers, its specific identity remains unknown. The animal characteristically has a red body with dark blotches towards the back of the upper surface and yellow coloration around the eye. It is moderately common in estuaries and along the open coast of New South Wales.

FAMILY LOLIGINIDAE
Squid

Loliginid squid have eight arms, each with two rows of suckers, and two much longer tentacular arms with club-like ends that have four rows of suckers. They also have a transparent membrane over the eyes, and the mantle is connected to the head by an interlocking ridge and groove structure. Nearly all species in the family are fast-swimming animals of the open ocean. Several other families of squid are also present in offshore waters. Some of the larger deepwater species have fearsome hooks interspersed among the tentacles and must be extremely formidable predators.

Sepioteuthis australis Quoy & Gaimard, 1833
Southern calamary

Habitat: Exposed sand, reef; 0–100 m depth.
Distribution: Dampier, WA, to Brisbane, Qld, and around Tas. Also New Zealand.
Maximum size: Mantle length to 380 mm.

Sepioteuthis australis has an appearance halfway between a squid and a cuttlefish, as the arms, head and body are typical of a squid but the side fins extend fully around the mantle rather than being diamond-shaped and located in the rear half of the body, as in most other species in the family. It also has the typical squid 'pen' running underneath the back, a translucent feather-shaped structure that is not calcified like cuttlebone but made of cartilage. Southern calamary is the most common squid found in coastal bays. The species is readily caught on squid jigs and often seen by divers in the evening. It grows rapidly, reaching maturity at a mantle length of about 160 mm and an age of one year. Spawning occurs in shallow water during the night, at which time females release and attach clusters of white cylindrical eggs to the seabed. At some sites spawning is presumably communal, as egg clusters carpeting the bottom can appear overnight.

Sepioteuthis australis, Bicheno, Tas.

FAMILY IDIOSEPIIDAE
Pygmy squid

The few pygmy squid species known have small cylindrical bodies with fins set at the rear. The upper surface between the fins is roughened into a sucking disc that enables the animal to attach itself to seagrass and seaweeds. Like other squids, the head has ten arms and a knob at the base connected into a cartilaginous socket on the mantle.

Idiosepius notoides Berry, 1821
Southern pygmy squid

Habitat: Sheltered seagrass, seaweed; 0–8 m depth.
Distribution: Cockburn Sound, WA, to southern Qld and around Tas.
Maximum size: Length to 20 mm.

Idiosepius notoides is a very small species of squid with the head half as long as the body and numerous fine black and blue spots covering a golden basal colour. The species occurs in great abundance in virtually all shallow seagrass beds along the southern coasts but is rarely noticed because of its small size.

Idiosepius notoides, Kettering, Tas.

FAMILY SEPIOLIDAE
Dumpling squids

Dumpling squids share many features with pygmy squids but are easily distinguishable by the short rounded bodies and oval fins attached midway along the sides of the body.

Sepioloidea lineolata, Cockburn Sound, WA. CLAY BRYCE

Sepioloidea lineolata (Quoy & Gaimard, 1832)
Lined dumpling squid

Habitat: Sheltered and moderately exposed sand, seagrass; 0–20 m depth.
Distribution: Southern WA to southern Qld.
Maximum size: Length to 50 mm.

Sepioloidea lineolata is unlikely to be confused with other cephalopods because of its distinctive black stripes down the body and its small rounded shape. The species is common on sand in estuaries and along the open coast. When disturbed, lined dumpling squid commence a spectacular display of colour and pattern changes. Females lay eggs in objects such as shells and tin cans and guard them until hatching occurs.

Euprymna tasmanica, Margate, Tas.

Euprymna tasmanica (Pfeffer, 1884)
Southern dumpling squid

Habitat: Sheltered and moderately exposed sand, seagrass; 0–15 m depth.
Distribution: Southern WA to Vic. and around Tas.
Maximum size: Length to 40 mm.

Euprymna tasmanica occurs commonly in sheltered bays and estuaries along the southern coast but remains hidden under sand during the day and is therefore generally seen only by divers on night dives. It has a typical dumpling squid body shape with iridescent green-yellow coloration and a covering of fine black spots. An almost identical species, ***Euprymna stenodactyla***, is reported from the New South Wales coast.

PHYLUM BRACHIOPODA

Brachiopods, lamp shells

Brachiopods superficially resemble bivalve molluscs in external appearance but have a completely different anatomy and are not closely related. Rather than having left and right valves, brachiopods have upper and lower valves, with a muscular stalk normally connecting the lower valve to the substrate. The naming of valves is somewhat confused because most brachiopods live with the lower, stalked valve uppermost. The stalk usually connects onto a large flange near the hinge of the valve, making the shells resemble Roman oil lamps when turned upside-down.

Enclosed within the valves is a lobed filament-bearing structure known as the lophophore, which is used for feeding and respiration. The synchronised beating of cilia located along the filaments produces a flow of water through the partly opened valves. Food particles suspended in the water current are trapped in mucous and conveyed down a groove to the mouth. Because structures similar to the lophophore of brachiopods are used for feeding by the phoronids (phylum Phoronida) and bryozoans (phylum Bryozoa), these three phyla are sometimes grouped together as 'lophophorates'.

The 350 or so species of brachiopods alive today represent only a small remnant of a group that was once dominant in seas. Sedimentary rocks often contain large deposits of fossilised brachiopod valves, more than 30,000 fossil species having been scientifically named.

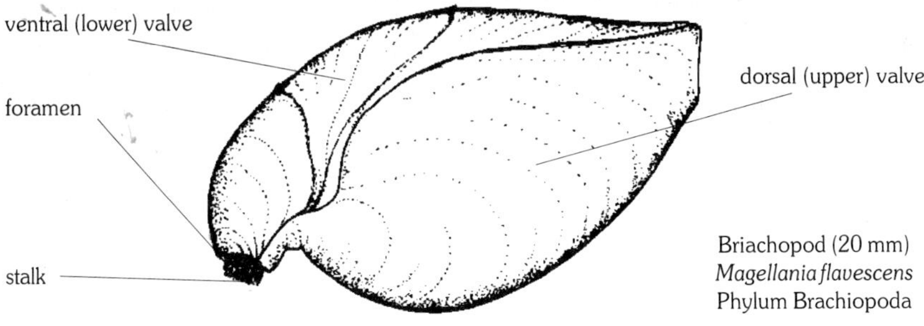

Briachopod (20 mm)
Magellania flavescens
Phylum Brachiopoda

Magellania flavescens (Lamarck, 1819)

Habitat: Moderately exposed reef; 0–15 m depth.
Distribution: Southern WA to NSW and northern Tas.
Maximum size: Length to 40 mm.

Magellania flavescens is the large species of brachiopod most commonly seen by divers. It can form large aggregations in localised areas of good water flow. The species can be recognised by the rounded shell with several faint grooves radiating down the valves, although these may be obscured by concentric growth lines and erosion on large animals.

Magellania flavescens, Busselton, WA

PHYLUM PHORONIDA

Phoronid worms

Phoronids are a small group of about 15 species of worm-like animals that live in tubes on the seabed. They superficially resemble sabellid worms but can usually be recognised by having the ciliated tentacles (the lophophore) arranged in a horseshoe pattern around the mouth. They also lack the segmentation and bristles of the polychaete worms and have a U-shaped gut with the anus located above the lophophore. Most phoronids release both sperm and eggs through excretory tubes in the sides of the body, and the eggs then adhere to the tentacles. After fertilisation and initial development, a free-living larva hatches and drifts among the plankton for several weeks. The larva then settles into an appropriate habitat and quickly forms a protective tube.

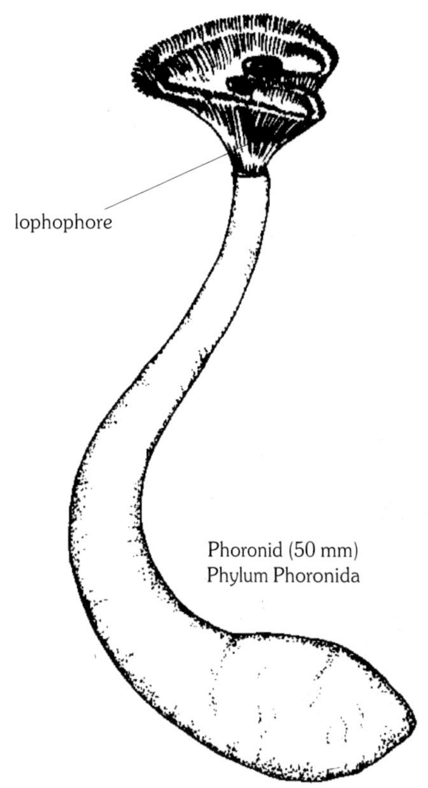

Phoronid (50 mm)
Phylum Phoronida

Phoronis australis, Woodmans Pt, WA

Phoronis australis Haswell, 1883

Habitat: Sheltered silt; 0–30 m depth.
Distribution: Perth, WA, to Moreton Bay, Qld.
Maximum size: Length to 200 mm.

Phoronis australis is a velvet black species which occurs abundantly in sheltered habitats. The tube is always attached under the sediment surface to the tube of *Cerianthus* anemones. This phoronid is somewhat unusual, in that the lophophore is not obviously U-shaped but is recurved into a spiral. At least three other species of phoronid are also wide-spread on soft sediments in sheltered locations (e.g. Port Phillip Bay) but are generally a light pink colour and rarely seen by divers.

PHYLUM BRYOZOA

Bryozoans, moss animals, lace corals

Bryozoans are minute colonial animals, which can form massive aggregations up to 1 m across. Well over 5,000 species exist, most of which occur attached to hard substrates in marine environments; however, one small class is found in fresh water, and a few species have modified stalks that allow them to live on sand.

Some colonies remain unattached, and a few are capable of moving over the sandy seabed. Colonies are often brightly coloured and exhibit a great variety of shapes, ranging from flat, encrusting sheets to erect plant-like and coral-like forms.

Bryozoan colonies consist of numerous zooids, small units about 1 mm long and often box-like in shape. The zooid is enclosed by calcareous or cuticular walls, with the side walls perforated to allow direct connections between zooids chambers throughout the whole colony. A large orifice in the upper wall allows a crown of feeding tentacles (the lophophore) to protrude. Long spines often protect the upper zooid surface, and a chitinous operculum may also be present to cover the aperture when the lophophore is withdrawn. Not all zooids have feeding tentacles; zooids may be modified to form joints or points of attachment in a colony, to form a brood chamber for the young, or equipped with bristles or pincers to prevent other organisms from settling. Much of the internal cavity of zooids is filled by a U-shaped gut, with the mouth at the centre of the lophophore and the anal opening just outside the crown of tentacles. They lack excretory organs or a blood circulatory system.

Bryozoan colonies grow by the asexual budding of zooids from the edge of the colony; zooids fuse walls if they contact other zooids from the same colony. New colonies arise from settling larvae and are the result of sexual reproduction. Colonies contain zooids with both male and female reproductive organs or in some species separate male and female zooids, and can occasionally self-fertilise. The fertilised eggs are sometimes released directly from the colony, but more often pass into a brood pouch where they undergo initial development. The growth and reproductive capacities of bryozoans are often very high, resulting in colonies quickly fouling exposed surfaces underwater. Some species are resistant to the anti-fouling paints used on ships' hulls and are therefore economically important because of the high cost required for their control.

Numerous bryozoan species can be found around Australia, including more than 500 species recorded from the southern and southeastern coasts. Many of their scientific names may be inappropriate, however, as they were applied in the nineteenth century without much assessment of the variation within a species. Some species can be reliably identified using the shape and colour of colonies, but many species differ substantially in appearance when growing in different habitats and the zooids therefore need to be closely examined for species identification.

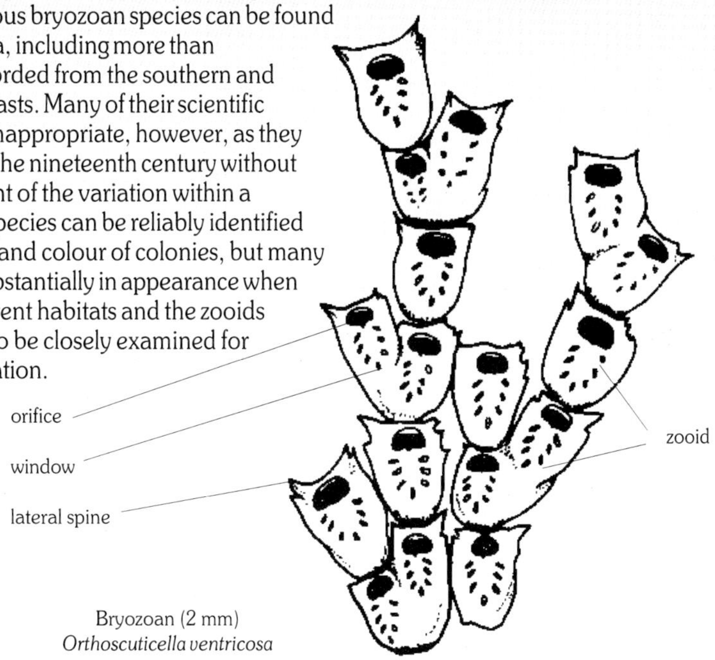

Bryozoan (2 mm)
Orthoscuticella ventricosa
Phylum Bryozoa

Lichenopora echinata (MacGillivray, 1884)

Habitat: Seaweeds, shells, seagrasses; 0–5 m depth.
Distribution: WA to Vic. and around Tas.
Maximum size: Colony width to 5 mm.

Lichenopora echinata is a unusual bryozoan that lives attached to marine plants and is common and widely distributed along the southern coast. The species forms small saucer-shaped colonies with the tubular zooids aggregated in the centre of the disc.

Lichenopora echinata, Blackmans Bay, Tas.

Hornera foliacea (MacGillivray, 1869)

Habitat: Moderately exposed reef; 5–30 m depth.
Distribution: Vic. and around Tas.
Maximum size: Colony length to 120 mm.

Hornera foliacea is a beautiful lace-like species with branches repeatedly divided and often connected by short crossbars. This bryozoan is moderately common on deeper reefs in locations protected from water turbulence.

Hornera foliacea, Bathurst Channel, Tas.

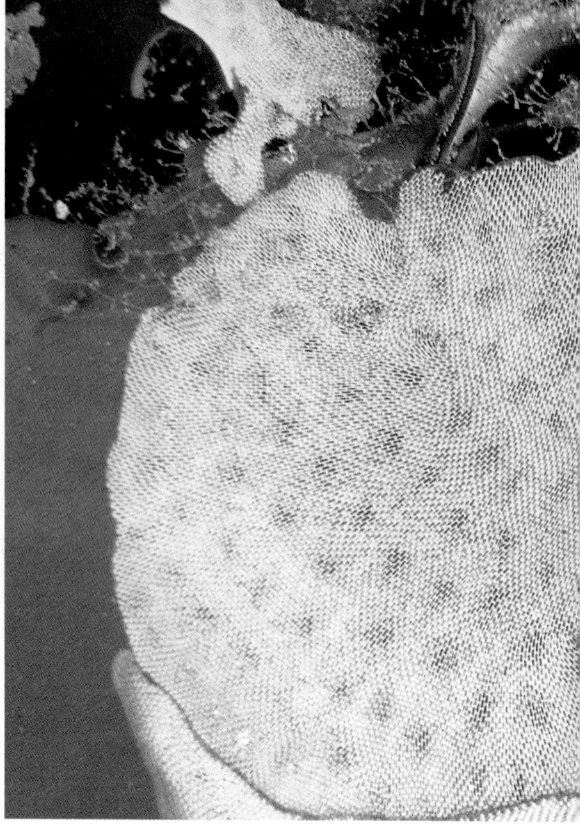

Membranipora membranacea, Low Head, Tas.

Membranipora membranacea (Linnaeus, 1758)

Habitat: Kelp fronds; 0–30 m depth.
Distribution: WA to NSW and around Tas. Also widespread overseas.
Maximum size: Colony length to 100 mm.

Membranipora membranacea forms thin, encrusting colonies over the surfaces of large brown algae, particularly the fronds of giant kelp (*Macrocystis* species). The zooids are rectangular and have only the side walls reinforced with calcium carbonate, producing a trellis-like pattern.

Biflustra perfragilis (MacGillivray, 1881)

Habitat: Moderately exposed reef; 8–20 m depth.
Distribution: SA to Vic. and northern Tas.
Maximum size: Colony length to 150 mm.

Biflustra perfragilis forms folded yellow-orange colonies made up of thin interconnected sheets with zooids on both sides. The zooids are aligned in rows, with the ends of each zooid adjacent to the centre of zooids in the next row. This bryozoan is moderately common on deep reefs in areas with good current flow. Crushed colonies produce a strong smell, which is sometimes noticed when dredges or trawls are pulled onto boats.

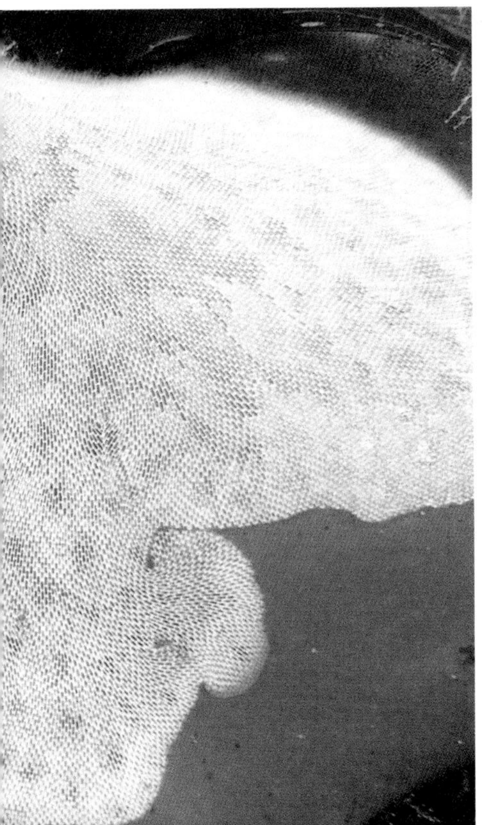

Biflustra perfragilis, Low Head, Tas.

Bugula dentata (Lamouroux, 1816)

Habitat: Sheltered and moderately exposed reef, jetty pylons; 1–40 m depth.
Distribution: WA to Qld and around Tas.
Maximum size: Colony length to 80 mm.

Bugula dentata forms bushy blue-green colonies made up of paired zooids aligned end on, to form filaments. Like other species in the genus *Bugula*, the walls of the zooids are not calcified, allowing the colony to flex with wave motion. *Bugula dentata* is one of the more common bryozoans at sheltered clear-water sites. The nudibranch *Tambja verconis* is often found feeding on this species.

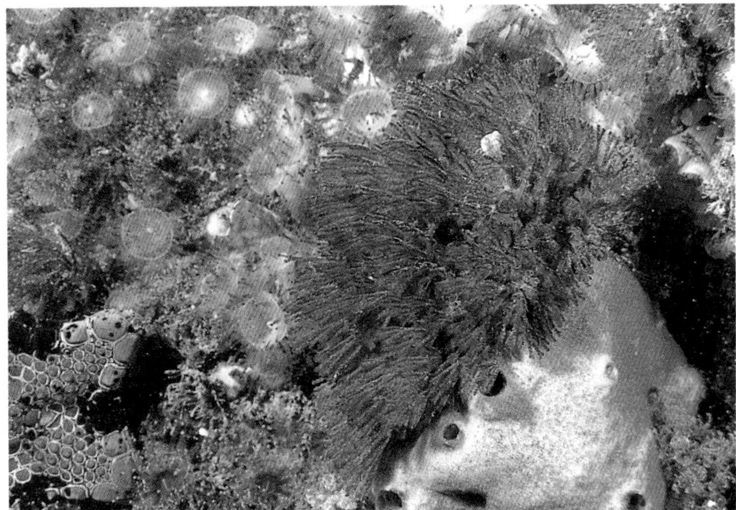

Bugula dentata, Rocky Cape, Tas.

Bugula cucullata (Busk, 1867)

Habitat: Moderately exposed reef; 1–10 m depth.
Distribution: Lacepede Bay, SA, to Vic. and around Tas.
Maximum size: Colony length to 50 mm.

Bugula cucullata is unlikely to be mistaken for other bryozoans as it has distinctive fan-shaped tufts of zooids spiralling up a central axis. The species is most abundant towards the south of Tasmania, where it occurs commonly in sheltered crevices on coastal reefs.

Bugula culcullata, Low Head, Tas.

Bugularia dissimilis (Busk, 1852)

Habitat: Moderately exposed reef; 5–20 m depth.
Distribution: Vic. and around Tas.
Maximum size: Colony length to 100 mm.

Bugularia dissimilis has flattened, flexible branches that regularly divide and expand in width away from the fork. The species is moderately common in sheltered areas of open coast.

Bugularia dissimilis, Ninepin Pt, Tas.

Cornucopina grandis (Busk, 1852)

Habitat: Moderately and submaximally exposed reef; 10–80 m depth.
Distribution: Vic. and around Tas.
Maximum size: Colony length to 100 mm.

Cornucopina grandis is a pink, densely tufted species with numerous flexible branches made up of paired zooids arranged in rows. The zooids are horn-shaped and have long spines. This species is normally found only on deep reefs in Victoria but enters comparatively shallow water in Tasmania.

Cornucopina grandis, Bicheno, Tas.

Mucropetraliella ellerii, Ricketts Point, Vic.

Mucropetraliella ellerii (MacGillivray, 1868)

Habitat: Sheltered reef, seaweeds; 0–5 m depth.
Distribution: SA to Vic. and around Tas.
Maximum size: Colony length to 20 mm.

Mucropetraliella ellerii is a bright red species that forms encrusting colonies on seaweeds (particularly *Sargassum* and *Cystophora*) and in crevices on reefs. There is some doubt about the level of zooid variation within this species; forms found on rock and seaweed may represent different species.

Adeona grisea, Marmion Lagoon, WA

Adeona grisea (Lamouroux, 1816)

Habitat: Moderately exposed reef; 8–35 m depth.
Distribution: WA to Vic. and northern Tas.
Maximum size: Colony length to 300 mm.

Adeona grisea forms rigid, dark-purple plates with zooids opening on both surfaces and which are interconnected and perforated by a regular series of holes. The species is moderately common in deep areas with currents, particularly in southwestern Australia.

Celleporaria sp.

Habitat: Moderately exposed reef; 5–15 m depth.
Distribution: SA to Vic. and northern Tas.
Maximum size: Colony length to 120 mm.

Celleporaria sp. is one of several poorly known species in the genus *Celleporaria*, which form flattened sheet-like colonies attached by the base to reef surfaces. Colonies extend by younger zooids growing upward over earlier generations. Examination of the zooids is needed to distinguish this species from another with similar form, *Cigclisula verticalis*.

Celleporaria sp., Rocky Cape, Tas.

Triphyllozoon moniliferum

(MacGillivray, 1860)

Habitat: Sheltered and moderately exposed reef; 3–20 m depth.
Distribution: WA to NSW and around Tas.
Maximum size: Colony length to 160 mm.

Triphyllozoon moniliferum and related species are often referred to as lace corals. Identification of the different species is generally difficult because of the profusion of old scientific names and lack of any comprehensive study. The zooids of *T. moniliferum* form folded, perforated sheets, which are usually about 5 mm apart. The species is common in sheltered waters that are not turbid.

Triphyllozoon moniliferum, Tinderbox, Tas.

Triphyllozoon umbonatum

(MacGillivray, 1884)

Habitat: Sheltered reef; 4-27 m depth.
Distribution: Kangaroo I, SA, to Vic. and around Tas.
Maximum size: Colony length to 80 mm.

Triphyllozoon umbonatum resembles *T. moniliferum* but differs by having more open folds and an obvious ridge running around the margins of the individual zooids. The species is less common than its relative and tends to occur in deeper water.

Triphyllozoon umbonatum, Bathurst Channel, Tas.

Iodictyum phoeniceum, D'Entrecasteaux Channel, Tas.

Iodictyum phoeniceum (Busk, 1854)

Habitat: Reef; 5–40 m depth.
Distribution: SA to Qld and around Tas.
Maximum size: Colony width to 100 mm.

Iodictyum phoeniceum is one of the more easily recognised bryozoans because of its lace-like structure and purple coloration. The species is moderately common in deep water on reefs along the open coast.

Orthoscuticella ventricosa (Busk, 1852)

Habitat: Moderately and submaximally exposed reef; 4–25 m depth.
Distribution: Encounter Bay, SA, to Vic. and around Tas.
Maximum size: Colony length to 120 mm.

Orthoscuticella ventricosa is a densely tufted bryozoan, with the orange-yellow branches composed of single zooids aligned end to end. The branches fork regularly and are noticeably curved at the ends, producing almost spherical structures with the zooids opening on the inside. The species occurs abundantly on exposed reefs, particularly in eastern Tasmania and Victoria.

Orthoscuticella ventricosa, Bicheno, Tas.

PHYLUM ENTOPROCTA

Entoprocts (endoprocts)

Entoprocts are a small phylum of about 60 species of bottom-attached animals, which are rarely noticed because of their small size (mostly about 1 mm). They superficially resemble hydroid polyps but have a completely different structure. The body is divided into a cup-shaped calyx, with an encircling row of 6–26 tentacles, and a stalk. The calyx contains a U-shaped gut, and both the mouth and the anus are located in the crown of tentacles. Food particles are trapped by cilia arranged on the inner surface of the tentacles and transported along a ciliated groove to the mouth. The calyx also contains the gonads and often carries fertilised eggs, which are brooded until free-swimming larvae are released.

Entoprocts were for a long time classed in the same phylum as bryozoans because of the crowns of small tentacles and a resemblance in their larvae. However, they have evolved along quite different stems of invertebrate evolution, as is indicated by the bryozoans having a body cavity (coelom), which the entoprocts lack. Other differences between the two groups are that in entoprocts the water current flows inward rather than outward through the tentacles, and the tentacles surround the anus as well as the mouth.

Apart from one small freshwater family (Urnatellidae), all entoprocts are marine. They occur attached to rock surfaces or, more often, to other invertebrates such as molluscs, tube-dwelling polychaete worms, bryozoans, ascidians or sponges. Marine entoprocts are divided into two families: the Pedicellinidae, which contains colonial forms originating from a common basal stolon, and the Loxosomatidae, which contains species attached directly to the substrate at the end of each stalk. Loxosomatids often multiply by budding and can therefore also produce a dense colony. A few species are not cemented in place but attached to the substrate by a sucking disc, enabling a limited degree of movement.

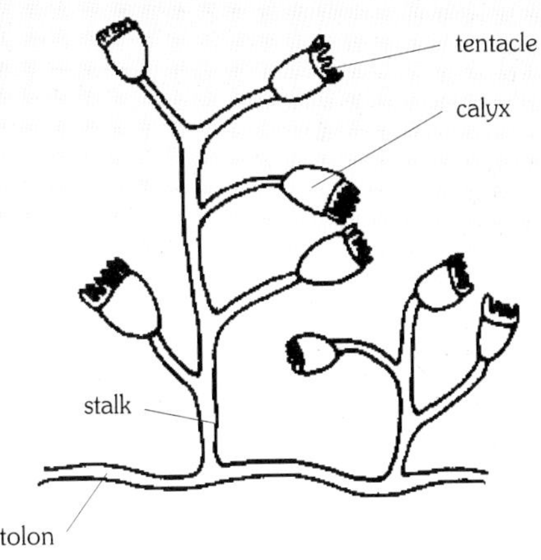

Entoproct (5 mm)
Phylum Entoprocta

Pedicellina sp.

Habitat: Invertebrates; 3–10 m depth.
Distribution: Eastern Tas.
Maximum size: Length to 5 mm.

Pedicellina sp. is a colonial species with numerous stalked calyces arising from a basal stolon. This entoproct is moderately common on the shells of abalone along the eastern Tasmanian coast. Its affinities are not known, but the species is probably also distributed widely along most of the southern Australian coast.

Pedicellina sp., Bruny I, Tas.

PHYLUM CHAETOGNATHA

Chaetognaths, arrow worms

Approximately 60 species of chaetognath form a small phylum, which is not closely related to any other. They are small animals, primarily less than 20 mm in length, with a vague resemblance to a feathered arrow in shape. The bodies are flattened, transparent and torpedo-shaped, with one or two pairs of fins on the sides and a tail fin. The front is slightly enlarged to form a head, which contains two eyes and spines in rows on either side of the mouth. Because of their relatively small body size, chaetognaths lack respiratory, circulatory and excretory organs; they have a straight, structurally simple digestive tract.

Chaetognaths are hermaphrodites (both male *and* female), and individuals in most species are able to fertilise their own eggs. Eggs may be released into the plankton or carried by the parent; they develop into adults without abrupt metamorphosis. All species are open-water carnivores, except for a few bottom-dwelling animals in the genus *Spadella*, which live among plants in shallow water. Chaetognaths feed by remaining motionless for a while and then quickly darting forward to seize planktonic copepods and other prey using the grasping spines on the head. The majority of species in the phylum belong to the genus *Sagitta*. They are extremely abundant in all seas.

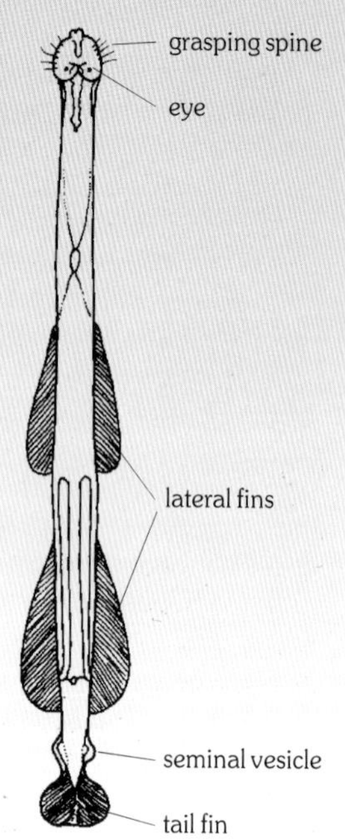

Chaetognath (10 mm)
Sagitta sp.
Phylum Chaetognatha

Spadella sp.

Habitat: Seaweeds on moderately exposed coasts; 0–10 m depth.
Distribution: WA to NSW and around Tas.
Maximum size: Length to 10 mm.

Spadella sp. has a short, wide body with conspicuous eyes and one pair of side fins located towards the rear. The tail fin has several adhesive papillae, which enable to animal to attach itself to seaweeds. This is the only genus of chaetognaths with bottom-dwelling species; all other genera occur in open water.

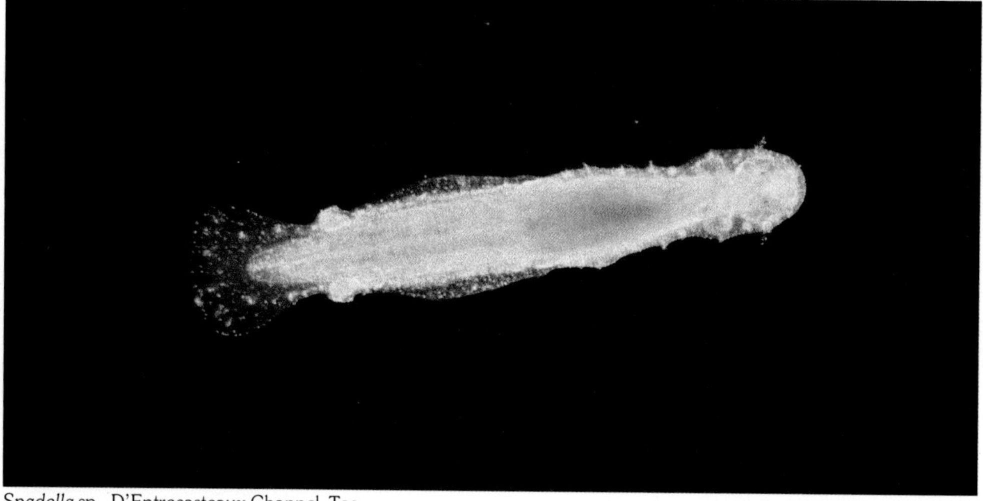

Spadella sp., D'Entrecasteaux Channel, Tas.

PHYLUM ECHINODERMATA

Echinoderms

Echinoderms are among the most conspicuous animals on the seashore, many of them being large, brightly coloured and having striking shapes. With more than 6000 species they form one of the most coherent phyla in the animal kingdom, having unique features and no strong relationship to other groups. Echinoderms were originally classed with anemones and jellyfish in a group of animals called the Radiata because they possessed structures radiating out from the central disc, but they are now thought to be more closely allied to vertebrate animals. Echinoderms and vertebrates are the only animals that have an internal calcareous skeleton. The name echinoderms ('spiny-skinned animals') derives from this feature, an arrangement of plates, spines or spicules underneath the surface skin. Because these skeletal elements resist decomposition and the phylum has been abundant since the Cambrian period (600–500 million years ago), echinoderms are well represented as fossils and are often used by geologists to characterise rock strata.

Most echinoderms have a body plan based on five or multiples of five, with five arms, five rows of tube feet, five pairs of gonads, etc. They lack a head but have an oral or mouth-bearing region, which is on either the upper or lower body surface relative to the seabed, depending on the class and species. A unique feature of echinoderms is the water vascular system, an arrangement of tubes carrying a watery liquid throughout the body. At the centre of the body is a circular canal with a major takeoff canal leading to the external surface, where a sieve-like structure (the madreporite) is usually present and forms a leaky barrier with the sea. The presence of the madreporite is probably a major reason why echinoderms have never colonised freshwater habitats; animals cannot maintain salt balance in fresh water because water floods into the body. Arising from the radial canal are five or more lateral canals with rows of tube feet that penetrate the body wall. These tube feet are specialised for a variety of purposes, including locomotion, food capture, adhesion, sensory detection and respiration. They are manipulated by valves and muscle layers varying water pressure in different sections of the body. The transport of liquid through the water vascular system is also aided by cilia.

Echinoderms have remarkable powers of regeneration. Many can grow new limbs and a new gut if damaged, and some deliberately shed arms in a process of asexual reproduction known as fission. Sexes are usually separate, and eggs are released and fertilised in the external environment. A few exceptional species, most of which live in cooler regions, release juvenile replicas of the adult, that are brooded in or under the body. Tropical and temperate species almost invariably have a planktonic larval phase lasting for a few days to a few weeks. Larval echinoderms are very distinctive in appearance.

Present-day echinoderms are divided into five classes: crinoids (feather stars), asteroids (sea stars), ophiuroids (brittle stars), echinoids (sea urchins) and holothurians (sea cucumbers). Several other classes once existed but are now extinct.

Class Crinoidea

Feather stars, crinoids, sea lilies

Feather stars, or crinoids, have long branched arms with a regular arrangement of small side appendages (the pinnules), producing a feather-like effect. In their normal feeding position, the arms and a centrally located mouth are held upwards. Because of a U-shaped gut, the anus is positioned on the same surface as the mouth but is offset somewhat from the centre. On the undersurface of the body is a ring of slender, jointed, calcareous appendages known as cirri, which are used for locomotion and to allow the animal to anchor to the substrate. Crinoids feed by trapping small planktonic organisms using modified tube feet that lack suckers. Food particles are transported in mucous strings down the arms along a ciliated food groove to the mouth.

Crinoids are a conspicuous group of animals on tropical reefs but are poorly represented in

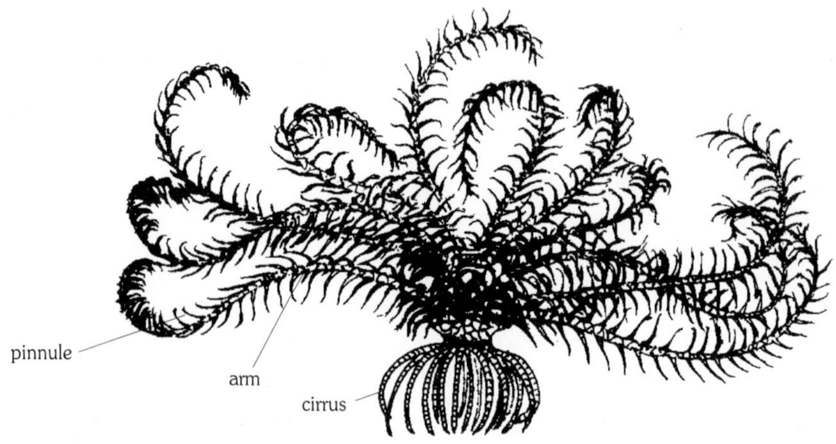

Feather star (200 mm)
Comatulata purpurea
Class Crinoidea

temperate Australian waters, as only about a dozen species are known. Nevertheless, within this area they can occur in extremely high densities at sites with tidal current flow.

FAMILY COMASTERIDAE

This is the largest Australian family of crinoids, containing most of the bright, conspicuous species. Members of the family have the pinnules nearer the disc modified at the tips into a curved, comb-like structure. The mouth is located towards the margin of the central disc region, and the anus is positioned almost centrally.

Cenolia trichoptera (Müller, 1846)

Habitat: Sheltered and moderately exposed reef; 0–70 m depth.
Distribution: Fremantle, WA, to Byron Bay, NSW, and around Tas.
Maximum size: Arm length to 230 mm.

Cenolia trichoptera is the largest and most conspicuous crinoid on shallow southern Australian reefs. It occurs in a variety of colour forms, most notably orange, yellow, purple, white and brown. These colours generally do not vary along the arms, in contrast to the mottled pattern of *C. tasmaniae*. The central disc of the body generally remains concealed in crevices or under rocks, while the arms are held up in the water column with the pinnules trapping passing plankton.

Cenolia trichoptera, Bicheno, Tas.

Cenolia tasmaniae (A.H. Clark, 1918)

Habitat: Sheltered and moderately exposed reef; 0–63 m depth.
Distribution: Fremantle, WA, to Byron Bay, NSW, and around Tas.
Maximum size: Arm length to 150 mm.

Cenolia tasmaniae is smaller than *C. trichoptera* and generally has more arms (about 37) and fewer cirri (about 20). It is most easily recognised by its mottled brown coloration, a lime-green disc and the densely compacted pinnules on the arms. This crinoid can occur in very high densities under rocks but is rarely noticed by the casual diver.

Cenolia tasmaniae, Tinderbox, Tas.

Comatula purpurea (Müller, 1843)

Habitat: Seagrass, sheltered reef; 0–15 m depth.
Distribution: Tropical Australia south to Fremantle, WA. Also widespread in the Indo-West Pacific region.
Maximum size: Arm length to 190 mm.

Comatula purpurea, Marmion Lagoon, WA

Comatula purpurea is a common crinoid associated with seagrasses in shallow water off Perth. It is aptly named because of its very dark purple coloration; the colour leaches from preserved specimens, turning the liquid almost black.

FAMILY ANTEDONIDAE

Species in this family have ten arms, a centrally located mouth, and cirri that are round in cross-section and relatively short. This is one of the largest families overseas but is poorly represented in southern Australia.

Antedon incommoda Bell, 1888

Habitat: Exposed reef; 0–68 m depth.
Distribution: Dampier Archipelago, WA, to Port Curtis, Qld, and around Tas.
Maximum size: Arm length to 50 mm.

Antedon incommoda is a small, ten-armed species with variably coloured arms, which are often pale brown or white. The species is associated with algae and other animals at sites with good current flow and will be found in most coastal areas.

Antedon incommoda, Bicheno, Tas.

Antedon loveni Bell, 1882

Habitat: Sheltered and moderately exposed reef; 0–18 m depth.
Distribution: Victor Harbor, SA, to Byron Bay, NSW, and around Tas.
Maximum size: Arm length to 30 mm.

Antedon loveni, Tinderbox, Tas.

Antedon loveni has a similar appearance to *A. incommoda* but is a more delicate species, and the segments of the cirri are longer than they are broad (unlike those of *A. incommoda*). The species tends to be patchily distributed among plants and animals on reefs, with high numbers in one area but none in apparently similar habitat nearby.

FAMILY APOROMETRIDAE

This distinctive family contains small species characterised by extremely long cirri, nearly as long as the arms. Only three species in one genus, *Aporometra*, are known, all of them restricted to southern Australia.

Aporometra occidentalis H.L. Clark, 1938

Habitat: Moderately exposed reef, seagrass; 0–30 m depth.
Distribution: Yanchep to Bass strait, Vic.
Maximum size: Arm length to 25 mm.

Aporometra occidentalis, the Western Australian species, has 39–61 cirrus segments, which are all broader than long. ***Aporometra paedophora***, the New South Wales species, has 25–35 cirrus segments, which are also all broader than long, while the South Australian, Victorian and Tasmanian species, ***Aporometra wilsoni***, has a number of cirri segments that are much longer than broad. Species of *Aporometra* are usually associated with macroalgae and seagrasses; more than 100 *Aporometra wilsoni* have been found on a single plant.

Aporometra occidentalis, Little I, WA

FAMILY PTILOMETRIDAE

Ptilometrids are unusual-looking crinoids with extremely long cirri and brittle arms with stiff, spike-like pinnules. They are sometimes called passion flowers by trawl fishermen. Only two species in the one genus are placed in this family, both of them restricted to temperate Australian waters.

Ptilometra australis (Wilton, 1843)

Habitat: Exposed reef, sponge gardens; 1–60 m depth.
Distribution: Eden, NSW, to the Capricorn Group, Qld. Also the Kent Group, Tas.
Maximum size: Arm length to 80 mm.

Ptilometra australis is characterised by the 18–23 arms and the typical 'passion flower' appearance of the family. The species is abundant in deep water and also enters the mouths of deep estuaries, where it is occasionally seen at sites with strong tidal current flow.

Ptilometra australis, Port Stephens, NSW

Ptilometra macronema (Müller, 1846)

Habitat: Exposed reef, sponge gardens; 16–120 m depth.
Distribution: Shark Bay, WA, to Port Phillip Bay, Vic.
Maximum size: Arm length to 80 mm.

Ptilometra macronema has similar habits and a similar general appearance to the closely related *P. australis.* It is most easily distinguished by the greater number of arms on mature specimens (25–31). *Ptilometra macronema* is most abundant in deep water, where it generally attaches itself to gorgonians and sponges.

Ptilometra macronema, Marmion Lagoon, WA

Class Asteroidea

Seastars, starfish

Asteroids have a star-shaped or pentagonal body with five or more stout arms. Each arm contains part of the digestive system and the gonads, one or more on each internal side wall. On the underside of the arm is an ambulacral groove lined by sensitive tube feet, which are often protected by a series of spines. In some burrowing species the tube feet are pointed, but more often they end in suction discs, which can grip strongly onto solid surfaces, enabling the animal to move about and capture and manipulate prey. The upper body surface has a network of calcareous plates embedded in the fleshy tissue of the body wall. Small balloon-like papulae project between some of the plates and are used in respiration. The upper surface often also has numerous pincer-like structures known as pedicellariae. These are used to remove foreign objects and to prevent other invertebrates from settling on and fouling the surface.

The mouth of asteroids is positioned at the centre of the undersurface. During feeding, the thin sack-like stomach is everted through the mouth and partially digests food outside the body. Some species feed on plant material, others on sessile invertebrates and many are scavengers, consuming whatever plant or animal material is locally available at the time. A few of the larger species are predators, capturing bivalve molluscs, echinoderms and other large prey. These species open large bivalves by pulling continuously on the valves for several hours, using relays of tube feet and resting other tube feet at the same time. A bivalve's adductor muscles can easily withstand the pressure exerted by tube feet for a short period but, like all muscle tissue, will fatigue and eventually relax if strained for too long.

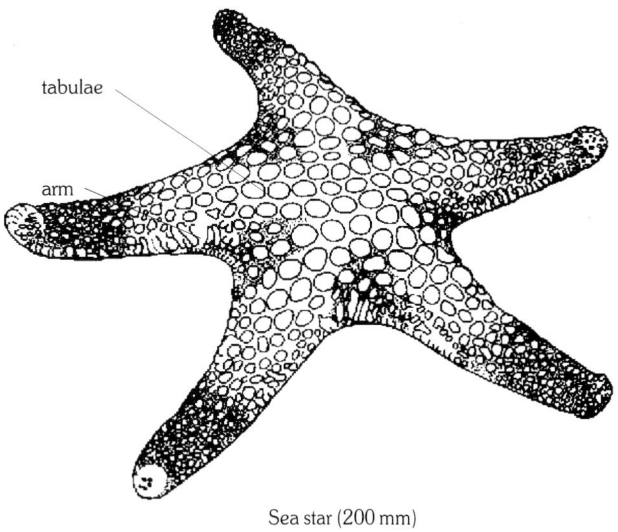

Sea star (200 mm)
Nectria ocellata
Class Asteroidea

FAMILY LUIDIIDAE

This family contains approximately 50 large species in the single genus *Luidia*, with eight species recorded around Australia. Tube feet are present in two rows and taper to a point rather than having suckers. Species in the family readily shed arms and are rarely captured without breaking into pieces.

Luidia australiae Döderlein, 1920

Habitat: Seagrass, sand, silt; 0–110 m depth.
Distribution: Dongara, WA, to Moreton Bay, Qld, and south to Bicheno, Tas.
Maximum size: Arm radius to 200 mm.

Luidia australiae is a large, conspicuous species with seven long arms, and is often first detected by its star-shaped imprint when buried in soft sediment. It has a mottled green and grey upper surface, covered by small plates. This species is common in sheltered waters but also occurs in deeper sand habitats off exposed coastal bays. It is an active predator, its diet consisting mainly of bivalves and heart urchins, which are engulfed whole.

Luidia australiae, Bicheno, Tas.

FAMILY ASTROPECTINIDAE

Astropectinids are related to the luidiids and have tube feet with pointed tips. They can usually be recognised by their pointed arms, which give the animals a star-shaped appearance, and by prominent rows of spines along the margins of the arms. Identification of species is primarily based on the arrangement of spines along the conspicuous upper plates around the outside of the body (the 'superomarginal plates') and the lower plates directly below these (the 'inferomarginal plates'). At least five similar-looking species in the family are recorded from temperate Australian waters. They all occur on soft sediments, where they remain buried through daylight hours, emerging after dark to feed.

Astropecten polyacanthus
Müller and Troschel, 1842

Habitat: Sand, silt; 0–185 m depth.
Distribution: Tropical Australia south to Sydney, NSW, and Cape Naturaliste, WA. Also widepread in the Indo-West Pacific region.
Maximum size: Arm radius to 90 mm.

Astropecten polyacanthus is the most widely distributed *Astropecten* species. It is generally easily recognised by the dark purple upper surface and deep orange colour below. The superomarginal plates are also distinctive, as they are situated largely along the sides of the arms and therefore appear longer than broad when viewed from above. (Other local species have the plates largely on top of the arms.) A large spine is also present on the innermost superomarginal plate, with the next one to three plates usually reduced and lacking spines, thereby creating a gap in the series of upward-pointing spines along the arms. At locations such as Pittwater, NSW, large numbers occasionally become stranded on sandflats at low-tide.

Astropecten polyacanthus, Pittwater, NSW

Astropecten preissei Müller and Troschel, 1843

Habitat: Sand, silt; 0–140 m depth.
Distribution: Shark Bay, WA, to Gulf St Vincent, SA.
Maximum size: Arm radius to 110 mm.

Astropecten preissei is the only southern species in the family lacking spines on the superomarginal plates and has a fawn to purplish colour. It is the largest and most abundant of the shallow-water species of *Astropecten* in southwestern Australian waters.

Astropecten preissei, Woodmans Point, WA

Astropecten triseriatus Müller and Troschel, 1843

Habitat: Sand, silt; 0–46 m depth.
Distribution: North West Cape to King George Sound, WA. Also widespread in the Indo-West Pacific region.
Maximum size: Arm radius to 110 mm.

Astropecten triseriatus is a heavily spined species of *Astropecten* that is similar to *A. vappa* but has three or more spines projecting from each of the upper plates around the outside of the body (compared with only one or two). This seastar was first described from specimens collected in southern Western Australia and is common in the Cockburn Sound and Albany areas. Since then, animals considered to belong to the same species have been collected from Fiji, Hawaii, Easter Island and Bass Strait — a strange distribution pattern.

Astropecten triseriatus, Albany, WA

Astropecten vappa Müller and Troschel, 1843

Habitat: Sand, silt; 0-128 m depth.
Distribution: Around the Australian mainland.
Maximum size: Arm radius to 125 mm.

Astropecten vappa occurs widely around the Australian continent but is patchily distributed. Like most other *Astropecten* species, it feeds mainly on small bivalve molluscs. The species is fawn to brown on the upper surface and cream below; each inferomarginal plate has a large upper spine, with a series of spines diminishing in size from top to bottom below.

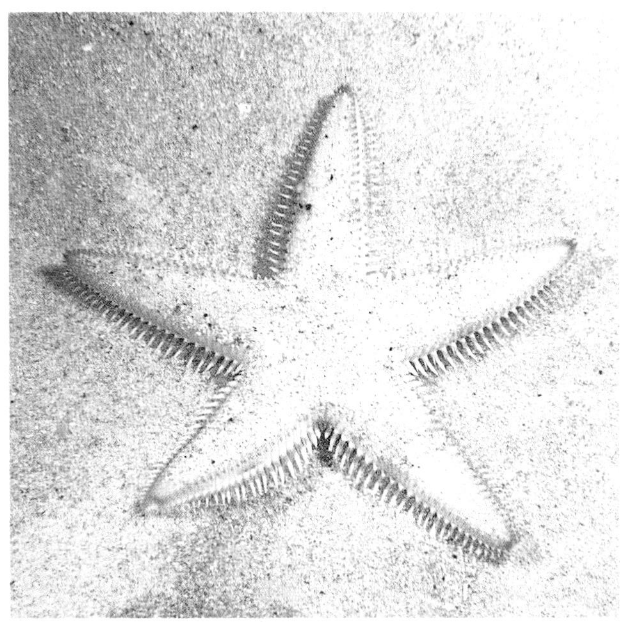

Astropecten vappa, Port Stephens, NSW. RUDIE KUITER

Bollonaster pectinatus (Sladen, 1883)

Habitat: Sand, silt; 2–280 m depth.
Distribution: Rottnest I, WA, to Newcastle, NSW, and around Tas.
Maximum size: Arm radius to 50 mm.

Bollonaster pectinatus is a small and colourful species that is characterised by a group of three to five similarly sized spines associated with each lower marginal plate, producing a comb-like effect along the body. The species is confined to deep water through much of its range but occurs off coastal beaches in Tasmania.

Bollonaster pectinatus, Cloudy Bay, Tas.

FAMILY ARCHASTERIDAE

Archasterids are a small family of seastars with five long arms, tube feet that end in sucking discs and very large plates along the upper and lower margins of the arms. The plates on the upper surface are covered by numerous small granules or spinelets, and large spines are present on the plates surrounding the mouth.

Archaster angulatus Müller and Troschel, 1842

Habitat: Sand; 0–50 m depth.
Distribution: Tropical Australia south to Cape Naturaliste, WA, and the Whitsunday I, Qld. Also widespread in the Indo-West Pacific region.
Maximum size: Arm radius to 80 mm.

Archaster angulatus, Busselton, WA

Archaster angulatus is a moderately common seastar found half-buried in sand off the southwestern Australian coast. The species appears a dull grey colour underwater, but oranges or reds are revealed when exposed to sunlight. The two species of *Archaster* are the only seastars known to entwine in pairs or larger groups when spawning.

FAMILY GONIASTERIDAE

Goniasterids belong to the same order as the archasterids. They are firm-bodied species, with numerous large plates on the upper surface producing a pavement-like effect. Most species in the family are flattened and star-shaped; a few are pentagonal.

Tosia magnifica (Müller and Troschel, 1842)

Habitat: Sheltered reef, silt, sand; 0–200 m depth.
Distribution: SA to eastern Vic. and around Tas.
Maximum size: Arm radius to 45 mm.

Tosia magnifica possesses 8 to 20 plates along each of the five body margins, in contrast to the six plates of *T. australis*. Square-bodied four-armed forms of both species are also relatively common. *Tosia magnifica* is particularly abundant in sheltered Tasmanian and Victorian bays, where it grazes in the open on small surface-living plants and microbes. In South Australia the species is found only in deep water.

Tosia magnifica, Bathurst Channel, Tas.

Tosia australis Gray, 1840

Habitat: Moderately exposed and sheltered reef, sand; 0–40 m depth.
Distribution: Fremantle, WA, to southern NSW and around Tas.
Maximum size: Arm radius to 50 mm.

Tosia australis has six (or rarely eight) large plates along each side of the body; on animals from wave-swept coasts the plates at the ends of the arms are greatly swollen. This species is found in slightly more exposed habitats than *T. magnifica* and feeds mainly on ascidians, sponges, bryozoans and algae.

Tosia australis, Spring Beach, Tas.

Tosia australis, Princess Royal Harbour, WA

Pentagonaster dubeni, Cape Portland, Tas.

Pentagonaster dubeni Gray, 1847

Habitat: Moderately exposed and sheltered reef; 0–200 m depth.
Distribution: Shark Bay, WA, to southern Qld and around Tas.
Maximum size: Arm radius to 75 mm.

While the relative length of the arms varies considerably between localities, *Pentagonaster dubeni* should be easily recognised because of its conspicuous yellow, orange or red plates separated by thin, white or yellow lines. This species is most often observed in shallow, sheltered bays and is particularly common in Bass Strait.

Stellaster inspinosus H.L. Clark, 1916

Habitat: Silt; 2–174 m depth.
Distribution: Barrow I to Mandurah, WA.
Maximum size: Arm radius to 70 mm.

Stellaster inspinosus, Bicton, WA.

Stellaster inspinosus is a striking pink to blood-red species, which varies little in shape throughout its range. The species' characteristic features include slightly rounded plates on the upper surface and pointed arms. Little is known of its biology.

FAMILY OREASTERIDAE

Oreasterids are large five-armed seastars with the central body generally elevated compared with the arms. They differ from the closely related goniasterids primarily by having superomarginal plates along the upper edges of the arms that are often embedded and inconspicuous, and arms that are generally rounded on the upper surface.

Goniodiscaster seriatus, Marmion Lagoon, WA

Goniodiscaster seriatus
(Müller and Troschel, 1843)

Habitat: Sand, seagrass; 0–30 m depth.
Distribution: Shark Bay to Cape Naturaliste, WA.
Maximum size: Arm radius to 80 mm.

Goniodiscaster seriatus is a distinctive Western Australian species with purple marginal plates, purple tubercles on the upper surface and rust-coloured patches. It is the most abundant seastar in seagrass beds off Perth, where it is found half-buried in sand.

Anthaster valvulatus (Müller & Troschel, 1843)

Habitat: Moderately exposed sand, reef; 0–40 m depth.
Distribution: Yanchep, WA, to Gulf St Vincent, SA.
Maximum size: Arm radius to 120 mm.

Anthaster valvulatus has five stumpy arms, with rounded tubercles on the dorsal surface becoming most prominent in a ring around the central region. The colour is mottled red and cream. This species is usually found in the open on sand or flat algal-covered rock. It is not regularly seen by divers but can be locally common in small areas.

Anthaster valvulatus, Two Peoples Bay, WA. RUDIE KUITER

Anthenea australiae Döderlain, 1915

Habitat: Silt, rock; 1–15 m depth.
Distribution: Broome to Fremantle, WA.
Maximum size: Arm radius to 95 mm.

Anthenea australiae is a large orange seastar that is locally abundant in the lower reaches of the Swan estuary. Little is known of the habits of this species; however, it is thought to feed on bacteria and other microbes associated with the surface of the sediment.

Anthenea australiae, Bicton, WA

Anthenea sidneyensis Döderlain, 1915

Habitat: Silt, 8–80 m depth.
Distribution: Eden, NSW, to Lindeman I, Qld.
Maximum size: Arm radius to 120 mm.

Anthenea sidneyensis can be recognised by its inflated shape and distinctive mottled green and rust coloration, which appears stable throughout its geographic range. This seastar occurs on the floor of large bays, harbours and estuaries and is more often collected in dredges and trawls than observed by divers. The species was known as *Anthenea edmondi* until recently.

Anthenea sidneyensis, Port Hacking, NSW. Neville Coleman/ Underwater Geographic

Nectria ocellata Perrier, 1876

Habitat: Exposed reef; 0–240 m depth.
Distribution: Eucla, WA, to northern NSW and around Tas.
Maximum size: Arm radius to 130 mm.

All six species in the genus *Nectria* are restricted to southern Australia, and five of them are found in shallow water. *Nectria ocellata* is the most common seastar on many exposed reefs in Victoria and Tasmania but in other states tends to be less common and occur in greater depths. It is a variable species, best separated from other *Nectria* species by the shape and arrangement of the granule-covered cylindrical structures on the central upper body. These 'tabulae' have a slightly convex upper surface and are separated by gaps in the central body region and gradually decrease in size towards the ends of the arms. Sessile invertebrates such as sponges and ascidians are the main food of this seastar.

Nectria ocellata, Ile des Phoques, Tas.

Nectria macrobrachia H.L. Clark, 1923

Habitat: Exposed reef; 0–180 m depth.
Distribution: Port Gregory, WA, to Wilsons Promontory, Vic., and King I and Kent Group, Tas.
Maximum size: Arm radius to 60 mm.

Nectria macrobrachia occurs commonly on exposed reefs throughout its range. It is the smallest of the *Nectria* species and can be recognised by the crowded tabulae, with concave upper surfaces, which extend to the ends of the arms. The colour is usually pale orange or pink, with purple (occasionally greenish) tips.

Nectria macrobrachia, Two Peoples Bay, WA

Nectria multispina, Esperance, WA

Nectria multispina H.L. Clark, 1928

Habitat: Moderately exposed reef; 0–25 m depth.
Distribution: Fremantle, WA, to Wilsons Promontory, Vic.
Maximum size: Arm radius to 90 mm.

Nectria multispina is the least common of the shallow-water *Nectria* species. It possesses crowded tabulae that have a smooth, outwardly rounded appearance and decrease rapidly in size away from the central body region. The colour pattern often includes a predominance of dark red interspersed with orange.

Nectria saoria Shepherd, 1967

Habitat: Exposed reef; 0–30 m depth.
Distribution: Fremantle, WA, to Port Phillip Bay, Vic.
Maximum size: Arm radius to 70 mm.

Nectria saoria, Port Lincoln, SA

Nectria saoria is the most common *Nectria* species on exposed rocky reefs in southwestern Australia. It is normally a bright orange colour and can be distinguished from other species by the large, rounded tabulae that extend to the tips of the arms.

Nectria wilsoni Shepherd & Hodgkin, 1965

Habitat: Moderately exposed reef, seagrass; 0–45 m depth.
Distribution: Beagle I, WA, to Lakes Entrance, Vic.
Maximum size: Arm radius to 100 mm.

Nectria wilsoni, Two Peoples Bay, WA

Nectria wilsoni possesses tabulae with concave upper surfaces and numerous small, rounded granules; the tabulae are well separated from each other by gaps and are restricted to the central section of the body. This species occurs in slightly more sheltered habitats than other *Nectria* species and is occasionally observed in seagrass meadows.

FAMILY ASTERODISCIDIDAE

Species within this family differ from oreasterids by having less well developed superomarginal plates along the sides of the arms and terminal plates that are often massive. They also differ by having spicules in the walls of the tube feet.

Asterodiscides truncatus (Coleman, 1911)

Habitat: Reef, silt; 14–800 m depth.
Distribution: Eucla, WA, to Solitary I, NSW. Also Kermadec Is.
Maximum size: Arm radius to 170 mm.

Asterodiscides truncatus, Bermagui, NSW. RUDIE KUITER

Asterodiscides truncatus is a striking species, immediately recognisable by the rounded tubercles on the upper body surface, large body size, and purple, red and orange coloration. It is occasionally sighted by divers on deep reefs and has also been collected by trawl from silt substrates in areas below normal diving depths.

FAMILY ASTEROPSEIDAE

The few species in this family have small surface plates covered by a smooth, tough skin and a central disc that is large in comparison with the size of the arms.

Petricia vernicina (Lamarck, 1816)

Habitat: Reef; 0–60 m depth.
Distribution: Houtman Abrolhos, WA, to Caloundra, Qld, and around Tas. Also Lord Howe I, Norfolk I and Kermadec Is.
Maximum size: Arm radius to 90 mm.

Petricia vernicina, Maria I, Tas.

Petricia vernicina is distinguished by its soft, rubbery appearance, reddish coloration and very large respiratory papulae, which are generally obvious on the upper surface of living animals. Dried specimens appear quite different from live animals as large marginal plates formerly hidden by the skin become apparent. The species occurs on sheltered and fully exposed reefs but is most common at moderately exposed sites. It feeds on encrusting invertebrates, particularly sponges, ascidians and bryozoans.

FAMILY OPHIDIASTERIDAE

This is a large family of primarily bright-coloured species that are most often found on tropical coral reefs. Ophidasterids have long arms that are almost round in cross-section and a small disc.

Fromia polypora H. L. Clark, 1916

Habitat: Exposed reef, 1–160 m depth.
Distribution: Houtman Abrolhos, WA, to Sydney, NSW, and around Tas.
Maximum size: Arm radius to 110 mm.

Fromia polypora is the most common species of seastar observed on southeastern Australian reefs with heavy wave exposure. Because of its long, bright orange arms flecked with black papulae, it is usually easy to see against the reef background. Like most of the other conspicuous seastars living on temperate reefs, its diet consists mainly of sedentary invertebrates such as sponges and ascidians.

Fromia polypora, Bicheno, Tas.

FAMILY ECHINASTERIDAE

Echinasterids have rounded plates that mesh end-on or side-on with gaps between, producing a net-like skeleton. They lack the large marginal plates that are typical of the preceding families. Most species have a small disc with five long arms that are almost round in cross-section and numerous spinelets on the plates.

Plectaster decanus (Müller & Troschel, 1843)

Habitat: Sheltered and moderately exposed reef; 0–200 m depth.
Distribution: Two Rocks, WA, to Byron Bay, NSW, and northern Tas.
Maximum size: Arm radius to 120 mm.

Plectaster decanus is a strikingly patterned species with rows of granules forming a network of orange ridges across the upper surface. Between the ridges are clusters of purple or red papules, forming a mosaic effect.

Plectaster decanus, Canal Rocks, WA

Plectaster decanus, Rocky Cape, Tas.

Echinaster arcystatus H.L. Clark, 1914

Habitat: Exposed reef; 0–40 m depth.
Distribution: Shark Bay, WA, to Montague I, NSW, and the Kent Group, Tas.
Maximum size: Arm radius to 180 mm.

Echinaster arcystatus resembles *Plectaster decanus* but grows to a larger size and has a paler, less distinctive network of small spines over the upper body surface and arms that are rounder in cross-section and flabby. It is an uncommon species that feeds mainly on encrusting sponges and other sessile animals.

Echinaster arcystatus, Busselton, WA

Echinaster varicolor H.L. Clark, 1938

Habitat: Sheltered and moderately exposed reef, seagrass; 1–50 m depth.
Distribution: Broome to Recherche Archipelago, WA.
Maximum size: Arm radius to 110 mm.

Echinaster varicolor is one of the largest and most colourful species found along the southern Western Australian coast. It has long arms, a reddish-brown

Echinaster varicolor, Twilight Cove, WA.

colour and black spots regularly arranged over the upper surface. The species is occasionally seen by divers but is not common.

Echinaster colemani Rowe & Albertson, 1987

Habitat: Exposed reef; 15–77 m depth.
Distribution: Ulladulla, NSW, to Moreton Bay, Qld. Also Norfolk I.
Maximum size: Arm radius to 140 mm.

Echinaster colemani can be recognised by the five long arms, plain red-brown surface coloration and numerous purple papulae. This is one of the rarer large seastars in temperate waters and is generally restricted to deep New South Wales reefs.

Echinaster glomeratus H.L. Clark, 1916

Habitat: Exposed reef; 0–40 m depth.
Distribution: Houtman Abrolhos, WA, to Cape Jervis, SA.
Maximum size: Arm radius to 150 mm.

Echinaster glomeratus is yellow to red, and has clusters of small spines embedded in the soft skin covering the upper surface. This seastar lives in the open but is not commonly seen.

Echinaster glomeratus, St Francis I., SA. NEVILLE COLEMAN/ UNDERWATER GEOGRAPHIC

Echinaster colemani, Terrigal, NSW

FAMILY ASTERINIDAE

This large family contains species covered by small plates without major gaps in the skeletal network. Nearly all plates bear short spinelets, with the spinelets on the undersurface often arranged in tufts or fans. Most asterinids are small and live concealed under rocks or in crevices during daylight.

Nepanthia troughtoni (Livingstone, 1934)

Habitat: Exposed reef; 0–70 m depth.
Distribution: Green Head, WA, to Wilsons Promontory, Vic., and King I and the Kent Group, Tas.
Maximum size: Arm radius to 70 mm.

Nepanthia troughtoni is one of the most common seastars on exposed reefs along the southern Australian coast. Throughout its geographic range, the species shows little variation in either shape or the light pink coloration. It feeds on encrusting animals, including sponges, and perhaps also algae.

Nepanthia troughtoni, Two Peoples Bay, WA

Nepanthia crassa (Gray, 1847)

Habitat: Sheltered and moderately exposed reef, silt; 0–38 m depth.
Distribution: Point Coates to Cape Naturaliste, WA.
Maximum size: Arm radius to 65 mm.

Nepanthia crassa generally has large green tubercles over the surface, contrasting with the reddish-brown background coloration. The species generally lives concealed under rocks during the day and moves about at night.

Nepanthia crassa, Bicton, WA

Paranepanthia grandis (H. L. Clark, 1928)

Habitat: Sheltered reef, 0–40 m depth.
Distribution: Point Peron, WA, to Sydney, NSW, and around Tas.
Maximum size: Arm radius to 70 mm.

Paranepanthia grandis is common throughout most of its geographic range but is rarely seen because it remains hidden during the day under rocks and in crevices. The most noticeable feature is the distinctly webbed arms. The species is brightly coloured pink or orange and, while sometimes blotched, usually lacks an obvious pattern.

Paranepanthia grandis, Gordon, Tas.

Asterina atyphoida H. L. Clark, 1916

Habitat: Under rocks; 0–40 m depth.
Distribution: Rottnest I, WA, to Wilsons Promontory, Vic., and around Tas.
Maximum size: Arm radius to 15 mm.

Asterina atyphoida, Edithburgh, SA

Asterina atyphoida is a small, five-sided seastar with a light brown or cream background coloration and distinctive green or blue tips at the ends of the arms. It is a cryptic animal, spending most of the day hidden under rocks.

Patiriella exigua (Lamarck, 1816)

Habitat: Rock pools; mid intertidal.
Distribution: Port Lincoln, SA, to southern Qld. and around Tas. Also South Africa.
Maximum size: Arm radius to 13 mm.

Patiriella exigua, Cloudy Lagoon, Tas.

Patiriella exigua is a small five-armed species, commonly observed in rockpools in the lower intertidal zone, where it moves about in the open during the day. It is brown to green-blue on the upper surface and a lighter green-blue underneath.

Patiriella calcar (Lamarck, 1816)

Habitat: Rock pools, sheltered reefs; mid intertidal to 10 m depth.
Distribution: Albany, WA, to Currumbin, Qld, and around Tas.
Maximum size: Arm radius to 50 mm.

Most casual observers to the seashore will have noticed *Patiriella calcar*, an abundant seastar with eight arms. It is a striking species because of the brilliant combination of reds, oranges, browns, greens and blues on the upper surface. This colour pattern is genetically controlled and can vary greatly between individuals living in the one rockpool. The species is omnivorous, feeding mainly on algae and detritus but also consuming mussels and other animals swept into rockpools by wave action.

Patiriella calcar, Ricketts Pt, Vic.

Patiriella gunnii (Gray, 1840)

Habitat: Under rocks; 0–30 m depth.
Distribution: Kalbarri, WA, to Byron Bay, NSW, and around Tas.
Maximum size: Arm radius to 40 mm.

Patiriella gunnii has a six-armed shape similar to *P. brevispina* but is more flattened and has slightly longer arms relative to the central section of the body. It generally has a mottled appearance, with combinations of two or more colours including brown, red, cream, green and blue. The species can be found under rocks in large numbers.

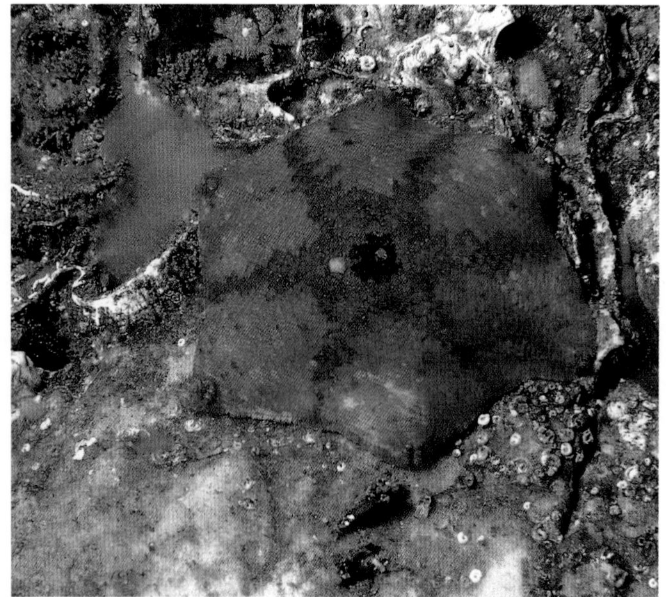
Patiriella gunniii, Rocky Cape, Tas.

Patiriella brevispina H. L. Clark, 1938

Habitat: Sheltered reef, seagrass; 0–15 m depth.
Distribution: Dongara, WA, to Collaroy, NSW, and northern Tas.
Maximum size: Arm radius to 65 mm.

A six-armed species, *Patiriella brevispina* can be recognised most easily underwater by the dark tan or purple body surface, which contrasts with bright orange tube feet. This seastar can be extremely abundant on the edge of sheltered reefs or seagrass beds, where animals lift their arms into the water column and attempt to trap drifting plant or animal material.

Patiriella brevispina, Princess Royal Harbour, WA

Patiriella vivipara Dartnall, 1969

Habitat: Sheltered rocky shores; low intertidal.
Distribution: Eaglehawk Neck to Margate, Tas.
Maximum size: Arm radius to 15 mm.

Patiriella vivipara and the very close relative *P. parvivipara* are unusual among seastars in brooding young within their bodies and releasing them directly through the upper body wall. Probably because they lack the dispersive planktonic stage of most other asteroids, these two species have extremely restricted ranges. *Patiriella vivipara* is known from only four small areas of rock platform in southeastern Tasmania, each no bigger than a hectare. It is the only species in the region with a uniform apricot colour.

Patiriella vivipara, Eaglehawk Neck, Tas.

Patiriella parvivipara Keough and Dartnall, 1978

Habitat: Moderately exposed rock pools; low intertidal.
Distribution: Ceduna to D'Anville Bay, SA.
Maximum size: Arm radius to 5 mm.

Patiriella parvivipara is the smallest seastar known in Australia, growing to a maximum diameter of less than 1 cm. Because of its small size and restricted distribution on the western Eyre Peninsula, the species was first recognised only in 1975. Like *P. vivipara* the species broods the young internally and releases them individually through the body wall (a newly released juvenile can be observed in the photo). The species is a pale orange colour; when held up to the light, developing young may be seen internally.

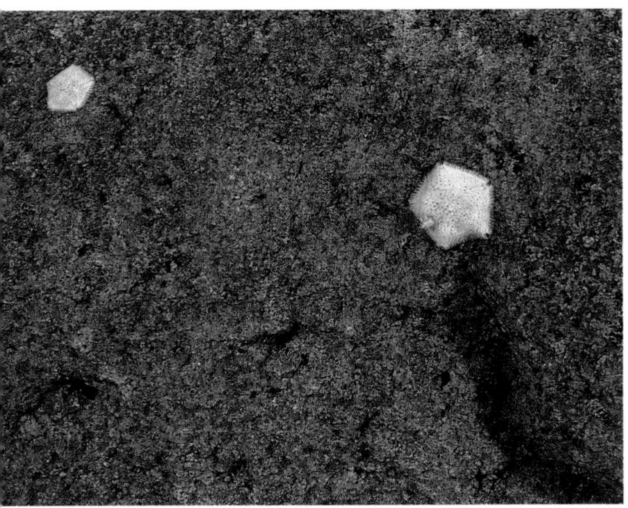

Patiriella parvivipara, Smooth Pool, SA

Patiriella regularis (Verrill, 1867)

Habitat: Sheltered rocky shores; mid intertidal to 5 m depth.
Distribution: Derwent estuary, Tas. Also New Zealand.
Maximum size: Arm radius to 35 mm.

Patiriella regularis is an olive green species with some similarity to the smaller intertidal species *P. exigua*, although that species has a more brownish coloration. Within Australia, *Patiriella regularis* has only been found in southeastern Tasmania but is a dominant species on intertidal rocks in that area and appears to outcompete other grazing seastars. It feeds on the film of algae and microbes coating rock surfaces. Like a number of other species (e.g. the screw shell *Maoricolpus roseus*, the chiton *Chiton glaucus* and the crab *Cancer novaezelandiae*), this species is believed to have been accidentally introduced into the country when transported to Tasmania with oysters early this century. The species is doubtfully recorded from Newcastle, NSW.

FAMILY ASTERIIDAE

The family Asteriidae contains species that lack large marginal plates, have numerous pedicellariae on the upper surface and have four rows of tube feet, in contrast to the two rows of tube feet in the preceding families. Most species have long arms, which merge into the central disc, and one or two rows of spines along the ambulacral grooves. This family is extremely diverse in the Northern Hemisphere but contains few species in southern Australia and only one species in the tropics.

Coscinasterias muricata Verrill, 1867

Habitat: Sheltered reef, silt, sand; 0–150 m depth.
Distribution: Houtman Abrolhos, WA, to southern Qld and around Tas. Also New Zealand.
Maximum size: Arm radius to 250 mm.

Patiriella regularis, Sandy Bay, Tas.

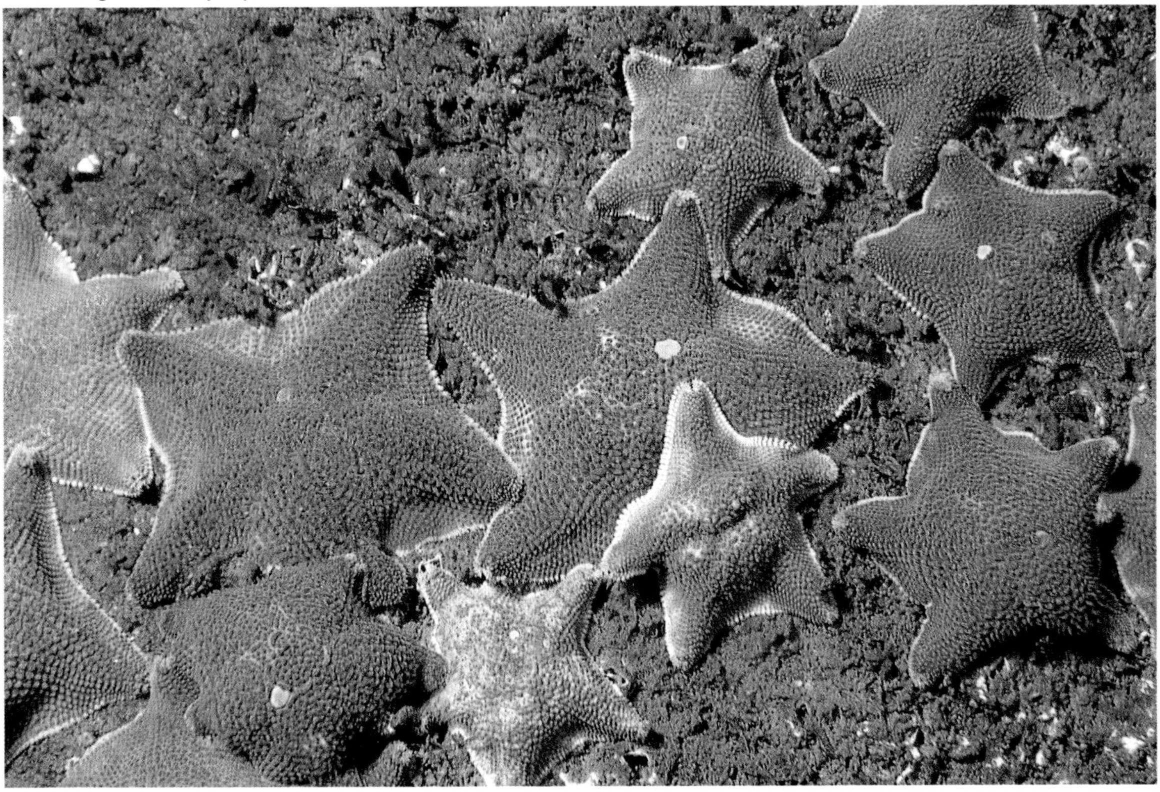

Coscinasterias muricata is the largest species of seastar found in southern Australia and occurs with great abundance in sheltered habitats. The species was called *Coscinasterias calamaria* until recently, a name now reserved for a close tropical relative, which has slightly differently shaped plates on the arms. *Coscinasterias muricata* has a mottled appearance, with rows of large spines surrounded by rings of crossed pedicellariae along its upper surface. The number of arms is usually eleven, but can vary from seven to fourteen. Each arm can regenerate into a complete animal if attached to a small piece of disc. While the species can also act as a scavenger, *C. muricata* is such an active predator of molluscs in sheltered marine habitats that it is considered a keystone species; it can alter community structure by preventing the establishment of beds of mussels, scallops, etc.

Astrostole scabra, Waterfall Bay, Tas.

Coscinasterias muricata, Sandy Bay, Tas.

Astrostole scabra (Hutton, 1872)

Habitat: Exposed reef, 3–146 m depth.
Distribution: Eddystone Point to Port Davey, Tas. Also New Zealand.
Maximum size: Arm radius to 220 mm.

Astrostole scabra is rarely recognised but occurs commonly in crevices on exposed reefs along the eastern Tasmanian coast. It is similar in appearance to *Coscinasterias muricata* but has seven arms only and bright orange tube feet. The species had not been recorded in Tasmania until late this century but is abundant in New Zealand and was probably introduced from that country.

Asterias amurensis Lütken, 1871

Habitat: Silt, sand, sheltered reef; 0–35 m depth.
Distribution: Port Phillip Bay, Vic., and Triabunna to Dover, Tas. Also Japan, China, Russia, Alaska.
Maximum size: Arm radius to 230 mm.

Asterias amurensis, Sandy Bay, Tas.

Asterias amurensis, Sandy Bay, Tas.

Asterias amurensis has been recently introduced into southeastern Tasmania, probably with ballast water on a ship from Japan or Korea. In appearance it can be confused only with *Uniophora granifera* but differs from that species by having distinctly pointed arms and two rows of spines (as opposed to one) along the ambulacral groove on the underside. Juvenile animals generally have blotches of purple on a yellowish background, but these tend to disappear as the animal matures. It is an active predator, preferring bivalve molluscs and heart urchins but also ingesting a variety of other food items. At present the species is largely confined to degraded habitats in the Derwent estuary and to shellfish farms in the D'Entrecasteaux Channel. Because of concern about the impact of this seastar on other species, any sightings outside this range should be reported to the local museum.

Uniophora granifera (Lamarck, 1816)

Habitat: Sheltered reef, silt, seagrass; 0–30 m depth.
Distribution: Spencer Gulf, SA, to Solitary I, NSW, and around Tas.
Maximum size: Arm radius to 120 mm.

Uniophora granifera is a variably coloured species with a smooth upper surface covered by blunt spines or rounded tubercles, which often form a zigzag pattern down the centre of each arm. The arrangement of these spines and tubercles is extremely variable, causing several forms to be originally described as different species. *Uniophora granifera* can be found in a variety of habitats but seems to be most common on sheltered rock surfaces.

Uniophora granifera, D'Entrecasteaux Channel, Tas.

Uniophora dyscrita (H.L. Clark, 1923)

Habitat: Sheltered reef, silt, seagrass; 2–185 m depth.
Distribution: Lancelin to Esperance, WA.
Maximum size: Arm radius to 70 mm.

Uniophora dyscrita, Busselton, WA

Uniophora dyscrita is very similar to *U. granifera*, hence, while presently recognised as different, may yet prove to be the Western Australian population of a single widely distributed species. *Uniophora dyscrita* is less common than *U. granifera* and is distinguished by the flattened shape of the spines on the lower side plates (inferomarginal plates). A third *Uniophora* species, ***Uniophora nuda***, with a smooth upper surface, occurs in South Australian waters. *Uniophora dyscrita* is rare in shallow water through most of its range but is occasionally seen in Cockburn Sound and Geographe Bay. The illustrated animal has lost an arm.

Allostichaster polyplax

(Muller & Troschel, 1844)

Habitat: Under rocks; 0–130 m depth.
Distribution: Houtman Abrolhos, WA, to Solitary I, NSW, and around Tas. Also New Zealand.
Maximum size: Arm radius to 44 mm.

Allostichaster polyplax is a small, long-armed seastar commonly found under rocks. The number of arms is generally eight but ranges from six to nine, and several of these arms are usually noticeably smaller than others. This species reproduces by dividing asexually as well as by normal sexual means; each half of the original animal grows new arms to replace those lost. Occasionally an animal is found with a single large arm and seven small, recently formed stumps. A related species with five regular arms (***Allostichaster regularis***) is found from South Australia to Southern Queensland.

Allostichaster polyplax, Bathurst Channel, Tas.

Smilasterias irregularis H.L. Clark, 1928

Habitat: Sheltered reef; 1–30 m depth.
Distribution: Nuyts Archpelago, SA, to Shellharbour, NSW, and northern Tas.
Maximum size: Arm radius to 65 mm.

Smilasterias irregularis is a five-armed species with a similar general appearance to *Allostichaster polyplax*, but with proportionately longer and thinner arms and without the spinelets on the upper surface forming a regular pattern. The colour is usually light pink, mottled with maroon. It is a cryptic species, generally remaining concealed under rock rubble during the day. Its distribution is highly patchy; in some locations it occurs abundantly, but through much of its geographic range the species is absent from apparently suitable areas.

Smilasterias irregularis, Port Victoria, SA

Smilasterias multipara

O'Loughlin & O'Hara, 1990

Habitat: Sheltered reef; 0–5 m depth.
Distribution: Cape Bridgewater to Wilsons Promontory, Vic., and north and east Tas.
Maximum size: Arm radius to 38 mm.

Smilasterias multipara is a recently described species with a small central disc and five long arms. It has a light background coloration and dark grey markings on the upper surface, which sometimes produce a banded appearance. In contrast to its close relative *S. irregularis*, *S. multipara* rarely loses its arms. It is predatory, feeding primarily on small molluscs. A third species in the genus, ***Smilasterias tasmaniae***, occurs in shallow waters in southeastern Tasmania. This species can be distinguished from the others by shorter and wider arms — the ratio of arm length/greatest arm width is less than 4:1 for *S. tasmaniae* and greater than 4:1 for the other two species.

Smilasterias multipara, Rocky Cape, Tas.

Smilasterias tasmaniae, Spring Beach, Tas.

Class Ophiuroidea

Brittle stars

Ophiuroids have a distinct central disc and five slender arms, which in some species are branched. The arms differ from the arms of asteroids because they are solid rather than hollow, lack internal reproductive and digestive organs, and although nerves and an extension of the water vascular system run along the underside, they have no obvious ambulacral groove. Each arm is constructed from small interlocking segments, which often have a vertical row of spines. Brittle stars move by the sinuous flexing of the arms rather than by the movement of tube feet. However, tube feet are present in a reduced form and are used for feeding, respiration and as sense organs. The mouth and madreporite (the plate covering the external opening of the water vascular system) are located on the undersurface among a complex arrangement of spines, papillae and plates. Ten internal respiratory chambers with slit-like openings (the bursae) are located between the jaw and the bases of the arms. Identification of brittle star species depends mainly on the arrangement of the various structural elements surrounding the jaws and on the shape and number of spines on the arms.

Most brittle star species feed on small organic particles, which are transported by tube feet along the arms. Some of the larger species capture worms and other bottom-dwelling prey. A few filter-feeding brittle stars are also known. These species, which include the basket stars, can occur in very high abundances at sites with appropriate conditions. They feed by raising arms into the current and capturing copepods and other planktonic organisms using the tube feet. If attacked by fishes or other predators, the arms of ophiuroids are readily sacrificed and can be quickly regenerated.

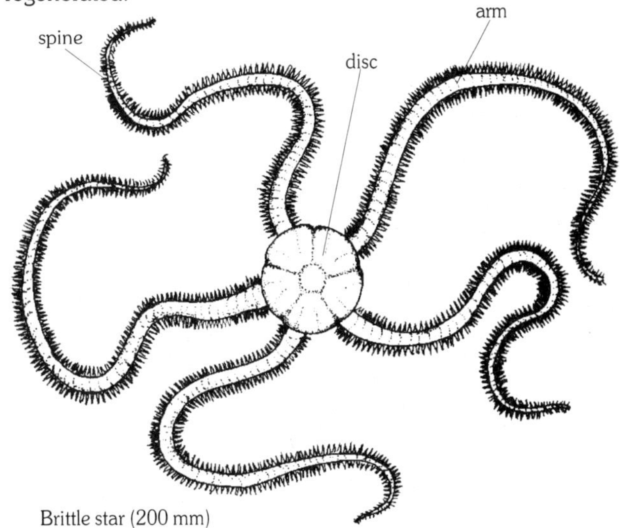

Brittle star (200 mm)
Ophionereis schayeri
Class Ophiuroidea

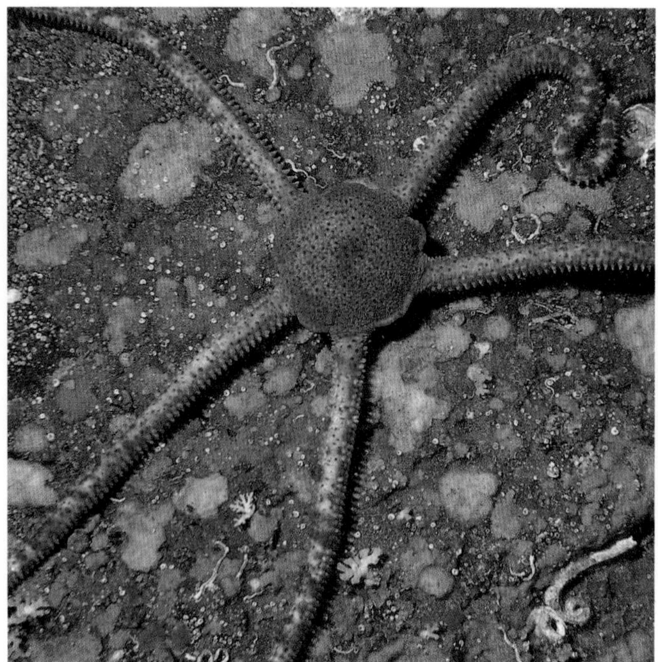

Ophiomyxa australis, Bathurst Channel, Tas.

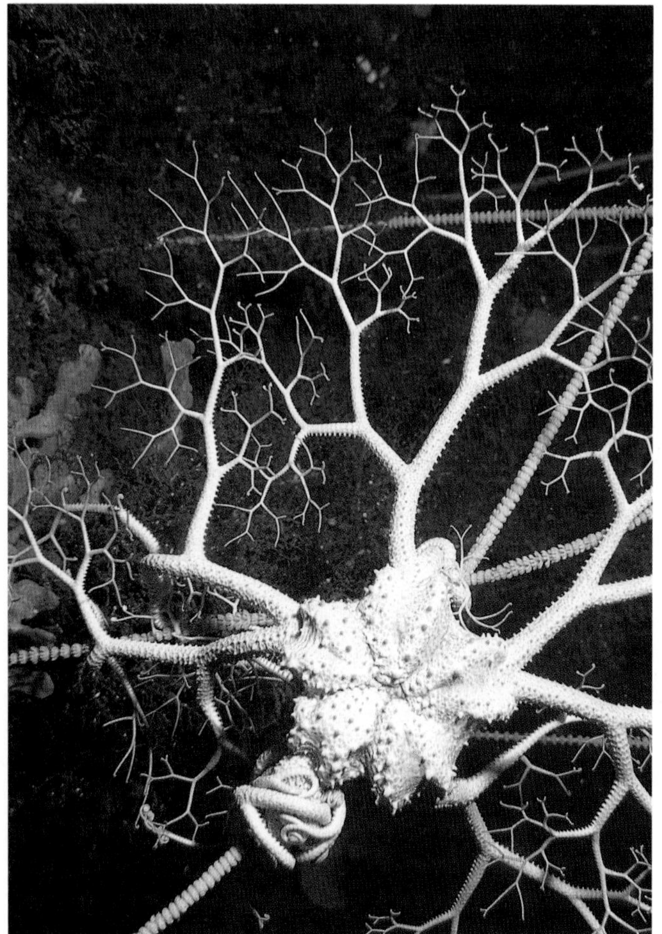

Conocladus australis, Bathurst Channel, Tas.

FAMILY OPHIOMYXIDAE

Ophiomyxids are a distinctive group of brittle stars with a thick skin covering on the disc and arms. Spines penetrate through the skin on the sides of the arms and are aligned in vertical rows. Only a single species is known from shallow Australian waters.

Ophiomyxa australis Lütken, 1869

Habitat: Under rocks; 0–1000 m depth.
Distribution: Around Australia, including Tas. Also through the Indo-West Pacific region.
Maximum size: Disc diameter to 35 mm, arm length to 140 mm.

Ophiomyxa australis can be recognised by the soft skin covering the plates on the disc and the upper arm surface, and by up to six short, sharp spines on each arm segment. Its pattern varies considerably between individuals, with some animals having inconspicuous fleck marks on the disc and others large spots or blobs. The colour is also highly variable, although reds and browns usually predominate.

FAMILY GORGONOCEPHALIDAE
Basket stars

This is the most easily recognised family of ophiuroids as it contains species with branched arms that are very flexible and capable of flexing up and down as well as from side to side. The body and arms are enclosed in a thick skin, and two or three spinelets are usually present on each arm side plate. Basket stars capture small planktonic animals and usually live attached to fixed animals and plants on reefs. During daylight they remain with their long arms enfolded; at night and on overcast days they expand the arms to feed.

Conocladus australis (Verrill, 1876)

Habitat: Exposed reef; 4–430 m depth.
Distribution: Jurien Bay, WA, to southern Qld, and around Tas.
Maximum size: Disc diameter to 55 mm, arm length to 150 mm.

Conocladus australis is the most abundant basket star found in temperate Australian waters and is commonly observed attached to sponges, gorgonians and sea whips on deep reefs. Its colour pattern usually consists of a light grey base with dark bands, although some specimens (such as the one illustrated) lack dark markings. Numerous raised tubercles on the disc and arms sometimes produce a ridged effect.

Astroboa ernae Döderlein, 1911

Habitat: Exposed reef; 0–80 m depth.
Distribution: Shark Bay, WA, to central SA.
Maximum size: Disc diameter to 50 mm, arm length to 150 mm.

Astroboa ernae has a dusky pink coloration with much finer granules over the disc and arms than *Conocladus australis*. During the day it tends to live on reefs or low on sponges or gorgonians and at night it moves onto a higher perch where it unfolds to feed on plankton.

Astroboa ernae, Esperance, WA

Astrosierra amblyconus (H.L. Clark, 1909)

Habitat: Exposed reef; 18–640 m depth.
Distribution: Sandon Bluffs, NSW, to Babel I, Tas.
Maximum size: Disc diameter to 50 mm, arm length to 150 mm.

Astrosierra amblyconus shows little variation in colour pattern, with a light pink basal colour and large tubercles over the disc and arms. The species feeds on planktonic crustaceans in a similar way to the other basket stars. It is occasionally seen by divers in deep water along the southern New South Wales coast and is probably common below normal diving depths.

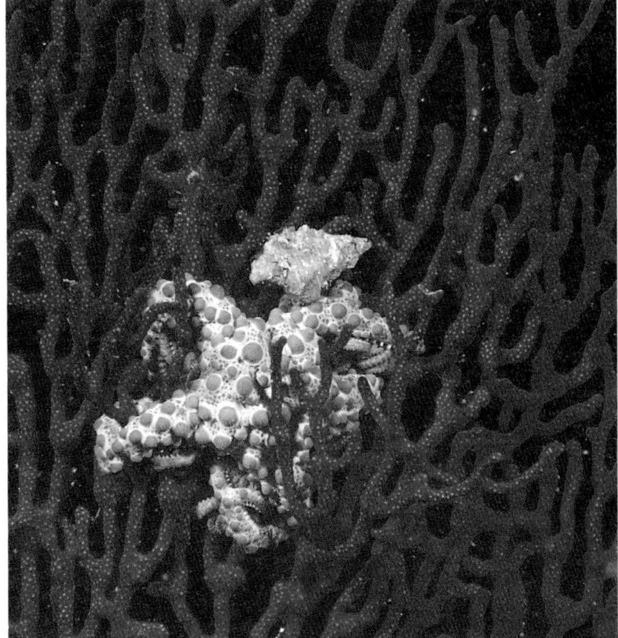

Astrosierra amblyconus, Bermagui, NSW. RUDIE KUITER

FAMILY OPHIACTIDAE

Ophiactids are characterised by the shape of the jaws, particularly the presence of a single broad plate at the end of each of the five sets of teeth. They have a well-developed arrangement of scales on the upper disc, often with a rosette of five radial plates arranged around a small central one. Most species have relatively short arms and live under rocks and in crevices.

Ophiactis resiliens Lyman, 1879

Habitat: Under rocks; 0–165 m depth.
Distribution: Rottnest I, WA, to southern Qld and around Tas. Also Lord Howe I and New Zealand.
Maximum size: Disc diameter to 9 mm, arm length to 50 mm.

Ophiactis resiliens generally has a patchy dark grey or brown disc with rectangular blotches along the upper surface of the arms and a cream undersurface of both disc and arms. The large scales (the radial shields) on the upper disc beside the base of the arms are elongate and have white outer edges; small spines occur on the edge of the disk between the arms. This species is common but not often noticed.

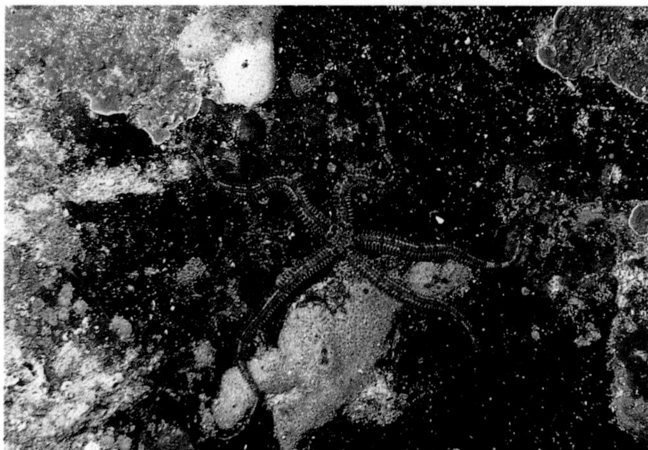

Ophiactis resiliens, Bicheno, Tas.

FAMILY OPHIOTRICHIDAE

Species in this family have the disc covered by thorny stumps or spines, and serrated arm spines that usually have a glassy appearance. Compared with other brittle star families, ophiotrichids exhibit little variation in jaw structure; the position of arm plates and spines and the arrangement of scales on the disc covering are the major features used in the identification of species. Most species in the family occur in the tropics, where they are commonly found entwined in corals and sponges.

Ophiothrix spongicola Stimpson, 1855

Habitat: Under rocks; 0–183 m depth.
Distribution: Houtman Abrolhos, WA, to southern Qld.
Maximum size: Disc diameter to 25 mm, arm length to 150 mm.

Ophiothrix spongicola is a large brittle star with sinuous arms and a general appearance similar to *Ophionereis schayeri*. However, unlike that species, the disc is covered by short spinelets except on the five paired triangular areas near the ends of the arms (the radial shields), and each arm segment has eight to ten serrated spines, which are as long as the arm width. The banding pattern on the arms, with alternate bands of purple (sometimes blue) edged with yellow and cream/pink, generally also allows the species to be recognised.

Ophiothrix spongicola, Esperance, WA

Ophiothrix caespitosa Lyman, 1879

Habitat: Bryozoans, sponges, algae; 0–137 m depth.
Distribution: Shark Bay, WA, to southern Qld and northern Tas.
Maximum size: Disc diameter to 10 mm, arm length to 50 mm.

Ophiothrix caespitosa occurs abundantly among plants and sessile animals on coastal reefs but is not often observed because of its preference for small cracks. The species is very spiny, with the disc covered by a field of small spinelets and eight to ten long, thin spines on each arm segment. The colour is usually pink and light brown with red stripes on the arms, but yellow animals are also sometimes found.

Ophiothrix caespitosa, Rocky Cape, Tas.

FAMILY OPHIOCOMIDAE

The disc and arm bases of ophiocomids are often obscured by skin. The disc scales are usually densely covered with granules or spinelets, and the arms have spines that are often solid and long. Compared with other brittle stars, ophiocomids species are generally large and active.

Clarkcoma canaliculata (Lütken, 1869)

Habitat: Under rocks; 0–40 m depth.
Distribution: Shark Bay, WA, to Sydney, NSW, and around Tas.
Maximum size: Disc diameter to 25 mm, arm length to 75 mm.

Clarkcoma canaliculata is abundant under rocks in the lower intertidal zone and in shallow depths; it is particularly common under large, unstable rocks that sit on smaller rocks or gravel. This brittle star has short arms and long arm spines, some of which are swollen at their tips. The colour is normally chocolate brown, dark purple or dark red.

Clarkcoma canaliculata, Ile des Phoques, Tas.

Clarkcoma pulchra, Esperance, WA

Clarkcoma pulchra (H.L. Clark, 1928)

Habitat: Under rocks; 0–40 m depth.
Distribution: Dongara, WA, to Byron Bay, NSW.
Maximum size: Disc diameter to 21 mm, arm length to 70 mm.

Until recently, *Clarkcoma pulchra* was considered to be a colour variant of *C. canaliculata*, but consistent differences in the size and density of granules on the undersurface and in the shape of the dorsal arm plates and arm spines indicate that the two species are distinct. *Clarkcoma pulchra* is found in a similar habitat to *C. canaliculata* but can be immediately recognised by the banded purple and cream arm spines. A third species in the genus, ***Clarkcoma bollonsi***, is found from Dongara, WA, to Mooloolaba, Qld, in deep water (9–630 m). It is an orange-brown colour, with the outer edge of each upper arm plate bearing a cream line.

FAMILY OPHIONEREIDIDAE

Ophionereids have a disc that overlies the arm bases, disc scales that generally lack spines, small oral shields, long arms that narrow slightly at the base, and prominent arm spines. The family contains relatively few species, nearly all of which are restricted to the tropics.

Ophionereis schayeri (Müller & Troschel, 1844)

Habitat: Under rocks; 0–183 m depth.
Distribution: Shark Bay, WA, to Collaroy, NSW, and around Tas.
Maximum size: Disc diameter to 30 mm, arm length to 150 mm.

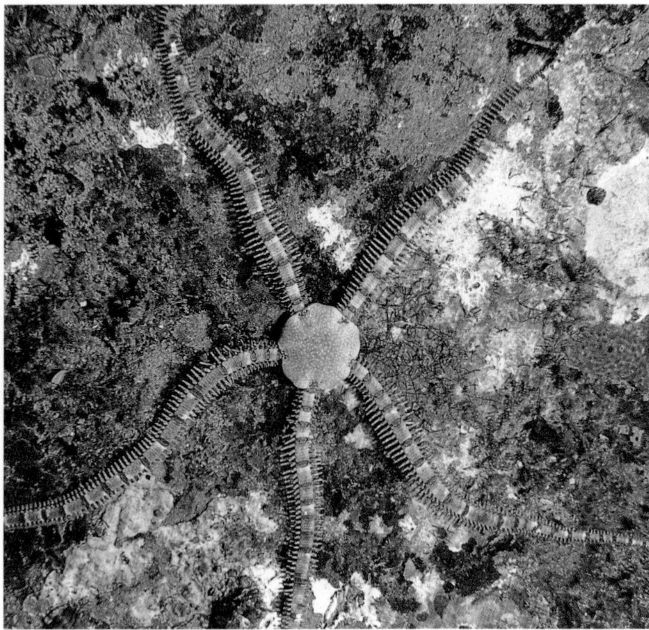

Ophionereis schayeri, Rocky Cape, Tas.

Ophionereis schayeri usually shows little variation in colour pattern; it has a greyish-brown disc with white spots, and snake-like arms with alternate dark grey (sometimes black), light grey and cream bands. This is the most commonly seen large brittle star and is abundant under large flat rocks in shallow water.

FAMILY OPHIODERMATIDAE

Ophiodermatids have the disc and arm bases covered by a layer of small, densely packed granules. These completely obscure the oral shields in some species and partially cover them in others. The arm spines are relatively short and lie pressed against the sides of the arms.

Ophiarachnella ramsayi (Bell, 1888)

Habitat: Under rocks; 0–73 m depth.
Distribution: Houtman Abrolhos, WA, to southern Qld and northern Tas.
Maximum size: Disc diameter to 35 mm, arm length to 150 mm.

Ophiarachnella ramsayi is found in the same habitat as *Ophionereis schayeri* and often under the same rocks. Numerous spines (up to 14) are present on each arm segment but they are very small and pressed closely against the arm. The species usually has a reddish disc and alternating brown and pink, or green and red, bands down the arm.

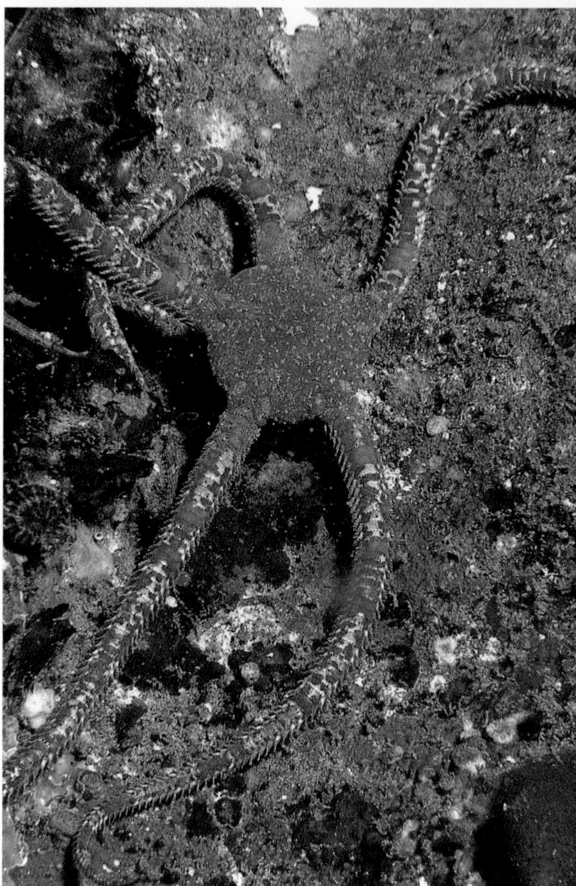

Ophiarachnella ramsayi, Esperance, WA

Ophiopsammus assimilis (Bell, 1888)

Habitat: Under rocks; 0–594 m depth.
Distribution: Dongara, WA, to Byron Bay, NSW.
Maximum size: Disc diameter to 30 mm, arm length to 90 mm.

Ophiopsammus assimilis can be recognised by the mottled pattern of reds, oranges and browns, the concave shape of the disc between the arms, the concealed radial shields and the very fine surface layer of granules that cover the disc. This brittle star can move very rapidly.

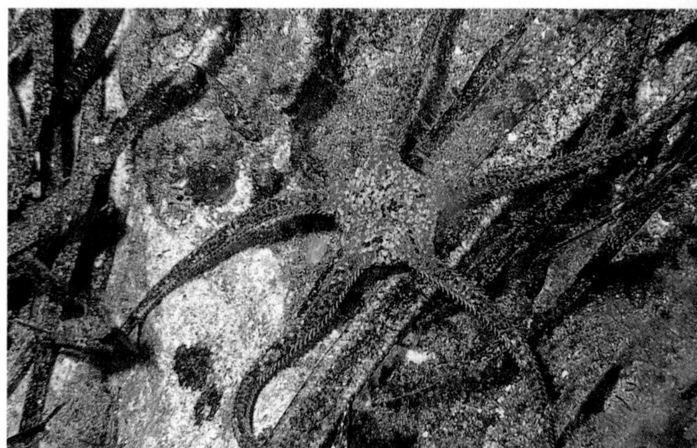

Ophiopsammus assimilis, Port Victoria, SA

Ophiopeza cylindrica (Hutton, 1872)

Habitat: Under rocks; 0–144 m depth.
Distribution: Dongara, WA, to Coffs Harbour, NSW. Also New Zealand.
Maximum size: Disc diameter to 12 mm, arm length to 35 mm.

Ophiopeza cylindrica resembles a small *Ophiopsammus assimilis* and is chiefly differentiated on the shape of radial shield plates hidden below the granulated disc surface. It is usually darkly coloured, with light bands on the arms, and the area around the mouth is cream. The species has been studied in New Zealand waters and found to bear live young.

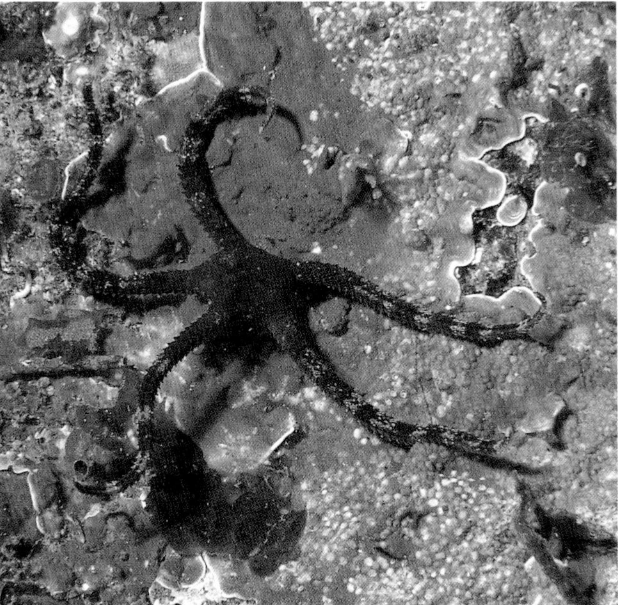

Ophiopeza cylindrica, Esperance, WA

FAMILY OPHIURIDAE

Temperate ophiurids are generally small and have short arms. The disc surrounds rather than overlies the arm bases and is covered by small scales. This is the dominant family in deep water, but only a small number of species occur at divable depths.

Ophioplocus bispinosus H.L. Clark, 1918

Habitat: Under rocks; 0–50 m depth.
Distribution: West I, SA, to Wilsons Promontory, Vic., and around Tas.
Maximum size: Disc diameter to 10 mm, arm length to 25 mm.

Ophioplocus bispinosus is a small grey brittle star with arms that are stiff and have a gradual taper. It differs from other species included here by having only two spines per arm segment; these spines are very small and not particularly noticeable. The species is rarely seen, but this may be because of its small size and cryptic rock-dwelling habit rather than low abundance.

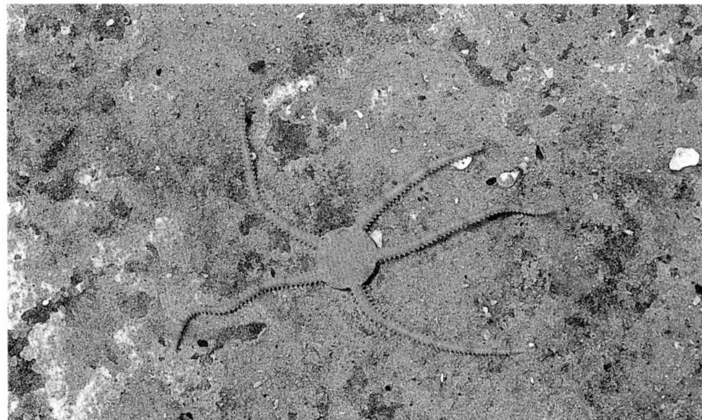

Ophioplocus bispinosus, Spring Beach, Tas.

Ophiura kinbergi (Ljungman, 1866)

Habitat: Sand, silt; 2–500 m depth.
Distribution: Around the Australian mainland and Tas. Also widespread in the Indo-West Pacific region.
Maximum size: Disc diameter to 10 mm, arm length to 15 mm.

Ophiura kinbergi is a small species with a similar general appearance to *Ophioplocus bispinosus* but differing by having three short narrow spines on each arm segment and combs of small spines around the bases of the arms. The upper surface is a mottled brown colour, and the undersurface is white. The species occurs abundantly in localised patches on soft sediments, where it can be seen skating quickly across the surface by rapidly flexing the leading arms.

Ophiura kinbergi, Sandy Bay, Tas.

Class Echinoidea

Sea urchins, sand dollars, heart urchins

Echinoids are globular or flattened animals with an outer shell (the test) made up of hundreds of interlocking calcareous plates. The test is covered by a thin skin and is rounded and globular in the sea urchins, rounded and flattened in the sand dollars, and heart-shaped and inflated in the heart urchins. In sea urchins and sand dollars the test is divided into five equal segments, each with a pair of vertical rows of plates bearing holes for tube feet (the ambulacral plates) and a pair of often larger plates lacking holes (the interambulacral plates). At the top of the test is an anus surrounded by small irregularly shaped plates and then ten large plates, five of which have pores for the release of sperm and eggs. The heart urchins and sand dollars have the anus located at the rear of the test or on the undersurface. They also have a star-shaped arrangement of pores with associated grooves (the petals) on the upper surface.

All echinoids have numerous spines projecting from the test. Several types of spines are usually present on sea urchins, with the large (primary) spines often having barbs and other sculpturing. Spines are moved by muscles and articulate with the test on knob-like processes on the plates, known as tubercles. Echinoids also possess pincer-like pedicellaria on the outer surface; these are used in defence and for the capture of food. The pedicellaria of several species are connected to poison sacs, and at least one tropical species with very large pedicellaria has caused human fatalities.

Sea urchins feed using a complex arrangement of rods and plates positioned behind the mouth, known as Aristotle's lantern. The tip of this structure consists of five beak-like teeth, which protrude from the mouth and grind food. Sediment-dwelling sand dollars have a different arrangement of teeth to help direct sand and silt into the mouth; heart urchins lack teeth and utilise the fine organic matter mixed with sediment for nutrition, aided (in some species) by symbiotic bacteria within the gut. Nearly all sea urchins are omnivorous scavengers, usually ingesting plants but also consuming animal material when available. Because large quantities of plant material are required by each animal for nutrition, species that occur in high densities are potentially able to destroy macroalgal or seagrass beds.

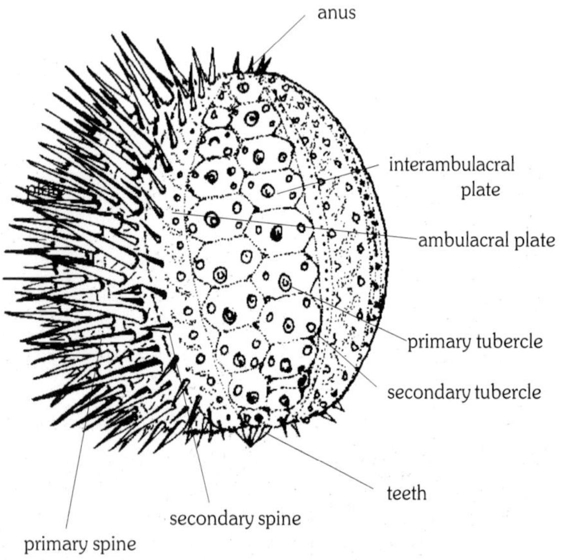

Sea urchin (100 mm)
Class Echinoidea

FAMILY CIDARIDAE

This is a widely distributed family of sea urchins that can be readily identified by the solid primary spines; only one primary spine is attached to each plate, and this spine often has a ring of secondary spines around the base. The family is well represented as fossils.

Goniocidaris tubaria (Lamarck, 1816)

Habitat: Sheltered and moderately exposed reef, silt; 0–630 m depth.
Distribution: Dongara, WA, to Ballina, NSW, and around Tas.
Maximum size: Test diameter to 60 mm, primary spines to 80 mm.

Goniocidaris tubaria is the most distinctive southern Australian sea urchin. It has large, serrated primary spines, which are often eroded and covered by sessile invertebrates, and platelike secondary spines, which form a corona-like structure around the base of the primary spines. This species is frequently seen in Tasmanian and Victorian waters and tends to occur at greater depth in the more northern section of its range.

Prionocidaris callista Rowe & Hoggett, 1986

Habitat: Reef, rubble; 1–200 m depth.
Distribution: Central NSW to southern Qld.
Maximum size: Test diameter to 70 mm, primary spines to 120 mm.

Goniocidaris tubaria, D'Entrecasteaux Channel, Tas.

Prionocidaris callista is a striking echinoid with purple coloration and large, serrated primary spines, which taper to a much finer point than the spines of *Goniocidaris tubaria*. This species is usually found in relatively deep water on the sides of channels in areas of strong current flow.

Prionocidaris callista, Port Stephens, NSW

Phyllacanthus parvispinus

Tenison-Woods, 1880

Eastern slate-pencil urchin

Habitat: Exposed reef; 0–80 m depth.
Distribution: Cape Howe, NSW, to Moreton Bay, Qld.
Maximum size: Test diameter to 90 mm, primary spines to 70 mm.

Phyllacanthus parvispinus, North Head, NSW

Phyllacanthus parvispinus is a solid dark-purple urchin with large rounded primary spines, which are usually eroded. Like *Goniocidaris tubaria,* the secondary spines are flat and most obvious around the base of the larger spines. The species uses its blunt primary spines to wedge rigidly into crevices during the day and thus can survive in areas with heavy wave action. It feeds at night on encrusting plants and animals scraped from the reef surface.

Phyllacanthus irregularis Mortensen, 1928

Western slate-pencil urchin

Habitat: Exposed reef; 1–20 m depth.
Distribution: Houtman Abrolhos, WA, to Gulf St Vincent, SA.
Maximum size: Test diameter to 110 mm, primary spines to 70 mm.

Phyllacanthus irregularis is very similar in general appearance to *P. parvispinus* and lives in a similar habitat. It can, however, be distinguished from the eastern species by possessing small pointed spinelets at the top of the test, rather than broad and scale-like spinelets. *Phyllacanthus irregularis* is most commonly found in shallow undercut caves in limestone reefs.

Phyllacanthus irregularis, Marmion Lagoon, WA

FAMILY DIADEMATIDAE

Diadematids have rounded, slightly flattened tests and primary spines that are long, slender, hollow and easily broken. The tubercles at the base of the primary spines usually have a ring with an undulating margin. Most species in the family are found in shallow tropical seas.

Centrostephanus rodgersii, Bicheno, Tas.

Centrostephanus rodgersii (Agassiz, 1863)

Habitat: Exposed reef; 0–35 m depth.
Distribution: Cape Everard, Vic., to Port Stephens, NSW, and south to Tasman Peninsula, Tas.
Maximum size: Test diameter to 100 mm, primary spines to 75 mm.

Centrostephanus rodgersii is the dominant sea urchin in shallow water along the New South Wales coast. When observed alive, the species has an iridescent turquoise sheen on most spine surfaces and a red sheen on individual spines when the observer is looking down the shaft. The spines of the two *Centrostephanus* species differ from those of other temperate Australian sea urchins (including the most common species, *Heliocidaris erythrogramma*) because they are hollow rather than having a solid core. *Centrostephanus rodgersii* generally occurs in large numbers and can alter community structure on reefs by eliminating kelps and other large macroalgae, causing barren areas of 'white rock'. The species seems to be spreading southwards along the Tasmanian coast; isolated specimens were first recognised in the northeast of the state only in 1978 but aggregations have now created barren areas in that region, and isolated specimens occur much further south.

Centrostephanus tenuispinus H.L. Clark, 1914

Habitat: Moderately exposed reef; 0–104 m depth.
Distribution: Shark Bay, WA, to Spencer Gulf, SA.
Maximum size: Test diameter to 90 mm, primary spines to 70 mm.

Centrostephanus tenuispinus, Esperance, WA

Centrostephanus tenuispinus has a general appearance similar to *C. rodgersii*, except for a slate grey rather than turquoise colour and thinner spines relative to their length. The species also tends to prefer concealment more than its relative and to remain wedged in crevices.

Diadema palmeri Baker, 1967

Habitat: Exposed reef; 10–60 m depth
Distribution: Montague I to Coffs Harbour, NSW. Also New Zealand.
Maximum size: Test diameter to 70 mm, primary spines to 150 mm.

The genus *Diadema* is largely restricted to tropical areas, where the various species with needle-sharp spines are the dominant sea urchins in shallow lagoons. However, *Diadema palmeri* is found only on the deeper temperate reefs off New South Wales and New Zealand. When observed underwater it has a dark appearance, but torchlight or sunlight reveals intense orange-red hues and, in the centre of the upper surface, a light-brown structure (the anal cone) with a black central spot.

FAMILY TEMNOPLEURIDAE

Temnopleurids can usually be recognised by the numerous short primary spines, which are small, solid and smooth. The pore-pairs in the test (through which tube feet pass) may be in one, two or three vertical series on ambulacral plates. About half the southern Australian sea urchin species are included in this family.

Amblypneustes ovum (Lamarck, 1816)

Habitat: Sheltered and moderately exposed reef; 0–70 m depth.
Distribution: Spencer Gulf, SA, to Cape Liptrap, Vic., and around Tas.
Maximum size: Test diameter to 60 mm, primary spines to 5 mm.

Sea urchins in the genus *Amblypneustes* are restricted to temperate Australian waters. They are distinguished from short-spined sea urchins in the genus

Diadema palmeri, Montague I, NSW. RUDIE KUITER

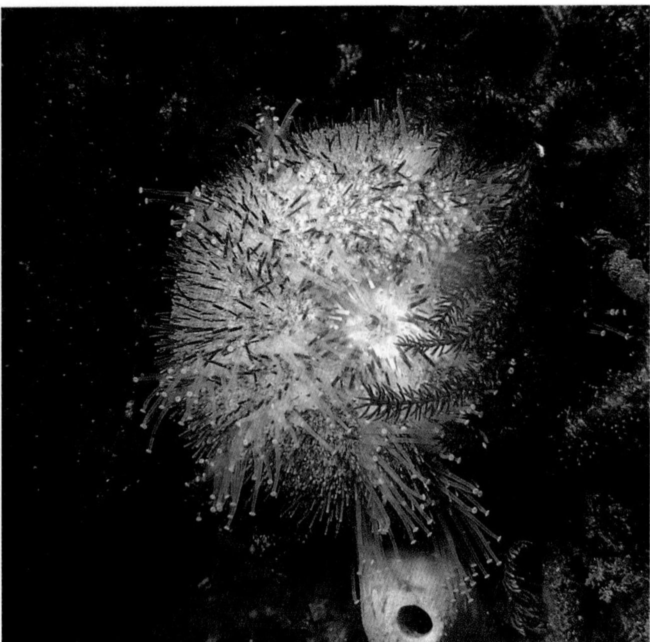
Amblypneutes ovum, Dennes Pt, Tas.

Holopneustes by possessing a single primary spine at the edge of each of the test plates with holes for tube feet (the ambulacral plates). In contrast, species of *Holopneustes* have a primary spine only at the edge of every second or third ambulactral plate. This is best observed on old broken tests because the ambulacral plates are easiest to distinguish on the inside of the test, and the tubercles at the base of primary spines are obvious only on the outer surface. At present, there is no consensus about the number of species of *Amblypneustes* in southern Australia because the species have not been studied as a group, and a number of different forms may or may not differ sufficiently to comprise separate species. *Amblypneustes ovum*, as originally described, has test width approximately equal to height, and the test pores through which tube feet pass are lined up in vertical series. Closely related species are ***Amblypneustes pachistus***, a southern Australian species with the test pores not in vertical series, and ***Amblypneustes grandis***, a large (to 85 mm diameter) southern Australian species with test width greater than height (a ratio of 1.2:1). Most species of *Amblypneustes* are commonly associated with macroalgal fronds but also can be found on bare reef surfaces.

Amblypneustes leucoglobus Döderlain, 1914

Habitat: Moderately exposed seagrasses, reef; 0–10 m depth.
Distribution: Geraldton to Eucla, WA.
Maximum size: Test diameter to 50 mm, primary spines to 5 mm.

Amblypneustes leucoglobus is a small sea urchin with light-coloured tube feet, dark green primary spines, and small white knobs on the ends of very short secondary spines. The species is occasionally detected by divers but generally remains concealed among plants.

Amblypneustes leucoglobus, Marmion Lagoon, WA

Amblypneustes pallidus (Lamarck, 1816)

Habitat: Sheltered and moderately exposed reef, seagrass; 1–180 m depth.
Distribution: Houtman Abrolhos, WA, to Port Willunga, SA.
Maximum size: Test diameter to 25 mm, primary spines to 4 mm.

Amblypneustes pallidus is a small, short-spined species with a distinctive appearance. The primary spines are yellow with pink tips, the secondary spines pink and the tube feet long and dark. Like a very closely related sea urchin found in the eastern states, ***Amblypneustes formosus***, the species has a distinctive zigzag pattern of diamond-shaped patches running down the interambulacral area of the test. *Amblypneustes pallidus* is rarely seen by divers, perhaps because of its small size, but is sometimes caught in dredge or trawl.

Amblypneustes pallidus, Little I, WA

Holopneustes porosissimus Agassiz & Desor, 1846

Habitat: Moderately exposed reef; 0–15 m depth.
Distribution: Houtman Abrolhos, WA, to Waratah Bay, Vic., and northern Tas.
Maximum size: Test diameter to 70 mm, primary spines to 3 mm.

Holopneustes porosissimus, Quarry Bay, WA

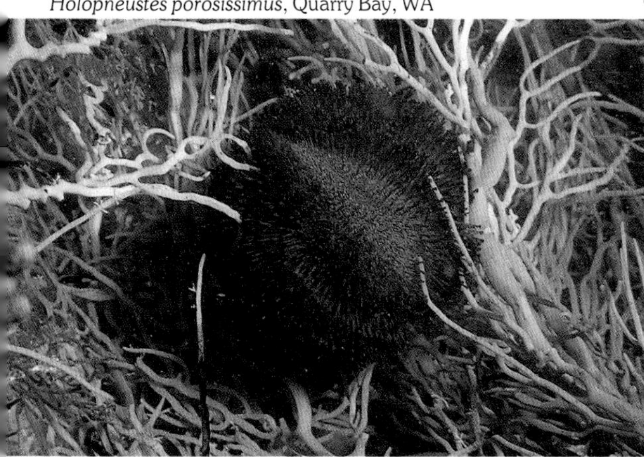

Holopneustes porosissimus is a common sea urchin that is rarely observed because of its habit of living wrapped in macroalgal fronds, particularly those of *Sargassum* and *Ecklonia* species. While the primary spines are a vivid red at the tips (khaki at the base) and the tube feet are purple, this brilliant coloration rarely stands out against the host alga because of the lack of red light at depth.

Holopneustes inflatus Lütken, 1872

Habitat: Exposed reef; 0–30 m depth.
Distribution: Fremantle, WA, to NSW and around Tas.
Maximum size: Test diameter to 70 mm, primary spines to 5 mm.

Holopneustes inflatus is an ovoid egg-shaped sea urchin, with the height often exceeding the width, and with uniform white to purple primary spines. The tube feet (and associated pores in the test through which the tube feet pass) form much wider bands than for *H. porosissimus*. The species generally occurs wrapped in fronds of the kelp *Ecklonia radiata* and feeds on the host plant.

Holopneustes inflatus, Spring Beach, Tas.

Holopneustes pycnotilus H.L. Clark, 1912

Habitat: Sheltered and moderately exposed reef; 0–8 m depth.
Distribution: Richmond R to Ulladulla, NSW.
Maximum size: Test diameter to 60 mm, primary spines to 4 mm.

Holopneustes pycnotilus is most easily identified by its brown test, pink spines and yellow suckers at the tips of the tube feet. Like the other two *Holopneustes* species, it is locally abundant below low-water mark but is easily overlooked because it generally remains concealed among algal fronds. Recent work indicates that an older name *Holopneustes purpurascens*, perhaps applies to this species.

Holopneustes pycnotilus, North Head, NSW

Holopneustes pycnotilus test, Bass Point, NSW

Salmacis belli Döderlein, 1902

Habitat: Exposed reef; 10–125 m depth
Distribution: Tropical Australia south to Port Walcott, WA, and Sydney, NSW. Also Indonesia.
Maximum size: Test diameter to 70 mm, primary spines to 5 mm.

Salmacis belli characteristically has a white test and bright red spines with yellow stripes at the tips and green bases. It occurs most often on steep reef walls in areas with good current flow but is not common.

Salmacis belli, Watsons Bay, NSW. RUDIE KUITER

FAMILY TOXOPNEUSTIDAE

This small family contains species similar in appearance to the temnopleurids as they have small primary spines that densely coat the surface of the test. However, the surface of the test is relatively smooth rather than having a sculpturing of pits, and the tubercles associated with the primary interambulacral spines are smooth rather than having an undulating surface around the central knob. The most characteristic feature is the presence of gill slits beside the soft-skinned mouth area.

Tripneustes gratilla (Linnaeus, 1758)

Habitat: Sheltered and moderately exposed reef; 0–75 m depth.
Distribution: Tropical Australia south to Margaret R, WA, and Montague I, NSW. Also widespread in the Indo-West Pacific region.
Maximum size: Test diameter to 145 mm, primary spines to 10 mm.

Tripneustes gratilla, North Head, NSW

Tripneustes gratilla has a skin that can vary in colour between orange and dark purple, and primary spines that are white and sometimes tipped with orange. The relative size of the spines and their arrangement are characteristic of the species. The test is often partly covered by shell and algal fragments, which are held in place by the tube feet. In some years the species is abundant in Sydney Harbour, but in other years rare, probably because of variation in the survival of larvae drifting south.

Pseudoboletia indiana (Michelin, 1862)

Habitat: Sheltered and moderately exposed reef, rubble; 5–100 m depth.
Distribution: Tropical Australia south to Houtman Abrolhos, WA, and Montague I, NSW. Also through the Indo-West Pacific region.
Maximum size: Test diameter to 75 mm, primary spines to 15 mm.

Pseudoboletia indiana is a white sea urchin with purple tips to the primary spines and shell or rock fragments generally attached to the test surface. It is shaped like a flattened egg with the lower section of the test wider than the upper section. This species can be the dominant echinoid in localised areas; it is most common on broken bottom near the sand edge of the deeper New South Wales reefs.

Pseudoboletia indiana, Bass Point, NSW

FAMILY ECHINOMETRIDAE

Echinometrids have a rounded or oval test with solid primary spines that are usually long and strong. Only one primary tubercle is present on each plate, and the pores for tube feet occur in oblique arcs. The family comprises many species in other parts of the world, with relatively few occurring in Australia.

Heliocidaris erythrogramma

(Valenciennes, 1846)

Habitat: Sheltered and moderately exposed reef; 0–35 m depth.
Distribution: Shark Bay, WA, to southern Qld, and around Tas.
Maximum size: Test diameter to 90 mm, primary spines to 25 mm.

Heliocidaris erythrogramma is the most common sea urchin in southern Australia and supports a commercially important fishery. A number of different colour variants are found, all made up of three colours (purple, green, white), which often differ between spines and test. The spines of animals on the west coast are much shorter than those in the east, causing animals from these two regions to appear quite different. Aggregations of *Heliocidaris erythrogramma* can remove larger macroalgae from reefs; in such areas the habitat is often overgrazed, resulting in poor growth rates and low reproductive capacity.

Heliocidaris erythrogramma, Tinderbox, Tas.

Heliocidaris erythrogramma, Little I, WA

Heliocidaris tuberculata (Lamarck, 1816)

Habitat: Exposed reef; 0–54 m depth.
Distribution: Ulladulla, NSW, to southern Qld. Also Lord Howe I and Kermadec Is.
Maximum size: Test diameter to 106 mm, primary spines to 25 mm.

Heliocidaris tuberculata occurs mixed with *H. erythrogramma* on the central New South Wales coast and is by far the most common sea urchin at Lord Howe Island. It is consistently coloured orange-red, and the spines are oval in cross-section and blunt at the tip. Large numbers are found in hollows on wave-swept reefs just below low-tide level.

Heliocidaris tuberculata, Bass Point, NSW

FAMILY CLYPEASTERIDAE

This family comprises flattened 'sand dollars' with rounded edges. The ambulacral plates that form the 'petals' on the upper surface are of two types: large primary plates and much smaller secondary plates that do not reach the ambulacral midline. The fine spines covering the upper surface have simple, pointed tips.

Clypeaster australasiae (Gray, 1851)

Habitat: Silt, sand, reef; 0–130 m depth.
Distribution: Port Phillip Heads, Vic., to Bowen, Qld, and northeastern Tas. Also Lord Howe I and Norfolk I.
Maximum size: Test length to 150 mm.

Clypeaster australasiae, North Head, NSW

Clypeaster australasiae is a cream to dark brown sand dollar with a slightly raised test and prominent petal-like markings. The surface is densely covered by numerous small spines and tubercles. The species can be locally abundant but is not often seen because it generally remains buried under sand and prefers deep water.

FAMILY LAGANIDAE

Laganids have a similar appearance to clypeasterids but the petals are formed from only one type of ambulacral plate, and each of the fine spines covering the upper surface ends in a crown-like tip. Like other sand dollars they live close to the sediment surface and feed unselectively on organic particles.

Peronella lesueuri (Agassiz, 1841)

Habitat: Silt, sand; 0–77 m depth.
Distribution: Tropical Australia south to Esperance, WA, and Bowen, Qld. Also Indonesia, Malaysia, Philippines.
Maximum size: Test length to 160 mm.

Peronella lesueuri is a large pink, orange or brown sand dollar that occurs commonly half-buried in soft sediments off Perth. Its test is covered by thousands of minute spines, which tend to obscure the star-shaped pattern of petals in the centre of the upper surface. A related but much smaller (to 45 mm) species, ***Peronella peroni***, occurs along the southern Australian coast from Western Australia to southern Queensland and northern and eastern Tasmania.

Peronella lesueuri, Bicton, WA

FAMILY LOVENIIDAE

This family includes species of echinoid that are heart-shaped when viewed from above and have a high test. They are primarily separated from other families of heart urchin, and subdivided into species, on the basis of the arrangement of pores, petals and grooves on the test and particularly the boundaries of grooves on the surface of the test. Loveniids can be recognised by a deep depression at the front of the test, the front series of ambulacral pores not forming a petal, and a band of minute spines forming a circular mark below the large anal hole.

Echinocardium cordatum (Pennant, 1777)

Heart urchin

Habitat: Silt, sand; 0–230 m depth.
Distribution: Around the Australian mainland and Tas. Also in temperate seas worldwide.
Maximum size: Test length to 60 mm.

Echinocardium cordatum, Bicheno, Tas.

Echinocardium cordatum test, Tinderbox, Tas.

Echinocardium cordatum is by far the most abundant of the heart-shaped echinoids in southern Australia. It has a general shape similar to several other local species but lacks a line of fine spines on the test around the petals. This heart urchin has an unusually wide distribution for an echinoderm; it is very common in European and American as well as Australian waters.

FAMILY SCHIZASTERIDAE

Heart urchins in this family have a deep longitudinal depression in the upper front of the test, petals that are considerably longer at front than at rear, and a band of minute spines around the petals.

Moira lethe Mortensen, 1930

Habitat: Moderately exposed sand; 6–18 m.
Distribution: Around the Australian mainland and Tas.
Maximum size: Test length to 50 mm.

Moira lethe is an ovoid heart urchin with a flat base and a very high test. The petals are unusually deeply sunken in this genus, and the test extends as a small cone around the anus. *Moira lethe* is widely distributed but rarely seen; it lives under a shallow layer of sediment on clean sand.

Moira lethe, Cloudy Bay, Tas.

FAMILY BRISSIDAE

Heart urchins in this family have a thin band of minute spines surrounding the petals, another surrounding the large anal hole and another forming a circle below the anus. The test is usually high and rounded, and the petals not deeply sunken.

Brissus latecarinatus (Leske, 1778)

Habitat: Sand; 0–50 m depth.
Distribution: Tropical Australia south to Ningaloo, WA, and Sydney, NSW. Also widespread in the Indo-West Pacific region.
Maximum size: Test length to 60 mm.

Brissus latecarinatus is a widespread tropical species that is moderately common along the central New South Wales coast. Like other heart urchins, living animals are most commonly collected by dredge, and only the empty tests are seen by divers. A related species with much the same range is ***Brissus agassizii***.

Brissus ?latecarinatus test, Jervis Bay, NSW

Class Holothuroidea

Holothurians, sea cucumbers, beche-de-mer

Holothurians are elongate, cucumber- or worm-like animals ranging in size from a few millimetres to a metre. Their bodies are soft because the spiny skeleton typical of other echinoderm groups has been reduced to small spicules embedded in the leathery body wall. Spicules may be shaped like perforated plates, wheels, stars or anchors; the shape of the spicule often uniquely identifies particular species. More than one type of spicule is often present in a single animal.

The basic five-sided symmetry of echinoderms is retained in holothurians even though the body lies parallel to the seabed. This pattern is sometimes masked because rows of tube feet are lost or modified in some species. Such adaptations are perhaps to be expected in animals that have evolved to move in a single direction.

The mouth of holothurians is located at one end of the body and surrounded by tentacles formed from modified tube feet. A convoluted gut passes through the body to an anus at the far end. Most species also have two highly branched internal organs that open into the hindgut and are used for respiration. These 'respiratory trees' can be expelled with the gut by some species as a means of defence. They are then quickly regenerated. Some holothurians also protect themselves from predators by releasing toxic white sticky threads.

The holothurian species with highly branched tentacles generally use these tentacles to capture plankton and other drifting food particles. However, the majority of species are unselective in their choice of food and will shovel large quantities of sediment through the gut in order to digest the small amount of organic matter present.

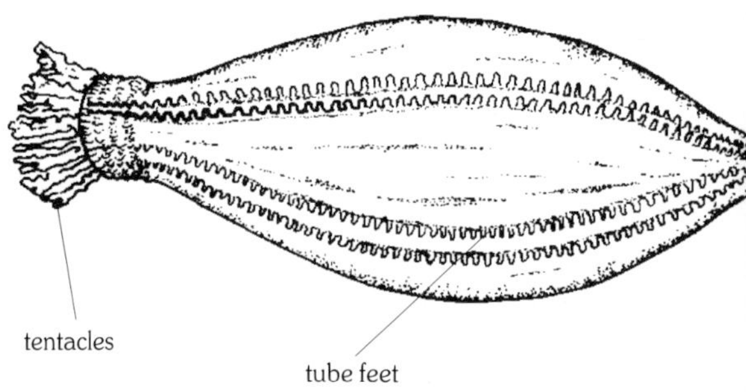

Holothurian (100 mm)
Cucumella mutans
Class Holothuroidea

FAMILY PHYLLOPHORIDAE

This is a large family of species with structures like tube feet (pedicels) on the body surface and tentacles that are repeatedly branched. The body is cylindrical or nearly so in shape, and has no distinct undersurface.

Lipotrapeza vestiens (Joshua, 1914)

Habitat: Sheltered reef, silt; 0–13 m depth.
Distribution: Perth, WA, to Waratah Bay, Vic., and northern Tas.
Maximum size: Length to 120 mm, diameter to 40 mm.

Lipotrapeza vestiens has a similar body form to *Neothyonidium ?dearmatum*; both are relatively large, brown species with numerous tube feet scattered over the body surface and twenty black tentacles arranged in inner and outer rings. *Lipotrapeza vestiens* has a curved body and is generally found under rocks with pieces of shell attached to the surface, rather than being buried in sediment.

Lipotrapeza vestiens, Ricketts Pt, Vic.

Neothyonidium ?dearmatum (Dendy & Hindle, 1907)

Habitat: Silt; 4–20 m depth.
Distribution: Vic. and Tas.
Maximum size: Length to 110 mm.

Neothyonidium ?dearmatum is a large holothurian with a body that remains buried in fine sediment. It has ten large branched tentacles surrounding ten smaller tentacles around the mouth. The large tentacles are held in the water column to trap plankton or wiped across the sediment and then moved one at a time across the mouth for the removal of the food particles. The body has numerous small tube feet (pedicels) sticking out from the sides of the body. There is some question about the identity of this species because of slight differences between the Australian population and the New Zealand species *Neothyonidium dearmatum*. The species is abundant in the D'Entrecasteaux Channel, Tas., and may extend around to Perth; holothurians with similar tentacles are commonly noticed by divers between these two locations.

Neothyonidium sp., D'Entrecasteaux Channel, Tas.

FAMILY CUCUMARIIDAE

Cucumariids are closely related to the phyllophorids, differing chiefly in lacking forked elongations on any of the calcareous plates that form a ring around the front of the gut. Spicules of the various species are quite variable in shape.

Cercodemas anceps (Selenka, 1867)

Habitat: Reef; 5–65 m depth.
Distribution: Tropical Australia south to Great Australian Bight, WA, and Sydney, NSW.
Maximum size: Length to 110 mm.

Cercodemas anceps, Fremantle, WA. CLAY BRYCE

Cercodemas anceps is a bright red and yellow holothurian with large tubercles on the body surface and a body that is almost square in cross-section. The species can occur abundantly in areas with good water flow and is often associated with wharves or wooden debris on the sea bed.

Plesiocolochirus ignava (Ludwig, 1875)

Habitat: Reef; 0–8 m depth.
Distribution: Houtman Abrolhos, WA, to Coffs Harbour, NSW, and around Tas.
Maximum size: Length to 30 mm.

Plesiocolochirus ignava, Portsea, Vic. RUDIE KUITER

Plesiocolochirus ignava has a solid box-like body with knobs along the edges and tube feet along the base. The surface is white or pale purple with orange markings. The species occurs commonly in localised areas and is often found climbing on algae and seagrasses.

FAMILY STICHOPODIDAE

Species in this family have leaf-shaped tentacles, well-developed respiratory trees and pedicels on the body surface. Two gonads are present internally, one on each side of the body. Like some of the holothuriids (described below), they do not bury in sediment but generally live on hard substrates.

Stichopus mollis (Hutton, 1872)

Habitat: Moderately exposed reef, seagrass, silt, sand; 0–140 m depth.
Distribution: Houtman Abrolhos, WA, to central NSW and around Tas. Also New Zealand.
Maximum size: Length to 200 mm.

Stichopus mollis, Princess Royal Harbour, WA

Stichopus mollis occurs abundantly throughout southern Australia and is the only species in this family commonly observed by divers. It has a cucumber shape with small dark spinelets on bumps, and tube feet on the undersurface only. The coloration is usually reddish-brown, but specimens can also be black or grey. This species generally remains hidden in crevices during the day and moves out to feed at night.

Stichopus ludwigi, Princess Royal Harbour, WA

Stichopus ludwigi Erwe, 1913

Habitat: Seagrass, sand; 2–25 m depth.
Distribution: Houtman Abrolhos, WA, to SA and southeastern Tas.
Maximum size: Length to 130 mm.

Stichopus ludwigi is a relatively uncommon species, most often found on the edge of seagrass beds in Western Australia. The coloration and pattern varies little between sites. The upper body has a bone-coloured base covered by small brown spots with three or four darker brown bands across the centre of the body. The lower body also has brown spots but in lower numbers and on a cream-coloured base. A number of short blunt spines, which are soft and very dark, occur around the upper edge of the body.

FAMILY HOLOTHURIIDAE

Holothuriids are identical to the stichopids in virtually all characteristics, except that they have only a single internal reproductive structure (on the left side of the body). This family is poorly represented in southern Australia but has numerous species in the tropics; it includes most of the large and brightly coloured species on coral reefs.

Holothuria hartmeyeri Erwe, 1913

Habitat: Rock rubble, seagrass, sand; 0–40 m depth.
Distribution: Houtman Abrolhos, WA, to Gulf St Vincent, SA.
Maximum size: Length to 250 mm.

Holothuria hartmeyeri superficially appears like a stretched version of *Stichopus ludwigi*, but the reproductive structures and the shape of spicules in the body wall indicate that the two species belong in different families. It can be distinguished from *S. ludwigi* by the darker and more irregular blotches on the upper surface as well as the more elongate shape. The species is moderately common in localised areas of broken bottom near seagrass beds.

Holothuria hartmeyeri, Princess Royal Harbour, WA

FAMILY SYNAPTIDAE

Synaptids have elongate bodies, which give them a worm-like appearance, and tentacles that end in finger-like processes. Embedded in the skin are anchor-like and perforated plate-like spicules.

Leptosynapta dolabrifera (Stimpson, 1855)

Habitat: Sheltered and moderately exposed reef, sand; 0–200 m depth.
Distribution: Houtman Abrolhos, WA, to southern Qld and around Tas. Also Lord Howe I.
Maximum size: Length to 150 mm.

Leptosynapta dolabrifera is one of the most common species of holothurian found under rocks in the intertidal zone and in shallow water. It has 12 tentacles, each with about seven paired finger-like lobes on the sides, and a translucent white body with numerous white clumps of spicules appearing as spots. The spicules are anchor-shaped and easily break through the fragile body surface to catch on skin, thereby making the animal feel sticky to the touch.

Leptosynapta dolabrifera, Busselton, WA

FAMILY CHIRIDOTIDAE

Chiridotids have an external appearance similar to synaptids but have wheel- or S-shaped spicules (sometimes both) in the skin. The tips of the tentacles are also slightly different, as they are leaf-shaped.

Chiridota gigas Dendy & Hindle, 1907

Habitat: Sheltered and moderately exposed reef, sand; 0–10 m depth.
Distribution: Cape Bridgewater, Vic., to Shellharbour, NSW, and around Tas. Also New Zealand.
Maximum size: Length to 250 mm.

Chiridota gigas can often be found in the same habitat and under the same rocks as *Leptosynapta dolabrifera*. Both species have similar-shaped bodies and tentacles, and lack tube feet on the body surface; however, *C. gigas* is easily recognised by its pink coloration and the numerous white spots on the body surface, which are actually clusters of wheel-shaped spicules.

Chiridota gigas, Bicheno, Tas.

PHYLUM HEMICHORDATA

Acorn worms, enteropneusts

This phylum contains about 100 species of worm-like animals with an acorn-shaped proboscis located on a fleshy collar, followed by a segmented trunk. The mouth is located between the proboscis and the collar, and a number of gill slits open into a groove at the front end of the trunk. The phylum was once included as a class in the phylum Chordata because of the gill slits and a central nervous system that has a similar initial development to the nervous system of chordates. They do not, however, possess a notochord, although a supporting rod in the collar has sometimes been thought analogous to this structure.

The phylum is divided into two classes, the Enteropneusta and the small, colonial Pterobranchia. Enteropneusts range in size from 50 mm to 2 m and generally live buried in U-shaped burrows or in tubes of cemented sand grains. They dig using the fleshy proboscis, which can be inflated or deflated.

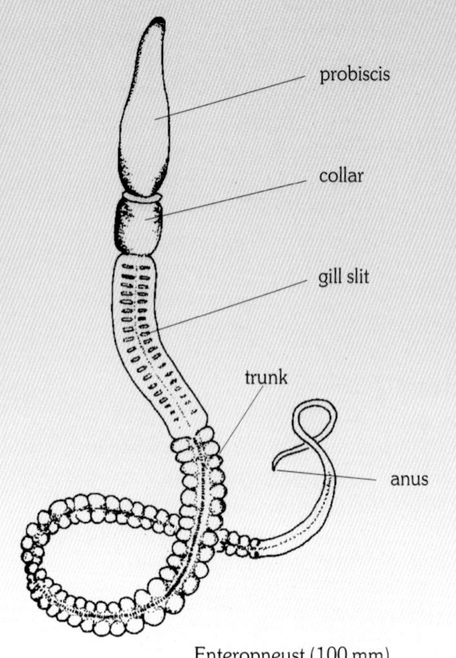

Enteropneust (100 mm)
Phylum Hemichordata

Ptychodera flava Eschscholtz, 1825

Habitat: Sheltered and moderately exposed sand; 0–5 m depth.
Distribution: Tropical Australia south to Rottnest I, WA. Also widespread in the Indo-West Pacific region.
Maximum size: Length to 200 mm.

Ptychodera flava is a yellow-brown species with wide flaps on the front half of the trunk, which contain the reproductive organs. This hemichordate occurs buried in sheltered pockets of coarse sand on exposed coasts and is locally common on the southern west coast. A second species with a longer trunk, ***Balanoglossus australiensis***, is found in the Sydney region.

Ptychodera flava, Rottnest I, WA. LOISETTE MARSH

PHYLUM CHORDATA

Chordates

Chordates share three features that may not always be obvious but appear at some stage in development. They have a nerve chord, part of which is expanded into a brain, on the upper side of the body. Below this is a rod-like supporting structure known as the notochord. They also generally have gill slits which connect the throat with the outside of the body.

The great majority of chordates are vertebrates, characterised by the presence of a backbone. Most vertebrates in marine environments are fishes. There are several chordate groups without backbones, however, and these all live in marine habitats.

Class Ascidiacea

Ascidians, sea squirts, tunicates

Ascidians are a diverse group of animals with complementary adult and larval stages that have little in common, either in appearance or in function. The adult ascidian is adapted for feeding and reproducing and remains fixed to the one spot. The body is characterised by a large perforated pharynx for filter feeding and a tough external protective covering made of cellulose-like material (the 'tunic'). It also possesses an inhalent siphon, which, in solitary species, is normally directed horizontally and downward. Water carrying microscopic food particles is pumped in via the inhalent siphon to the sieve-like pharynx. After passing the pharynx, filtered water is ejected through an exhalent siphon that is generally directed upwards and away from the inhalent siphon in solitary species. In many compound species, a communal exhalent siphon pumps away waste and food-depleted water generated by several individual units called zooids, each of which has an inhalent siphon and gut. The filtration system of ascidians is extremely efficient, removing particles as small as bacteria.

Ascidian larvae do not feed but are adapted solely for dispersal. They are small and tadpole-shaped, live for a maximum of a few hours and are free-swimming. On finding a suitable place to settle they attach by the head, absorb their tail, twist their mouth around away from the substratum and expand their upper body. One of the most interesting features of ascidians is the rudimentary backbone that the larvae use for support, as it is this 'notochord' that provides the evidence that ascidians are more closely related to fishes and other vertebrates than to invertebrates. Ascidian eggs are readily manipulated in the laboratory and develop rapidly as embryos, making this group, and echinoderms, the standard organisms used in studies of early embryo development for the past century. Almost all ascidians are hermaphroditic; some species release eggs for external fertilisation in the water, and others are fertilised internally by free-swimming sperm.

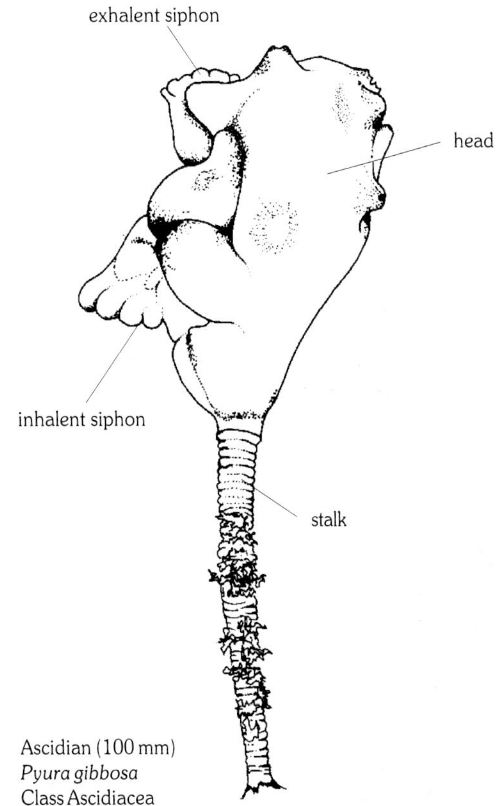

Ascidian (100 mm)
Pyura gibbosa
Class Ascidiacea

Although only the brightly coloured species are generally noticed by divers, and only cungevoi is widely recognised by fishermen and shore fossickers, ascidians are common virtually everywhere on rocky reefs. Approximately 1500 species are known worldwide, with about 300 recorded from southern Australia.

FAMILY ASCIDIIDAE

Species in this family are solitary (rather than compound, or colonial) ascidians, with regular rows of straight perforations in the pharynx wall and a gut that loops around the gonads on the left side of the body. Most species have a firm body covering (the tunic) and are moderately large.

Ascidia challengeri Herdman, 1882

Habitat: Reef; 0–600 m depth.
Distribution: Southern Tas. Also Heard I, Kerguelen I and Antarctica.
Maximum size: Length to 200 mm.

Ascidia challengeri is a cylindrical ascidian with a rigid translucent tunic and flat siphons. It has an unusual distribution because few other animals or plants are known from the shores of southern Tasmania *and* from deep water around the Antarctic continent. The species is rare in Tasmania but occurs commonly on the continental shelf further south.

Ascidia challengeri, Bathurst Channel, Tas.

Ascidia sydneiensis Stimpson, 1855

Habitat: Mud, sand; 2–50 m depth.
Distribution: Around the Australian mainland and Tas. Also widely distributed overseas.
Maximum size: Height to 200 mm.

Ascidia sydneiensis is one of the largest and most wide ranging of ascidians and is one of the few to prefer soft sediments in which to live. It can usually be recognised by the pleats (about six) in the two siphon apertures and by short processes that project from the body surface and are often coated in mud. The apertures have a fine fringe around their edges.

Ascidia sydneiensis, Bathurst Channel, Tas.

Phallusia obesa (Herdman, 1880)

Habitat: Sheltered reef; 1–15 m depth.
Distribution: Port Hedland, WA, to Cape Melville, Qld.
Maximum size: Height to 160 mm.

Phallusia obesa is a solid ascidian with a body that is longer than wide and with 10–12 pleats around the siphon apertures. The body surface has several raised ridges and is usually flecked by numerous dark pigment spots. This species can occur extremely abundantly in sheltered bays with high levels of nutrients and good water flow.

Phallusia obesa, Princess Royal Harbour, WA

FAMILY STYELIDAE

Styelids usually have tough, leathery bodies and a surface that is often encrusted with plants, animals or embedded sand. Most are solitary, although a few species (e.g. *Botrylloides leachi*) multiply asexually to form colonies. An expanded stomach with a surface creased by numerous longitudinal folds is present towards the front of the gut. Gonads occur on both sides of the body and may be numerous.

Cnemidocarpa radicosa (Herdman, 1882)

Habitat: Moderately exposed reef, sand; 0–50 m depth.
Distribution: Perth, WA, to Tallebudgera, Qld, and around Tas.
Maximum size: Height to 100 mm.

Cnemidocarpa radicosa is a large solitary ascidian with a cream to yellow surface. Its external surface is grooved with furrows, particularly near the long inhalent siphon. The species is common in Tasmania but relatively rare in warmer areas.

Cnemidocarpa radicosa, Bathurst Channel, Tas.

Polycarpa clavata Hartmeyer, 1919

Habitat: Moderately exposed reef, seagrass; 2–40 m depth.
Distribution: Tropical Australia south to central SA and Cairns, Qld. Also New Caledonia.
Maximum size: Height to 80 mm.

Polycarpa clavata can be recognised by its bright orange coloration, lobed tunic and a stalk with numerous circular pits; in large individuals the stalk becomes as long as the head. This is the most conspicuous species attached to seagrasses in the Perth region and is also found on reefs.

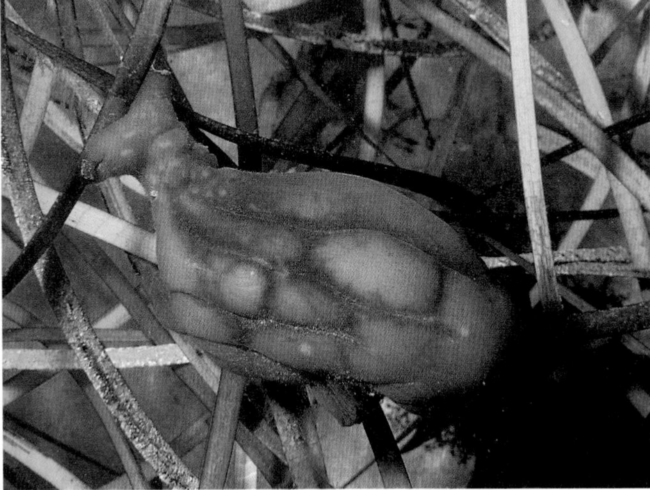

Polycarpa clavata, Marmion Lagoon, WA

Polycarpa viridis Herdman, 1880

Habitat: Silt, seagrass; 3–10 m depth.
Distribution: Perth, WA, to Sydney, NSW.
Maximum size: Height to 50 mm.

Polycarpa viridis has a smooth cream or yellow body, with four purple markings usually present on the inside of each siphon. It is generally found embedded in soft sediment and maintains anchorage with the support of a sand-encrusted stalk, which may be as long as the body. The species can occur in high densities in areas with good water flow.

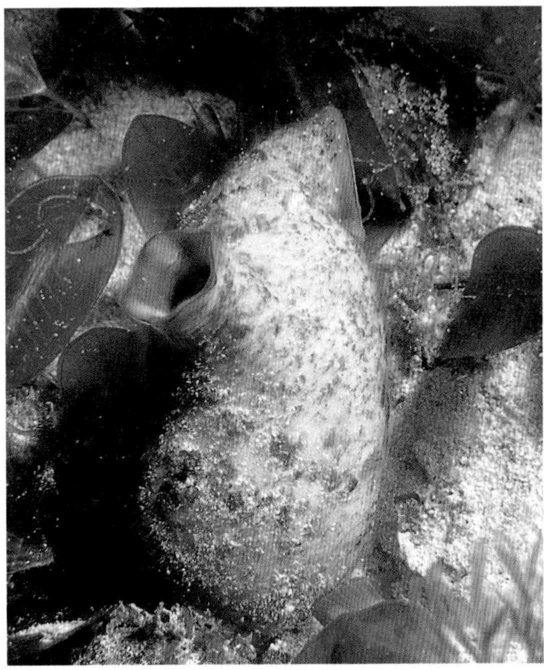

Polycarpa viridis, Horseshoe Reef, WA

Amphicarpa meridiana Kott, 1985

Habitat: Sheltered reef; 3–82 m depth.
Distribution: Gulf St Vincent, SA, to Solitary I, NSW, and around Tas.
Maximum size: Height to 10 mm.

Amphicarpa meridiana is a small cylindrical species that occurs in aggregations and often has several individuals attached to the one basal stalk. The tunic is thin and encrusted with sand except around the siphonal openings, which are either orange or red and do not have lobes. This ascidian is commonly found on jetty pylons.

Botrylloides magnicoecum, Bathurst Channel, Tas.

Amphicarpa meridiana, Pearson I, SA

Botrylloides magnicoecum, Terrigal, NSW

Botrylloides magnicoecum Hartmeyer, 1912

Habitat: Sheltered and moderately exposed reef; 3–20 m depth.
Distribution: Shark Bay, WA, to Gladstone, Qld, and around Tas. Also widespread overseas.
Maximum size: Height to 30 mm.

Botrylloides magnicoecum is one of the most magnificent of all ascidians when it forms large colonies. These can be up to 300 mm wide and are a mosaic of blue and yellow. The individual zooids are very small (1–2 mm) and usually lie in parallel double rows down the sides of thumb-shaped lobes, with a communal exhalent siphon forming the centre of the thumb. In tropical waters the species occurs in encrusting sheets without well-developed lobes.

Botrylloides leachi (Savigny, 1816)

Habitat: Sheltered reef; 0–25 m depth.
Distribution: Dampier Archipelago, WA, to Cape Flattery, Qld, and around Tas. Also widespread overseas.
Maximum size: Height to 2 mm, colony width to 50 mm.

Botrylloides leachi is one of the most variable of all ascidian species and has confused zoologists to the extent that it has been given 26 different scientific names in the past. It is an encrusting species and can occur in virtually all combinations of colours. The species has double rows of zooids and communal exhalent siphons, which sometimes have a rosette of zooids around them.

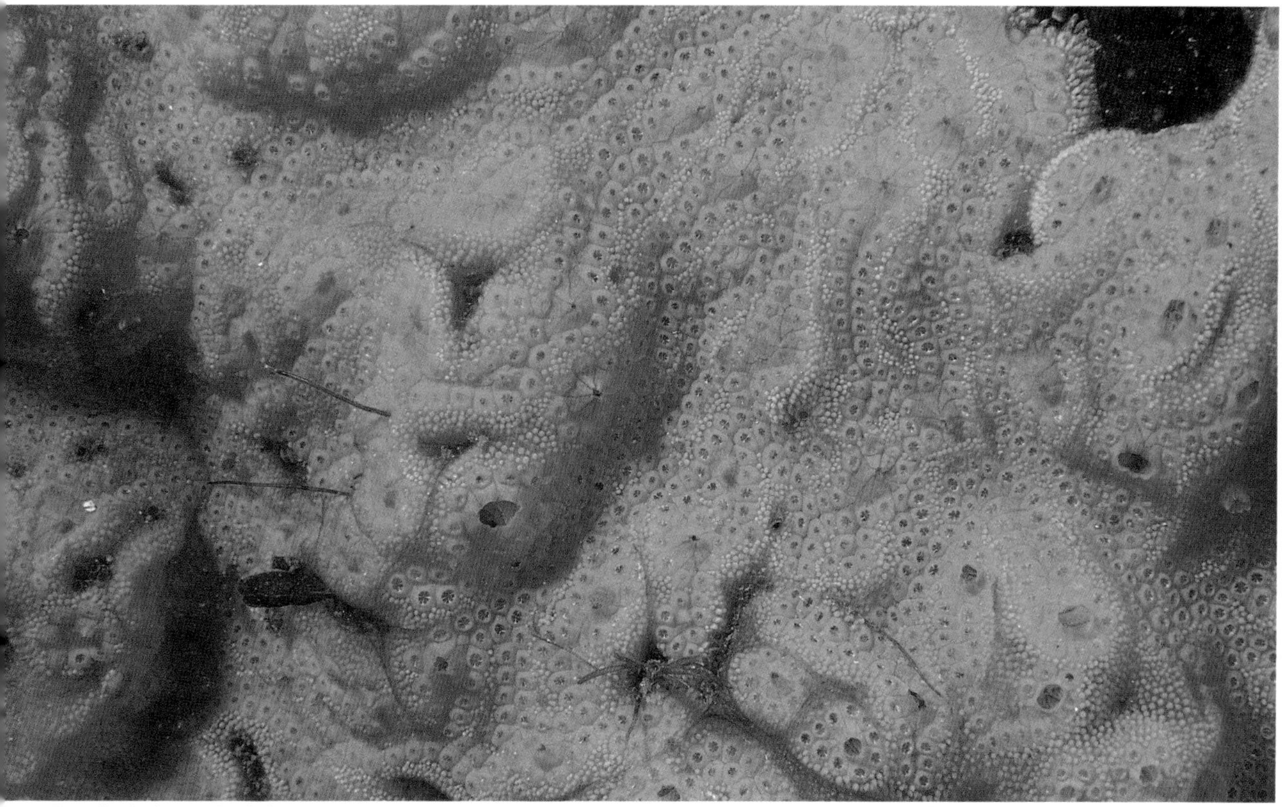

Botrylloides leachi, Tinderbox, Tas

Botrylloides leachi, Ile des Phoques, Tas

Botrylloides perspicuum, Marmion Lagoon, WA

Botrylloides perspicuum Herdman, 1886

Habitat: Seagrass, reef; 1–12 m depth.
Distribution: Dampier Archipelago, WA, to Hervey Bay, Qld, and around Tas. Also widespread in the Indo-West Pacific region.
Maximum size: Height to 10 mm, colony width to 100 mm.

Botrylloides perspicuum varies greatly in colour and is easily confused with *B. leachi* but differs from that species in being firm rather than soft to the touch and having raised ridges between the rows of zooids. The species commonly forms large gelatinous masses attached to seagrasses.

Botrylloides perspicuum, Two Peoples Bay, WA

FAMILY PYURIDAE

Pyurids are solitary ascidians, almost all of which have tough, opaque bodies and one gonad on each side of the body cavity. Associated with the base of the inhalent siphon are branched, tentacular structures, and the siphon is usually lined by spine-like or plate-like spicules.

Herdmania momus (Savigny, 1816)

Habitat: Reef, seagrass; 0–100 m depth.
Distribution: Broome, WA, to Lizard I, Qld, and around Tas. Also widespread overseas.
Maximum size: Height to 200 mm.

Herdmania momus is the most common ascidian observed subtidally in southern Australia. The characteristic feature of this species is a circular red line around the edges of the two siphons, although in the largest specimens this ring is difficult to see. Large animals have a tough wrinkled surface usually covered by encrusting organisms, and they are often half-buried among sponges and other animals on the reef surface. Small individuals have a more rounded shape and a white translucent tunic and can be found attached to seagrasses as well as on reefs.

Herdmania momus, Esperance, WA

Herdmania momus, Low Head, Tas.

Pyura australis, Marmion Lagoon, WA

Pyura australis (Quoy & Gaimard, 1834)

Habitat: Moderately exposed reef, seagrass; 2–20 m depth.
Distribution: Dongara, WA, to Shellharbour, NSW, and around Tas.
Maximum size: Height to 300 mm.

Pyura australis is one of the group of ascidians known as sea tulips because they possess long stalks and rounded heads. This species is distinguished from others in the group mainly by the internal structure of the stalk and by the arrangement of tubercles in ridges along the side of the head. However, this last feature is not completely reliable because some animals have inconspicuous tubercles or none at all.

Pyura gibbosa (Heller, 1878)

Habitat: Exposed reef; 3–25 m depth.
Distribution: Perth, WA, to Moreton Bay, Qld, and around Tas.
Maximum size: Height to 300 mm.

Pyura gibbosa occurs in two different forms. The eastern Australian form (the subspecies *Pyura gibbosa gibbosa*) has yellow ridges with tubercles along the sides, contrasting with the orange-red tunic. The tubercles on the western form (the subspecies *Pyura gibbosa draschii*) are generally more spiny and the stalk is relatively thin.

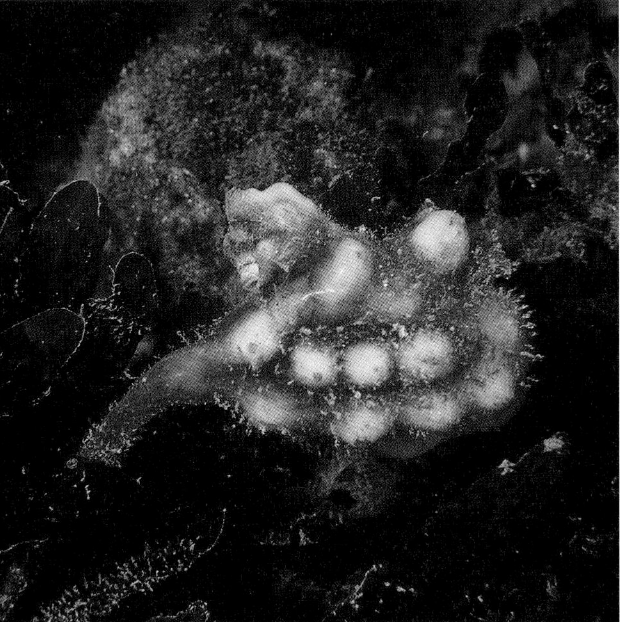

Pyura gibbosa gibbosa, North Head, NSW

Pyura gibbosa draschii, Bicheno, Tas.

Pyura spinifera (Quoy & Gaimard, 1834)

Habitat: Exposed reef; 2–80 m depth.
Distribution: Carnarvon, WA, to Solitary I, NSW, and Deal I, Tas.
Maximum size: Height to 320 mm.

Pyura spinifera is easily identified because of the pink or yellow encrusting sponge *Halisarca australiensis*, which invariably coats its surface. This ascidian is one of the most conspicuous species on deeper New South Wales reefs and usually occurs as a group of stalked animals, with another species of sponge-encrusted ascidian (*Cnemidocarpa pedata*) at the base.

Pyura spinifera, Bass Point, NSW

Pyura stolonifera (Heller, 1878)
Cunjevoi

Habitat: Reef, sand; 0–12 m depth.
Distribution: Shark Bay, WA, to Noosa, Qld, and around Tas. Also widespread in the Southern Hemisphere.
Maximum size: Height to 300 mm.

Pyura stolonifera forms large mats over intertidal rock platforms and also carpets many wharf pylons. The species can be distinguished from other species in the same genus by its hard tunic, a flat upper surface surrounded by a ridge, and two siphons that lie close together and project slightly above the flat surface. The opening of the siphons usually remains tightly closed at low-tide, causing water to project in a thin stream for a considerable distance if the animal is trodden on. On rock platforms close to populated areas, large numbers of cunjevoi are used as bait by rock fishermen, who remove the orange internal organs and leave the tunic with its shiny grey inner surface. The same species is eaten and sold as a food

Pyura stolonifera, Balmoral, NSW

item in Chile; it was similarly used by Australian Aboriginal people, including a tribe in the Gosford area who gave it the name cunjevoi.

FAMILY DIAZONIDAE

Diazonids are a small family of species that have translucent, gelatinous tests and six-lobed siphons. Nearly all species are colonial, with numerous zooids embedded together in the one structure. As in the following families, the zooid body is divided into two parts: a thoracic section containing the siphons, pharynx and nerve structures, and an abdominal section containing the gut loop, heart and gonads.

Pseudodiazona claviformis (Kott, 1963)

Habitat: Reef; 10–100 m depth.
Distribution: Great Australian Bight, SA, to Sydney, NSW.
Maximum size: Height to 60 mm.

Pseudodiazona claviformis forms gelatinous colonies that can take the shape of eggs, fans or clubs. The individual zooids, each with paired inhalent and exhalent siphons, can be seen clearly through the transparent matrix.

Pseudodiazona claviformis, Merimbula, NSW

FAMILY CLAVELINIDAE

Clavelinids are a group of colonial or solitary species with translucent gelatinous tests and siphons with a smooth, rounded margin. Gonads are present towards the rear of the gut loop and can often be detected by large eggs protruding from the walls.

Clavelina meridionalis (Herdman, 1891)

Habitat: Sheltered and moderately exposed reef; 2–16 m depth.
Distribution: Tropical Australia south to Houtman Abrolhos, WA, and Sydney, NSW. Also Indonesia.
Maximum size: Height to 200 mm.

Clavelina meridionalis is a solitary species with a head about as long as the stalk. The head is transparent and has conspicuous yellow markings, which contrast with a light mauve tint to the body. The species occurs most commonly in sheltered sites with good current flow.

Clavelina meridionalis, Port Stephens, NSW

Clavelina ostrearum (Michaelson, 1930)

Habitat: Moderately and submaximally exposed reef; 5–15 m depth.
Distribution: Albany, WA, to Pearson I, SA.
Maximum size: Height to 110 mm.

Clavelina ostrearum, Pearson I, SA

Clavelina ostrearum resembles *C. meridionalis* but has a deep blue head and white stalk. The siphonal openings flare considerably, with the inhalent siphon bent almost vertically downwards.

Clavelina cylindrica (Quoy & Gaimard, 1834)

Habitat: Reef; 5–12 m depth.
Distribution: Shark Bay, WA, to Bowen, Qld, and around Tas.
Maximum size: Height of colony to 600 mm.

Clavelina cylindrica occurs in distinctive grape-like clusters with numerous 10–20 mm zooids attached to a central stalk. The zooids are generally an opaque rather than transparent blue and have dark pigmented patches between the siphons.

Clavelina cylindrica, Waterfall Bay, Tas.

Clavelina pseudobaudinensis (Kott, 1976)

Habitat: Reef; 4–10 m depth.
Distribution: Houtman Abrolhos, WA, to Jervis Bay, NSW, and around Tas. Also Lord Howe I.
Maximum size: Height to 80 mm.

Clavelina pseudobaudinensis has transparent zooids that are half embedded in a common base with a short stalk. The zooids are often flecked with fine white spots and have a blue, generally crescent-shaped marking between the two siphons and blue spots below. A species with similar markings, ***Clavelina australis***, overlaps *C. pseudobaudinensis* in its range but can be distinguished because the zooids join very close to their bases or directly to the stalk rather than being fused together from at least half-way down.

Clavelina pseudobaudinensis, Bicheno, Tas.

Clavelina molluccensis (Sluiter, 1904)

Habitat: Reef; 3–12 m depth.
Distribution: Around Australian mainland. Also widespread in the Indo-West Pacific region.
Maximum size: Height to 60 mm.

The surface of *Clavelina molluccensis* is light blue yet sufficiently transparent to show the circular bands of muscle around the pharynx within. Each zooid has three blue spots in a transverse line between the two siphons and additional blue markings above and below the siphons. At South Australian sites where the species has been studied through the year, it has been found to disappear during summer and autumn.

Clavelina molluccensis, Busselton, WA

FAMILY PYCNOCLAVELLIDAE

This family is very close to the family Clavelinidae, and until recently the two were classified together. Pycnoclavellids differ chiefly in larval characteristics, particularly the presence of two or three tubular, invaginated adhesive organs on the head.

Pycnoclavella aurantia Kott, 1990

Habitat: Moderately exposed algal beds; 6–15 m depth.
Distribution: Cape Naturaliste, WA, to Port Lincoln, SA.
Maximum size: Height to 14 mm.

Pycnoclavella aurantia is a distinctive golden ascidian that occurs in clusters attached to the tips of plants. Each zooid has a swollen head, a long stalk and an abdomen that is embedded in a common mass on the plant surface. The species is not often seen but is most often found growing on the brown alga *Scaberia agardhii*.

Pycnoclavella aurantia, Bunker Bay, WA

Pycnoclavella diminuta (Kott, 1957)

Habitat: Reef; 3–30 m depth.
Distribution: Tropical Australia south along WA to Gulf St Vincent, SA. Also Lord Howe I, Philippines and New Caledonia.
Maximum size: Height to 30 mm.

Pycnoclavella diminuta occurs on reef surfaces in densely packed colonies that may extend up to 250 mm across. Each zooid has a relatively short lightbulb-like head at the end of a stalk 20 mm long, with the stalks arising from a common base. The colour of this species is variable, with whites, oranges and blues predominating.

Pycnoclavella diminuta, Pearson I, SA

FAMILY HOLOZOIDAE

Holozoids form soft colonies with numerous zooids embedded deeply within the fleshy mass. The rim of the inhalent siphon has six lobes, while the exhalent siphon may either be six-lobed or a large, rounded communal opening with a lip. The stomach is located about half-way down one loop of the gut rather than at the lower end as in the preceding family.

Sigillina australis Savigny, 1816

Habitat: Rock; 2–20 m depth.
Distribution: Montebello I, WA, to Port Stephens, NSW, but absent from Vic. Also New Zealand.
Maximum size: Height to 560 mm.

Sigillina australis is a stalked, colonial species with the head initially smaller than the stalk but growing proportionately longer as the colony develops. The head consists of a mass of individual zooids, each about 3 mm long, and is orange or pink.

Sigillina cyanea (Herdman, 1899)

Habitat: Reef; 4–150 m depth.
Distribution: Tropical Australia south to Albany, WA, and Sydney, NSW.
Maximum size: Height to 900 mm.

Sigillina cyanea is easily distinguished from *S. australis* because of its dark blue colour; otherwise, the colonies appear almost identical. Because colour is rarely a sufficiently important character to separate species, the two ascidians would probably be grouped together if not for the tadpole-shaped larvae that differ between species in size and shape.

Sigillina australis, Marmion Lagoon, WA

Sigillina cyanea, Horseshoe Reef, WA

Sycozoa cerebriformis (Quoy & Gaimard, 1834)

Habitat: Reef; 5–50 m depth.
Distribution: Shark Bay, WA, to Mooloolabah, Qld, and around Tas.
Maximum size: Height to 100 mm.

Sycozoa cerebriformis is a commonly observed species that is variable in colour (red, pink, orange, yellow or blue) and in shape. Small colonies are flat and fan-shaped with an obvious stalk, but the fan becomes greatly twisted as it lengthens in large colonies, producing a highly convoluted form reminiscent of the lobes of the brain. Common exhalent siphons occur along the thin outer margins of the colony, and the zooids lie in paired parallel rows down the upper part of each side.

Sycozoa cerebriformis, Bathurst Channel, Tas.

Sycozoa cerebriformis, Port Victoria, SA

Sycozoa pulchra (Herdman, 1886)

Habitat: Sheltered sand, silt; 5–15 m depth.
Distribution: Dongara, WA, to Torres Strait, Qld, and around Tas. Also Indonesia.
Maximum size: Height to 330 mm.

Sycozoa pulchra has a long, narrow stalk with a mass of root-like hairs at the base for attachment to the sediment. The head is vase-shaped with about eight rows of 20–50 paired zooids down the sides. The species is common in sheltered areas with good current flow and can reach densities of 2000 heads per square metre.

Sycozoa pulchra, Albany, WA

Sycozoa pedunculata (Quoy & Gaimard, 1834)

Habitat: Sheltered reef, sand; 4–10 m depth.
Distribution: Perth, WA, to Western Port, Vic., and around Tas.
Maximum size: Height to 110 mm.

Sycozoa pedunculata is easily confused with *S. pulchra* but has a thicker stalk, denser arrangement of zooids in the head, more rounded head and no hairs at the base of the stalk. An uncommon Antarctic species that is occasionally found in southern Australia, *Sycozoa sigillinoides* , also resembles these two species; it is orange, has relatively large zooids and

Sycozoa pedunculata, Woodmans Point, WA

has a single large exhalent siphon in the centre of each head rather than several siphons around the outer margin of the head.

FAMILY POLYCITORIDAE

Polycitorids are colonial animals with numerous retractible zooids usually embedded together within a test. Each zooid has a separate inhalent and exhalent siphon with six lobes around the opening. The zooids are often arranged in a circle, with the exhalent siphons lying close together in the centre.

Polycitor giganteus (Herdman, 1899)

Habitat: Moderately exposed reef; 0–400 m depth.
Distribution: Port Hedland, WA, to Mooloolabah, Qld, and northern Tas.
Maximum size: Height to 300 mm.

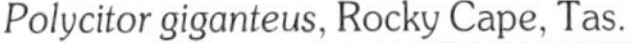

Polycitor giganteus, Rocky Cape, Tas.

Polycitor giganteus, Merimbula, NSW

Polycitor giganteus has a firm gelatinous consistency with tubular zooids embedded in a transparent matrix. The zooids are either white or orange and can be seen as streaks radiating towards the centre of the matrix. They retract deeply within the test when disturbed.

Cystodytes dellachiajei (Della Valle, 1877)

Habitat: Moderately exposed reef; 0–736 m depth.
Distribution: Around the Australian mainland and Tas. Also widespread overseas.
Maximum size: Width of colony to 100 mm.

Cystodytes dellachiajei forms small encrusting colonies on rock surfaces. Zooids are arranged in small circles around exhalent siphons and can be seen through the translucent gelatinous test. The species is very common but not often noticed because of its nondescript appearance.

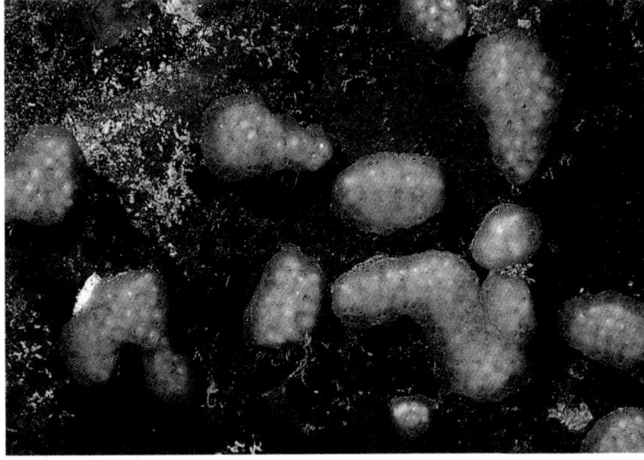

Cystodytes dellachiajei, Tinderbox, Tas.

FAMILY POLYCLINIDAE

Ascidians in this family are characterised by the gonads being located at the base of the abdomen and by having communal outlets for water and waste products rather than individual exhalent siphons.

Synoicum citrum Kott, 1992

Habitat: Reef; 5–25 m depth.
Distribution: Port MacDonnell, SA, to Wilsons Promontory, Vic., and around Tas.
Maximum size: Height to 20 mm.

Synoicum citrum is a greenish-yellow colonial ascidian with zooids arranged in a circular pattern in groups of about ten around communal exhalent siphons. The species was described from squashed, poorly preserved colonies, and so there is some uncertainty about the identity of the illustrated colony. The characteristic outwardly flared apertures of the exhalent siphon and the circular arrangement of inhalent siphons were not mentioned in the original description.

Synoicum ?citrum, Bathurst Channel, Tas.

Synoicum sacculum Kott, 1992

Habitat: Sheltered and moderately exposed reef; 2–425 m depth.
Distribution: Elliston, SA, to Flinders, Vic., and around Tas.
Maximum size: Height to 25 mm.

Synoicum sacculum is a bright red colonial species composed of numerous small lobes (about 10 mm diameter) arising from a basal mass. Numerous circular groups of seven to ten zooids, arranged around a central flanged exhalent siphon, form each lobe. The abundance of this species varies greatly between seasons and between years.

Synoicum sacculum, Waterfall Bay, Tas.

Aplidium clivosum Kott, 1992

Habitat: Jetty piles, reef; 3–10 m depth.
Distribution: Port Hedland, WA, to Heron I, Qld, but not recorded from Vic.
Maximum size: Height to 40 mm.

Aplidium clivosum is a red colonial ascidian that is characterised by a crater-like form. Zooids form double rows leading across the crater floor to very large communal apertures through which processed water and waste are ejected. Several crater-like structures are generally coalesced together in the one colony. This ascidian is a prominent feature of jetty pylons in southwestern and southern Australia.

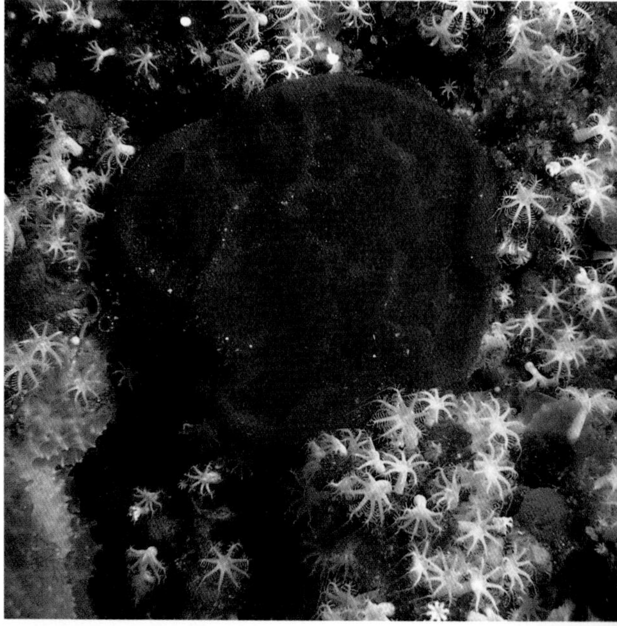

Aplidium clivosum, Busselton, WA

Aplidium multiplicatum Sluiter, 1909

Habitat: Sheltered reef; 2–10 m depth.
Distribution: Tropical Australia south to Gulf St Vincent, SA, and to Jervis Bay, NSW.
Maximum size: Height to 10 mm.

Aplidium multiplicatum forms sheet-like colonies up to 70 mm across over hard surfaces. Zooids occur in double rows along either sides of canals that empty into large exhalent siphons. The colour of this species varies considerably but is usually red or orange.

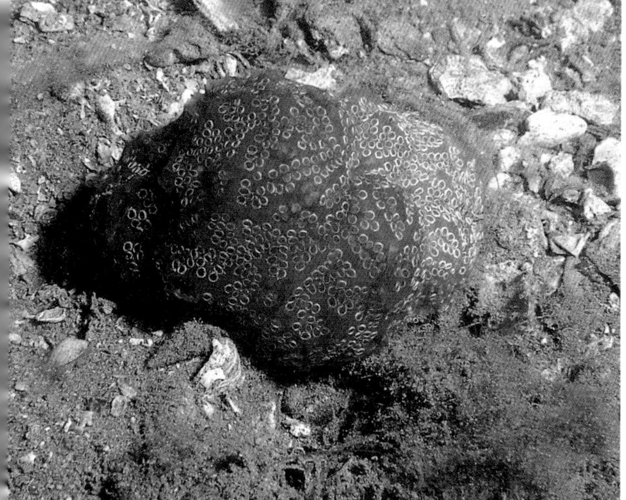

Aplidium multiplicatum, Bicton, WA

FAMILY RITTERELLIDAE

This family of colonial ascidians is closely related to the Polyclinidae, as gonads are located in the lower abdomen. However, individual zooids have separate exhalent siphons with six lobes around the opening, and the zooids are attached basally and can contract away from the surface of the colony.

Ritterella pedunculata (Herdman, 1899)

Habitat: Sheltered reef; 2–12 m depth.
Distribution: Great Australian Bight, SA, to Arrawarra, NSW, and around Tas.
Maximum size: Height to 50 mm.

Ritterella pedunculata is one of the more distinctive species of ascidian. Colonies consist of numerous sand-encrusted stalks with flattened plate-like ends and are often entangled. The species occurs on shallow sand-scoured reefs and is most abundant in areas with tidal currents.

Ritterella pedunculata, Rocky Cape, Tas.

FAMILY DIDEMNIDAE

The didemnids are a brightly coloured group of ascidians with small zooids, which lack a posterior abdomen, and well-developed outlet chambers into which filtered water and waste products are released. The body wall is often rigid because of the presence of star-shaped calcareous spicules.

Didemnum mosleyi (Herdman, 1886)

Habitat: Moderately exposed reef; 5–30 m depth.
Distribution: Around the Australian mainland and Tas. Also widespread in the Indo-West Pacific region.
Maximum size: Colony width to 250 mm.

Didemnum mosleyi is a thin encrusting species that occurs in large colonies on shaded surfaces on reefs. This ascidian is variable in colour and has a regular

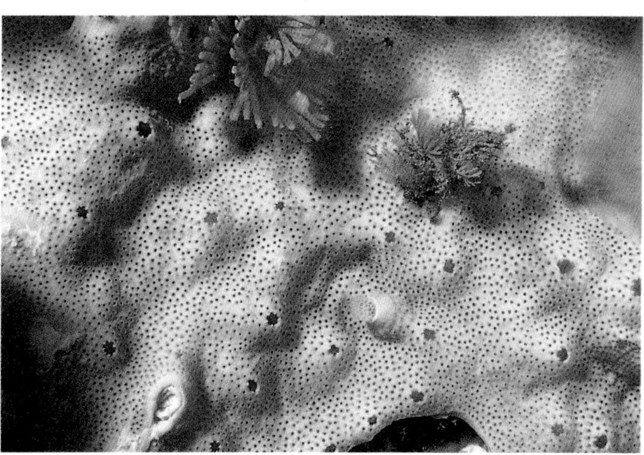

Didemnum mosleyi, Canal Rocks, WA

arrangement of small holes for inlet siphons, large outlet holes, and a brittle, lightly calcified test. It differs from several closely related species by having regular star-shaped spicules (0.02 to 0.05 mm in diameter) and dark zooids, and small, spicule-filled papillae are often present on the surface.

Didemnum spongioides Sluiter, 1909

Habitat: Sheltered and moderately exposed reef; 0–12 m.
Distribution: Rottnest I, WA, to Western Port, Vic., and eastern Tas. Also widespread in the Indo-West Pacific region.
Maximum size: Colony width to 400 mm.

Didemnum spongioides has a firm test with conical lobes surrounding the outlet apertures. It is common on rock and wood surfaces and is variably coloured. This ascidian is often mistaken for a sponge.

Didemnum ?spongioides, Canal Rocks, WA

Unidentified didemnid ascidian, Bathurst Channel, Tas.

Class Thaliacea

Salps, thaliaceans

Thaliaceans, or salps, are pelagic animals that generally have semi-transparent, barrel-shaped bodies. Many species form colonies in particular phases of their life-histories, in which case the typical barrel-shape is distorted. They move by the contraction and relaxation of prominent muscle bands surrounding the test, a process that causes water to be drawn in the front of the body and forcibly ejected from the rear. As the water passes through gill slits, food particles are removed.

The life cycles are complex and often involve alternate sexual and asexual generations. Sexual reproduction sometimes results in short-lived tadpole-like larvae, which resembles adult appendicularians. Salps are renowned for their ability to rapidly grow and increase in numbers; huge swarms can quickly appear in the ocean during periods of favourable weather. Most of the 70-odd species are most abundant in tropical and subtropical seas, but more than 20 have been recorded from southern Australia.

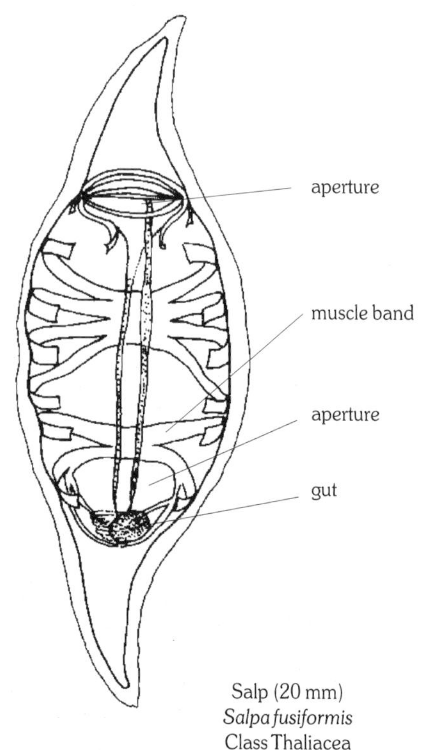

Salp (20 mm)
Salpa fusiformis
Class Thaliacea

Pyrosoma atlanticum Peron, 1804

Habitat: Ocean; 0–500 m depth.
Distribution: WA to southern Qld and around Tas. Also widespread overseas.
Maximum size: Length of colonies to 500 mm.

Pyrosoma atlanticum is a colonial species, with individual zooids rapidly reproducing asexually to form large cylindrical structures. These colonies are almost transparent and can luminesce brightly. In southeastern Australia *Pyrosoma atlanticum* is most abundant at water depths greater than 250 m, but the species is regularly seen in shallow water off the Tasmanian coast.

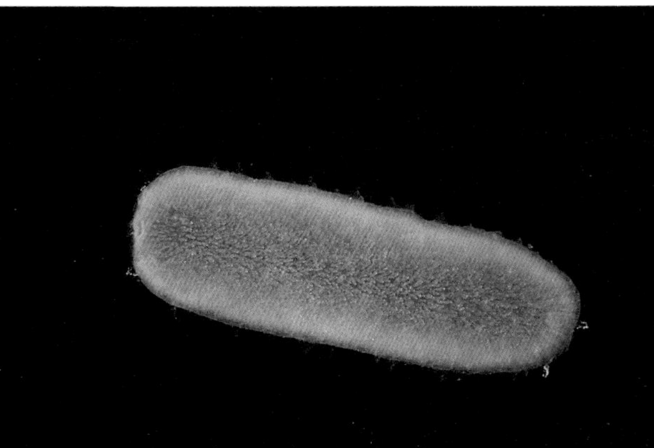

Pyrosoma atlanticum, Waterfall Bay, Tas.

Pegea confoederata Forsskål, 1775

Habitat: Ocean; 0–100 m depth.
Distribution: Around the Australian mainland and Tas. Also widespread overseas.
Maximum size: Length to 80 mm.

Pegea confoederata occurs in two forms, either as a solitary cylindrical animal (as illustrated) or in aggregated chains of smaller, pear-shaped zooids. Both forms are characterised by two X-shaped sets of muscle bands. The species is moderately common in all tropical and temperate seas.

Pegea confoederata, D'Entrecasteaux Channel, Tas.

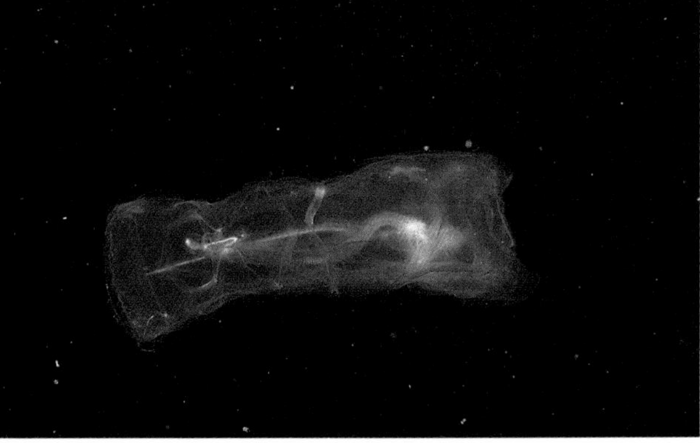

Class Larvacea

Appendicularians, larvaceans

This class contains about 60 species of transparent, planktonic animals with small, tadpole-shaped bodies. The body is divided into two parts, an ovoid trunk, which contains the head and gut, and a relatively long tail, which contains the notochord. The tail is set at a sharp angle to the main axis of the head. Appendicularians drift through the sea enclosed in large, gelatinous 'houses'. Each house is extremely delicate and will be abandoned if damaged. Movement of the tail generates a current through the house and propels the animal forward. Appendicularians feed on small phytoplankton cells and large bacteria, which are trapped in a fine-meshed mucous net placed across the internal current. In some sheltered areas, appendicularians seasonally occur in swarms and provide most of the biomass in plankton samples.

Oikopleura sp.

Habitat: Estuarine and coastal waters; 0–5 m depth.
Distribution: Tas.
Maximum size: Length to 3 mm.

A number of species in the genus *Oikopleura* occur around Australia, most of them with a similar general appearance. The illustrated species occurs abundantly in southern Tasmania during the warmer months and is one of the major components of inshore plankton.

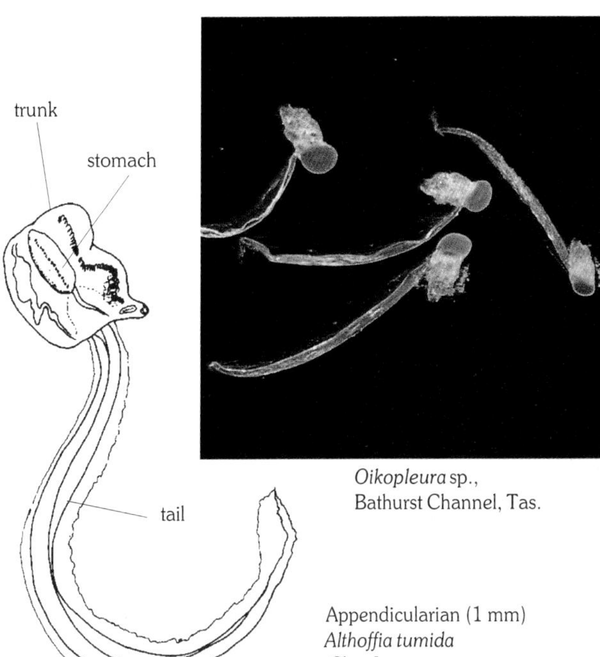

Oikopleura sp., Bathurst Channel, Tas.

Appendicularian (1 mm)
Althoffia tumida
Class Larvacea

Class Cephalaspidomorphi

Jawless fishes

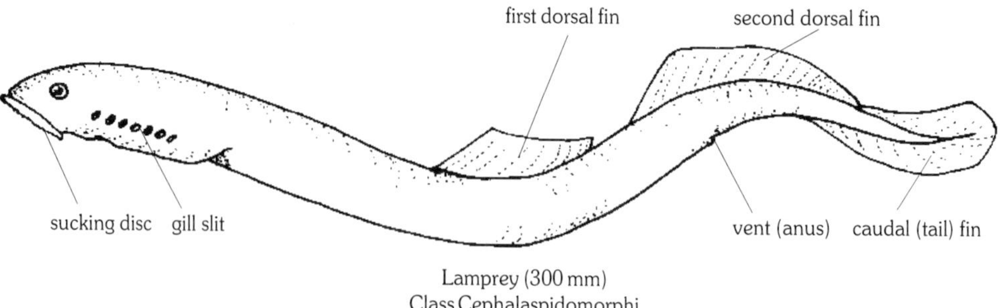

Lamprey (300 mm)
Class Cephalaspidomorphi

Four surviving classes of vertebrate animals — Cephalaspidomorphi (lampreys), Pteraspidomorphi (hagfishes), Chondrichthyes (sharks) and Osteichthyes (bony fishes) — are collectively known as fish because of the presence of fins and other adaptations for an aquatic life. This grouping is somewhat artificial, because mammals diverged from the bony fishes in much more recent geological times than the bony fishes diverged from the sharks, and so the bony fishes are more closely related to mammals; however, mammals have become greatly modified for life on land during a period when the bony fishes and sharks have changed little. The term 'fish' is used by biologists to denote one or more animals belonging to a single species, whereas the term 'fishes' refers to a group containing two or more species.

The class Cephalapidomorphi contains few living species but was once very important as it includes the jawless fishes that were dominant in seas about 300 million years ago.

FAMILY PETROMYZONTIDAE
Lampreys

Lampreys have an eel-like body, a sucking-disc mouth that has numerous teeth in circular rows (but no jaws), a single nostril on top of the head and seven gill slits. They have a cartilaginous rather than bony skeleton and lack paired fins and scales.

Geotria australis Gray, 1851
Pouched lamprey

Habitat: Open sea, rivers.
Distribution: Moore River, WA, to Lakes Entrance, Vic., and around Tas. Also New Zealand and South America.
Maximum size: Length to 600 mm.

The pouched lamprey differs from the only other southern lamprey, ***Mordacia mordax***, by having a large mouth fringed with fleshy papillae and eyes on the side of the head. It lives at sea for only part of its life, migrating into rivers at the subadult stage. Once in fresh water, animals mature without feeding; they then spawn and die. Newly hatched lampreys complete a larval stage within rivers and then migrate to sea. Little is known of the marine stage. They feed on other fishes by attaching themselves using the suctoral mouth and then rasping and sucking the body tissues.

Geotria australis, Badger Ck, Vic. RUDIE KUITER

Class Chondrichthyes

Cartilaginous fishes (sharks, rays)

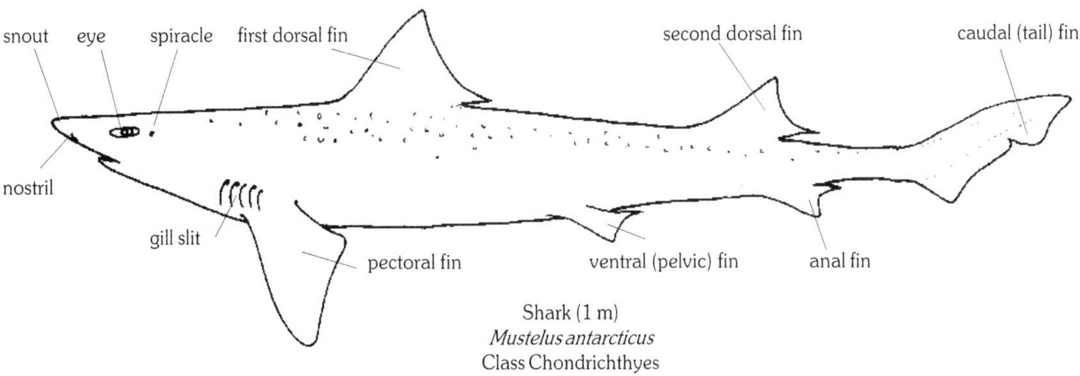

Shark (1 m)
Mustelus antarcticus
Class Chondrichthyes

This class contains jawed fishes that have a skeleton constructed from cartilage rather than bone and, with the exception of the ghost sharks, have five to seven gill slits on each side of the body. Sharks and rays reproduce by the male passing sperm to the female using modified ventral fins known as claspers. Some species produce large egg cases, which attach to the sea bed, but most species bear live young.

FAMILY HETERODONTIDAE
Port Jackson sharks, bullhead sharks

Heterodontids are characterised by a blunt rounded head with raised ridges over the eyes, two dorsal fins with associated spines, and a characteristic arrangement of sharp teeth at the front of each jaw and rounded teeth behind. Only eight species in the one genus are known in the family.

Heterodontus portusjacksoni (Meyer, 1793)
Port Jackson shark

Habitat: Sheltered and moderately exposed reef, seagrass; 1–275 m depth.
Distribution: Houtman Abrolhos, WA, to Byron Bay, NSW, and around Tas.
Maximum size: Length to 1.65 m.

The Port Jackson Shark has a distinctive appearance and occurs commonly, so is well known to most divers and fishermen in southern Australia. It can be confused only with the crested Port Jackson shark ***Heterodontus galeatus***, a species that occurs in New South Wales and southern Queensland and has high crests above the eyes and broad dark bars rather than oblique lines down the sides. Port Jackson sharks have spirally flanged egg cases, which are twisted into reef crevices and in which the young develop over a period of a year. Hatchlings require about ten years to grow to maturity, which they reach at about 800 mm length. Adult female *H. portusjacksoni* from New South Wales migrate southwards as far as Tasmania during the summer months. The species is not dangerous but should be handled with caution because of a venomous barb in front of each dorsal fin. It also has strong jaws with plate-like teeth that are used for crushing bivalve molluscs.

Heterodontus portusjacksoni, Jervis Bay, NSW. KELVIN AITKEN

FAMILY PARASCYLLIDAE
Collared catsharks

Collared catsharks are a small family of bottom-dwelling sharks with small heads, sinuous bodies, two spineless dorsal fins, nasal barbels near the corners of the mouth, and a groove joining the nostrils to the mouth. They are mainly nocturnal, remaining hidden in reef crevices during the day.

Parascyllium ferrugineum McCulloch, 1911
Rusty catshark

Habitat: Moderately and submaximally exposed reef; 5–150 m depth.
Distribution: Albany, WA, to Gabo I, Vic., and around Tas.
Maximum size: Length to 800 mm.

The rusty catshark is an elongate species of shark with a grey-brown background colour and numerous regularly spaced dark brown dots on the body and fins. The species is rarely seen by divers or fishermen except in cooler Tasmanian waters.

Parascyllium variolatum, Recherche Archipelago, WA. CLAY BRYCE.

Parascyllium ferrugineum, Erith I, Tas.

Parascyllium variolatum (Duméril, 1853)
Varied catshark

Habitat: Moderately exposed reef; 3–180 m depth.
Distribution: Dongara, WA, to Lakes Entrance, Vic., and King I, Tas.
Maximum size: Length to 900 mm.

The varied catshark can be recognised by its sinuous snake-like appearance, the pattern of large white spots on a dark brown background and the characteristic black collar punctuated by small white spots that lies just behind the head. This catshark is relatively common within its range but is not often sighted by divers because it remains concealed among kelp and in crevices during the day.

FAMILY SCYLIORHINIDAE
Catsharks

This is a large family of sharks that closely resemble the collared catsharks but generally lack nasal barbels and have a mouth extending back behind the eyes. Most of the 90 or so species are restricted to the tropics.

Cephaloscyllium laticeps (Duméril, 1853)
Draughtboard shark, swell shark

Habitat: Exposed reef, sand; 3–60 m depth.
Distribution: Recherche Archipelago, WA, to Jervis Bay, NSW, and around Tas.
Maximum size: Length to 1.5 m.

The draughtboard shark is a harmless slow-moving shark with an inflatable stomach, the reason why one of its common names is the 'swell shark'. The species

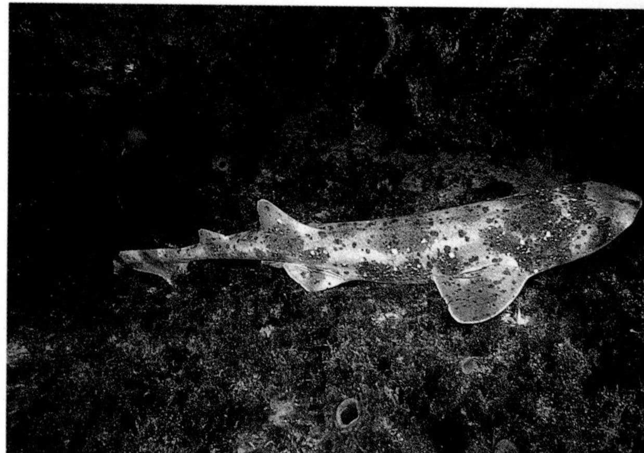

Cephaloscyllium laticeps, Wilsons Prom., Vic, KELVIN AITKEN

Cephaloscyllium laticeps egg case, D'Entrecasteaux Channel, Tas.

occurs commonly on Tasmanian reefs but is usually found in deeper water around the mainland. It often enters lobster pots, a surprising feat given that large animals almost completely fill the pot.

FAMILY ORECTOLOBIDAE
Wobbegongs

Wobbegongs are flattened sharks that sit immobile for long periods waiting for passing prey. They have characteristic fleshy lobes projecting down from the upper lip, two dorsal fins of similar size and an anal fin just in front of the tail. Only about eight species are known in the family, most of them occurring in tropical and temperate Australian waters.

Orectolobus ornatus (De Vis, 1883)

Ornate wobbegong

Habitat: Reef; 2–50 m depth.
Distribution: Around the Australian mainland and Flinders I, Tas.
Maximum size: Length to 3 m.

Orectolobus ornatus, Port Stephens, NSW

The ornate wobbegong is the most common wobbegong in southern Australian waters and can be recognised by the blotches surrounded by black spots over the body and fins. Like other wobbegong species, the upper body is covered by mottled browns, greys and greens, and leafy skin flaps are present around the lip. Wobbegongs have probably caused more shark bites in southern Australia than all other sharks combined. Their long pointed teeth can inflict a painful wound but are generally used only if the animal is molested.

Orectolobus maculatus (Bonnaterre 1788)

Spotted wobbegong

Habitat: Exposed reef; 4–110 m depth.
Distribution: Fremantle, WA, to Moreton I, Qld.
Maximum size: Length to 3.2 m.

The spotted wobbegong resembles the ornate wobbegong in size and shape but has circular blotches surrounded by rings of white spots on the upper body surface. It is less often seen by divers on eastern coastal reefs than the ornate wobbegong. It is also less common than another wobbegong, the western wobbegong ***Orectolobus* sp.**, in Western Australia. The western wobbegong can be recognised by its dark background colour and fewer and smaller skin flaps on the upper lip.

Orectolobus maculatus, Jervis Bay, NSW. KELVIN AITKEN

FAMILY ODONTASPIDIDAE
Grey nurse sharks

Grey nurses are large, heavy-bodied sharks with two high dorsal fins of approximately equal size and a large anal fin. Four species in two genera are known in the family, with only one recorded from southern Australian coastal waters.

Carcharias taurus, Seal Rocks, NSW. Kelvin Aitken

Carcharias taurus Rafinesque, 1810

Grey nurse shark

Habitat: Exposed reef; 1–190 m depth.
Distribution: Around the Australian mainland. Also widespread overseas.
Maximum size: Length to 3.2 m.

The grey nurse shark is the only large species of shark seen regularly on coastal reefs in southern Australia. The species can be quickly identified by the two large dorsal fins. Grey nurse sharks are now considered harmless unless antagonised but were once considered maneaters, probably largely because they swim with their long teeth exposed. After a period of needless slaughter the species is now fully protected in New South Wales. Population growth of grey nurse sharks is extremely slow, partly because of the low birth rate. Juveniles develop teeth within the uterus at about 100 mm size and then hunt and eat each other there, with only the fittest animal surviving from each litter to be released into the sea.

FAMILY LAMNIDAE
Makos

The five species in this family of primarily oceanic sharks have approximately equal-sized upper and lower lobes on the tail and a pronounced keel along the side of the body in front of the tail.

Carcharodon carcharias (Linnaeus 1758)

Great white shark, white pointer

Habitat: Open water; 0–1280 m depth.
Distribution: North West Cape, WA, to southern Qld and around Tas. Also widespread overseas.
Maximum size: Length to 6.4 m.

The great white shark is massive, with a high first dorsal fin and very small second dorsal and anal fins. It has a blue-grey upper body, which changes abruptly

Carcharodon carcharias, Port Lincoln, SA. Kelvin Aitken

to white on the under surface. The white pointer has a deservedly fearsome reputation, and few of the divers who have observed the species underwater without a cage would like to repeat the experience. Animals smaller than 3 m in length feed mainly on fish, but at larger sizes marine mammals become an important component of the diet. The world population of great white sharks appears to be steadily declining, with very few pregnant females reported worldwide during the past fifty years.

FAMILY TRIAKIDAE
Houndsharks

The triakids are small streamlined sharks closely related to the whaler sharks. They have long snouts, two dorsal fins that lack spines, and a tail with a large upper lobe that is distinctly notched. About 30 species are known, with three recorded from temperate Australia.

Mustelus antarcticus (Günther, 1870)
Gummy shark

Habitat: Sand, reef; 1–350 m depth.
Distribution: Shark Bay, WA, to Port Stephens, NSW, and around Tas.
Maximum size: Length to 1.75 m.

Gummy sharks are slender grey sharks with white spots and flat plate-like teeth for crushing molluscs. Together with the school shark, ***Galeorhinus galeus***, a free-swimming relative which has sharp teeth and no spots, the gummy shark provides much of the 'flake' used in fish and chip shops. This species grows slowly and is thought to have been substantially overfished, hence the commercial catch is now heavily regulated.

FAMILY CARCHARHINIDAE
Whaler sharks

Whaler sharks can be recognised by their streamlined bodies, large first dorsal fin placed slightly forward of midway along the back, small second dorsal fin in

Mustelus antarcticus, Port Phillip Bay, Vic. Rudie Kuiter

Carcharhinus brachyurus, Neptune I, SA. Kelvin Aitken

front of the tail, five gill slits (the last above the pectoral fins) and mouth set well back under the head. Included among the 50-odd species are many of the world's most dangerous sharks.

Carcharhinus brachyurus (Günther, 1870)
Bronze whaler

Habitat: Open water, sand, reef; 0–100 m depth.
Distribution: Jurien Bay, WA, to Coffs Harbour, NSW, and northern Tas.
Maximum size: Length to 3.25 m.

The bronze whaler has a torpedo-shaped body with large first dorsal fin and small second dorsal and anal fins. It has a general appearance similar to several other more tropical whaler sharks but can usually be identified by its bronze upper coloration on live specimens and the lack of a ridge of skin running between the dorsal fins. The species is, however, often confused with the black whaler ***Carcharhinus obscurus***, a second whaler shark found in southern Australian waters. The black whaler has black or white tips to the pectoral fins and a more rounded apex to the dorsal fin. Both temperate whalers are potentially dangerous and have a liking for speared fish, but more often the bronze whaler feeds on schooling pelagic fishes such as Australian salmon, and the black whaler feeds on bottom-dwelling organisms.

FAMILY SQUATINIDAE
Angelsharks

Angelsharks are intermediate in characteristics between sharks and rays; their head is incompletely joined to the wide pectoral fins. Only 13 species in one genus are known.

Squatina australis, Montague I, NSW. RUDIE KUITER

Squatina australis (Regan, 1906)
Angelshark, monkfish

Habitat: Moderately exposed sand; 2–130 m depth.
Distribution: Rottnest I, WA, to Port Stephens, NSW, and northern Tas.
Maximum size: Length to 1.52 m.

The angelshark is a large species with a light grey upper surface covered by numerous white spots. It is sometimes detected buried under a thin layer of sand near reef edges or seagrass beds, but is not common.

FAMILY RHINOBATIDAE
Guitarfishes

Species in this family have characteristics of both sharks and skates. They possess a large disc formed by the fusion of the head and pectoral fins, and a long tail with two large dorsal fins and a terminal fin. Guitarfishes sit on the seabed and feed on benthic crustaceans and molluscs. Most of the 50 or so species are found in shallow tropical areas.

Aptychotrema vincentiana (Haake, 1885)
Western shovelnose ray

Habitat: Sheltered and moderately exposed sand; 1–32 m depth.
Distribution: Port Hedland, WA, to Wilsons Promontory, Vic., and Kent Group, Tas.
Maximum size: Length to 1.2 m.

The western shovelnose ray is occasionally seen by divers or caught in nets off sheltered beaches in southern Australia. A similar species with a slightly longer snout and less obvious blotches on the body, the eastern shovelnose ray ***Aptychotrema rostrata***, is fairly common on the coast from central New South Wales to southern Queensland. Both species feed actively on crustaceans and molluscs that live on or under sand.

Aptychotrema vincentiana, Edithburgh, SA. RUDIE KUITER

Trygonorrhina fasciata Müller & Henle, 1841
Fiddler ray, banjo ray

Habitat: Sheltered and moderately exposed sand, reef; 0–50 m depth.
Distribution: Eden, NSW, to southern Qld.
Maximum size: Length to 1.2 m.

Trygonorrhina fasciata, Narooma, NSW. RUDIE KUITER

Two species of fiddler ray occur in temperate Australian waters: *Trygonorrhina fasciata*, confined to New South Wales and southern Queensland waters; and ***Trygonorrhina guanerius***, found west of eastern Bass Strait. Until recently, these two species were considered regional forms of the one species. They are mainly distinguished by differences in the ornate dorsal markings, with *T. fasciata* possessing a triangle and *T. guanerius* three short longitudinal stripes immediately behind the eyes. Fiddler rays frequently enter extremely shallow water to forage over sandflats.

FAMILY TORPEDINIDAE
Numbfishes, electric rays

Torpedinids have flabby, rounded discs with short to moderate-length tails and rounded dorsal and tail fins. Their most characteristic feature is a pair of kidney-shaped electric organs located on the sides of the disc. About 40 species are known, two of which occur in southern Australia.

Narcine tasmaniensis Richardson, 1840
Tasmanian numbfish

Habitat: Sheltered mud, sand; 3–640 m depth.
Distribution: Beachport, SA, to Coffs Harbour, NSW, and around Tas.
Maximum size: Length to 460 mm.

Narcine tasmaniensis, D'Entrecasteaux Channel, Tas.

The Tasmanian numbfish has a rounded tan to dark brown disc, a tail longer than the disc, two large dorsal fins, and white undersurface. The species is one of the most common fishes on soft sediments in the deeper sheltered bays of southern Tasmania, but it occurs mainly on the continental shelf in water depths of 200–640 m off the mainland. The Tasmanian numbfish will produce a mild electric shock if handled.

Hypnos monopterygium
(Shaw & Nodder 1795)
Numbfish

Habitat: Moderately exposed sand; 2–220 m depth.
Distribution: Broome, WA, to Caloundra, Qld.
Maximum size: Length to 690 mm.

The numbfish has a distinctive double-lobed shape with very short tail. The species should be well known to most New South Wales and Western Australian divers because of the severe electric shock produced on contact. In many cases, divers receive shocks when placing a hand on apparently bare sand — the only sign of a concealed ray is its two fringed nostrils open at the sediment surface. The numbfish feeds on comparatively large fish, which are stunned and pounced on, the lobes wrapping around and engulfing the victim. The species is very rarely found in Victorian waters.

Hypnos monopterygium, Port Stephens, NSW

FAMILY RAJIDAE
Skates

Skates comprise a large group of ray-like fishes that are usually found in deep offshore waters. They usually have numerous thorn-like spines over the body and tail, two small dorsal fins near the end of the tail, and lack large venomous spines.

Raja lemprieri Richardson, 1845
Thornback skate

Habitat: Sand, mud; 0–170 m depth.
Distribution: Beachport, SA, to Jervis Bay, NSW, and around Tas.
Maximum size: Length to 520 mm.

Although most species in the family are restricted to deep water, the thornback skate commonly enters shallow estuaries in southern Tasmania. The most characteristic features of this species are the dark patch underneath the snout and thorns around the eyes.

Raja lemprieri, D'Entrecasteaux Channel, Tas.

Raja whitleyi, Bicheno, Tas. RUDIE KUITER

Raja whitleyi Iredale, 1938
Whitley's skate

Habitat: Sand, mud; 1–170 m depth.
Distribution: Albany, WA, to Wollongong, NSW, and around Tas.
Maximum size: Length to 1.7 m.

Whitley's skate is the largest skate found in Australian waters and can reach a weight of 50 kg. The features distinguishing this species are its long tail, broad fins, lack of spines beside the eyes and a grey upper surface spotted with white flecks. This skate is commonly entangled in the graball nets used in Tasmania and is difficult to extract because of its large size and the numerous short spines along the tail.

FAMILY DASYATIDIDAE
Stingrays

Stingrays have a rounded or diamond-shaped disc formed by the fusion of the head and pectoral fins, and a long thin tail which carries one or two venomous barbs. Dorsal and tail fins are absent, although folds of skin are sometimes present on the tail. Species generally cruise slowly along the seabed searching for invertebrate prey but are very strong swimmers and can move quickly. Large animals are potentially dangerous if threatened.

Dasyatis brevicaudata, Cloudy Lagoon, Tas.

Dasyatis brevicaudata (Hutton, 1875)
Smooth stingray

Habitat: Sand, reef; 0–100 m depth.
Distribution: Shark Bay, WA, to Maroochydore, Qld, and around Tas. Also New Zealand and southern Africa.
Maximum size: Length to 4.3 m.

The smooth stingray is the largest of all stingrays, reaching a weight of 350 kg. It resembles another massive southern Australian ray, the black stingray ***Dasyatis thetidis***, but has a series of small white spots across the flaps and lacks spines down the middle of the back. The smooth stingray is not aggressive but can be inquisitive, so should be treated with great caution as the large venomous spine on the tail can cause fatal wounds.

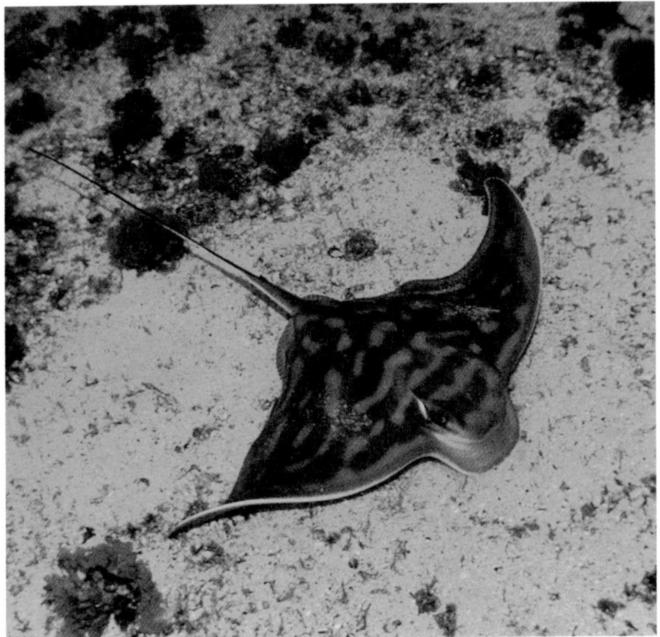

Myliobatis australis, Sydney, NSW. RUDIE KUITER

FAMILY MYLIOBATIDAE
Eagle rays

Eagle rays can be recognised by the pointed wing flaps, bulbous head and whip-like tail, which is often broken. The tail has a single dorsal fin at the front, followed by a venomous spine. While eagle rays should be treated warily, none of the 25 species in the family are considered as dangerous as stingrays.

Myliobatis australis Macleay, 1881
Eagle ray

Habitat: Sand, seagrass, reef; 0–85 m depth.
Distribution: Jurien Bay, WA, to Moreton Bay, Qld, and around Tas.
Maximum size: Length to 2.41 m.

The eagle ray is the only species in the family found in southern Australia. Its upper surface has numerous blue spots and crescents arranged in a regular pattern across an olive-green background. Eagle rays are often seen foraging across estuarine sandflats for crabs and molluscs in water so shallow that the wings protrude above the water surface.

FAMILY UROLOPHIDAE
Stingarees

Stingarees are generally similar in appearance to stingrays but are smaller in size and have a rounded fin at the end of the tail. They possess one or two venomous spines on the tail and, despite their small size, should be considered dangerous. Australia is the centre of diversity for this family, with about half the approximately 40 species restricted to this country and at least 10 species present in temperate waters.

Urolophus cruciatus (Lacepede, 1804)
Banded stingaree

Habitat: Sand, reef; 0–160 m depth.
Distribution: Beachport, SA, to Tathra, NSW, and around Tas.
Maximum size: Length to 500 mm.

Urolophus cruciatus, Bicheno, Tas.

The banded stingaree is by far the most common species found in shallow Tasmanian waters and can occur in very large aggregations in small areas of sandy reef. The pattern of dark bands on the disk is distinctive.

Urolophus paucimaculatus Dixon, 1969
Sparsely spotted stingaree

Habitat: Sand; 1–150 m depth.
Distribution: Lancelin, WA, to Crowdy Head, NSW, and around Tas.
Maximum size: Length to 440 mm.

The sparsely spotted stingaree is most easily recognised in southern waters because of its pattern of white spots on the upper surface; however, these spots become less distinct or are absent in specimens seen in deeper water and towards the north of its range. The species is more aggressive than other southern stingarees and has been known to attack divers. It is sometimes captured by trawlers in large quantities.

Urolophus paucimaculatus, Cloudy Bay, Tas.

Urolophus paucimaculatus, Rocky Cape, Tas.

Urolophus sp.

Habitat: Sand; 7–35 m depth.
Distribution: Bermagui to Jervis Bay, NSW.
Maximum size: Length to 400 mm.

Urolophus sp. is a moderately common stingaree that until recently was confused with *Urolophus cruciatus*. While both species have a banded appearance, the markings of the two differ: this species has a transverse stripe between the eyes, and *Urolophus cruciatus* a longitudinal stripe. This species is found on sand near the edge of reefs or seagrass beds.

Urolophus sp., Jervis Bay, NSW

Trygonoptera testacea Müller & Henle, 1841
Common stingaree

Habitat: Sheltered sand, mud; 0–135 m depth.
Distribution: Cape Howe, NSW, to Caloundra, Qld.
Maximum size: Length to 470 mm.

The common stingaree is a medium-sized ray with a dark brown to grey upper surface. In front of the barbs there is a very small dorsal fin, which in some individuals is only the size of a skin fold. The common stingaree, as its name suggests, is the most abundant species in the family along the New South Wales coast, particularly in estuaries.

Trygonoptera mucosa (Whitley, 1939)
Western stingaree

Habitat: Sheltered sand, mud; 0–120 m depth.
Distribution: Dongara, WA, to Port Phillip Bay, Vic.
Maximum size: Length to 800 mm.

The western stingaree occurs in two forms, which may represent different species: a small western form, which extends to Adelaide, and a larger eastern form, which is mainly confined to Victoria. Both forms differ from *Trygonoptera testacea* in lacking the small dorsal fin on the tail. The western stingaree is most commonly seen in shallow sheltered bays near seagrass beds.

Trygonoptera testacea, Narooma, NSW

Trygonoptera mucosa, Albany, WA

Class Osteichthyes

Bony fishes

Compared with the cartilaginous fishes, the bony fishes have evolved quite recently but are now the predominant vertebrate group, with more than 20 000 living species. This great diversity is probably one consequence of the rapidity with which populations evolve into different species if geographically separated. Bony fishes are characterised by a skeleton of bone and also have a single gill opening on each side of the head. They also generally have a distinctive row of scales with sensory pits along the sides of the body; these are used for sensing slight changes in water pressure, thereby providing information on the location of objects in their new vicinity. Most species produce eggs rather than bearing live young.

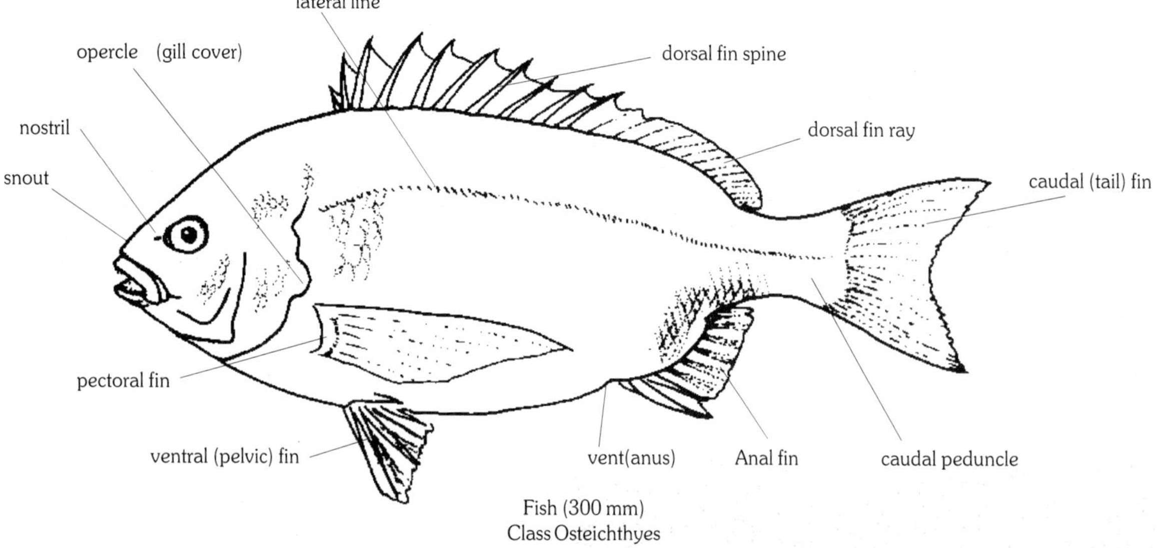

Fish (300 mm)
Class Osteichthyes

FAMILY MURAENIDAE
Moray eels

Morays are powerful eels with the lateral line reduced to a few pores above and in front of the small gill opening. They have a single fin, which extends from the head around the tail to the anus, and can also usually be recognised by the skin having a ridged appearance behind the head. The family comprises at least 150 species, but the exact number is uncertain because of confusion in classifying the many tropical species.

Gymnothorax prasinus (Richardson, 1848)

Green moray

Habitat: Reef; 0–20 m depth.
Distribution: Shark Bay, WA, to southern Qld and south to Maria I, Tas. Also New Zealand.
Maximum size: Length to 970 mm.

The green moray is the species of moray eel most often seen in southern Australian waters. It has a yellowish-brown humped head, blending into a green body. The species generally remains concealed in crevices during the day and moves about in the open when feeding at night. A second temperate moray eel, the speckled moray ***Gymnothorax obesus***, occurs along the New South Wales coast. This eel is easily

Gymnothorax prasinus, Seal Rocks, NSW. RUDIE KUITER

distinguished by colour pattern, as it has numerous cream speckles scattered over a brown body. A few tropical moray eels also occasionally occur down the New South Wales and Western Australian coasts but are rarely encountered.

FAMILY CONGRIDAE
Conger eels

Conger eels are large and muscular like the morays but differ by having pectoral fins and a smooth skin. They also have a full lateral line, and the gill openings form a slit rather than a hole. Around 150 species are known, most of them found in areas with a soft silt bottom.

Conger wilsoni (Bloch & Sneider, 1801)
Short-finned conger eel

Habitat: Sheltered reef; 0–10 m depth.
Distribution: Geraldton, WA, to Kangaroo I, SA, and Bermagui, NSW, to southern Qld. Also New Zealand and southern Africa.
Maximum size: Length to 1.5 mm.

The short-finned conger eel is a large grey eel with a dorsal fin that commences slightly behind the pectoral fin tips and is continuous with the tail and anal fins. It occurs most commonly near the mouths of sheltered estuaries among seabed debris, particularly near wharf pylons. The species remains in crevices during the day and moves about at night. Conger eels are not usually aggressive but will defend themselves if caught by spear, line or lobster pot.

Conger wilsoni, Merimbula, NSW

Conger verreauxi, Bathurst Channel, Tas.

Conger verreauxi Kaup, 1856
Southern conger eel

Habitat: Sheltered and moderately exposed reef; 0–80 m depth.
Distribution: Beachport, SA, to eastern Vic. and around Tas.
Maximum size: Length to 2 m.

The southern conger eel occurs in the section of the southern Australian coast where the short-finned conger eel is absent. It differs from that species by having a slightly longer dorsal fin (starting above rather than just behind the tip of the pectoral fin) and lacking the pale coloration of the short-finned conger eel under the head. During the day it remains hidden in caves, with the tip of the tail often protruding.

FAMILY OPHICHTHIDAE
Snake eels, worm eels

Ophichthids are long, thin, rounded eels with reduced fins and usually a pointed tip in place of the tail. They have extremely muscular bodies for their size and generally live buried in sand. This is the most diverse of the eel families, with over 250 species.

Ophisurus serpens (Linnaeus 1758)
Serpent eel

Habitat: Sand, silt; 0–50 m depth.
Distribution: Lancelin, WA, to Noosa River, Qld, and northeastern Tas. Also widespread overseas.
Maximum size: Length to 2.5 m.

The serpent eel occurs commonly on soft sediments in estuaries but is rarely observed or captured because it remains hidden in burrows with only the head protruding. The species can usually be identified by the slender pointed mouth, the arrangement of pores on the head and the sandy brown colour. It has sharp teeth and is a surprisingly strong animal when speared or captured on a line, so is best left alone. Juveniles may be found in shallow water, but the adults live offshore.

Ophisurus serpens, Terrigal, NSW

Muraenichthys breviceps Günther, 1876
Short-headed worm-eel

Habitat: Silt, sand; 0–70 m depth.
Distribution: Rottnest I, WA, to Vic. and around Tas. Also New Zealand.
Maximum size: Length to 630 mm.

The several species of worm-eel in southern Australian waters differ from the serpent eel by lacking a pectoral fin. The short-headed worm-eel is long and thin with a brown-green back and pale belly. It remains buried under sediment during the day and moves about at night looking for prey. When feeding over sand this animal is interesting to watch; it probes deeply in the sediment with its sharply pointed tail until it contacts an alpheid or ghost shrimp and then twists around and follows the tail with the head to locate the prey.

Muraenichthys breviceps, Margate, Tas.

FAMILY ANGUILLIDAE
Freshwater eels

Freshwater eels are long muscular eels with small pectoral fins, a well-developed lateral line, small gill openings, and a mosaic of minute oval scales embedded in the skin. The common name of the family is somewhat misleading because, in addition to living in rivers, they spend the juvenile and late adult stages of their lives at sea. About 15 species are known.

Anguilla australis Richardson, 1841
Short-fin eel

Habitat: Freshwater, open sea; 0–300 m depth.
Distribution: Bremer R, SA, to Brisbane R, Qld, and around Tas. Also New Zealand.
Maximum size: Length to 1.1 m.

Anguilla australis, Douglas River, Tas.

Short-fin eels have a multiphase life cycle. Eels in the youngest phase look nothing like adult eels but are thin, transparent and leaf-like, and drift south in the open ocean with the East Australian Current. Before their relationship to the adult was known, these juvenile eels were given the genus name *Leptocephalus*, a term still used to refer to that phase of the life cycle. The leptocephali transform into transparent worm-like glass eels, which move into rivers. On reaching the first rapid in the river, the glass eels begin taking on pigment and quickly change into miniature replicas of the adult, known as elvers. The elvers develop and mature into adults in rivers and then start the long migration (which may exceed 3000 km) to the Coral Sea, where they spawn and die, leaving a new generation of sea-going leptocephali. Short-fin eels are caught commercially in Victorian and Tasmanian rivers, and most of the catch is exported to Germany.

Anguilla reinhardtii Steindachner, 1867
Long-fin eel

Habitat: Freshwater, estuary, open sea; 0–300 m depth.
Distribution: Melbourne, Vic., to Cape York, Qld, and northern and eastern Tas. Also Lord Howe I and New Caledonia.
Maximum size: Length to 1.6 m.

Anguilla reinhardtii, Douglas River, Tas.

Adult long-fin eels occur in many of the same rivers as short-fin eels, and the juvenile leptocephali drift in the same currents. However, the two species are easily distinguished because the dorsal fin of the long-fin eel commences well in front of the anal fin and not approximately level with it, and the body is heavily spotted or blotched. Long-fin eels also grow to a much larger size and are more aggressive than short-fin eels, and prefer flowing rivers and creeks to calm ponds and lakes.

FAMILY CLUPEIDAE
Herrings, sardines, pilchards

This family contains about 180 species of schooling fishes that have a scaleless head and sides that are covered by reflective, weakly attached scales. Southern Australian species in this group have small ventral and anal fins, the first located about mid-way along the body and a single dorsal fin with soft rays. This and the tuna family Scombridae are by far the most commercially important families worldwide with millions of tonnes caught in productive seas every year.

Sardinops neopilchardus
(Steindachner, 1879)
Pilchard, sardine, mulie

Habitat: Bays, open sea; 0–100 m depth.
Distribution: Cape Cuvier, WA, to Rockhampton, Qld, and northern and eastern Tas. Also New Zealand.
Maximum size: Length to 250 mm.

The pilchard is the most common clupeid in southern Australian waters and reaches the largest size. It has a green-blue upper surface and is silver below, with a series of dark spots high on the sides. Schools shoal and spawn near the water surface in spring and summer in South Australia, and in summer and autumn in New South Wales, and move into deeper water in the other seasons. Other related fishes that occur commonly are the blue sprat ***Spratelloides robustus***, a species with dark blue on the upper half and a horse-shoe mark at the base of the tail, and the Australian anchovy ***Engraulis australis***, a species in the related family Engraulidae, with a very long mouth extending back behind the eye.

Sardinops neopilchardus, Seal Rocks, NSW. Rudie Kuiter

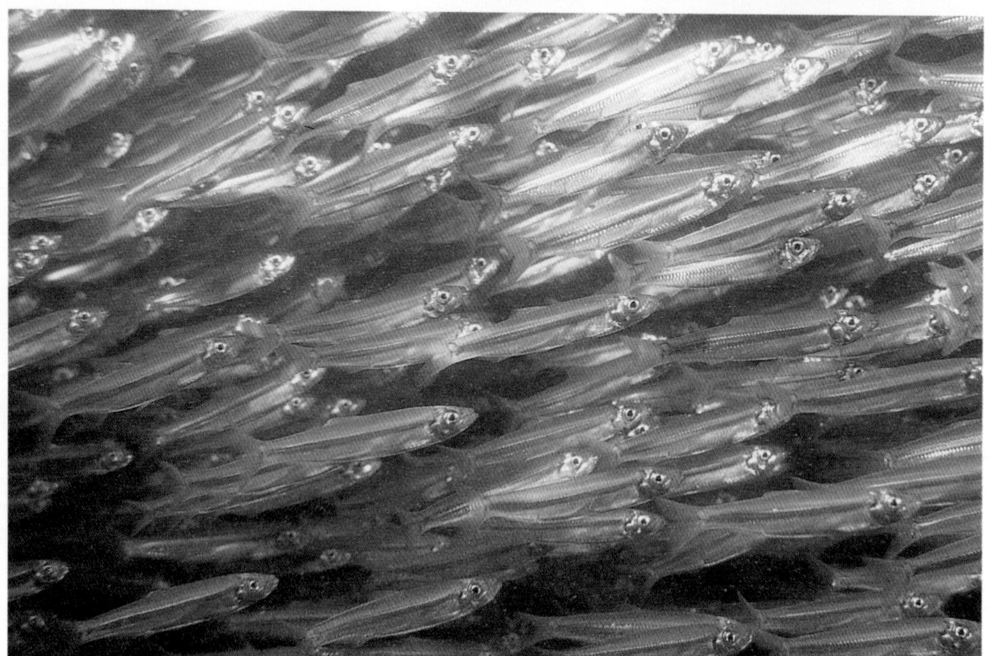

Hyperlophus vittatus, Flinders, Vic. RUDIE KUITER

Hyperlophus vittatus (Castelnau, 1875)
Sandy sprat

Habitat: Bays, estuaries; 0–5 m depth.
Distribution: Kalbarri, WA, to Moreton Bay, Qld.
Maximum size: Length to 100 mm.

Sandy sprat are small schooling fish, which occur abundantly in sheltered bays and are sold occasionally as bait. The species can be recognised by the sandy colour and broad silver stripe along the side. It also has a slightly serrated edge along the belly and in front of the dorsal fin, caused by overlapping scales.

FAMILY SALMONIDAE
Salmon, trout

Salmonids are a Northern Hemisphere family of about 70 fishes, some of which, during the past two centuries, have been introduced to all continents of the world with the exception of Antarctica. They have small scales, a large dorsal fin with a short base set about midway along the back, an adipose fin in front of the tail that is spotted in the same way as the dorsal fin, and low pectoral fins.

Salmo trutta Linnaeus, 1758
Brown trout

Habitat: Rivers, lakes, estuaries, continental shelf.
Distribution: Southwestern WA to NSW and around Tas. Also widely distributed overseas.
Maximum size: Length to 1.4 m.

Salmo trutta, Douglas River, Tas.

The brown trout is a European species keenly sought by anglers in rivers and lakes but also occurring in estuarine and marine waters, where it is known as 'sea-run trout'. The rainbow trout ***Oncorhyncus mykiss*** is also occasionally taken in marine water by fishermen; this species differs from the brown trout by having rows of large spots extending across the tail. The Atlantic salmon ***Salmo salar*** also resembles the brown trout, the main difference being a slightly forked tail and a relatively small mouth not extending back past the eyes. Atlantic salmon that have escaped from aquaculture cages are now frequently caught in gillnets in southeastern Tasmania, but such escapees are not well adapted for feeding away from captivity and are often in poor condition. The depth limits of trout at sea are poorly known because they can readily avoid trawl nets.

FAMILY GALAXIIDAE
Mountain trout, native trout

The galaxiids are a family of small Southern Hemisphere fishes closely related to the true trouts and salmons. About 46 species are known worldwide, with 20 species in Australia, most of them confined to freshwater lakes and rivers. They are distinguished by a lack of scales and a dorsal fin set well back above the anal fin.

Galaxias truttaceus Valenciennes, 1846
Spotted galaxias, mountain trout

Habitat: Rivers, estuaries, sea; 0–4 m depth.
Distribution: Albany, WA, and Otway Ranges to Lakes Entrance, Vic., and around Tas.
Maximum size: Length to 200 mm.

Adult spotted galaxias live in rivers, but during autumn they spawn and release eggs, which drift out to sea. Little is known of the marine stage of the life cycle. Juveniles about 65 mm long migrate back into rivers from the sea in spring, when they can be collected in large numbers. In some Tasmanian rivers other species (notably Tasmanian whitebait *Lovettia sealei* and common jollytail *Galaxias maculatus*) also join in this migration of juvenile fish. This run of 'whitebait' was once exploited as a substantial fishery.

Galaxias truttaceus, Douglas River, Tas.

Galaxias maculatus, Apsley River, Tas.

Galaxias maculatus (Jenyns, 1842)
Common jollytail, native trout

Habitat: Rivers, estuaries, sea; 0–5 m depth.
Distribution: Albany, WA, to southern Qld and around Tas. Also Lord Howe I, New Zealand and South America.
Maximum size: Length to 190 mm.

Common jollytail have more elongate bodies than spotted galaxias and lack spots on the sides of the body, possessing weak, wavy vertical bars instead. The two species often occur in the same river systems, with the common jollytail predominant in the lower reaches and estuary. Both species have similar life histories.

FAMILY PROTOTROCTIDAE
Southern graylings

The southern graylings differ from related families by lacking a lateral line and having scales, a dorsal fin that starts behind the ventral fin and ends before the start of the anal fin, and a small fleshy adipose fin in front of the tail. The family contains two species, one of which is extinct.

Prototroctes maraena Günther, 1864
Australian grayling, cucumber fish

Habitat: Rivers, estuaries, sea; 0–4 m depth.
Distribution: Port MacDonnell, SA, to Nowra, NSW, and around Tas.
Maximum size: Length to 330 mm.

Like the galaxiid fishes, Australian grayling remain in fresh water as adults but have a marine juvenile stage which lasts until they reach about 50 mm in length. This species was once very common but has declined in numbers to only a few stable adult populations, so

Prototroctes maraena, Douglas River, Tas.

the species is considered threatened. Part of the reason for concern about this species' survival is that the only other species in the family, the New Zealand grayling *Prototroctes oxyrhynchus*, suffered a rapid population crash early in the twentieth century and is now extinct.

FAMILY PLOTOSIDAE
Eel-tailed catfish

Eel-tailed catfish have long tapering bodies with several barbels around the mouth. They also have venomous spines at the front of the dorsal and pectoral fins that can cause an extremely painful wound. Most of the approximately 40 species in the family are tropical.

Cnidoglanis macrocephalus

(Valenciennes, 1840)
Estuary catfish, cobbler

Habitat: Sand, seagrass, reef; 0–15 m depth.
Distribution: Houtman Abrolhos, WA, to southern Qld and northern Tas.
Maximum size: Length to 910 mm.

The estuary catfish is a large, dark catfish that usually has pale mottled patches over the back and sides. It is highly rated for its taste and is one of the most expensive fish species in Western Australia, where it is known as cobbler; however, in New South Wales the species is rarely eaten and is generally regarded as a nuisance when caught. A related tropical species, the white-lipped catfish ***Paraplotosus albilabris***, occurs with the estuary catfish on the southern west coast but can be recognised because it lacks a small tentacle at the back of the lip. The estuary catfish is attracted to large clumps of drift seagrass or kelp plants on sand and remains concealed in this habitat during the day. Fish hidden in this way commonly cause painful injuries to people wading in shallow water.

Cnidoglanis macrocephalus, Narooma, NSW

Plotosus lineatus (Thunberg, 1791)

Striped catfish

Habitat: Sand, seagrass, reef; 0–15 m depth.
Distribution: Tropical Australia south to Esperance, WA, and Sydney, NSW. Also widespread in the Indo-West Pacific region.
Maximum size: Length to 350 mm.

Juvenile striped catfish occur in closely packed balls, which from a distance look like a single amorphous organism. Within each ball, the lower animals feed by pecking invertebrates from the substratum while the upper animals wait their turn. Each individual has

Plotosus lineatus, Sydney Harbour, NSW. RUDIE KUITER

cream and black stripes, which are most distinctive in the juveniles, and several barbels around the mouth. Like the estuary catfish, this species has venomous spines.

FAMILY AULOPODIDAE
Sergeant bakers, threadsails

Aulopids are related to the salmonid group of fishes, as is evident by the small fleshy adipose fin in front of the tail. They are elongate fishes with soft-rayed fins and a large mouth. Eight species in a single genus are known, most of them confined to deep water.

Aulopus purpurissatus Richardson, 1843
Sergeant baker

Habitat: Exposed reef; 2–248 m depth.
Distribution: Coral Bay, WA, to Laguna Bay, Qld, and northern Tas.
Maximum size: Length to 690 mm.

The sergeant baker has a mottled red coloration and flathead-like shape. The two sexes differ in the shape of the dorsal fin; in males the second ray projects out for a distance of nearly half the body length. Sergeant baker are occasionally caught by line on shallow coastal reefs in southern Western Australia and New South Wales, and in deeper water in the other states.

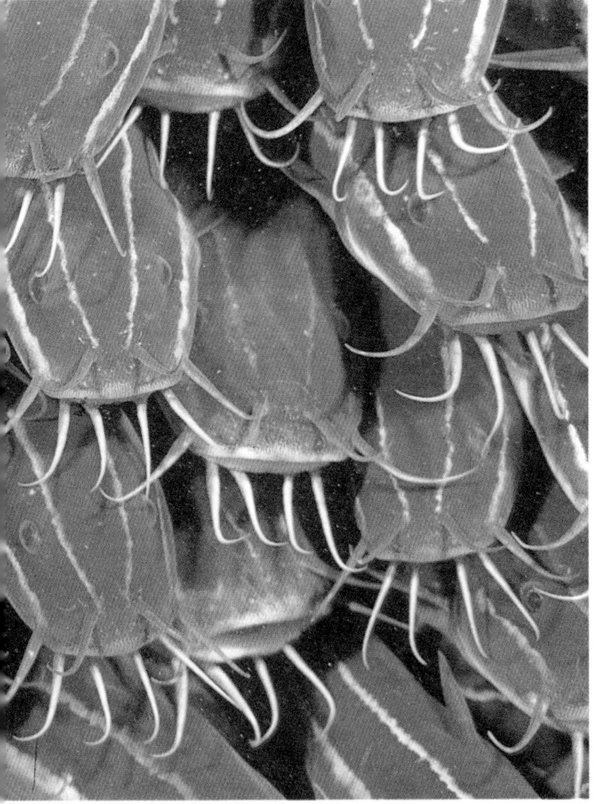

Aulopus purpurissatus, Bass Point, NSW

The fish would be considered good-eating if not for numerous small bones. Sergeant baker are often noticed by divers, because they are inquisitive and relatively common, and perch high on the reef.

FAMILY GONORYNCHIDAE
Beaked salmon

This family comprises several species in a single distinctive genus. Beaked salmon have a rounded, protrusible mouth with a small barbel on the upper lip, long flat-sided bodies and a soft-rayed dorsal fin that is set well back along the body.

Gonorynchus greyi (Richardson, 1845)
Beaked salmon

Habitat: Sheltered and moderately exposed sand; 0–160 m depth.
Distribution: Shark Bay, WA, to southern Qld.
Maximum size: Length to 500 mm.

Juvenile beaked salmon occur commonly on white sand in southern Australia, particularly in the channels of estuaries, but are rarely noticed because of their habit of quickly burying when disturbed. Adults are generally confined to deeper water offshore.

Gonorynchus greyi, Flinders I, Tas.

FAMILY SYNODONTIDAE
Lizard fishes

This family contains elongate, bottom-living fishes with large ventral fins, small pectoral fins, a short-based dorsal fin and pointed snout. They spend most of their time perched on the ventral fins, waiting for relatively large prey, which they ambush and hold using needle-like teeth. Nearly all of the 35 species are tropical, but several commonly range southwards to New South Wales and Western Australia.

Synodus dermatogenys Fowler, 1912
Two-spot lizardfish

Habitat: Moderately exposed sand; 5–25 m depth.
Distribution: Tropical Australia south to southern NSW.
Maximum size: Length to 220 mm.

The two-spot lizardfish is often seen perched on sand near reefs in the Sydney area and buries quickly when disturbed. It is distinguished from related species by the dark rounded markings that lie below a bluish-grey stripe on the sides, and two black spots in front of the eyes.

Synodus dermatogenys, Camp Cove, NSW. RUDIE KUITER

FAMILY BATRACHOIDIDAE
Frogfishes

Frogfishes are a group of about 50 species of scaleless fishes, which are well camouflaged for life on the bottom. They usually have fleshy projections on the head, a mottled coloration, three lateral lines and a long dorsal fin. The three spines at the start of the dorsal fin may be venomous, and so these fishes should be handled with great care. The common name refers to the croaking sound produced by the swim bladder when animals are captured.

Batrachomoeus rubricephalus
Hutchins, 1976
Pinkheaded frogfish

Habitat: Moderately exposed reef; 2–10 m depth.
Distribution: Houtman Abrolhos to Eucla, WA.
Maximum size: Length to 310 mm.

Batrachomoeus rubricephalus, Trigg Reef, WA. CLAY BRYCE

The pinkheaded frogfish is unlikely to be confused with other fishes in southern Western Australia, but a similar species, the eastern frogfish ***Batrachomoeus dubius***, is present in New South Wales. The pinkheaded frogfish is a lighter colour than its eastern relative and has pinkish bands between the eyes and on the sides of the head. Because of their cryptic appearance both species are more often caught on line than seen by divers. They have an expandable mouth that can accommodate very large prey. Females guard their eggs, which are placed on the ceiling of rock crevices.

FAMILY ANTENNARIDAE
Anglerfishes

Anglerfishes are an interesting family of about 40 species with pectoral fins modified for crawling, the first dorsal spine usually modified into a device for luring prey, and the second and third spines long and separated. They have large extendable mouths and expandable stomachs, which are adaptations for feeding on relatively large fish prey. Anglerfishes remain immobile until another fish approaches closely, and the prey is then sucked up whole.

Antennarius striatus (Shaw & Nodder, 1794)

Striped anglerfish

Habitat: Sheltered reef, sponge gardens; 0–200 m depth.
Distribution: Tropical Australia south to Wollongong, NSW, and Geraldton, WA.
Maximum size: Length to 250 mm.

The striped anglerfish occurs commonly in the Sydney area and, like the other anglerfishes, is an expert at camouflage. It is among the most variably coloured of all fish species, with white, yellow, orange, brown, green and jet black animals known. Nearly all have a pattern of dark, oblique stripes on the body.

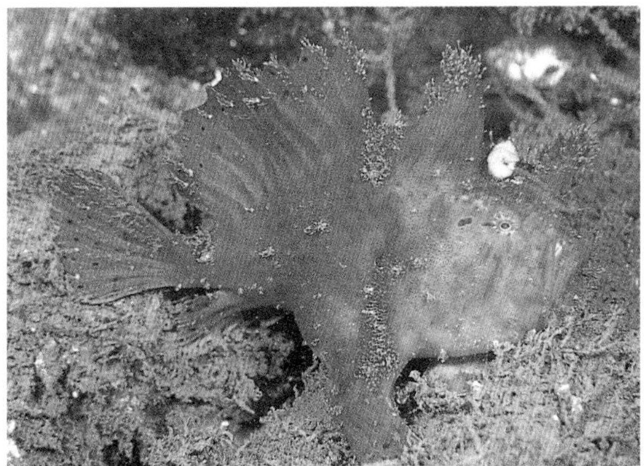

Antennarius striatus, Watsons Bay, NSW. RUDIE KUITER

Echinophryne crassispina

McCulloch & Waite, 1918
Prickly anglerfish

Habitat: Sheltered and moderately exposed reef; 1–20 m depth.
Distribution: Albany, WA, to Jervis Bay, NSW, and northern Tas.
Maximum size: Length to 70 mm.

The prickly anglerfish differs from other southern anglerfishes by having a dense covering of forked spinelets on the skin including over most of the fins. The species is probably quite common in ledges and under rocks but is rarely seen because of its cryptic appearance.

Echinophryne crassispina, Port Phillip Bay, Vic. RUDIE KUITER

Rhycherus filamentosus, Boat Harbour, Tas. MALCOLM WELLS

Rhycherus filamentosus (Castelnau, 1872)
Tasselled anglerfish

Habitat: Moderately exposed reef; 2–60 m depth.
Distribution: Gulf St. Vincent, SA, to Lakes Entrance, Vic., and northern Tas.
Maximum size: Length to 230 mm.

The tasselled anglerfish is easily identified by the numerous filaments scattered over the body surface and the prominent U-shaped lure that is attached to a long rod-like base. The species is moderately common on reefs but is rarely seen by divers because of its disruptive camouflage and preference for small crevices.

FAMILY BRACHIONICHTHYIDAE
Handfishes

Brachionichthyids are a small family of fishes that are very closely related to the anglerfishes but differ by having the second and third dorsal spines joined into a single fin rather than being separated. As in the anglerfishes, the first dorsal spine forms a lure, and the pectoral fins are used like legs for walking over the bottom. The gills are concealed under skin; after water has passed over the gills it is expelled through a large pore on each side of the body. This family of fishes is confined to southern Australia, with most of the seven or so species restricted to Tasmanian waters.

Brachionichthys hirsutus (Lacépède, 1804)
Spotted handfish

Habitat: Sheltered sand, mud; 2–30 m depth.
Distribution: Southeastern Tas.
Maximum size: Length to 120 mm.

Brachionichthys hirsutus, Sandy Bay, Tas.

The spotted handfish has a cream background with a dense covering of orange-brown spots over the skin and fins. This handfish was once commonly seen in the deeper bays of southeastern Tasmania, but the population seems to have virtually disappeared during recent years and is considered endangered. Sightings should be reported to local Fisheries officers. Other handfish species are also very rare.

Brachionichthys verrucosus
(McCulloch & Waite, 1918)
Warty handfish

Habitat: Sheltered sand; 5–110 m depth.
Distribution: Gulf St Vincent, SA, to Mallacoota, Vic.
Maximum size: Length to 80 mm.

Brachionichthys verrucosus, Portsea, Vic. KELVIN AITKEN

The warty handfish has a short lure and numerous small, wart-like processes on the surface of the skin. The sides of the body are mottled brown and white, providing the animal with excellent camouflage. This handfish is rarely seen by divers; most specimens have been collected by scallop dredge in depths greater than 20 m.

FAMILY GOBIESOCIDAE
Clingfishes, shore-eels

This family contains two very different-looking groups of fishes that until recently were classified in different orders. Although related, the inclusion of these two groups together in the one family is ridiculous, given the small amount of variation between some other fish families. The shore-eels include four species of small eel-like fishes that lack pectoral fins; the dorsal, ventral and tail fins lack finrays and are joined together. The clingfishes are a group of more than 100 species of small fishes with flattened bodies, ventral suckers and separate dorsal, tail and anal fins. Clingfish are often very difficult to detect among the algae and broken reef on which they live, and many species in southern Australia are yet to be scientifically named.

Alabes dorsalis (Richardson, 1845)
Common shore-eel

Habitat: Sheltered and moderately exposed reef; 0–30 m depth.
Distribution: Southern WA to southern Qld and around Tas.
Maximum size: Length to 120 mm.

The common shore-eel is not often seen because of its small size but is one of the most abundant fishes among algae, rocks and shells in shallow water. The species can be identified by an opaque body, rudimentary ventral fin and dark circular blotches that are nearly always present on the sides.

Alabes dorsalis, Ricketts Pt, Vic. RUDIE KUITER

Aspasmogaster tasmaniensis (Günther, 1861)
Tasmanian clingfish

Habitat: Under rocks on sheltered reef; 0–10 m depth.
Distribution: Southern WA to Vic. and around Tas.
Maximum size: Length to 80 mm.

The Tasmanian clingfish is probably the most common fish species living under rocks in sheltered Victorian and Tasmanian reef habitats. It has a light pink body with about 20 dark pink or brown bands across the upper surface and a large skin fold across the top of the snout. A related species with a similar appearance but lacking the dark bands, the smooth-snout clingfish ***Aspasmogaster liorhyncha***, is very abundant under sea urchins in circular depressions on sandstone reefs in New South Wales.

Aspasmogaster tasmaniensis with eggs, Ricketts Pt, Vic.

Cochleoceps bicolor Hutchins, 1991
Western cleaner clingfish

Habitat: Moderately exposed reef; 5–40 m depth.
Distribution: Southern WA to Port Phillip Bay, Vic.
Maximum size: Length to 70 mm.

The western cleaner clingfish has 12–15 blue lines across the top and sides of the body and is covered with numerous tightly packed red and purple dots, which are darker towards the tail. A close eastern Victorian and New South Wales relative, the eastern cleaner clingfish ***Cochleoceps orientalis***, has red dots of a constant colour and blue lines which do not descend fully down the sides of the body. Both species are found in association with sponges, kelp or ascidians in relatively deep water. They are named cleaner clingfish because they sometimes cling to larger fishes such as morwongs and boxfishes and pick off the parasites living there.

Cochleoceps bicolor, Recherche Archipelago, WA. CLAY BRYCE

FAMILY MORIDAE
Morid cods

The morid cod family is the Southern Hemisphere counterpart of the commercially important true cod family (Gadidae) of the Northern Hemisphere. Australian species of morid cod have a barbel under the chin, long second dorsal and anal fins separated from the tail fin, and ventral fins under the back of the head. Most species in the family are common only in deep water, but several live close inshore along the southern Australian coast.

Lotella rhacina (Bloch & Schneider, 1801)
Beardie

Habitat: Exposed reef; 2–90 m depth.
Distribution: Lancelin, WA, to Byron Bay, NSW, and around Tas. Also New Zealand.
Maximum size: Length to 660 mm.

Beardies occur commonly in and near caves at depths below 10 m but also forage into much shallower water at night. They can be recognised by the thin white line around the fin edges.

Lotella rhacina, Bass Point, NSW

Pseudophycis bachus (Bloch & Schneider, 1801)
Red cod

Habitat: Sheltered and moderately exposed sand, silt, reef; 0–375 m depth.
Distribution: Coffin Bay, SA, to Wilsons Promontory, Vic., and around Tas. Also New Zealand.
Maximum size: Length to 800 mm.

Pseudophycis bachus, Taroona, Tas.

The red cod is the most common of the morid cods in Victorian and Tasmanian waters. There is some uncertainty about the identity of this species because it has a characteristic dark blotch at the base of the pectoral fin, which seems to differ in position from the blotch on the New Zealand fishes originally given the scientific name. Like other local cods, the flesh of the red cod is soft and does not store well. The species is rarely seen or captured on line during the day, as it generally begins to move about only at nightfall.

Pseudophycis barbata Günther, 1863
Bearded cod

Habitat: Exposed reef; 1–275 m depth.
Distribution: Rottnest I, WA, to Sydney, NSW, and around Tas.
Maximum size: Length to 640 mm.

Pseudophycis barbata, Ninepin Pt, Tas.

The bearded cod is often confused with the red cod but has wider black marking around the fins, lacks the black patch at the base of the pectoral fin, and has a rounded rather than straight outer edge to the tail. The two species also have different habitat requirements, the bearded cod preferring open coast rather than sheltered habitats and being seen less often.

FAMILY OPHIDIIDAE
Lings

The lings are related to the cods but have a more eel-like body and ventral fins that are reduced to the size of feelers (if present at all). Of more than 150 species in the family worldwide, very few occur in shallow water.

Genypterus tigerinus Klunzinger, 1872
Rock ling

Habitat: Reef, seagrass; 0–60 m depth.
Distribution: Garden I, WA, to Newcastle, NSW, and around Tas.
Maximum size: Length to 1.2 m.

The rock ling is a large, mottled eel-like species that is closely related to the cods. The dorsal and anal fins are continuous with the tail, and the ventral fins lie below the head and are used as feelers. During the day, adult rock ling remain in caves, where they are often mistaken for conger eels, while juvenile animals are observed in sheltered seagrass habitats. Captured animals are difficult to handle because of a heavy coating of slime but are well regarded as food. Rock ling are highly susceptible to spearfishing and gillnetting and seem to have virtually disappeared from much of the southern coast.

Genypterus tigerinus, Maria I, Tas.

FAMILY HEMIRAMPHIDAE
Garfishes, halfbeaks

The garfishes are a distinctive group of slender, open-water fishes with a triangular upper jaw and long needle-like lower jaw. About 80 species are known worldwide.

Hyporhamphus melanochir
(Valenciennes, 1846)
Southern sea garfish

Habitat: Open water; 0–2 m depth.
Distribution: Lancelin, WA, to eastern Vic. and around Tas.
Maximum size: Length to 520 mm.

The southern sea garfish is the largest species in the family found in southern Australia and is the only one commonly found in marine waters. A species once mistaken for the southern sea garfish, the eastern sea garfish ***Hyporhamphus australis*** of New South Wales, differs in the number of lateral line scales

Hyporhamphus melanochir, Popes Eye, Vic. Rudie Kuiter

(58–60 cf. 52–57). There are also several other species of garfish associated with estuaries, particularly along the warmer sections of coast. The southern sea garfish has an unusual diet as it is virtually the only species in southern Australia to consume seagrass in any quantity. During the day adults feed on seagrass; at night they consume planktonic crustaceans and stray insects landing on the water surface. The species is exploited by recreational and commercial fishers because of its sweet, firm flesh, although small individuals are quite bony.

FAMILY ATHERINIDAE
Hardyheads, silversides

Hardyheads are a family of small elongate fishes with two separated dorsal fins. They lack a lateral line but have a silver or reddish stripe along the side. A large number of the approximately 120 species in the family occur in fresh water or are associated with sheltered bays or estuaries.

Leptatherina presbyteroides
(Richardson, 1843)
Silverfish, prettyfish, Tamar hardyhead

Habitat: Sheltered sand, seagrass; 0–5 m depth.
Distribution: Houtman Abrolhos, WA, to southern NSW and around Tas.
Maximum size: Length to 110 mm.

Silverfish are probably the most abundant of all fishes in shallow marine environments along the southern coast. They occur in schools of tens of thousands close to the water's edge, where they feed on both bottom-living and planktonic prey. The schools are sometimes mixed with another abundant species, the small-mouthed hardyhead ***Atherinasoma microstoma***, although that species tends to live in the less saline reaches of estuaries. Silverfish can be distinguished from related species by the evenly spaced line of semicircular scales along the centre of the upper surface behind the head. The anus is also situated just in front of the tip of the ventral fin, when that fin is flattened along the body, whereas in *A. microstoma* it is situated just behind.

Kestratherina esox (Klunzinger, 1872)
Pike-headed hardyhead

Habitat: Sheltered sand, seagrass; 0–1 m depth.
Distribution: Kangaroo I, SA, to Western Port, Vic., and around Tas.
Maximum size: Length to 150 mm.

The pike-headed hardyhead is the largest of the southern hardyheads. It occurs most commonly in very shallow water in sheltered southern Tasmanian bays near beds of the seagrass *Heterozostera tasmanica*. The species can be recognised by its comparatively long and pointed snout. The pike-headed hardyhead and a species in the same genus with a shorter more-rounded head, the short-headed

Leptatherina presbyteroides, Sandy Bay, Tas.

Kestratherina esox, Cloudy Lagoon, Tas.

Atherinason hepsetoides, Bicheno, Tas.

hardyhead ***Kestratherina brevirostris***, also differ from the other local hardyheads in having the anus a long way behind the tip of the ventral fin (nearly half-way back to the anal fin).

Atherinason hepsetoides (Richardson, 1843)
Deepwater hardyhead

Habitat: Moderately exposed sand; 0–30 m depth.
Distribution: Kangaroo I, SA, to Sydney, NSW, and around Tas.
Maximum size: Length to 90 mm.

Atherinason hepsetoides can be distinguished from other temperate hardyheads by the relatively large number of small scales along the back. It also differs in behaviour from other species, as it occurs off the coast in depths to 30 m during the day, moving up into the shallows to feed at night.

FAMILY MONOCENTRIDAE
Pineapple fishes

The three species in this family have distinctive rounded bodies, which are covered by a mosaic of yellow plate-like scales with heavy backward-directed spines and black lines between.

Cleidopus gloriamaris De Vis, 1882
Knight fish, pineapple fish

Habitat: Moderately exposed reef, silt; 3–250 m depth.
Distribution: Shark Bay to Great Australian Bight, WA, and Eden, NSW, to Capricorn Group, Qld.
Maximum size: Length to 280 mm.

Knight fish have a red luminescent organ on the lower jaw, which houses light-emitting bacteria; the green light produced by the bacteria is used at night to detect and possibly attract prey. Juveniles are found in comparatively shallow water in caves on reefs and also sometimes enter estuaries. Adults generally inhabit deep water, where they are occasionally trawled.

Cleidopus gloriamaris, Seal Rocks, NSW. RUDIE KUITER

FAMILY TRACHICHTHYIDAE
Roughies, sawbellies

This is a family of predominantly deepwater fishes with large bony heads and a row of serrated scales along the belly between the ventral and anal fins. About 30 species are known, with five species entering shallow temperate waters.

Trachichthys australis Shaw & Nodder, 1799
Roughy

Habitat: Moderately exposed reef; 1–30 m depth.
Distribution: Kalbarri, WA, to southern Qld.
Maximum size: Length to 180 mm.

Trachichthys australis, Busselton, WA.

The roughy is easily recognised by its rounded body, reddish-brown colour and white and dark markings on opercles and fins. It is often seen by divers hovering around the entrance to caves on shallow coastal reefs and is occasionally caught by line. The species releases a toxic white substance through pores in the skin as a defensive measure when captured.

Optivus sp.
Violet roughy

Habitat: Sheltered and moderately exposed reef; 3–50 m depth.
Distribution: Port Phillip Bay, Vic., to Moreton Bay, Qld, and northern Tas.
Maximum size: Length to 120 mm.

The violet roughy is a common species on New South Wales reefs, inhabiting caves and deep ledges. It can be recognised by its square shape and the coloured lines along the upper and lower sections of the tail. This species has yet to be named because it was confused until recently with the slender roughy *Optivus elongatus* of New Zealand. A second undescribed species of *Optivus* occurs below 30 m depth from Perth to the Great Australian Bight.

Optivus sp., Watsons Bay, NSW

Paratrachichtys sp.
Sandpaperfish

Habitat: Exposed reef; 5–220 m depth.
Distribution: Perth, WA, to Port Stephens, NSW, and northern Tas.
Maximum size: Length to 250 mm.

The sandpaper fish was confused until recently with the New Zealand species *Paratrachichthys trailli* but differs in fin counts. It has a deeper body than the violet roughy, and a dark ring around the anus that generates light. The species is restricted to deep water on the mainland but is quite common in shallow caves in Tasmania.

Paratrachichtys sp., Bathurst Channel, Tas.

FAMILY BERYCIDAE
Red snapper

Red snapper species all have a similar general appearance, with a red or orange body, deeply forked tail and large mouth and eyes. Nine species are known worldwide.

Centroberyx affinis (Günther, 1859)
Nannygai

Habitat: Exposed reef, silt; 4–150 m depth.
Distribution: Eastern Vic. to Newcastle, NSW, and northeastern Tas. Also New Zealand.
Maximum size: Length to 510 mm.

Centroberyx affinis, Merimbula, NSW. KEN HOPPEN

The nannygai is the only common species in the family found in shallow water along the New South Wales coast. It is often seen by divers in midwater above steeply sloping reefs along the exposed coast, although juveniles are known to enter estuaries such as Botany Bay. Large quantities of the species are commercially trawled.

Centroberyx lineatus (Cuvier, 1829)

Swallowtail

Habitat: Exposed reef; 12–300 m depth.
Distribution: Lancelin, WA, to Bermagui, NSW.
Maximum size: Length to 430 mm.

The swallowtail is best recognised by the deeply forked tail. The species occurs in large schools, which are common in depths greater than 30 m along the southern coast. These schools occasionally move into shallow water on the edge of dropoffs.

Centroberyx gerrardi (Günther, 1887)

Red snapper

Habitat: Exposed reef; 5–300 m depth.
Distribution: Lancelin, WA, to Port Phillip Bay, Vic.
Maximum size: Length to 660 mm.

Centroberyx lineatus, Albany, WA. CLAY BRYCE

Centroberyx gerrardi, Investigator Group, SA

Centroberyx gerrardi is a bright orange-red species with a prominent white line along the side of the body and red eyes. It is common on offshore reefs near the Great Australian Bight but becomes less common away from this central part of its range. Unlike other members of the family found locally, the red snapper is usually a solitary species found near caves.

FAMILY ZEIDAE
Dories

The nine species of dory are compressed, rounded fishes with a large head, silver body, small scales and protrusible mouth. Most occur in deep water, with only the john dory and occasionally the silver dory entering divable depths in Australia.

Zeus faber Linnaeus, 1758
John dory

Habitat: Sand, reef; 1–170 m depth.
Distribution: Port Hedland, WA, to Qld and around Tas.
Maximum size: Length to 750 mm.

Zeus faber, Clovelly, NSW. RUDIE KUITER

The john dory has a characteristic spot on the side of the body, which folklore suggests is a thumbprint imprinted by St Peter. It occurs most abundantly in deep offshore waters, although individuals occasionally enter shallow estuaries, particularly along the New South Wales coast. The john dory is one of the most expensive fishes because of its good eating qualities, and is trawled in moderate quantities. Most of the dory on the market is, however, king or mirror dory caught in deepwater trawls. These species have a similar texture and taste. Silver dory ***Cyttus australis*** is smaller than John dory, has an orange head and fins, and enters shallow water in Tasmania.

FAMILY SYNGNATHIDAE
Pipefishes, pipehorses, seahorses, seadragons

Syngnathids are a distinctive family of fishes with armour-coated bodies surrounded by a series of rings. Most are slow-moving species that rely heavily on camouflage for survival among the seagrasses, seaweeds and encrusting animals in which they live. About 30 of the more than 200 species in the family occur in temperate Australian waters.

Stigmatopora argus (Richardson, 1840)
Spotted pipefish

Habitat: Sheltered seagrass, algae; 0–8 m depth.
Distribution: Shark Bay, WA, to Sydney, NSW, and around Tas.
Maximum size: Length to 260 mm.

Species with relatively straight bodies in the syngnathid family are commonly called pipefishes, a term alluding to a fanciful resemblance in shape to

Stigmatopora argus, Cloudy Lagoon, Tas.

pipecleaners. The spotted pipefish and its relative, the wide-bodied pipefish *Stigmatopora nigra*, are the only two species of pipefish in southern Australia that lack a tail fin. They are also the most abundant species. Although rarely seen because they match eelgrass leaves in shape and colour, large numbers will be captured by hauling a small seine net through virtually any seagrass bed. The spotted pipefish can be recognised by its olive-green colour and black spots along the upper surface. Like other pipefishes, the colour becomes most intense in females during the breeding season when they are competing for mates.

Stigmatopora nigra Kaup, 1856
Wide-bodied pipefish

Habitat: Sheltered seagrass, algae; 0–35 m depth.
Distribution: Rottnest I, WA, to Tangalooma, Qld, and around Tas. Also New Zealand.
Maximum size: Length to 160 mm.

The wide-bodied pipefish is a relatively small species that lacks a tail fin, has a long snout and a pattern of extremely fine black dots covering the body. It is easily confused with the spotted pipefish but differs from that species in having the dorsal fin further forward on the body (originating on the fifth to seventh trunk ring, rather than on the ninth to thirteenth). The name wide-bodied refers to the swelling of the trunk that occurs in females during the breeding season; at other times of the year this species is one of the thinnest pipefishes. Wide-bodied pipefish occur in enormous abundance in eelgrass beds (*Heterozostera tasmanica*), but individuals are also frequently found attached to small pieces of floating algae.

Filicampus tigris (Castelnau, 1879)
Tiger pipefish

Habitat: Sheltered reef, sand, silt; 2–30 m depth.
Distribution: Broome, WA, to Spencer Gulf, SA, and Sydney, NSW, to Moreton Bay, Qld.
Maximum size: Length to 300 mm.

The tiger pipefish is one of the largest pipefish species and is easily recognised by the colour pattern, especially the markings on the head and the regular vertical patches down the body. It is commonly seen resting motionless on rubble bottom near the entrance to deep estuaries from Sydney northwards.

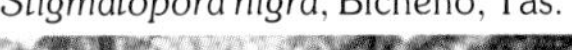

Stigmatopora nigra, Bicheno, Tas.

Filicampus tigris, Port Stephens, NSW

Festucalex cinctus (Ramsay, 1882)
Girdled pipefish

Habitat: Sheltered reef, sand; 3–30 m depth.
Distribution: Tropical Australia south to Sydney, NSW.
Maximum size: Length to 160 mm.

The girdled pipefish is a small species with a short snout and has either a dark silver-spotted body or is cream with about 15 broken bands. It is one of the most common pipefish occurring in Sydney Harbour and is usually seen resting on a rubble bottom or on coarse sand.

Heraldia nocturnia Paxton, 1975
Upsidedown pipefish

Habitat: Exposed reef; 2–30 m depth.
Distribution: Geographe Bay, WA, to Seal Rocks, NSW, and around Tas.
Maximum size: Length to 100 mm.

The upsidedown pipefish has only recently been identified but is widely distributed along the southern coast. Much of the reason for its late discovery is that it lives deep in caves, often with another species of pipefish, the serrated pipefish ***Maroubra perserrata***, which has the rings forming a corrugated pattern along the back. *Heraldia nocturnia* is brown or tan with blotches and has a characteristic tail fin with projecting tips to the rays.

Heraldia nocturnia, Ile des Phoques, Tas.

Hippocampus abdominalis Lesson, 1827
Big-bellied seahorse

Habitat: Sheltered and moderately exposed reef, silt; 0–12 m depth.
Distribution: Kangaroo I, SA, to Sydney, NSW, and around Tas.
Maximum size: Length to 250 mm.

Festucalex cinctus, North Head, NSW

The big-bellied seahorse is the largest and most commonly seen species of seahorse in southern Australian waters. It has 23–31 rays on the dorsal fin and is generally a yellowish colour with dark spots. Adults occur most abundantly in areas of broken reef near the entrance to estuaries; however, they can also occur in a wide range of other habitats, including on boat-mooring chain and on kelp. As with most other members of the seahorse and pipefish family, the males incubate eggs in a pouch and eventually release young that look like miniature replicas of the adult. There is some concern about the possible overexploitation of big-bellied seahorses, because large numbers of dried animals have recently been exported to Asia for use as aphrodisiacs.

Hippocampus abdominalis, Bicheno, Tas.

Hippocampus breviceps Peters, 1870
Short-headed seahorse

Habitat: Sheltered algae, seagrass; 0–5 m depth.
Distribution: Lancelin, WA, to Sydney, NSW, and around Tas.
Maximum size: Length to 80 mm.

Short-headed seahorses are rarely seen because of good camouflage but can be common in localised areas. They are generally found attached to the fronds of brown algae (particularly *Sargassum* and *Cystophora*). The species differs from other temperate Australian seahorses by having 19–22 fin rays on the dorsal fin but can also be distinguished by the pale blue spots over the body and the relatively short snout.

Hippocampus breviceps, Cloudy Lagoon, Tas.

Hippocampus whitei Bleeker, 1855
White's seahorse

Habitat: Sheltered seagrass, reef; 0–20 m depth.
Distribution: SA to Noosa, Qld.
Maximum size: Length to 150 mm.

White's seahorse has 15–17 rays in the dorsal fin and a long snout. The colour is variable, with browns and yellows predominant, and the body is usually flecked with fine white spots that are much smaller and more

Hippocampus whitei, North Head, NSW

numerous than the spots on the short-headed seahorse. The species is common in estuarine *Posidonia* beds and is particularly abundant in Sydney Harbour, but in southern waters only vagrants associated with drifting algae have been found.

Hippocampus angustus Günther, 1870
Western Australian seahorse

Habitat: Sheltered reef, seagrass; 0–10 m depth.
Distribution: North West Cape to Augusta, WA.
Maximum size: Length to 220 mm.

The Western Australian seahorse has a distinctive series of brown lines down the snout but otherwise is very similar to White's seahorse. It is abundant on broken bottom and *Posidonia* seagrass in Cockburn Sound, WA, but is not often seen elsewhere.

Hippocampus angustus, Woodmans Pt, WA

Phyllopteryx taeniolatus (Lacepède, 1804)
Common seadragon, weedy seadragon

Habitat: Moderately to submaximally exposed reefs; 1–50 m depth.
Distribution: Geraldton, WA, to Port Stephens, NSW, and around Tas.
Maximum size: Length to 460 mm.

Phyllopteryx taeniolatus, Partridge I, Tas.

Seadragons are closely related to seahorses but have elongate, non-prehensile tails, and the male holds eggs under the tail rather than carrying them in a brood pouch. Living individuals have an astonishing colour pattern, consisting principally of an orange-red background colour, iridescent blue stripes on the chest and numerous white spots and yellow markings. Eggs remain under the tail of the adult male for about two months; then hatched juveniles grow rapidly to a length of about 70 mm after three weeks on a diet mainly composed of mysid crustaceans. The juveniles are most abundant on the sandy edge of reefs at the mouths of bays. Adults live among the larger algae on exposed reefs and tend to be found in relatively deep water in the northern section of their range.

Phycodurus eques (Günther, 1865)

Leafy seadragon

Habitat: Moderately exposed reefs; 4–30 m depth.
Distribution: Lancelin, WA, to Wilsons Promontory, Vic.
Maximum size: Length to 430 mm.

The leafy seadragon is perhaps the most spectacularly shaped of all fishes, with numerous branched appendages arising from the edges of the body. The leaf-like outline of this species blends in so well with seaweed in its local environment that most divers, as well as predator and prey species, will pass within a metre of the animal without noticing it. This seadragon is common at a few locations in South Australia and is a fully protected species in that state.

Solegnathus spinosissimus (Günther, 1870)

Spiny pipehorse

Habitat: Silt, sand; 3–400 m depth.
Distribution: Vic., NSW and around Tas. Also New Zealand.
Maximum size: Length to 470 mm.

The spiny pipehorse is an attractively coloured species with a pink or orange body, yellow stripes and a red patch around the anus. The species lacks the leaf-like appendages of the sea dragons but has a similar method of carrying eggs under the tail. It is usually restricted to deep water near the Australian mainland and is noticed only when dead animals are washed ashore, although divers in the D'Entrecasteaux Channel, Tas., often seen them living near sea whips.

Solegnathus spinosissimus, Zuidpool Rock, Tas.

Phycodurus eques, Victor Harbor, SA. RUDIE KUITER

FAMILY PEGASIDAE
Sea moths, dragon fishes

Sea moths have one of the most distinctive of fish body shapes, with a long snout, broad pectoral fins, long tail and body encased in bony plates. Only five species are recognised in the family.

Pegasus lancifer Kaup, 1861
Sculptured seamoth

Habitat: Sheltered silt, sand; 0–55 m depth.
Distribution: Great Australian Bight, WA, to Lakes Entrance, Vic., and around Tas.
Maximum size: Length to 110 mm.

The sculptured seamoth is occasionally seen in sheltered inlets, where it uses its pectoral fins to crawl over soft sediments searching for buried crustaceans and worms. Males have small coloured patches at the rear of the pectoral fins, which are raised and displayed to potential mates.

Pegasus lancifer, Mornington, Vic. RUDIE KUITER

Pegasus volitans Linnaeus, 1758
Slender seamoth

Habitat: Sheltered sand; 3–75 m depth.
Distribution: Tropical Australia south to Cockburn Sound, WA, and Bermagui, NSW.
Maximum size: Length to 160 mm.

The slender seamoth differs from the sculptured seamoth by having a longer snout and narrower body. Juveniles swim in open water, whereas adults lack a swim bladder and are only found on the seabed, often on a coarse sand bottom where there is moderate current flow.

Pegasus volitans, Bicton, WA

FAMILY SCORPAENIDAE
Scorpion fishes

The scorpion fishes are a diverse group of several hundred bottom-dwelling fishes that have large heads with spiny ridges and long venomous spines. Included in this family is the infamous stonefish of the tropics. The recommended procedure if stung by any of the scorpion fishes is to immerse the wound in very hot water, as the venom will break down when heated.

Centropogon australis (White, 1790)
Eastern fortescue

Habitat: Sheltered reef, sand, seagrass; 0–30 m depth.
Distribution: Lakes Entrance, Vic., to Hervey Bay, Qld.
Maximum size: Length to 140 mm.

The eastern fortescue is a relatively small species with pale body and dark black bars when adult and mottled colour pattern while juvenile. Two quite different colour forms (illustrated here) are both common. The species is one of the most abundant fishes in sheltered bays along the New South Wales coast and is well known to most prawn fishermen because of the painful sting inflicted by its venomous dorsal spines. A closely related species, the western fortescue ***Centropogon latifrons***, occurs in southern Western Australia in much the same habitat but is less common.

Centropogon australis, Port Stephens, NSW

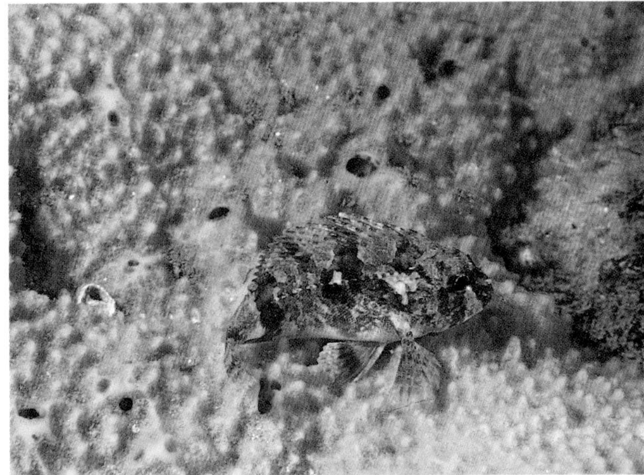

Centropogon australis (dark form), Merimbula, NSW

Gymnapistes marmoratus (Cuvier, 1829)
Soldierfish, cobbler

Habitat: Sheltered seagrass, sand; 0–26 m depth.
Distribution: Fremantle, WA, to Sydney, NSW, and around Tas.
Maximum size: Length to 230 mm.

The soldierfish has a mottled black and white pattern which, from a distance, can be mistaken for that of a fortescue; however, the two species are easily separated on close inspection because the soldierfish has smooth skin with no scales. Soldierfish occur abundantly in almost all southern Australian eelgrass (*Heterozostera tasmanica*) beds, where they pose a hazard to barefoot bathers because of the venomous spines. In late winter and early spring adult soldierfish leave these shallow seagrass beds to congregate in deeper water in huge concentrations, presumably for spawning. The species is quite slow growing and large soldierfish are considerably older (more than 10 years) than most other species at the same size.

Gymnapistes marmoratus, Princess Royal Harbour, WA

Maxillicosta scabriceps Whitley, 1935
Little scorpion fish

Habitat: Sheltered and moderately exposed sand; 2–40 m depth.
Distribution: Exmouth Gulf, WA, to Western Port, Vic., and south to Tinderbox, Tas.
Maximum size: Length to 120 mm.

The little scorpion fish is a pale species with mottled brown and red markings. It is commonly trawled in scallop beds and occasionally seen by divers at night; during the day it remains buried in sand with just the eyes protruding.

Maxillicosta scabriceps, Edithburgh, SA

Neosebastes scorpaenoides Guichenot, 1842
Common gurnard perch

Habitat: Moderately and submaximally exposed reef, sand; 2–140 m depth.
Distribution: Ceduna, SA, to Sydney, NSW, and around Tas.
Maximum size: Length to 400 mm.

Neosebastes scorpaenoides, Ninepin Pt, Tas.

The common gurnard perch is the largest of the scorpion fishes regularly encountered by divers, anglers and gillnet fishers in southern Australia. It has a mottled red-brown colour and large pectoral fins that are blotched red and green. The very long spines at the beginning of the dorsal fin have caused numerous painful wounds. The species is usually found on broken bottom near the edge of reefs and is occasionally caught on line or in gillnets. Its flesh is firm and tasty.

Neosebastes pandus (Richardson, 1842)
Gurnard perch

Habitat: Moderately and submaximally exposed reef, sand; 10–200 m depth.
Distribution: Houtman Abrolhos, WA, to Gulf St Vincent, SA.
Maximum size: Length to 400 mm.

Neosebastes pandus, Busselton, WA. CLAY BRYCE

The gurnard perch differs from the common gurnard perch by having larger pectoral fins extending well past the start of the anal fin. It is usually a darker colour than the common gurnard perch, with small black spots on the head and upper body. It is most abundant on broken reef bottom but is not often seen.

Helicolenus percoides (Richardson, 1842)
Red gurnard perch, sea perch, ocean perch

Habitat: Exposed reef, silt; 10–750 m depth.
Distribution: Albany, WA, to Newcastle, NSW, and around Tas. Also New Zealand.
Maximum size: Length to 470 mm.

Helicolenus percoides, Bicheno, Tas.

The red gurnard perch differs from other gurnard perches in having three brown bands across the body and fewer spines on the cheek. Adults are most abundant in deep waters on the continental slope, with smaller animals more common on the continental shelf, where they are trawled commercially. Juveniles also sometimes occur on much shallower Tasmanian reefs adjacent to deep water. This large range of depths is unusual, and it is possible that two or more similar-looking fishes are being confused as a single species.

Scorpaena cardinalis Richardson, 1842
Red rock cod, eastern red scorpion cod

Habitat: Reef; 1–40 m depth.
Distribution: Eastern Vic. to Noosa Head, Qld. Also New Zealand.
Maximum size: Length to 400 mm.

The red rock cod occurs commonly in a wide range of habitats along the New South Wales coast and is one of the species most frequently captured by line. It can be recognised by its large head, black spots on the belly and small filaments on the sides of the body. The colour varies from mud-brown to bright red.

Scorpaena cardinalis, Bass Point, NSW

Scorpaena papillosa (Bloch & Schneider, 1801)

Southern rock cod, red rock cod, southern red scorpion cod

Habitat: Reef; 1–130 m depth.
Distribution: Port Lincoln, SA, to Newcastle, NSW, and around Tas. Also New Zealand.
Maximum size: Length to 360 mm.

The southern rock cod lacks filaments on the side of the body and, although a variably coloured species, can nearly always be recognised by a white collar behind the eye and a white patch behind the anal fin. Small animals are very common on coastal reefs in Victoria and Tasmania, with the largest animals living mainly in deep water.

Scorpaena papillosa, Bicheno, Tas.

Scorpaena sumptuosa, Rottnest I, WA. CLAY BRYCE

Scorpaena sumptuosa Castelnau, 1875

Western scorpionfish, western red scorpion cod

Habitat: Reef; 5–40 m depth.
Distribution: Point Quobba to Esperance, WA.
Maximum size: Length to 400 mm.

Western scorpionfish differ from the other two southern Australian species of *Scorpaena* by having a deeper chasm behind the eye and a deeper body. They are often seen by divers on moderately exposed reefs in Western Australia and are also occasionally taken by handline.

Dendrochirus brachypterus (Cuvier, 1829)
Dwarf lionfish

Habitat: Sheltered and moderately exposed reef; 5–40 m depth.
Distribution: Tropical Australia south to Houtman Abrolhos, WA, and Montague I, NSW. Also widespread in the Indo-West Pacific region.
Maximum size: Length to 150 mm.

A number of tropical species of lionfish extend into temperate waters, the dwarf lionfish being the most common. None of these species breed in the region but they are carried as eggs and long-lived larvae from more northern areas in southward-flowing currents. The dwarf lionfish can be distinguished from close relatives by its small size, curved bands on the pectoral fins, and lack of rays projecting out from the membrane on the pectoral fins.

Dendrochirus brachypterus, Port Stephens, NSW

Glyptauchen panduratus (Richardson, 1850)
Goblinfish

Habitat: Sheltered and moderately exposed reef; 3–60 m depth.
Distribution: Rottnest I, WA, to Sydney, NSW, and around Tas.
Maximum size: Length to 200 mm.

The goblinfish is an unusual species with a highly distinctive head. It is possibly common on rubbly bottom but is rarely noticed because the shape and colour pattern provide excellent camouflage. At night goblinfish emerge from crevices and move slowly about.

Glyptauchen panduratus, Portsea, Vic. KEN HOPPEN

FAMILY TRIGLIDAE
Gurnards

The gurnards are an interesting group of fishes with squarish heads and colourful wing-like pectoral fins. Three of the rays of the pectoral fins are free and thickened and are used as fingers for walking over the seafloor and probing for prey. Most of the estimated 120 species in the family occur in deep water, with about eight species entering shallow temperate Australian waters at least occasionally, most often in southern Tasmania.

Lepidotrigla papilio (Cuvier, 1829)
Spiny gurnard

Habitat: Sheltered and moderately exposed sand; 2–50 m depth.
Distribution: Perth, WA, to eastern Vic. and around Tas.
Maximum size: Length to 180 mm.

The spiny gurnard is occasionally encountered in shallow coastal waters and estuaries. It is characterised by having the lateral line and rows on either side of the dorsal fin formed from relatively large scales with spines. A New South Wales species, the eastern spiny gurnard ***Lepidotrigla pleuracanthica***, differs slightly by being more reddish and having a jagged-looking rather than continuous membrane across the top of the dorsal fin.

Lepidotrigla papilio, Sandy Bay, Tas.

Lepidotrigla vanessa (Richardson, 1839)

Butterfly gurnard, cocky gurnard

Habitat: Sand, silt; 10–100 m depth.
Distribution: Great Australian Bight, WA, to Newcastle, NSW, and around Tas.
Maximum size: Length to 280 mm.

The butterfly gurnard has a dark spot on the dorsal fin, large pectoral fins, which usually reach well past the tips of the ventral fin, and 64–69 scales along the lateral line. Although juveniles occasionally enter estuaries, the species is not often seen by divers because animals usually remain in water depths greater than 20 m.

Lepidotrigla vanessa, Bicheno, Tas.

Pterygotrigla polyommata (Richardson, 1839)

Latchet, sharp-beaked gurnard

Habitat: Sand, silt; 5–420 m depth.
Distribution: Rottnest I, WA, to southern NSW and around Tas.
Maximum size: Length to 620 mm.

The latchet is the only gurnard entering shallow water with long spines projecting forward from the head and equally long spines projecting back from the opercle. Like several other fishes that are trawled commercially on the continental shelf, juvenile latchets occasionally enter the deeper southern and eastern Tasmanian estuaries during autumn.

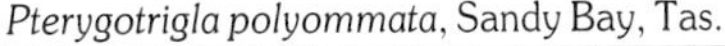

Pterygotrigla polyommata, Sandy Bay, Tas.

FAMILY PATAECIDAE
Prowfishes

The three species in the prowfish family are all restricted to temperate Australian waters. They lack ventral fins and scales but have a soft skin covering the body and fins. The dorsal fin is high and extends from the front of the head to the tail.

Aetapcus maculatus (Günther, 1861)
Warty prowfish

Habitat: Sheltered and moderately exposed reef; 3–30 m depth.
Distribution: Shark Bay, WA, to Wilsons Promontory, Vic., and south to Maria I, Tas.
Maximum size: Length to 220 mm.

The warty prowfish can be recognised by shape and by its flabby skin covered by wart-like lumps. The skin is shed in a single piece at regular intervals, an important process for a fish that remains immobile for most of its life, as it prevents the build-up of fouling organisms. The warty prowfish is difficult to detect in its natural habitat because it closely resembles the sponges among which it lives.

Aetapcus maculatus, Maria I, Tas.

FAMILY GNATHANACANTHIDAE
Red velvetfishes

This family contains a single species that differs from the prowfishes by having large pectoral fins and a deeply notched dorsal fin.

Gnathanacanthus goetzeei Bleeker, 1855
Red velvetfish

Habitat: Moderately exposed reef; 2–30 m depth.
Distribution: Jurien Bay, WA, to Wilsons Promontory, Vic., and around Tas.
Maximum size: Length to 460 mm.

The red velvetfish is one of the most striking fishes when removed from the sea, as it is bright orange and has large floppy fins. In its natural habitat, however, the fish is difficult to detect because the colour is quite dull (red light being rapidly absorbed in seawater) and the animal sways with the surge in the same way as nearby kelp plants. Red velvetfish are most often seen in Tasmanian waters, where they are occasionally caught in gillnets. Being spiked by the red velvetfish is said to cause excruciating pain, which can last for many hours.

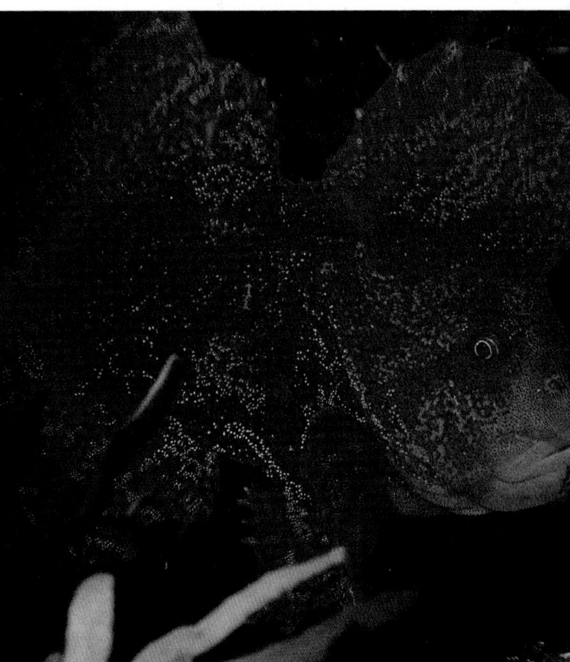

Gnathanacanthus goetzeei, Port Davey, Tas. PETER MOONEY

FAMILY APLOACTINIDAE
Velvetfishes

The velvetfishes are distinguished by prickly scales over the body, giving the fish a velvety appearance, and by bony knobs in rows on the sides of the head. An estimated 25 species are present worldwide, but most of these species are known from only a few widely distributed specimens.

Aploactisoma milesii (Richardson, 1850)
Velvetfish

Habitat: Sheltered and moderately exposed reef, seagrass; 1–30 m depth.
Distribution: Shark Bay, WA, to Sydney, NSW, and northern Tas.
Maximum size: Length to 200 mm.

Aploactisoma milesii, Bass Point, NSW. RUDIE KUITER

The velvetfish is a reasonably common species in southern Australia but is not often seen because of its cryptic appearance. It lives among broken rock bottom, sponges and seagrasses, and is most abundant in deep estuaries.

FAMILY PLATYCEPHALIDAE
Flathead

Flathead form a well-defined group related to the scorpion fishes. They have crocodile-shaped bodies with relatively broad pectoral and pelvic fins. Most of the 60 or so known species are found in Australia, making this region the centre of diversity for the family. The various species have distinctive arrangements of spots, blotches and lines on the tail, and they raise this fin as a flag to signal other animals. They live on the seabed and wait in ambush for relatively large-sized prey such as fish, crabs, shrimp or squid to pass nearby.

Platycephalus bassensis Cuvier, 1829
Sand flathead

Habitat: Sheltered sand, silt; 0–100 m depth.
Distribution: Bremer Bay, WA, to Jervis Bay, NSW, and around Tas.
Maximum size: Length to 460 mm.

Platycephalus bassensis, Dunalley, Tas.

The sand flathead is the most frequently caught species in Victorian and Tasmanian waters, where it occurs in great abundance in shallow bays. It is sandy coloured with dark spots and bands and has a tail with brown blotches in the upper half and a large black mark sometimes broken by a white line in the lower half.

Platycephalus speculator Klunzinger, 1872
Yank flathead, Castelnau's flathead, southern blue-spotted flathead

Habitat: Moderately exposed sand; 1–30 m depth.
Distribution: Kalbarri, WA, to eastern Vic. and northern Tas.
Maximum size: Length to 900 mm.

The yank flathead is very similar in appearance to the sand flathead but is lighter in colour and has three or four well-defined black spots surrounded by white in the lower half of the tail. Behind the eye it has two long adjoining spines which are about the same length, whereas in the sand flathead the lower spine is

Platycephalus speculator, Canal Rocks, WA

considerably longer than the upper. The yank flathead is common on patches of sand adjacent to seagrass beds.

Platycephalus caeruleopunctatus

McCulloch, 1922

Eastern blue-spotted flathead

Habitat: Moderately exposed sand; 5–100 m depth.
Distribution: Lakes Entrance, Vic., to Moreton Bay, Qld.
Maximum size: Length to 680 mm.

The eastern blue-spotted flathead is very similar to the yank flathead, and its geographic range starts at the end of the yank flathead's range. It can be distinguished from that species by the elongate rather than rounded black spots on the lower section of the tail.

Platycephalus caeruleopunctatus, Terrigal, NSW

Platycephalus fuscus Cuvier, 1829

Dusky flathead

Habitat: Sheltered sand, silt, reef; 0–25 m depth.
Distribution: Wilsons Promontory, Vic., to Mackay, Qld.
Maximum size: Length to 1.2 m.

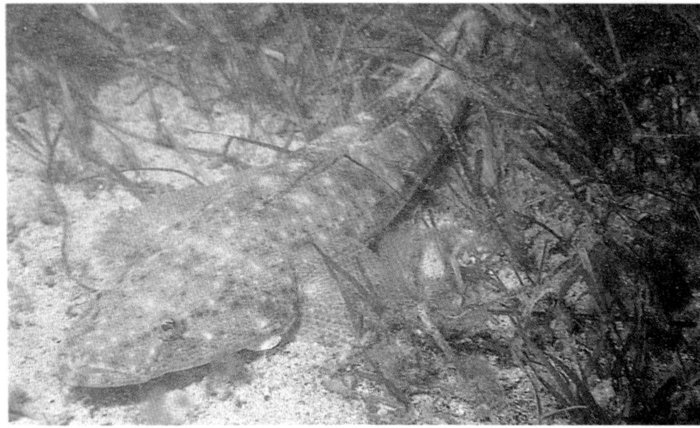

Platycephalus fuscus, Terrigal, NSW

The dusky flathead can be recognised by the rows of fine brown spots along the rays of the pectoral fins and by the spotted upper section and plain lower section of the tail with a dark blotch between. It can also be recognised by its great size; this is the largest of all flathead species, growing to more than 15 kg in weight. It is the species most often captured by New South Wales anglers, as it occurs abundantly in estuaries and also sheltered bays along the open coast.

Platycephalus endrachtensis

Quoy & Gaimard, 1824

Bar-tailed flathead

Habitat: Sheltered silt, sand; 0–20 m depth.
Distribution: Tropical Australia south to Fremantle, WA, and Port Hacking, NSW.
Maximum size: Length to 760 mm.

The bar-tailed flathead has numerous fine spots over the body and fins and a tail with three black stripes on a white background and a short yellow stripe above. The species occurs abundantly in the lower reaches of the Swan River estuary near Perth.

Platycephalus endrachtensis, Bicton, WA

Platycephalus laevigatus (Cuvier, 1829)

Rock flathead, grass flathead

Habitat: Sheltered and moderately exposed seagrass, reef; 0–20 m depth.
Distribution: Geographe Bay, WA, to Nowra, NSW, and around Tas.
Maximum size: Length to 500 mm.

The rock flathead has a dark mottled appearance, a rounded body and several rows of dark spots along the rays of the tail. It occurs commonly in seagrass beds and on flat vegetated reefs, particularly in the larger Victorian bays. The rock flathead is the most highly regarded of flathead species for its flavour.

Platycephalus laevigatus, Stanley, Tas. MALCOLM WELLS

Leviprora inops (Jenyns, 1840)
Long-headed flathead

Habitat: Sheltered seagrass, reef; 0–10 m depth.
Distribution: Shark Bay, WA, to Kangaroo I, SA.
Maximum size: Length to 610 mm.

The long-headed flathead has a very large head in relation to the rest of the body, a mottled back with a dark band across the eyes and a brown stripe running obliquely down the outer half of the first dorsal fin. The species is commonly found among seagrass and macroalgae along the southern Western Australian coast. Like the rock flathead, it sits on sand rather than burying.

Neoplatycephalus richardsoni
(Castelnau, 1872)
Tiger flathead

Habitat: Exposed sand, silt; 10–160 m depth.
Distribution: Vic. to Sydney, NSW, and around Tas.
Maximum size: Length to 650 mm.

The tiger flathead has long, conspicuous spines behind the eye and bright orange spots over the upper body surface. A few orange spots extend onto the upper section of the tail, but the lower section of the tail has no markings. The tiger flathead occurs abundantly in depths below 30 m, with only the occasional individual moving into shallow water. This species is the most valuable flathead commercially trawled in Victoria and Tasmania.

Neoplatycephalus richardsoni, Bicheno, Tas.

Leviprora inops, Princess Royal Harbour, WA

Thysanophrys cirronasus (Richardson, 1848)
Tassel-snouted flathead, rock flathead

Habitat: Moderately exposed reef, sand; 5–35 m depth.
Distribution: Lancelin, WA, to eastern SA and Montague I, NSW, to Caloundra, Qld.
Maximum size: Length to 380 mm.

The tassel-snouted flathead is the most distinctive Australian flathead because it has a large, ridged head that lacks scales. The markings on the body are predominantly brown with an unusual mauve hue. Tassel-snouted flathead are occasionally seen on broken coastal reef, usually sitting motionless on patches of sand.

Onigocia spinosa
(Temminck & Schlegel, 1842)
Spiny flathead

Habitat: Sheltered and moderately exposed sand, mud; 2–25 m depth.
Distribution: Tropical Australia south to Cockburn Sound, WA. Also widespread in the Indo-West Pacific region.
Maximum size: Length to 90 mm.

The spiny flathead is a small species with a broad, spiny head and pelvic fins that are distinctively black with yellow and white tips. The species is the most abundant flathead in Cockburn Sound but is rarely noticed.

Thysanophrys cirronasus, Coogee, NSW. RUDIE KUITER

Suggrundus japonica (Tilesius, 1812)
Rusty flathead

Habitat: Sheltered silt; 4–20 m depth.
Distribution: Tropical Australia south to Fremantle, WA. Also widespread in the Indo-West Pacific region.
Maximum size: Length to 200 mm.

The rusty flathead can be identified by the brown stripes across the upper lip and along the lower part of the head, and numerous black spots on the tail. It occurs abundantly on soft sediments in the lower reaches of the Swan estuary near Perth. An almost identical species, the mud flathead ***Suggrundus jugosus***, is common in muddy estuaries from Sydney northwards along the eastern coast.

Suggrundus japonica, Bicton, WA

Onigocia spinosa, Woodmans Point, WA

FAMILY SERRANIDAE
Rock cods, seaperches

The Serranidae is one of the largest families of fishes, with more than 400 species worldwide. Included in the family are bottom-dwelling and schooling species, exhibiting a great range of colours, shapes and behaviour patterns.

Caesioperca lepidoptera
(Bloch & Schneider, 1801)
Butterfly perch

Habitat: Exposed reef; 4–100 m depth.
Distribution: Albany, WA, to Byron Bay, NSW, and around Tas. Also New Zealand.
Maximum size: Length to 300 mm.

Butterfly perch have a pink body with a round black spot on the side of adults and blue markings around the eyes. They feed on plankton and occur in large schools near the edge of dropoffs on coastal reefs. The species occurs in relatively shallow water in Tasmania but in New South Wales is usually associated with reefs deeper than 30 m. They sleep at night in crevices between rocks.

Caesioperca lepidoptera, Ninepin Pt, Tas.

Caesioperca rasor (Richardson, 1839)
Barber perch

Habitat: Sheltered and moderately exposed reef; 2–100 m depth.
Distribution: Albany, WA, to Wilsons Promontory, Vic., and around Tas.
Maximum size: Length to 260 mm.

Barber perch differ from butterfly perch in having a bar rather than a round blotch on the body in adults, a greater proportion of blue in the coloration, and a

Caesioperca rasor, Rocky Cape, Tas.

narrower body shape. Juveniles usually have a mauve head and pink body. The barber perch occurs in mixed schools with butterfly perch in some areas but generally prefers more sheltered and shallow habitats.

Hypoplectrodes annulatus (Günther, 1859)
Yellow-banded seaperch

Habitat: Exposed reef; 10–100 m depth.
Distribution: Wilsons Promontory, Vic., to southern Qld.
Maximum size: Length to 300 mm.

The yellow-banded seaperch has a distinctive pattern of black bands on a yellow background but is rarely seen by divers because of its cryptic habits. It generally lives upside down against the roof of caves.

Hypoplectrodes annulatus, La Perouse, NSW. RUDIE KUITER

Hypoplectrodes maccullochi (Whitley, 1929)
Half-banded seaperch

Habitat: Moderately to submaximally exposed reef; 5–50 m depth.
Distribution: Wilsons Promontory, Vic., to Byron Bay, NSW, and south to Bicheno, Tas.
Maximum size: Length to 200 mm.

The half-banded seaperch is a small pink fish with yellowish stripes on the sides; these stripes narrow on the upper body but become diffuse lower down. The species is commonly found on reefs, generally half-hiding among sponges and soft corals.

Hypoplectrodes maccullochi, Bicheno, Tas.

Hypoplectrodes nigrorubrum (Cuvier, 1828)
Black-banded seaperch

Habitat: Sheltered and moderately exposed reef; 3–35 m depth.
Distribution: Kalbarri, WA, to The Entrance, NSW, and northern Tas.
Maximum size: Length to 280 mm.

Hypoplectrodes nigrorubrum, Little I, WA

The black-banded seaperch is the most frequently observed seaperch in southern Australia. It has four broad dark stripes down the body, with the last of these at the base of the tail. The background colour varies between animals and includes pink, red, green, brown and white, with red forms predominating. The species is usually seen in the open but also inhabits caves.

Epinephelides armatus (Castelnau, 1875)
Breaksea cod, black-arse cod, tiger cod

Habitat: Exposed reef; 4–35 m depth.
Distribution: Shark Bay to Recherche Archipelago, WA.
Maximum size: Length to 550 mm.

The breaksea cod is more commonly encountered by anglers and divers than other large serranid cods in southern Australia. It inhabits caves but is also inquisitive and will move out to approach divers. The species has three flat spines on the opercles, a plain-coloured body that lacks spots or stripes, and a black patch around the anus. The flesh is barely edible.

Epinephelides armatus, Esperance, WA

Othos dentex (Cuvier, 1828)
Harlequin fish

Habitat: Moderately to submaximally exposed reef; 2–30 m depth.
Distribution: Jurien Bay, WA, to Victor Harbor, SA.
Maximum size: Length to 760 mm.

The harlequin fish is a brilliantly coloured species with an orange-red body, blue spots on the upper surface and yellow spots below. It is normally found resting

Othos dentex, Leander Reef, WA

alone on reef or in caves and will follow a diver at a distance.

Epinephelus rivulatus (Valenciennes, 1830)
Chinaman cod

Habitat: Reef, seagrass; 2–30 m depth.
Distribution: Kimberleys to Rottnest I, WA.
Maximum size: Length to 460 mm.

The chinaman cod can be recognised by yellow tips to the dorsal fin and a black patch at the base of the pectoral fins. It usually has four or five dark bands across the body. The species is most abundant on deeper offshore reefs in the tropics but also occurs at the edges of shallow reefs near Perth.

Epinephelus rivulatus, Seven Mile Beach, WA

Acanthistius ocellatus (Günther, 1859)
Eastern wirrah, old boot

Habitat: Exposed reef; 4–100 m depth.
Distribution: Eastern Vic. to southern Qld and northeastern Tas. Also Lord Howe I.
Maximum size: Length to 640 mm.

Acanthistius ocellatus, Bass Point, NSW

The eastern wirrah has a greenish-brown coloration with dark blue-centred spots and 13 spines at the start of the dorsal fin. It is one of the more common large fishes on deeper New South Wales reefs, where it is usually found sheltering near caves. It is often caught on line but is not highly regarded by anglers for its taste.

Acanthistius serratus (Cuvier, 1828)
Western wirrah

Habitat: Exposed reef; 0–40 m depth.
Distribution: Shark Bay, WA, to Ceduna, SA.
Maximum size: Length to 500 mm.

Acanthistius serratus. Barry Hutchins

The western wirrah has a paler body than its eastern namesake and relatively small spots which coalesce into lines on the head. The species is moderately common in southwestern Australia but is not often seen by divers because of its preference for caves. The flesh is poor quality.

FAMILY CALLANTHIIDAE

This small family contains one genus and about eight species of plankton-eating fishes, which generally occur on deep reefs. They are closely related to the serranids and were included in that family until recently, but differ by having a lateral line that runs very high on the body below the dorsal fin, and a row of modified scales with pits running along the centre of the body.

Callanthius australis, Montague I, NSW. Rudie Kuiter

Callanthius australis Ogilby, 1899
Splendid perch, rosy perch

Habitat: Exposed reef; 17–180 m depth.
Distribution: Shark Bay, WA, to Port Macquarie, NSW, and around Tas.
Maximum size: Length to 490 mm.

The splendid perch is a brilliantly coloured species with intense yellows, oranges, pinks and purples arranged over the body and fins. Juveniles are more elongate and less vividly coloured than adults and have a conspicuous orange spot behind the head.

FAMILY PLESIOPIDAE
Blue devilfishes, hulafishes

The family Plesiopidae contains both perch-like species, which occur as solitary individuals, and elongate species in the genus *Trachinops*, which form dense schools. All species have a lateral line broken in two parts and ventral fins with one spine and four rays. About 20 species are known worldwide, with a large proportion restricted to southern Australia.

Paraplesiops meleagris (Peters, 1869)
Western blue devil

Habitat: Exposed reef; 5–40 m depth.
Distribution: Houtman Abrolhos, WA, to Port Phillip Bay, Vic.
Maximum size: Length to 360 mm.

The western blue devil is immediately recognisable by the iridescent blue spots densely packed over the body. It occurs commonly on offshore reefs. When observed underwater the species shows little fear of divers but retreats slowly into a refuge, generally either a ledge or a cave.

Paraplesiops bleekeri (Günther, 1861)
Eastern blue devil

Habitat: Exposed reef; 3–30 m depth.
Distribution: Montague I, NSW, to Gold Coast, Qld.
Maximum size: Length to 400 mm.

The eastern blue devil has a similar shape to the western blue devil but with three broad white bands down the body and yellow markings at the base of the tail and on the fins. It lives in much the same habitat as the western blue devil but is less abundant, and is now fully protected in New South Wales.

Paraplesiops meleagris, Dongara, WA

Paraplesiops bleekeri, Clovelly, NSW. RUDIE KUITER

Trachinops caudimaculatus McCoy, 1890

Southern hulafish, blotched-tailed trachinops

Habitat: Sheltered and moderately exposed reef; 1–35 m depth.
Distribution: Investigator Group, SA, to Wilsons Promontory, Vic., and around Tas.
Maximum size: Length to 100 mm.

In terms of numbers, the southern hulafish is probably the most abundant species on Tasmanian reefs, as huge swarms are found over sheltered reefs in the southern part of its range. On the mainland it is less abundant and generally occurs in caves at moderate depths (>10 m). The species has projecting rays in the centre of the tail and differs from others in the genus by having a large black blotch at the base of the tail.

Trachinops caudimaculatus, D'Entrecasteaux Channel, Tas.

Trachinops noarlungae Glover, 1974

Noarlunga hulafish, yellow-headed hulafish

Habitat: Sheltered and moderately exposed reef; 4–30 m depth.
Distribution: Houtman Abrolhos, WA, to Gulf St Vincent, SA.
Maximum size: Length to 150 mm.

Noarlunga hulafish differ from southern hulafish by having more scales (73–90 cf. 45–51 in the front segment of lateral line) and a yellow tail with a blue margin. The species is common on reefs and can occur in large schools near the entrance to caves.

Trachinops noarlungae, Port Noarlunga, SA. RUDIE KUITER

Trachinops brauni Allen, 1977
Blue-lined hulafish, Brauns hulafish

Habitat: Moderately and submaximally exposed reef; 3–35 m depth.
Distribution: Houtman Abrolhos to Recherche Archipelago, WA.
Maximum size: Length to 80 mm.

The blue-lined hulafish has an elongate filament projecting from the tail, which is longer and thinner than on others in the genus, and is also easily recognised by the electric blue stripe along each side. The species is often mixed with the Noarlunga hulafish in groups of 5–20 at the mouths of small caves and crevices.

Trachinops brauni, Rottnest I, WA

Trachinops taeniatus Günther, 1861
Eastern hulafish

Habitat: Moderately exposed reef; 5–25 m depth.
Distribution: Cape Conran, Vic., to Noosa Head, Qld.
Maximum size: Length to 100 mm.

Trachinops taeniatus, Narooma, NSW

The eastern hulafish is similar in body proportions to the blue-lined hulafish but clearly differs in its red and yellow striped coloration. It congregates in groups feeding on zooplankton at the entrance to caves.

FAMILY PSEUDOCHROMIDAE
Dottybacks

Dottybacks are a tropical group of small and colourful fishes with a slender-bodied appearance similar to the plesiopids. They can be recognised by a dorsal fin with up to three spines, an anal fin with three spines and a lateral line that is broken into two sections.

Labracinus lineatus (Castelnau, 1875)
Lined dottyback

Habitat: Moderately exposed reef; 3–30 m depth.
Distribution: Tropical Australia south to Jurien Bay, WA. Also widespread in the Indo-West Pacific region.
Maximum size: Length to 210 mm.

Labracinus lineatus, Seven Mile Beach, WA

The lined dottyback has characteristic lines of blue dots down the body and pink spots on the fins. This fish is primarily a tropical species but is also often seen by divers in caves along the central Western Australian coast, where it can been mistaken for a species of blue devilfish.

FAMILY GLAUCOSOMATIDAE
Pearl perches

This is a small family of deep-bodied fishes with large head, eyes and mouth. The dorsal fin has a low spinous section in front and high rayed section behind. The head is covered with scales.

Glaucosoma hebraicum Richardson, 1845
Westralian jewfish, West Australian jewfish, jewie, dhufish

Habitat: Exposed reef; 5–200 m depth.
Distribution: Beagle I to Recherche Archipelago, WA.
Maximum size: Length to 1.22 m.

The Westralian jewfish can be recognised by its shape and the characteristic black line through the eye. The dorsal fin of adults tapers to a projecting point; juveniles have six black stripes along the body. The species is the most highly prized of the bottom-dwelling fishes caught by line in Western Australia. Adults normally occur in deepwater but they also congregate on reefs in water depths of about 20 m during the spawning season from December to March. Animals mature after three or four years at about 500 mm length. A similarly shaped relative occurs on the east coast, the pearl perch ***Glaucosoma scapulare***.

Glaucosoma hebraicum, Rottnest I, WA. BARRY HUTCHINS

FAMILY TERAPONTIDAE
Grunters

The grunters are a family of fishes with a perch-like appearance, two spines on each opercle and a swim bladder attached by muscles to the back of the skull. Grunters contract and expand these muscles when stressed, producing a croaking sound. Most of the 40 or so species in the family occur in tropical estuaries, rivers or lakes.

Pelates sexlineatus (Quoy & Gaimard, 1824)
Eastern striped trumpeter

Habitat: Sheltered seagrass, sand, reef; 1–30 m depth.
Distribution: Narooma, NSW, to southern Qld.
Maximum size: Length to 200 mm.

Pelates sexlineatus, Port Stephens, NSW

The eastern striped trumpeter has a silver body, five or six stripes along the sides and slight spotting at the base of the tail. It occurs most abundantly in weedy areas near the mouth of estuaries and is also present on sheltered coastal reefs.

Pelates octolineatus (Jenyns, 1842)
Striped trumpeter, striped perch, shitty

Habitat: Sheltered seagrass, sand; 0–15 m depth.
Distribution: Broome, WA, to Gulf St Vincent, SA.
Maximum size: Length to 280 mm.

The striped trumpeter closely resembles the eastern striped trumpeter but has a smaller and more rounded head and three-pointed teeth. It also has five to eight stripes along the sides and a fully spotted tail. The

Pelates octolineatus, Woodmans Point, WA

species is very abundant in sheltered seagrass beds, consuming large quantities of algae growing on the seagrass as a part of its diet.

Pelsartia humeralis (Ogilby, 1899)
Sea trumpeter

Habitat: Sheltered and moderately exposed seagrass; 1–12 m depth.
Distribution: Houtman Abrolhos, WA, to Kangaroo I, SA.
Maximum size: Length to 380 mm.

The sea trumpeter differs from other grunters by having a dark patch behind the opercle, three or four dark bands down the body and spotted dorsal, anal and tail fins. It commonly occurs in schools on coastal seagrass beds in southern Western Australia, with a few stragglers recorded from South Australia.

Pelsartia humeralis, Rottnest I, WA. Barry Hutchins

FAMILY APOGONIDAE
Cardinalfishes, gobbleguts

The cardinalfishes are a diverse family of small fishes with large mouths in which they brood their eggs (hence the alternate name, gobbleguts). They have two dorsal fins, which are occasionally joined at the base, and only two spines in the anal fin. Of the estimated 250 species about ten occur in shallow temperate Australian waters.

Apogon victoriae Günther, 1859
Red-striped cardinalfish

Habitat: Moderately exposed reef; 2–20 m depth.
Distribution: Shark Bay to Cape Leeuwin, WA.
Maximum size: Length to 140 mm.

The red-striped cardinalfish has several reddish-brown stripes along the body and black blotches at the base of the pectoral and tail fins. It is frequently seen by divers in caves and ledges on shallow Western Australian reefs.

Apogon victoriae, Horseshoe Reef, WA

Apogon limenus Randall & Hoese, 1988
Sydney cardinalfish

Habitat: Sheltered and moderately exposed reef; 1–30 m depth.
Distribution: Merimbula, NSW, to Yeppoon, Qld.
Maximum size: Length to 140 mm.

The Sydney cardinalfish has a similar but darker colour pattern to the red-striped cardinalfish and lacks the half stripe from the top of the eye to below the rear of the dorsal fin. It is one of the more common

Apogon limenus, Watsons Bay, NSW

reef-dwelling species in deep New South Wales estuaries and is abundant in Sydney Harbour.

Apogon rueppellii Günther, 1859
Gobbleguts

Habitat: Sheltered and moderately exposed seagrass, reef, sand; 0–10 m depth.
Distribution: Arnhem Land, NT, to Albany, WA.
Maximum size: Length to 120 mm.

The gobbleguts has a pale body with a series of black spots along the lateral line and a diagonal stripe behind the eye. It is the most abundant fish species in shallow seagrass beds around Perth, with extremely high numbers of juveniles present over the summer months.

Apogon rueppellii, Seven Mile Beach, WA

Vincentia conspersa (Klunzinger, 1872)
Southern cardinalfish

Habitat: Exposed reef; 1–65 m depth.
Distribution: Ceduna, SA, to Wilsons Promontory, Vic., and around Tas.
Maximum size: Length to 140 mm.

Several closely related species in the genus *Vincentia* occur in southern Australia, with the southern cardinalfish the common species in Victorian and Tasmanian waters. This fish differs from the closely related scarlet cardinalfish ***Vincentia badia***, a species distributed along the southern coast west of Gulf St Vincent, by having 26 rather than 23–24 scales along the lateral line. The southern cardinalfish remains hidden in caves during the day and flits about after planktonic crustaceans at night.

Vincentia conspersa, Edithburgh, SA

Vincentia punctata (Klunzinger, 1879)
Orange cardinalfish

Habitat: Exposed reef; 5–30 m depth.
Distribution: Rottnest I, WA, to Kangaroo I, SA.
Maximum size: Length to 150 mm.

The orange cardinalfish has been confused until recently with the southern cardinalfish but differs by having two spines and ten rays in the anal fin rather than two spines and seven to nine rays. It also has a relatively long distance between the end of the second dorsal fin and the start of the tail fin. The orange cardinalfish is most often seen by divers at night when it moves out from caves to feed.

Vincentia punctata, Princess Royal Harbour, WA

FAMILY DINOLESTIDAE
Long-finned pike

This family contains a single species, the long-finned pike. Somewhat surprisingly given its barracuda-like shape, this species is most closely related to the cardinalfishes.

Dinolestes lewini (Griffith, 1834)
Long-finned pike

Habitat: Exposed reef; 0–60 m depth.
Distribution: Rottnest I, WA, to Port Macquarie, NSW, and around Tas.
Maximum size: Length to 900 mm.

The long-finned pike is abundant on southern reefs, sometimes in schools of hundreds of animals but more often alone or in pairs. It can be confused with the unrelated striped seapike or perhaps with the snook, but the squatter body, yellow tail and long anal fin distinguish it from those species.

Dinolestes lewini, Port Phillip Bay, Vic. RUDIE KUITER

FAMILY SILLAGINIDAE
Whiting

Members of the family Sillaginidae are elongate, bottom-dwelling fishes with pointed snouts, small mouths and long dorsal and anal fins. Although they are commonly known as whiting in Australia, they are unrelated to the European whiting, a species of merluccid cod. Most species occur on shallow sandflats, where they pick at half-buried prey. About 25 species are known, most of them restricted to the tropical Indo-Pacific region and nearby temperate coasts.

Sillago flindersi McKay, 1985
School whiting

Habitat: Sand, silt; 1–170 m depth.
Distribution: Wilsons Promontory, Vic., to Moreton Bay, Qld, and eastern Tas.
Maximum size: Length to 320 mm.

The school whiting differs only slightly from a close relative along the southern Australian coast, the southern school whiting *Sillago bassensis*, by having a pale rather than silver belly, an indistinct rather than a distinct silvery line along the side, and pale brown blotches on the side at about the level of the lateral line. Both species have oblique brown lines across the upper sides of the body, although in many animals these are difficult to see. Adult school whiting generally live in deep water and rarely enter estuaries; juveniles occur in large schools on clean sand.

Sillago flindersi, Ulladulla, NSW

Sillago maculata Quoy & Gaimard, 1824
Trumpeter whiting, winter whiting

Habitat: Sand, silt; 0–30 m depth.
Distribution: Tropical Australia south to Geographe Bay, WA, and Narooma, NSW.
Maximum size: Length to 300 mm.

Sillago maculata, Port Stephens, NSW

Trumpeter whiting possess a number of obvious brown blotches on the sides of the body and a black spot at the base of the pectoral fin. The species is abundant in sheltered estuaries on both the eastern and western coasts of Australia.

Sillaginodes punctata (Cuvier, 1829)

King George whiting, spotted whiting, South Australian whiting

Habitat: Sand, silt, seagrass; 0–25 m depth.
Distribution: Jurien Bay, WA, to northern NSW and northern Tas.
Maximum size: Length to 690 mm.

Adult King George whiting are usually easily recognised because of their large size and the pattern of small round spots in irregular wavy lines on the body. They also have much smaller scales (more than 120 along the lateral line) than other whiting species (less than 80 along lateral line). Juveniles less than 100 mm long are found abundantly in patches of sand among shallow seagrass, while adults normally live and feed in bare sand habitat. This is the largest species in the family, reaching a maximum weight of nearly 5 kg. It is an excellent eating fish and is the most valuable scalefish caught in South Australia.

Sillaginodes punctata, Flinders, Vic. RUDIE KUITER

FAMILY POMATOMIDAE
Tailor, bluefishes

The three recognised species in this family are powerful fishes with streamlined bodies, relatively small scales, and a second dorsal fin that is similar to the anal fin but slightly larger.

Pomatomus saltatrix (Linnaeus 1766)

Tailor, chopper

Habitat: Open sea, estuaries; 0–15 m depth.
Distribution: Onslow, WA, to Fraser I, Qld, and around Tas. Also widely distributed overseas.
Maximum size: Length to 1.2 m.

The tailor occurs in warm temperate seas on all continents and supports an important fishery in the United States, where it is known as bluefish. It is an open-water migratory species, moving south from subtropical areas in spring and northward again in autumn. Relatively few animals are caught on the southern Australian coast and only the odd vagrant in Tasmania. The tailor is a voracious feeder on small fish, getting its name from its ability to cut nets and lines with the sharp teeth. The locations of beaches with feeding schools can usually be identified from a distance because of the associated crowd of anglers.

Pomatomus saltatrix, Clovelly, NSW. RUDIE KUITER

FAMILY CARANGIDAE
Trevally

The family Carangidae contains about 140 species, mainly restricted to the tropics. Most are streamlined, fast-swimming, schooling fish with deeply forked tails and a row of spiny scutes extending forward along the body from the centre of the tail.

Pseudocaranx dentex (Bloch & Schneider, 1801)
Silver trevally, white trevally, skipjack trevally, skippy

Habitat: Open water, estuaries; 0–120 m depth.
Distribution: North West Cape, WA, to southern Qld and around Tas. Also widely distributed overseas.
Maximum size: Length to 940 mm.

The silver trevally occurs in large schools in coastal waters and occasionally enters deep estuaries. It has a reflective silver body with a black spot on the margin of the gill cover and a yellow stripe sometimes present along the midline. Juveniles also have six or seven pale vertical bands on the sides. This species is unusual in being an open-water swimming fish that feeds on bottom-living prey. It is the only species of trevally commercially caught in southern Australia. Much of the fish served in restaurants as trevally is in fact trevalla and therefore belongs in the unrelated family Centrolophidae (see page 497).

Pseudocaranx dentex (juvenile), Sandy Bay, Tas.

Pseudocaranx wrighti (Whitley, 1931)
Skipjack trevally, sand trevally

Habitat: Open water; 0–30 m depth.
Distribution: Houtman Abrolhos, WA, to southern NSW and around Tas. Also Lord Howe I.
Maximum size: Length to 700 mm.

Pseudocaranx wrighti, Canal Rocks, WA

The skipjack trevally has long been confused with the silver trevally, and there is still doubt about the distributions of the two species. The skipjack trevally is distinguished by having fewer scales along the lateral line (67–79 cf. 96–115) and a rounded, jet-black spot on the opercle edge behind the eye, rather than a more elongate and diffuse black spot. The species occurs in large schools along the open coast.

Trachurus novaezelandiae Richardson, 1843
Yellowtail, yellowtail mackerel, yellowtail scad, yellowtail horse mackerel

Habitat: Open water, estuaries; 0–500 m depth.
Distribution: North West Cape, WA, to Wide Bay, Qld. Also Lord Howe I and New Zealand.
Maximum size: Length to 500 mm.

The yellowtail has an elongate shape, prominent scutes along the lateral line, and a bright yellow tail. It occurs in huge schools of similar-sized fish, with the smaller animals most common in inshore areas and the larger animals associated with deep water. This species is very commonly caught by line off jetties in New South Wales.

Trachurus novaezelandiae, Tathra, NSW

Trachurus declivis, Bicheno, Tas. RUDIE KUITER

Trachurus declivis (Jenyns, 1841)

Jack mackerel, horse mackerel, scad, cowanyoung

Habitat: Open water; 0–500 m depth.
Distribution: Shark Bay, WA, to southern Qld and around Tas. Also New Zealand.
Maximum size: Length to 540 mm.

The jack mackerel has a similar body shape to yellowtail but a greenish-grey tail, fewer scales (usually less than 76 along the lateral line), and a straight rather than slightly curved front section to the lateral line. It occurs in large schools, which remain deep on the continental shelf except when surface water temperatures fall below 17°C. Fish mature at a size of approximately 270 mm when three or four years old and have a maximum age of about 15 years. A commercial fishery taking up to 40 000 tonnes per year of the species recently commenced in Tasmania. This catch compares with a combined Australian catch of all other fish species of about 100 000 tonnes per year. Most of the jack mackerel caught is used as fish meal for the salmon-farming industry and is worth only about 10c per kilogram.

Seriola lalandi Valenciennes, 1833

Yellowtail kingfish

Habitat: Open water; 0–50 m depth.
Distribution: Perth, WA, to Capricorn Group, Qld, and northern Tas.
Maximum size: Length to 1.93 m.

The yellowtail kingfish can be identified by its large size, blue-green coloration on the upper part of the body and yellow stripe along the midline. The species occurs in large schools on coastal reefs, particularly

Seriola lalandi, Leander Reef, WA

near deep dropoffs, and also occasionally enters estuaries. It is the largest of the pelagic fishes commonly seen by divers in New South Wales waters. It is also one of the fastest-growing fishes, reaching maturity after two years when about 500 mm long. The flesh of yellowtail kingfish from northern areas is often heavily infected with a parasitic worm, which turns the flesh mushy when cooked.

FAMILY ARRIPIDAE
Australian salmon

This small family contains only three species, all of them restricted to southern Australia and New Zealand. They resemble the tailor in shape but have a single dorsal fin with the spinous and rayed sections joined by a low notch. The term 'Australian salmon' is a poor choice of name, except for fish marketers, because these fishes are not closely related to the true salmon of the Northern Hemisphere.

Arripis truttacea (Cuvier, 1829)

Western Australian salmon, cocky salmon, blackback salmon, bay trout, salmon trout

Habitat: Open water; 0–30 m depth.
Distribution: Kalbarri, WA, to Eden, NSW, and around Tas.
Maximum size: Length to 960 mm.

Arripis truttacea, Esperance, WA. RUDIE KUITER

The Western Australian salmon is the largest species in the family and supports a substantial beach seine fishery taking about 2500 tonnes per year. The flesh is somewhat coarse and soft, with most used for canning. Fish spawn only along the southern Western Australian coast during autumn, after which most of the juvenile fish population drift eastwards during the first year. The Victorian and Tasmanian population grows more slowly than the western population and migrates westward for spawning after four to six years at about 500 mm in length.

Arripis trutta (Bloch & Schneider, 1801)

Eastern Australian salmon, cocky salmon, blackback salmon, bay trout, salmon trout

Habitat: Open water; 0–30 m depth.
Distribution: Port Phillip Bay, Vic., to Brisbane, Qld, and around Tas. Also Lord Howe I and New Zealand.
Maximum size: Length to 890 mm.

Arripis trutta, Port Phillip Bay, Vic. RUDIE KUITER

The eastern Australian salmon has been recognised only recently as different from the western Australian salmon. These two fishes cannot be reliably distinguished by external appearance, and therefore need to be collected for identification in Victoria and Tasmania where the two species commonly overlap. The major feature differentiating the species is the presence of more gillrakers (the bony tooth-like processes on the inside of the gill arches) in the eastern Australian salmon (33–40 on the first gill arch, cf. 25–31 for western Australian salmon). Both species occur in large schools along the open coast, with juveniles found in very shallow water in estuaries. Eastern Australian salmon spawn during summer in the region between Lakes Entrance and Bermagui. The commercial catch of this species is smaller than for the other two species in the family (about 1000 tonnes per year).

Arripis georgiana, Portsea, Vic. RUDIE KUITER

Arripis georgiana Valenciennes, 1831

Tommy ruff, Tommy rough, Australian herring, sea herring

Habitat: Open water; 0–30 m depth.
Distribution: Shark Bay, WA, to Lakes Entrance, Vic.
Maximum size: Length to 410 mm.

Tommy ruff have a similar body shape to juvenile Australian salmon but have obvious black markings on the tips of the tail. The species occurs in large schools in sheltered bays, migrating as the fish mature in February and March to spawning grounds at the southwest corner of Western Australia. The tommy ruff supports a commercial fishery taking about 1500 tonnes per year, most fish being marketed whole but some being frozen for rock lobster bait.

FAMILY GERREIDAE
Silverbellies

The silverbellies are a family of silver-coloured fishes with pointed heads, downwardly protrusible mouths, and long dorsal fins that often have a black margin. Most of the 40 or so species in the family occur in North American waters.

Parequula melbournensis (Castelnau, 1872)

Silverbelly, lowfin

Habitat: Sand, mud; 1–100 m depth.
Distribution: Rottnest I, WA, to Merimbula, NSW, and around Tas.
Maximum size: Length to 220 mm.

The silverbelly differs from most other fishes in the family by having the first spines in the dorsal fin relatively short rather than elevated. The species is abundant on soft sediment in a variety of habitats, from sheltered estuaries to deep sandy bottom along the exposed coast. During the day they generally occur in schools, which disperse at night.

Parequula melbournensis, Fisher I, Tas.

Gerres subfasciatus Cuvier, 1830

Silverbiddy, roach, common silverbelly

Habitat: Silt, sand; 3–40 m depth.
Distribution: Tropical Australia south to Albany, WA, and Wollongong, NSW.
Maximum size: Length to 220 mm.

The silverbiddy has elongate spines at the start of the dorsal fin and a black fin margin. The species lives in large schools in sheltered bays along the New South Wales coast and occurs in even higher densities in estuaries. Silverbiddy are caught in small quantities by beach seine net, with about 150 tonnes per year marketed in New South Wales.

Gerres subfasciatus, Bicton, WA

FAMILY SPARIDAE
Breams

This family contains 41 species of perch-like fishes with strong fin spines and a distinctive arrangement of canine and molar teeth. Most are restricted to southern Africa and the Mediterranean, but four species live in southern Australia. These species can occur in great abundance and are extremely important to both recreational and commercial fishers.

Acanthopagrus australis (Owen, 1853)

Yellowfin bream, bream, silver bream

Habitat: Sheltered and moderately exposed sand, reef; 1–30 m depth.
Distribution: Lakes Entrance, Vic., to Townsville, Qld.
Maximum size: Length to 660 mm.

Acanthopagrus australis, Port Stephens, NSW

The yellowfin bream has a silver to olive-green body and yellow pelvic and anal fins. The species spawns during late autumn or winter at the entrance to estuaries. Most eggs drift to sea, and the small juveniles return into estuaries after one month at about 13 mm length. Adult fish occur in high numbers in both estuaries and shallow coastal waters, the estuarine animals having darker-coloured bodies. Near Sydney, yellowfin bream reach maturity at about 240 mm length and an age of three to four years. Much of the male population changes sex to female after the first spawning season.

Acanthopagrus butcheri (Munro, 1949)
Black bream, bream, silver bream

Habitat: Sheltered sand, mud, seagrass; 0–15 m depth.
Distribution: Shark Bay, WA, to Mallacoota, Vic., and around Tas.
Maximum size: Length to 540 mm.

Black bream have darker pelvic and anal fins and more scales along the lateral line (52–58 cf. 43–46) than yellowfin bream but are otherwise very similar in appearance. Both species are heavily targeted by anglers and commercial fishers. The black bream is largely confined to estuaries, where small juveniles are most abundant over shallow seagrass beds and larger animals frequent the deeper holes. Growth of black bream is slightly slower than for yellowfin bream. Fish in Victoria mature after five years at a size of about 230 mm, while those in South Australia and Western Australia take about three years to reach the same size.

Acanthopagrus butcheri, Port Phillip Bay, Vic. RUDIE KUITER

Rhabdosargus sarba (Forsskål, 1775)
Tarwhine

Habitat: Sheltered and moderately exposed sand, reef; 0–20 m depth.
Distribution: Coral Bay to Albany, WA, and Lakes Entrance, Vic., to Qld. Also widespread overseas.
Maximum size: Length to 800 mm.

Tarwhine differ from the two bream species by having six rather than four rows of scales above the lateral line, and distinct yellow lines following the scale rows along the body. The species occurs on shallow coastal reefs and also regularly enters estuaries. It is caught by line and occasionally seen by divers but is not as abundant as bream or snapper.

Rhabdosargus sarba, Port Stephens, NSW

Chrysophrys auratus (Schneider, 1801)
Snapper, cockney bream, red bream, squire, old man

Habitat: Reef; 1–200 m depth.
Distribution: Barrow I, WA, to Hinchinbrook I, Qld, and northern Tas. Also New Zealand, Japan and the Indo-Malayan region.
Maximum size: Length to 1.3 m.

Chrysophrys auratus, Port Stephens, NSW

Snapper are pink in colour and when adult have a more hump-headed appearance than other Australian members of the family Sparidae. They also have fewer soft rays in the dorsal fin (9–10 cf. 10–14). Juvenile snapper are commonly called cockney bream and have numerous blue spots over the sides of the body. Snapper spawn after forming schools in shallow water at whatever time of year water temperatures exceed 18°C. Spawning thus occurs during summer in Victoria and during winter in Queensland and central Western Australia. Growth is slow, many of the larger fish being more than 20 years old. The species is probably the most prized reef fish caught in southern and southeastern Australian waters.

FAMILY SCIAENIDAE
Croakers, drum

Fishes in this family have elongate bodies with a long single dorsal fin composed of two parts, the first just connected to the base of the second, and a lateral line that continues onto the tail. In other countries they are commonly known as croakers or drum because they have muscles attached to the swimbladder producing sounds that resonate long distances underwater. About 200 species are known worldwide, many of them commercially important.

Argyrosomus hololepidotus (Lacepéde, 1802)
Mulloway, jewfish, river kingfish, soapy, butterfish

Habitat: Reef, sand, mud; 2–150 m depth.
Distribution: Exmouth Gulf, WA, to Brisbane, Qld. Also southern Africa.
Maximum size: Length to 2 m.

The mulloway is a large species of sciaenid with a silver to steel-grey colour and a series of white spots along the lateral line. A second species of sciaenid that is also highly regarded by anglers, the teraglin ***Atractoscion aequidens***, is found in deep water off New South Wales; it differs from the mulloway by having an indented rather than slightly rounded tail. Mulloway spawn outside the surf zone of coastal beaches. The larvae then drift at sea for several months and move into estuaries when about 100 mm long. Fish aged one or two years are abundant in estuaries, where they are known as soapies. They grow rapidly and mature at about 700 mm length (7 kg weight) at an age of six years. The croaking of mulloway is one of the characteristic sounds heard along the Swan estuary near Perth on still nights.

Argyrosomus hololepidotus, Sydney, NSW. RUDIE KUITER

FAMILY HAEMULIDAE
Sweetlips

Species of sweetlip can usually be recognised by their relatively large size, long dorsal fin, small mouth and large rubbery lips. The family is diverse and abundant in the tropics, with about 120 species, but only one species commonly ranges south to temperate waters.

Plectorhinchus flavomaculatus
(Ehrenberg, 1830)
Gold-spotted sweetlips, netted morwong

Habitat: Moderately exposed reef; 1–30 m depth.
Distribution: Tropical Australia south to Geographe Bay, WA, and Moruya, NSW. Also widespread in the Indo-West Pacific region.
Maximum size: Length to 600 mm.

Plectorhinchus flavomaculatus, Seven Mile Beach, WA

Gold-spotted sweetlips are moderately common on coastal reefs with broken bottom, most often in close proximity to seagrass beds in Western Australia. They have a blue body with numerous yellow spots in wavy lines along the sides.

FAMILY NEMIPTERIDAE
Spinecheeks

The spinecheeks are a tropical group with about 65 species. They have elongate or deep bodies, a long dorsal fin with ten spines, an anal fin with three spines, large eyes and small mouth.

Pentapodus vitta Quoy & Gaimard, 1824
Western Australian butterfish

Habitat: Moderately exposed seagrass, sand; 1–15 m depth.
Distribution: Dampier Archipelago to Geographe Bay, WA.
Maximum size: Length to 310 mm.

The Western Australian butterfish characteristically lives in small schools near patchy meadows of the seagrasses *Heterozostera tasmanica* and *Halophila ovata* along the Western Australian coast. The species has a dark stripe bordered by blue lines running through the eye and down the body.

Pentapodus vitta, Cliff Head, WA

FAMILY MULLIDAE
Goatfishes, red mullet

The goatfish family is easily recognised because all species have two long barbels below the chin, used as feelers for probing into soft sediments for prey. Many of the estimated 60 species are called red mullet because animals take on a bright red colour at night, when stressed, or after death.

Upeneichthys lineatus
(Bloch & Schneider, 1801)
Blue-lined goatfish, blue-striped goatfish, red mullet

Habitat: Sheltered and moderately exposed sand, reef; 3–100 m depth.
Distribution: Mallacoota, Vic., to southern Qld.
Maximum size: Length to 310 mm.

Upeneichthys lineatus, Merimbula, NSW

Upeneichthys lineatus (night colouration), Port Stephens, NSW

The blue-lined goatfish is a relatively large goatfish that has blue spots forming lines along the sides of the body. It is commonly seen in sheltered bays and open estuaries in New South Wales. Mobs of several animals are usually found together and sometimes follow in the wake of larger fishes that disturb the sediment.

Upeneichthys vlamingii (Cuvier, 1829)

Southern goatfish, blue-spotted goatfish, red mullet

Habitat: Sheltered and moderately exposed sand, reef; 2–40 m depth.
Distribution: Jurien Bay, WA, to Wilsons Promontory, Vic., and around Tas.
Maximum size: Length to 350 mm.

Upeneichthys vlamingii, Cape Portland, Tas.

The southern goatfish is difficult to distinguish from the blue-lined goatfish, and these two fishes were long considered the one species. The southern goatfish has a slightly longer snout than the blue-lined goatfish and a dark stripe along the side in living animals. However, this stripe cannot be clearly seen on animals during their red colour phase. Juvenile fish form small schools in sheltered bays, while adults are more commonly found on their own near the edge of reefs.

Parupeneus signatus (Günther, 1867)

Black-spotted goatfish

Habitat: Sheltered and moderately exposed sand, reef; 1–25 m depth.
Distribution: Tropical Australia south to Geographe Bay, WA, and Mallacoota, Vic. Also New Zealand and New Guinea.
Maximum size: Length to 470 mm.

Parupeneus signatus, North Head, NSW

Black-spotted goatfish have alternating red and white bands along the body and a distinctive black spot at the rear of the body behind the dorsal fin. This spot is usually preceded by an area of white. Although a tropical species, schools of juveniles are often seen by divers on sand beside reefs in sheltered bays near Sydney and Perth.

Upeneus tragula Richardson, 1846
Bartailed goatfish

Habitat: Sheltered silt, sand; 2–20 m depth.
Distribution: Tropical Australia south to Perth, WA, and Merimbula, NSW. Also widespread in the Indo-West Pacific region.
Maximum size: Length to 280 mm.

The bartailed goatfish is a tropical species that also occurs commonly on the silty bottom of larger estuaries in New South Wales and Western Australia. It can be recognised by the small brown blotches over the sides and the reddish-brown bars on the fins. The species has a characteristic swimming motion at night; it sits motionless on the bottom for a while and then darts quickly to a new location.

Upeneus tragula, Bicton, WA

FAMILY MONODACTYLIDAE
Pomfrets

The pomfrets are a small family containing five species of deep-bodied fish with symmetric dorsal and anal fins that are elongate near the front and sweep in a crescent back towards the tail. They have very small ventral fins.

Schuettea woodwardi (Waite, 1905)
Woodward's pomfret

Habitat: Moderately exposed reef; 1–15 m depth.
Distribution: Shark Bay, WA, to Ceduna, SA.
Maximum size: Length to 24 mm.

Woodward's pomfret commonly occurs in large schools along the southern section of the west coast. It lives in caves during the day and feeds in the open at night on planktonic crustaceans. This species has a less common relative at similar latitudes on the east coast, the eastern pomfret ***Schuettea scalaripinnis***, a species with a yellow upper surface and a thin dark bar at the back of the head.

Schuettea woodwardi, Seven Mile Beach, WA

FAMILY PEMPHERIDIDAE
Bullseyes, sweepers

Bullseyes are closely related to the pomfrets but are a larger family of about 20 species and have a comparatively small dorsal fin. Their large eyes are used at night for visually locating relatively small planktonic prey.

Pempheris multiradiata Klunzinger, 1879
Common bullseye, large-scaled bullseye

Habitat: Reef; 0–30 m depth.
Distribution: Jurien Bay, WA, to Terrigal, NSW, and around Tas.
Maximum size: Length to 280 mm.

The common bullseye is one of the most widespread and abundant fishes on southern Australian reefs. Juveniles generally live at the entrance to caves near

Pempheris multiradiata, Bicheno, Tas.

the sand edge in shallow water, where they can be recognised by distinctive yellow pelvic fins with black tips. Adults occur in smaller groups on deeper reefs and have nine to eleven rows of bronze-coloured scales.

Pempheris klunzingeri McCulloch, 1911

Rough bullseye, Klunzinger's bullseye

Habitat: Moderately and submaximally exposed reef; 0–20 m depth.
Distribution: Shark Bay, WA, to Gulf St Vincent, SA.
Maximum size: Length to 210 mm.

The rough bullseye has small scales, a characteristic orange bar at the back of the head, and diffuse black markings along the edges of the dorsal and anal fins. It occupies the same habitat as the common bullseye and is often seen together with that species in caves, the common bullseye predominating in south coast locations and the rough bullseye predominating in the west.

Pempheris compressa (Shaw, 1790)

Small-scale bullseye

Habitat: Moderately and submaximally exposed reef; 5–30 m depth.
Distribution: Eden to Byron Bay, NSW.
Maximum size: Length to 200 mm.

Pempheris klunzingeri, Seven Mile Beach, WA

Pempheris compressa, Coogee, NSW. RUDIE KUITER

The small-scale bullseye is the eastern counterpart of the rough bullseye. It differs by having a reddish bar behind the head, a smaller reddish marking below the eye and a thin black line along the leading margin of the dorsal fin. The species is abundant in caves on offshore reefs, with juveniles generally occurring in shallower water, particularly near the entrances to estuaries.

Pempheris affinis McCulloch, 1911
Black-tipped bullseye

Habitat: Moderately and submaximally exposed reef; 4–30 m depth.
Distribution: Montague I, NSW, to Hervey Bay, Qld.
Maximum size: Length to 170 mm.

Pempheris affinis, Long Bay, NSW. RUDIE KUITER

The black-tipped bullseye is often seen in mixed schools with the small-scale bullseye on reefs along the east coast and is most abundant towards the north of New South Wales. It is easily distinguished by the black markings at the tips of the dorsal and tail fins and by the silver lateral line.

Parapriacanthus elongatus (McCulloch, 1911)
Slender bullseye

Habitat: Exposed reef; 2–60 m depth.
Distribution: Perth, WA, to Disaster Bay, NSW, and around Tas.
Maximum size: Length to 130 mm.

The slender bullseye usually occurs in large schools in deep water, and occasionally strays into shallow areas of reef. The species has a more slender appearance than other temperate bullseyes and lacks scales on the base of the anal fin.

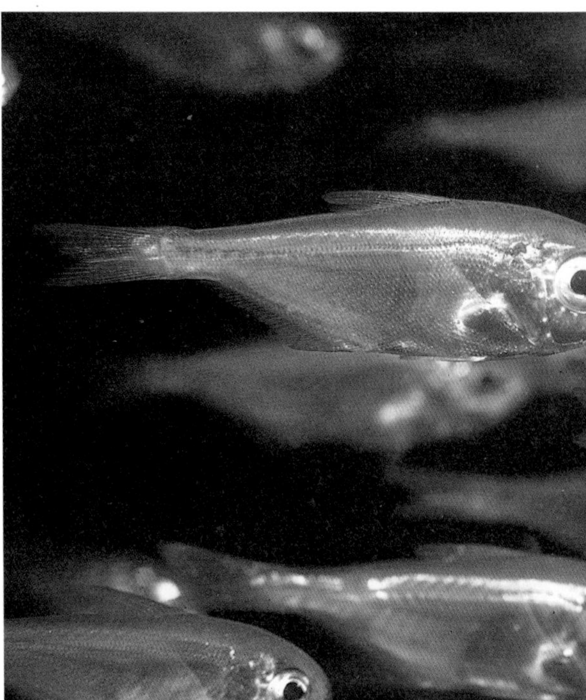

Parapriacanthus elongatus, Flinders, Vic. RUDIE KUITER

FAMILY KYPHOSIDAE
Drummers, rudderfish

The ten drummer species are solid, oval-shaped fishes with small mouths and usually 11 spines at the start of the dorsal fin. They feed largely on seaweed and, possibly for this reason, have a distinctive and unusual arrangement of teeth.

Kyphosus sydneyanus, Esperance, WA. Clay Bryce

Kyphosus cornelii, Houtman Abrolhos, WA. Clay Bryce

Kyphosus sydneyanus (Günther, 1886)

Silver drummer, buffalo bream, buff bream, Sydney drummer

Habitat: Exposed reef; 0–30 m depth.
Distribution: Shark Bay, WA, to Moreton Bay, Qld, and northern Tas. Also Lord Howe I and New Zealand.
Maximum size: Length to 860 mm.

The silver drummer is most often found as solitary individuals along the east and south coasts but forms impressive schools, which inhabit the shallow surge zone, around reefs in Western Australia. It has a silver body with indistinct lines along the scale rows, a black outer section of the tail and a small black spot below the pectoral fin. Despite its large size and the recent trend for exotic seafood, most people agree that this fish and related species are inedible.

Kyphosus cornelii (Whitley, 1944)

Western buffalo bream

Habitat: Exposed reef; 0–20 m depth.
Distribution: Coral Bay to Cape Leeuwin, WA.
Maximum size: Length to 600 mm.

The western buffalo bream occurs in mixed schools with the silver drummer on the west coast. It differs from the silver drummer by having a more forked tail, and lacking the black edge to the tail fin and the moustache-like marking under the eye. Although both species feed predominantly on seaweeds, the diets of the two species differ, the western buffalo bream eating mainly red algae and the silver drummer preferring brown algae

FAMILY GIRELLIDAE
Blackfishes

The family Girellidae is sometimes included within the drummer family Kyphosidae; however, blackfish have more dorsal fin spines than drummer and a different arrangement of teeth. The family comprises only one genus with ten species worldwide.

Girella tricuspidata (Quoy & Gaimard, 1824)
Luderick, blackfish, nigger

Habitat: Reef; 0–20 m depth.
Distribution: Adelaide, SA, to Hervey Bay, Qld, and northern Tas.
Maximum size: Length to 620 mm.

Girella tricuspidata, Port Stephens, NSW

Luderick have a grey body with about 10 thin dark lines down the sides. Adults occur abundantly in estuaries and on shallow coastal reefs, while juveniles are normally associated with estuarine seagrasses during the first year and then move into deeper channels nearby. Fish mature at about 250 mm length and an age of about three years. They spawn in the surf zone, particularly near the entrance of estuaries. Luderick are intensively fished by both commercial and recreational fishers. The flesh provides reasonable eating, provided that captured animals are bled immediately. The recreational fishery for luderick is probably the only one worldwide where plants are used as fish bait.

Girella elevata Macleay, 1881
Eastern rock blackfish, black drummer

Habitat: Submaximally and maximally exposed reef; 0–25 m depth.
Distribution: Wilsons Promontory, Vic., to Noosa Head, Qld, and eastern Tas. south to St Helens. Also Lord Howe I.
Maximum size: Length to 760 mm.

Girella elevata, Montague I, NSW. RUDIE KUITER

The eastern rock blackfish is similar in shape to the luderick but has an overall bluish-black colour with no obvious markings. It is not seen often, probably partly because it remains hidden for most of the day in caves in shallow habitats with wave surge. The related western rock blackfish ***Girella tephraeops***, a species found from Carnarvon to Esperance, has much fewer scales along the lateral line (80–86 cf. 50–58) and a mottled appearance.

Girella zebra (Richardson, 1846)
Zebra fish

Habitat: Reef; 0–20 m depth.
Distribution: Jurien Bay, WA, to Sydney, NSW, and northern Tas.
Maximum size: Length to 540 mm.

The zebra fish has a similar shape to other *Girella* species but is easily recognised because of the yellow fins and the nine dagger-shaped bars down the body. It occurs abundantly in schools of 5–30 animals on shallow sheltered reefs, particularly near boulder fields.

Girella zebra, Port Phillip Bay, Vic. RUDIE KUITER

FAMILY SCORPIDIDAE
Sweeps

The sweeps are deep-bodied fishes related to the drummers. They have scales over most of the body, including the sides of the head and the fin bases. About half of the species belonging to the family live in temperate Australian waters.

Scorpis aequipinnis Richardson, 1848
Sea sweep, snapjack

Habitat: Exposed reef; 1–25 m depth.
Distribution: Shark Bay, WA, to Jervis Bay, NSW, and around Tas.
Maximum size: Length to 560 mm.

The sea sweep is one of the largest species in the family, reaching a maximum weight of nearly 4 kg. It has symmetrically placed dorsal and anal fins like the pomfrets, a grey body, yellow markings on the lower lip and two faint bands on the sides of the body. The sea sweep occurs in open water, most commonly in shallow turbulent areas beside reefs. It is sometimes caught by line and is good eating.

Scorpis aequipinnis, Albany, WA

Scorpis georgiana Valenciennes, 1832
Banded sweep

Habitat: Moderately exposed reef; 2–35 m depth.
Distribution: Coral Bay, WA, to Kangaroo I, SA.
Maximum size: Length to 460 mm.

The banded sweep differs from the sea sweep by having dark black bands across the body and a less strongly forked tail. It is less active than the other sweeps and tends to remain close to caves and ledges in the reef, sometimes retreating within. This species can be caught by line but is not often eaten because of its poor flavour.

Scorpis georgiana, Albany, WA

Scorpis lineolata Kner, 1865
Sweep, silver sweep

Habitat: Reef; 1–30 m depth.
Distribution: Port Phillip Bay, Vic., to Noosa Head, Qld, and around Tas. Also Lord Howe I and New Zealand.
Maximum size: Length to 370 mm.

Sweep are found in great abundance in shallow water above New South Wales reefs but decline rapidly in numbers south of this area. Juveniles are also occasionally found near the entrances of estuaries. They are darker and less rounded than the other local species in the genus and do not have the first few spines of the dorsal and anal fins greatly elevated.

Scorpis lineolata, Merimbula, NSW

Neatypus obliquus Waite, 1905
Footballer sweep, western footballer

Habitat: Submaximally and maximally exposed reefs; 8–200 m depth.
Distribution: Shark Bay, WA, to Flinders I, SA.
Maximum size: Length to 240 mm.

The footballer sweep is unlikely to be confused with any other species because of its distinctive yellow stripes, which obliquely cross the body. It occurs in large schools near offshore reefs in Western Australia and is very inquisitive, approaching and encircling divers.

Atypichthys strigatus, Merimbula, NSW

Neatypus obliquus, Seven Mile Beach, WA

Microcanthus strigatus, Houtman Abrolhos, WA

Atypichthys strigatus (Günther, 1860)
Mado

Habitat: Reef; 0–30 m depth.
Distribution: Apollo Bay, Vic., to Noosa Head, Qld, and south to Tasman Peninsula, Tas. Also Lord Howe I.
Maximum size: Length to 250 mm.

Mado are easily recognised by the elongate silver body with yellow fins and black stripes along the sides. It is one of the most abundant species on New South Wales coastal reefs and is also caught under jetties in large numbers for use as bait.

Microcanthus strigatus (Cuvier, 1831)
Stripey, footballer

Habitat: Sheltered and moderately exposed reef; 2–15 m depth.
Distribution: Exmouth Gulf to Cape Leeuwin, WA, and Merimbula, NSW, to Capricorn Group, Qld. Also Japan, China and Hawaii.
Maximum size: Length to 160 mm.

The stripey has evenly spaced black and yellow stripes along the body and fins. It also has a slightly hump-backed appearance because the snout and eyes are very low on the body. The species commonly occurs in small schools on sheltered reefs and under jetties.

Tilodon sexfasciatus (Richardson, 1842)
Moonlighter, six-banded coral fish, butterfish

Habitat: Moderately and submaximally exposed reef; 2–30 m depth.
Distribution: Jurien Bay, WA, to Port Phillip Bay, Vic., and Wynyard, Tas.
Maximum size: Length to 400 mm.

The moonlighter has a rounded body, six dark bands down the sides including one at the base of the tail, and a yellowish tint to the dorsal fins and upper body. Juvenile moonlighter are easily mistaken for butterfly fishes because, in addition to the other features, they have a pointed snout and large black spots near the rear of the body on the dorsal and anal fins. Adult moonlighter are generally seen on coastal reefs in pairs. Juveniles occur in shallow water, where they move about picking at prey on their own.

Tilodon sexfasciatus, Albany, WA

Amphichaetodon howensis, Montague I, NSW. RUDIE KUITER

FAMILY CHAETODONTIDAE
Butterflyfishes

The butterflyfishes are a group of about 120 species that are mainly restricted to coral reefs. The family is well known to most divers and aquarists because of the striking and colourful appearances of the various species. Three species complete their lifecycles in temperate Australian waters, although vagrant individuals of a number of other species drift south as eggs and larvae from subtropical areas and partially complete their lives on southeastern and southwestern Australian reefs.

Amphichaetodon howensis (Waite, 1903)
Lord Howe butterflyfish

Habitat: Submaximally exposed reef; 5–150 m depth.
Distribution: Merimbula, NSW, to southern Qld. Also Lord Howe I and New Zealand.
Maximum size: Length to 180 mm.

The Lord Howe butterflyfish is occasionally sighted in pairs on deep New South Wales rocky reefs. It has five black bands down the sides and a yellow tint to the upper body and fins.

Chelmonops curiosus Kuiter, 1986
Western talma, truncate coralfish, squareback butterflyfish

Habitat: Sheltered and moderately exposed reef; 2–40 m depth.
Distribution: Shark Bay, WA, to Robe, SA.
Maximum size: Length to 200 mm.

Chelmonops curiosus, Investigator Group, SA

The western talma is an unmistakeable resident of sheltered coastal reefs in southwestern Australia. It has a silver body with five black bands down the sides and a blue line inside the rear edge of the high dorsal and anal fins. The species commonly occurs in pairs, which move slowly over the reef picking at small invertebrates.

Chelmonops truncatus (Kner, 1859)
Eastern talma, truncate coralfish

Habitat: Moderately exposed reef; 8–70 m depth.
Distribution: Merimbula, NSW, to Noosa Head, Qld.
Maximum size: Length to 220 mm.

The eastern talma is unlikely to be confused with the western talma because of their different geographic ranges, but the two species are almost identical in general appearance. The main distinguishing characteristic of the eastern talma is the shorter and less

Chelmonops truncatus, Jervis Bay, NSW

pointed dorsal and anal fins. It is not as common as its western relative but is regularly seen in the Jervis Bay area.

Chaetodon guentheri Ahl, 1913
Günthers butterflyfish

Habitat: Moderately exposed reef; 8–70 m depth.
Distribution: Merimbula, NSW, to Capricorn Group, Qld.
Maximum size: Length to 220 mm.

Günthers butterflyfish is probably the most abundant of the subtropical butterfly fishes that drift south as larvae with the East Australian Current and settle on New South Wales reefs over summer. Specimens as far south as Montague Island grow to almost adult size but usually disappear from reefs by the end of winter. Günthers butterflyfish differs from other species that have approximately the same shape by the black stripe through the eye, fine purple spots on sides, yellow coloration at the rear of the body, and black and blue trim to the fins.

Chaetodon guentheri, Port Stephens, NSW

FAMILY ENOPLOSIDAE
Old wife

This family contains a single Australian species, the old wife, which resembles the butterflyfishes but has two dorsal fins.

Enoplosus armatus (Shaw, 1790)
Old wife

Habitat: Sheltered and moderately exposed reef, seagrass; 0–100 m depth.
Distribution: Kalbarri, WA, to Noosa Head, Qld, and northern Tas.
Maximum size: Length to 310 mm.

The old wife occurs in pairs or as large solitary individuals on coastal reefs, but more often is seen in large schools in sheltered habitats such as over seagrass beds or beside jetty pylons. This species should be carefully handled when captured, as the spines in the first dorsal fin are venomous. The name 'old wife' is derived from the grating sound that the fish makes when stressed.

Enoplosus armatus, Albany, WA

FAMILY PENTACEROTIDAE
Boarfishes

Boarfishes are a family of 14 predominantly deepwater species with pointed snouts and heads encased in bony plates. They also have strong spines, which are venomous in some species, so these fishes should be handled carefully.

Pentaceropsis recurvirostris (Richardson, 1845)
Long-snouted boarfish

Habitat: Exposed reef; 4–260 m depth.
Distribution: Rottnest I, WA, to Sydney, NSW, and around Tas.
Maximum size: Length to 610 mm.

The long-snouted boarfish is the only species to be regularly seen in shallow Australian waters, usually near caves or ledges. It is easily speared and entangled in gillnets, and is therefore rare near heavily fished coasts. The species has dark stripes running obliquely across the body, long venomous spines at the start of the dorsal fin, and extended dorsal, pelvic and anal fins. Juveniles have numerous dark spots over the sides of the body. The long-snouted boarfish is one of very few fish species that feeds on brittle stars.

Pentaceropsis recurvirostris, Three Hummock I, Tas

Parazanclistius hutchinsi, Port Phillip Bay, Vic. RUDIE KUITER

Parazanclistius hutchinsi Hardy, 1983
Short boarfish, Hutchins' boarfish

Habitat: Exposed reef; 10–79 m depth.
Distribution: Rottnest I, WA, to Port Phillip Bay, Vic.
Maximum size: Length to 340 mm.

The short boarfish was discovered only recently and seems to be a rare inhabitant of southern Australian reefs. It has a black spot in a white ring on the dorsal fin and differs from another uncommon species, the black-spotted boarfish ***Zanclistius elevatus***, by having rounded dorsal, pelvic and anal fins.

FAMILY POMACENTRIDAE
Damselfishes

This is a large family of approximately 300 fishes, usually associated with coral reefs. Damselfish are generally small and brightly coloured and have large scales and two spines at the start of the anal fin, the first being much shorter than the second.

Parma victoriae (Günther, 1863)
Scalyfin, Victorian scalyfin, rock perch

Habitat: Sheltered and moderately exposed reef; 0–25 m depth.
Distribution: Dongara, WA, to Wilsons Promontory, Vic., and northern Tas.
Maximum size: Length to 250 mm.

The scalyfin is one of the largest damselfishes, and because it is territorial it aggressively defends the area around its home cave. This area will include a crop of algae, which is continually grazed by the fish. Adult

Parma victoriae, Albany, WA

scalyfin can be distinguished from related species by the relatively plain body with blue tips to the fins and the light grey crescent-shaped markings under the eye and on the opercles. Juveniles are difficult to identify because they have an orange body, blue-ringed black spot on the dorsal fin and neon blue streaks, all features shared with juvenile fish of other species in the genus.

Parma microlepis Günther, 1862
White ear

Habitat: Exposed reef; 0–30 m depth.
Distribution: Port Phillip Bay, Vic., to Byron Bay, NSW, and south to Maria I, Tas.
Maximum size: Length to 200 mm.

The white ear gets its name from the characteristic white patch at the back of the head, which contrasts with the dark body; this patch is present even during the colourful juvenile phase. White ear occur extremely abundantly on coastal reefs in New South Wales. Males become very aggressive during the breeding season and usually develop additional light-coloured patches on the head at that time.

Parma microlepis, Three Hummock I., Tas.

Parma mccullochi Whitley, 1929
McCulloch's scalyfin, common scalyfin

Habitat: Exposed reef; 2–35 m depth.
Distribution: Houtman Abrolhos to Recherche Archipelago, WA.
Maximum size: Length to 300 mm.

McCulloch's scalyfin is the most abundant damselfish in southwestern Australia, where it occurs in high densities on coastal reefs. Adults have a dark mottled appearance with blue trim around the edges of the fins. Juveniles have a yellow body with a darker, blue-lined back.

Parma mccullochi, Canal Rocks, WA

Parma occidentalis Allen & Hoese, 1975
Western scalyfin

Habitat: Exposed reef; 1–10 m depth.
Distribution: Coral Bay to Cape Leeuwin, WA.
Maximum size: Length to 300 mm.

The western scalyfin occurs on many of the same southwestern reefs as McCulloch's scalyfin but is a less abundant species. Adults of the two species are difficult to distinguish because they have a similar colour pattern; however, the head of the western scalyfin has a much steeper profile and the mouth projects slightly more. The juveniles are readily distinguished because of vertical white bars on the western scalyfin.

Parma occidentalis, Jurien Bay, WA. BARRY HUTCHINS

Parma unifasciata (Steindachner, 1867)
Girdled scalyfin, girdled parma

Habitat: Exposed reef; 1–25 m depth.
Distribution: Montague I, NSW, to Noosa Head, Qld.
Maximum size: Length to 200 mm.

The girdled scalyfin occurs abundantly along the central New South Wales coast and generally prefers a boulder habitat with wave surge. Adults have an obvious white vertical band across the centre of the body; the yellow and blue juveniles also carry the band but it is much less distinct.

Parma unifasciata, Bass Point, NSW

Chromis hypsilepis (Günther, 1867)
One-spot puller

Habitat: Exposed reef; 1–40 m depth.
Distribution: Mallacoota, Vic., to Byron Bay, NSW, and the Kent Group, Tas. Also Lord Howe I, Norfolk I and New Zealand.
Maximum size: Length to 150 mm.

Chromis hypsilepis, Ulladulla, NSW

The one-spot puller is among the most abundant species on southern New South Wales coastal reefs. It has a blue body with a distinctive white spot below the end of the dorsal fin. The species feeds on zooplankton and unless threatened swims in large aggregations high above the bottom. Adults nest communally by depositing eggs together on the tops of reefs.

Chromis klunzingeri Whitley, 1929
Blackheaded puller

Habitat: Exposed reef; 5–40 m depth.
Distribution: Houtman Abrolhos to Recherche Archipelago, WA.
Maximum size: Length to 120 mm.

The blackheaded puller is the most distinctive of the southern Australian damselfish, with yellow sides to the body above the lateral line, white below, and a dark black patch across the head. It generally feeds in the open on plankton and is particularly common along the southern Western Australian coast.

Chromis klunzingeri, Esperance, WA

FAMILY CIRRHITIDAE
Hawkfishes

Hawkfishes are a family of about 30 small fishes that can be recognised by having tufts of filaments at the ends of the dorsal spines and by a characteristic perching behaviour on reefs.

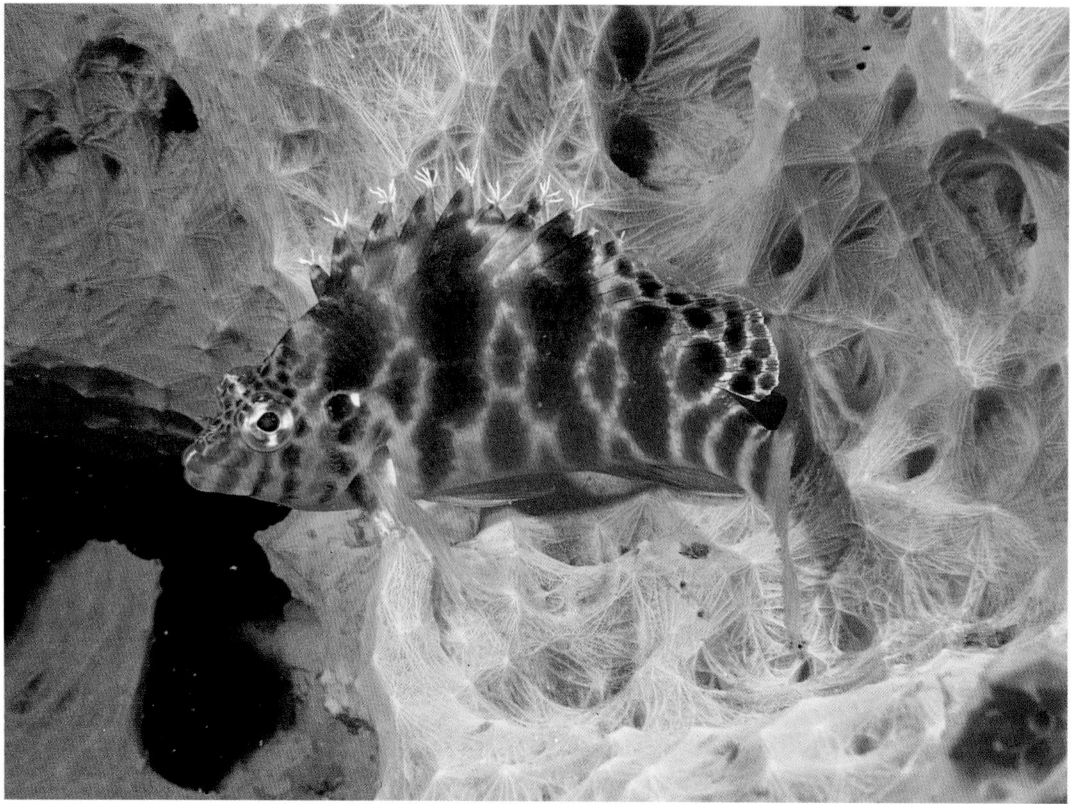

Cirrhitichthys aprinus, Coogee, NSW. RUDIE KUITER

Cirrhitichthys aprinus (Cuvier, 1829)
Blotched hawkfish

Habitat: Sheltered and moderately exposed reef; 5–30 m depth.
Distribution: Tropical Australia south to Houtman Abrolhos, WA, and Merimbula, NSW. Also widespread in the Indo-West Pacific region.
Maximum size: Length to 120 mm.

The blotched hawkfish is primarily a tropical species, but also occurs commonly in deep estuaries along the central New South Wales coast. It sits perched on thickened lower rays of the pectoral fins among sponges and other reef growth, waiting for prey.

FAMILY CHIRONEMIDAE
Kelpfish

Kelpfish are closely related to both the hawkfish and morwong families. They are a small group of species with strengthened pectoral fins to enable them to wedge among rocks in the kelp zone along exposed coasts.

Chironemus marmoratus Günther, 1860
Eastern kelpfish

Habitat: Exposed reef; 0–20 m depth.
Distribution: Mallacoota, Vic., to Byron Bay, NSW, and northeastern Tas. Also New Zealand.
Maximum size: Length to 400 mm.

The eastern kelpfish has a mottled green, brown and light grey pattern, with small white spots on most of the scales. It occurs commonly in the surge zone of

Chironemus marmoratus, Terrigal, NSW

coastal reefs and is sometimes confused with the rock cale *Crinodus lophodon*, a species in a related family (described below), with a rounded head but generally similar appearance. A closely related species, the western kelpfish ***Chironemus georgianus***, occurs along the southern coast. The western kelpfish has tufts of filaments on the dorsal spines and lacks white spots on the head and scales. It behaves differently from the eastern kelpfish, as it is a more secretive species that spends much of its time in caves and ledges.

FAMILY APLODACTYLIDAE
Sea carps

Sea carps can be recognised by their mottled coloration, rounded heads and fleshy lower rays to the pectoral fins. Only five species are included in the family, three of them in temperate Australian waters.

Aplodactylus arctidens Richardson, 1839
Southern sea carp, marble fish, stinky groper

Habitat: Exposed reef; 1–40 m depth.
Distribution: Investigator Group, SA, to Cape Conran, Vic., and around Tas. Also New Zealand.
Maximum size: Length to 600 mm.

Aplodactylus arctidens, Popes Eye, Vic. RUDIE KUITER

The southern sea carp is a large seaweed-eating species found in large numbers among kelp plants on shallow coastal reefs in southeastern Australia. A small commercial catch is exported live from Tasmania to Sydney markets, although it is difficult to believe that anyone could eat this fish, as the flesh is light green with a ripe smell.

Aplodactylus westralis, Esperance, WA

Aplodactylus westralis Russell, 1987
Western sea carp, cockatoo morwong

Habitat: Exposed reef; 1–20 m depth.
Distribution: Rottnest I to Recherche Archipelago, WA.
Maximum size: Length to 630 mm.

The western sea carp has a more rounded head than its eastern relative and also differs by having pale blue spots over the body and head. This species is quite common in shallow water on the southern coast of Western Australia but is not often seen on the west coast. Like other species in the family, the western sea carp feeds mainly on brown algae.

Crinodus lophodon (Günther, 1859)
Rock cale, cockatoo fish, rock cocky, joey

Habitat: Exposed reef; 0–10 m depth.
Distribution: Mallacoota, Vic., to Byron Bay, NSW.
Maximum size: Length to 450 mm.

Crinodus lophodon, Bass Point, NSW

The rock cale is the most abundant large fish seen in and just below the surge zone on exposed coastal reefs in New South Wales. It usually sits on a coralline algal turf and can also wedge itself in crevices during large wave sets. The species is distinguished from related fishes by the small rounded head and white spots on the fins.

FAMILY CHEILODACTYLIDAE
Morwongs

Morwong are large fishes with rubbery lips and the lower four to seven rays of the pectoral fin unbranched, thickened and at least one greatly elongated. About 20 species are present in the family, the majority occurring in southern Australia. Morwong are frequently speared because of their abundance, size and slow-moving habits, but they rarely take a hook.

Cheilodactylus fuscus Castelnau, 1879
Red morwong

Habitat: Exposed reef; 0–30 m depth.
Distribution: Eastern Bass Strait, Vic., to Hervey Bay, Qld. Also New Zealand.
Maximum size: Length to 650 mm.

The red morwong is the most common morwong on New South Wales reefs and is one of the most abundant of large fishes there. The species has a distinctive red upper body with pale bands near the tail and a pair of small horns in front of the eyes.

Cheilodactylus fuscus, Bass Point, NSW

Cheilodactylus nigripes Richardson, 1850
Magpie perch

Habitat: Sheltered and moderately exposed reef; 1–60 m depth.
Distribution: Albany, WA, to Kiama, NSW, and south to Bruny I, Tas.
Maximum size: Length to 410 mm.

Magpie perch usually have two wide black bands across the body; however, the second band is light grey at some sites and becomes paler at night. Juveniles have a reddish tail, which darkens as animals mature. The species is very common on reefs along the southern coast but is not often caught by line because it feeds on small invertebrates that are sucked off the bottom in mouthfuls of sediment.

Cheilodactylus nigripes, Ninepin Pt, Tas.

Cheilodactylus rubrolabiatus
Allen & Heemstra, 1976
Red-lipped morwong

Habitat: Moderately and submaximally exposed reef; 2–30 m depth.
Distribution: Coral Bay, WA, to Ceduna, SA.
Maximum size: Length to 750 mm.

Cheilodactylus rubrolabiatus, Lucky Bay, WA. RUDIE KUITER

The red-lipped morwong has a pattern of oblique brown bands across the body, spots between the bands, and red markings on the lips, opercle edge and pectoral and pelvic fins. It is the morwong most commonly seen by divers on the west coast and generally lives in shallow weedy areas of reef.

Cheilodactylus spectabilis Hutton, 1872
Banded morwong, carp

Habitat: Exposed reefs; 3–50 m depth.
Distribution: Robe, SA, to Seal Rocks, NSW, and around Tas. Also New Zealand.
Maximum size: Length to 1 m.

The banded morwong is abundant on deep reefs in eastern and western Tasmanian waters, but is less common north of Bass Strait. It generally congregates in small groups in large caves. The brown bands on a light red background are characteristic, although in the largest animals the bands blend into the brick-red coloration between. This species has recently been targeted by gillnet fishers, who receive a high price for live-caught animals.

Cheilodactylus gibbosus, Busselton, WA

Cheilodactylus spectabilis, Ile des Phoques, Tas.

Cheilodactylus gibbosus Richardson, 1841
Western crested morwong, magpie morwong

Habitat: Sheltered and moderately exposed reef; 2–20 m depth.
Distribution: Shark Bay to Recherche Archipelago, WA.
Maximum size: Length to 350 mm.

The western crested morwong has the fourth spine of the dorsal fin greatly elevated, and the following spines gradually diminishing in size. It is most often found on reefs near sand in sheltered coastal bays and occasionally enters estuaries.

Cheilodactylus vestitus (Castelnau, 1879)
Eastern crested morwong, magpie morwong

Habitat: Sheltered and moderately exposed reef; 1–20 m depth.
Distribution: Port Hacking, NSW, to Capricorn Group, Qld. Also Lord Howe I and New Caledonia.
Maximum size: Length to 350 mm.

The eastern crested morwong differs in only minor features from the western crested morwong; it has an extension of the upper black bar to the bottom tip of the tail and has yellow coloration behind the eye and under the dorsal fin. It is not abundant but is seen most often just inside the entrances of the deeper estuaries.

Cheilodactylus vestitus, Port Stephens, NSW.

Nemadactylus macropterus
(Bloch & Schneider, 1801)
Jackass morwong, sea bream, silver perch

Habitat: Exposed sand, silt; 5–400 m depth.
Distribution: Rottnest I, WA, to Moreton Bay, Qld, and around Tas. Also New Zealand, southern Africa and South America.
Maximum size: Length to 700 mm.

The jackass morwong has a silver body with a black crescent-shaped marking at the back of the head. It usually occurs in water deeper than 50 m depth, but schools sometimes enter relatively shallow water in Tasmania and juveniles are found in deep estuaries. The species is important commercially, as about 1000 tonnes per year are trawled in southeastern Australia. Maturity is reached at an age of three years and a size of about 250 mm in length. Adults then grow slowly, with fish at 500 mm being about 15 years old. Some fish in New Zealand have been aged at more than 50 years.

Nemadactylus macropterus (night coloration), Sandy Bay, Tas.

Nemadactylus douglasii (Hector, 1875)
Blue morwong, grey morwong, rubberlip perch

Habitat: Exposed sand, reef; 10–100 m depth.
Distribution: Wilsons Promontory, Vic., to Moreton Bay, Qld, and south to Storm Bay, Tas. Also New Zealand.
Maximum size: Length to 740 mm.

The blue morwong has a similar shape to the jackass morwong but is easily recognised by the distinctive blue coloration, particularly on the fins. While the species is occasionally seen over sand beside reefs in New South Wales, the largest schools occur below divable depths and are commercially trawled.

Nemadactylus douglasii, Montague I, NSW. ALISON KUITER

Nemadactylus valenciennesi (Whitley, 1937)
Queen snapper, blue morwong

Habitat: Exposed reef; 3–240 m depth.
Distribution: Shark Bay, WA, to Wilsons Promontory, Vic., and King I, Tas.
Maximum size: Length to 610 mm.

The queen snapper differs from other morwong in having wavy yellow and blue lines radiating from the eye. Juveniles also have several yellow lines along the body and a black blotch on the side; however, these fade and become indistinct in larger individuals. The species is good eating.

Nemadactylus valenciennesi, Esperance, WA

Dactylophora nigricans (Richardson, 1850)
Dusky morwong, strongfish

Habitat: Sheltered and moderately exposed seagrass, reef, sand; 1–30 m depth.
Distribution: Lancelin, WA, to Port Phillip Bay, Vic.
Maximum size: Length to 1.2 m.

The dusky morwong is the largest and most elongate of the morwongs and is also the largest fish species commonly seen in seagrass beds and on nearby sand patches. Adult fish have a uniform green-brown colour, while juveniles have brown spots and bars on the upper body and tail. The flesh is much less palatable than that of other morwongs.

Dactylophora nigricans, Rapid Bay, SA. RUDIE KUITER

FAMILY LATRIDIDAE
Trumpeter

Trumpeter are a small Southern Hemisphere family comprising only four species. They are closely related to morwongs but have a deeply notched dorsal fin and relatively small pectoral fins.

Latridopsis forsteri (Castelnau, 1872)
Bastard trumpeter

Habitat: Exposed reef, sand; 0–60 m depth.
Distribution: Robe, SA, to Sydney, NSW, and around Tas.
Maximum size: Length to 650 mm.

The bastard trumpeter is the only trumpeter commonly seen by divers and is distinguished by a perch-like shape and bronze coloration in the upper half of the body. It is one of the more popular species caught by gillnet and spear in Tasmania. Most of the animals caught in shallow water are less than five years old and 1 kg in weight; mature animals of up to 30 years age occur in deeper water. Small juveniles are commonly referred to as paper fish because of an extremely thin and semitransparent body.

Latridopsis forsteri, Ile des Phoques, Tas.

Latris lineata (Bloch & Schneider, 1801)
Tasmanian trumpeter, stripey trumpeter

Habitat: Exposed reef; 0–300 m depth.
Distribution: Albany, WA, to Montague I, NSW, and around Tas. Also New Zealand and Amsterdam I.
Maximum size: Length to 1.2 m.

The Tasmanian trumpeter has a pointed snout and three olive-green stripes along the upper sides of the body. It was once among the most commonly caught species around Tasmania but during the past half-century the population has been almost eliminated from shallow water. The species is now found primarily in deep water or along remote sections of the southern and western Tasmanian coasts. It is considered one of the best eating fishes.

Latris lineata, Mutton Bird I, Tas.

FAMILY MUGILIDAE
Mullet

Mullet can usually be recognised by their small heads and distinctive shape. They have two dorsal fins of similar size set well apart, a small mouth and large scales, and they lack a clearly defined lateral line. Many of the estimated 100 species in the family are prized as food fish overseas, but in Australia mullet are among the lowest priced fishes.

Aldrichetta forsteri (Valenciennes, 1836)
Yellow-eye mullet, Coorong mullet

Habitat: Sheltered sand, seagrass; 0–20 m depth.
Distribution: Shark Bay, WA, to Newcastle, NSW, and around Tas.
Maximum size: Length to 500 mm.

The yellow-eye mullet is by far the most common mullet in southern Australia and is best recognised by the yellow eye and relatively long mouth. It is extremely abundant in southern Australian estuaries; about 1000 tonnes per year are caught commercially. The species changes diet with age; juveniles feed on planktonic animals, medium-size fish feed on benthic crustaceans and molluscs, and the larger fish feed almost exclusively on algae.

Aldrichetta forsteri, Cloudy Lagoon, Tas.

Mugil cephalus Linnaeus, 1758
Sea mullet

Habitat: Sheltered and moderately exposed sand, reef; 0–20 m depth.
Distribution: Around the Australian mainland and Tas. Also widespread overseas.
Maximum size: Length to 790 mm.

Mugil cephalus, Sorrento, Vic. RUDIE KUITER

The sea mullet differs from other local species by having a transparent eyelid covering each eye and eight rather than 9–13 segmented rays plus three spines in the anal fin. It occurs very abundantly in the warmer part of its range but is rare in Tasmania. Juveniles live in estuaries, while adults are often seen schooling along the coast picking at food on algal-covered rocks. Animals reach maturity after three years, at a size of about 330 mm.

FAMILY LABRIDAE
Wrasses

The wrasse family includes more than 400 species with a huge range of sizes and shapes. Behavioural patterns vary greatly between species. For most species, behaviour controls the sex of animals; juveniles join a female harem that is dominated by a single male, and they transform into a male only if they are dominant among the females and the male has disappeared.

Achoerodus viridis (Steindachner, 1866)
Eastern blue groper

Habitat: Exposed reef; 0–40 m depth.
Distribution: Wilsons Promontory, Vic., to Hervey Bay, Qld.
Maximum size: Length to 1 m.

Two species of groper occurs in temperate Australian waters. The eastern blue groper differs from the western blue groper ***Achoerodus gouldii***, a species extending from Western Australia to Victoria, by having more scales along the lateral line (41–45 cf. 33–37) and blue scribbles around the eye. The two also differ in colour, with the male eastern blue groper having a blue body and the female a brown body

Achoerodus viridis, Bermagui, NSW. RUDIE KUITER

ather than the predominant green of the western blue groper. Both species are inquisitive and sometimes ollow divers, a fatal characteristic for a fish that is also arge and tasty. Because local populations are quickly lecimated by spear fishers, the eastern blue groper is protected in New South Wales. Western blue groper are less common than their eastern relatives and are only seen in large numbers along the remoter sections of the south coast.

Austrolabrus maculatus (Macleay, 1881)
Blackspotted wrasse

Habitat: Exposed reef; 3–40 m depth.
Distribution: Shark Bay, WA, to Victor Harbor, SA, and Montague I to Byron Bay, NSW.
Maximum size: Length to 170 mm.

Austrolabrus maculatus, Esperance, WA. RUDIE KUITER

The blackspotted wrasse has a dull but distinctive colour pattern with a red-brown, black-spotted upper body and white belly. Juveniles and females also have a white bar in front of the tail and a white-edged black spot below the end of the dorsal fin. The species does not occur in the Victorian region, and the southwestern and eastern Australian populations have diverged and acquired slightly different characteristics. Southwestern fish are common in shallow depths among seaweeds on reefs, whereas New South Wales fish are rarely seen in shallow water but occur among sponges at depths greater than 20 m.

Bodianus frenchii (Klunzinger, 1880)
Western foxfish

Habitat: Exposed reef; 10–40 m depth.
Distribution: Houtman Abrolhos, WA, to southern NSW.
Maximum size: Length to 490 mm.

The western foxfish is a bright red species with a large yellow blotch on the upper surface about midway along the body and another below the end of the dorsal fin. It occurs commonly on deep offshore reefs, often swimming back and forth at cave entrances. A closely related foxfish, ***Bodianus* sp.**, occurs on deep reefs from southern Queensland to eastern Tasmania. It has yellow pectoral and tail fins and blotches on the side which are white rather than yellow. These blotches are also slightly further forward on the body than those on the western foxfish.

Bodianus frenchii, Leander Reef, WA

Choerodon rubescens (Günther, 1862)

Baldchin groper

Habitat: Exposed reef, seagrass; 2–40 m depth.
Distribution: Coral Bay to Geographe Bay, WA.
Maximum size: Length to 900 mm.

The baldchin groper has a variable background colour, which ranges from greenish-brown to pinkish-gray. The species is best recognised by the rounded head, small eye and white chin. Large animals are generally confined to deep reefs, while juveniles live in shallow seagrass and algal beds. This is the best-tasting of the temperate wrasses and is targeted by anglers along the central Western Australian coast.

Choerodon rubescens, Rottnest I, WA. Barry Hutchins

Coris auricularis (Valenciennes, 1838)

Western king wrasse

Habitat: Moderately exposed reef; 1–45 m depth.
Distribution: Coral Bay to Recherche Archipelago, WA.
Maximum size: Length to 400 mm.

Male and female *Coris auricularis* have a similar body shape but have such different patterns that they are often mistaken for separate species. The male has white and dark bars behind the pectoral fin, yellow coloration at the base of the pectoral fin, a blue and yellow patch at the end of the operculum, and a white chin and red cheek. The female has a dark red stripe extending through the eye to the base of the tail and numerous fine red stripes along the sides. Juveniles have two dark stripes along the side of the body, separated by a thin white stripe through the base of the eye. Juveniles and small females set up cleaner stations on reefs where they pick parasites off larger fish. They are grouped into a harem controlled by a single dominant male, and if the male disappears for more than a few days the largest female will change sex. The species occurs very commonly on the edge of reef close to sand and seagrass.

Coris auricularis (male), Horseshoe Reef, WA

Coris auricularis (juvenile), Canal Rocks, WA

Coris sandageri Phillips, 1927
Eastern king wrasse, Sandager's wrasse

Habitat: Exposed reef; 5–40 m depth.
Distribution: Eastern Vic. to Broughton I, NSW. Also New Zealand.
Maximum size: Length to 500 mm.

The eastern king wrasse is less abundant and tends to occur in deeper water than its western relative. It utilises a similar behavioural strategy, with a single large male controlling a harem of females. Males are easily identified by the two large black bars edged by white and yellow behind the head, whereas females lack the bars and are more drably coloured. Juveniles have a thin body with a golden stripe down the side that ends at a black spot on the base of the tail. The species is active only during daylight; at night it sleeps buried under sand.

Coris sandangeri (male), Montague I, Nsw. Rudie Kuiter

Coris picta (Bloch & Schneider, 1801)
Combfish

Habitat: Exposed reef, sand; 1–25 m depth.
Distribution: Eastern Vic. to Moreton Bay, Qld.
Maximum size: Length to 220 mm.

Coris picta, Bass Point, NSW

Adult combfish have a characteristic comb-like stripe along the body and red markings on the top of the head. Juveniles have a wide black stripe along the side of the body, continuing to the end of the tail. The species is very common on New South Wales reefs, where it feeds either by cleaning parasites off other fish or by picking at small invertebrates from the seabed.

Ophthalmolepis lineolata Valenciennes, 1839
Maori wrasse

Habitat: Exposed reef; 1–30 m depth.
Distribution: Houtman Abrolhos, WA, to southern Qld, and Kent Group, Tas.
Maximum size: Length to 410 mm.

Maori wrasse can usually be recognised by the dark brown back, white stripe along the side and yellow-green belly. Large animals also have conspicuous blue lines radiating from the eyes, resembling Maori tattoos, and males have an additional dark stripe along the side. The species is abundant on reefs in moderate water depths. It is an inquisitive species and will circle divers.

Ophthalmolepis lineolata, Canal Rocks, WA

Halichoeres brownfieldi (Whitley, 1945)
Brownfield's wrasse

Habitat: Moderately exposed seagrass, reef; 0–30 m depth.
Distribution: Coral Bay to Recherche Archipelago, WA.
Maximum size: Length to 150 mm.

Brownfield's wrasse is lime-green with iridescent spots and stripes, particularly near the head. Large catches are taken in small seine nets in *Posidonia* seagrass meadows along the southwestern Australian coast, indicating that the species is one the most abundant fishes there. The species is not often noticed, however, because of its small size and good camouflage.

Halichoeres brownfieldi, Rottnest I, WA. Barry Hutchins

Dotalabrus aurantiacus (Castelnau, 1872)

Castelnau's wrasse, pretty polly

Habitat: Moderately exposed reef, seagrass; 1–47 m depth.
Distribution: Rottnest I, WA, to Montague I, NSW, and northern and eastern Tas.
Maximum size: Length to 150 mm.

Castelnau's wrasse is a variably patterned species that can usually be recognised by four broken bars across the body and dark radiating lines below the eye. The species is most easily recognised underwater by a characteristic bobbing motion, as it swims obliquely up from the seabed and then settles back down, only to repeat the process. The species is very common among brown seaweeds and seagrass but is often mistaken for the juvenile stage of other wrasse species.

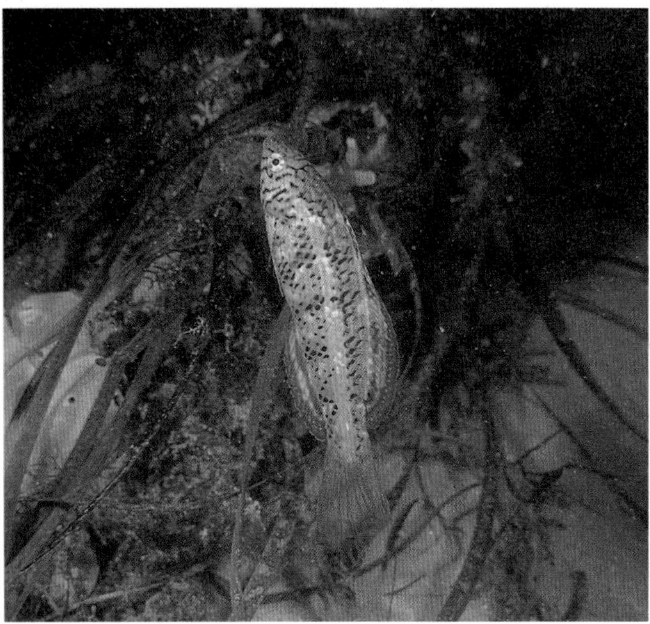

Dotalabrus aurantiacus, Kangaroo I, SA. Rudie Kuiter

Eupetrichthys angustipes

Ramsay & Ogilby, 1888
Snakeskin wrasse

Habitat: Exposed reef; 4–40 m depth.
Distribution: Houtman Abrolhos, WA, to Solitary Islands, NSW, and Kent Group, Tas.
Maximum size: Length to 200 mm.

The snakeskin wrasse is quite similar to Castelnau's wrasse but has a more elongate body with the light-coloured belly abruptly darkening above, and with darker stripes down the sides. The two species also have similar swimming styles, moving in short bursts up from the bottom. When resting, the snakeskin wrasse lies on its side with the head turned at an angle. The species occurs commonly in boulder habitats near sand in New South Wales waters and is moderately common on seaweed-covered reefs in Western Australia but is rarely seen along the southern coast.

Eupetrichthys angustipes, Bermagui, NSW. Rudie Kuiter

Notolabrus gymnogenis (Günther, 1862)

Crimson-banded wrasse

Habitat: Exposed reef; 4–40 m depth.
Distribution: Mallacoota, Vic., to southern Qld. Also Lord Howe I.
Maximum size: Length to 490 mm.

The crimson-banded wrasse occurs very commonly on New South Wales coastal reefs. Males are brightly

Notolabrus gymnogenis (male), Terrigal, NSW

Notolabrus gymnogenis (female), La Perouse, NSW. RUDIE KUITER

coloured with a characteristic red band across the body and red dorsal and anal fins, while females are a reddish colour with numerous horizontal rows of white spots. Juveniles are drably coloured, with rows of white spots set against a green-brown background.

Notolabrus tetricus (Richardson, 1840)

Blue-throated wrasse, bluenose, parrot fish, kelpie, winter bream, bluehead

Habitat: Reef; 1–160 m depth.
Distribution: Ceduna, SA, to Sydney, NSW, and around Tas.
Maximum size: Length to 500 mm.

Juvenile blue-throated wrasse initially have a nondescript green or brown appearance but as they mature into females they gain a black stripe followed by white stripe across the body. Large females transform into males and develop a rounded bluish head and yellow pectoral and pelvic fins. This species is the most abundant wrasse found on Victorian and Tasmanian reefs. The largest animals tend to live in relatively deep and exposed habitats, while juveniles occur in large numbers on shallow seaweed-dominated reefs. The species is very commonly caught on line and in gillnet. Although the flesh is not highly regarded, a small industry has recently developed based on the sale of live fish.

Notolabrus tetricus, Hope I, Tas.

Notolabrus parilus (Richardson, 1850)

Brown-spotted wrasse, orange-spotted wrasse

Habitat: Moderately and submaximally exposed reef; 2–20 m depth.
Distribution: Shark Bay, WA, to Queenscliff, Vic.
Maximum size: Length to 490 mm.

Female and juvenile brown-spotted wrasse have a drab greenish-brown appearance and are difficult to distinguish from related *Notolabrus* species. Males have an orange-brown background with a white stripe along the side and numerous small golden spots. This species is abundant on vegetated reefs in southwestern Australia but is less frequently seen in South Australia and is extremely rare in Victoria.

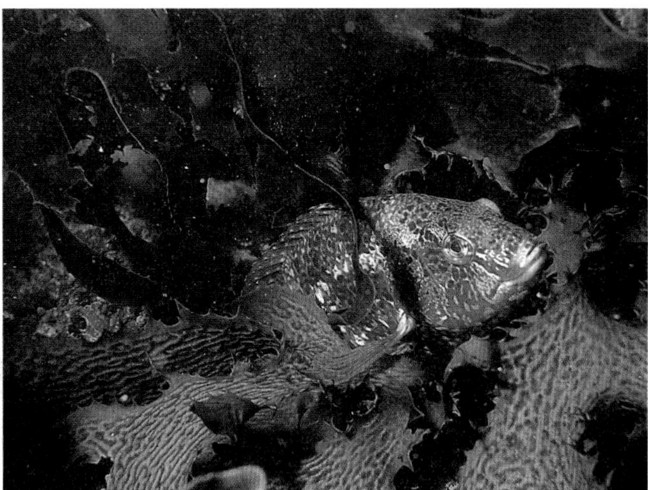

Notolabrus parilus, Horseshoe Reef, WA

Notolabrus fucicola (Richardson, 1840)

Purple wrasse, kelpie, parrot fish, winter bream, saddled wrasse

Habitat: Exposed reef; 0–90 m depth.
Distribution: Kangaroo I, SA, to Montague I, NSW, and around Tas. Also New Zealand.
Maximum size: Length to 400 mm.

Purple wrasse have a blue, green or brown background colour with five yellow dots underneath the dorsal fin. Unlike closely related species, males do not differ substantially from females although they are

Notolabrus fucicola, Port Davey, Tas.

more intensely coloured. This species is extremely abundant in shallow water among kelps on fully exposed Tasmanian and Victorian reefs. It also occurs with the blue-throated wrasse on moderately exposed reefs and sometimes mates with that species, producing distinctive hybrids.

Pseudolabrus psittaculus (Richardson, 1840)

Rosy wrasse

Habitat: Exposed reef; 2–218 m depth.
Distribution: Albany, WA, to Sydney, NSW, and around Tas.
Maximum size: Length to 250 mm.

Rosy wrasse are a pink, narrow-bodied species with some yellow coloration on males and a black spot at the rear of the dorsal fin on females and juveniles. Most of the population lives below normal diving depths, where the species is sometimes trawled by commercial boats. Small animals are quite common near shallow caves on exposed Tasmanian and Victorian reefs.

Pseudolabrus psittaculus, Ile des Phoques, Tas.

Pseudolabrus luculentus (Richardson, 1848)

Luculentus wrasse

Habitat: Exposed reef; 10–50 m depth.
Distribution: Mallacoota, Vic., to Byron Bay, NSW. Also Lord Howe I, Norfolk I and New Zealand.
Maximum size: Length to 250 mm.

Luculentus wrasse is occasionally seen along the New South Wales coast but is much more common at Lord Howe Island. Males can be recognised by several black and white blotches at the base of the dorsal fin, while females look very similar to rosy wrasse except for a more pointed snout and white stripes across the chin.

Pseudolabrus luculentus, Bermagui, NSW. RUDIE KUITER

Pseudolabrus biserialis (Klunzinger, 1879)

Red-banded wrasse

Habitat: Moderately and submaximally exposed reef; 3–20 m depth.
Distribution: Houtman Abrolhos to Recherche Archipelago, WA.
Maximum size: Length to 250 mm.

Pseudolabrus biserialis, Canal Rocks, WA

Male and female red-banded wrasse have red bodies with distinctive white stripes along the sides; the female has black spots along the back, and the male has brighter fins. They are common on exposed seaweed-covered reefs in southwestern Australia.

Pictilabrus laticlavius (Richardson, 1939)
Senator wrasse

Habitat: Moderately exposed reef; 0–30 m depth.
Distribution: Houtman Abrolhos, WA, to Byron Bay, NSW, and around Tas.
Maximum size: Length to 300 mm.

Male and female senator wrasse have similar shapes but very different patterns. Males have a green background colour with violet stripes along the sides, whereas the females and juveniles are a reddish colour. The senator wrasse is one of the most abundant wrasses on temperate reefs and also one of the most inquisitive. It generally lives close to the seabed among kelp and other large algae.

Pictilabrus laticlavius, Canal Rocks, WA

Suezichthys aylingi Russell, 1985
Crimson cleaner wrasse, crimson wrasse, butcher's dick

Habitat: Submaximally and maximally exposed reef; 20–100 m depth.
Distribution: Eastern Vic. to Seal Rocks, NSW, and eastern Tas. Also New Zealand.
Maximum size: Length to 120 mm.

The crimson cleaner wrasse is the most intensely coloured local wrasse species, particularly the terminal-phase male. The body is a scarlet colour with a white line along the side; purple lines are present along the base of the fins and on the head. This

Suezichthys aylingi, Bermagui, NSW. Rudie Kuiter

species is not often seen by divers but is common on deep reefs. It is sometimes observed picking parasites off other fishes.

FAMILY ODACIDAE
Rock whiting, weed whiting

Odacids are closely related to the family Labridae and are occasionally included in that family. They differ in internal bone structure, by having teeth that are partially fused into a beak, and by having four rays in the ventral fin, except in one species (*Siphonognathus argyrophanes*) where the ventral fins are absent. As in the Labridae the females are generally drab in appearance and transform into brightly coloured males if behavioural cues provided by the male are missing. The 12 species in the family are restricted to southern Australian and New Zealand waters. Although commonly called rock whiting, this name is misleading because all species are associated with seaweeds or seagrasses rather than bare rocky reefs.

Odax acroptilus (Richardson, 1846)
Rainbow fish

Habitat: Moderately exposed reef, seagrass; 2–20 m depth.
Distribution: Kalbarri, WA, to Newcastle, NSW, and south to Maria I, Tas.
Maximum size: Length to 290 mm.

The rainbow fish shows pronounced sexual differences in shape: males are brightly coloured with two long dorsal spines, while females have a dull appearance to blend in among seagrasses and macroalgae. Both sexes have teeth fused into a beak in a similar way to the parrot fishes. Rainbow fish are common in

Odax acroptilus (male), Deal I, Tas. SIMON TALBOT

1202 *Odax acroptilus* (female), Cape Portland, Tas.

seagrass beds and on reefs but generally remain hidden among plants, and are therefore difficult to observe.

Odax cyanomelas (Richardson, 1850)
Herring cale

Habitat: Exposed reef; 0–30 m depth.
Distribution: Kalbarri, WA, to Coffs Harbour, NSW, and south to Tasman Peninsula, Tas.
Maximum size: Length to 510 mm.

Herring cale are long, flexible fishes, which move with a sinuous motion through kelp beds. Juveniles and females are a mottled greenish-brown colour, while males are dark with bright blue stripes along the top and bottom of the tail. This species feeds on the large brown algae *Ecklonia radiata, Phyllospora comosa* and *Lessonia corrugata* and is very abundant in the surge zone among these plants.

Odax cyanomelas, Bermagui, NSW. RUDIE KUITER

Siphonognathus attenuatus (Ogilby, 1897)
Slender weed whiting

Habitat: Moderately exposed reef, sand; 5–25 m depth.
Distribution: Rottnest I, WA, to Wilsons Promontory, Vic., and south to Freycinet Peninsula, Tas.
Maximum size: Length to 140 mm.

The slender rock whiting is a long thin fish with relatively short snout, pale belly and prominent white-edged black spot on the tail. The preferred habitat of this species is along the boundary between reef and sand. It is not often seen, perhaps because it occurs in deeper water than most other odacids.

Siphonognathus attenuatus, Palana, Tas.

Siphonognathus beddomei (Johnston, 1885)
Pencil weed whiting, pencil rock whiting, pygmy rock whiting

Habitat: Exposed reef; 1–15 m depth.
Distribution: Dongara, WA, to Wilsons Promontory, Vic., and around Tas.
Maximum size: Length to 140 mm.

Siphonognathus beddomei, Trousers Pt, Tas.

The pencil rock whiting has an extended body like the slender rock whiting, but the snout is long and pointed. The sides of the body generally carry thin blue stripes, which are particularly conspicuous during the breeding season. Small aggregations of this species are very common above beds of *Phyllospora comosa* and other large brown algae on exposed reefs but are not often noticed by divers because of the animals' small size.

Neoodax balteatus (Valenciennes, 1840)

Little rock whiting, ground mullet, little weed whiting

Habitat: Sheltered and moderately exposed seagrass, reef; 0–20 m depth.
Distribution: Fremantle, WA, to Sydney, NSW, and around Tas.
Maximum size: Length to 140 mm.

The great majority of little rock whiting in any area are juveniles and females and have a dark stripe along the side, a brown upper body and pale belly. The few males differ by having deeper, reddish-brown bodies, blue trim to the fins and blue stripes along the head.

Neoodax balteatus (male), Cloudy Lagoon, Tas.

Neoodax balteatus, Maria I, Tas.

This is one of the most abundant fishes in seagrass beds along the southern coast. Females also occur among large algae at moderately exposed marine locations.

Haletta semifasciata (Valenciennes, 1840)

Blue rock whiting, grass whiting, blue weed whiting, stranger, blue-arsed whiting

Habitat: Sheltered and moderately exposed seagrass, reef; 0–15 m depth.
Distribution: Fremantle, WA, to Sydney, NSW, and around Tas.
Maximum size: Length to 410 mm.

The blue rock whiting has a similar general shape to the little rock whiting but can be recognised by the longer and more pointed snout, silver stripe along the side in juveniles, dark markings across the body in adults and distinctive blue patch around the anus. It grows to a much larger size than the little rock whiting and is occasionally sold in Victorian fish markets. The blue rock whiting is usually associated with seagrass beds and is one of the largest fish species found there. A major component of its diet is small gastropods.

Haletta semifasciata, Cloudy Lagoon, Tas.

FAMILY PINGUIPEDIDAE
Grubfishes, weevers

Grubfishes are elongate fishes with long dorsal and anal fins, and a body rounded in cross-section. They are generally easy to recognise underwater because of their distinctive habit of sitting on the seabed perched on the strong ventral fins. Most of the 50 or so species in the family live in the tropics, but two species occur on the southern coast in shallow water.

Parapercis haackei (Steindachner, 1884)
Wavy grubfish

Habitat: Sheltered and moderately exposed sand, rock; 1–35 m depth.
Distribution: Point Quobba, WA, to Gulf St Vincent, SA.
Maximum size: Length to 110 mm.

The body of the wavy grubfish is divided into a pale lower section and light brown upper section, with a dark wavy line extending along the upper body between. The species is very common among rubble near the sand edge of reefs and is highly inquisitive.

Parapercis haackei, Busselton, WA

Parapercis ramsayi Steindachner, 1884
Spotted grubfish

Habitat: Sheltered and moderately exposed sand, mud, rock; 5–80 m depth.
Distribution: Perth, WA, to Kangaroo I, SA, and Montague I to Byron Bay, NSW.
Maximum size: Length to 200 mm.

The spotted grubfish has a distinctive arrangement of dark blotches aligned along the side of the white body, and thin lines of spots along the upper body surface. It is found in a variety of habitats in estuaries and coastal bays, almost always close to a rock refuge. The species is less common than the wavy grubfish in shallow water and more inclined to retreat into a refuge if approached. It is most abundant below 40 m depth.

Parapercis ramsayi, Jervis Bay, NSW

FAMILY BOVICHTIDAE
Thornfishes

Bovichtids are elongate fishes with flattened heads and large eyes set close together near the top of the body. They have two dorsal fins, the first of which is short and spiny, and strong ventral fins under the head used for perching. The family is closely related to the Antarctic ice fishes and has a similar southern distribution. The seven recognised species all occur on coasts adjoining the Southern Ocean.

Bovichtus angustifrons (Regan, 1913)
Dragonet, thornfish, marblefish

Habitat: Exposed reef; 0–20 m depth.
Distribution: Ceduna, SA, to Eden, NSW, and around Tas.
Maximum size: Length to 280 mm.

Dragonets are small fishes that can usually be recognised by the large spine projecting back from the rear of the head. Juvenile dragonet have a drab grey-brown appearance, making them difficult to see in rockpools and on the shallow reefs where they live. Adults generally live in caves in deeper water and often have a bright red background coloration, which blends in with nearby coralline algal-encrusted rock. With Macleay's threefin, this is the most abundant small fish living on exposed Victorian and Tasmanian

Bovichtus angustifrons (juvenile), Cloudy Lagoon, Tas.

Bovichtus angustifrons (adult), Bicheno, Tas.

reefs. It also occurs in sheltered habitats on jetty pylons and on shallow reefs. Until recently this species was called *Bovichtus variegatus*, a name now restricted to a related New Zealand species.

Pseudophritis urvillii (Valenciennes, 1831)

Congolli, freshwater flathead, sandy, tupong

Habitat: Sheltered sand, seagrass, freshwater; 0–4 m depth.
Distribution: Streaky Bay, SA, to Bega, NSW, and around Tas.
Maximum size: Length to 360 mm.

The congolli is a mottled fish with a flathead-like shape. It lives mainly in the lower reaches of streams but is also common in estuaries and is occasionally seen in fully marine embayments and far upstream. Mature animals migrate down rivers to spawn in estuaries.

Pseudophritis urvillii, Douglas River, Tas.

FAMILY BLENNIDAE
Blennies

This is a large family comprising more than 300 small fishes, most of which are restricted to the tropics. They are characterised by long dorsal and anal fins, teeth in a characteristic comb-like row near the edge of the jaw, and a coating of mucous rather than scales on the body surface.

Parablennius tasmanianus (Richardson, 1849)

Tasmanian blenny

Habitat: Sheltered reef; 0–10 m depth.
Distribution: Ceduna, SA, to Eden, NSW, and around Tas.
Maximum size: Length to 130 mm.

The Tasmanian blenny can be recognised by its small size, long fringed tentacles over the eye and a fine stippling of dots across the body. Related species with larger black dots on the head occur north and west of the distribution of this species but have not yet been

Parablennius tasmanianus (female), Portsea, Vic.

Parablennius tasmanianus (male), Dunalley, Tas.

scientifically named. The Tasmanian blenny is very common in sheltered habitats along the southeastern coast, where it makes a home in small rock crevices, shells or discarded bottles and cans. During the spawning season females guard clusters of eggs, which are attached to the sides of their nests.

Petroscirtes lupus (De Vis, 1886)
Brown sabretooth blenny

Habitat: Sheltered reef, seagrass; 0–10 m depth.
Distribution: Merimbula, NSW, to southern Qld. Also New Caledonia.
Maximum size: Length to 130 mm.

The brown sabretooth blenny has a mottled brown body with six to eight dark saddles in the upper region and a dorsal fin with a first spine that projects slightly above the rest. This fish occupies much the same habitat among boulders and debris in estuaries as is used by the Tasmanian blenny further south. Its diet is somewhat unusual, as large quantities of plant material are included.

Petroscirtes lupus, North Head, NSW

Plagiotremus rhinorhynchos (Bleeker, 1852)
Blue-lined sabretooth blenny

Habitat: Sheltered reef; 2–20 m depth.
Distribution: Tropical Australia south to Walpole, WA, and Merimbula, NSW. Also widespread in the Indo-West Pacific region.
Maximum size: Length to 120 mm.

The blue-lined sabretooth blenny has a flexible, elongate body with two thin blue stripes commencing either side of the eye and passing along the sides. It can be confused with the blue-lined hula fish in Western Australia and sometimes occurs in schools of that species, but the tail is normal rather than elongated at the centre. This is the most common of several colourful sabretooth blennies that live primarily in the tropics but are occasionally carried south by currents. They mimic cleaner wrasse by approaching large fish (and divers) as if to remove parasites. When close enough, they dart forward and remove a piece of flesh using two sharp fangs.

Plagiotremus rhinorhynchos, Seven Mile Beach, WA

FAMILY TRIPTERYGIIDAE
Threefins

The tripterygids are a large family of about 130 species, which resemble the blennies but have three dorsal fins and relatively large scales. All southern Australian species are small and live concealed on reefs.

Helcogramma decurrens

McCulloch & Waite, 1918
Black-throated threefin, yellowback threefin

Habitat: Sheltered and moderately exposed reef; 0–15 m depth.
Distribution: Point Quobba, WA, to Victor Harbor, SA.
Maximum size: Length to 70 mm.

This species receives its common names from the characteristic yellow upper and black lower coloration of the male. The female is drab by comparison, possessing a lighter-coloured body spotted with red, brown or mustard-coloured flecks. This is one of the most abundant fish species present on reefs in South Australia and southern Western Australia but is not often noticed by divers because of its small size.

Helcogramma decurrens, Horseshoe Reef, WA

Norfolkia clarkei (Moreton, 1888)

Common threefin, Macleay's threefin

Habitat: Reef; 0–30 m depth.
Distribution: Rottnest I, WA, to Coffs Harbour, NSW, and around Tas.
Maximum size: Length to 80 mm.

The common threefin has a pink or brown body with a prominent stripe below the eye. It is perhaps the most abundant fish on coastal reefs but is difficult to observe because it generally remains in caves or under ledges. The species also occurs in estuaries, where it is often found around jetty pylons. Two almost identical species with similar coloration and a stripe below the eye have also been recorded from the south coast. ***Norfolkia incisa***, a very small species (<30 mm) found between Esperance and Wilsons Promontory, has a first dorsal fin with the webbing between the spines deeply indented. The rare South Australian species ***Norfolkia cristata*** has a first dorsal fin higher than the second, whereas it is lower in *Norfolkia clarkei*.

Norfolkia clarkei, Maria I, Tas.

Forsterygion varium

(Forster in Bloch & Schneider, 1801)
Many-rayed threefin

Habitat: Sheltered reef; 0–10 m depth.
Distribution: Eastern Tas. Also New Zealand.
Maximum size: Length to 150 mm.

Many-rayed threefin are relatively large threefins with mottled brown, green and pink bodies and a first dorsal fin with six to seven spines in contrast to the three of most other local species in the family. Males are brighter than females and have bluish tips to the fins. This species is very abundant on shallow reefs in the Derwent Estuary and D'Entrecasteaux Channel

Forsterygion varium, Tinderbox, Tas.

but has not been recorded outside eastern Tasmania. A closely related but uncommon species, ***Forsterygion gymnotum***, is also found on the same reefs in the Derwent Estuary. That species differs from the many-rayed threefin by having a more bulbous head and the first spine in the first dorsal fin longer than the next few spines, rather than shorter.

Lepidoblennius marmoratus (Macleay, 1878)
Jumping blenny

Habitat: Sheltered and moderately exposed reef; 0–5 m depth.
Distribution: Cape Naturaliste, WA, to Cape Jervis, SA.
Maximum size: Length to 130 mm.

The jumping blenny has a blunt head, pale belly and irregular dark markings along the upper body. The first dorsal fin is considerably longer in males than in females. The species is common near low-tide level on sheltered reefs and is also occasionally observed sitting on dry rocks. An almost identical species with greater number of scales along the lateral line (44–60 cf. 33–40), ***Lepidoblennius haplodactylus***, occurs commonly in a similar habitat in New South Wales.

Lepidoblennius marmoratus, Albany, WA

FAMILY CLINIDAE
Weedfishes

Clinids, or weedfishes, are a group of small fishes with modified finger-like ventral fins positioned below the back of the head. Most have the first few spines of the dorsal fin connected by an indented membrane to the rayed section. There is, however, one aberrant group of elongate species, the snakeblennies, that do not have this feature. Clinids are generally associated with seaweeds or seagrasses and are very common in southern Australia. More than one-third of the 100 or so clinids known worldwide are restricted to this region, most of them yet to be scientifically named. Species in the family are somewhat unusual among bony fishes by giving birth to live young rather than releasing eggs.

Cristiceps australis Valenciennes, 1836
Southern crested weedfish

Habitat: Sheltered and moderately exposed seagrass, seaweed; 0–10 m depth.
Distribution: Geraldton, WA, to southern Qld and around Tas.
Maximum size: Length to 230 mm.

The southern crested weedfish is one of three species of *Cristiceps*, a genus characterised by an elongate, three-spined first dorsal fin, which commences near the eyes. This fin on *Cristiceps australis* commences level with the centre of the eye and is not directly connected to the base of the second dorsal fin. The species is abundant in seagrass and algal beds with slight wave action but is not common in the most sheltered estuarine seagrass beds.

Cristiceps australis, Portsea, Vic. RUDIE KUITER

Heteroclinus perspicillatus

(Valenciennes, 1836)
Common weedfish

Habitat: Sheltered reef, seagrass; 0–10 m depth.
Distribution: Port Lincoln, SA, to Merimbula, NSW, and around Tas.
Maximum size: Length to 200 mm.

The common weedfish is one of about 20 small species of clinid known from southern Australia and is distinguished from others by having three spines and 31–34 rays regularly arranged along the dorsal fin and by the shape of the tentacles and arrangement of pores on the top of the head. The species can also usually be recognised by pattern, as it typically has a rounded blotch on each side near the start of the dorsal fin, and the body immediately in front of the tail is equally divided into dark upper and white lower sections. As the name suggests, the common weedfish is the most abundant clinid in southern Australia and is common in a large range of habitats.

Heteroclinus perspicillatus, Cloudy Lagoon, Tas.

Heteroclinus nasutus (Günther, 1861)

Largenose weedfish

Habitat: Sheltered and moderately exposed reef; 0–8 m depth.
Distribution: Port Phillip Bay, Vic., to Minnie Water, NSW.
Maximum size: Length to 90 mm.

The largenose weedfish is a small species with a similar shape to the common weedfish but with a thin, elongate tentacle above each eye and a branched tentacle near the end of the snout. Although the colour is quite variable, the body is usually flecked with white spots and the dorsal and anal fins tipped with white. This species occurs commonly along the New South Wales coast among shallow algae on sheltered reefs.

Heteroclinus tristis (Klunzinger, 1872)

Forster's weedfish, longnose weedfish

Habitat: Moderately exposed reef; 0–10 m depth.
Distribution: Recherche Archipelago, WA, to Sydney, NSW, and around Tas.
Maximum size: Length to 300 mm.

Forster's weedfish is one of the more easily recognised species of weedfish, as it is a large species with a flattened body, pointed snout, long unbranched pair of tentacles on top of the eye and psychedelic pattern of swirls on the side. The species was known as *Heteroclinus forsteri* until recently. It is very common

Heteroclinus nasutus, North Head, NSW

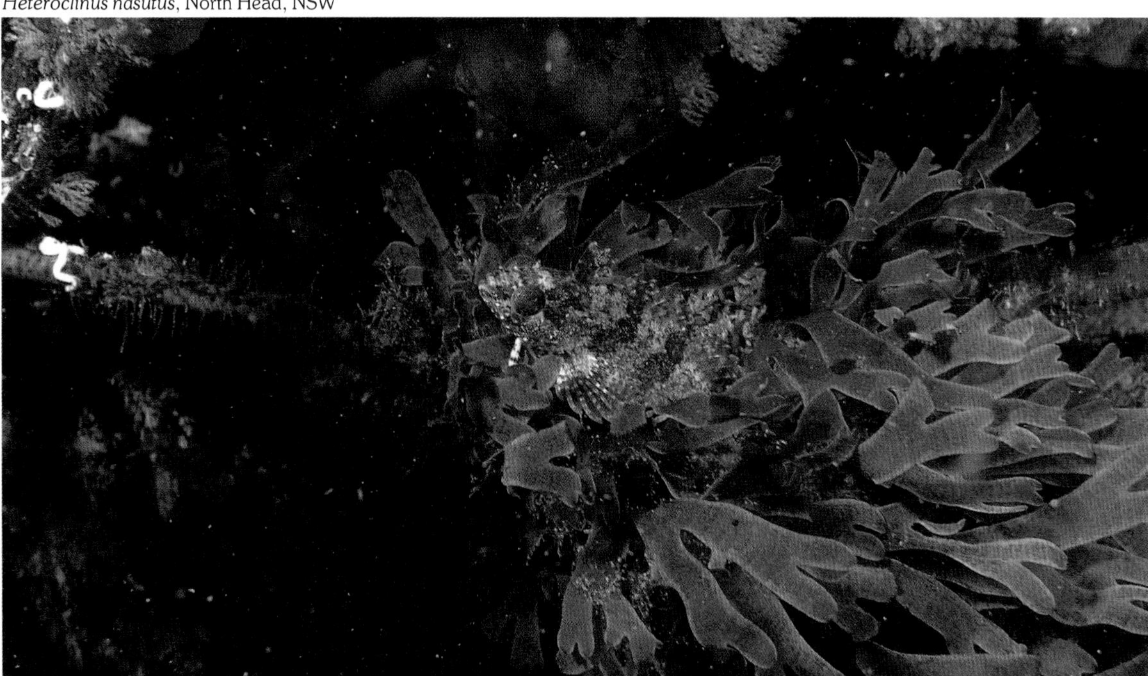

Heteroclinus tristis, Flinders, Vic. RUDIE KUITER

among large seaweeds on moderately exposed southeastern reefs but because of the good camouflage is only occasionally seen by divers.

Heteroclinus johnstoni (Saville-Kent, 1886)
Johnston's weedfish

Habitat: Exposed reef; 0–50 m depth.
Distribution: Kangaroo I, SA, to Port Phillip Bay, Vic., and around Tas.
Maximum size: Length to 400 mm.

Johnston's weedfish can be identified by its large size, prominent branched tentacles projecting forward from the front of the head, and seven large, rounded eyespots on the side of the body below the dorsal fin. The species is most abundant in Tasmania, where it is commonly seen lying on reef below a covering of kelp. It occurs in habitats with greater wave turbulence than other weedfish.

Ophiclinus gracilis Waite, 1906
Blackback snakeblenny

Habitat: Sheltered reef; 0–10 m depth.
Distribution: Rottnest I, WA, to Sydney, NSW, and around Tas.
Maximum size: Length to 110 mm.

Heteroclinus johnstoni, Stinking Bay, Tas. SIMON TALBOT

Ophiclinus gracilis, Ricketts Pt, Vic.

The blackback snakeblenny is a small sinuous species with a dark upper body and prominent white blotches towards the tail. It is common under rocks in sheltered habitats, particularly at sites with large accumulations of macroalgal debris.

Ophiclinus gabrieli Waite, 1906
Gabriel's snakeblenny, frosted snakeblenny

Habitat: Sheltered reef; 0–10 m depth.
Distribution: Kangaroo I, SA, to Wilsons Promontory, Vic., and northern Tas.
Maximum size: Length to 180 mm.

Gabriel's snakeblenny has a lower dorsal fin with more rays (52–55 cf. 44–49) than the blackback snakeblenny and a different colour pattern. The sides are dark brown with flecks of silver concentrated towards the rear and in a line midway across the body. The species occurs under rocks and in seagrass beds but is not often seen.

Ophiclinus gabrieli, Flinders, Vic. RUDIE KUITER

FAMILY CALLIONYMIDAE
Stinkfish, dragonets

Callionymids are an easily recognised group of fishes with eyes close together on top of the head, a small downward-projecting mouth, a large tailfin, large fan-shaped ventral fins, and a gill opening reduced in size to a small pore. They also lack scales and have a slimy skin with a foul taste, thus providing the family with the name stinkfish. Males are generally much more colourful than females and can possess very long fins or rays. About 130 species are known worldwide, most of them occurring in the tropics.

Pseudocalliurichthys goodladi (Whitley, 1944)
Goodlad's stinkfish, longspine stinkfish

Habitat: Sheltered and moderately exposed sand, silt; 3–20 m depth.
Distribution: Exmouth Gulf to Esperance, WA.
Maximum size: Length to 220 mm.

Goodlad's stinkfish has a speckled upper surface and pale belly and a flattened body shape somewhat similar to flatheads. The two sexes differ substantially in form, with males having the first two spines of the dorsal fin greatly extended. This species is abundant in Cockburn Sound and the lower reaches of the Swan River but is rarely seen by divers outside this area.

Pseudocalliurichthys goodladi, Bicton, WA

Eocallionymus papilio (Günther, 1864)
Painted stinkfish

Habitat: Sheltered and moderately exposed reef, sand; 1–50 m depth.
Distribution: Kalbarri, WA, to Port Stephens, NSW, and around Tas.
Maximum size: Length to 130 mm.

The painted stinkfish can usually be recognised by the presence of cream blotches with fine blue margins on the back and streaks down the side of the body. The species is small and inconspicuous and usually remains immobile on the seabed unless disturbed. It occurs moderately commonly, most often on broken bottom close to the edge of reefs. The form found in estuaries, which may perhaps prove to be a different species, is larger and more elongate than the form found on coastal reefs.

Eocallionymus papilio (female), Bicheno, Tas.

Foetorepus calauropomus, Port Phillip Bay, Vic. RUDIE KUITER

Eocallionymus papilio (males), Portsea, Vic.

Foetorepus calauropomus (Richardson, 1844)
Common stinkfish

Habitat: Sand, silt; 1–100 m depth.
Distribution: Perth, WA, to southern Qld and around Tas.
Maximum size: Length to 350 mm.

The common stinkfish is the largest stinkfish found in southern Australia and has an extremely long tailfin. Males are very colourful with a pink tinge to the body, blue markings on the fins and side of the head, and yellow lips. Females have a drab body except for blue wavy lines on the head and fine blue spots on the fins. The species is common in deep bays and is often taken by trawlers, but rarely enters shallow water and so is not often seen by divers.

Repomucenus calcaratus (Macleay, 1881)
Spotted dragonet

Habitat: Sand; 5–100 m depth.
Distribution: WA to Kangaroo I and southern NSW to Qld.
Maximum size: Length to 280 mm.

Less colourful than most other dragonets, the spotted dragonet has a flecked, sand-coloured upper surface and pale belly. The most distinctive feature is a black patch on the first dorsal fin. The species is moderately common in coastal bays near reef margins in New South Wales but seems to be restricted to water depths over 20 m elsewhere. There is some doubt about the distribution of this species; animals found in south-western Australia may comprise a different species.

Repomucenus calcaratus, Terrigal, NSW

FAMILY GOBIIDAE
Gobies

The gobies are small, bottom-dwelling fishes, which can usually be recognised by having the ventral fins fused together into a distinctive cup-shaped disc. However, a few species, particularly among the pelagic and hovering forms, have the ventral fins separate. This is the largest family of marine fishes, with more than 1500 species known.

Arenigobius bifrenatus (Kner, 1865)
Bridled goby

Habitat: Sheltered sand, mud; 0–2 m depth.
Distribution: Fremantle, WA, to Moreton Bay, Qld, and around Tas.
Maximum size: Length to 150 mm.

The bridled goby is one of the larger and more colourful gobies found along the southern coast. It can be recognised by the short, rounded head, light grey body and two black stripes that commence at the eye, extend backward across the head and break into spots along the sides. A closely related species with an identical shape, the half-bridled goby ***Arenigobius frenatus***, has a darker body with indistinct bars across the sides and large black spots on the top of the head. *Arenigobius frenatus* is found from Western Port to Queensland. Both species occur abundantly just below low-tide level on mudflats near seagrass beds. They feed partly on plant material.

Arenigobius bifrenatus, Bermagui, NSW. RUDIE KUITER

Bathygobius kreffti (Steindachner, 1866)
Frayed-fin goby, Krefft's goby

Habitat: Sheltered mud, sand; 0–6 m depth.
Distribution: Spencer Gulf, SA, and southern NSW to southern Qld.
Maximum size: Length to 90 mm.

The frayed-fin goby is distinguished from other local gobies by its rounded head and dark black patches across the sides and back of the body. The species is abundant near the mouths of estuaries along the New South Wales coast and is often associated with seagrass beds. The South Australia population appears to be isolated from the eastern population.

Bathygobius kreffti, Merimbula, NSW

Favonigobius lateralis (Macleay, 1881)
Long-finned goby

Habitat: Sheltered sand, mud; 0–7 m depth.
Distribution: Shark Bay, WA, to central Qld and around Tas.
Maximum size: Length to 80 mm.

The long-finned goby is most easily recognised by the numerous thin white stripes running vertically across the lower half of the body behind the pectoral fins. Other features are a relatively flattened head, a long anal fin with the tip nearly reaching the tail fin, and black blotches on the side of the body. The species is very abundant in a range of sheltered habitats and is the goby most commonly noticed by divers in estuaries.

Favonigobius lateralis, Spencer Gulf, SA

Nesogobius hindsbyi (McCulloch & Ogilby, 1919)
Orange-spotted goby

Habitat: Sheltered silt; 0–60 m depth.
Distribution: Port Phillip Bay, Vic., and eastern, southern and western Tas.
Maximum size: Length to 75 mm.

Nearly all species in the genus *Nesogobius* have been discovered only in recent years, and the ten known species are restricted to temperate Australian waters. The orange-spotted goby is one of only two *Nesogobius* species that have been given scientific names so far. This goby can be recognised by the translucent body and numerous rust-coloured flecks on the back. It is abundant in southern Tasmanian estuaries but rare elsewhere.

Nesogobius hindsbyi, Bathurst Channel, Tas.

Nesogobius pulchellus (Castelnau, 1872)
Castelnau's goby

Habitat: Sheltered and moderately exposed sand, seagrass, reef; 0–10 m depth.
Distribution: Fremantle, WA, to Sydney, NSW, and around Tas.
Maximum size: Length to 60 mm.

Castelnau's goby is one of the more easily recognised *Nesogobius* species because of its relatively dark coloration, particularly near the tail, and the red spots forming stripes on the dorsal fin. The first dorsal fin in the male is elevated and used as a flag to signal other animals. This species is common on sand near the edge of reefs and seagrass beds.

Nesogobius pulchellus, Tinderbox, Tas.

Nesogobius sp. 1
Girdled goby

Habitat: Sand; 0–5 m depth.
Distribution: Eastern SA to eastern Vic. and around Tas.
Maximum size: Length to 90 mm.

Nesogobius sp. 1, Cloudy Lagoon, Tas.

The girdled goby and the orange-spotted goby are the only two *Nesogobius* species that have scales on the top of the head behind the eye, with the girdled goby also possessing dark rectangular markings on the side of the body below the midline. This is the most abundant goby in Tasmanian and Victorian waters and is present in huge numbers off almost all but the most exposed sandy beaches. The species is often noticed darting away on shallow sandflats and is frequently mistaken for juvenile flathead.

Nesogobius sp. 2

Groove-cheek goby

Habitat: Exposed sand; 8–30 m depth.
Distribution: Rottnest I, WA, to Sydney, NSW.
Maximum size: Length to 85 mm.

The groove-cheek goby differs from other species of *Nesogobius* by having a groove on the side of the opercle. It can also generally be recognised by the narrow translucent body with ginger flecks on the upper body and broken light-blue stripe on the side. This species occurs in more exposed habitats than other local gobies and is most often seen in deep coastal bays.

Nesogobius sp. 2, Bass Point, NSW.

Tasmanogobius gloveri Hoese, 1991

Marine goby

Habitat: Sheltered sand, silt; 0–8 m depth.
Distribution: Kangaroo I, SA, to Western Port, Vic., and around Tas.
Maximum size: Length to 65 mm.

The genus *Tasmanogobius* contains three southeastern Australian species that lack scales on the head. The marine goby has bulbous eyes and a cream body, with a characteristic stripe and five or six squarish blotches along the sides. This fish is locally common in estuaries, where it sits near the entrance of burrows.

Tasmanogobius gloveri, Margate, Tas.

FAMILY URANOSCOPIDAE
Stargazers

Stargazers are large bottom-dwelling fishes with a bulldog appearance. They have eyes and mouth on top of a rounded, bony head, a large spine projecting rearward from just above the base of each pectoral fin, and fleshy skin. Most of the 30 or so species are restricted to deep water. They usually bury themselves in sand, waiting for relatively large-sized prey, which are sucked in by the protrusible mouth.

Kathetostoma laeve (Bloch & Schneider, 1801)

Common stargazer

Habitat: Sheltered and moderately exposed sand, silt; 0–60 m depth.
Distribution: Esperance, WA, to northern NSW and around Tas.
Maximum size: Length to 750 mm.

Kathetostoma laeve, Port Phillip Bay, Vic. RUDIE KUITER

The common stargazer has a distinctive greyish body with pale underside and two dark vertical bands across the body that fade with age. It is the only stargazer regularly seen by divers in southeastern Australia but is uncommon. As the appearance suggests, this species is quite pugnacious and has been known to attack divers.

FAMILY LEPTOSCOPIDAE
Sandfishes, sand stargazers

The family Leptoscopidae comprises only about seven species, restricted to Australia and New Zealand. They are closely related to the stargazers but are generally more elongate, lack the strong spine projecting from the back of the head and have widely separated ventral fins. Australian sandfishes live half-buried in sand off beaches.

Crapatalus munroi Last & Edgar, 1987
Munro's pygmy-stargazer

Habitat: Moderately exposed sand; 1–18 m depth.
Distribution: Vic. and around Tas.
Maximum size: Length to 120 mm.

Munro's pygmy-stargazer has a sand-coloured pattern on the upper body, matching the shape and colour of surrounding sediment. The species differs from another common leptoscopid, ***Lesueurina platycephala***, by having a deeper body and scales on the base of the pectoral fin. These two species also differ slightly in habitat as *L. platycephala* occurs in the area of breaking waves off moderately exposed beaches, whereas *C. munroi* occurs in slightly deeper water.

Crapatalus munroi, Popes Eye, Vic. RUDIE KUITER

FAMILY GEMPYLIDAE
Gemfishes

Gemfishes are nearly all large, elongate fishes with fang-like front teeth, a deeply forked tail, rows of small finlets behind the dorsal and anal fins, and very small scales or none at all. Most of the estimated 20 species are active carnivores, preying on fish in offshore waters.

Thyrsites atun (Euphrasen 1791)
Barracouta, snoek, couta

Habitat: Open sea, coastal bays; 0–200 m depth.
Distribution: Shark Bay, WA, to Moreton Bay, Qld, and around Tas. Also occurs widely around the Southern Hemisphere in temperate latitudes.
Maximum size: Length to 1.4 m.

The barracouta is an elongate, silver-coloured fish that occurs in schools and has a superficial resemblance to the baracudas (a tropical group, family Sphyraenidae, which is not closely related). Adult barracouta are commonly taken on trolled lures near the Victorian and Tasmanian coasts, while small schools of juveniles sometimes enter sheltered bays. The species was once a mainstay of the fish and chip trade, but stocks crashed in the mid-1970s and are yet to recover. Fillets of this fish are often infested with a parasitic tapeworm, which, although harmless to humans, turns the flesh soft and milky.

Thyrsites atun, Margate, Tas.

FAMILY CENTROLOPHIDAE
Trevallas

The trevallas are a group of variably shaped fishes that can usually be recognised by a rounded scaleless head with numerous pores, indistinct ridges radiating from the eyes, and a single row of very fine teeth in each jaw. Adults of most species live in deep water, whereas juveniles are usually found under drifting objects such as logs and jellyfish, near the surface of the open ocean. Species in the family are highly regarded as food fish.

Seriolella brama (Günther, 1860)
Warehou, snotgall trevalla, snotty-nose trevalla, blue warehou, Portland hake

Seriolella brama, Port Phillip Bay, Vic. Rudie Kuiter

Habitat: Open water; 0–120 m depth.
Distribution: SA to NSW and around Tas. Also New Zealand.
Maximum size: Length to 90 mm.

The warehou is a rounded, silver-grey fish with a large black patch above the pectoral fin base. Schools of this trevalla occur moderately commonly around the Tasmanian coast but are not often seen along the mainland coast. Another member of the family, the spotted trevalla ***Seriolella maculata***, also occurs in shallow southern waters as an adult. That species has a more slender body, a series of dark spots along the middle of the sides and dusky markings behind the eye.

FAMILY SCOMBRIDAE
Mackerels and tunas

Scombrids (mackerels and tunas) are powerful, streamlined fishes with two dorsal fins that depress into grooves, a row of short finlets behind the second dorsal and anal fins, and keels on either side of the body in front of the tail. Most species occur in schools in the open sea, where they are voracious predators of smaller fishes, squids and crustaceans. The family is extremely important commercially, with more than 5 million tonnes caught annually worldwide.

Scomber australasicus Cuvier, 1832
Blue mackerel, slimy mackerel

Habitat: Open water; 0–200 m depth.
Distribution: Around the Australian mainland and Tas. Also widespread in southwest Pacific waters.
Maximum size: Length to 500 mm.

Scomber australasicus, Bermagui, NSW. Rudie Kuiter

Blue mackerel can be recognised by their streamlined bodies with wavy bars along the back, spots in the lower region of the sides, and five to six finlets in front of the tail. Adults occur in large schools off the southern Australian coastline, but the smallest animals may be found inshore. The species has an oily flesh and is generally used as bait or for canning rather than eaten fresh.

Sarda australis (Macleay, 1881)

Australian bonito

Habitat: Open water; 0–100 m depth.
Distribution: Eastern Vic. to southern Qld and eastern Tas.
Maximum size: Length to 1 m.

Sarda australis, Seal Rocks, NSW. Rudie Kuiter

The Australian bonito has a striped body and a very similar appearance to the widespread tropical bonito ***Sarda orientalis*** and occurs mixed with that species on the east coast. It differs by having stripes (sometimes indistinct) on the lower half of the body and 18–22 gill rakers on the first gill arch (cf. 8–13 in *S. australis*). The Australian bonito is occasionally caught by lure cast from rocks along the New South Wales coast. The meat is not highly regarded.

Thunnus maccoyi Castelnau, 1872

Southern bluefin tuna

Habitat: Open ocean.
Distribution: WA to southern Qld and around Tas. Also widespread in the Southern Hemisphere.
Maximum size: Length to 1.87 m.

Thunnus maccoyi. Ken Hoppen

The southern bluefin tuna is an open water species that occurs in large schools in subtropical and temperate waters. Two other tunas also regularly occur in the region, the albacore ***Thunnus alalunga***, a species with very long pectoral fins extending back behind the second dorsal fin, and the yellowfin tuna ***Thunnus albacares***, a species with yellow dorsal and anal fins. The southern bluefin tuna spawns in the Indian Ocean off northwestern Australia, with juvenile fish migrating down the western and then along the southern coasts, gaining in size as they travel. Heavy fishing along this migratory route during the past two decades is thought to have greatly reduced stocks.

FAMILY SIGANIDAE
Rabbitfishes, spinefeet

Siganids are rounded fishes with a small mouth and numerous spines in the dorsal and anal fins. The ventral fins are unusual because a spine is present at each end and three rays are located between. The spines in the fins are venomous, providing several species with the ironic name of 'happy moments'. The pain from a sting of these fishes can be reduced by placing the affected limb in hot water. Nearly all of the 30 species in the family are restricted to the tropical Indo-Pacific region.

Siganus nebulosus (Quoy & Gaimard, 1824)
Black spinefoot, black rabbitfish, happy moments

Habitat: Sheltered and moderately exposed reef, seagrass; 0–15 m depth.
Distribution: Shark Bay to Fremantle, WA, and Eden, NSW, to Yeppon, Qld.
Maximum size: Length to 410 mm.

The black spinefoot has a variable pattern of spots and blotches across the sides and a large black blotch usually present behind the top of the gill cover. This is the only species in the family regularly found in warm temperate Australian waters and is moderately common in areas of broken rock and weed bottom. It was confused with similar tropical species until recently.

FAMILY BOTHIDAE
Left-eyed flounders

This family contains well over 100 species of fishes that have eyes on the left side of the head and a typical flounder shape. The larvae, like those of other flatfishes, swim normally and have an eye on each side of the body, but at about the time a larva settles onto the bottom, one eye gradually shifts around or through the head and the two eyes become positioned together. Included in the family are many of the larger flatfish species, all of which are good eating.

Pseudorhombus jenynsii (Bleeker, 1855)
Small-toothed flounder

Habitat: Sheltered and moderately exposed silt, sand; 0–50 m depth.
Distribution: Fremantle, WA, to southern Qld.
Maximum size: Length to 350 mm.

Small-toothed flounder can be recognised by the gold-speckled dark blotches on the upper body, the relatively large size, and the large eyes protruding above the surface of the head. This flounder is present in muddy estuaries around most of the southern coast and is also caught on offshore trawling grounds. It possibly does not occur in the Bass Strait region.

Siganus nebulosus, Seven Mile Beach, WA.

Pseudorhombus jenynsii, Albany, WA

FAMILY PLEURONECTIDAE
Right-eyed flounders

Pleuronectids are similar to the family Bothidae, except that the eyes are located on the right side of the body. The left side of the body lacks pigment and remains permanently underneath. More than 100 species are known, nearly half of them living around Japan. Eight species are known from temperate Australian waters.

Ammotretis rostratus (Günther, 1862)
Long-snouted flounder, sole

Habitat: Sheltered and moderately exposed sand, silt; 0–80 m depth.
Distribution: Augusta, WA, to NSW and around Tas.
Maximum size: Length to 340 mm.

The long-snouted flounder has a rounded body with finely spotted upper surface that varies in colour from brown to grey. The snout is short and hook-like. The species is common in sheltered Victorian and Tasmanian bays and estuaries, where the smallest juveniles live near the water's edge and move in and out with the tide.

Ammotretis lituratus (Richardson, 1843)
Spotted flounder, sole

Habitat: Moderately exposed sand; 0–80 m depth.
Distribution: Spencer Gulf, SA, to eastern Vic. and around Tas.
Maximum size: Length to 320 mm.

Ammotretis rostratus, Sandy Bay, Tas.

The spotted flounder can be distinguished from the long-snouted flounder, a species with similar shape, by the presence of a small rounded lump near the end of the left (underside) pectoral fin, and by distinctive orange spots that are normally present on the upper surface. It also prefers a slightly different habitat, living on clean sand in moderately exposed conditions. The species occurs at shallower depths in Tasmania than on the mainland but is uncommon.

Ammotretis elongatus (McCulloch, 1914)
Elongate flounder

Habitat: Sheltered and moderately exposed sand; 0–20 m depth.
Distribution: Geraldton, WA, to eastern Vic. and Goose I, Tas.
Maximum size: Length to 220 mm.

The elongate flounder is narrower than related species and has a pale upper surface with gold and bluish-black speckles that closely resemble the texture of

Ammotretis lituratus, Cloudy Lagoon, Tas.

Ammotretis elongatus, Woodmans Point, WA

shelly sediments nearby. The species is moderately common in shallow, sheltered bays in southwestern Australia.

Rhombosolea tapirina (Günther, 1862)
Greenback flounder

Habitat: Sheltered sand; 0–100 m depth.
Distribution: Southern WA to southern NSW and around Tas. Also New Zealand.
Maximum size: Length to 450 mm.

The greenback flounder can be identified by the blotchy green-brown pattern, pointed head and hooked snout. It is the only flatfish in southern Australia that is large and abundant enough to be commercially exploited. The largest animals are generally found on sand in the deeper channels of estuaries, but they are also plentiful on sandflats, mudflats and the lower reaches of rivers. Juveniles live on sandflats in water less than a metre deep. Although often seen to remain stationary for long periods, greenback flounder tend to capture polychaetes and other prey by digging rather than waiting as an ambush predator.

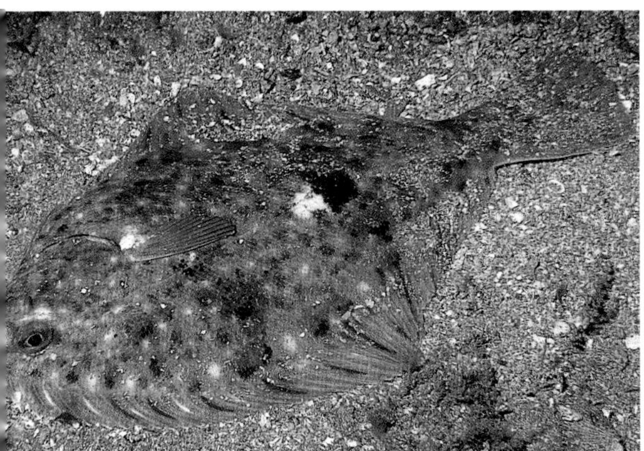
Rhombosolea tapirina, D'Entrecasteaux Channel, Tas.

FAMILY SOLEIDAE
True soles

The soles are oval-shaped fishes with eyes on the right side of the head and long dorsal and anal fins that often connect with the tail; pectoral fins are either greatly reduced in size or absent entirely. They also usually have a small mouth and a dense scattering of fine papillae on the underside of the head. Eight of the 120 or so species in the family are known from southern Australian waters.

Synaptura nigra Macleay, 1880
Black sole

Habitat: Sheltered silt; 0–20 m depth.
Distribution: Port Phillip Bay, Vic., to southern Qld.
Maximum size: Length to 350 mm.

The black sole has a light grey or black upper surface and a distinctive oval shape because the tail is connected to the dorsal and anal fins. The body surface is coated with mucus and therefore feels slimy. This species is moderately common in estuaries and coastal bays. It is the only local species of sole to reach edible size and is considered good eating.

Synaptura nigra, Merimbula, NSW

Aseraggodes haackeanus (Steindachner, 1883)
Southern sole

Habitat: Sheltered silt; 1–30 m depth.
Distribution: Perth, WA, to Gulf St Vincent, SA.
Maximum size: Length to 350 mm.

The southern sole has a general appearance similar to the elongate flounder but is easily distinguished by the row of small cirri around the margin of the head. The

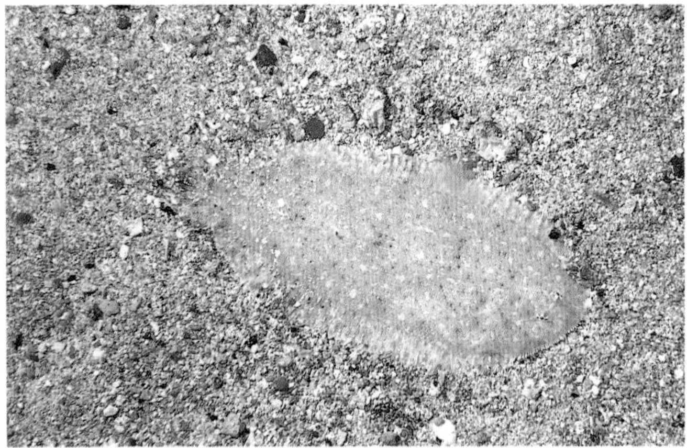
Aseraggodes haackeanus, Edithburgh, SA

species is common in the South Australian gulfs but is not often seen elsewhere.

Aseraggodes sp.
Peppered sole

Habitat: Sheltered silt; 1–30 m depth.
Distribution: NSW.
Maximum size: Length to 350 mm.

The peppered sole was until recently considered identical to the southern sole but differs in colour pattern and generally has fewer scales on the lateral line and more rays in the dorsal fin. The species is moderately common on coarse sand in the deeper New South Wales estuaries and also occurs in coastal bays.

Aseraggodes sp., Port Stephens, NSW

Paraplagusia unicolor, Terrigal, NSW

FAMILY CYNOGLOSSIDAE
Tongue soles

Tongue soles have eyes on the left of the head, like the family Bothidae, but differ by lacking pectoral fins and by having a leaf-like shape, and the dorsal and anal fins are connected into the tail.

Cynoglossus broadhursti Waite, 1905
Southern tongue sole

Habitat: Sheltered sand; 0–45 m depth.
Distribution: Carnarvon, WA, to Gulf St Vincent, SA.
Maximum size: Length to 300 mm.

Cynoglossus broadhursti, Bicton, WA

The southern tongue sole has a small head and elongate body that tapers to a point. The upper surface is uniformly light brown and lower surface white. Divers occasionally see this species sliding over sandy sediments at night, leaving an obvious trail across the sand in its wake.

Paraplagusia unicolor (Macleay, 1881)
Lemon tongue sole

Habitat: Sheltered sand; 2–36 m depth.
Distribution: Tropical Australia south to Mandurah, WA, and southern NSW.
Maximum size: Length to 330 mm.

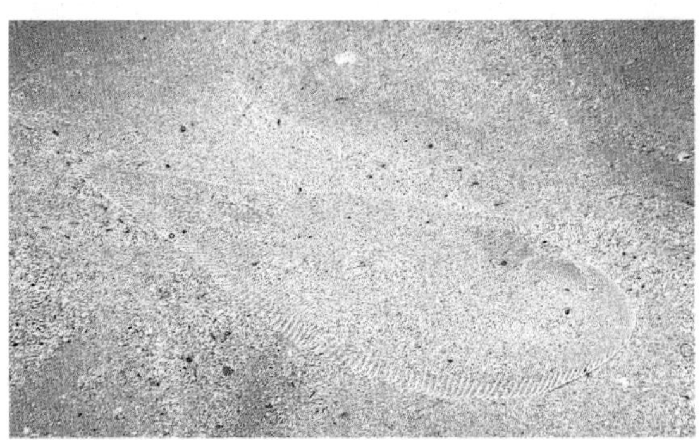

The lemon tongue sole can be mistaken for the southern tongue sole but differs by having a narrower tail, relatively large hook-shaped snout and small tentacles on the lips. Although primarily a tropical species, this flatfish is regularly seen near Fremantle and Sydney.

FAMILY MONACANTHIDAE
Leatherjackets, filefishes

Leatherjackets are an easily identified group of fishes with a long spine over the eye and a leathery skin that includes numerous tiny embedded scales. The main spine of most species can be depressed into a groove or locked into place by a small spine located just behind. Australia is the centre of diversity for this family, as more than half of the estimated 90 species occur here, generally in temperate waters.

Acanthaluteres spilomelanurus (Quoy & Gaimard, 1824)
Bridled leatherjacket

Habitat: Sheltered seagrass, reef; 0–10 m depth.
Distribution: Fremantle, WA, to Sydney, NSW, and around Tas.
Maximum size: Length to 140 mm.

The bridled leatherjacket is one of the smallest Australian leatherjackets. Males are readily identified by the black stripes in front of the eyes, blue spots on the sides of the body and a black crescent-shaped marking near the edge of the tail. Females and juveniles have a mottled-brown pattern and are very difficult to distinguish from juvenile toothbrush leatherjackets, particularly if the bridle-like stripes at the front of the head are absent or indistinct. These two species are best separated by the presence of numerous black spots on the sides of the body in bridled leatherjackets, whereas juvenile toothbrush leatherjackets have a pattern of small white blotches. The bridled leatherjacket is abundant in seagrass beds, particularly towards the south of its range, and is also common among *Sargassum* and *Cystophora* plants on sheltered reefs.

Acanthaluteres spilomelanurus (male), Cloudy Lagoon, Tas.

Acanthaluteres vittiger (Castelnau, 1873)
Toothbrush leatherjacket

Habitat: Reef, seagrass; 0–40 m depth.
Distribution: Jurien Bay, WA, to Coff's Harbour, NSW, and around Tas.
Maximum size: Length to 320 mm.

Male toothbrush leatherjackets have a characteristic set of bristles on each side of the rear of the body. Females have a less distinctive appearance but can be recognised by the shape of the body, a light brown colour pattern and a dorsal spine that fits completely into a groove when depressed. Both sexes occur abundantly on moderately and submaximally exposed reefs in Tasmania and Victoria. Juveniles live in schools in sheltered and moderately exposed habitats, often alongside bridled leatherjackets, and are very similar in appearance to that species.

Acanthaluteres vittiger (female), Seven Mile Beach, WA

Acanthaluteres brownii (Richardson, 1846)
Spiny-tailed leatherjacket

Habitat: Sheltered and moderately exposed reef; 2–25 m depth.
Distribution: Rottnest I, WA, to Kangaroo I, SA.
Maximum size: Length to 460 mm.

Acanthaluteres brownii (female), Esperance, WA

Acanthaluteres brownii (male), Port Noarlunga, SA. RUDIE KUITER

The spiny-tailed leatherjacket can be recognised by the blue spots and lines on the sides and the orange or yellow patch with spines in front of the tail. This leatherjacket is commonly seen by divers in southern Western Australia and occurs abundantly in that region on coastal reefs and over seagrass beds.

Bracheluteres jacksonianus

(Quoy & Gaimard, 1824)
Pygmy leatherjacket

Habitat: Sheltered and moderately exposed reef, seagrass; 0–25 m depth.
Distribution: Lancelin, WA, to Moreton Bay, Qld, and around Tas.
Maximum size: Length to 90 mm.

This is the most distinctive of the Australian leatherjackets because of its small size and rounded shape. It is also unusual, in that the dorsal spine lacks a secondary locking spine and can therefore be easily depressed. Pygmy leatherjackets are common in all southern states in seagrass and brown algal habitats. At night they often sleep while attached by the mouth to seaweed fronds.

Brachaluteres jacksonianus, Jervis Bay, NSW

Thamnaconus degeni (Regan, 1903)

Degen's leatherjacket

Habitat: Moderately exposed reef, silt; 4–80 m depth.
Distribution: Great Australian Bight, WA, to Wilsons Promontory, Vic., and around Tas.
Maximum size: Length to 290 mm.

Thamnaconus degeni (male), Orford, Tas. PETER LAST

The male Degen's leatherjacket has an elongate body with large blue spots forming lines on the head and sides. Females resemble toothbrush leatherjackets by having a light brown body but differ in the shape of the spine, which is slender and has minute barbs. Degen's leatherjacket is generally confined to low reef, sponge gardens and silty sediment in depths between 30 and 70 m. Along the east coast of Tasmania near Orford they are occasionally seen on shallow reefs.

Monacanthus chinensis, Cliff Head, WA

Monacanthus chinensis (Osbeck 1765)
Fan-bellied leatherjacket

Habitat: Sheltered reef, seagrass; 0–50 m depth.
Distribution: Tropical Australia south to Geographe Bay, WA, and Western Port, Vic. Also widespread in the Indo-West Pacific region.
Maximum size: Length to 380 mm.

The fan-bellied leatherjacket has a number of distinctive features, including an extendible flap on the belly, fine filaments over the body surface, and six small spines in front of the tail. Although primarily a tropical species, it occurs commonly in warm temperate marine estuaries and is often associated with seagrass beds.

Scobinichthys granulatus
(Ramsay & Ogilby, 1886)
Rough leatherjacket

Habitat: Sheltered and moderately exposed reef; 0–30 m depth.
Distribution: Shark Bay, WA, to Maroochydore, Qld, and northern Tas.
Maximum size: Length to 300 mm.

The rough leatherjacket has a coarse skin with fine filaments, large dorsal spine, extendable flap of skin on the belly, and a characteristic pattern on the tail fin. The body pattern is somewhat variable, but often includes a dark patch above and just behind the pectoral fin and a network of small polygonal blotches. This leatherjacket is common in seagrass beds and on estuarine reefs in southern Australia and is abundant in New South Wales.

Scobinichthys granulatus, Bass Point, NSW

Meuschenia australis (Donovan, 1824)
Brown-striped leatherjacket, southern leatherjacket

Habitat: Moderately and submaximally exposed reef; 0–20 m depth.
Distribution: Robe, SA, to Wilsons Promontory, Vic., and around Tas.
Maximum size: Length to 320 mm.

Male brown-striped leatherjackets are readily identified by the yellow-green body, blue line below the dorsal fin, blue tail with a black margin, and bluish-green dorsal and anal fins. Females have a pattern of brown stripes along the body similar to those on six-spined leatherjackets but with dark spots on the belly and head. The brown-striped leatherjacket is uncommon on the Australian mainland but is commonly seen on kelp-covered Tasmanian reefs.

Meuschenia australis (female), Rocky Cape, Tas.

Meuschenia australis (male), Rocky Cape, Tas.

Meuschenia flavolineata Hutchins, 1977
Yellow-striped leatherjacket

Habitat: Moderately exposed reef; 2–30 m depth.
Distribution: Dongara, WA, to Broughton I, NSW, and northern Tas.
Maximum size: Length to 300 mm.

Yellow-striped leatherjackets have dark bodies with a characteristic yellow or orange patch in front of the tail. They occur widely in southern Australian waters and are moderately common throughout but generally do not move far from reefs with caves. Pairs of yellow-striped leatherjackets are often seen moving about together, the female with the yellow patch extended onto the tail and the male with small spines.

Meuschenia flavolineata (female at front), Preservation I, Tas.

Meuschenia freycineti (Quoy & Gaimard, 1824)
Six-spined leatherjacket

Habitat: Sheltered and moderately exposed reef, seagrass; 0–50 m depth.
Distribution: Jurien Bay, WA, to Broughton I, NSW, and around Tas.
Maximum size: Length to 550 mm.

Six-spined leatherjackets can usually be recognised by the network of fine blue lines on the head, and yellow dorsal and anal fins. The species exhibits a considerable amount of colour variation, with the most colourful males occurring along the New South Wales coast and having a large orange patch on the side. Six strong spines are situated in front of the tail on males, but these are much reduced on females. Mature animals are common in seagrass beds and on sheltered coastal reefs; juveniles are abundant in seagrass beds.

Meuschenia freycineti (male), Cloudy Lagoon, Tas.

Meuschenia galii, Albany, WA

Meuschenia freycineti (female), Flinders I, Tas.

Meuschenia trachylepis, Merimbula, NSW

Meuschenia galii (Waite, 1905)
Blue-lined leatherjacket

Habitat: Moderately exposed reef; 2–30 m depth.
Distribution: Shark Bay, WA, to Wilsons Promontory, Vic.
Maximum size: Length to 350 mm.

The blue-lined leatherjacket is closest in appearance to the six-spined leatherjacket but lacks spines in front of the tail and has stronger stripes and spots on the body. The orange tail has a distinctive pattern of blue stripes extending partway down. This species is abundant on seaweed-covered reefs in southwestern Australia, becoming less common towards Victoria.

Meuschenia trachylepis (Günther, 1870)
Yellow-finned leatherjacket

Habitat: Sheltered and moderately exposed reef; 1–40 m depth.
Distribution: Eastern Vic. to southern Qld.
Maximum size: Length to 350 mm.

The yellow-finned leatherjacket occurs in the same sheltered habitat as the six-spined leatherjacket and resembles that species, but can be distinguished by the presence of scribbles on the side of the body, fine filaments projecting from the skin, and a different pattern on the tail. The species is abundant near the entrances to New South Wales estuaries and is occasionally also seen on coastal reefs.

Meuschenia hippocrepis
(Quoy & Gaimard, 1824)
Horseshoe leatherjacket

Habitat: Moderately exposed reef; 3–18 m depth.
Distribution: Houtman Abrolhos, WA, to Wilsons Promontory, Vic., and northern Tas.
Maximum size: Length to 500 mm.

The horseshoe leatherjacket is a colourful species with blue, green, black and yellow markings on the head and body, and characteristic horseshoe-shaped marks on the sides. It is moderately common throughout its range and is locally abundant in Bass Strait. It often occurs with the yellow-striped leatherjacket in the east

Meuschenia hippocrepis, Busselton, WA

and the blue-lined leatherjacket in the west. If threatened, the horseshoe leatherjacket retreats into caves.

Meuschenia venusta Hutchins, 1977

Stars and stripes leatherjacket

Habitat: Moderately exposed reef; 5–20 m depth.
Distribution: Shark Bay, WA, to Sydney, NSW, and northern Tas.
Maximum size: Length to 210 mm.

The stars and stripes leatherjacket is an easily recognised species with a pointed snout, prominent lines on the head, and rows of spots along the body. Although this leatherjacket is widely distributed in southern Australia, it is regularly seen only at clear-water sites on deep offshore reefs.

Meuschenia venusta, Rocky Cape, Tas.

Meuschenia scaber

(Forster in Bloch & Schneider, 1801)
Velvet leatherjacket, cosmopolitan leatherjacket

Habitat: Exposed reef; 6–200 m depth.
Distribution: Cape Naturaliste, WA, to Sydney, NSW, and around Tas. Also New Zealand.
Maximum size: Length to 310 mm.

The velvet leatherjacket has a pointed head with two characteristic stripes radiating down below the eye and dark blotches on the sides. This species is commonly seen on deep reefs along the eastern coast, most often in water depths exceeding 20 m. It is the most aggressive of the local leatherjackets, sometimes biting divers.

Meuschenia scaber, Bicheno, Tas.

Nelusetta ayraudi (Quoy & Gaimard, 1824)

Chinaman leatherjacket

Habitat: Reef, seagrass, sand; 2–350 m depth.
Distribution: North West Cape, WA, to southern Qld.
Maximum size: Length to 710 mm.

The chinaman leatherjacket has an elongate, ovate body with a relatively long, thin dorsal spine and three dark stripes running along the sides. The stripes are obvious on juveniles but indistinct on adults. The largest animals are restricted to deep water, whereas schools of juveniles commonly approach divers in estuaries and sheltered bays, particularly along the New South Wales coast. This is by far the largest species of leatherjacket in temperate waters.

Nelusetta ayraudi, Jervis Bay, NSW

Eubalichthys bucephalus (Whitley, 1931)

Black reef leatherjacket, Whitley's leatherjacket

Habitat: Exposed reef; 4–250 m depth.
Distribution: Houtman Abrolhos, WA, to Broughton I, NSW.
Maximum size: Length to 400 mm.

The black reef leatherjacket has a distinctive white eye, which contrasts noticeably with the dark body. The species is moderately common on coastal reefs in New South Wales, where cohabiting pairs are sometimes found associated with particular caves. Black reef leatherjackets are restricted to deep water around the southern and southwestern coasts and are caught by trawl rather than being seen by divers in that region.

Eubalichthys bucephalus, Terrigal, NSW

Eubalichthys gunnii (Günther, 1870)

Gunn's leatherjacket, velvet leatherjacket

Habitat: Moderately exposed reef; 4–150 m depth.
Distribution: Port Lincoln, SA, to Wilsons Promontory, Vic., and around Tas.
Maximum size: Length to 450 mm.

Eubalichthys gunnii, Ninepin Pt, Tas.

Gunn's leatherjacket is best recognised by the chickenwire-like network of patches on the side. Uncommon around the mainland, the species is sighted occasionally by divers or caught in gillnet on Tasmanian reefs. It rarely moves far from caves.

Eubalichthys mosaicus (Ramsay & Ogilby, 1886)

Mosaic leatherjacket

Habitat: Sheltered and moderately exposed reef; 1–80 m depth.
Distribution: Dongara, WA, to Noosa Head, Qld, and northern Tas.
Maximum size: Length to 600 mm.

Juvenile mosaic leatherjackets have a distinctive and colourful arrangement of yellows, oranges and blues on the sides of a rounded body. As they age the oranges darken to black, the blues become paler and the body elongates. The smallest juveniles are common under large jellyfish in offshore waters, settling onto reefs in estuaries and sheltered bays. Adults are occasionally found in divable depths but are mainly confined to deep water.

Eubalichthys mosaicus, Esperance, WA

FAMILY ARACANIDAE
Temperate boxfishes

The temperate boxfishes are a small family of 11 species. All of them have a rigid outer box-like covering, which is formed from large, fused triangular plates. This outer covering, the carapace, is ridged along the belly and usually has additional ridges along the back and upper sides. Dorsal and ventral fins lie opposite each other at the rear of the body. When feeding, these fishes often blow a jet of water at sediment to expose the prey hidden beneath.

Aracana aurita (Shaw 1798)
Shaw's cowfish

Habitat: Sheltered and moderately exposed reef, seagrass; 0–200 m depth.
Distribution: Dongara, WA, to southern NSW and around Tas.
Maximum size: Length to 250 mm.

Shaw's cowfish is the most common species of boxfish on reefs in southeastern Australia. Males and females differ substantially in colour pattern, with females having a pattern of scribbled orange, black and white markings over the body, and the less common males having a distinctive arrangement of yellow, blue and white dots and stripes.

Aracana aurita (female), Taroona, Tas.

Aracana aurita (male), Cape Portland, Tas.

Aracana ornata (Gray, 1838)
Ornate cowfish

Habitat: Sheltered seagrass, reef; 1–60 m depth.
Distribution: Esperance, WA, to Mallacoota, Vic., and around Tas.
Maximum size: Length to 150 mm.

The male ornate cowfish differs from the closely related Shaw's cowfish by having narrower spines on the back, a prominent bump in front of the eye and a regular arrangement of blue-centred black spots on the yellow sides of the body. The female ornate cowfish is more difficult to distinguish because it has red, white and black striped sides, but the body is deeper with narrower spines on the back than female Shaw's cowfish, and the lines along the sides are more regularly arranged. The ornate cowfish is most often sighted near seagrass beds.

Aracana ornata (male), Cape Portland, Tas.

Aracana ornata (female), Fosters Islet, Tas.

Anoplocapros amygdaloides
Fraser-Brunner, 1941
Western smooth boxfish

Habitat: Moderately exposed seagrass, reef; 2–100 m depth.
Distribution: Shark Bay, WA, to Great Australian Bight, SA.
Maximum size: Length to 390 mm.

The western smooth boxfish has a rounded, spine-less body with numerous dark blotches on the back. Females are moderately common on shallow coastal reefs, particularly near seagrass beds, while large males are normally restricted to deepwater.

Anoplocapros inermis (Fraser-Brunner, 1935)
Eastern smooth boxfish, blue boxfish, robust boxfish

Habitat: Moderately exposed reef; 10–300 m depth.
Distribution: Western Port, Vic., to southern Qld.
Maximum size: Length to 350 mm.

The eastern smooth boxfish differs slightly from its western relative: the female has lighter brown blotches on the back and the male has a blue body with golden sides. There is also a large bump on the snout between the mouth and eye. The species is locally common around Sydney and frequently taken in trawls but is uncommon in shallow water through most of its geographic range.

Anoplocapros amygdaloides, Cliff Head, WA

Anoplocapros inermis, Port Stephens, NSW

Anoplocapros lenticularis (Richardson, 1841)
Humpback boxfish, white-barred boxfish

Habitat: Moderately and submaximally exposed reef; 10–40 m depth.
Distribution: Dongara, WA, to Lorne, Vic.
Maximum size: Length to 200 mm.

The humpback boxfish is a distinctive species with a high back and concave upper profile on the snout. The sides are orange-red lined with white, and additional black markings are present on the upper bodies of juveniles and females. The species occurs moderately commonly near coastal reefs and jetty pylons but is most often seen in trawl catches.

Anoplocapros lenticularis, Little I, WA

FAMILY OSTRACIIDAE
Tropical boxfishes, cowfishes, trunkfishes

Ostraciids are a tropical family of about 20 species, which differ from the family Aracanidae in several minor features, including lacking a ridge under the body and having the anal fin placed more posteriorly. Some authors consider the two families to be merely subfamilies of a single family. The skin of some ostaciids contains a toxic substance, which can kill other small fish if they are confined together in an aquarium.

Tetrasomus concatenatus (Bloch, 1786)
Turretfish

Habitat: Sheltered sand, seagrass; 1–30 m depth.
Distribution: Tropical Australia south to Albany, WA, and Jervis Bay, NSW.
Maximum size: Length to 220 mm.

The body of the turretfish is triangular in cross-section, with two distinctive spines projecting from the ridge along the back. Hexagonal markings and blue spots, which increase in size with age, are present on the flat sides. This tropical species is common in sheltered New South Wales bays but is rarely seen in southwestern Australia.

Tetrasomus concatenatus, North Head, NSW

FAMILY TETRAODONTIDAE
Toadfishes, pufferfishes

Toadfishes are a large, easily recognised group of about 100 species with torpedo-shaped bodies, rounded dorsal and anal fins set at the back of the body, soft skin lacking scales but sometimes with small embedded spines, and teeth fused into a beak. Their distinctive appearance is fortunate, because a lethal poison, tetrodotoxin, is present in the skin and internal organs of most species. They should not be eaten, except perhaps in parts of Asia where there is a long cultural history associated with their use. Even in Japan where great care is taken in the preparation of these fishes, many people die from poisoning each year after eating the tetraodontid delicacy *fugu*.

Omegophora armilla (Waite & McCulloch, 1915)
Ringed toadfish

Habitat: Sheltered and moderately exposed reef, sand; 4–146 m depth.
Distribution: Lancelin, WA, to Botany Bay, NSW, and around Tas.
Maximum size: Length to 250 mm.

The ringed toadfish has a rounded body with a distinctive fawn patch encircled by a black line at the base of the pectoral fin. This species has an unusual geographic distribution, as it is moderately common in shallow water in the northern section of its range in Western Australia but generally occurs only in trawlable depths in cooler southeastern Australian waters. The western animals have a less rounded body than southern animals and fine blue spots on the back, so perhaps two species are involved.

Omegophora armilla, Busselton, WA

Omegophora armilla, Cloudy Bay, Tas.

Omegophora cyanopunctata Hardy & Hutchins, 1981
Blue-spotted toadfish

Habitat: Moderately exposed reef; 3–25 m depth.
Distribution: Rottnest I, WA, to Gulf St Vincent, NSW.
Maximum size: Length to 180 mm.

The blue-spotted toadfish differs from the closely related ringed toadfish by having a blue line surrounding the round patch beside the pectoral fin, large blue spots over the upper body surface, and prominent white makings on the lower sides. This toadfish is common on shallow reefs and around jetty pylons in southwestern Australia.

Omegophora cyanopunctata, Canal Rocks, WA

Contusus brevicaudus Hardy, 1981
Prickly toadfish

Habitat: Sheltered sand, seagrass; 0–20 m depth.
Distribution: Rottnest I, WA, to Jervis Bay, NSW, and around Tas.
Maximum size: Length to 250 mm.

The prickly toadfish has an inflated body with several large black blotches on the back. It occurs moderately commonly in estuaries. A closely related species, the barred toadfish ***Contusus richei***, has an almost identical pattern and occurs in much the same habitat, particularly in the most southern section of the range. That species can be recognised by the more elongate body in front of the tail, with the dorsal and anal fins not reaching near the base of the tail fin.

Contusus brevicaudus, Flinders I, Tas.

Tetractenos glaber (Freminville, 1813)
Smooth toadfish

Habitat: Sheltered mud, sand, seagrass; 0–10 m depth.
Distribution: Port Lincoln, SA, to Moreton Bay, Qld, and around Tas.
Maximum size: Length to 160 mm.

The smooth toadfish is one of the most abundant fishes in muddy estuaries along the southeastern coast, with some animals entering the lower reaches of rivers. The species can be recognised by the red tail and the pattern of large black spots with well-defined margins on the upper body. A New South Wales species, ***Tetractenos hamiltoni***, has a similar pattern but can be recognised by a covering of small spines over the body surface.

Tetractenos glaber, Flinders I, Tas.

Torquigener pleurogramma (Regan, 1903)
Banded toadfish, weeping toado

Habitat: Sheltered and moderately exposed sand; 0–27 m depth.
Distribution: Coral Bay, WA, to Adelaide, SA, and Narooma, NSW, to Hervey Bay, Qld. Also Lord Howe I.
Maximum size: Length to 220 mm.

The banded toadfish has a distinctive horizontal line along the sides and several vertical lines on the lower section of the head. This species occurs abundantly in schools along the southwestern coast and is also common in New South Wales. Despite its small size, this species has been known to attack spear fishers, so should be treated warily.

Torquigener pleurogramma, Cliff Head, WA

Torquigener squamicauda (Ogilby, 1911)
Brushtail toadfish, scaly tailed toadfish

Habitat: Sheltered and moderately exposed sand; 0–10 m depth.
Distribution: Wollongong, NSW, to Yeppon, Qld.
Maximum size: Length to 150 mm.

The brushtail toadfish is a relatively small species with prominent spines on the body and a line along the side, but lacking lines on the head. It is moderately common in sheltered coastal environments in the Sydney area, although more abundant further north.

Torquigener squamicauda, Terrigal, NSW

FAMILY DIODONTIDAE
Porcupine fishes

This is a distinctive group of about 20 slow-moving fishes with bodies covered in large spines. These spines, formed from modified scales, are fixed in some species and movable in others. As with the closely related family Tetraodontidae, porcupine fishes can greatly inflate their body by ingesting water or air. This defensive mechanism causes eaten fish to become wedged in the throat of predators.

Diodon nicthemerus Cuvier, 1818
Globe fish, porcupine fish

Habitat: Sheltered and moderately exposed reef, sand; 0–50 m depth.
Distribution: Dongara, WA, to Seal Rocks, NSW, and around Tas.
Maximum size: Length to 280 mm.

The globe fish is an unmistakeable species with a dark-grey back, black blotches on the sides, a white belly and yellow spines. When threatened, the fish inflates its body rapidly into a sphere with outwardly radiating spines. The species occurs in a range of habitats along the southern coast and is most abundant on sheltered coastal reefs.

Dicotylichthys punctulatus Kaup, 1855
Three-barred porcupine fish

Habitat: Reef, sand; 0–50 m depth.
Distribution: Southern NSW to Qld and Flinders I, Tas.
Maximum size: Length to 430 mm.

The three-barred porcupine fish differs from other local diodontids, including a few tropical species that occasionally drift south, by the regular pattern of small black spots over the body. The species is common in New South Wales and occurs both in estuaries and along the open coast.

Dicotylichthys punctulatus, Merimbula, NSW

Diodon nicthemerus, Waterfall Bay, Tas.

Class Reptilia

Reptiles

Reptiles are cold-blooded animals, which breathe air and are primarily adapted for life on land. Most produce shelled eggs to minimise water loss, and their bodies have four legs and a scaly skin. The class is divided into four orders: Testudinata (turtles), Squamata (snakes and lizards), Crocodilia (crocodiles) and Rhynchocephalia (the New Zealand tuatara). The Testudinata, Squamata and Crocodilia all have marine representatives in the tropics, but only a single turtle resides in any of the world's temperate seas. A number of other reptiles are not fully marine but have marine affinities. These include the metallic skink *Niveoscincus metallicus*, which regularly forages for crustaceans and other animals in the intertidal zone in southern Tasmania. Several species of sea snakes periodically drift south into temperate seas from the tropics and occasionally become stranded on beaches.

Dermochelys coriacea (Vandelli, 1761)

Leathery turtle, luth

Habitat: Inshore and offshore waters.
Distribution: Around the Australian mainland and Tas. Also widespread overseas.
Maximum size: Length to 3 m.

The leathery turtle is the largest and most distinctive sea turtle and is classified in its own family. Among the unique features are large paddle-shaped limbs (which lack claws), small bones embedded in the leathery skin and ridges running down the body. Although primarily nesting in the tropics, the leathery turtle is also unusual among turtles for spending most of its time feeding on jellyfish in temperate waters. Several other sea turtles have also been recorded as far south as Tasmania but are rare stray visitors that are almost invariably in poor condition. The most southern recorded nesting site for the leathery turtle is near Ballina, NSW.

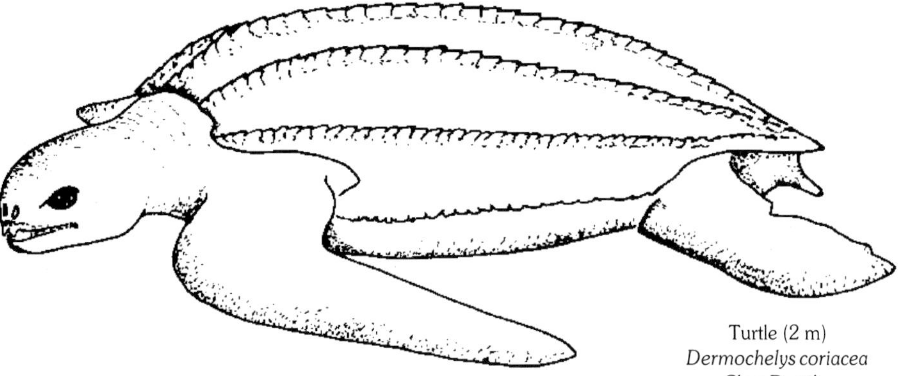

Turtle (2 m)
Dermochelys coriacea
Class Reptilia

Dermochelys coriacea nesting, Rantau Abang, Malaysia.

Class Aves

Birds

Birds are an immediately recognisable group of about 8100 species which all possess feathers, wings and a beak. Although sometimes linked with the mammals because they are warm-blooded, these two vertebrate groups have different reptilean ancestry and are now not thought to be closely related. About 100 of the 750-odd Australian species are associated with temperate Australian coasts. These include estuarine foragers such as stints, knots, pelicans, swans, gulls, eagles, ibis and egrets, and coastal species such as terns, shearwaters, gannets, albatross, prions, oyster-catchers, penguins and petrels. These birds are well described in other publications, and so only two representative species are discussed here. The small number of species included does not imply that birds are a relatively unimportant group of marine animals; birds play a key role as predators and grazers in many shallow-water marine and estuarine food webs.

Penguin (300 mm)
Eudyptula minor
Class Aves

Eudyptula minor (Forster, 1781)

Little penguin, fairy penguin

Habitat: Inshore waters.
Distribution: Fremantle, WA, to Mooloolabah, Qld, and around Tas. Also New Zealand.
Maximum size: Length to 330 mm.

Penguins are the birds most highly adapted for life at sea, possessing streamlined bodies, scale-like feathers, an insulating layer of down, and the ability to 'fly' through water using flipper-like wings. The little penguin is the smallest of the 18 recognised species of penguin and is readily distinguished from others by its small size, blue-grey back, white belly and black beak. It is also the only species to breed in Australia, nesting in burrows or rock crevices. Females in southeastern Australia generally lay two eggs in late winter or early spring and, with assistance from the male, incubate them for five weeks. Hatchlings are fed by the parents, who initially alternate on a daily basis between fishing at sea and tending the young. After about two months the young leave the nest and disperse along the coast. The adults follow to rebuild fat reserves, but return to their burrows after about six weeks to moult. The Australian population has been dwindling in recent times, presumbly because of coastal land-clearing and predation by feral animals, and possibly also because of diminishing stocks of pilchards, anchovies and other prey fish species.

Eudyptula minor, Bruny I, Tas.

Puffinus tenuirostris (Temminck, 1835)
Muttonbird, short-tailed shearwater, moonbird, squab

Habitat: Ocean.
Distribution: St Francis I, SA, to Broughton I, NSW, and around Tas. Migrates to North Pacific.
Maximum size: Length to 400 mm.

The muttonbird has a dark grey to black body, a long, thin beak, and pointed, sickle-shaped wings. Flocks of thousands are sometimes seen in offshore waters during daylight, returning to nesting burrows on tussock-covered headlands at dusk. These flocks ingest thousands of tonnes of krill (*Nyctiphanes australis*) annually, presumably having a substantial effect on the krill population and affecting other marine species that also consume this prey. The muttonbird, or short-tailed shearwater, is exceptional even among birds for its seasonal migration over tens of thousands of kilometres. During the southern winter, it forages near the Alaskan and Russian coasts in the North Pacific. In late September adult birds return to the nests of the previous year, initially reconstructing the nests, and then laying eggs within a few days of 25 November. The young hatch after an incubation period averaging 53 days and grow very rapidly to a weight substantially greater than the adults. On some Bass Strait islands, young are harvested for human consumption at this time (March/April). Both adults and juveniles leave on their northern migration in late April or early May. Fewer than half of the fledglings survive the round-trip to return.

Puffinus tenuirostris, Bruny I, Tas.

Class Mammalia

Mammals

Mammals are a relatively small group of about 4500 species that suckle their young with milk and have hair, regulated body temperatures and a four-chambered heart. Nearly all mammals live on land, but species in three orders are adapted for life at sea. The Sirenia, an order that includes the dugongs and manatees, is confined to the tropics, while the Pinnipedia (seals) and Cetacea (whales) are prevalent in temperate and polar waters. Several other orders include species that live on land but forage at sea. The most noticeable of these in southern Australian waters is the eastern water rat *Hydromys chrysogaster*, a rodent that regularly feeds in shallow waters leaving accumulations of crab fragments on the shore to mark its presence.

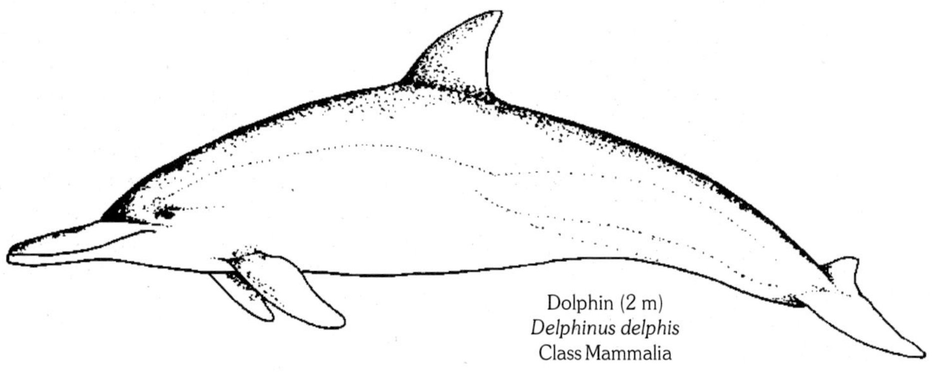

Dolphin (2 m)
Delphinus delphis
Class Mammalia

Neophoca cinerea, Perth, WA. CLAY BRYCE

Order Pinnipedia
Seals, sea lions

Pinnipeds have stream-lined bodies, forelimbs modified as flippers, webbed hindlimbs and a tail reduced to the size of a small stump. They are adapted both for spending most of their lives in water, feeding on fish and other marine life, and for crawling around land or ice to breed, give birth and moult. This order is divided into three families: Odobenidae (the Northern Hemisphere walrus), Phocidae (true seals) and Otariidae (eared seals, including the sea lions and fur seals). Eared seals spend a greater proportion of time on land than phocid seals and are less structurally modified for an aquatic life. They have ear lobes, longer flippers, a more flexible neck and hindlimbs that can be turned forward. Three species breed in Australian waters. No phocid seals are locally resident, although the elephant seal *Mirounga leonina* formed large breeding colonies on King Island in Bass Strait until the nineteenth century, when the population was exterminated by hunters. The few elephant seals seen now are summer stragglers from the subantarctic islands. A number of other phocid species also arrive occasionally on our coasts but are well outside their usual ranges in the Antarctic.

Neophoca cinerea (Péron, 1816)
Australian sea lion

Habitat: Exposed coast, sand beaches.
Distribution: Houtman Abrolhos, WA, to Kangaroo I, SA.
Maximum size: Length to 2.3 m.

Sea lions, or hair seals, are characterised by a body covering of stout guard hairs, whereas the other group of phocid seals, the fur seals, have a pelt of softer fur hairs located close to the skin in addition to the guard hairs. Male Australian sea lions differ substantially in appearance from females. They have a solid, dark-brown body with an light-coloured mane of stiff hairs on the head. Females and juveniles have a silvery-grey back merging into a light yellow belly. Australian sea lions rarely move far from the place they were born and spend much of their lives ashore on sandy beaches. They generally live in colonies on offshore islands, although two mainland colonies are also known. The total population is currently estimated to be about 5000 animals. Breeding occurs mainly in spring, although pups can be born well outside this season in some years. Few animals live longer than ten years.

Arctocephalus pusillus, Hogan I, Tas. SIMON TALBOT

Arctocephalus pusillus (Schreber, 1976)
Australian fur seal

Habitat: Exposed coast.
Distribution: Lady Julia Percy I, Vic., to Seal Rocks, NSW, and around Tas. Also Southern Africa.
Maximum size: Length to 2.3 m.

The Australian fur seal is the only seal commonly seen in southeastern Australian waters. It is virtually identical in appearance to the New Zealand fur seal but differs in tooth structure, as it has large teeth with three cusps rather than the small teeth with one cusp of its relative. The Australian fur seal also differs in breeding habitat, as it prefers exposed rocky shores rather than the sheltered boulder beaches used by the New Zealand fur seal. Birth and mating occur in November and December, with pups reaching maturity after four to five years and rarely surviving for longer than ten years. The species is a good climber on rocks and an excellent swimmer, reaching depths in excess of 130 m while searching for fish and large invertebrate prey. The population of this species was almost eliminated by sealers hunting for pelts in the early nineteenth century but now numbers about 25 000 animals.

Arctocephalus forsteri, Kangaroo I, SA. KELVIN AITKEN

Arctocephalus forsteri (Lesson, 1828)
New Zealand fur seal

Habitat: Exposed coast.
Distribution: Albany, WA, to eastern SA and Maatsuyker I and the Friars, Tas. Also New Zealand and associated subantarctic islands.
Maximum size: Length to 2.5 m.

The New Zealand fur seal has a brown back with a slightly lighter belly and a relatively long and pointed snout. The species was not distinguished locally from the Australian fur seal until recently. Identification of the two species is greatly aided by the small area of overlap in their distributions. Although the New Zealand fur seal is the most widely distributed seal in Australia, it has a smaller total population (about 8000 animals) than the Australian fur seal. The life histories of the two species do not differ greatly.

Order Cetacea
Whales, dolphins

The 80-odd species of whales and dolphins are so well adapted for life at sea that they resemble fishes much more than terrestrial mammals. They all have stream-lined bodies, which merge into the tail, and many species also have a dorsal fin near the centre of the back. Under the skin they have a uniform layer of fat, the blubber, which provides insulation and food storage. The hindlimbs and associated pelvis, which are prominent on seals and sea lions, are reduced to small internal vestiges. One interesting aspect of whales and dolphins is their intelligence, which is widely considered to be equivalent to that of primate mammals. Cetaceans are divided into two suborders: the Mysticeti (baleen whales) and the Odontoceti (toothed whales). Baleen whales feed by filtering large quantities of plankton using modified hairs that form sieve plates around the mouth. This group includes the largest animal known to have ever lived, the blue whale *Balaenoptera musculus*. Most toothed whales are dolphins and porpoises, but the group also includes the killer whale and sperm whales. Toothed whales generally feed on fish and squid.

Megaptera novaeangliae, Tonga. KELVIN AITKEN

Megaptera novaeangliae Borowski, 1781
Humpback whale

Habitat: Ocean.
Distribution: Around Australian mainland and Tas. Also widespread overseas.
Maximum size: Length to 18 m.

The humpback whale is readily identified by the extremely long, white flippers. It also has a stout body compared with other whales, a broad head with a series of knobs on the top, a small dorsal fin and a tail with a scalloped rather than smooth rear edge. The behaviour pattern is also distinctive, as these whales are spectacular leapers, often rolling in mid-air and crashing back into the water on their backs. Humpbacks whales feed in Antarctica during the spring, summer and autumn months and then migrate along the eastern and western Australian coasts to subtropical and tropical grounds where they calve in summer. Southward-moving animals are in relatively poor condition, as they do not feed while at the calving grounds. Humpback whales communicate using complex songs, which can travel hundreds of kilometres underwater given suitable conditions.

Eubalaena australis Desmoulins, 1822
Southern right whale

Habitat: Coastal bays, ocean.
Distribution: Southern and eastern mainland of Australia and Tas. Also widespread in the Southern Hemisphere.
Maximum size: Length to 18 m.

The southern right whale lacks a dorsal fin and has an curved mouth with long baleen plates. Unlike other local baleen whales, it lacks pleats on the throat. Its name derives from early whalers who considered this was the 'right' kind of whale to hunt because it lives close inshore, floats when dead and produces copious amounts of oil. The species quickly changed from being a hazard to shipping in places such as Hobart, to being virtually extinct. However, the right whale population is making a belated recovery in Australia, as the number of females migrating to Australia to calve in spring has increased significantly during the past two decades. Some authorities consider this species to be the same as the northern right whale *Eubalaena glacialis*, because animals in the Northern and Southern Hemispheres differ little in appearance despite the 8000 km gap between their ranges.

Eubalaena australis, Bicheno, Tas. MALCOLM WELLS

Orcinus orca (Linnaeus, 1758)
Killer whale, orca

Habitat: Ocean.
Distribution: Western, southern and eastern mainland of Australia and Tas. Also widespread overseas.
Maximum size: Length to 9 m.

The killer whale is a very large member of the dolphin family and is distinguished from other dolphins by the rounded head, the dorsal fin which is very high and pointed in adult males, the paddle-like flippers, and white patch above the eyes. The species usually frequents offshore waters in southern Australia, although pods are occasionally seen inshore along the eastern Tasmanian and southern New South Wales coasts. Despite its fearsome reputation, there is no confirmed account of a killer whale fatally attacking a human. The species sometimes feeds on marine mammals, but more often feeds on squid and fish.

Orcinus orca, Tasman Peninsula, Tas. SIMON TALBOT

Globicephalus melas (Traill, 1806)
Long-finned pilot whale

Habitat: Ocean.
Distribution: Southern and eastern mainland of Australia and Tas. Also widespread overseas.
Maximum size: Length to 6.5 m.

The long-finned pilot whale is a dark brownish-grey animal with a bulbous head and rounded dorsal fin. An almost identical species, the short-finned pilot whale ***Globicephala macrorhynchus***, also occurs in this region but is relatively rare and has shorter flippers (less than a fifth of body length). Both species are not often seen at sea and would be little known, except that large pods frequently strand themselves on ocean beaches.

Globicephalus melas, Hawaii. KELVIN AITKEN

Tursiops truncatus (Montagu, 1821)
Bottlenose dolphin

Habitat: Sheltered bays, ocean.
Distribution: Around Australian mainland and Tas. Also widespread overseas.
Maximum size: Length to 4 m.

The bottlenose dolphin is a large dolphin with a relatively short beak, a hooked dorsal fin, a curved mouth permanently shaped into a grin, and a grey back, gradually blending into white on the belly. This species moves into estuaries more often than other dolphins and usually lives in groups of five to 20 animals. Bottlenose dolphins are inquisitive, approaching divers and moving into very shallow water at Monkey Mia (Shark Bay, WA) to interact with waders.

Tursiops truncatus, Port Phillip Bay, Vic. KEN HOPPEN

Delphinus delphis, Merimbula, NSW. KELVIN AITKEN

Delphinus delphis Linnaeus, 1758
Common dolphin

Habitat: Sheltered bays, ocean.
Distribution: Around the Australian mainland and Tas. Also widespread overseas.
Maximum size: Length to 2.5 m.

The common dolphin differs from the bottlenose dolphin by having a longer beak and dorsal fin, and by the distinctive grey, oval-shaped markings on the sides, overlapping near the centre of the body. The species occurs in large schools, which can exceed 1000 animals, and is the classical dolphin illustrated on ancient Mediterranean frescos. Common dolphins often follow boats but are wary of divers and are rarely glimpsed underwater.

Glossary

abdomen the segmented section of the body, located behind the thorax on an arthropod.
ambulacral groove the narrow groove on the underside of echinoderm arms.
ambulacral plates a series of calcareous plates on an echinoid test with holes to allow tube feet to pass through.
anal fin a fin attached to the lower edge of a fish behind the anus.
antennule the first antenna of crustaceans.
aperture the entrance to the internal cavity of a gastropod shell.
apical cell the terminal cell on a branch.
apothecia the cup-shaped reproductive bodies on fungi that release spores.
Aristotle's lantern the feeding structure of echinoids that is formed from several calcareous elements and includes the jaws.
auricle elongate leaf-like or string-like projections from the body of some ctenophores.
barbel a fleshy, whisker-like process that projects from the lip or underside of the head of a fish.
benthos plants and animals that live on the seabed or under sediment.
binary fission an asexual method of reproduction that involves cells splitting into two parts of approximately equal size.
bursa (pl. **bursae**) a slit-like opening to ophiuroid respiratory chamber; it is located between the jaw and the arm base.
byssal threads the fine threads extruded by bivalves to attach the animal to the seabed.
calcareous composed of calcium carbonate.
calcite a crystalline form of calcium carbonate.
calyx the main body of an entoproct; it is connected to the substrate by a stalk.
carapace an extension of the body wall that extends behind the head of crustaceans to protect part or all of the thorax.
caudal fin the tail fin of a fish.
cellulose a fibrous organic compound that provides structural support in plants.
ceratum (pl. **cerata**) a projection extending from the upper body surface of opisthobranchs.
cheliped the first walking limb of a crustacean if modified into a grasping claw.
chemotroph an organism that utilises inorganic molecules to obtain energy.
cilium (pl. **cilia**) a short whip-like process that extends in groups from the surface of a cell.
cirrus (pl. **cirri**) a limb of a barnacle that extends and contracts during feeding; also a slender, jointed appendage that projects from the base of a feather star and is used for attachment or locomotion.
columella the central column of a gastropod shell, including the inner lip of the aperture.
conceptacle a pit containing reproductive organs located on the surface of macroalgal fronds.
cuticle a waxy surface layer on insects, leaves, etc..
dorsal fin a fin attached to the upper edge of a fish.
dorsal region the high central region of the valve of a chiton.
ectoderm the outer layer of cells.
ectoplasm the outer dense layer of protoplasm within a cell.
endoderm the inner layer of cells.
endoplasm the inner less-dense layer of protoplasm within a cell.
epiphyte a plant that grows attached to another plant.
eukaryote an organism (e.g. plant or animal) with cells containing at least one distinct nucleus bounded by a membrane.
exoskeleton the rigid outer covering of arthropods.
flagellum (pl. **flagella**) a long whip-like process that extends from the surface of a cell.
girdle the tough outer mantle of chitons, often with a covering of spines or scales.
gonotheca the outer capsule of the reproductive structures on hydroids.
hermaphrodite a plant or animal with both male and female sexual organs.
holdfast the basal structure on macroalgae that anchors the plant to the seabed.
hypha (pl. **hyphae**) a strand of a fungus.
infero-marginal plates the large plates that lie along the lower outer edge of seastar arms.
interambulacral plates a series of calcareous plates on an echinoid test that lack holes for tube feet.
invertebrate an animal without a backbone at any stage of development.
lateral line the row of scales with sensory pits along the side of the body of fishes.
lateral region the raised fan-shaped area towards the sides of the valve of a chiton.
leaf sheath a covering that encases the base of a seagrass leaf.
lophophore a feeding structure formed from a convoluted row of ciliated tentacles surrounding the mouth of a brachiopod, bryozoan or phoronid.
macroalga (pl. **macroalgae**) a large alga that grows attached to the seabed (commonly known as a seaweed).
mantle a fold of the body wall that covers all or part of a mollusc.
medusa (pl. **medusae**) a free-swimming animal shaped like an inverted saucer, with tentacles projecting from the undersurface.
metabolism the chemical processes that occur within the cell.
nacre an iridescent coating on the internal surface of some mollusc shells.
nematocyst a stinging cell of a cnidarian.
nucleus (pl. **nuclei**) a large, membrane-bound organelle within a cell that contains the genetic material.
operculum (= **opercle**, pl. **opercula**) a rounded structure used to seal the entrance to gastropod shells or polychaete tubes when the animal withdraws; also refers to the gill covers of fish.
oral shield large plate located on the under surface of a brittle star disc between the bases of the arms.
organelle a distinctive structural component of a cell.
oscule the exhalent opening of a sponge.
outer lip the outer edge of the aperture.
ovate oval-shaped but flattened.
ovoid egg-shaped.
pallets the feather-like structures attached to the rear of some boring bivalves; and used to seal the entrance to the hole.
palps blunt sensory or manipulative appendages attached to the head.
papilla (pl. **papillae**) a small pimple-like process on the body surface.
papula (pl. **papulae**) a balloon-like extension of the echinoderm water vascular system that generally projects from the upper surface and is used for respiration.
parapodium (pl. **parapodia**) a side lobe that extends outwards from the foot of opisthobranchs or the body wall of polychaetes.
pectoral fins the paired fins attached to the sides of a fish behind the head.
pedicel tube-foot-like structure on the side of a holothurian.
pedicellaria a stalked, pincer-like structure projecting from the surface of asteroids and echinoids.
pelagic actively swimming.

pelvic fins (= **ventral fins**) the paired fins attached near the lower edge of a fish immediately behind the head.
perennial an organism that can survive for several years.
periostracum the thin, brown, protective layer formed on the outside of mollusc shells.
petals the flower-shaped system of grooves on the upper surface of heart-urchins and related echinoids.
petiole the small stalk attached at the base of leaves of some seagrass species.
photosynthesis the process by which light energy is used to synthesis complex organic molecules from carbon dioxide and water.
phototroph an organism (e.g. a plant) that utilises the energy of sunlight to synthesise organic chemicals.
phytoplankton small plants that drift in open water.
pinnule a small jointed appendage that extends from the side of the arm of a feather star.
plankton plants and animals that live in open water and are primarily transported by currents.
planula (pl. **planulae**) a mobile invertebrate larva that is small, flattened and covered by cilia.
pleopod a swimming or respiratory appendage that is located on the underside of crustaceans.
pleural region the low triangular area intermediate between the dorsal and lateral regions on the valve of a chiton.
polyp a cup-shaped animal that is usually attached at the base, with a row of tentacles surrounding the upper rim.
prokaryote a simple unicellular organism (e.g. bacteria) that has genetic material distributed within the cell as filaments rather than contained in a nucleus.
protoplasm the organic material within a cell.
pseudopodium (pl. **pseudopodia**) a temporary foot-like protrusion of the cell wall that is used to engulf particles or for locomotion.
radial shield a triangular structure on the upper disc of ophiuroids that is located in pairs near the base of each arm.
radula the replaceable teeth of molluscs; they are usually arranged in regular rows on a belt-like structure within the mouth.
ramuli a small branchlet that generally terminates algal branching.
receptacle a branch of an alga that bears reproductive organs.
rhinophore a protruding, tentacle-like structure located behind the eye on many opisthobranchs.
rhizoid a hair-like process that extends from the roots, rhizome or stolon of a plant.
rhizome an underground, horizontally spreading stem of a plant.
rostrum a projection that extends forward from the head between the eyes.
sclerite a calcareous structure that provides internal skeletal support.
septum (pl. **septa**) an internal partition of a cnidarian.
sessile attached to the seabed.
seta (pl. **setae**) a bristle projecting from the body wall of annelid worms.
siliceous composed of silica (silicon dioxide), the material of glass.
siphonal canal the groove extending away from the aperture and which contains the siphon.
spicule a calcareous or siliceous structure that provides internal support to an animal.
spire the pointed section of a gastropod shell that lies above the aperture.
spongin a fibrous protein that is used as skeletal material in sponges.
spore a single-celled product of reproduction that can divide and develop into a new individual.
stipe an unbranched section of a macroalga that connects the holdfast to the frond.
stolon the runner of a seagrass plant or cnidarian; it extends along the seabed, connecting leaf clusters or polyps.
supero-marginal plates the large plates that lie along the upper outer edge of seastar arms.
symbiosis a relationship between two organisms that results in mutual benefit.
tabula (pl. **tabulae**) a rounded, table-shaped plate on the upper surface of seastars.
telson the remnant of a segment located at the rear of the abdomen of some crustaceans.
test the outer shell of an echinoid or foraminiferan.
thallus (pl. **thalli**) the body of a plant.
thorax the central section of an arthropod body; it consists of several segments behind the head and in front of the abdomen.
tube foot an external extension of the water vascular system of echinoderms, generally located in a row and terminating in a suction disc.
tubercle small wart-shaped projection on the surface of an animal.
tunic a tough outer covering over the body of ascidians.
umbone (= **umbo**) the apex of a bivalve shell near the hinge.
uropod one of the paired appendages extending from the last segment of isopods or the last three segments of amphipods.
utricle a small, sausage-shaped structure that is generally compacted with others to form the plant surface of *Codium* and related green algae.
valve the shell of a brachiopod, chiton or bivalve.
ventral fins (= **pelvic fins**) the paired fins attached near the lower edge of the body immediately behind the head.
vertebrate an animal possessing a backbone.
vesicle a bubble-like structure such as the float on an alga.
water vascular system a water-filled system of tubes that is used for respiration, locomotion and excretion in echinoderms.
zooid an individual unit that is the basic building block of a bryozoan or ascidian colony.
zooplankton small animals that drift in open water.

Selected bibliography

Although most of the large plants and animals that are commonly noticed in southern Australian waters are described in this book, these species comprise only a small proportion of the total species in the area. For a number of groups, such as sponges, hydroids and polychaetes, only a few representative species have been included here. The following books or articles should be consulted for accurate species identification; however, even using these publications, an unsatisfactorily large number of animal species remain unstudied and unnamed. Many of the scientific names used in the older publications listed below are outdated and will therefore differ from the names provided in the text.

BACTERIA

The definitive publication that covers the identification of bacteria using traditional Linnaean methods is Holt (1984), while Cropp & Garland (1988) describe methods and a scheme for identifying marine species.

Cropp, C.M. & C.D. Garland (1988) A scheme for the identification of marine bacteria. Australian Microbiologist Vol. 9, pp 27-34.

Holt, J.G. (1984) Bergey's Manual of Systematic Bacteriology. 4 vols. Williams & Wilkins, Baltimore.

PROTISTS

Amoebas, ciliates

The amoebas and ciliates have not been studied in any detail in southern Australia. Most species in these groups are widely distributed worldwide, so the publications of Boror (1973), Bovee & Sawyer (1979), Lee *et al.* (1985) and Carey (1991) are useful for placing local animals into genera, and Capriulo (1990) lists a number of relevant taxonomic papers.

Foraminiferans

Illustrated guides to common local species of foram are provided by McKenzie (1962) and Albani (1979), while an older publication illustrating foraminiferan genera worldwide by Cushman (1933) remains useful.

Unicellular algae

The taxonomic literature on unicellular algae is large and dispersed. Clayton & King (1990) and Capriulo (1990) provide information on the various divisions of unicellular algae and list important publications that should be consulted to access more specific literature.

Benthic algae

The comprehensive volumes produced by Womersley are the major references for identifying green algae (Womersley, 1984), brown algae (Womersley, 1987) and many of the larger red algae (Womersley, 1994). Unfortunately, this series remains to be completed, with two further volumes on red algae pending. For identification of these groups it is necessary to consult Kraft & Woelkerling (1990) for a list of scientific papers with recent information on the taxonomy of different red algal genera. Womersley's monographs omit Western Australian and New South Wales species that do not reach the south coast. Useful references for these areas are Huisman & Walker (1990), Farrant & King (1989) and Millar & Kraft (1993). Identification of nongeniculate coralline algae requires Woelkerling (1988). Fuhrer *et al.* (1981) provide a photographic guide to about 150 common benthic species.

Albani, A.D. (1979) Recent shallow water Foraminiferida from New South Wales. Australian Marine Sciences Association Handbook no. 3, pp. 1–51.

Borror, A.C. (1973) Marine flora and fauna of the Northeastern United States. Protozoa: Ciliophora. NOAA Technical Report NMFS Circular, vol. 378, pp. 1–62.

Bovee, E.C. & T.K.Sawyer (1979) Marine flora and fauna of the Northeastern United States. Protozoa: Sarcodina: Amoeba. NOAA Technical Report NMFS Circular, vol. 419, pp. 1–57.

Capriulo, G.M. (1990) Ecology of Marine Protozoa. Oxford University Press, New York.

Carey, P. (1991) Marine Interstitial Ciliates: An Illustrated Key. Chapman & Hall, London.

Clayton, M.N. & R.J. King (1990) Biology of Marine Plants. Longman Cheshire, Melbourne.

Cushman, J.A. (1933) An illustrated key to the genera of the Foraminifera. Cushman Laboratory for Foraminiferal Research, Special Publication no. 5, Sharon, Mass.

Farrant, P.A. & R.J. King (1989) The Dictyotales (Algae: Phaeophyta) of New South Wales. Proceedings of the Linnean Society of New South Wales, vol. 110 (4), pp. 369–406.

Fuhrer, B., I.G. Christianson, M.N. Clayton & B.M. Allender (1981) Seaweeds of Australia. Reed, Sydney.

Huisman, J.M. & D.I. Walker (1990) A catalogue of the marine plants of Rottnest Island, Western Australia, with notes on their distribution and biogeography. Kingia, vol. 1, pp. 349–459.

Lee, J.J., S.H.Hutner & E.C. Bovee (1985) An Illustrated Guide to the Protozoa. Society of Protozoologists and Allen Press, Lawrence, Kansas.

McKenzie, K.G. (1962) A record of the Foraminifera from Oyster Harbour, near Albany, Western Australia. Journal of the Royal Society of Western Australia, vol. 45, pp. 117–132.

Millar, A.J.K. & G.T. Kraft (1993) Catalogue of marine and freshwater red algae (Rhodophyta) of New South Wales, including Lord Howe Island, south-western Pacific. Australian Systematic Botany, vol. 6, pp. 1–90.

Woelkerling, W.J. (1988) The Coralline Red Algae: An Analysis of Genera and Subfamilies of Nongeniculate Corallinaceae. British Museum (Natural History), Oxford University Press, London.

Womersley, H.B.S. (1984) The Marine Benthic Flora of Southern Australia. Part I. Government Printer, Adelaide.

Womersley, H.B.S. (1987) The Marine Benthic Flora of Southern Australia. Part II. Government Printer, Adelaide.

Womersley, H.B.S. (1994) The Marine Benthic Flora of Southern Australia. Part IIIA. Australian Biological Resources Study, Canberra.

FUNGI

The taxonomy of marine fungi is described by Kohlmeyer & Kohlmeyer (1979) and Moss (1986), while Austin (1988) lists all genera of fungi, including yeasts, which have been recorded from the marine environment.

Austin, B. (1988) Marine Microbiology. Cambridge University Press, Cambridge.

Kohlmeyer, J. & E. Kohlmeyer (1979) Marine Mycology: The Higher Fungi. Academic Press, New York.

Moss, S.T. (1986) The Biology of Marine Fungi. Cambridge University Press, Cambridge.

LICHENS

Lichens on temperate Australian shores have never been studied as a group. Identifying species in many common genera (e.g. *Caloplaca*) is a taxonomic nightmare as it requires wading through the dispersed primary literature, which contains many synonyms and cosmopolitan taxa. Filson (1988) provides a checklist of Australian lichen species. Keys are provided by Rogers (1992) which allow the identification of lichens to genera.

Filson, R.B. (1988) Checklist of Australian Lichens. 3rd edition. National Herbarium of Victoria, Melbourne.

Rogers, R.W. (1992) Keys to Australian lichen genera. Flora of Australia, vol. 54, pp. 65–94.

SEAGRASSES

A complete key to Australian seagrasses and discussion of seagrass taxonomy is provided by Kuo & McComb (1989). Robertson (1984) gives detailed information on many southern Australian species; however, a number of additional species have been described since 1984. Aston (1973) and Lanyon (1986) are helpful for identifying tropical species that extend south.

Aston, H.I. (1973) Aquatic Plants of Australia. Melbourne University Press, Melbourne.

Kuo, J. & A.J. McComb (1989) Seagrass taxonomy, structure and development. pp. 6–73, in Biology of Seagrasses: A Treatise on the Biology of Seagrasses with Special Reference to the Australian Region, A.W.D. Larkum, A.J. McComb & S.A. Shepherd (eds), Elsevier, Amsterdam.

Lanyon, J. (1986) Seagrasses of the Great Barrier Reef. Great Barrier Reef Marine Park Authority, Townsville.

Robertson, E.L. (1984) Seagrasses. pp. 57–122, in The Marine Benthic Flora of Southern Australia. Part I, H.B.S. Womersley (ed.), Government Printer, Adelaide.

SALTMARSH PLANTS

Bridgewater *et al.* (1981) provide the only publication dealing collectively with Australian saltmarsh plants.

Bridgewater, P.B., C. Rosser & A. de Corona (1981) The Saltmarsh Plants of Southern Australia. Monash University, Melbourne.

SPONGES

The major source of information on southern Australian sponges is the recent catalogue by Hooper & Wiedenmayer (1994). An overview of the genera of sponges found in this region is given by Bergquist & Skinner (1982), with many of these diagnoses expanded in Bergquist (1978). The only recent paper describing the sponge fauna in a particular area (Bass Strait) is Wiedenmayer (1989), while Bergquist & Kelly-Borges (1991) describe several of the local *Tethya* species.

Bergquist, P.R & I.G. Skinner (1982) Sponges. pp. 38–72, in Marine Invertebrates of Southern Australia. Part I, S.A. Shepherd & I.M. Thomas (eds), Government Printer, Adelaide.

Bergquist, P.R. (1978) Sponges. Hutchinson, London.

Bergquist, P.R. & M. Kelly-Borges (1991) An evaluation of the genus *Tethya* (Porifera: Demospongiae) with descriptions of new species from the southwest Pacific. Beagle, vol. 8, pp. 37–72.

Hooper, J.N.A. & F. Wiedenmayer (1994) Zoological Catalogue of Australia. vol. 12. Porifera. CSIRO, Melbourne.

Wiedenmayer, F. (1989) Demospongiae (Porifera) from northern Bass Strait, southern Australia. Memoirs of the Museum of Victoria, vol. 50, pp. 1–242.

CNIDARIANS

Hydrozoans

The best general coverage of hydroids is Watson (1982), with older papers on Tasmanian hydroids by Hodgson (1950) and Watson (1956) also useful as they include many widely distributed species.

Anthozoans

Much of the southern Australian anthozoan fauna remains undescribed, including a number of common anemones, soft corals and gorgonians. The only overview of the group are the chapters in Shepherd (1982), although caution should be used when identifying gorgonians as many of the species listed by Grasshoff (1982) do not occur in this region. Older scientific papers of relevance are Carlgren (1949, 1950, 1954), Cutress (1971) and Verseveldt (1977), while Cairns & Parker (1992) provide a comprehensive coverage of the temperate scleractinian corals and Carter (1995) recently described new ceriantharians.

Scyphozoans

Southcott (1982) includes descriptions and diagrams of virtually all of the common southern Australian scyphozoan species, with many of these species also included in Kramp (1965). The most comprehensive descriptions of scyphozoans worldwide are found in Mayer (1910) and Kramp (1961), with the first of these publications containing beautiful illustrations of hundreds of species.

Cairns, S.D. & S.A. Parker (1992) Review of the Recent Scleractinia (stony corals) of South Australia, Victoria and Tasmania. Records of the South Australian Museum, vol. 3, pp. 1–82.

Carlgren, O. (1949) A survey of the Ptychodactiaria, Corallimorpharia and Actiniaria. Kunglica Svenska Vetenskapsakademiens Handlingar Ser. 4, vol. 1, pp. 1–121.

Carlgren, O. (1950) Actiniaria and zoantharia from South Australia. Kunglica Fysiografiska Sällskapets i Lund Förhandlingar, vol. 20, pp. 1–15.

Carlgren, O. (1954) Actiniaria and zoantharia from south and west Australia with comments upon some Axiniaria from New Zealand. Archiv für Zoologi, vol. 6, pp. 571–595.

Carter, S. (1995) *Pachycerianthus* (Anthozoa: Ceriantharia: Cerianthidae), two newly described species from Port Jackson, Australia. Records of the Australian Museum, Vol. 47, pp. 1-6.

Cutress, C.E. (1971) Corallimorpharia, Actiniaria and Zoanthidea. Memoirs of the National Museum of Victoria, vol. 32, pp. 83–92.

Grasshoff, M. (1982) Gorgonians or sea fans (Order Gorgonacea). pp. 198–207, in Marine Invertebrates of Southern Australia. Part I, S.A. Shepherd & I.M. Thomas (eds), Government Printer, Adelaide.

Hodgson, M. (1950) A revision of the Tasmanian Hydroida. Papers and Proceedings of the Royal Society of Tasmania, vol. 1949, pp. 1–65.

Kramp, P.L. (1961) Synopsis of the medusae of the world. Journal of the Marine Biological Association of the United Kingdom, vol. 40, pp. 1–469.

Kramp, P.L. (1965) Some medusae (mainly Scyphomedusae) from Australian coastal waters. Transactions of the Royal Society of South Australia, vol. 89, pp. 257–278.

Mayer, A.G. (1910) Medusae of the World. Carnegie Institute, Washington, DC.

Southcott, R.V. (1982) Jellyfishes (Classes Scyphozoa and Hydrozoa). pp. 115–159, in Marine Invertebrates of Southern Australia. Part I, S.A. Shepherd & I.M. Thomas (eds), Government Printer, Adelaide.

Verseveldt, J. (1977) Australian Octocorallia. Australian Journal of Marine and Freshwater Research, vol. 28, pp. 171–240.

Watson, J.E. (1956) Hydroids of Bruny Island, southern Tasmania. Transactions of the Royal Society of South Australia, vol. 99, pp. 157–176.

Watson, J.E. (1982) Hydroids (Class Hydrozoa). pp. 77–114, in Marine Invertebrates of Southern Australia. Part I, S.A. Shepherd & I.M. Thomas (eds), Government Printer, Adelaide.

CTENOPHORES

The only publication that includes local ctenophores is O'Sullivan (1986), which illustrates most species recorded from the Southern Ocean. The most useful publications dealing with ctenophores overseas are Moser (1903), Mayer (1912) and Ralph (1949).

Mayer, A.G. (1912) Ctenophores of the Atlantic Coast of North America. Carnegie Institute, Washington, DC.

Moser (1903) Ctenophoren der Deutscher Südpolar-Expedition. Deutscher Südpolar-Expedition, vol. 11, pp. 1–192.

O'Sullivan, D.O.S. (1986) A guide to the Ctenophores of the Southern Ocean and adjacent waters. ANARE Research Notes, vol. 36, pp. 1–43.

Ralph, P.M. (1949) Ctenophores from the waters of Cook Strait and Wellington Harbour. Transactions of the Royal Society of New Zealand, vol. 78, pp. 70–82.

PLATYHELMINTHS

The more important guides to identifying tubellarian, triclad and polyclad platyhelminths are Cannon (1986), Sluys (1989), Sluys & Ball (1989) and Prudhoe (1982a,b), with Faubel *et al.* (1994) listing papers in which free-living Australian species are described.

Cannon, L.R.G. (1986) Turbellaria of the World: A Guide to Families and Genera. Queensland Museum, Brisbane.

Faubel, A., D. Blome & L.R.G. Cannon (1994) Sandy beach meiofauna of eastern Australia (southern Queensland and New South Wales). I. Introduction and Macrostomida (Platyhelminthes). Invertebrate Taxonomy, vol. 8, pp. 989–1007.

Prudhoe, S. (1982a) Polyclad flatworms (Phylum Platyhelminthes). pp. 220–227, in Marine Invertebrates of Southern Australia. Part I, S.A. Shepherd & I.M. Thomas (eds), Government Printer, Adelaide.

Prudhoe, S. (1982b) Polyclad turbellarians from the southern coasts of Australia. Records of the South Australian Museum, vol. 18, pp. 361–384.

Sluys, R. (1989) A Monograph of the Marine Triclads. Balkema, Rotterdam.

Sluys, R. & I.R. Ball (1989) A synopsis of the marine triclads of Australia and New Zealand. Invertebrate Taxonomy, vol. 2, pp. 915–959.

NEMERTEANS

The only recent publication dealing with several species of southern Australian nemerteans is Gibson (1990). Gibson (1972) provides an overview of the families and Gibson (1995) lists all known species..

Gibson, R. (1972) Nemerteans. Hutchinson, London.

Gibson, R. (1990) The macrobenthic nemertean fauna of the Albany region, Western Australia. pp. 89–194, in Proceedings of the Third International Marine Biological Workshop: The Marine Flora and Fauna of Albany, Western Australia, F.E. Wells, D.I. Walker, H. Kirkman & R. Lethbridge (eds), Western Australian Museum, Perth.

Gibson, R. (1995) Nemertean genera and species of the world: an annotated checklist of orginal names and description citations, synonyms, current taxonomic status, habitats and recorded zoogeographic distribution. Journal of Natural History, vol. 29, pp. 271 62.

NEMATODES

Very little material is available to aid in the identification of marine nematodes. The best publications for placing nematodes into genera are Platt & Warwick (1983, 1988). These two manuals form a series, with the concluding volume due to be released in 1995. A checklist of Australian marine nematodes is provided by Greenslade (1989), with more recent species descriptions listed in Faubel *et al.* (1994; see Platyhelminths).

Greenslade, P. (1989) Checklist of free-living nematodes from Australia, Macquarie Island and Heard Island. Records of the South Australian Museum, vol. 23, pp. 7–19.

Platt, H.M. & R.M. Warwick (1983) Free living marine nematodes. Part I, British enoplids. Synopses of the British Fauna (New Series). no. 28. Cambridge University Press, Cambridge.

Platt, H.M. & R.M. Warwick (1988) Free living marine nematodes. Part II, British chromadorids. Synopses of the British Fauna (New Series). no. 38. Cambridge University Press, Cambridge.

ANNELIDS

Oligochaetes, leeches

Substantive regional accounts of southern Australian marine oligochaetes are provided in the recent studies of Erséus (1990a, b, 1993), Coates (1990) and Coates & Stacey (1993). No recent local study of marine leeches has been undertaken.

Polychaetes

The authoritative if slightly outdated guide to placing the world's polychaetes into genera is Fauchald (1977). The two-volume monograph of Day (1967) on South African polychaetes contains numerous illustrations and is very helpful for identifying local polychaetes to genera; however, this work has limited value for determining species names because many species considered by Day to be distributed worldwide are now thought to have much more localised distributions. The only local publication with a broad coverage of polychaetes is Hutchings (1982); this provides diagnoses of polychaete families but was not intended for general species identification as relatively few species are included. Day & Hutchins (1979) produced a checklist of all Australian species known up to that time, but many of the species included in the checklist are questionable as they relate to overseas species that were once thought to have worldwide distributions. A number of recent papers on families and genera in Australia are scattered through the scientific literature (e.g., Knight-Jones *et al.*, 1974; Rainer & Hutchings, 1977; Hutchings & Turvey, 1982; Hutchings, 1984; Hutchings & McRae, 1993), while Hutchings & Murray (1984) describe a large proportion of the estuarine New South Wales species and also provide an extensive bibliography.

Coates, K.A. (1990) Marine Enchytraeidae (Oligochaeta) of the Albany area, Western Australia. pp. 13–42, in Proceedings of the Third International Marine Biological Workshop: The Marine Flora and Fauna of Albany, Western Australia, F.E. Wells, D.I. Walker, H. Kirkman & R. Lethbridge (eds), Western Australian Museum, Perth.

Coates, K.A. & D.F. Stacey (1993) The marine Enchytraetidae (Oligochaeta, Annelida) of Rottnest Island, Western Australia. pp. 391–414, in Proceedings of the Fifth International Marine Biological Workshop: The Marine Flora and Fauna of Rottnest Island, Western Australia, F.E. Wells, D.I. Walker, H. Kirkman & R. Lethbridge (eds), Western Australian Museum, Perth.

Day, J.H. (1967) A Monograph of the Polychaetes of Southern Africa. Part I, Errantia. Part 2, Sedentaria. British Museum, London.

Day, J.H. & P.A. Hutchings (1979) An annotated checklist of Australian and New Zealand Polychaeta, Archiannelida and Myzostomidae. Records of the Australian Museum, vol. 32, pp. 80–161.
Erséus, C. (1990a) Marine Tubificidae (Oligochaeta) of Victoria, Australia, with descriptions of six new species. Memoirs of the Museum of Victoria, vol. 50, pp. 275–285.
Erséus, C. (1990b) The marine Tubificidae and Naididae (Oligochaeta) of south-western Australia. pp. 43–88, in Proceedings of the Third International Marine Biological Workshop: The Marine Flora and Fauna of Albany, Western Australia, F.E. Wells, D.I. Walker, H. Kirkman & R. Lethbridge (eds), Western Australian Museum, Perth.
Erséus, C. (1993) The marine Tubificidae (Oligochaeta) of Rottnest Island, Western Australia. pp. 331–390, in Proceedings of the Fifth International Marine Biological Workshop: The Marine Flora and Fauna of Rottnest Island, Western Australia, F.E. Wells, D.I. Walker, H. Kirkman & R. Lethbridge (eds), Western Australian Museum, Perth.
Fauchald, K. (1977) The polychaete worms: Definitions and keys to the orders, families and genera. Natural History Museum of Los Angeles, Science Series, vol. 28, pp. 1–188.
Hutchings, P.A. (1982) Bristleworms (Phylum Annelida). pp. 228–298, in Marine Invertebrates of Southern Australia. Part I, S.A. Shepherd & I.M. Thomas (eds), Government Printer, Adelaide.
Hutchings, P.A. (1984) The Spionidae of South Australia (Annelida: Polychaeta). Transactions of the Royal Society of South Australia, vol. 108, pp. 1–20.
Hutchings, P.A. & J. McRae (1993) The Aphroditidae (Polychaeta) from Australia, together with a redescription of the Aphroditidae collected during the Siboga Expedition. Records of the Australian Museum, vol. 45, pp. 279–363.
Hutchings, P.A. & A. Murray (1984) Taxonomy of polychaetes from the Hawkesbury River and the southern estuaries of New South Wales, Australia. Records of the Australian Museum Supplement, vol. 3, pp. 1–118.
Hutchings, P.A. & S.P. Turvey (1982) The Nereididae of South Australia. Transactions of the Royal Society of South Australia, vol. 106, pp. 93–144.
Knight-Jones, E.W., P. Knight-Jones & L.C. Llewellyn (1974) Spirorbinae (Polychaeta: Serpulidae) from southeastern Australia: notes on their taxonomy, ecology and distribution. Records of the Australian Museum, vol. 29, pp. 107–151.
Rainer, S.F. & P.A. Hutchings (1977) Nephtyidae (Polychaeta: Errantia) from Australia. Records of the Australian Museum, vol. 31 (8), pp. 307–347.

SIPUNCULANS, ECHIURANS

These two phyla have been unusually well studied in southern Australian waters, thanks to the research of Edmonds (1980, 1982a, b) and Stephen & Edmonds (1972).

Edmonds, S.J. (1980) A revision of the systematics of Australian sipunculans (Sipuncula). Records of the South Australian Museum, vol. 18, pp. 1–74.
Edmonds, S.J. (1982a) Sipunculans (Phylum Sipuncula). pp. 299–311, in Marine Invertebrates of Southern Australia. Part I, S.A. Shepherd & I.M. Thomas (eds), Government Printer, Adelaide.
Edmonds, S.J. (1982b) Echiurans (Phylum Echiura). pp. 312–318, in Marine Invertebrates of Southern Australia. Part I, S.A. Shepherd & I.M. Thomas (eds), Government Printer, Adelaide.
Stephen, A.C. & S.J. Edmonds (1972) The Phyla Sipuncula and Echiura. Trustees of the British Museum (Natural History), London.

PYCNOGONIDS

The only major revision of Australian pycnogonids is an outdated publication by Clark (1963). Higher order systematics and a key to the families are included in King (1973).

Clark, W.C. (1963) Australian Pycnogonida. Records of the Australian Museum, vol. 26, pp. 1–81.
King, P.E. (1973) Pycnogonids. Hutchinson, London.

MITES

Bartsch (1993a, b, c) provides the only substantive taxonomic account of southern Australian halacarid mites. The publication of Balogh & Balogh (1992) is widely used to place oribatid mites into genera, although this work has some deficiencies (see Hunt, 1994).

Balogh, J. & P. Balogh (1992) The Orabatid Mites Genera of the World, vols I and II. Hungarian Natural History Museum, Budapest.
Bartsch, I. (1993) Arenicolous Halacaridae (Acari) from south-western Australia. pp. 73–103, in Proceedings of the Fifth International Marine Biological Workshop: The Marine Flora and Fauna of Rottnest Island, Western Australia, F.E. Wells, D.I. Walker, H. Kirkman & R. Lethbridge (eds), Western Australian Museum, Perth.
Bartsch, I. (1993) *Halacarus* (Halicaridae, Acari) from south-western Australia. pp. 45–71, in Proceedings of the Fifth International Marine Biological Workshop: The Marine Flora and Fauna of Rottnest Island, Western Australia, F.E. Wells, D.I. Walker, H. Kirkman & R. Lethbridge (eds), Western Australian Museum, Perth.
Bartsch, I. (1993) Rhombognathine mites (Halicaridae, Acari) from Rottnest Island, Western Australia. pp. 19–43, in Proceedings of the Fifth International Marine Biological Workshop: The Marine Flora and Fauna of Rottnest Island, Western Australia, F.E. Wells, D.I. Walker, H. Kirkman & R. Lethbridge (eds), Western Australian Museum, Perth.
Hunt, G.S. (1994) Orabatids: a mite biodiverse (Acarina). Memoirs of the Queensland Museum, vol. 36, pp. 107–114.

INSECTS

The comprehensive guide to Australian insects is CSIRO (1991). A wordwide review of the various marine insect groups is provided by Cheng (1976).

Cheng, L. (1976) Marine Insects. North-Holland Publishing Company, Amsterdam.
CSIRO (1991) The Insects of Australia. 2 vols. Melbourne University Press, Melbourne.

CRUSTACEANS

The two general guides to crustaceans are Hale (1927–29) and Jones & Morgan (1994). Both have limitations when used to identify local species: Hale (1927–29) because of its age and the exclusion of barnacles, cladocerans and copepods, and Jones & Morgan (1994) because most of the examples used are tropical species. Jones & Morgan (1993) have produced a useful checklist of Rottnest Island crustaceans, many of them widely distributed in southern Australia.

Cladocerans

Smirnov & Timms (1983) describe all of the known Australian cladoceran species; however, relatively few of these are marine.

Barnacles

A checklist of Australian barnacle species is provided by Jones *et al.* (1990), while comprehensive regional descriptions of species are contained in Jones (1990, 1993). A key to species in the *Elminius* complex is provided by Bayliss (1994).

Calanoid and cyclopoid copepods
Regional illustrated guides to temperate planktonic copepods have been published for New South Wales (Dakin & Colefax, 1940), eastern Tasmania (Nyan Taw, 1978) and Bass Strait (Watson & Chaloupka, 1982).

Harpacticoid copepods
Very few southern Australian harpacticoid copepods have been described. The most useful manual for placing harpacticoid copepods into genera was published by Wells (1976). The standard illustrated reference is the classic monograph of Lang (1948).

Parasitic copepods
No guide is available for identifying local parasitic copepods; however, nearly all can be placed into genera using the publications of Kabata (1992) and Gotto (1993).

Ostracods
The majority of temperate ostracod species remain undescribed and unknown. The most comprehensive illustrated accounts of local shallow-water species are McKenzie (1967), Yassini & Wright (1988) and Yassini & Jones (1995).

Stomatopods
Virtually all known temperate Australian stomatopod species are included in Hale (1927–29). A recent key to the world's genera was published by Manning (1980).

Cumaceans
Herbert Hale published a large and comprehensive series of papers on Australian cumaceans in the Transactions of the Royal Society of South Australia (see, for example, Hale, 1953) and the Records of the South Australian Museum (see, for example, Hale, 1945).

Tanaids
The taxonomy of temperate tanaids is a mess, with the exception of species in the Tanaidae, an important family revised by Sieg (1980). Genera in the other abundant tanaidomorph family, Leptocheliidae, are discussed by Lang (1973). Sieg (1993) lists apseudomorph tanaids recorded from Australian waters, with all relevant references; however, only four of these are shallow-water temperate species.

Mysids
Most local mysids have been included in the unpublished thesis of Fenton (1985), while Mauchline (1980) reviews information on species worldwide.

Isopods
The ancient monograph of Hale (1927–29) remains the most useful publication for identifying isopod species, although many of the genera have since changed. Three of the most important isopod families, the Cirolanidae, Limnoriidae and Idoteidae, have been recently revised by Bruce (1986), Cookson (1990) and Poore & Lew Ton (1993), respectively, while Harrison & Ellis (1991) provide a key to the genera of Sphaeromatidae, the largest local family.

Amphipods
Identification of gammaridean amphipods firstly requires placing the specimen into family and genus using the worldwide monograph of Barnard & Karaman (1991). This work also lists all species known at that time, and provides a comprehensive bibliography. Many Australian families and genera have been revised in recent years, with the more substantial of these studies being Barnard (1972, 1974), Barnard & Drummond (1978, 1979, 1982), Moore (1981, 1987), Myers & Moore (1983), Lowry & Poore (1985) and Myers (1988). Hyperiid amphipods have been recently investigated by Zeidler (1992), and older keys to hyperiid families and genera are provided by Bowman & Gruner (1973). Few caprellid amphipods have been described from southern Australia. Guiler (1954) illustrates nine caprellid species, although several of the names he uses are not now appropriate. The most useful illustrated work on caprellids worldwide is a Japanese monograph (Arimoto, 1976).

Euphausids
Euphausids are best identified using Baker *et al.* (1990), Dakin & Colefax (1940) and Nyan Taw (1978).

Shrimps, prawns
All known inshore Australian species of penaeid prawn are illustrated and described in Grey *et al.* (1983). Carid shrimps are less comprehensively covered, with Hale (1927–29) remaining the major illustrated reference for this group (although many of the genera have now changed). The other important local publication on carid shrimps is Wadley (1978), a study of Moreton Bay species but which also contains illustrations of many temperate animals. The comprehensive monograph for identifying carid shrimp to genera is Holthuis (1993), with the older work of Burukovsky (1983) still useful. Temperate alpheid and thalassinid shrimps are well described and illustrated in the publications of Banner & Banner (1982), Poore & Griffin (1979) and Poore (1994).

Anomuran and brachyuran crabs
Nearly all temperate crabs can be reliably identified using Hale (1927–29), Griffin & Yaldwyn (1971) and Marine Research Group of Victoria (1984). The major deficiency with these works is the hermit crabs, many of which have been described only recently (see Morgan, 1989, 1993). Important papers on particular crab families are Tyndale-Biscoe & George (1962) on leucosiids, Griffin (1966) and Griffin & Tranter (1986) on majids, Lucas (1980) on hymenosomatids, Stephenson (1972) on portunids, and Griffin (1966) on grapsids and ocypodids. A useful checklist of temperate Western Australian decapods has also been collated by Morgan & Jones (1990).

Arimoto, I. (1976) Taxonomic studies of caprellids (Crustacea, Amphipoda, Caprellidae) found in the Japanese and adjacent waters. Seto Marine Biological Laboratory, Special Publications Series III, pp. 1–229.

Baker, A.C., B.P. Boden & E. Brinton (1990) A Practical Guide to the Euphausiids of the World. Natural History Museum Publications, London.

Banner, D.M. & A.H. Banner (1982) The alpheid shrimp of Australia. Part III: the remaining alpheids, principally in the genus *Alpheus*, and the family Ogyrididae. Records of the Australian Museum, vol. 34, pp. 1–357.

Barnard, J.L. (1972) Gammaridean Amphipoda of Australia, Part I. Smithsonian Contributions to Zoology, vol. 103, pp. 1–333.

Barnard, J.L. (1974) Gammaridean Amphipoda of Australia, Part V: Superfamily Haustoriodea. Smithsonian Contributions to Zoology, vol. 139, pp. 1–148.

Barnard, J.L. & M.M. Drummond (1978) Gammaridean Amphipoda of Australia, Part III: The Phoxocephalidae. Smithsonian Contributions to Zoology, vol. 245, pp. 1–551.

Barnard, J.L. & M.M. Drummond (1979) Gammaridean Amphipoda of Australia, Part IV. Smithsonian Contributions to Zoology, vol. 269, pp. 1–69.

Barnard, J.L. & M.M. Drummond (1982) Gammaridean Amphipoda of Australia, Part V: Superfamily Haustoriodea. Smithsonian Contributions to Zoology, vol. 360, pp. 1–148.

Barnard, J.L. & G.S. Karaman (1991) The families and genera of marine gammaridean Amphipoda. Records of the Australian Museum Supplement, vol. 13, pp. 1–866.
Bayliss, D.E. (1994) Description of three new barnacles of the genus *Elminius* (Cirripedia: Thoracica) from South Australia, with a key to species of the Elminiidae. Transactions of the Royal Society of South Australia, vol. 118, pp. 115–124.
Bowman, T.E. & H.E. Gruner (1973) The families and genera of Hyperiidea (Crustacea- Amphipoda). Smithsonian Contributions to Zoology, vol. 146, pp. 1–64.
Bruce, N. (1986) Cirolanidae (Crustacea: Isopoda) of Australia. Records of the Australian Museum Supplement, vol. 6, pp. 1–239.
Burukovsky, R.N. (1983) Key to Shrimps and Lobsters. Russian Translation Series 5. Balkema, Rotterdam.
Cookson, L.J. (1990) Australasian species of Limnoriidae (Crustacea: Isopoda). Memoirs of the Museum of Victoria, vol. 52, pp. 137–262.
Dakin, W.J. & A.N. Colefax (1940) The plankton of the Australian coastal waters off New South Wales. Monograph. Department of Zoology, University of Sydney, vol. 1, pp. 1–215.
Fenton, G.E. (1985) Ecology and taxonomy of mysids (Mysidacea: Crustacea). Ph.D. Thesis, University of Tasmania.
Gotto, V. (1993) Commensal and parasitic copepods associated with marine invertebrates (and whales). Synopses of the British Fauna (New Series), no. 46. Cambridge University Press, Cambridge.
Grey, D.L., W. Dall & A. Baker (1983) A Guide to the Australian Penaeid Prawns. Northern Territory Printing Office, Darwin.
Griffin, D.J.G. (1966) A review of the Australian majid spider crabs (Crustacea, Brachyura). Australian Zoologist, vol. 13, pp. 259–298.
Griffin, D.J.G. (1966) The taxonomy, ecology and social behaviour of the Tasmanian shore crabs (Crustacea, Brachyura) of the families Grapsidae and Ocypodidae. Ph.D. thesis, University of Tasmania.
Griffin, D.J.G. & H.A. Tranter (1986) The Decapoda Brachyura of the Siboga Expedition, Part VIII, Majidae. Siboga Expedition Monograph no. XXXIX, C4, pp. 1–112.
Griffin, D.J.G. & J.C. Yaldwyn (1971) Brachyura (Crustacea), Decapoda). Memoirs of the National Museum of Victoria, vol. 32, pp. 43–63.
Guiler, E.R. (1954) Some collections of caprellids from Tasmania. Annals and Magazine of Natural History, vol. 12, vii, pp. 531–553.
Hale, H.M. (1927–1929) The Crustaceans of South Australia. Parts I and II. Government Printer, Adelaide.
Hale, H.M. (1945) Australian Cumacea. no. 9 The family Nannastacidae. Records of the South Australian Museum no. VIII (2), pp. 145–218.
Hale, H.M. (1953) Australian Cumacea. no. 18. Notes on the distribution and collecting with artificial light. Transactions of the Royal Society of South Australia, vol. 76, pp. 70–76.
Harrison, K. & J.P. Ellis (1991) The genera of the Sphaeromatidae (Crustacea: Isopoda): a key and distribution list. Invertebrate Taxonomy, vol. 5, pp. 915–952.
Holthuis, L.B. (1993) The recent genera of the caridean and stenopodidean shrimps (Crustacea, Decapoda), with an appendix on the order Amphionidacea. Backhuys, Rotterdam.
Jones, D.S. (1990) The shallow-water barnacles (Cirripedia: Lepadomorpha, Balanomorpha) of southern Western Australia. pp. 333–437, in Proceedings of the Third International Marine Biological Workshop: The Marine Flora and Fauna of Albany, Western Australia, F.E. Wells, D.I. Walker, H. Kirkman & R. Lethbridge (eds), Western Australian Museum, Perth.
Jones, D.S. (1993) The barnacles of Rottnest Island, Western Australia, with descriptions of two new species. pp. 113–133, in Proceedings of the Fifth International Marine Biological Workshop: The Marine Flora and Fauna of Rottnest Island, Western Australia, F.E. Wells, D.I. Walker, H. Kirkman & R. Lethbridge (eds), Western Australian Museum, Perth.
Jones, D.S., J.T. Anderson & D.T. Anderson (1990) A checklist of the Australian Cirripedia. Technical Reports of the Australian Museum, vol. 3, pp. 1–38.
Jones, D.S. & G.J. Morgan (1993) An annotated checklist of Crustacea from Rottnest Island, Western Australia. pp. 135–162, in Proceedings of the Fifth International Marine Biological Workshop: The Marine Flora and Fauna of Rottnest Island, Western Australia, F.E. Wells, D.I. Walker, H. Kirkman & R. Lethbridge (eds), Western Australian Museum, Perth.
Jones, D.S. & G.J. Morgan (1994) A Field Guide to the Crustaceans of Australian Waters. Reed, Sydney.
Kabata, Z. (1992) Copepods parasitic on fishes: Keys and notes for the identification of species. Synopses of the British Fauna (New Series). no. 47. Cambridge University Press, Cambridge.
Lang, K. (1948) Monographie der Harpactiden. Lund, Sweden.
Lang, K. (1973) Taxonomische und phylogenetische Untersuchungen über die Tanaidaceen (Crustacea). 8. Die Gattungen *Leptochelia* Dana, *Paratanais* Dana, *Heterotanais* G.O. Sars und *Nototanais* Richardson. Dazu eininge Bemerkungen über die Monokonophora und ein Nachtrag. Zoologica Scripta, vol. 2, pp. 197–229.
Lowry, J.K. & G.C.B. Poore (1985) The ampeliscid amphipods of South-eastern Australia (Crustacea). Records of the Australian Museum, vol. 36, pp. 259–298.
Lucas, J.S. (1980) Spider crabs of the family Hymenosomatidae (Crustacea; Brachyura) with particular reference to Australian species: systematics and biology. Records of the Australian Museum, vol. 33 (4), pp. 148–257.
McKenzie, K.G. (1967) Recent Ostracoda from Port Phillip Bay, Victoria. Proceedings of the Royal Society of Victoria, vol. 80, pp. 61–106.
Manning, R. (1980) The superfamilies, families and genera of Recent stomatopod Crustacea, with diagnoses of six new families. Proceedings of the Biological Society of Washington, vol. 93, pp. 362–372.
Marine Research Group of Victoria (1984) Coastal Invertebrates of Victoria: An Atlas of Selected Species. Marine Research Group of Victoria in association with the Museum of Victoria, Melbourne.
Mauchline, J. (1980) The biology of mysids. Advances in Marine Biology, vol. 18, pp. 3–373.
Moore, P.G. (1981) Marine Amphipoda (Crustacea) new to science from the Tasmanian phytal fauna. Journal of Natural History, vol. 15, pp. 939–964.
Moore, P.G. (1987) Taxonomic studies on Tasmanian phytal amphipods (Crustacea): the families Anamixidae, Leucothoidae and Sebidae. Journal of Natural History, vol. 21, pp. 239–262.
Morgan, G.J. (1989) The hermit crabs (Decapoda: Anomura: Diogenidae, Paguridae) of southwestern Australia, with descriptions of two new species. Records of the Western Australian Museum, vol. 14, pp. 391–417.
Morgan, G.J. (1993) Three new species of *Pagurixus* (Crustacea, Decapoda, Paguridae) from Western Australia, with notes on other Australian species. pp. 163–181, in Proceedings of the Fifth International Marine Biological Workshop: The Marine Flora and Fauna of Rottnest Island, Western Australia, F.E. Wells, D.I. Walker, H. Kirkman & R. Lethbridge (eds), Western Australian Museum, Perth.
Morgan, G.J. & D.S. Jones (1990) Checklist of marine decapod Crustacea of southern Western Australia. pp. 483–497, in Proceedings of the Third International Marine Biological Workshop: The Marine Flora and Fauna of Albany, Western

Australia, F.E. Wells, D.I. Walker, H. Kirkman & R. Lethbridge (eds), Western Australian Museum, Perth.

Myers, A.A. (1988) The genera *Archaeobemlos* n.gen., *Bemlos* Shoemaker, *Protolembos* Myers and *Globosolembos* Myers (Amphipoda, Aoridae, Aorinae) from Australia. Records of the Australian Museum, vol. 40, pp. 265–332.

Myers, A.A. & P.G. Moore (1983) The New Zealand and SE Australian species of *Aora* Kröyer (Amphipoda, Gammaridea). Records of the Australian Museum, vol. 35, pp. 167–180.

Nyan Taw (1978) Some common components of the zooplankton of the south-eastern coastal waters of Tasmania. Papers and Proceedings of the Royal Society of Tasmania, vol. 112, pp. 69–136.

Poore, G.C.B. (1994) A phylogeny of the families of Thalassinidea (Crustacea: Decapoda) with keys to families and genera. Memoirs of the Museum of Victoria, vol. 54, pp. 79–120.

Poore, G.C.B. & D.J.G. Griffin (1979) The Thalassinidea (Crustacea: Decapoda) of Australia. Records of the Australian Museum, vol. 32 (6), pp. 217–321.

Poore, G.C.B. & H.M. Lew Ton (1993) Idoteidae of Australia and New Zealand (Crustacea: Isopoda: Valvifera). Invertebrate Taxonomy, vol. 7, pp. 197–278.

Sieg, J. (1980) Taxonomische Monographie der Tanaidae Dana, 1849 (Crustacea, Tanaidacea). Abhandlungen der Senckenbergischen Naturforschenden Gesellschaft, vol. 537, pp. 1–267.

Sieg, J. (1993) Remarks on the Tanaidacea (Crustacea: Isopoda) of Australia: on *Bilobatus crenulatus* gen. et sp. nov., from Port Darwin. Beagle, vol. 10, pp. 45–54.

Smirnov, N.N. & B.V. Timms (1983) A revision of the Australian Cladocera (Crustacea). Records of the Australian Museum Supplement, vol. 1, pp. 1–132.

Stephenson, W. (1972) An annotated checklist and key to the Indo-West Pacific swimming crabs (Crustacea: Decapoda: Portunidae). Royal Society of New Zealand Bulletin, vol. 10, pp. 1–64.

Tyndale-Biscoe, M. & R.W. George (1962) The Oxystomata and Gymnopleura (Crustacea, Brachyura) of Western Australia with descriptions of two new species from Western Australia and one from India. Journal of the Royal Society of Western Australia, vol. 45, pp. 65–96.

Wadley, V.A. (1978) A checklist and illustrated key to the epibenthic shrimps (Decapoda: Natantia) of Moreton Bay, Queensland. CSIRO Australia, Division of Fisheries and Oceanography Report, vol. 51, pp. 1–24.

Watson, G.F. & M.V. Chaloupka (1993) Zooplankton of Bass Strait: species composition, systematics and artificial key to species. Victorian Institute of Marine Sciences Technical Report no. 1, pp. 1–128.

Wells, J.B.J. (1976) Keys to Aid in the Identification of Marine Harpacticoid Copepods. Aberdeen University Press, UK.

Yassini, I. & A.J. Wright (1988) Distribution and ecology of Recent ostracodes from Port Hacking, New South Wales. Proceedings of the Linneological Society of New South Wales, vol. 110, pp. 159–174.

Zeidler, W. (1992) Hyperiid amphipods (Crustacea: Amphipoda: Hyperiidea) collected recently from eastern Australian waters. Records of the Australian Museum Supplement, vol. 44, pp. 85–133.

MOLLUSCS

Chitons

Worldwide classifications of chitons are provided by Kaas & van Belle (1980) and van Belle (1983). Southern Australian chitons are discussed and figured by Macpherson & Gabriel (1962), Cotton (1964), Marine Research Group of Victoria (1984) and Ludbrook & Gowlett-Holmes (1989); however, no substantive work on Western Australian or New South Wales chitons has been published since Iredale & Hull (1927). The numerous Australian species in the genus *Ischnochiton* were revised by Kaas & van Belle (1990).

Shelled gastropods

The megagastropod fauna of southern Australia is well covered by a number of recent publications (Wells & Bryce, 1986; Ludbrook & Gowlett-Holmes, 1989; Richmond, 1990, 1992; Wilson, 1993, 1994). The micromollusc fauna is primarily described in scientific journals and the older monographs of Macpherson & Gabriel (1962) and May (1958).

Opisthobranchs

The major publications describing and illustrating southern Australian opisthobranchs are Willan & Coleman (1984), Burn (1989) and Wells & Bryce (1993).

Bivalves

The best general guide to most of the families of bivalves is Lamprell & Whitehead (1992); Cotton (1961) describes the South Australian fauna but many of his names have since changed. Common bivalve species are included in several general works on molluscs: Macpherson & Gabriel (1962), Wells & Bryce (1986), Ludbrook & Gowlett-Holmes (1989) and Richmond (1990, 1992).

Cephalopods

The only recent general treatment of Austalian cephalopods is Zeidler & Norris (1989); however, the octopuses have been substantially revised since that time (see Stranks, 1990; Stranks & Norman, 1992). The most comprehensive worldwide monograph detailing cephalopod species is Nesis (1987).

Scaphopods, aplacophorans

No general works are available on these groups specific to southern Australia. Small sections on scaphopods are included in Macpherson & Gabriel (1962) and Wells & Bryce (1986), while Scheltema (1989) describes a number of southern Australian aplacophorans found in offshore waters.

van Belle, R.A. (1983) The systematic classification of the chitons (Mollusca: Polyplacophora). Informations Societe Belge de Malacologie no. XI, pp. 1–178.

Burn, R. (1989) Opisthobranchs (subclass Opisthobranchia). pp. 725–788, in Marine Invertebrates of Southern Australia. Part II, S.A. Shepherd & I.M. Thomas (eds), Government Printer, Adelaide.

Cotton, B.C. (1959) South Australian Mollusca. Archaeogastropoda. Government Printer, Adelaide.

Cotton, B.C. (1961) South Australian Mollusca. Pelycypoda. Government Printer, Adelaide.

Cotton, B.C. (1964) South Australian Mollusca. Chitons. Government Printer, Adelaide.

Iredale, T. & A.F.B. Hull (1927) A Monograph of the Australian Loricates. Royal Zoological Society of New South Wales, Sydney.

Kaas, P. & R.A. van Belle (1980) Catalogue of Living Chitons. Backhuys, Rotterdam.

Kaas, P. & R.A. van Belle (1990) Monograph of Living Chitons. vol. 4. Brill, Leiden.

Lamprell, K. & T. Whitehead (1992) Bivalves of Australia. Crawford House Press, Bathurst, NSW.

Ludbrook, N.H. & K.L. Gowlett-Holmes (1989) Chitons, gastropods and bivalves. pp. 504–724, in Marine Invertebrates of Southern Australia. Part II, S.A. Shepherd & I.M. Thomas (eds), Government Printer, Adelaide.

Macpherson, J.H. & C.J. Gabriel (1962) Marine Molluscs of Victoria. Melbourne University Press, Melbourne.

Marine Research Group of Victoria (1984) Coastal Invertebrates of Victoria: An Atlas of Selected Species. Marine Research Group of Victoria in association with the Museum of Victoria, Melbourne.

May, W.L. & J.H. Macpherson (1958) Illustrated Index of Shells. Tasmanian Government Printer, Hobart.

Nesis, K.N. (1987) Cephalopods of the World. TFH Publications, Neptune City, NJ.

Richmond, M.H. (1990) Tasmanian Seashells Common to Other States. Richmond Printers, Devonport.

Richmond, M.H. (1992) Tasmanian Seashells. vol. 2. Richmond Printers, Devonport.

Scheltema, A.H. (1989) Australian aplacophoran molluscs: I. Chaetodermomorpha from Bass Strait and the continental slope off south-eastern Australia. Records of the Australian Museum, vol. 41, pp. 43–62.

Stranks, T.N. (1990) Three new species of *Octopus* (Mollusca: Cephalopoda) from south-eastern Australia. Memoirs of the Museum of Victoria, vol. 50, pp. 457–465.

Stranks, T.N. & M.D. Norman (1992) Review of the *Octopus australis* complex from Australia and New Zealand, with descriptions of a new species (Mollusca: Cephalopoda). Memoirs of the Museum of Victoria, vol. 53, pp. 345–373.

Wells, F.E. & C.W. Bryce (1986) Seashells of Western Australia. Western Australian Museum, Perth.

Wells, F.E. & C.W. Bryce (1993) Sea Slugs of Western Australia. Western Australian Museum, Perth.

Willan, R.C. & N. Coleman (1984) Nudibranchs of Australasia. Australian Marine Photographic Index, Sydney.

Wilson, B. (1993) Australian Marine Shells. Prosobranch gastropods. Part 1. Odyssey Publishing, Perth.

Wilson, B. (1994) Australian Marine Shells. Prosobranch gastropods. Part 2 (Neogastropods). Odyssey Publishing, Perth.

Zeidler, W. & K.H. Norris (1989) Squids, cuttlefish and octopuses (Class Cephalopoda). pp. 789–822, in Marine Invertebrates of Southern Australia. Part II, S.A. Shepherd & I.M. Thomas (eds), Government Printer, Adelaide.

BRACHIOPODS

No guide is available for identifying Australian brachiopods. Species found in South Australia are discussed and partly figured by Verco (1910), and a few species illustrated in May & Macpherson (1958).

May, W.L. & J.H. Macpherson (1958) Illustrated Index of Australian shells. Tasmanian Government Printer, Hobart.

Verco, J.C. (1910) The brachiopods of South Australia. Transactions and Proceedings of the Royal Society of South Australia, vol. 34, pp. 89–99.

PHORONIDS

Australian phoronids are best identified using Emig *et al.* (1977), with recent records listed in Emig (1992) and descriptions of all the world's species in Emig (1979).

Emig, C.C. (1979) British and other phoronids. Synopses of the British Fauna no. 13. Cambridge University Press, Cambridge.

Emig, C.C., D.F. Boesch & S. Rainer (1977) Phoronida from Australia. Records of the Australian Museum, vol. 30, pp. 455–474.

Emig, C.C. & C. Roldán (1992) The occurrence in Australia of three species of Phoronida (Lophophorata) and their distribution in the Pacific area. Records of the South Australian Museum, vol. 26, pp. 1–8.

BRYOZOANS

The only recent guide to southern Australian bryozoans is Bock (1982).

Bock, P.E. (1982) Bryozoans (Phylum Bryozoa or Ectoprocta). pp. 319–394, in Marine Invertebrates of Southern Australia. Part I, S.A. Shepherd & I.M. Thomas (eds), Government Printer, Adelaide.

CHAETOGNATHS

A key to Australian chaetognaths is provided by Thomson (1947), with descriptions of Tasmanian and southern species included in Nyan Taw (1978) and O'Sullivan (1982).

Nyan Taw (1978) Some common components of the zooplankton of the south-eastern coastal waters of Tasmania. Papers and Proceedings of the Royal Society of Tasmania, vol. 112, pp. 69–136.

O'Sullivan, D.O.S. (1982) A guide to the chaetognaths of the Southern Ocean and adjacent waters. ANARE Research Notes, vol. 2, pp. 1–57.

Thomson, J.M. (1947) The Chaetognatha of Southeastern Australia. Bulletin of the Council for Scientific and Industrial Research Melbourne, vol. 222, pp. 1–43.

ECHINODERMS

The major reference to southern Australian echinoderms is Shepherd & Thomas (1982), with the publication of the Marine Research Group of Victoria (1984) useful for descriptions and diagrams of many common species. Regional checklists of the southwestern Western Australia echinoderm fauna provided by Marsh (1990, 1993) are also helpful; however, for much of the Western Australian fauna and for all of the New South Wales fauna it is necessary to consult the sometimes-outdated monograph by Clark (1946) and the primary literature. Keys to tropical species are given by Clark & Rowe (1971), and Tasmanian species by Dartnall (1980).

Clark, A.M. (1966) Port Phillip Bay Survey 1957–1963. Echinodermata. Memoirs of the National Museum of Victoria, vol. 27, pp. 289–351.

Clark, A.M. & F.W.E. Rowe (1971) Monograph on Shallow-water Indo-west Pacific Echinoderms. British Museum, London.

Clark, H.L. (1946) The echinoderm fauna of Australia, its composition and its origin. Publications of the Carnegie Institute, Washington, vol. 566, pp. 1–567.

Dartnall, A. (1980) Tasmanian Echinoderms. Fauna of Tasmania Handbook no. 3, pp. 1–82.

Marine Research Group of Victoria (1984) Coastal Invertebrates of Victoria: An Atlas of Selected Species. Marine Research Group of Victoria in association with the Museum of Victoria, Melbourne.

Marsh, L.M. (1990) Shallow water echinoderms of the Albany region, south-western Australia. pp. 439–482, in Proceedings of the Third International Marine Biological Workshop: The Marine Flora and Fauna of Albany, Western Australia, F.E. Wells, D.I. Walker, H. Kirkman & R. Lethbridge (eds), Western Australian Museum, Perth.

Marsh, L.M. (1993) Echinoderms of Rottnest Island. pp. 279–304, in Proceedings of the Fifth International Marine Biological Workshop: The Marine Flora and Fauna of Rottnest Island, Western Australia, F.E. Wells, D.I. Walker, H. Kirkman & R. Lethbridge (eds), Western Australian Museum, Perth.

Shepherd, S.A. & I.M. Thomas (1982) Marine Invertebrates of Southern Australia. Part I. Government Printer, Adelaide.

ASCIDIANS, SALPS, APPENDICULARIANS

Recent revisions of Australian ascidians have been made by Kott (1985, 1990, 1992) with the fourth and final group studied in this series, the didemnids, to be described soon. The major publication for identifying salps and appendicularians is Thompson (1948), with regional information also contained in Dakin & Colefax (1940) and Nyan Taw (1978).

Kott, P. (1985) The Australian Ascidiacea Part 1, Phlebobranchia and Stolidobranchia. Memoirs of the Queensland Museum, vol. 23, pp. 1–440.
Kott, P. (1990) The Australian Ascidiacea Part 2, Aplousobranchia (1). Memoirs of the Queensland Museum, vol. 29, pp. 1–266.
Kott, P. (1992) The Australian Ascidiacea Part 3, Aplousobranchia (2). Memoirs of the Queensland Museum, vol. 32, pp. 375–620.
Thompson, H. (1948) Pelagic Tunicates of Australia. CSIRO, Melbourne.

FISHES

Fishes are more easily identified than other groups of animals, thanks to recent publications covering southern Australia (Hutchins & Swainson, 1986; Gomon *et al.*, 1994), New South Wales (Kuiter, 1993), Tasmania (Edgar *et al.*, 1983; Last *et al.*, 1984) and Western Australia (Hutchins & Thompson, 1983). Sharks and rays are comprehensively illustrated and described in Last & Stevens (1994).

Edgar, G.J., P.R. Last & M.W. Wells (1983) Coastal Fishes of Tasmania and Bass Strait. Cat & Fiddle Press, Hobart.
Gomon, M.F., J.C.M. Glover & R.H. Kuiter (1994) The Fishes of Australia's South Coast. State Printer, Adelaide.
Hutchins, B. & R. Swainston (1986) Sea Fishes of Southern Australia. Swainston Publishing, Perth.
Hutchins, B. & M. Thompson (1983) The Marine and Estuarine Fishes of South-western Australia. Western Australian Museum, Perth.
Kuiter, R.H. (1993) Coastal Fishes of Southeastern Australia. Crawford House Press, Bathurst, NSW.
Last, P.R., E.O.G. Scott & F.H. Talbot (1983) Fishes of Tasmania. Tasmanian Fisheries Development Authority, Hobart.
Last, P.R. & J. Stevens (1994) Sharks and Rays of Australia. CSIRO, Melbourne.

REPTILES, BIRDS and MAMMALS

A large number of publications are available which can be used to identify the higher vertebrates. Useful local books are Cogger (1992) for marine reptiles, Readers Digest (1976) for birds, and Baker (1983), Ridgeway & Harrison (1981, 1985) and Jefferson et al. (1993) for marine mammals.

Baker, A.N. (1983) Whales and Dolphins of New Zealand and Australia: An identification guide. Victoria University Press, Wellington.
Cogger, H.G. (1992) Reptiles and Amphibians of Australia. Reed, Sydney.
Jefferson, T.A., S. Leatherwood & M.A. Webber (1993) Marine Mammals of the World. FAO Species Identification Guide, UNEP, Rome.
Readers Digest (1976) Complete Book of Australian Birds. Readers Digest, Sydney.
Ridgeway, S.H. & R. Harrison (1981) Handbook of Marine Mammals. vol. 1. The Walrus, Sea lions, Fur seals and Sea Otter. Academic Press, London.
Ridgeway, S.H. & R. Harrison (1985) Handbook of Marine Mammals. vol. 3. The Sirenians and Baleen Whales. Academic Press, London.

Index